ILLUSTRATED GREAT DECISIONS OF THE
SUPREME COURT

"Authority of Law," by sculptor James Earle Fraser, sits on the right side of the Supreme Court's front stairway.

Source: Lois Long, Collection of the Supreme Court of the United States.

ILLUSTRATED GREAT DECISIONS OF THE
SUPREME COURT

TONY MAURO | SECOND EDITION

CQ PRESS

A Division of Congressional Quarterly Inc.
Washington, D.C.

CQ Press
1255 22nd Street, NW, Suite 400
Washington, DC 20037

Phone: 202-729-1900; toll-free, 1-866-427-7737 (1-866-4CQ-PRESS)

Web: www.cqpress.com

Cover design: Jeffrey M. Hall, ION Graphic Design Works

Cover photos: Top, left to right: file photo; Library of Congress; file photo; Reuters
           Bottom: file photo

♾ The paper used in this publication exceeds the requirements of the American National Standard for Information Sciences—Permanence of Paper for Printed Library Materials, ANSI Z39.48-1992.

Printed and bound in the United States of America

09 08 07 06 05   1 2 3 4 5

Library of Congress Cataloging-in-Publication Data

Mauro, Tony.
  Illustrated great decisions of the Supreme Court / Tony Mauro.— 2nd ed.
    p. cm.
  Includes bibliographical references and index.
  ISBN 1-56802-964-0 (cloth : alk. paper)
  1. Constitutional law—United States—Cases. I. Title.

  KF4549.M334 2006
  347.73'260264—dc22   2005030474

To Bob Dubill and Peter Watson

My mentors and friends

CONTENTS

CASES ARRANGED ALPHABETICALLY

Cases are followed in parentheses by the name of the section in which they appear.

PREFACE

A case argued in early 2000 before the Supreme Court concerned whether Colorado had gone too far in enacting a law that restricted the ability of protesters to demonstrate outside abortion clinics. When Justice Antonin Scalia wondered aloud whether a similar law could have been written to restrict labor union picketing, a government lawyer made the mistake of asserting that labor disputes, unlike abortion protests, had not caused violence in Colorado.

Chief Justice William Rehnquist reacted angrily to the assertion. There *had* been violence in Colorado labor disputes, he countered. "Read *Moyer v. Peabody*," Rehnquist told the lawyer. The case Rehnquist cited was a minor one decided in 1909, but it was nonetheless revealing in that Rehnquist, in correcting a lawyer's misstatement of history, admonished her to read a Supreme Court decision, not a history book. The opinion, written by Justice Oliver Wendell Holmes Jr., would tell the lawyer all she needed to know.

Supreme Court decisions, in addition to resolving disputes, also tell stories. They are snapshots of U.S. history, each one capturing a situation that has a background, a set of facts, and a sifting of legal theories and precedents current at the time. Once issued, they cast a shadow forward, establishing principles and standards that are incorporated or elaborated on when the Court next decides a case in that field of law.

Illustrated Great Decisions of the Supreme Court, second edition, contains a series of those snapshots, presenting 108 of the pivotal, far-reaching decisions of the Supreme Court. Through them, a reader can view the broad sweep of U.S. history or simply focus on the factual background, decision, highlights, and impact of a single case.

The book is meant as an introduction to the work of the Supreme Court, though not a cursory one. Supreme Court justices often criticize those who write about the Court for focusing only on the outcome of the case—which side won or which side lost. The entries in this book go beyond the outcome, detailing how the Court reached its decisions as well as what went before and what came after. Like other political institutions, the Supreme Court often changes its perspective. Because much depends on who is sitting on the bench and the cases that come before it, decisions are sometimes revisited. The case descriptions in this book inform the reader about the latest interpretations of some of the Court's oldest cases.

In the twenty-five years that I have covered the Supreme Court as a journalist, I have often gone back to read these decisions in isolation, but I have sometimes wondered about the context in which they were written and what happened in their aftermath. This book, I hope, will provide some of that context in addition to the detail of what the Court actually said in some of its more important and interesting decisions.

Supreme Court scholars will quickly notice that not all the hoary decisions that lawyers must learn about are included here. The selection of cases is weighted toward the modern era, with an emphasis on civil rights and First Amendment cases that might be of particular interest to students and the general public. *Bob Jones University v. United States* (1983) and *New Jersey v. T.L.O.* (1985) probably would not be on any list of the top Supreme Court cases, but the issues they raise—official searches of student belongings at school and tax-exempt status for a university that discriminates against minorities—can trigger thought-provoking debate about basic constitutional issues. *Chandler v. Florida* (1981), which opened the door to widespread camera coverage of the courts, may not be a landmark case, but as demonstrated by the O.J. Simpson trial, it relates to an issue that is still hotly disputed: whether the presence of cameras distorts the judicial process to the point where a defendant's right to a fair trial is damaged. *Loving v. Virginia* (1967), which struck down laws against interracial marriage, may not be in the pantheon of top civil rights decisions, but its still-current subject matter—and its ironically apt title—make it worthy of discussion. Likewise, *United States v. The Schooner Amistad* (1841) is not usually counted as a pivotal civil rights decision, but the 1997 movie about the case, in which the late justice Harry Blackmun appeared in a cameo role, justified its inclusion in the book.

Also heavily represented in these pages are other cases in which Jehovah's Witnesses, gays, racists, pornographers, as well as Japanese Americans and other minorities sought to vindicate fundamental rights. These, too, make for compelling stories that reveal much about tolerance and intolerance in U.S. life. *Buck v. Bell* (1927), for example, is given full treatment here because it evokes a dark period when those with disabilities were treated as outcasts. The Cherokee Cases (1831 and 1832) are included because they similarly reveal how the Supreme Court played a role in shaping the nation's policies, in this case toward Native Americans.

Society's treatment of Jehovah's Witnesses has produced nearly two dozen Supreme Court decisions, several of which are included in this volume. Justice Harlan Fiske Stone once stated that Jehovah's Witnesses "ought to have an endowment in view of the aid which they give in solving the legal problems of civil liberties." Many of those legal issues persist to this day, which is why they are covered here.

I have also tried to include most of the cases that are essential building blocks for any comprehensive study of the Supreme Court. *Marbury v. Madison* (1803), *Ex parte Milligan* (1866), *Humphrey's Executor v. United States* (1935), *Youngstown Sheet and Tube Co. v. Sawyer* (1952), and *Baker v. Carr* (1962) are all here. Other lesser-known corners of the law are treated in several entries. Environmental law, based mainly on statutory rather than constitutional provisions, has produced few landmark decisions, but one, *Sierra Club v. Morton* (1972) is included because it illuminates the entire field of environmental law. *Village of Euclid v. Ambler Realty Co.* (1926) was similarly included, to cover the modern constitutional view of zoning, part of everyday municipal life across the United States.

The twenty new cases presented in this second edition cover more than a dozen areas of law, but establishment of religion decisions figure prominently. Cases on copyright and the right to trial by jury, two areas not addressed in the first edition, have also been added.

A few words about the organization of the book: In the first edition, the cases were arranged alphabetically, but in this edition they are grouped by twenty-four subject areas—each opening with a brief introduction—to enable the reader to see the progression of the Court's jurisprudence on a range of issues, such as freedom of the press or the commerce power. For ease of reference, an alphabetical listing of the cases is also provided after the main table of contents. In addition, the volume contains useful reference material, including the U.S. Constitution, justices' biographies, a succession chart of Supreme Court seats, a thumbnail sketch of the Court's history, and a glossary of common legal terms. The many illustrations throughout the book bring the cases to life.

In writing this book, I am indebted to many people who assisted and inspired me. The late Bernard Schwartz, the prolific historian of the Supreme Court, told me not long before he died that I ought to write a book, and I am sorry he is not alive to see that I acted on his advice. Schwartz showed that it is possible to take an investigative approach to writing about the Supreme Court without slighting its status as a majestic and admirable institution.

Others who helped me in the selection and research, as well as in other aspects of the book, include, in alphabetical order, Kathleen Arberg, Tom Baker, Martin Belsky, David Burns, Ron Collins, Joseph Conn, Bruce Fein, Victor Gaberman, David Garrow, David Hudson, Kenneth Jost, Lisa Keen, Edward Lazarus, Joyce Murdoch, Shawn Francis Peters, David Pride, Bruce Sanford, John Stanton, the Stepp family, Tiffany Villager, and J. Harvie Wilkinson III. Among the books I found most helpful were several written or edited by Joan Biskupic and Elder Witt, Warren Burger, John Garraty, Kermit Hall, Peter Irons, Richard Kluger, Edward Lazarus, Jethro Lieberman, Sandra Day O'Connor, David Rabban, William Rehnquist, Cass Sunstein, Bernard Schwartz, Mark Tushnet, Melvin I. Urofsky, and Bob Woodward and Scott Armstrong.

I also could not have written this book without the patience and understanding of my colleagues first at *USA Today* and, more recently, at *Legal Times* and American Lawyer Media. They encouraged me to write and tolerated my prolonged absences from work. Thanks go to Rich Barbieri, Bob Dubill, Ed Foster-Simeon, Fred Gaskins, Linda Mathews, Jim Oliphant, Aric Press, and Eva Rodriguez.

At CQ Press, I was very lucky to have patient, careful, and knowledgeable editors: January Layman-Wood, Doug Goldenberg-Hart, Molly Lohman, and Gwenda Larsen. Most of all, I want to thank the three women I love and cherish in my life, all of whom helped me immeasurably: my mother, Josephine Mauro, whose keen librarian's eye caught errors and imprecision in early drafts; my wife, Kathy Cullinan; and my daughter, Emily Mauro.

INTRODUCTION

*J*ustice Sandra Day O'Connor spoke with little emotion on June 28, 2004, when she announced the Supreme Court's historic decision in *Hamdi v. Rumsfeld*. "A state of war is not a blank check for the President when it comes to the rights of the Nation's citizens," O'Connor stated matter-of-factly in one of four decisions issued that day stemming from the United States' "war on terror."

The decision made headlines worldwide and no doubt confounded foreign readers. How could the United States' highest court, in the middle of a war, repudiate the position of the commander-in-chief on the detention of so-called "enemy combatants"? Not many of the world's governments would have tolerated such second-guessing in wartime.

But for O'Connor and the Supreme Court, it was all in a day's work. The justices had quietly played their constitutional role of keeping the other branches of government in their place. In this instance, it was the executive branch that had overstepped its bounds under the Constitution. On another day, the Court might be reining in Congress or a state.

Whether the subject is wartime powers or prayers at commencement ceremonies or the privacy of a student's backpack, the Supreme Court plays a pivotal role in our everyday lives. The cacophony of voices we hear, the individual rights we enjoy, the racial diversity and tensions we experience, the economy we work in, and the government that supervises it all have been shaped, fostered, or impeded at some crucial point in their development by decisions of the Supreme Court.

But, except for rare periods in history, the Supreme Court has exerted its influence without much public fanfare or notice. It is the least-visible branch of government and, by all accounts, its members like it that way. Often the Court is a reluctant arbiter of disputes that it wishes had been resolved by others. At times the Supreme Court has mirrored or even lagged behind changes in society, rather than acting as the engine for change. At other times, however, the Court startles the nation with a bold stroke. As central as its role has been, the modern Supreme Court is sometimes self-deprecating. "Why should

anyone care what we think?" Justice Antonin Scalia once asked, only half-jokingly, in a speech.

The Supreme Court views its role as that of a border patrol. It impartially polices the boundaries of power between the president and Congress, the federal government and the states, and all governments and the individual, to ensure that the Constitution's masterly array of checks and balances operates as the Framers intended.

Because the Court's members are not elected and have life tenure, the Supreme Court also believes it can perform that function apart from, and somewhat above, the political fray. Justices often call the judiciary the "nonpolitical branch" of the national government; its members are insulated from political pressures and election-year accountability for their decisions. That is one of the reasons why the justices steadfastly oppose the televising of their proceedings: They do not want to become part of the media-political culture of Washington, D.C.

One process, however, always thrusts the Court into the limelight: the nomination and confirmation of a new justice. Clashes over the nomination of Robert Bork, who did not make it, and Clarence Thomas and John Roberts Jr., who did, demonstrate that politics and publicity are unavoidable parts of the judicial process. By selecting one person over another, the president seeks to influence the Court's future politically, at least in a general sense. And by questioning nominees and expressing concerns, senators try to deliver a political message to the Court with the justices they confirm.

Once on the Court, the justices themselves also act politically, and not necessarily in the negative sense of that word. They take great pains to explain their decisions in a way that will win public acceptance and legitimacy. On issues ranging from capital punishment to race relations, the Court often makes reference to public opinion and political and social trends. As Justice Ruth Bader Ginsburg has put it on numerous occasions, the Court should not concern itself with the "weather" of any given day, but it should be mindful of the "climate" of the era.

At times, the Court cannot avoid being swept into the center of a political storm. That is in part because of how the

Supreme Court operates. Unlike the other branches of government, the Supreme Court does not—with rare exceptions—set out to tackle an issue that is bothering the U.S. public. Instead, because the Constitution commands that the Court decide "cases or controversies," the justices must await cases that arrive on their doorstep in the form of appeals from lower court rulings. The cases that come to the Court must pose a real conflict between real parties, not a hypothetical dispute or a request for advice on whether a law, in the abstract, is constitutional.

Those restrictions do not mean the justices are entirely passive or helpless in shaping their agenda or docket. Roughly 7,000 cases are presented to the Court each year, presenting a full array of issues from which to choose. Especially during the more activist periods of the Court's history, trends in the Court's selection of cases can be discerned: an emphasis on property rights early in the twentieth century, for example, or an interest in the rights of criminal defendants during the Warren Court era.

This aspect of the Court's history has political dimensions, as well. Justices, by and large, reflect the political bent of the presidents who nominated them. For a president who has the opportunity to name several justices—Franklin D. Roosevelt, for example—appointments to the Court can extend his political legacy decades beyond his own tenure. The current Court's conservatism, in many respects, can be traced to President Ronald Reagan, who left office in 1989. There have been notable exceptions to the theory that justices reflect the views of the presidents who appointed them. The liberalism of the Warren Court was driven in large part by two appointees of Republican president Dwight D. Eisenhower, namely Earl Warren and William J. Brennan Jr.

HOW THE COURT WORKS

Most cases that make it to the Supreme Court's docket are appealed from lower federal courts or from the highest court of the fifty states. If the party that lost in the lower court seeks to have the decision overturned, it files what is known as a *certiorari* petition with the Supreme Court. This is a request for the Court to "certify" the case for review, which, if granted, means that the Court will read briefs and listen to oral arguments in the case before deciding whether the lower court ruling should be overturned or upheld.

The Court also considers a small number of cases under its original jurisdiction, meaning that the Supreme Court is the first, not the last, stop for litigants. These cases are usually in the form of a lawsuit by one state against another, often over boundaries. The 1998 case of *New York v. New Jersey,* for example, asked the Supreme Court to referee a longstanding dispute over which of the two states has jurisdiction over Ellis Island. In such a case, the Court itself does not conduct a trial but instead appoints a special master who hears the evidence and makes a recommendation to the justices.

With all other cases filed at the Court, the justices and their law clerks look at the appeals to decide whether they merit full attention. In the past, each justice's law clerks, usually three or four clerks, reviewed the cases and summarized them for his or her boss. Today, clerks for most justices combine their efforts: they divide up incoming petitions and write summaries for the justices in the pool. As a result, the Court will often turn down an appeal before more than one or two justices actually reads the petitions.

At regularly scheduled private conferences, the justices discuss the cases they or their clerks have recommended for consideration. No one but the nine justices attends these conferences. The justices zealously guard the secrecy of these conferences so they can discuss the cases freely. If four or more justices vote to accept a case, it is placed on the docket. Sometimes this process is complicated by the recusal of one or more justices. For reasons that are almost never spelled out, justices will occasionally announce they have not participated in the decision to grant or deny review in a given case. Often, the reason is a financial conflict of interest—the justice owns stock in a company that is one of the parties in the case, for example. But sometimes family connections cause a justice to recuse. In 1996, for example, Justice Clarence Thomas did not participate in *United States v. Virginia,* involving the male-only admissions policy at Virginia Military Institute. Thomas's son Jamal was enrolled at VMI at the time.

In the vast majority of cases, the Court decides not to review the decision of the lower court. When that happens, the lower court decision takes effect as the law governing the case and other similar cases in the same jurisdiction. For this reason, "deciding to decide" is one of the most important functions of the Court. In capital punishment cases, this preliminary screening role of the Supreme Court can literally make the difference between life and death. If the Court declines to review a death row inmate's case, the execution can proceed.

What motivates the Court to accept one case for review but reject another? The Court rarely explains its reasoning in a specific case, but, in general, justices say that an important factor is whether lower courts in different parts of the country have ruled in opposite ways on the same issue. The Court may then accept a petition for review with an eye toward producing a uniform national rule that will help resolve future disputes. But this is not always the case: With increasing regularity, the Court has been willing to tolerate disagreements among lower courts, causing consternation among national companies and others who have to live with different legal rules in different parts of the country.

In deciding whether to review a case, justices also consider the hard-to-define factor of national importance. When a lower court strikes down a federal law, that is a virtual guarantee that the Court will take up the appeal. On some other hard-fought issues, the Court will sometimes agree to intervene promptly, even when not many lower courts have been involved. Other times, however, the Court passes up hotly contested issues. For example, the Court has not accepted a case directly involving the controversial Second Amendment right to bear arms since 1939. In the late 1990s several cases challenging the Pentagon policy on homosexuals in the military went to the Supreme Court, but the justices declined to review any of them.

But in roughly seventy to ninety cases each term, the Court grants the petition for review. Once the announcement is made that the Court will decide a case, the case takes on new importance and prominence. Lawyers shift into high gear as they write briefs and prepare for oral argument. Other organizations with an interest in the case file briefs as amicus curiae—friend of the court—to alert the justices to an aspect of the case they might not otherwise consider.

Two parts of the process are conducted in public: oral argument and, months later, the announcement of the decision. In the Court's early years, oral argument could last for days. The 1824 case of *Gibbons v. Ogden* was argued over five days; one of the advocates, the legendary Daniel Webster, later described the experience as an "intellectual pleasure."

But now, in almost all cases, momentous or trivial, each side has a half hour to make its case. Much of the time is taken up with answering questions from the justices who want to clarify the record or to emphasize a point for the benefit of their colleagues. Little time is left for rhetorical flourishes, and the half hour can be grueling for the lawyers. Early in the tenure of the late Chief Justice William Rehnquist he upbraided lawyers who did not address him as "Mr. Chief Justice." Later, he corrected lawyers' pronunciation or grammar. A small but powerful group of lawyers has developed a specialty of arguing before the Supreme Court. But many cases are still argued, with mixed results, by the hometown lawyers who handled them from the start.

Oral arguments are scheduled in two-week cycles beginning when the term starts on the legendary first Monday in October and running through April. Throughout that period and continuing through the end of June or early July, the justices evaluate incoming cases and write and issue opinions in cases that have been argued. During the three-month summer recess, many justices travel or teach overseas while still keeping up with the steady flow of incoming cases.

Soon after cases are argued, the justices confer privately and cast tentative votes. If the chief justice is on the winning side, he or she will assign the task of writing the decision to another justice in the majority or to himself. If the chief justice is in the minority, the senior justice in the majority does the assigning. The assignment power is one of the roles that makes the chief justice the "first among equals."

In most instances, the justice assigned to write the opinion asks one of his or her law clerks to prepare the first draft. Some justices revise the drafts heavily, while others make few changes. When the justice is satisfied with the opinion, it is circulated to the other justices for revisions and negotiation. Once they see a draft opinion, some justices find it so convincing that they actually switch sides. Others condition their vote on a change in wording that the author may or may not be willing to make. Justice William Brennan Jr. sent Chief Justice Earl Warren a twenty-one-page list of proposed changes in Warren's draft of the landmark decision *Miranda v. Arizona.* Some have labeled the process horse-trading, but more often it appears to be a sincere effort to arrive at an opinion that is agreeable to as many justices as possible.

Sometimes, however, efforts at compromise fail, and justices write separate concurring and dissenting opinions. The opinion-writing process can take months, and it is not unusual for a case argued in October to be finally resolved the next April or later.

Writing dissents is a time-honored tradition on the Supreme Court. They have no formal purpose because the law of the case is laid down in the majority decision. Justice Oliver Wendell Holmes Jr., who later wrote many notable dissents, described them as "useless" early in his career. Still, most justices believe they are important, partly because they force the majority to deal with questions about the decision's rationale or impact. Dissents also serve the role of laying down principles that the Court might return to years or decades later. When the Court upheld "separate but equal" public accommodations for blacks and whites in the 1896 case of *Plessy v. Ferguson,* Justice John Marshall Harlan's dissent declared that "our Constitution is color-blind"—a view that the Court finally embraced fifty-eight years later in *Brown v. Board of Education.*

Once the opinions and dissents are finished, the decisions are printed and released at the same time that the author announces them from the bench in open court. Justices used to read their opinions word for word, sometimes taking several hours to do so. On the current Court, justices usually briefly summarize their decisions. Printed decisions are released to the press and public immediately, and within minutes the texts are also available on the Internet. Because of security concerns, the Court did not launch its own Web site (www.supremecourtus.gov) until April 2000, but now that site is frequently used and usually provides full texts of decisions within an hour of their release. Law professors, bloggers, and other Court-watchers also quickly post new decisions along with commentary. (One site where opinions and other Supreme Court resources can be found is *www.findlaw.com,* and the URLs are provided for all the cases in this book.)

The number of cases the Supreme Court has agreed to decide has ranged from more than 1,800 per year in the 1890s to fewer than 100 a century later. Congress helped reduce the Court's caseload by passing several laws that gave justices greater discretion in picking the cases they want to decide. Several current justices have said that limiting the number to fewer than 100 cases per term is optimal in terms of the pace and quality of the opinions written.

THE EVOLVING COURT

Even though today's Court exercises a great deal of discretion over its agenda, there have been times in its history when issues have almost forced their way onto the docket. Early cases involving the regulation of interstate commerce in the new nation, such as *Gibbons v. Ogden,* and the question of slavery, as in 1857 in *Scott v. Sandford*—the Dred Scott case—would have been difficult for the Court to avoid. In the twentieth century, the justices could not ignore the issue of New Deal economic regulation, as in *Schechter Poultry Corp. v. United States* and race, again, in *Brown v. Board of Education.* Recent scholarship on the Warren Court of the 1950s and 1960s also indicates that justices sometimes sought out cases to resolve certain issues relating to the rights of criminal defendants, as in *Gideon v. Wainwright.*

The early Supreme Court did not play as central a role in U.S. political life as today's Court. It began its existence in 1790 in the shadow of the other two branches of government, with no building of its own and little clear idea of what it was to do. Few cases of consequence came its way, and the decision in one of them—*Chisholm v. Georgia* in 1793—was actually reversed with the adoption of the Eleventh Amendment. It was not until the case of *Marbury v. Madison* in 1803 that Chief Justice John Marshall defined the Court's role as the institution that would decide whether acts of Congress conformed to the Constitution and set them aside if they did not. Thwarting the will of the majority of the people as expressed by its representatives in Congress is a remarkable power, but Marshall's opinion made it clear the Court would not hesitate to put the executive branch in its place as well—as the Court has done to virtually every president since, up to and including George W. Bush.

Marshall's vision was to use the power of judicial review to foster an effective national government. In *McCulloch v. Maryland* (1819) and *Gibbons v. Ogden,* the Court applied that vision. *Gibbons v. Ogden,* in particular, made it clear that the national government had the power to sweep away state rivalries

and obstacles that could hamper the development of a national economy.

The Supreme Court has not always operated with a broad national vision, however. Its decision in *Scott v. Sandford* denied citizenship to blacks and said Congress could not bar slavery in the territories. Chief Justice Charles Evans Hughes later described that ruling as a "self-inflicted wound" that sullied the Court's reputation for generations.

After the Civil War, Congress tried to repair the damage done by the Court's decision in *Scott* by passing the Fourteenth Amendment to the Constitution, which first granted citizenship to all persons born or naturalized in the United States, and then said that states could not deny equal protection of the laws or due process of law to their people or deny their citizens the privileges or immunities of citizenship. The Fourteenth Amendment, one of three post–Civil War amendments, may not be as well known as the First Amendment or the Fifth, but it is the well-spring of most of the protections of civil rights asserted during the twentieth century, exerting an extraordinary influence over society today. Supreme Court historian Bernard Schwartz called the Fourteenth Amendment "the cornerstone of American constitutionalism."

At first, however, the Fourteenth Amendment was interpreted narrowly. In late nineteenth century rulings known as the Slaughterhouse Cases and the Civil Rights Cases, the Court rendered the Civil War amendments virtually useless for protecting individual rights. The *Plessy* decision continued the trend. Even though slavery had ended, the Court's actions allowed Jim Crow laws to flourish and segregation to persist well into the twentieth century. In *Yick Wo v. Hopkins* (1886), however, the Court used the Fourteenth Amendment to protect immigrants from discriminatory treatment by government.

After World War II the Court began to give the Fourteenth Amendment a more expansive interpretation in cases of racial discrimination. In *Shelley v. Kraemer* (1948) the Court invoked the Fourteenth Amendment to bar government from enforcing racial restrictions in the sale of housing. And in *Brown v. Board of Education,* one of the landmark cases of the twentieth century, the Court directed the power of the Fourteenth Amendment at school segregation.

The other sweeping change wrought by the Fourteenth Amendment was the protection of individual liberties—the freedoms of speech, press, and religion, as well as the rights of criminal defendants—from state as well as federal restrictions. Even a woman's right to have an abortion, articulated in *Roe v. Wade* (1973), is rooted in the Supreme Court's view that the Fourteenth Amendment protects women from state invasions of their personal privacy.

Along with this more expansive view of the Fourteenth Amendment, the Supreme Court in the twentieth century breathed life into the First Amendment. If one of the major trends of the century was the expansion of individual freedoms, the Court's interpretation of the First Amendment was one of the chief engines behind it. In *Near v. Minnesota* (1931), *New York Times v. Sullivan* (1964), and *New York Times v. United States* (1971), the Court gave broad protection to freedom of speech and freedom of the press. More recently, the Court in *Reno v. American Civil Liberties Union* (1997) gave its First Amendment blessing to the rapidly expanding Internet.

For the first half of the century, the Court was less tolerant of political dissent, reflecting wartime and cold war nervousness about subversive speech. From *Schenck v. United States* (1919) to *Dennis v. United States* (1951), the Court supported government restrictions on political speech. As the nation became more confident of its strength, however, the Supreme Court showed more tolerance toward controversial speech. In *Texas v. Johnson* the Court in 1989 even upheld the right of protesters to burn the American flag, a cherished national symbol. Efforts in Congress to prohibit flag-burning through a constitutional amendment—which the Supreme Court would have to heed—have so far been unsuccessful.

The religion clauses of the First Amendment have generated dozens of difficult cases for the Supreme Court. In general the Court has kept the wall of separation between church and state high. The Court's decisions on school prayer, in particular, have placed it in the center of controversy, although in recent years the justices have ruled more favorably toward public aid to religious schools. The tension between the two religion clauses—one barring the establishment of religion, the other protecting free exercise of religion—continues to confound the Court, however. Enhancing the power of one clause, it seems, inevitably infringes on the other.

The Court has also played a powerful role in the economic life of the nation. In the Granger Cases of 1877 (including *Munn v. Illinois*) the Court said that states could, in the "public interest," regulate fees charged by grain elevators and warehouses. But at the beginning of the twentieth century, the Court launched the so-called Lochner era (named for a 1905 case, *Lochner v. New York*), in which reformist and labor-oriented regulations of businesses were struck down. In *Hammer v. Dagenhart,* the Court in 1918 threw out the first federal law aimed at ending industry's use of child labor. The law barred the interstate shipment of products made in factories or mines that employed children under the age of fourteen. The Court said the law exceeded congressional power to regulate interstate commerce.

When the Court's economic theories came into conflict with President Franklin D. Roosevelt's New Deal legislation, which was designed to fight the Great Depression, Roosevelt responded by trying to "pack" the Court with his own appointees. Roosevelt's plan was one of the sharpest political challenges to the Court's legitimacy in U.S. history. It was roundly criticized, and the plan faded when the Court suddenly reversed course and began upholding Roosevelt's legislation.

Since that time the Supreme Court's decisions ending school desegregation, barring teacher-led prayer in schools, declaring a woman's right to an abortion, and in effect deciding the outcome of the 2000 presidential election have subjected the institution to criticism from some quarters and praise from others. Despite the controversy, the Court enjoys a high level of respect from the public. In many opinion polls It often comes out on top among government institutions, even though most members of the public cannot name more than a single justice. Some even argue that the Court is popular *because* it is so little known, and they use that questionable proposition to urge that the Court remain in the shadows.

Whatever the justices' personal preferences, however, the Supreme Court cannot stay out of the limelight. As this book was going to press, the justices had taken on new cases involving physician-assisted suicide, religious use of illegal drugs, and abortion rights for minors. Further cases stemming from the war on terror are likely to make their way back to the high court. In the decades to come, issues relating to privacy, new technology, and medical and genetic advances are sure to bubble to the surface and command the Court's attention.

Throughout history the Supreme Court has been described both as the "least dangerous" branch, as Alexander Hamilton put it, and as the "storm center" of political controversy, in Justice Holmes's words. Both labels, at various times, have been apt. In the Court's role as constitutional arbiter, it may be destined to shuttle back and forth between both roles—or, as has occurred more often, to chart a course down the middle.

AFFIRMATIVE ACTION

*A*ffirmative action programs, which give minorities and women a boost in admissions, contracting, and other government programs, became widespread in the 1960s as a way to help remedy the effects of centuries of unequal treatment. But affirmative action gradually became politically unpopular, partly because it was viewed as unfair to qualified whites and partly because of the words of the Fourteenth Amendment to the Constitution. That post–Civil War amendment bars unequal treatment under the law for anyone in the United States, and it does not explicitly make an exception for unequal treatment to help a previously disadvantaged group. The Supreme Court has grappled with the difficult constitutional issue in several landmark cases.

Other related cases mentioned in the Affirmative Action section

Brown v. Board of Education of Topeka (1954) (see p. 243)
United Steelworkers v. Weber (1979)
Fullilove v. Klutznick (1980)
Firefighters Local Union No. 1794 v. Stotts (1984)
Wygant v. Jackson Board of Education (1986)
Johnson v. Santa Clara County (1987)
Richmond v. J.A. Croson Co. (1989)
Adarand Constructors v. Pena (1995)

Regents of the University of California v. Bakke

Decided June 28, 1978
438 U.S. 265
laws.findlaw.com/US/438/265.html

DECISION

A state university medical school admissions program that reserves a certain number of slots for minority students violates the 1964 Civil Rights Act, which prohibits excluding anyone from federally funded programs on the basis of race. Programs that consider race as one of many factors in admission are not unconstitutional because they can be justified as a way of remedying past discrimination.

BACKGROUND

"Affirmative action" is a phrase that encompasses a variety of programs and policies that take race or gender into account as a positive factor in admissions, employment, contracting, and other benefits. These programs began in the 1960s as part of the civil rights movement. Congress had passed laws prohibiting racial discrimination in employment and public accommodations, but some civil rights and political leaders felt that was not enough. The effects of centuries of past discrimination could not be erased overnight with a simple guarantee of equality; temporarily, at least, minorities might need a boost.

In a 1966 speech at Howard University, President Lyndon B. Johnson put the case for affirmative action simply: "You do not take a person who, for years, has been hobbled by chains and liberate him, bring him up to the starting line, and then say, 'you are free to compete with all the others,' and still justly believe that you have been completely fair. . . . It is not enough to open the gates of opportunity. All our citizens must have the ability to walk through those gates."

Under Democratic and Republican presidents alike, government programs that set aside a certain percentage of government business for minority contractors proliferated. By the late 1970s, by one estimate, the federal government had about thirty programs of this kind in operation. Similar set-asides or preferences were enacted in state universities and in a range of workplaces. The programs were seen as a way of compensating minorities for the inequities they and their ancestors had suffered.

But as soon as these programs took effect, they generated controversy—especially in "zero-sum" situations where giving a boost to a minority person meant that a specific white person was disadvantaged. To the whites, usually far removed from the racism that had harmed minorities in the past, the programs seemed to violate fundamental fairness, as well as the equal protection clause of the Fourteenth Amendment.

One of those aggrieved whites was Allan Bakke. Son of a mailman and a teacher, Bakke was a graduate of the University of Minnesota and the father of three children. Although he was making a comfortable salary in California as an aerospace engineer, Bakke wanted to become a physician. He took premed courses and volunteered in an emergency room. In 1973, at age thirty-three, he applied to several medical schools, but was turned down. He was especially upset about being rejected two years in a row by the University of California at Davis. He learned that the university had set aside sixteen of the one hundred places in its entering class for blacks, Hispanics, Asian Americans, and Native Americans. Those sixteen spaces were filled through a separate admission process. In 1973 the school had 2,464 applicants for the 100 vacancies, and in 1974, there were 3,737 applications. Bakke's grades and medical school admission test scores were significantly better than those of the applicants admitted to the minority slots, although there was disagreement over whether he would have been admitted even if the sixteen slots had not been reserved for minorities.

Bakke filed suit against the university, claiming he was a victim of "reverse discrimination." California courts sided with him. The California Supreme Court ruled that the university admission policy violated the Fourteenth Amendment and ordered that Bakke be admitted. The university appealed to the U.S. Supreme Court, setting the stage for a major confrontation on race.

As oral arguments approached, the case attracted widespread attention. More than fifty separate amicus curiae (friend of the court) briefs descended on the Supreme Court. Among those briefs was one from the Justice Department, which had been deeply divided over the issue. The Justice Department brief argued against strict quotas, but said the university was entitled to take race into account to remedy past discrimination against minorities in society.

Archibald Cox, who served as solicitor general under Presidents John F. Kennedy and Lyndon B. Johnson, represented the University of California. At oral argument Cox said the Court's decision "will determine, perhaps for decades," whether minority students will have "meaningful access" to university and professional education. Bakke's lawyer, Reynold Colvin, countered that "race is an improper classification" in state university admissions. Wade McCree, representing the

Justice Department, told the Court, "To be blind to race today is to be blind to reality."

The Court was deeply split on the issue, and Justice Powell held the key to the decision. Partly to gain more time for a decision, the Court asked for additional briefs. At first, Powell was determined to strike down the Davis admission program outright, but on narrower grounds than the California court had used. Powell believed that a program such as Harvard University's, which used race as one of many factors to achieve diversity, could be constitutional. According to Court historian Bernard Schwartz, Justice Brennan suggested that Powell vote to affirm the California ruling in part and reverse it in part. Powell accepted the suggestion. But the outcome of the case still awaited a decision by Justice Blackmun, who was hospitalized for surgery during the winter after the *Bakke* case was argued. Blackmun finally agreed to uphold the Davis program, establishing a 4–4 divide with Powell as the tiebreaker. It was not until late June, eight months after it was first argued, that the *Bakke* decision came down. When Powell announced it from the bench, he acknowledged that "we speak today with a notable lack of unanimity."

VOTE

5–4, with Justice Lewis F. Powell Jr. announcing the Court's judgment. Joining him for parts of the ruling were Justices Byron R. White, William J. Brennan Jr., Thurgood Marshall, and Harry A. Blackmun, who also dissented in part. Justices John Paul Stevens, Potter Stewart, William Rehnquist, and Chief Justice Warren E. Burger joined other parts of the Powell opinion, also dissenting in part.

HIGHLIGHTS

Justice Powell's opinion, in its entirety, won the support of only one justice: Powell himself. But because four other justices concurred with different parts of it, and no other opinion commanded a majority of five justices, Powell's opinion spoke for the Court.

Powell's first task was to meet the unavoidable challenge of reconciling the university's affirmative action admissions program with the words of Title VI of the Civil Rights Act of 1964. Its text seemed clear enough: "No person in the United States shall, on the ground of race, color, or national origin, be excluded from participation in . . . any program or activity receiving Federal financial assistance." The law does not say "no black person" or "no minority person."

Powell's opinion addressed that point by arguing that no matter what the words said, the law was intended to protect the same rights that the Fourteenth Amendment protected. That amendment, Powell argued, did not necessarily require

the kind of completely color-blind treatment that Bakke was demanding. Powell acknowledged, however, that the university program was "undeniably a classification based on race and ethnic background." Minority applicants were eligible for one hundred spots in the school's incoming class, while whites could compete for only eighty-four.

As such, the Court agreed, the state program had to be judged using the highest level of scrutiny, a level that usually results in the program being struck down. "When a classification denies an individual opportunities or benefits enjoyed by others solely because of his race or ethnic background, it must be regarded as suspect."

The state's justifications for the program were not sufficient for the program to meet that high standard. Helping the victims of societal discrimination did not warrant harming individuals such as Bakke who were not responsible for that discrimination, Powell said. The state's goal of educational diversity was the only justification that was constitutionally permissible, Powell said. "An otherwise qualified medical student with a particular background—whether it be ethnic, geographic, culturally advantaged or disadvantaged—may bring to a professional school of medicine experiences, outlooks, and ideas that enrich the training of its student body and better equip its graduates to render with understanding their vital service to humanity."

The separate admissions program for minorities, Powell said, was not the only effective way of reaching that goal, so it could not be upheld. In effect, Powell was saying that some programs that take race into account are permissible, but not the one before the Court.

Justice Brennan wrote separately to underscore the "positive" aspects of the Powell decision that embraced affirmative action. "The Court today, in reversing in part the judgment of the Supreme Court of California, affirms the constitutional power of Federal and State Governments to act affirmatively to achieve equal opportunity for all. . . . Government may take race into account when it acts not to demean or insult any racial group, but to remedy disadvantages cast on minorities by past racial prejudice, at least when appropriate findings have been made by judicial, legislative, or administrative bodies with competence to act in this area." That remedial goal would have justified using a lower level of scrutiny to assess the Davis program, Brennan argued, but that view did not prevail.

In a separate opinion Justice Marshall voiced mixed feelings about the decision. "While I applaud the judgment of the Court that a university may consider race in its admissions process, it is more than a little ironic that, after several hundred years of class-based discrimination against Negroes, the Court is unwilling to hold that a class-based remedy for that discrimination is permissible."

Allan Bakke is followed by reporters after his first day at the medical school of the University of California at Davis in 1978. Originally denied admission, Bakke sued the university over its affirmative action program, which he claimed disadvantaged white applicants. In *Regents of the University of California v. Bakke* (1978), a divided Supreme Court rejected racial quotas but allowed race to be considered as one of many factors in admissions. Bakke was subsequently admitted. *Source: AP/Wide World Photos/Walt Zeboski.*

Justice Blackmun voiced what turned out to be a naive hope that affirmative action would be needed for a only short period of time. "I yield to no one in my earnest hope that the time will come when an 'affirmative action' program is unnecessary and is, in truth, only a relic of the past. I would hope that we could reach this stage within a decade at the most. But the story of *Brown v. Board of Education,* decided almost a quarter of a century ago, suggests that that hope is a slim one. . . . In order to get beyond racism, we must first take account of race. There is no other way. And in order to treat some persons equally, we must treat them differently."

EXCERPTS

From Justice Powell's majority opinion: "The special admissions program is undeniably a classification based on race and ethnic background. To the extent that there existed a pool of at least minimally qualified minority applicants to fill the 16 special admissions seats, white applicants could compete only for 84 seats in the entering class, rather than the 100 open to minority applicants. Whether this limitation is described as a quota or a goal, it is a line drawn on the basis of race and ethnic status. . . .

"Petitioner urges us to adopt for the first time a more restrictive view of the Equal Protection Clause and hold that discrimination against members of the white 'majority' cannot be suspect if its purpose can be characterized as 'benign.' The clock of our liberties, however, cannot be turned back to 1868. It is far too late to argue that the guarantee of equal protection to all persons permits the recognition of special wards entitled to a degree of protection greater than that accorded others. . . .

". . . Preferential programs may only reinforce common stereotypes holding that certain groups are unable to achieve success without special protection based on a factor having no relationship to individual worth. . . . [T]here is a measure of inequity in forcing innocent persons in respondent's position to bear the burdens of redressing grievances not of their making. . . .

"The fourth goal asserted by petitioner is the attainment of a diverse student body. This clearly is a constitutionally permissible goal for an institution of higher education. Academic freedom, though not a specifically enumerated constitutional right, long has been viewed as a special concern of the First Amendment. The freedom of a university to make its own judgments as to education includes the selection of its student body. . . .

"The fatal flaw in petitioner's preferential program is its disregard of individual rights as guaranteed by the Fourteenth Amendment. Such rights are not absolute. But when a State's distribution of benefits or imposition of burdens hinges on ancestry or the color of a person's skin, that individual is entitled to a demonstration that the challenged classification is necessary to promote a substantial state interest. Petitioner has failed to carry this burden. For this reason, that portion of the California court's judgment holding petitioner's special admissions program invalid under the Fourteenth Amendment must be affirmed."

IMPACT

Television and radio networks flashed news of the long-awaited ruling to the public as soon as it was announced. But because of its length, and the odd lineup of justices, many of the initial reports were inaccurate. Bakke had won admission to the medical school, but what else had the Court said about affirmative action? It was not immediately clear.

By day's end, it appeared to most analysts that the Court had achieved a solomonic compromise, striking down the university's specific quota-like program, but allowing race to be considered as one of many factors in future programs. One headline the next day read "No One Lost." Attorney General Griffin Bell said, "I think the whole country ought to be pleased."

Some criticized Powell's opinion for lacking a solid, consistent theory behind it. "The solution may seem statesmanlike, but as constitutional argument, it leaves you hungry an hour later," said conservative scholar Robert Bork, who later would be nominated to succeed Powell. Some civil rights leaders also were angry at the decision's bottom line: that Bakke, a white man who they felt did not need a helping hand from government, would be going to medical school. (Bakke ultimately graduated and became an anesthesiologist in Minnesota, where he has avoided publicity about his role in the case.)

But others more optimistically pointed out that *Bakke* was a quarrel over how to help minorities achieve equality, not over whether that was a worthy goal. "*Bakke* was not only a symbol of how far toward racial justice we still have to go, but of how very far since *Brown* [*v. Board of Education*] we had come," wrote J. Harvie Wilkinson III in the book *From Brown to Bakke*.

After Justice Powell retired from the bench, he described the *Bakke* decision as the most important of his tenure. Indeed it has framed the debate over affirmative action ever since, even if it failed to resolve that debate.

For years after *Bakke,* the Court issued similarly fractured opinions on the issue, with Powell always in the majority, whatever that happened to be. Generally, the Court upheld affirmative action programs. In *United Steelworkers v. Weber* (1979) the Court approved a 50 percent set-aside for blacks in a private steel industry training program. In *Fullilove v. Klutznick* (1980) the Court said a federal program aiding minority contractors was constitutional. In *Johnson v. Santa Clara County* (1987) a program that benefited women as well as minorities was approved.

While generally approving programs that gave preference to minorities and women for future positions or benefits, the Court disapproved of affirmative action plans that resulted in whites losing jobs they already had. In *Firefighters Local Union No. 1794 v. Stotts* (1984) and *Wygant v. Jackson Board of Education* (1986), the Court struck down policies that exposed white workers to being laid off during budget cutbacks even though they had more seniority than minorities.

After Powell retired, and Reagan and Bush appointees dominated the Court, the Court grew more hostile toward affirmative action. In 1989 the Court in *Richmond v. J.A. Croson Co.* applied strict scrutiny to a local program that required city contractors to give 30 percent of their subcontracting work to minority firms. The 6–3 decision said the city had not provided evidence of past discrimination in the area of the economy that was the plan targeted.

The retirement of Justice Marshall in 1991 and the arrival of Clarence Thomas, a conservative black justice, meant further trouble for affirmative action. Thomas once offered the view that voting in favor of affirmative action would violate his personal religious beliefs, because it meant treating people unfairly. He argues that affirmative action programs stigmatize the minority individuals who benefit from them.

In an important decision in 1995, the Court scrutinized one of the many federal set-aside programs that had flourished since the *Fullilove* decision. The 5–4 decision in *Adarand Constructors v. Pena* again applied strict scrutiny and said race-based classifications had to be narrowly tailored to further a compelling state interest. "In the eyes of government," wrote Justice Antonin Scalia, "we are all one race here. It is American." The Court sent the case back to lower courts for further review, and in 1997 a judge ruled in favor of Adarand, a white-owned company that claimed the set-aside program was discriminatory. The *Adarand* decision was a major setback for affirmative action. President Bill Clinton sought to salvage the concept with a "mend it, don't end it" approach.

In an ironic footnote to the *Bakke* case, California voters in 1996 approved Proposition 209, ending all affirmative action programs in government hiring and contracts as well as in state university admissions. The incoming class at the University of California-Davis medical school in 1998 included five black and three Hispanic students.

That kind of dip in enrollment, as well as the Court's increasing disenchantment with affirmative action, led political leaders to begin searching for other ways to achieve greater diversity. One approach that seemed promising in state university admissions was to accept the top 10 percent of the graduating class of any school in the state, regardless of race.

In 2003 the issue of affirmative action returned to the Supreme Court in the case of *Grutter v. Bollinger,* a challenge to the University of Michigan Law School's affirmative action program. To the surprise of many, the Court by a 5–4 vote upheld the program, stating that achieving a diverse student body was in fact a valid goal for a state university. The fact that the law school viewed race as one of many factors in a "holistic" assessment of applicants, as well as the endorsement of affirmative action by major corporations and the military, appeared to sway the justices. On the same day, however, the Court issued a ruling in a companion case, *Gratz v. Bollinger,* involving the affirmative action program used in Michigan's undergraduate admissions. That program, which gave minority students a numerical bonus, struck the Court as a form of a quota and was deemed unconstitutional.

Grutter v. Bollinger

Decided June 23, 2003
539 U.S. 306
laws.findlaw.com/US/000/02-241.html

DECISION

The limited use of race as a factor in admitting students to a state-run law school does not violate the Constitution's equal protection clause if it is aimed at the valid goal of attaining a diverse student body.

BACKGROUND

The Supreme Court's fractured decision in the 1978 case *Regents of the University of California v. Bakke* never ended the debate over affirmative action; in fact, the ruling may have kept it alive, at least in the context of public university admissions. Justice Lewis Powell Jr. wrote the decisive opinion in the *Bakke* case upholding affirmative action, breaking a 4–4 tie, but the fact that no other justice joined in his opinion left it vulnerable to attack and left university officials uncertain about how extensively they could use race as a positive factor in admissions or in other government benefits or programs.

This uncertainty increased as federal appeals courts and the Supreme Court became increasingly hostile toward affirmative action. In 1996, in a lawsuit brought by white student Cheryl Hopwood, the U.S. Court of Appeals for the Fifth Circuit ruled that the affirmative action program used to give black and Hispanic applicants a boost at the University of Texas was a form of unconstitutional race discrimination. This ruling meant that affirmative action programs could not be used in Texas, Louisiana, and Mississippi—the states in the jurisdiction of the fifth circuit court—while they were legal elsewhere in the country. More than two decades after *Bakke,* it became time for the Supreme Court to look at the issue again.

The vehicle for that reexamination was a lawsuit brought by Barbara Grutter, who was rejected for admission into the University of Michigan Law School in 1997. The state-run law school is highly competitive, accepting only about one in ten people who apply. Since 1992 it had used a "flexible" admissions policy that used typical criteria like grade point average and Law School Admissions Test results, along with other factors including race. Its stated goal was to admit a "critical mass" of students from underrepresented minorities to enrich the learning experience at the law school. Although not a quota or a specific numerical goal, the term "critical mass" implied enough members of a given minority that each person in that group would not feel isolated or be viewed as a "spokesperson" for that minority.

In her lawsuit against then–university president Lee Bollinger, Grutter claimed that her rejection was the direct result of the university's "racially discriminatory procedures and practices." The university responded that it has used race as a factor, but only "as part of a broad array of qualifications and characteristics."

A U.S. district court judge in Michigan, invoking *Bakke,* struck down the program as a form of illegal race discrimination. The U.S. Court of Appeals for the Sixth Circuit reversed, also citing *Bakke,* but this time to uphold the program. The appeals court accepted evidence that without using race as a plus factor, the percentage of minorities in the student body entering the law school in 2000 would have been 4 percent instead of 14 percent. Achieving diversity in its student body, the court ruled, was a valid goal for the University of Michigan.

As the *Grutter* case made its way to the Supreme Court, both sides in the affirmative action debate portrayed it as either the death knell or the salvation of such policies. Dozens of briefs flowed into the Supreme Court from groups extolling or attacking affirmative action. The Bush administration sided with opponents of the Michigan program, though it did not flatly oppose affirmative action in all circumstances.

One indication of the importance of the case was how the Supreme Court handled a parallel case brought by white applicants to the University of Michigan's undergraduate program. Jennifer Gratz and Patrick Hamacher challenged the undergraduate affirmative action program, which differed from the law school program in that it assigned a point value to an applicant's minority status. A district court judge struck down the

Left to right, Barbara Grutter and Jennifer Gratz, two plaintiffs in the University of Michigan affirmative action cases, leave a news conference in 2003. The Supreme Court's fractured decision *Regents of the University of California v. Bakke* (1978) left university officials uncertain about the use of race in admissions and in other government programs. This uncertainty led to reexamination of the issue in *Grutter v. Bollinger* (2003) and *Gratz v. Bollinger* (2003).
Source: AP/Wide World Photos/Paul Sancya.

undergraduate program for many of the same reasons that the law school system was also overruled. When the undergraduate case went to the appeals court, for reasons that have not been explained, it was never ruled on. The Supreme Court, apparently interested in ruling on both programs at the same time, took the unusual step of reaching down to the district court level to add the *Gratz* case to its docket, even though the appeals court had not ruled.

VOTE

5–4, with Justice Sandra Day O'Connor writing for the majority, joined by Justices John Paul Stevens, David Souter, Ruth Bader Ginsburg, and Stephen Breyer. Chief Justice William Rehnquist and Justices Antonin Scalia, Anthony Kennedy, and Clarence Thomas dissented in whole or in part.

HIGHLIGHTS

Justice O'Connor was viewed as the pivotal justice who would decide the case for an otherwise divided court. Many briefs and arguments were directed at winning her vote, but in the end it was the late Justice Powell who swayed her toward approving affirmative action. It was no surprise that O'Connor's touchstone—the starting point for her decision—was Powell's opinion in *Bakke*. Justice O'Connor viewed Powell as her mentor on the Court. Before he died in 1998, Powell often boasted that he was the first Supreme Court justice to have danced with

another justice—namely O'Connor, the Court's first female member.

Since Bakke, she said, "Public and private universities across the Nation have modeled their own admissions programs on Justice Powell's views on permissible race-conscious policies." After analyzing his opinion at length, O'Connor concluded, "Today we endorse Justice Powell's view that student body diversity is a compelling state interest that can justify the use of race in university admissions."

O'Connor's next step was to analyze the Michigan law school program using "strict scrutiny"—the standard that is hardest for government programs to meet.

Achieving diversity was a goal that served not only the University of Michigan's needs, but society's as well, O'Connor wrote. She cited briefs filed by major corporations as well as by high-ranking retired military officers who claimed that affirmative action programs were still necessary to fill the ranks of their workforce with qualified and diverse employees. The negative consequences for society of putting an abrupt end to affirmative action altogether appeared to weigh heavily in O'Connor's decision.

Finally, O'Connor analyzed the specifics of the law school program to find that "it bears the hallmarks" of a narrowly tailored plan—another key part of the strict scrutiny test. As the Court had in *Bakke,* O'Connor said an actual quota for minority applicants would not be acceptable. But by making race one of many factors in an individualized, "holistic" assessment of each applicant, Michigan law school had achieved the narrow tailoring the Court was looking for. She rejected the Bush administration's view that all race-neutral alternatives had to be tried first before affirmative action could be employed.

O'Connor offered her own bit of tailoring to university affirmative action programs, announcing that they should not last indefinitely. Twenty-five years hence—or fifty years after the *Bakke* decision—affirmative action should no longer be necessary to achieve the goals that Michigan and other schools had in adopting them, O'Connor said.

Dissenting justices said that no matter what the intentions of the program, government institutions like Michigan's law school should not be treating people of different races differently under the Constitution. Chief Justice Rehnquist offered statistics to support his view that the law school program does in fact amount to a quota. "Stripped of its 'critical mass' veil, the law school's program is revealed as a naked effort to achieve racial balancing," Rehnquist wrote. Justice Clarence Thomas approved of O'Connor's twenty-five-year time limit on affirmative action in higher education, but added, "I believe that the law school's current use of race violated the Equal Protection Clause and that the Constitution means the same thing today as it will in 300 months."

EXCERPTS

From Justice O'Connor's majority opinion: "In order to cultivate a set of leaders with legitimacy in the eyes of the citizenry, it is necessary that the path to leadership be visibly open to talented and qualified individuals of every race and ethnicity. All members of our heterogeneous society must have confidence in the openness and integrity of the educational institutions that provide this training. . . . Access to legal education (and thus the legal profession) must be inclusive of talented and qualified individuals of every race and ethnicity, so that all members of our heterogeneous society may participate in the educational institutions that provide the training and education necessary to succeed in America. . . .

"We are mindful, however, that '[a] core purpose of the Fourteenth Amendment was to do away with all governmentally imposed discrimination based on race.' . . . Accordingly, race-conscious admissions policies must be limited in time. This requirement reflects that racial classifications, however compelling their goals, are potentially so dangerous that they may be employed no more broadly than the interest demands. . . . We expect that 25 years from now, the use of racial preferences will no longer be necessary to further the interest approved today."

IMPACT

On the same day the Court handed down *Grutter*, it also decided *Gratz v. Bollinger*, the separate challenge to the undergraduate Michigan affirmative action program. By a 6–3 vote, the Court struck down that program, finding that by assigning a specific number of points to minority status, it veered too closely to a forbidden quota for minority applicants. Most minorities were virtually guaranteed of admission, the Court found, in contrast to the law school's individualized judgment.

The combination of the two rulings on the same day gave both sides in the affirmative action debate something to cheer about. Even President Bush, who had filed a brief in the case against the university's programs, said, "I applaud the Supreme Court for recognizing the value of diversity on our Nation's campuses. . . . Today's decisions seek a careful balance between the goal of campus diversity and the fundamental principle of equal treatment under the law."

But most commentators suggested that in the long run the *Grutter* decision involving the law school had more lasting significance. After twenty-five years, a period when affirmative action programs often seemed doomed, a majority of the justices had signed onto the once-solitary views of Justice Powell. Affirmative action programs had been endorsed by corporate America, the military, and now the Supreme Court itself. In the brief period since the ruling, it appears that at least some of the passion has gone out of the debate over affirmative action.

The rulings were largely welcomed in academia for providing a clearer blueprint for the kind of affirmative actions programs that were acceptable. Some larger universities complained that the "holistic" assessment of applicants the Court seemed to prefer would require much more money and staff. The Center for Individual Rights, which provided legal help to the white students in both Michigan cases, promised to monitor state universities to ensure they did not ignore the high court's limits on affirmative action.

CAPITAL PUNISHMENT

$\mathcal{F}$ew issues have been more troubling for the Supreme Court—and for the nation—than capital punishment. Prisoners have been executed for their crimes since before the founding of the nation. But beginning in the last half of the twentieth century and continuing into the twenty-first, capital punishment has been questioned in a variety of ways. Pointing to the high percentage of minorities and lower-income inmates on death rows nationwide, some question whether death penalties are imposed fairly. In recent years DNA testing has made it possible to demonstrate that some inmates awaiting execution are actually innocent. But it is the Eighth Amendment's prohibition against "cruel and unusual" punishment that keeps the debate going before the Court, as the justices measure capital punishment procedures and methods against changing laws and sentiment in the United States and abroad.

Other related cases mentioned in the Capital Punishment section

Trop v. Dulles (1958)
Maxwell v. Bishop (1968)
Gregg v. Georgia (1976)
Woodson v. North Carolina (1976)
Coker v. Georgia (1977)
Enmund v. Florida (1982)
Ford v. Wainwright (1986)
McCleskey v. Kemp (1987)
Stanford v. Kentucky (1989)
Herrera v. Collins (1993)
Callins v. Collins (1994)
Atkins v. Virginia (2002)

Furman v. Georgia

Decided June 29, 1972
408 U.S. 238
laws.findlaw.com/US/408/238.html

DECISION

Capital punishment, as it is imposed and carried out, violates the Eighth Amendment to the Constitution, which prohibits "cruel and unusual" punishments.

BACKGROUND

The death penalty has been part of the U.S. justice system since the earliest days. The First Congress in 1790 made murder, forgery, robbery, and rape punishable by death. The Fifth Amendment to the Constitution presumed the death penalty's existence by guaranteeing due process of law before a criminal defendant could be deprived "of life or limb."

But that history has not prevented capital punishment from being a constitutional flashpoint in the Supreme Court's history. The primary reason is the Eighth Amendment, which says that "cruel and unusual punishments" shall not be inflicted. Unlike other commands of the Constitution, these words have seemed unusually subjective, hard to define without reference to shifting public sentiment. Flogging may have seemed neither cruel nor unusual in colonial days, but now most would agree that it is both, as well as anachronistic.

After World War II other nations began abolishing the death penalty. In the United States the civil rights movement also created abolitionist pressure because death sentences were meted out disproportionately to black defendants. One 1966 study found that of 119 convicted rapists in the South who were executed after World War II, 110 were black.

The NAACP Legal Defense and Educational Fund and the American Civil Liberties Union (ACLU) launched a campaign to challenge death sentences in all of the forty-two jurisdictions that had death penalty laws. The aim was to slow down executions to the point of a virtual moratorium. In 1968 the goal was reached: it was the first year in the nation's history in which no one was executed.

That was also the year in which the Supreme Court came close to striking down a death penalty law for the first time. In *Maxwell v. Bishop,* six of the nine justices voted to reject Alabama's death penalty law because it did not call for separate consideration of the death penalty after a finding of guilt. In other words, the same jury that found a defendant guilty had wide leeway to simultaneously sentence the defendant to death. Many legal experts had argued the finding of guilt and the sentencing should be separate, partly to enable a defen-

dant to testify in favor of a lower sentence without exposing himself or herself to questioning about guilt.

A 6–3 vote in that case would have dramatically weakened death penalty laws nationwide. But it never came to pass. According to *The Brethren* by Bob Woodward and Scott Armstrong, Justice Douglas wrote an overly broad ruling, which scared off a justice, making it a 5–4 vote. Justice Abe Fortas then resigned, turning it into a 4–4 tie. By the time the case was reargued, two Nixon appointees had joined the Court, and the tide shifted in favor of the death penalty.

But public sentiment seemed to be turning the other way. Former attorney general Ramsey Clark came out against the death penalty, declaring, "It is the poor, the sick, the ignorant, the powerless, and the hated who are executed."

The continuing tide of death penalty appeals made it inevitable that the Court would take up the issue again. In June 1971 the Court agreed to consider two Georgia cases and one from Texas that challenged the constitutionality of the death penalty.

They became known collectively as *Furman v. Georgia,* taking the name of the case of William Furman, a twenty-six-year-old black man convicted of murdering a white woman while he was burglarizing her house. He claimed it was an accidental shooting, but because it occurred during a felony, Furman was sentenced to the electric chair. The other two cases involved black defendants sentenced to death for raping white women. Although the cases posed many of the issues of racial bias and arbitrariness upon which death penalty opponents were pinning their hopes, chances of defeating the death penalty were widely viewed as slim.

VOTE

5–4, with an unsigned (per curiam) opinion. In the majority were Justices William O. Douglas, William J. Brennan Jr., Potter Stewart, Byron R. White, and Thurgood Marshall. Dissenting were Chief Justice Warren E. Burger and Justices Harry A. Blackmun, Lewis F. Powell Jr., and William Rehnquist.

HIGHLIGHTS

The basic holding of the Court, declaring capital punishment unconstitutional, is contained in a one-paragraph unsigned opinion of the Court. All nine justices wrote separately to express their views, making it clear that this case caused consid-

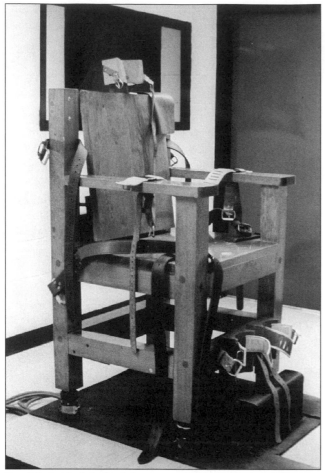

Georgia's electric chair. After being sentenced to the electric chair, William Furman, a twenty-six-year-old black man convicted of murdering a white woman, challenged the constitutionality of the death penalty. In *Furman v. Georgia* (1972), the justices ruled the imposition and carrying out of capital punishment a violation of the Eighth Amendment's prohibition on "cruel and unusual" punishment.

Source: Reuters.

erable strife within the Court. According to *The Brethren,* Justice Stewart later told friends he had lost sleep over the case, sobered by the knowledge that the decision would affect the lives of more than 700 people on death row.

The justices in the majority had the challenging task of justifying a constitutional end to capital punishment when it was acknowledged in the Constitution. And the fact that a vast majority of states had not overturned the death penalty made it hard to argue that society viewed it as cruel and unusual.

On the first problem, Justice Brennan's separate opinion conceded the point that the Constitution contemplated capital punishment. "We can thus infer that the Framers recognized the existence of what was then a common punishment. We cannot, however, make the further inference that they intended to exempt this particular punishment from the express prohibition of the Cruel and Unusual Punishments Clause."

On the second problem, Brennan insisted that there was no way to look at capital punishment as anything but cruel and unusual. "In comparison to all other punishments today, then, the deliberate extinguishment of human life by the State is uniquely degrading to human dignity. I would not hesitate to hold, on that ground alone, that death is today a 'cruel and unusual' punishment, were it not that death is a punishment of longstanding usage and acceptance in this country." His answer to that was that, even though it is accepted, it is not ordinary or usual. "When a country of over 200 million people inflicts an unusually severe punishment no more than 50 times a year, the inference is strong that the punishment is not being regularly and fairly applied."

Justice Marshall, who had challenged the death penalty as a civil rights lawyer before joining the Court, voiced similar views that the death penalty was in all respects unconstitutional. He cited a non–death penalty case from 1958 that said the limits of the Eighth Amendment ban on cruel and unusual punishment depended on "evolving standards of decency." Marshall went on to assert that capital punishment is ineffective, arbitrarily meted out, and occasionally puts an innocent man to death. It was "morally unacceptable," he said.

The other three justices in the majority struck down the death penalty on narrower grounds, viewing it as rarely and arbitrarily applied and ineffective. Stewart said the death penalty was used in a "freakish" manner. But by not saying it was unconstitutional in all cases, these justices implied that if death penalty laws were revised and improved, they could be made constitutional.

Dissenting justices in general deferred to the judgment of the legislators who had enacted death penalty laws and said that out of respect for federal-state relations, the Court should not be second-guessing them.

"If we were possessed of legislative power, I would either join with Mr. Justice Brennan and Mr. Justice Marshall or, at the very least, restrict the use of capital punishment to a small category of the most heinous crimes," wrote Chief Justice Burger. Justice Powell also noted the Court's own "unswerving" support for capital punishment over the decades as evidence that it could not be viewed as unconstitutional now.

"The most expansive reading of the leading constitutional cases does not remotely suggest that this Court has been granted a roving commission," said Rehnquist, ". . . to strike down laws that are based upon notions of policy or morality suddenly found unacceptable by a majority of this Court."

EXCERPTS

From the per curiam (unsigned) opinion: "The Court holds that the imposition and carrying out of the death penalty in these cases constitute cruel and unusual punishment in violation of the Eighth and Fourteenth Amendments." (All nine justices wrote separate opinions, none of which represented the views of the Court. Because of this unusual arrangement, excerpts from the nine opinions follow.)

Justice Douglas's concurrence: "[W]e deal with a system of law and of justice that leaves to the uncontrolled discretion of judges or juries the determination whether defendants committing these crimes should die or be imprisoned. Under these laws no standards govern the selection of the penalty. People live or die, dependent on the whim of one man or of 12. . . .

"[T]hese discretionary statutes are unconstitutional in their operation. They are pregnant with discrimination and discrimination is an ingredient not compatible with the idea of equal protection of the laws that is implicit in the ban on 'cruel and unusual' punishments."

Justice Brennan's concurrence: "Death is an unusually severe and degrading punishment; there is a strong probability that it is inflicted arbitrarily; its rejection by contemporary society is virtually total; and there is no reason to believe that it serves any penal purpose more effectively than the less severe punishment of imprisonment. The function of these principles is to enable a court to determine whether a punishment comports with human dignity. Death, quite simply, does not."

Justice Stewart's concurrence: "These death sentences are cruel and unusual in the same way that being struck by lightning is cruel and unusual. For, of all the people convicted of rapes and murders in 1967 and 1968, many just as reprehensible as these, the petitioners are among a capriciously selected random handful upon whom the sentence of death has in fact been imposed."

Justice White's concurrence: "The imposition and execution of the death penalty are obviously cruel in the dictionary sense. But the penalty has not been considered cruel and unusual punishment in the constitutional sense because it was thought justified by the social ends it was deemed to serve. At the moment that it ceases realistically to further these purposes, however, the emerging question is whether its imposition in such circumstances would violate the Eighth Amendment. . . .

"[T]his point has been reached with respect to capital punishment as it is presently administered under the statutes involved in these cases."

Justice Marshall's concurrence: "There is but one conclusion that can be drawn from all of this—i.e., the death penalty is an excessive and unnecessary punishment that violates the Eighth Amendment. . . .

"In addition, even if capital punishment is not excessive, it nonetheless violates the Eighth Amendment because it is morally unacceptable to the people of the United States at this time in their history. . . .

"I believe that the following facts would serve to convince even the most hesitant of citizens to condemn death as a sanc-

tion: capital punishment is imposed discriminatorily against certain identifiable classes of people; there is evidence that innocent people have been executed before their innocence can be proved; and the death penalty wreaks havoc with our entire criminal justice system. . . .

"In striking down capital punishment, this Court does not malign our system of government. On the contrary, it pays homage to it."

Chief Justice Burger's dissent: "There are no obvious indications that capital punishment offends the conscience of society to such a degree that our traditional deference to the legislative judgment must be abandoned. It is not a punishment such as burning at the stake that everyone would ineffably find to be repugnant to all civilized standards. Nor is it a punishment so roundly condemned that only a few aberrant legislatures have retained it on the statute books."

Justice Blackmun's dissent: "Cases such as these provide for me an excruciating agony of the spirit. I yield to no one in the depth of my distaste, antipathy, and, indeed, abhorrence, for the death penalty, with all its aspects of physical distress and fear and of moral judgment exercised by finite minds. That distaste is buttressed by a belief that capital punishment serves no useful purpose that can be demonstrated. . . . Were I a legislator, I would vote against the death penalty for the policy reasons argued by counsel for the respective petitioners and expressed and adopted in the several opinions filed by the Justices who vote to reverse these judgments. . . .

"I do not sit on these cases, however, as a legislator, responsive, at least in part, to the will of constituents. Our task here, as must so frequently be emphasized and reemphasized, is to pass upon the constitutionality of legislation that has been enacted and that is challenged. This is the sole task for judges."

Justice Powell's dissent: "In terms of the constitutional role of this Court, the impact of the majority's ruling is all the greater because the decision encroaches upon an area squarely within the historic prerogative of the legislative branch—both state and federal—to protect the citizenry through the designation of penalties for prohibitable conduct. It is the very sort of judgment that the legislative branch is competent to make, and for which the judiciary is ill-equipped. . . .

"It seems to me that the sweeping judicial action undertaken today reflects a basic lack of faith and confidence in the democratic process."

Justice Rehnquist's dissent: "[T]oday's holding necessarily brings into sharp relief the fundamental question of the role of judicial review in a democratic society. How can government by the elected representatives of the people co-exist with the power of the federal judiciary, whose members are constitutionally insulated from responsiveness to the popular will, to declare invalid laws duly enacted by the popular branches of government?"

IMPACT

The Court's decision in *Furman v. Georgia* caused what one commentator called a "constitutional earthquake." In a single decision the Court invalidated all existing capital punishment laws and removed the threat of death for hundreds of prison inmates. Anthony Amsterdam, who had argued before the Court against capital punishment in the case, said the ruling represented "the biggest step forward that criminal justice has taken in a 1,000 years."

As sweeping as the decision was, scholars often view it as a failure. When the Court made a similarly sweeping decision in 1954 in *Brown v. Board of Education* declaring an end to segregated public schools, it did so in a relatively brief, forceful, and unanimous decision. In *Furman,* by contrast, no two justices could completely agree on a rationale for abolishing the death penalty, or preserving it, for that matter. All nine justices wrote separately, producing one of the longest Supreme Court decisions in history at 234 pages.

"Not one of the justices in the majority thought to reconsider his vote rather than march forward in total disarray," wrote Edward Lazarus in the 1998 book *Closed Chambers.* Without a clear statement of its reasoning, the Court failed to win public support for its decision. Support for capital punishment actually increased after the ruling, according to polls that showed public resentment toward the Court.

Legislators moved quickly to follow the roadmap provided by the dissenting justices in *Furman* to devise new death penalty laws that would pass constitutional muster. Burger had written, "Since there is no majority of the Court on the ultimate issue presented in these cases, the future of capital punishment in this country has been left in an uncertain limbo. . . . The legislatures are free to eliminate capital punishment for specific crimes or to carve out limited exceptions to a general abolition of the penalty, without adherence to the conceptual strictures of the Eighth Amendment."

Some legislatures enacted laws that made the death penalty mandatory for certain crimes, hoping to remove the arbitrariness that had upset the Court majority. Others took a nearly opposite approach, passing laws that called for "guided discretion," forcing juries to consider specific mitigating and aggravating circumstances before sentencing anyone to death. Many states separated the sentencing process from the finding of guilt.

As thirty-five states began enforcing these new laws, appeals started up again, and again the Supreme Court ruled. This time, in *Gregg v. Georgia* and two companion cases from Florida and Texas in 1976, the Court endorsed "guided discretion" and separate proceedings for finding guilt and sentencing. The 7–2 decision also found that capital punishment did not in all circumstances violate the Eighth Amendment.

"The concerns expressed in *Furman* that the penalty of death not be imposed in an arbitrary or capricious manner can be met by a carefully drafted statute that ensures that the sentencing authority is given adequate information and guidance," Justice Stewart wrote in *Gregg.*

In a separate ruling on the same day, the Court in *Woodson v. North Carolina* struck down laws that made the death penalty automatic for certain crimes. Such statutes, said Stewart, treat individual defendants as a "faceless, undifferentiated mass to be subjected to the blind infliction of the penalty of death."

The *Gregg* decision meant that after a four-year interruption, capital punishment was again constitutional. Utah inmate Gary Gilmore, who gave up his appeals, ended what amounted to a ten-year moratorium on the death penalty when he was executed by a firing squad in January 1977. Since then, more than 500 death row inmates have been executed. Nearly 3,500 people await execution in the nation's prisons.

With a resumption of the death penalty came a resumption of the Court's handling of more routine death penalty cases that in some instances limited the scope of capital punishment. In *Coker v. Georgia* (1977) the Court said death was too harsh a penalty for the crime of rape, and in *Enmund v. Florida* (1982) the Court said death could not be imposed on a murder accomplice who did not pull the trigger or witness the crime. After limiting capital punishment to convicted murderers, the Court then began carving out exceptions that made capital punishment unconstitutional for specific categories of murderers: the insane (*Ford v. Wainwright,* 1986), the mentally retarded (*Atkins v. Virginia,* 2002) or the too-young (*Roper v. Simmons,* 2005). The *Roper* decision said no one younger than eighteen at the time of the crime could be sentenced to death.

At the same time, as the Court became more conservative in the 1990s, it began to reject many procedural challenges to the death penalty and it streamlined procedures to shorten the time—often upwards of ten years—between a defendant's death sentence and the actual execution. In an important 1987 case, *McCleskey v. Kemp,* the Court rejected statistical evidence indicating that black defendants who had killed whites were the most likely to be sentenced to death. Such a disparity, the Court held, did not make the system unconstitutional. In 1993 the Court ruled in *Herrera v. Collins* that a defendant's last-minute claim of innocence did not entitle him to federal review of his sentence.

Even as the Court continued to support the death penalty, Justices Marshall and Brennan held to their view that the death

penalty was in all circumstances unconstitutional. After they retired, Justice Blackmun, who had struggled with the issue since
Furman, reached the same conclusion as Marshall and Brennan. Dissenting in 1994 from the Court's decision not to review
Callins v. Collins, Blackmun wrote, "From this day forward, I no
longer shall tinker with the machinery of death." He continued,
"I feel morally and intellectually obligated simply to concede
that the death penalty experiment has failed." Blackmun retired
later that year, leaving behind a Court that had no members who
were categorically opposed to capital punishment.

Thompson v. Oklahoma

Decided June 29, 1988
487 U.S. 815
laws.findlaw.com/US/487/815.html

DECISION

Executing someone who was younger than sixteen at the time
of the crime for which he or she is being punished amounts to
"cruel and unusual" punishment, which is barred by the Eighth
Amendment to the Constitution.

BACKGROUND

William Wayne Thompson was fifteen when he, along with
three older friends, brutally murdered his former brother-in-law
in 1983 in Oklahoma. All four defendants were tried separately
for the murder, and all four were sentenced to death.

Because Thompson was still a child in the eyes of the law,
before the trial the district attorney went through a legal procedure aimed at determining if Thompson was mentally competent to stand trial and whether he understood that murder was
wrong. After a hearing, the trial judge ruled that Thompson
could stand trial.

On appeal, Thompson's conviction and sentence were upheld. Oklahoma's highest criminal appeals court ruled that
"once a minor is certified to stand trial as an adult, he may
also, without violating the Constitution, be punished as an
adult."

The case arrived at the Supreme Court at a time when it
was still trying to sort out a number of ramifications of its 1976
revival of capital punishment in *Gregg v. Georgia.* Cases testing
whether it was appropriate to execute the mentally disabled or
to take racial factors into consideration were making their way
to the Court. The Court had never before ruled on whether it
was appropriate to execute convicted murderers who were juveniles when they committed the crime.

VOTE

5–3, with Justice John Paul Stevens writing the majority opinion. Joining him were Justices William J. Brennan Jr., Thurgood
Marshall, and Harry A. Blackmun. Justice Sandra Day O'Connor
wrote a separate opinion concurring in the judgment. Dissenting were Chief Justice William Rehnquist and Justices Byron R.
White and Antonin Scalia. Justice Anthony M. Kennedy did not
participate.

HIGHLIGHTS

The Eighth Amendment bars "cruel and unusual" punishment,
but never defines what that phrase means. Since 1958 the
Court has determined that both factors—cruel and unusual—
were subjective terms that had to be defined in terms of the
laws and sensibilities of the time. Punishment that was viewed
as neither cruel nor unusual two centuries ago—such as public
flogging or beheading—could be viewed entirely differently
today, and the Court struggled with how to make that determination. As the Court put it in the 1958 decision *Trop v. Dulles,*
the meaning of the Eighth Amendment has to be judged according to "evolving standards of decency that mark the
progress of a maturing society."

In *Thompson v. Oklahoma,* as with other Eighth Amendment cases, the Court assessed the relevant "standards of decency" by looking at many factors, some of which may sound
like taking a popularity poll, but which the Court defends as fulfilling the command of the Eighth Amendment. Looking at legislation in Oklahoma and nationwide, the Court determined
that there was virtual unanimity in treating young people under
sixteen as children for most purposes—ranging from voting to
serving on juries. In all states, Justice Stevens noted, the jurisdiction of juvenile courts reaches up to age sixteen. "All of this
legislation is consistent with the experience of mankind, as
well as the long history of our law, that the normal 15-year-old
is not prepared to assume the full responsibilities of an adult."

More relevant to the case at hand, the Court found that all
of the eighteen states that set a minimum age for the death

penalty require that the defendant have passed his or her sixteenth birthday at the time of the crime. The laws of other nations follow the same pattern.

The Court also looked at the behavior of juries. Stevens noted that the last time someone had been executed for a crime committed under the age of sixteen was 1948.

Another basic tenet of death penalty law is that it is a punishment reserved for those who can truly be held culpable or blameworthy for their crime. In a civilized society, executing someone who cannot fully understand the seriousness of his or her crime or the gravity of the punishment would be inhumane, akin to killing an innocent animal. So the question for the Court was whether someone who is younger than sixteen could have the full awareness necessary to be executed for his or her crime. The Court decided that fifteen-year-olds do not pass that test.

One of the major justifications for the death penalty, deterring others from committing similar crimes, is also nonexistent for juveniles, Stevens said. "The likelihood that the teenage offender has made the kind of costbenefit [sic] analysis that attaches any weight to the possibility of execution is so remote as to be virtually nonexistent."

In dissent, Justice Scalia pointed to the laws of nineteen states that set no minimum age for executions. From that, he concluded that the national consensus would affirm, not contradict, what Oklahoma did in the *Thompson* case. "The statistics of executions demonstrate nothing except the fact that our society has always agreed that executions of 15-year-old criminals should be rare, and in more modern times has agreed that they (like all other executions) should be even rarer still. There is no rational basis for discerning in that a societal judgment that no one so much as a day under 16 can ever be mature and morally responsible enough to deserve that penalty; and there is no justification except our own predilection for converting a statistical rarity of occurrence into an absolute constitutional ban."

In a concurrence, Justice O'Connor struck a middle position. She said the Court could not be sure what the consensus is on juveniles unless it was clear that individual states had actually considered the issue and established a minimum age. Therefore, she said, juvenile executions should be banned only in those states in which the legislature has not established a minimum age. "The conclusion I have reached in this unusual case is itself unusual," she wrote. "I believe, however, that it is in keeping with the principles that have guided us in other Eighth Amendment cases. . . . By leaving open for now the broader Eighth Amendment question that both the plurality and the dissent would resolve, the approach I take allows the ultimate moral issue at stake in the constitutional question to be addressed in the first instance by those best suited to do so, the people's elected representatives."

EXCERPTS

From Justice Stevens' majority opinion: "The line between childhood and adulthood is drawn in different ways by various States. There is, however, complete or near unanimity among all 50 States and the District of Columbia in treating a person under 16 as a minor for several important purposes. . . .

"The conclusion that it would offend civilized standards of decency to execute a person who was less than 16 years old at the time of his or her offense is consistent with the views that have been expressed by respected professional organizations, by other nations that share our Anglo-American heritage, and by the leading members of the Western European community. . . .

"The road we have traveled during the past four decades—in which thousands of juries have tried murder cases—leads to the unambiguous conclusion that the imposition of the death penalty on a 15-year-old offender is now generally abhorrent to the conscience of the community. . . .

"The Court has already endorsed the proposition that less culpability should attach to a crime committed by a juvenile than to a comparable crime committed by an adult. The basis for this conclusion is too obvious to require extended explanation. Inexperience, less education, and less intelligence make the teenager less able to evaluate the consequences of his or her conduct while at the same time he or she is much more apt to be motivated by mere emotion or peer pressure than is an adult. The reasons why juveniles are not trusted with the privileges and responsibilities of an adult also explain why their irresponsible conduct is not as morally reprehensible as that of an adult."

IMPACT

Thompson v. Oklahoma was not the Court's final word on the subject of executing juveniles. The Court had ended executions for those under sixteen, but what about those who were between their sixteenth and eighteenth birthdays? One year later, in *Stanford v. Kentucky,* the Court answered that question, ruling that it was constitutional to execute someone who was seventeen at the time of the crime. This, the Court said, did not violate "evolving standards of decency."

The issue returned to the Court in 2005. The Court had just found capital punishment unconstitutional for the mentally retarded, and many of the same reasons—lack of maturity and knowledge of the seriousness of their acts—seemed to apply to juveniles as well. And in the fifteen years since *Stanford v. Kentucky,* executing juveniles had lost favor in the United States and worldwide. In *Roper v. Simmons* the Court by a 5–4 vote put an end to executing juveniles in the United States.

Roper v. Simmons

Decided March 1, 2005
No. 03-633
laws.findlaw.com/US/000/03-633.html

DECISION

The Eighth Amendment's prohibition against "cruel and unusual punishment" is violated when someone younger than eighteen at the time of his or her crime is executed. Capital punishment should be reserved for the worst offenders; juveniles, because of their immaturity and lack of judgment, cannot be placed in that category.

BACKGROUND

One day when seventeen-year-old Christopher Simmons was a junior in high school, he announced to his friends that he wanted to kill somebody. Accompanied by a friend on the night of September 8, 1993, Simmons did just that. They broke into the suburban St. Louis home of Shirley Crook and tied her up with duct tape. They took her to a nearby state park, reinforced the tape with wire, and threw her from a bridge into the Meramec River. She drowned, and the next day two fishermen found her body.

Meanwhile Simmons was bragging to school friends about the murder, and soon police arrested him. At the police station in Fenton, Missouri, Simmons confessed to the murder. The state charged him with burglary, kidnapping, and murder and urged jurors to impose the death penalty at his trial in adult court.

Simmons' guilt was never in doubt, but his lawyers did argue against the death penalty. At age seventeen, they argued, Simmons could not buy alcohol or see certain movies because lawmakers believe young people that age are not responsible enough. Similarly, they argued that Simmons could not be held responsible enough to be executed for his crime. The jury sentenced Simmons to death anyway.

After a series of appeals, the Missouri Supreme Court in 2003 did something unusual; it set aside Simmons's death penalty and sentenced him to life in prison instead, in defiance of a fairly recent precedent of the U.S. Supreme Court. In a 1989 case called *Stanford v. Kentucky,* the U.S. Supreme Court, which earlier had struck down the death penalty for anyone younger than

fifteen, upheld the death penalty for sixteen and seventeen year olds. But the Missouri high court determined that since then "a national consensus has developed" against executing juveniles younger than seventeen. Also, the Missouri justices noted that in 2002 the U.S. Supreme Court had ruled against the execution of the mentally retarded, for reasons that were analogous to the case of juveniles.

The state of Missouri, in the name of Donald Roper, the superintendent of the prison where Simmons was incarcerated, appealed the Missouri decision to the U.S. Supreme Court. Fifteen years after it had ruled on the issue, the Court agreed to take another look—in legal terms, an unusually short period of time.

VOTE

5–4, with Justice Anthony Kennedy writing the majority opinion. Joining him were Justices John Paul Stevens, David Souter, Ruth Bader Ginsburg, and Stephen Breyer. Justices Sandra Day

Former Missouri death row inmate Christopher Simmons murdered a woman when he was seventeen years old. In *Roper v. Simmons* (2005) the Court ruled that the Eighth Amendment's prohibition against "cruel and unusual punishment" made it unconstitutional to execute someone who was under the age of eighteen at the time he or she committed a crime.
AP/Wide World Photos/Missouri Department of Corrections.

O'Connor, Antonin Scalia, Clarence Thomas, and Chief Justice William Rehnquist dissented.

HIGHLIGHTS

In the earlier case of *Stanford v. Kentucky,* Justice Kennedy had joined the majority that upheld the execution of offenders ages sixteen and seventeen. But now, in the case of Christopher Simmons, Kennedy changed his mind.

Kennedy cited two main reasons for the shift. The first was that, as with the execution of the mentally retarded, the national consensus had shifted in recent years away from the practice of executing juveniles. Since the Stanford ruling, five states had abandoned juvenile executions—a "significant" trend, Kennedy said, though not as dramatic as the shift away from execution of the mentally retarded. The trend on the execution of juveniles is also seen internationally, Kennedy said, noting the "stark reality" that the United States is the only country in the world that still officially allows execution of juveniles. The trend lines at home and abroad, Kennedy said, were relevant in determining what kinds of punishments should be viewed as "cruel and unusual" under the Eighth Amendment.

The second main reason Kennedy cited was his view, supported by scientific research, that juveniles lack the judgment, maturity, and character of adults. As a result, Kennedy said, they can simply not be held responsible for their reckless acts in the same way that adults can. In addition, their immaturity means that the threat of capital punishment is unlikely to deter or prevent them from committing crimes. Deterrence has long been viewed as a major justification for capital punishment.

Dissenting justices questioned the validity of the consensus that Kennedy cited. Justice O'Connor said that while juveniles in general are less mature than adults, juries should be able to determine in individual cases whether some seventeen-year-olds are mature enough to deserve the death penalty. Justice Scalia also criticized the majority for making the Court "the sole arbiter of our nation's moral standards" instead of leaving such judgments to elected officials.

EXCERPTS

From Justice Kennedy's majority opinion: "Because the death penalty is the most severe punishment, the Eighth Amendment applies to it with special force. . . . Capital punishment must be limited to those offenders who commit 'a narrow category of the most serious crimes' and whose extreme culpability makes them 'the most deserving of execution.' . . .

"In recognition of the comparative immaturity and irresponsibility of juveniles, almost every State prohibits those under 18 years of age from voting, serving on juries, or marrying without parental consent. . . .

"Their own vulnerability and comparative lack of control over their immediate surroundings mean juveniles have a greater claim than adults to be forgiven for failing to escape negative influences in their whole environment. . . ."

IMPACT

The decision had the immediate consequence of saving the lives of some seventy death row inmates nationwide. They, like Simmons, were awaiting execution as punishment for murders they committed when they were juveniles.

Some death penalty opponents who celebrated the decision said that some of Kennedy's language in the ruling could be useful in further legal challenges to the death penalty. Because none of the nine Supreme Court justices opposes the death penalty in all cases, it appears unlikely that the Court will, anytime soon, declare capital punishment unconstitutional. As a result, opponents' best strategy may be to chip away at the death penalty by convincing the Court that it is an inappropriate punishment for certain classes of prisoners, as it has ruled for the mentally retarded and now juveniles. Using Kennedy's rationale, some have said that capital punishment for those who were under the influence of drugs at the time of their crimes, for example, could be attacked—though that would probably be a much tougher case to make.

In the aftermath of the Roper decision, Justice Kennedy came under sharp attack from conservatives for using such vague standards as international consensus in his decision. The decision fueled angry debate over whether it is appropriate to cite international and foreign laws and norms in deciding U.S. constitutional matters. Justice Scalia criticized Kennedy on this point, asserting that the meaning of the Eighth Amendment should not be determined "by the subjective views of five members of this Court and like-minded foreigners."

CIVIL RIGHTS

The Fourteenth Amendment to the Constitution was passed after the Civil War to set the ground rules for southern states reentering the United States. But in a few short phrases guaranteeing that states could not deprive anyone of "life, liberty or property" without the "due process of law" and the "equal protection of the laws," the amendment launched what one author has called "a second constitutional revolution" that is still felt today. It formed the legal basis for the civil rights movement but did not affect only racial minorities. The Supreme Court has interpreted the amendment ever since its enactment both narrowly and expansively in ways that have profoundly affected other groups, ranging from persons with mental retardation to immigrants to welfare recipients.

Other related cases mentioned in the Civil Rights section

Scott v. Sandford (1857) (see p. 231)
Yick Wo v. Hopkins (1886) (see p. 237)
Skinner v. Oklahoma (1942)
Saenz v. Roe (1999)

Slaughterhouse Cases

(The Butchers' Benevolent Association of New Orleans v. The Crescent City Livestock Landing and Slaughterhouse Co.; Esteben v. Louisiana)

Decided April 14, 1873
83 U.S. 36
laws.findlaw.com/US/83/36.html

DECISION

The privileges or immunities clause of the Fourteenth Amendment does not protect the right to labor. Therefore, a state is not in violation of the Fourteenth Amendment if it grants monopolies to businesses. The Fourteenth Amendment's due process clause also does not guarantee the right to carry on a business.

BACKGROUND

Congress had framed the post–Civil War amendments—the Thirteenth, Fourteenth, and Fifteenth Amendments—primarily to end slavery and its oppressive effects on black Americans. It was ironic, then, that the first major Supreme Court case testing the meaning of those amendments involved, not former slaves but white Louisiana businessmen.

The Reconstruction "carpetbag" legislature of Louisiana passed a law in 1869 that gave one company the exclusive right to operate a meat slaughterhouse in the city. In the days before modern refrigeration and sanitation, this government-regulated monopoly was to promote public health and reduce the dumping of animal waste into the Mississippi River. Opponents of the law charged that legislators had been bribed by wealthy businessmen to give the monopoly to the Crescent City Livestock Landing and Slaughterhouse Company.

Competing butchers also objected to the law, which forced them to use the government slaughterhouse and to pay for the privilege of doing so. They sued to challenge the law. One of their lawyers was John Campbell, a former Supreme Court justice from Alabama. Campbell, despite his moderate views on slavery, had resigned his seat when his state seceded from the Union. In addition to a range of other legal arguments, Campbell argued that the law violated the new Fourteenth Amendment to the Constitution. The right of the butchers to do business, he claimed, was one of the "privileges or immunities" of citizenship that the amendment protected.

In his capacity as a circuit judge, Justice Joseph Bradley agreed with Campbell that the Louisiana law violated the Fourteenth Amendment. The amendment gave the federal government the power to protect basic rights at the state level, including the right to labor, he said. His ruling was appealed to the Supreme Court. Three separate lawsuits involving the Louisiana law were consolidated before the Court and became known, collectively, as the Slaughterhouse Cases.

VOTE

5–4, with Justice Samuel F. Miller writing the majority opinion. Joining him were Justices Nathan Clifford, David Davis, William Strong, and Ward Hunt. Dissenting were Chief Justice Salmon P. Chase and Justices Stephen J. Field, Joseph P. Bradley, and Noah H. Swayne.

HIGHLIGHTS

The part of the Fourteenth Amendment at issue in the case says, "No State shall make or enforce any law which shall abridge the privileges or immunities of citizens of the United States." Some historians say the writers of the Fourteenth Amendment clearly intended these words to make the federal Bill of Rights binding on the states. At the very least, some scholars say, the sponsors of the Fourteenth Amendment wanted to create one citizenship enjoyed by blacks and whites and protected by the federal Constitution. The amendment had been passed to counteract the Supreme Court's decision in *Scott v. Sandford,* which was based in part on the notion that U.S. citizenship was distinct from state citizenship. (See *Scott v. Sandford.*)

But in the Slaughterhouse decision, Justice Miller found just the opposite meaning in the Fourteenth Amendment. For him and the majority of the Court, the amendment maintained the distinction between state and national citizenship and protected only the limited "privileges or immunities" of national citizenship. The rights of state citizens—far broader and more basic—would be interpreted and protected at the state level, without federal intervention.

The Fourteenth Amendment, according to the Court, gave the federal government a very limited role in protecting most of the individual rights people enjoy. To interpret the Fourteenth Amendment otherwise, Miller said, would be "to fetter and degrade the State governments by subjecting them to the control of Congress, in the exercise of powers heretofore universally

When Louisiana granted a twenty-five-year monopoly to one slaughterhouse, every butcher in New Orleans was forced to use it. The butchers sued, basing their claim on the Fourteenth Amendment, which forbids states from passing laws that "abridge the privileges or immunities" of U.S. citizens. In the Slaughterhouse Cases (1873) the Supreme Court upheld the Louisiana law.

Source: Courtesy of the Historic New Orleans Collection, Museum/Research Center.

conceded to them of the most ordinary and fundamental character," and would also radically change "the whole theory of the relations of the State and Federal governments to each other and of both these governments to the people."

Miller did not define what the rights of national citizenship were; that task, he said, would await a future case. But, as examples, he said the Fourteenth Amendment would protect the right of a U.S. citizen to travel to Washington, D.C., and to use navigable waters of the United States.

Apart from these kinds of rights, the Court said the main purpose of the Fourteenth Amendment was to prohibit state laws that discriminated against emancipated slaves. Under Section 5 of the Fourteenth Amendment, the Court said, Congress was authorized to enact laws to enforce that mandate.

"We doubt very much whether any action of a State not directed by way of discrimination against the negroes as a class, or on account of their race, will ever be held to come within the purview of this provision," Miller wrote. Under Miller's analysis of the Fourteenth Amendment, the Louisiana law could not be overturned by the Supreme Court or by any part of the federal government. Unless it had to do with the rights of blacks or the limited privileges of national citizenship, a state's action did not bring the Fourteenth Amendment into play.

The dissenting justices sharply disagreed. Justice Field said the case presents an issue "of the gravest importance not merely to the parties here, but to the whole country. It is nothing less than the question whether the recent amendments to the Federal Constitution protect the citizens of the United States against the deprivation of their common rights by State legislation. In my judgment, the fourteenth amendment does afford such protection, and was so intended by the Congress which framed and the States which adopted it." If the Four-

teenth Amendment had only the limited meaning that the majority attached to it, Field said, "it was a vain and idle enactment, which accomplished nothing."

Justice Bradley also wrote a dissent, asserting that national citizenship was primary and state citizenship secondary, in the constitutional scheme bolstered by the Fourteenth Amendment. "A citizen of the United States has a perfect constitutional right to go to and reside in any State he chooses, and to claim citizenship therein, and an equality of rights with every other citizen, and the whole power of the nation is pledged to sustain him in that right," said Bradley. "He is not bound to cringe to any superior, or to pray for any act of grace, as a means of enjoying all the rights and privileges enjoyed by other citizens."

Among the privileges protected by the amendment, said Bradley, is the right to "choose one's calling," which the Louisiana slaughterhouse monopoly law infringed. Bradley added, "To say that these rights and immunities attach only to State citizenship, and not to citizenship of the United States, appears to me to evince a very narrow and insufficient estimate of constitutional history and the rights of men, not to say the rights of the American people."

Justice Swayne also wrote a dissent, attacking the Louisiana law for similar reasons. "A more flagrant and indefensible invasion of the rights of many for the benefit of a few has not occurred in the legislative history of the country," Swayne said.

EXCERPTS

From Justice Miller's majority opinion: "The most cursory glance at these articles discloses a unity of purpose, when taken in connection with the history of the times, which cannot fail to have an important bearing on any question of doubt concerning their true meaning. Nor can such doubts, when any reasonably exist, be safely and rationally solved without a reference to that history, for in it is found the occasion and the necessity for recurring again to the great source of power in this country, the people of the States, for additional guarantees of human rights; additional powers to the Federal government; additional restraints upon those of the States. Fortunately, that history is fresh within the memory of us all, and its leading features, as they bear upon the matter before us, free from doubt. . . .

". . . Under the pressure of all the excited feeling growing out of the war, our statesmen have still believed that the existence of the State with powers for domestic and local government, including the regulation of civil rights—the rights of person and of property—was essential to the perfect working of our complex form of government, though they have thought proper to impose additional limitations on the States, and to confer additional power on that of the Nation.

"But whatever fluctuations may be seen in the history of public opinion on this subject during the period of our national existence, we think it will be found that this court, so far as its functions required, has always held with a steady and an even hand the balance between State and Federal power, and we trust that such may continue to be the history of its relation to that subject so long as it shall have duties to perform which demand of it a construction of the Constitution, or of any of its parts."

IMPACT

Today the distinction between state and federal citizenship has little practical meaning. But at the time of the Slaughterhouse Cases, the difference was important. The Court's controversial decision went a long way toward reassuring states' rights supporters that state citizenship still meant something.

The immediate meaning of the decision was, as Court scholar Bernard Schwartz has said, that the recently enacted privileges or immunities clause of the Fourteenth Amendment was "all but read out of the amendment" just a few short years later. An important tool that could have accelerated the protection of individual rights at the state as well as federal level was rendered useless. In Justice Swayne's evocative phrase, the majority opinion turned "what was meant for bread into a

stone." It took decades for the Court, in piecemeal fashion, to extend the reach of the Bill of Rights to the states, and it had to use other provisions of the Fourteenth Amendment to do it.

The Slaughterhouse decision had considerable impact on civil rights as well. Michael Kent Curtis, author of *No State Shall Abridge,* a book on the Fourteenth Amendment, says that even though the majority said the amendment was meant to protect blacks, "it was cited to justify decisions denying them a wide range of rights." The Slaughterhouse decision gave energy to states' rights, which as the years went by became a vehicle for Jim Crow laws and statutes that ignored the Bill of Rights.

In Supreme Court jurisprudence, the privileges or immunities clause was largely ignored for more than 125 years. Scholars occasionally expressed renewed interest in it as the source for some new or old right. Suddenly, in a 1999 decision for the Court, Justice John Paul Stevens invoked the clause and triggered new debate over the Slaughterhouse decision. In *Saenz v. Roe* Stevens cited the privileges or immunities clause in support of his view that California could not give a different level of welfare benefits to newcomers to the state.

The Court said the right of a newly arrived citizen to enjoy the same privilege or immunities of other citizens of the state was clearly protected by the Fourteenth Amendment, "despite fundamentally differing views concerning the coverage of the privileges or immunities clause of the Fourteenth Amendment, most notably expressed in the majority and dissenting opinions in the *Slaughter-House Cases.*"

Justice Clarence Thomas, who dissented in *Saenz,* said the demise of the clause was responsible for the "disarray" in the Court's Fourteenth Amendment decisions. "I would be open to reevaluating its meaning in an appropriate case," Thomas said, but the *Saenz* case was not the one. In a footnote Thomas also said, "legal scholars agree on little beyond the conclusion that the clause does not mean what the Court said it meant in 1873."

Some of those scholars reacted positively to the *Saenz* decision, expressing hope that it would result in a revival of the privileges or immunities clause, which, some argue, could provide a more straightforward foundation for economic rights and other individual rights than other parts of the Fourteenth Amendment.

Buck v. Bell

Decided May 2, 1927
274 U.S. 200
laws.findlaw.com/US/274/200.html

DECISION

A Virginia law that allows the sterilization of so-called "mental defectives" who are institutionalized in state facilities is constitutional. Noting the extensive procedure of hearings and appeals that must take place before sterilization is approved, the Court said that the law violates neither the due process clause nor the equal protection clause of the Fourteenth Amendment.

BACKGROUND

The "eugenics" movement, which was in vogue in the early part of the twentieth century, advanced the view that the human species could be improved through selective breeding and other methods that would weed out "undesirables." One of those methods was sterilization through surgery on men or women to make them unable to produce children. An enthusiastic supporter of the movement was Dr. Albert Priddy, superintendent of the State Colony for Epileptics and Feeble-Minded in Lynchburg, Virginia. He sterilized many patients in the institution, until a court in 1918 discouraged the practice because no law specifically allowed it. The Virginia legislature solved that problem in 1924 by enacting a law that spelled out the steps, including the appointment of a guardian, that would be followed for patients deemed to be candidates for sterilization. Once sterilized, the inmates would be eligible for release. The law was based on the premise that certain kinds of mental illness could be inherited.

Carrie Buck was an eighteen-year-old whose mother had once been confined to the Virginia institution presided over by Priddy. Carrie was judged to have the mental capacity of a nine-year-old, about the same level as her mother. Carrie was committed to the institution after she was raped. She gave birth to a girl, who was also diagnosed as mentally retarded. Her history, in the view of state officials, made her a prime candidate for sterilization under the new law.

Carrie took advantage of the law's safeguards and obtained a guardian who then hired a lawyer to plead her case. But lower courts endorsed the plan to have her sterilized, including one court that said it would be a "blessing" for Carrie and others like her. One judgment found that Carrie Buck "is the probable potential parent of socially inadequate offspring, likewise afflicted."

Before the Supreme Court, her lawyer did not argue with the procedure laid out by the law, but said that forced sterilization could never be justified. He also argued that because the law subjected only institutionalized people to possible sterilization and not those outside institutions, it violated equal protection principles.

VOTE

8–1, with Justice Oliver Wendell Holmes Jr. writing the majority opinion. He was joined by Chief Justice William Howard Taft and Justices Willis Van Devanter, James C. McReynolds, Louis D. Brandeis, George Sutherland, Edward T. Sanford, and Harlan Fiske Stone. Justice Pierce Butler dissented without explanation.

HIGHLIGHTS

Justice Holmes was eighty-six years old when he wrote *Buck v. Bell*. As with many Holmes decisions, it was tersely written, with simple and direct prose. The decision is best remembered for one of its blunt sentences about Carrie Buck's family: "Three generations of imbeciles are enough."

Holmes deferred to the judgment of the legislators in deciding that society would benefit from sterilizing inmates like Carrie Buck, in the same way that vaccinating people benefits society.

As for the due process argument, Holmes recounted the "very careful provisions by which the act protects the patients from possible abuse. . . . There is no doubt that [Buck] has had due process at law," Holmes wrote. He also dismissed the equal protection claim out of hand, calling it "the last resort of constitutional arguments."

EXCERPTS

From Justice Holmes's majority opinion: "We have seen more than once that the public welfare may call upon the best citizens for their lives. It would be strange if it could not call upon those who already sap the strength of the State for these lesser sacrifices, often not felt to be such by those concerned, in order to prevent our being swamped with incompetence. It is better for all the world if, instead of waiting to execute degenerate offspring for crime or to let them starve for their imbecility, society can prevent those who are manifestly unfit from continuing their kind. The principle that sustains compulsory vaccination is broad enough to cover cutting the Fallopian tubes. Three generations of imbeciles are enough."

IMPACT

By 1930 twenty-four states, encouraged by the Court's opinion, had enacted laws similar to Virginia's. An estimated 20,000 men and women were sterilized during this period. In Virginia alone, 8,300 people were sterilized between 1922 and 1972, when the practice was discontinued.

Today the harsh judgment of *Buck v. Bell* seems not only outdated but also completely at odds with society's attitudes toward those with mental disabilities. It is also seen as a blemish on the reputation of Justice Holmes, who is otherwise regarded by most scholars as one of the greatest justices of all time. One biographer described Holmes as a "true believer" in the eugenics movement long before the case came to the Court.

Legally speaking, the modern view of individual rights makes it difficult to imagine that today's Court would decide *Buck v. Bell* as did the Court in 1927. Some justices might be tempted, as Holmes was, to defer to the wisdom of elected officials in enacting laws like Virginia's. But recent precedent has given special protection to personal decisions about matters as intimate as having children.

Medically, the eugenics movement fell out of favor in part because it was embraced by Nazi Germany, although echoes of the debate can be heard in current discussions about genetic engineering. In the Nuremberg war crimes trials after World War II, *Buck v. Bell* was invoked by Nazi defendants to justify their actions aimed at "improving" the human race.

As for Carrie Buck, she was sterilized in 1927 and left the institution. Recent research has cast doubt on whether she, her mother, or her daughter were as impaired as the state contended they were. Carrie Buck was said to be an avid reader in her later years, and her daughter, who lived to the age of eight, performed well in school. The research suggests that the three generations of Buck women may have been victimized by zealots of the eugenics movement.

Carrie Buck and her mother, Emma Buck, were at the center of the debate over the "eugenics" movement in the 1920s, when Carrie Buck challenged a Virginia law permitting the sterilization of persons with mental disabilities. In *Buck v. Bell* (1927) Justice Oliver Wendell Holmes, writing for the majority, likened the social benefits of sterilization to vaccination and held that the law violated neither the equal protection clause nor the due process clause of the Fourteenth Amendment.

Source: Arthur Estabrook Papers, M.E. Grenander Department of Special Collections and Archives, University at Albany Libraries.

Buck v. Bell has never been overturned outright, but a 1942 decision, *Skinner v. Oklahoma,* has probably robbed it of most of its force. In *Skinner* the Court struck down an Oklahoma law that authorized sterilization of habitual criminals. The Court said the right to have children was fundamental, but it did not strike the law down on that basis. Instead, it said the law violated equal protection principles because it exempted people who committed certain kinds of crimes.

In 2002 Virginia took note of the seventy-fifth anniversary of *Buck v. Bell* by dedicating a road marker to Carrie Buck. Both the Virginia General Assembly and Virginia governor John Warner apologized for the state's participation in the eugenics movement. "The eugenics movement was a shameful effort in which state government never should have been involved," Warner said.

Goldberg v. Kelly

Decided March 23, 1970
397 U.S. 254
laws.findlaw.com/US/397/254.html

DECISION

Before a city or state may cut off benefits to a person receiving welfare, that recipient is entitled to a hearing. At the hearing, the recipient can dispute the government's claim of ineligibility by calling and challenging witnesses and evidence. This right is based on the due process guarantees of the Fourteenth Amendment to the U.S. Constitution and on the fact that welfare benefits are "a matter of statutory entitlement for persons qualified to receive them."

BACKGROUND

The growth of the modern U.S. welfare state after World War II was accompanied by an assortment of arbitrary policies and procedures at the local and state levels. Recipients in many areas could have benefits cut off without any hearings, or they could be cut off first and given an opportunity to appeal later. As the number of Americans receiving welfare approached 10 million, a fledgling "welfare rights" movement in the 1960s sought to secure rights and safeguards for welfare recipients.

The welfare rights movement in many ways mirrored efforts to expand rights for other minorities. Some advocates sought to have the courts declare that poor people were a protected class of citizens, which would subject laws treating poor people differently to "strict scrutiny," a high standard in law that had been used to strike down racially discriminatory statutes. Yale law professor Charles Reich also advanced the view that welfare benefits should be regarded as a form of "property" that could not be withdrawn easily by government.

Justice William Brennan Jr., one of the Court's leading liberals, was in sympathy with this movement. Late in his life he told an interviewer, "I was looking for a 'new property' case" that would become a vehicle for exploring welfare rights. *Goldberg v. Kelly,* which originated in New York City, proved to be just such a case.

The city's welfare regulations and procedures gave more recognition to the rights of recipients than did those in most of the rest of the country. If a caseworker felt that a recipient was no longer entitled to benefits, the recipient was notified in writing and given a chance to respond and to request a hearing. Benefits could be terminated in the meantime. Even Justice Brennan later called the regulations a "model of rationality."

But lawyers for a group of welfare recipients whose benefits had been cut off said the procedures gave insufficient due process, primarily because benefits could be terminated before an appeal was heard. This, they said, could endanger lives and make the appeal a hollow right.

The individual stories of welfare recipients in the case, including John Kelly, a homeless black man, were compelling. For example, an erroneous report that Esther Lett had a job led a caseworker to cut off her benefits. While her appeal was pending, she and her four nieces nearly starved and had to be hospitalized at one point. Another recipient had been cut off after he was robbed of $20, which a caseworker said amounted to "mismanagement of funds." A suit was filed against city welfare commissioner Jack Goldberg.

VOTE

5–3, with Justice William J. Brennan Jr. writing for the majority. Joining him were Justices William O. Douglas, John M. Harlan, Byron R. White, and Thurgood Marshall. Chief Justice Warren E. Burger and Justices Hugo L. Black and Potter Stewart dissented.

HIGHLIGHTS

One remarkable feature of the majority opinion is that it assessed not just the words of New York City's regulation but the real-life impact of those regulations. For example, Brennan says that allowing a recipient to appeal a benefit cutoff after the fact may sound fair, but in reality it "may deprive an eligible recipient of the very means by which to live while he waits. . . . His need to concentrate upon finding the means for daily subsistence, in turn, adversely affects his ability to seek redress."

Another regulation, requiring the recipient to appeal in writing, is also impractical, Brennan wrote. "The opportunity to be heard must be tailored to the capacities and circumstances of those who are to be heard. Written submissions are an unrealistic option for most recipients, who lack the educational attainment necessary to write effectively and who cannot obtain professional assistance."

The closest Brennan came to achieving the goals of the welfare rights movement was a footnote citing Reich's works and adding, "It may be realistic today to regard welfare entitlements as more like 'property' than a 'gratuity.'" He also described welfare benefits as an "entitlement" for those who qualify.

EXCERPTS

From Justice Brennan's majority decision: "From its founding, the Nation's basic commitment has been to foster the dignity and well-being of all persons within its borders. We have come to recognize that forces not within the control of the poor contribute to their poverty. This perception, against the background of our traditions, has significantly influenced the development of the contemporary public assistance system. Welfare, by meeting the basic demands of subsistence, can help bring within the reach of the poor the same opportunities that are available to others to participate meaningfully in the life of the community. At the same time, welfare guards against the societal malaise that may flow from a widespread sense of unjustified frustration and insecurity. Public assistance, then, is not mere charity, but a means to 'promote the general Welfare, and secure the Blessings of Liberty to ourselves and our Posterity.' The same governmental interests that counsel the provision of welfare, counsel as well its uninterrupted provision to those eligible to receive it; pre-termination evidentiary hearings are indispensable to that end."

IMPACT

The decision in *Goldberg v. Kelly* has been acclaimed—and criticized—for launching the "due process revolution" in which standards of fairness were applied to the myriad benefits and regulations that flow from government. It was also something of a high-water mark. The Court never went any further in describing welfare as a property right than it did in *Goldberg,* and in several subsequent decisions it gave government more leeway in reducing benefits and changing the rules. But even in the early 1990s, when President Bill Clinton proclaimed an end to "welfare as we know it," the *Goldberg* decision stood as a reminder that welfare recipients still retain procedural safeguards.

The *Goldberg* decision has also been cited as a prime example of judicial activism, a case in which a justice's social or political goals drove the outcome. Brennan himself cited the ruling as "an expression of the importance of passion in governmental conduct, in the sense of attention to the concrete human realities at stake."

Plyler v. Doe

Decided June 15, 1982
457 U.S. 202
laws.findlaw.com/US/457/202.html

DECISION

States may not refuse to pay for the education of illegal aliens and may not prevent their enrollment in public schools. A Texas law that sought to deny education to illegal aliens violates the equal protection clause of the Fourteenth Amendment, which prohibits states from denying equal treatment to "any person within its jurisdiction."

BACKGROUND

The number of foreigners entering the United States illegally and staying despite their illegal status continues to grow. In the early 1980s the federal government estimated that between 3 million and 6 million illegal aliens were residing in the United States; others put the number at two or three times that figure. The growing alien population put a strain on local government services and schools, especially in the parts of Texas near the U.S. border with Mexico.

In 1975 Texas revised its education laws to deny money to local school districts for the education of illegal alien children. One section of the law also authorized local schools to deny admission to such children.

The law was challenged in court on behalf of a group of school-aged illegal alien children from Mexico, under the name of "Doe." These children, who lived in Smith County, sued school superintendent James Plyler, claiming that their exclusion from public education in the Tyler Independent School District violated the Fourteenth Amendment, which guarantees equal protection of the laws to all. A federal district court and appeals court agreed.

The history of the Supreme Court shows a mixed record on the rights of aliens. As early as 1886 in *Yick Wo v. Hopkins,* the Court determined that the Fourteenth Amendment protected all persons within a state's jurisdiction, not just citizens (see *Yick Wo v. Hopkins*). But the Court at various times since then had approved some state laws that reserve certain jobs and privileges to citizens.

The Court also has recognized that the Constitution gives Congress complete power to admit or exclude aliens. Therefore, the Court occasionally has allowed Congress to pass laws treating aliens differently, in ways that states might not be able to because of the Fourteenth Amendment.

VOTE

5–4, with Justice William J. Brennan Jr. writing the majority opinion. Joining him were Justices Thurgood Marshall, Harry A. Blackmun, Lewis F. Powell Jr., and John Paul Stevens. Dissenting were Chief Justice Warren E. Burger and Justices Byron R. White, William Rehnquist, and Sandra Day O'Connor.

HIGHLIGHTS

The Court began by reaffirming its long-held view that the Fourteenth Amendment does not just protect citizens. "Whatever his status under the immigration laws, an alien is surely a 'person' in any ordinary sense of that term. Aliens, even aliens whose presence in this country is unlawful, have long been recognized as 'persons' guaranteed due process of law by the Fifth and Fourteenth Amendments. The Equal Protection Clause was intended to work nothing less than the abolition of all caste-based and invidious class-based legislation."

That does not mean that illegal aliens are entitled to every benefit available to citizens, the Court said. But two factors made the claim by the Texas illegal aliens particularly compelling, according to the majority. First, those most affected by the Texas law were children, who could not reasonably be held accountable because of the illegal acts of their parents.

"Those who elect to enter our territory by stealth and in violation of our law should be prepared to bear the consequences, including, but not limited to, deportation. But the children of those illegal entrants are not comparably situated," the Court said. "Legislation directing the onus of a parent's misconduct against his children does not comport with fundamental conceptions of justice."

The second important factor was that the alien students were being deprived of an education, not something of lesser importance. "Public education is not a 'right' granted to individuals by the Constitution," the Court said. "But neither is it merely some governmental 'benefit' indistinguishable from other forms of social welfare legislation. Paradoxically, by depriving the children of any disfavored group of an education, we foreclose the means by which that group might raise the level of esteem in which it is held by the majority."

The justices struggled to define the level of scrutiny that should be applied to laws that discriminate against aliens. In examining cases that restrict fundamental rights of racial minorities, for example, the Court applies "strict scrutiny," a high standard that very few laws can survive. But here, the Court said that because education is not a fundamental right and the aliens bear responsibility for their illegal status, a lower level of

scrutiny applied. Nevertheless, government had to provide a substantial justification for restricting aliens' access to education, the Court decided.

"If the State is to deny a discrete group of innocent children the free public education that it offers to other children residing within its borders, that denial must be justified by a showing that it furthers some substantial state interest," the Court said. "No such showing was made here."

The dissenters, led by Chief Justice Burger, a conservative, attacked the majority for making policy, rather than sound constitutional decisions. The Court should not be considering factors such as the cost to society of leaving alien children uneducated, Burger said. That kind of judgment is for legislators to make, not the Supreme Court, in his view.

"Were it our business to set the Nation's social policy, I would agree without hesitation that it is senseless for an enlightened society to deprive any children—including illegal aliens—of an elementary education," Burger wrote. "However, the Constitution does not constitute us as 'Platonic Guardians,' nor does it vest in this Court the authority to strike down laws because they do not meet our standards of desirable social policy, 'wisdom,' or 'common sense.' We trespass on the assigned function of the political branches under our structure of limited and separated powers when we assume a policymaking role as the Court does today."

Burger accused the Court of the kind of judicial activism that goes beyond the proper role of the courts. "The Constitution does not provide a cure for every social ill, nor does it vest judges with a mandate to try to remedy every social problem."

EXCERPTS

From Justice Brennan's majority opinion: "Sheer incapability or lax enforcement of the laws barring entry into this country, coupled with the failure to establish an effective bar to the employment of undocumented aliens, has resulted in the creation of a substantial 'shadow population' of illegal migrants—numbering in the millions—within our borders. This situation raises the specter of a permanent caste of undocumented resident aliens, encouraged by some to remain here as a source of cheap labor, but nevertheless denied the benefits that our society makes available to citizens and lawful residents. The existence of such an underclass presents most difficult problems for a Nation that prides itself on adherence to principles of equality under law. . . .

". . . In determining the rationality of [the Texas law] we may appropriately take into account its costs to the Nation and to the innocent children who are its victims. In light of these countervailing costs, the discrimination contained in [the law] can hardly be considered rational unless it furthers some substantial goal of the State. . . .

"Appellants argue that the classification at issue furthers an interest in the 'preservation of the state's limited resources for the education of its lawful residents.' Of course, a concern for the preservation of resources standing alone can hardly justify the classification used in allocating those resources. . . .

". . . It is difficult to understand precisely what the State hopes to achieve by promoting the creation and perpetuation of a subclass of illiterates within our boundaries, surely adding to the problems and costs of unemployment, welfare, and crime. It is thus clear that whatever savings might be achieved by denying these children an education, they are wholly insubstantial in light of the costs involved to these children, the State, and the Nation."

IMPACT

The *Plyler* majority decision was a powerful and controversial declaration that the Constitution protects everyone—even those who came to the United States illegally.

States continue to struggle with providing education and other services to illegal aliens, and the cost continues to be a political issue. In 1994 voters in California approved Proposition 187, which was aimed at denying a variety of services, including education, to illegal aliens. The ballot initiative was immediately challenged in court and was never implemented. In March 1998 a federal judge declared the proposition unconstitutional. The main reason was that it amounted to a state immigration policy, which runs against the constitutional provision giving Congress sole authority over immigration matters. But the judge also cited *Plyler v. Doe* as justification for striking down the part of Proposition 187 that would deny schooling to aliens.

California governor Gray Davis, who said during his election campaign in 1998 that he opposed Proposition 187, angered immigration rights advocates when he announced that he would submit the issue to mediation before the U.S. Court of Appeals for the Ninth Circuit. In July 1999, however, Davis announced he was dropping all appeals aimed at resurrecting Proposition 187.

PGA Tour v. Martin

Decided May 29, 2001
532 U.S. 661
laws.findlaw.com/US/532/661.html

DECISION

The Americans with Disabilities Act prohibits the Professional Golf Association (PGA) Tour from denying access to its golf tours to golfer Casey Martin because of his disability. Martin's request to use a golf cart during part of a qualifying match would not cause a fundamental alteration of the game and is a reasonable accommodation under the law.

BACKGROUND

Casey Martin is a talented golfer in spite of a disorder he has had from birth, Klippel-Trenaunay-Weber syndrome, which restricts the flow of blood from his right leg to his heart. The disorder causes pain and makes it difficult for him to walk.

As a child Martin won several amateur golf awards in Oregon, and he played golf for Stanford University. But his disease progressed, and in his last few years at Stanford he was unable to walk an entire eighteen-hole course without pain and risk to his health. Because of this problem, in college he was able to obtain waivers from rules that require players to walk the course and carry their own clubs.

But when Martin turned pro and sought a similar waiver for the final part of a qualifying match in which he was playing, the PGA Tour said no. Martin sued the PGA Tour under Title III

of the Americans with Disabilities Act, which in general prohibits discrimination on the basis of disability at "public accommodations" including golf courses. The law defines discrimination as failing to make "reasonable modifications" for the disabled person, unless the modification would "fundamentally alter" the service provided.

PGA Tour claimed that allowing Martin to use a golf cart while other players had to walk would fundamentally alter the game, because the stamina required in walking the course was part of what goes into winning the match. But the district court and U.S. Court of Appeals disagreed, ruling that allowing Martin to use the golf cart was a reasonable accommodation. The district court noted that Martin's disability was a test of his stamina that was equal to that faced by other golfers who could walk the course. PGA Tour appealed to the Supreme Court.

VOTE

7–2, with Justice John Paul Stevens writing the majority opinion. Joining him were Chief Justice William Rehnquist and Justices Sandra Day O'Connor, Anthony Kennedy, David Souter, Ruth Bader Ginsburg, and Stephen Breyer. Justice Antonin Scalia, joined by Justice Clarence Thomas, dissented.

HIGHLIGHTS

It is rare for golf—or any sport, for that matter—to be scrutinized so closely by the Supreme Court. Sports usually cause disagreements outside the realm of courts.

But in this case, because of the comprehensive nature of the Americans with Disabilities Act (ADA), how the PGA Tour treated one of its players became fair game for judicial decision making. The ADA, passed in 1990, was meant to cover a wide range of activities that often shut out those with disabilities. It could not cover strictly private places like homes and clubs, but like other civil rights laws it did cover "public accommodations" like hotels that offer services to the general public. Golf courses were specifically mentioned in the law as examples of a public accommodation.

Though at earlier stages PGA Tour argued that it was a private club, at the Supreme Court it acknowledged that it operated a public accommodation when it ran golf matches on golf courses. But it argued that Martin was not a consumer of its services. Instead, it said that Martin was a provider of the services offered to consumers at the golf course—akin to an actor in a play at a public theater, rather than an audience member at the play. As such, he was not protected by that part of the ADA and was not covered by any other provision either, because he was an independent contractor, not an employee.

Justice Stevens did not buy that argument. He said the PGA Tour offers services to golfers who participate as well as to customers who watch, so Martin is covered by the law.

The question of whether letting Martin use a golf cart would "fundamentally alter" the game of golf led Stevens to closely examine the history and rules of the sport. Stevens determined that the essence of the game is getting the ball in the hole in as few shots as possible – an endeavor that has nothing to do with using or not using a golf cart. He also noted that PGA rules allow the use of golf carts in a variety of circumstances, including tours involving senior players. So, he said, giving Martin a golf cart did not change the game significantly.

In a caustic dissent, Justice Scalia said not only that the majority was misinterpreting the law, but that it had embarked on a "long and misguided journey" that included deciding what is the fundamental nature of golf—a question that neither the Supreme Court nor any other court is qualified to answer.

EXCERPTS

From Justice Stevens's majority opinion: "Under the ADA's basic requirement that the need of a disabled person be evaluated on an individual basis, we have no doubt that allowing Martin to use a golf cart would not fundamentally alter the nature of petitioner's tournaments. As we have discussed, the purpose of the walking rule is to subject players to fatigue, which in turn may influence the outcome of tournaments. Even if the rule does serve that purpose, it is an uncontested finding of the District Court that Martin 'easily endures greater fatigue even with a cart than his able-bodied competitors do by walking.' . . . A modification that provides an exception to a peripheral tournament rule without impairing its purpose cannot be said to 'fundamentally alter' the tournament. What it can be said to do, on the other hand, is to allow Martin the chance to qualify for and compete in the athletic events petitioner offers to those members of the public who have the skill and desire to enter. That is exactly what the ADA requires."

From Justice Scalia's dissent: "It has been rendered the solemn duty of the Supreme Court of the United States . . . to decide What Is Golf. I am sure that the Framers of the Constitution, aware of the 1457 edict of King James II of Scotland prohibiting golf because it interfered with the practice of archery, fully expected that sooner or later the paths of golf and government, the law and the links, would once again cross, and that the judges of this august Court would some day have to wrestle with that age-old jurisprudential question, for which their years

Golfer Casey Martin hits a shot during a practice round at the 1998 U.S. Open. Martin, who has a rare circulatory disorder, sued the Professional Golfers' Association when it refused to allow him to use a golf cart while playing. In *PGA Tour v. Martin* (2001) the Court ruled that the Americans with Disabilities Act entitled him to reasonable accommodation under the law.
Source: AP/Wide World Photos/Eric Risberg.

of study in the law have so well prepared them: Is someone riding around a golf course from shot to shot *really* a golfer? The answer, we learn, is yes. The Court ultimately concludes, and it will henceforth be the Law of the Land, that walking is not a 'fundamental' aspect of golf. Either out of humility or out of self-respect (one or the other) the Court should decline to answer this incredibly difficult and incredibly silly question."

IMPACT

Though critics of the decision warned that it would spoil the game and lead to exceptions being made for golfers with bad backs and other problems, that trend has not materialized.

And the ruling has not been widely applied to other sports either, apparently. In a 2005 decision the Supreme Judicial Court of Massachusetts said that the *Casey* decision did not require a fitness club to open its racquetball competitions to a wheelchair-bound player. Doing so would fundamentally alter the game and was not required, the court said.

As for Martin, he has continued to play golf, most recently in the Canadian Tour, and with a cart. In an April 2005 article the *Toronto Sun* quoted Martin as saying, "I believe that, in my lifetime, there will be another player who will need [the golf cart], but the idea that it would open the floodgates was ridiculous."

COMMERCE POWER

*A*lthough Congress today seems to involve itself in all issues facing the United States—from steroid use by athletes to telemarketing—the Constitution spells out a limited list of its duties. Whenever Congress passes a law, in theory, it must connect the legislation to one of these "enumerated powers." The power that is invoked to justify a broad range of legislation is contained in the so-called commerce clause, namely, the power to "regulate commerce with foreign nations, and among the several states." Since the early days of the nation, how the Supreme Court has interpreted that power—narrowly or broadly—has played a key role in determining how strong the national government is.

Other related cases mentioned in the Commerce Power section

Civil Rights Cases (1883) (see p. 234)
United States v. E.C. Knight Co. (1895)
Northern Securities Co. v. United States (1904)
Swift and Co. v. United States (1905)
Lochner v. New York (1905) (see p. 219)
West Coast Hotel v. Parrish (1937)
Wickard v. Filburn (1942)
Reed v. Reed (1971)
Frontiero v. Richardson (1973)
Printz v. United States (1997)
Clinton v. New York (1998)
United States v. Morrison (2000)

Gibbons v. Ogden

Decided March 2, 1824
22 U.S. 1
laws.findlaw.com/US/22/1.html

DECISION

Congress has broad powers under Article I, Section 8, of the Constitution, which says, "Congress shall have power to regulate commerce with foreign nations, and among the several States, and with the Indian tribes." The Court interpreted this grant to cover all conceivable forms of commerce, including navigation, except if the commerce takes place entirely within a state. Moreover, the power to regulate interstate commerce is exclusive—not to be shared with any state.

BACKGROUND

The need to regulate commerce on a national basis was one of the main reasons for creation of the Constitution. Trade barriers between states had been a major obstacle to the development of a strong national economy. But it was not until more than thirty-five years later that the Supreme Court was called on to interpret the scope of that regulatory power.

The case concerned a dispute that stemmed from the invention of the steamboat by Robert Fulton at the beginning of the nineteenth century. Fulton and his partner Robert Livingston obtained a license from the state of New York that gave them a monopoly over steam navigation in New York waters. They in turn licensed Aaron Ogden to run ferryboats between New York City and Elizabethtown, New Jersey. The monopoly provoked just the sort of interstate squabbling the Constitution's Framers had sought to prevent. Connecticut, New Jersey, and Ohio closed their waters to vessels licensed under the New York monopoly. Other states permitted creation of other monopolies within their boundaries.

The New York monopoly also did not keep ambitious competitors from trying to break into the business. One competitor was Thomas Gibbons, who, under federal license, operated competing boats named the *Stoudinger* and the *Bellona* between New York and New Jersey without New York's permission. Ogden sued to stop him.

Gibbons, a wealthy southern planter, spent freely to win his case. He hired Daniel Webster, probably the best and best-known lawyer of the time, to argue his case. The battle also became personal. Gibbons went to Ogden's house to challenge him to a duel, and Ogden responded by suing him for trespass.

The Supreme Court agreed to resolve the dispute over the conflicting licenses. Webster urged the Court to give a broad interpretation to the commerce power and to make that power exclusive to the national government. Lawyers for Ogden argued that the states should have equal power over commerce with the national government.

VOTE

6–0, with Chief Justice John Marshall writing for the Court. He was joined by Justices Bushrod Washington, William Johnson, Thomas Todd, Gabriel Duvall, and Joseph Story.

HIGHLIGHTS

The Court gave an expansive interpretation of federal power over commerce as it nullified Ogden's monopoly. The federal law under which Gibbons was licensed took precedence over the state monopoly, the Court said.

On the broader issue of the meaning of the commerce clause, the Court interpreted the word *commerce* in the widest possible way—not just referring to commercial transactions, but to "every species of commercial intercourse," including, as in the case before the Court, navigation.

The Court gave an equally broad meaning to the word *regulate*. Marshall wrote, "It is the power to regulate, that is, to prescribe the rule by which commerce is to be governed. This power, like all others vested in Congress, is complete in itself, may be exercised to its utmost extent, and acknowledges no limitations other than are prescribed in the constitution."

The opinion did not, however, leave states without a role in regulating commerce. "It is not intended to say that these words comprehend that commerce, which is completely internal, which is carried on between man and man in a State, or between different parts of the same State, and which does not extend to or affect other States. Such a power would be inconvenient, and is certainly unnecessary."

The decision sidestepped knottier problems that might arise if states regulate in areas on which the federal government has been silent. If state and federal regulation conflicted, however, the Court said the federal regulation is supreme.

EXCERPTS

From Justice Marshall's majority opinion: "The genius and character of the whole government seem to be, that its action is to be applied to all the external concerns of the nation, and to those internal concerns which affect the States generally, but not to those which are completely within a particular State, which do not affect other States, and with which it is not necessary to interfere, for the purpose of executing some of the general powers of the government. The completely internal commerce of a State, then, may be considered as reserved for the State itself.

"But, in regulating commerce with foreign nations, the power of Congress does not stop at the jurisdictional lines of the several States. It would be a very useless power, if it could not pass those lines. The commerce of the United States with foreign nations, is that of the whole United States. Every district has a right to participate in it. The deep streams which penetrate our country in every direction, pass through the interior of almost every State in the Union, and furnish the means of exercising this right. If Congress has the power to regulate it, that power must be exercised whenever the subject exists. If it exists within the States, if a foreign voyage may commence or terminate at a port within a State, then the power of Congress may be exercised within a State. . . .

". . . [I]t has been contended that if a law passed by a State, in the exercise of its acknowledged sovereignty, comes into conflict with a law passed by Congress in pursuance of the constitution, they affect the subject, and each other, like equal opposing powers.

"But the framers of our constitution foresaw this state of things, and provided for it, by declaring the supremacy not only of itself, but of the laws made in pursuance of it. The nullity of any act, inconsistent with the constitution, is produced by the declaration that the constitution is the supreme law. The appropriate application of that part of the clause which confers the same supremacy on laws and treaties, is to such acts of the State Legislatures as do not transcend their powers, but, though enacted in the execution of acknowledged State powers, interfere with, or are contrary to the laws of Congress made in pursuance of the constitution, or some treaty made under the authority of the United States. In every such case, the act of Congress, or the treaty, is supreme; and the law of the State, though enacted in the exercise of powers not controverted, must yield to it."

IMPACT

The Court's opinion was widely acclaimed because it broke up the unpopular steamboat monopoly. Democratic-Republicans such as Thomas Jefferson, however, criticized the decision for overwhelming the rights of states.

Congress itself did not immediately take advantage of its broad grant of power. And the expansiveness with which the Court has interpreted federal commerce power and *Gibbons v. Ogden* has ebbed and flowed depending on other political currents. But it is undeniable that Marshall's opinion was one of the building blocks of the modern-day vision of a strong—some would say intrusive—national government. Antitrust regulations, labor laws, even some aspects of modern civil rights legislation, are based on the commerce power.

In *Swift and Co. v. United States* (1905), for example, the Court said price-fixing could be barred under antitrust laws because of the commerce power. The federal law governing labor-management relations was upheld on commerce clause grounds in 1937 (see *National Labor Relations Board v. Jones and Laughlin Steel Corp.*). In 1964 the Court said the federal government could prohibit racial discrimination in public accommodations because of its impact on interstate commerce (see *Heart of Atlanta Motel v. United States*).

The latest swing of the pendulum came in 1995 when, for the first time, the Supreme Court struck down a federal law that had been passed by Congress under the commerce power. The

The lawsuit of one-time business partners Thomas Gibbons, left, and Aaron Ogden, right, led to a landmark Commerce Clause decision in 1824. Chief Justice John Marshall's opinion in *Gibbons v. Ogden* defined commerce to include transportation and navigation and stated that Congress has the exclusive power to regulate interstate commerce.

Sources: left, Georgia Historical Society; right, Collection of The New-York Historical Society (accession number 1878.1, negative number 6359).

law, which prohibited possession of a firearm in school zones, could not be justified, the Court said, because "in no sense" did the law relate to interstate commerce. The Court's decision in *United States v. Lopez* was the touchstone for a series of decisions in which the Court curtailed congressional power. (See *United States v. Lopez.*) But in the 2005 decision *Gonzales v.*

Raich, the Court upheld the enforcement of federal antidrug laws against sick people in California who were authorized by state law to use marijuana for medical purposes. (See *Gonzales v. Raich.*) To some commentators, the decision ran counter to *Lopez* and represented something of a return to the principles first articulated in *Gibbons v. Ogden.*

Muller v. Oregon

Decided February 24, 1908
208 U.S. 412
laws.findlaw.com/US/208/412.html

DECISION

A state may limit the number of hours a woman can work. The Court said states can use their police power and their responsibility to protect the health of citizens to enact laws in this area, even if the laws interfere to some degree with contract and property rights.

BACKGROUND

In response to the growth of industry in the nation, many states passed legislation designed to protect workers, especially women, from long working hours and dangerous working conditions. At the same time, the Supreme Court was giving greater weight to contract and property rights in decisions that tended to favor big business. In the landmark *Lochner v. New York* (1905) the Court struck down a New York law limiting bakery workers to ten hours of labor per day. The law infringed on the "liberty of contract," the Court said. (See *Lochner v. New. York.*)

In 1908 the Court was required to reconcile these conflicting principles of business regulation. Curt Muller, the owner of the Grand Laundry in Portland, Oregon, was arrested for requiring a Mrs. Elmer Gotcher to work for more than ten hours on September 4, 1905. That violated a 1903 Oregon law that made it a crime to require a woman to work in a factory or laundry for more than ten hours a day. Muller was fined $10. Mindful of the *Lochner* decision, Muller appealed. The state supreme court upheld the fine, setting the stage for review by the U.S. Supreme Court.

To defend the law Oregon, with the help of the National Consumers' League, hired the noted lawyer—and future Supreme Court justice—Louis Brandeis. The consumers' group was interested in the case in part because similar laws protecting women from long hours had been enacted in nineteen other jurisdictions.

Brandeis decided to take a new approach in arguing in favor of the Oregon law. Given the Court's skepticism toward laws that restricted the freedom of contracts, Brandeis felt the Court needed to be informed of relevant social, economic, and medical research that would buttress the arguments in favor of restricting women's working hours.

The result was a legal brief that spent two pages arguing the law and more than one hundred pages summarizing the research. The findings here and abroad, Brandeis said, were nearly unanimous in showing that work quality improved with shorter workdays, and that women were ill equipped to work long hours, especially in their childbearing years.

VOTE

9–0, with Justice David J. Brewer writing the opinion of the Court. Joining him were Chief Justice Melville W. Fuller and Justices John Marshall Harlan, Edward D. White, Rufus W. Peckham, Joseph McKenna, Oliver Wendell Holmes Jr., William R. Day, and William H. Moody.

HIGHLIGHTS

The challenge for Justice Brewer was to explain how the *Muller* case was different from the Court's decision three years earlier in *Lochner v. New York,* in which the Court struck down a ten-hour workday limit for male bakery workers. The New York law was invalidated as a violation of the Fourteenth Amendment, which the *Lochner* Court believed protects the right to contract for the sale of one's labor.

The laundry owner cited *Lochner* as the main justification for also striking down the Oregon law. Brewer acknowledged that women enjoy the right to contract for their labor just as much as men, but said Muller's argument "assumes that the difference between the sexes does not justify a different rule respecting a restriction of the hours of labor." Citing the Brandeis brief by name, Brewer reported "a widespread belief that woman's physical structure, and the functions she performs in consequence thereof, justify special legislation restricting or

When Oregon imposed a sixty-hour maximum work week for women, laundry owner Curt Muller (with arms folded) argued that the law violated his rights. In *Muller v. Oregon* (1908) Justice David J. Brewer wrote the opinion for a unanimous Supreme Court upholding the validity of state maximum working hour laws. The Court accepted sociological arguments about the effects of long hours on women's health and reproductive systems.

Source: Courtesy of Mrs. Neill Whisnant and the Portland Chamber of Commerce.

qualifying the conditions under which she should be permitted to toil."

As a result, the Court agreed that because women were in a special category, "legislation designed for her protection may be sustained, even when like legislation is not necessary for men, and could not be sustained." Having made that distinction, the Court upheld the Oregon law, Brewer said, "without questioning in any respect the decision in *Lochner v. New York.*"

EXCERPTS

From Justice Brewer's majority opinion: "That woman's physical structure and the performance of maternal functions place her at a disadvantage in the struggle for subsistence is obvious. This is especially true when the burdens of motherhood are upon her. Even when they are not, by abundant testimony of the medical fraternity continuance for a long time on her feet at work, repeating this from day to day, tends to injurious effects upon the body, and, as healthy mothers are essential to vigorous offspring, the physical well-being of woman becomes

an object of public interest and care in order to preserve the strength and vigor of the race. . . .

". . . The two sexes differ in structure of body, in the functions to be performed by each, in the amount of physical strength, in the capacity for long continued labor, particularly when done standing, the influence of vigorous health upon the future well-being of the race, the self-reliance which enables one to assert full rights, and in the capacity to maintain the struggle for subsistence. This difference justifies a difference in legislation, and upholds that which is designed to compensate for some of the burdens which rest upon her."

IMPACT

Today the language of *Muller v. Oregon* sounds antiquated, even offensive toward women. At the time, however, legislation treating women differently was viewed as a progressive reform. Now, however, such a law would be so constitutionally suspect that it almost certainly would not be allowed to stand.

In the 1971 case *Reed v. Reed*, for example, and in *Frontiero v. Richardson* two years later, the Supreme Court struck down laws that gave men favorable treatment in the administration of estates and in military benefits, respectively. In these and other cases the Court gave notice that laws treating men and women differently would be scrutinized under the Fourteenth Amendment—although the exact level of scrutiny has been a matter of debate.

Some commentators believed at first that the *Muller* decision had overturned *Lochner* without saying so directly. And for several years the *Muller* decision encouraged reformers to urge passage of, and defend, labor laws. Brandeis often assisted them, until he was nominated to a seat on the Court in 1916.

But *Muller* turned out to have done little to shorten the Court's *Lochner* era, in which the justices usually struck down laws restricting businesses.

The *Muller* case is remembered among justices and Supreme Court advocates for another reason. Brandeis's brief, with its emphasis on research that went beyond the specific facts of the case, had a powerful impact on the Court. A brief that incorporates such material has become known as a "Brandeis brief," and is often used in cases involving race discrimination or other issues where advocates feel the Court needs to know the broader context.

Standard Oil Co. of New Jersey v. United States

Decided May 15, 1911
221 U.S. 1
laws.findlaw.com/US/221/1.html

DECISION

Federal antitrust law should be interpreted to prohibit only those combinations of businesses and trade practices that are "unreasonable." Under this "rule of reason," the Standard Oil monopoly must be broken up.

BACKGROUND

As the nation became more highly industrialized, single companies or groups of companies called "trusts" dominated certain segments of the economy. They combined to make it harder for competitors to stay in business, and, as they grew, they controlled production generally to maintain higher prices to the consumer. At the turn of the twentieth century, steel, oil, tobacco, sugar, and meatpacking were among the industries that trusts or monopolies dominated.

Congress in 1890 tried to deal with this threat to free and open markets by passing the Sherman Antitrust Act, which barred "every contract, combination in the form of trust or otherwise, or conspiracy, in restraint of trade or commerce among the several states, or with foreign nations."

Although based on the Constitution's grant of power to Congress to regulate interstate commerce, the antitrust law represented a major escalation of Congress's role in regulating the economy. At first the Supreme Court treated it warily. In *United States v. E.C. Knight Co.* (1895) the Court rejected the government's effort to break up the sugar trust under the Sherman Act. The Court ruled that the manufacture of sugar had only an indirect impact on interstate commerce, so was subject to state, not federal, authority. For several years, the *Knight* ruling rendered the Sherman Act virtually powerless.

President Theodore Roosevelt, elected as a reformer, persisted in his campaign of "trust-busting," and in 1904 the Court took a broader view of the scope of the law. In *Northern Securities Co. v. United States* the Court found that a holding company aimed at monopolizing the railroad industry did indeed affect interstate commerce. In *Swift and Co. v. United States* the next year, the Court applied the Sherman Act to the meatpacking industry, finding that many business activities within a state created a "course of commerce" that was interstate and therefore subject to regulation under the Sherman Act.

The *Northern Securities* ruling emboldened the Roosevelt administration to take on two even bigger targets: Standard Oil and American Tobacco, companies that epitomized monopolistic practices. Standard Oil controlled more than 90 percent of the nation's refining capacity, and muckraking journalists such as Ida Tarbell had exposed its abuses. As the lawsuits that stemmed from enforcement of the Sherman Act against those two companies headed to the Supreme Court, the *Harvard Law Review* said public attention was focused on the Court "to a greater extent than ever before in its history." *Harper's Weekly* said, "the financial markets have virtually stood still awaiting their settlement."

VOTE

9–0, with Chief Justice Edward D. White writing the majority opinion. Joining him were Justices Oliver Wendell Holmes Jr., Joseph McKenna, William R. Day, Horace H. Lurton, Charles Evans Hughes, Willis Van Devanter, and Joseph R. Lamar. Justice John Marshall Harlan concurred in part and dissented in part.

In this 1904 cartoon John D. Rocke-feller's Standard Oil Company is depicted as an octopus with a stranglehold on government and industry alike. In *Standard Oil Co. v. United States* (1911) the Supreme Court said the trust violated the Sherman Antitrust Law. Chief Justice Edward D. White's opinion drew a line between trusts that placed "unreasonable" limits on competi-tion and those that monopolized markets through fair competition, a doctrine known as "the rule of reason."

Source: Library of Congress.

HIGHLIGHTS

In a lengthy opinion, Chief Justice White argued that Congress could not have meant the Sherman Act to reach and prohibit all business contracts that restrained free and competitive trade. Reviewing economic regulations going back to precolonial times in England, the Court said that while business practices restraining competition have long been illegal, "if the restraint was partial in its operation and was otherwise reasonable, the contract was held to be valid." Monopolies that resulted in in-flated prices to consumers also have long been outlawed, White noted, but not all monopolies have been banned.

The language of the Sherman Act seemed to be much more sweeping, barring all business practices that restrained trade. White got around that problem simply by insisting that no matter what Congress said, it must have meant that some judgment had to be used to decide which practices were pro-hibited by the law and which were not.

"Not specifying but indubitably contemplating and requir-ing a standard, it follows that it was intended that the standard of reason which had been applied at the common law and in this country in dealing with subjects of the character embraced by the statute was intended to be the measure used for the purpose of determining whether, in a given case, a particular act had or had not brought about the wrong against which the statute provided," the Court said.

White dismissed allegations that this rule of reason would place too much power in the hands of the courts because they would always have to interpret what was reasonable.

Having decided the standard to apply, the Court then had to determine whether Standard Oil's domination of the oil in-dustry was reasonable or not. This was not an easy task, the Court said after reviewing a "jungle of conflicting testimony covering a period of forty years."

The story of the Rockefellers' nationwide expansion of Standard Oil leads inevitably to the conclusion that their ac-tions were not reasonable, the Court said. "We think no disin-terested mind can survey the period in question without being irresistibly driven to the conclusion that the very genius for commercial development and organization which it would seem was manifested from the beginning soon begot an intent and purpose to exclude others," White wrote. The company's practices, he added, "necessarily involved the intent to drive others from the field and to exclude them from their right to trade, and thus accomplish the mastery which was the end in view." The Court upheld the lower court's decree breaking up the company.

Justice Harlan wrote a separate opinion, agreeing with the Court that Standard Oil's monopoly violated the Sherman Act. But he dissented from the "rule of reason" interpretation White had placed on the law. He said the Court had indulged in judi-cial legislation by inserting the word *unreasonable* into the act, something the Court had declined to do in a case just fifteen years earlier.

Amending an act of Congress goes beyond the Court's constitutional duties, Harlan said. "The Courts have nothing to do with the wisdom or policy of an act of Congress. Their duty is to ascertain the will of Congress, and if the statute embody-ing the expression of that will is constitutional, the Courts must respect it. They have no function to declare a public policy, nor to amend legislative enactments."

EXCERPTS

From Justice White's majority opinion: "[T]he criteria to be resorted to in any given case for the purpose of ascertaining whether violations of the section have been committed is the rule of reason guided by the established law and by the plain duty to enforce the prohibitions of the act, and thus the public policy which its restrictions were obviously enacted to subserve. And it is worthy of observation, as we have previously remarked concerning the common law, that although the statute, by the comprehensiveness of the enumerations embodied in both the 1st and 2d sections, makes it certain that its purpose was to prevent undue restraints of every kind or nature, nevertheless, by the omission of any direct prohibition against monopoly in the concrete, it indicates a consciousness that the freedom of the individual right to contract, when not unduly or improperly exercised, was the most efficient means for the prevention of monopoly, since the operation of the centrifugal and centripetal forces resulting from the right to freely contract was the means by which monopoly would be inevitably prevented if no extraneous or sovereign power imposed it and no right to make unlawful contracts having a monopolistic tendency were permitted. In other words, that freedom to contract was the essence of freedom from undue restraint on the right to contract. . . .

". . . To hold to the contrary would require the conclusion either that every contract, act, or combination of any kind or nature, whether it operated a restraint on trade or not, was within the statute, and thus the statute would be destructive of all right to contract or agree or combine in any respect whatever as to subjects embraced in interstate trade or commerce, or, if this conclusion were not reached, then the contention would require it to be held that, as the statute did not define the things to which it related, and excluded resort to the only means by which the acts to which it relates could be ascertained—the light of reason—the enforcement of the statute was impossible because of its uncertainty."

IMPACT

The "rule of reason" was a creation of Chief Justice White, and it was an artful compromise between progressives who wanted a strict interpretation of the law and business interests who wanted a looser reading. Justice Holmes remarked to a law clerk, "The moment I saw that in the circulated draft, I knew he [White] had us. How could you be against that without being for a rule of unreason?" The *Standard Oil* decision was probably White's most significant opinion as chief justice. Two weeks later the Court also ordered the breakup of the American Tobacco Company.

The ruling's bottom line—the breakup of Standard Oil—was popular. But progressives attacked the "rule of reason" for watering down the law and giving businesses too much leeway. Business interests complained that the rule was too vague to give them clear guidance on what they could or could not do. Antitrust issues continued to dominate U.S. politics, and in 1914 Congress passed the Clayton Act and created the Federal Trade Commission partly to wrest back to itself control over the issue.

The rule of reason continued to be the guiding principle of the Court's antitrust decisions for several decades, sometimes resulting in probusiness decisions and sometimes not. In the late 1930s the Court began adopting more definitive rules, finding that certain practices were presumed to violate the law, no matter how reasonable they might seem in a given situation. Meanwhile, antitrust enforcement waxed and waned, depending on who was elected president. In recent years a more conservative Supreme Court has made use of both the rule of reason and "per se" rules in judging antitrust cases.

As for Standard Oil, the Court's decision meant that the thirty-three companies in its holding company had to become separate, competing entities. Many of them became familiar names in their own right: Mobil, Amoco, and Chevron, among others. In 1972 what was left of the original Standard Oil Company of New Jersey changed its name to Exxon Corporation.

Schechter Poultry Corp. v. United States

Decided May 27, 1935
295 U.S. 495
laws.findlaw.com/US/295/495.html

DECISION

A federal law aimed at regulating and stimulating the economy in the wake of the Great Depression is unconstitutional. The National Industrial Recovery Act, which imposed codes of competition on many industries, gives too much power to the president and regulates aspects of the economy that only indirectly affected interstate commerce.

BACKGROUND

Helping the nation climb out of the Great Depression was the main task of government in the early 1930s. President Herbert Hoover made a start by boosting federal spending on public works to create jobs and establishing a federal loan agency to help businesses return to health. But Hoover stopped short of government-imposed controls on prices and production. He felt that kind of government intervention would ultimately harm the national economy.

That approach was rejected in the 1932 presidential election when Franklin D. Roosevelt soundly defeated Hoover. Roosevelt believed he had a mandate from the voters for "bold, persistent experimentation." One of these experiments was the National Industrial Recovery Act (NIRA), which, through a variety of controls, sought to increase wages and spending power for workers while also raising prices and controlling production to benefit companies. Business groups and associations were allowed to draw up codes of fair competition that could be approved or rejected by the president. Once approved, the codes would have the force of federal law. The NIRA was an unprecedented expansion of federal power over the economy, which supporters said was necessary to bring about a recovery.

By February 1934 more than 700 codes of competition had been established for the benefit of a wide range of industries with millions of employees. One of the newly regulated industries was the wholesale poultry trade in New York City. The code imposed a minimum wage of fifty cents an hour and a maximum workweek of forty-eight hours, as well as several health and marketing regulations. The four brothers who ran the Schechter Poultry Company were accused of violating the code by paying wages that were too low and by selling thousands of pounds of diseased chickens at artificially low prices. They were fined and sentenced to jail, but appealed their convictions, setting up a test case of the constitutionality of the law.

To make its case, the government argued that the sale of chickens in New York City was inseparable from interstate commerce, bringing it under the power to regulate commerce "among the several States" that the Constitution gives to Congress. But lawyers for the Schechter brothers argued that the chickens had "come to rest" in New York and no longer had anything to do with interstate commerce.

VOTE

9–0, with Chief Justice Charles Evans Hughes writing the opinion of the Court. Joining him were Justices Willis Van Devanter, James C. McReynolds, Louis D. Brandeis, George Sutherland, Pierce Butler, Harlan Fiske Stone, Owen J. Roberts, and Benjamin N. Cardozo.

HIGHLIGHTS

The Court made it clear that it was unimpressed by arguments that the Great Depression justified setting aside constitutional rules. "The recuperative efforts of the federal government must be made in a manner consistent with the authority granted by the Constitution," Hughes wrote.

A. L. A. Schechter, center, with his lawyers, Joseph Heller, left, and Frederick Wood. In *Schechter Poultry Corp. v. United States* (1935), known as the "sick chicken" case, the Court declared portions of the National Industrial Recovery Act unconstitutional, giving Schechter and his poultry business a victory.
Source: ©Bettmann/CORBIS.

Hughes was also unswayed by the government's defense of the law. Detailing the extraordinary powers the recovery act gave to the executive branch, he concluded, "Such a delegation of legislative power is unknown to our law, and is utterly inconsistent with the constitutional prerogatives and duties of Congress."

In a concurring opinion, Justice Cardozo underlined Hughes's criticism of the law in a now-classic line. "If that conception shall prevail, anything that Congress may do within the limits of the commerce clause for the betterment of business may be done by the President upon the recommendation of a trade association by calling it a code. This is delegation running riot."

The Court's second reason for striking down the law was that the local chicken business operated by the Schechter brothers did not have enough of a relationship to interstate commerce to allow federal intervention. The ruling established a "direct-indirect" test for deciding if Congress had the power to regulate a certain business activity.

"Where the effect of intrastate transactions upon interstate commerce is merely indirect, such transactions remain within the domain of state power," Hughes wrote. "If the commerce clause were construed to reach all enterprise and transactions which could be said to have an indirect effect upon interstate commerce, the federal authority would embrace practically all the activities of the people, and the authority of the state over its domestic concerns would exist only by sufferance of the federal government."

Added Cardozo, "Activities local in their immediacy do not become interstate and national because of distant repercussions. What is near and what is distant may at times be uncertain. There is no penumbra of uncertainty obscuring judgment here. To find immediacy or directness here is to find it almost everywhere. If centripetal forces are to be isolated to the exclusion of the forces that oppose and counteract them, there will be an end to our federal system."

EXCERPTS

From Justice Hughes's majority opinion: "Extraordinary conditions do not create or enlarge constitutional power. The Constitution established a national government with powers deemed to be adequate, as they have proved to be both in war and peace, but these powers of the national government are limited by the constitutional grants. Those who act under these grants are not at liberty to transcend the imposed limits because they believe that more or different power is necessary. . . .

"Such a sweeping delegation of legislative power finds no support in the decisions upon which the Government especially relies. . . .

". . . Much is made of the fact that almost all the poultry coming to New York is sent there from other states. But the code provisions, as here applied, do not concern the transportation of the poultry from other states to New York, or the transactions of the commission men or others to whom it is consigned, or the sales made by such consignees to defendants. . . .

". . . The mere fact that there may be a constant flow of commodities into a State does not mean that the flow continues after the property has arrived and has become commingled with the mass of property within the state. . . . So far as the poultry here in question is concerned, the flow in interstate commerce had ceased. The poultry had come to a permanent rest within the state. . . .

". . . [T]he authority of the federal government may not be pushed to such an extreme as to destroy the distinction, which the commerce clause itself establishes, between commerce 'among the several States' and the internal concerns of a state. The same answer must be made to the contention that is based upon the serious economic situation which led to the passage of the Recovery Act—the fall in prices, the decline in wages and employment, and the curtailment of the market for commodities. Stress is laid upon the great importance of maintaining wage distributions which would provide the necessary stimulus in starting 'the cumulative forces making for expanding commercial activity.' Without in any way disparaging this motive, it is enough to say that the recuperative efforts of the federal government must be made in a manner consistent with the authority granted by the Constitution."

IMPACT

The "sick chicken" case, as it came to be known, was another striking reminder of the independence of the judiciary. Neither political pressure nor the memory of the deprivations of the Depression would sway the Court to bend its view of the Constitution. Congress, urged on by President Roosevelt, had gone too far, in the Court's view, and no one except the justices could bring them back.

As the administration canceled the codes of competition in response to the decision, some businesses celebrated the return of voluntary efforts to restore the economy. President Roosevelt, however, was furious with the decision. Holding up telegrams from those businesses that were concerned about the demise of the beneficial regulations, Roosevelt said the Court had imposed a "horse-and-buggy definition of interstate commerce" on the nation. Solving the nation's economic problems would be hampered by differing regulations in each of the forty-eight states, he argued. Roosevelt said the ruling was probably the most important since the *Dred Scott* case, the infamous 1857 decision that said blacks could not be citizens.

In several subsequent opinions, the Court continued to give the administration trouble, so two years later, Roosevelt proposed increasing the number of justices in a controversial plan aimed at neutralizing the Court's anti–New Deal slant. At just about the same time, however, the Court changed its tune, taking a broader view of the definition of interstate commerce, and New Deal legislation began to fare better with the Court. That aspect of the *Schechter* precedent was short-lived.

The Court's narrow view of when and how much power Congress could cede to the president also has had limited impact. Even when the Supreme Court, in the 1998 case *Clinton v. New York,* struck down the line-item veto law because Congress had given the president too much power, the majority opinion did not cite the *Schechter* case.

National Labor Relations Board v. Jones and Laughlin Steel Corp.

Decided April 12, 1937
301 U.S. 1
laws.findlaw.com/US/301/1.html

DECISION

The National Labor Relations Act of 1937 is constitutional. Congress's power to regulate interstate commerce includes the power to regulate activities within a state that have a close relationship to interstate commerce, including labor disputes that could disrupt interstate commerce.

BACKGROUND

The year 1937 was one of high drama at the Supreme Court. President Franklin Roosevelt was frustrated that the conservative Court had found many of his New Deal laws unconstitutional. To neutralize the Court's uncooperative majority, Roosevelt sent to Congress a proposal to reorganize the Court. The plan called for adding a justice for each sitting justice who refused to resign after turning seventy. The plan, immediately derided as "Court-packing," was, however, perfectly legal—Congress had changed the size of the Supreme Court several times before. Although doomed to failure, Roosevelt's plan focused intense scrutiny and pressure on the Supreme Court.

Five days after Roosevelt announced his plan, the Court heard arguments in a set of cases that ultimately would set it in a new direction, satisfying Roosevelt and New Deal advocates and defusing the Court-packing campaign.

The lead case was *National Labor Relations Board v. Jones and Laughlin Steel Corp.* It involved a challenge to the National Labor Relations Act, then known as the Wagner Act for its sponsor, New York senator Robert Wagner. Congress passed the law in 1935 to bolster the labor movement in its effort to unionize U.S. workers. It prohibited a series of unfair labor practices by employers, including firing workers for union activities and refusing to bargain with a union. But even as Congress passed the law, many supporters believed the Supreme Court would find it unconstitutional.

There were several reasons for predicting the law's demise. The conservative Court believed in the "liberty of contract," which included the right of employers to bargain with employees without government interference. The Court at the time also had a very narrow view of the power of Congress to regulate anything that did not directly involve commerce "among the several States," in the words of the Constitution. Labor disputes inside a factory would probably not meet the Court's definition of interstate commerce that could be regulated by Congress. But the Roosevelt administration decided to defend the law vigorously through some test cases in federal court.

The Jones and Laughlin dispute was a classic example of practices the law was passed to prevent. Jones and Laughlin was the nation's fourth largest steel producer, with 22,000 workers at plants in South Pittsburgh and Aliquippa, Pennsylvania. Aliquippa was a company town, meaning that it was tightly controlled by Jones and Laughlin. In July 1935, just a few days after President Roosevelt signed the Wagner Act into law, the company fired ten workers who had organized fellow employees into a union. The National Labor Relations Board (NLRB), created by the law, ordered the company to reinstate the workers and pay them the wages they lost because of the firings. The company challenged the order, and a federal appeals court ruled that the Wagner Act was unconstitutional.

The case went to the Supreme Court, along with four other suits on the same issue. The Court was crowded for the three days of argument in the cases. The lawyers for the employers asserted that the labor disputes had nothing to do with interstate commerce.

VOTE

5–4, with Chief Justice Charles Evans Hughes writing the majority opinion. Joining him were Justices Louis D. Brandeis, Harlan Fiske Stone, Owen J. Roberts, and Benjamin N. Cardozo. Dissenting were Justices Willis Van Devanter, James C. McReynolds, George Sutherland, and Pierce Butler.

HIGHLIGHTS

Chief Justice Hughes began by paying his respects to the federal system, under which states and the federal government are supposed to coexist. "The authority of the federal government may not be pushed to such an extreme as to destroy the distinction, which the commerce clause itself establishes, between commerce 'among the several States' and the internal concerns of a state. That distinction between what is national and what is local in the activities of commerce is vital to the maintenance of our federal system."

But that did not make the Wagner Act unconstitutional, Hughes said, arguing that the law should be given as favorable an interpretation as possible. "The cardinal principle of statutory construction is to save and not to destroy," Hughes wrote.

The Court swept aside its earlier narrow definition of interstate commerce, broadening it to include business activities that occur entirely within one state. "Although activities may be intrastate in character when separately considered, if they have such a close and substantial relation to interstate commerce that their control is essential or appropriate to protect that commerce from burdens and obstructions, Congress cannot be denied the power to exercise that control."

The Court also dismissed the argument that the law interfered with "the right of contract" under the due process clause of the Fifth Amendment. This right had been interpreted in the past as protecting the right of employers to choose their employees and deal with them without the government getting involved. "The Act does not interfere with the normal exercise of the right of the employer to select its employees or to discharge them," Hughes wrote. "The employer may not, under cover of that right, intimidate or coerce its employees with respect to their self-organization and representation, and, on the other hand, the Board is not entitled to make its authority a pretext for interference with the right of discharge when that right is exercised for other reasons than such intimidation and coercion."

The dissenters, Justices McReynolds, Van Devanter, Sutherland, and Butler, were known as the Four Horsemen of the Apocalypse for their consistently negative reaction to Roosevelt's New Deal legislation. In this case, their usual ally, Justice Roberts, voted against them.

McReynolds read his angry dissent from the bench. He said the majority's broadened definition of the commerce power of Congress would eventually sweep in everything, leaving nothing beyond the reach of regulations. He offered some rhetorical examples in the form of questions: "May a mill owner be prohibited from closing his factory or discontinuing his business because so to do would stop the flow of products to and from his plant in interstate commerce? May employees in a factory be restrained from quitting work in a body because this will close the factory and thereby stop the flow of commerce? May arson of a factory be made a Federal offense whenever this would interfere with such flow? . . . If the ruling of the Court just announced is adhered to these questions suggest some of the problems certain to arise."

McReynolds wanted to cling to the old distinction between manufacturing and commerce, which would have placed the labor dispute outside the scope of congressional regulations. "The things inhibited by the Labor Act relate to the management of a manufacturing plant—something distinct from commerce and subject to the authority of the state. And this may not be abridged because of some vague possibility of distant interference with commerce."

With *National Labor Relations Board v. Jones and Laughlin Steel Corp.* (1937) the Supreme Court abandoned its narrow view of the federal power to regulate interstate commerce. The decision came barely two months after President Franklin D. Roosevelt submitted a plan to Congress to enlarge the Court. Roosevelt hoped that new members would, as depicted in this editorial cartoon, "reflect" his views.
Source: ©1937, The Washington Post. Reprinted with permission.

EXCERPTS

From Justice Hughes's majority opinion: "The congressional authority to protect interstate commerce from burdens and obstructions is not limited to transactions which can be deemed to be an essential part of a 'flow' of interstate or foreign commerce. Burdens and obstructions may be due to injurious action springing from other sources. The fundamental principle is that the power to regulate commerce is the power to enact 'all appropriate legislation' for 'its protection and advancement.' . . .

". . . [T]he stoppage of those operations by industrial strife would have a most serious effect upon interstate commerce. In view of respondent's far-flung activities, it is idle to say that the effect would be indirect or remote. It is obvious that it would be immediate and might be catastrophic. We are asked to shut our eyes to the plainest facts of our national life and to deal with the question of direct and indirect effects in an intellectual vacuum. . . . When industries organize themselves on a national scale . . . how can it be maintained that their industrial labor relations constitute a forbidden field into which Congress may not enter when it is necessary to protect interstate commerce from the paralyzing consequences of industrial war?"

IMPACT

The *Jones and Laughlin* decision, along with *West Coast Hotel v. Parrish* (upholding a state minimum wage law) decided a month earlier, marked the end of an era in the life of the Supreme Court. During the *Lochner* era, named after the 1905 case *Lochner v. New York,* the Court had viewed the federal government as a limited government that was meant to stay out of the way of free enterprise. This *laissez-faire* approach ended with the 1937 Court taking a much bolder view of the role the government could take in monitoring and regulating the economy to make sure it operated for the benefit of the public. The Court continued in this direction through the New Deal, issuing decisions such as *Wickard v. Filburn* (1942), which upheld a penalty assessed against a farmer who produced more grain than the law allotted him. (See *Lochner v. New York.*)

The decisions in 1937 took much of the steam out of Roosevelt's Court-packing plan, as did the vacancies that occurred during the next several years. Roosevelt finally had the chance he was waiting for to reshape the Court.

Political lore has it that the justices had Roosevelt's plan in mind when they ruled in his favor in *Jones and Laughlin.* Justice Roberts, in particular, had opposed New Deal legislation in prior cases, but voted with the majority to uphold the NLRB. His change of mind has been called "the switch in time that saved nine," although some scholars have suggested more recently that Roberts had already changed his mind before the Roosevelt plan was unveiled.

Justice Robert Jackson later described the *Jones and Laughlin* decision as the most far-reaching victory ever won by the labor movement. It gave federal protection to the right of unions to organize and bargain collectively, and unions grew with that protection.

The decision was also, as Court scholar Bernard Schwartz has described, "the foundation of what turned out to be a virtual constitutional revolution." Like *Gibbons v. Ogden* in 1824, it offered an expansive view of the national economy that was not just the province of the states but could be regulated—and encouraged—on a national scale. "With effect on commerce as the test, the radius of federal power becomes as broad as the economic life of the nation."

With this new precedent in place, the Court upheld virtually every federal regulation of business that Congress enacted. During the mid-1990s a more conservative Court began to question whether Congress was applying the interstate commerce power too liberally. In *United States v. Lopez* (1995) the Court struck down a federal law that made it a crime to possess a firearm near a school. (See *United States v. Lopez.*) The law had been based on the commerce power, but the Court said having a gun near a school had no conceivable relationship to interstate commerce. Several other decisions since *Lopez* have breathed new life into other aspects of states' rights at the expense of federal power. In *Printz v. United States* (1997), for example, the Court said Congress overstepped its authority when it passed a measure requiring state officials to gather handgun registration information for federal purposes.

Heart of Atlanta Motel v. United States

Decided December 14, 1964
379 U.S. 241
laws.findlaw.com/US/379/241.html

DECISION

Congress has the power, through regulation of interstate commerce, to prohibit racial discrimination in privately owned hotels and motels. The Court upheld a portion of the Civil Rights Act of 1964 that prohibits bias on the basis of race, religion, or national origin in public accommodations.

BACKGROUND

Even as late as 1964, many hotels and other public accommodations nationwide—not merely in the South—were segregated. Blacks who traveled from one city to another on business or for pleasure often had to go miles out of their way to find places to sleep.

Thirty-two states had enacted laws making public accommodations open to all, but enforcement was spotty and no national law or policy on the subject existed. In fact, at the national level, as far as Supreme Court precedent was concerned, any effort by Congress to prohibit discrimination in private establishments was unconstitutional. In the so-called Civil Rights Cases of 1883, the Court had struck down an 1875 federal law banning race discrimination in inns and other businesses. The effect was to foreclose civil rights legislation for more than three-quarters of a century. (See Civil Rights Cases.)

President Lyndon B. Johnson sought to correct this injustice in 1964. Knowing that Congress would be kindly disposed toward him following the assassination of President John F. Kennedy—at least for a little while—Johnson pushed for comprehensive civil rights legislation. After signing the law, Johnson, a Democrat, told an aide that he had probably delivered the southern states to the Republican Party for a generation.

One section of the law states "All persons shall be entitled to the full and equal enjoyment of the goods, services, facilities, privileges, advantages, and accommodations of any place of public accommodation . . . without discrimination or segregation on the ground of race, color, religion, or national origin."

Because this provision in essence affected private business relationships that are usually beyond government regulation, Congress had to justify the law in terms of one of its enumerated or specified powers under the Constitution—prefer-

ably something other than the Fourteenth Amendment, which the Supreme Court in 1883 had said did not justify a similar law.

Instead, Congress invoked Article 1, Section 8, of the Constitution, which gives it exclusive power "to regulate Commerce . . . among the several States." At hearings that led up to the legislation, evidence was given to show that discrimination in hotels and restaurants had a significant impact on interstate commerce in part because it discouraged black people from traveling. The head of the Federal Aviation Administration testified, for example, that "air commerce is adversely affected" by racial discrimination in hotel accommodations.

The law was challenged by the Heart of Atlanta Motel, a 216-room establishment located in downtown Atlanta near several interstate highways. The motel clearly solicited interstate travelers through billboards and advertisements in national publications. It acknowledged that about three-fourths of its patrons were from out of state. Nevertheless, the owners argued that they should be able to continue their policy of refusing rooms to blacks.

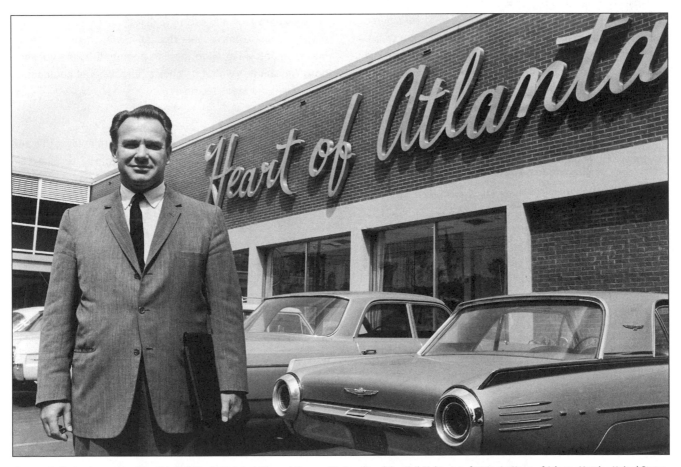

Moreton Rolleston Jr., owner of the Heart of Atlanta Motel, challenged the constitutionality of the Civil Rights Act of 1964. In *Heart of Atlanta Motel v. United States* (1964) a unanimous Supreme Court upheld the law, saying that Congress may use its powers to regulate interstate commerce to prohibit racial discrimination in privately owned public accommodations.

Source: ©Bettmann/CORBIS.

The motel owners claimed that Congress had overstepped its commerce powers in enacting the law. They also argued that the law violated the Fifth Amendment because it amounted to the government "taking" their property without compensation or due process. A lower federal court upheld the law and ordered the motel to accept blacks, setting the stage for the appeal to the Supreme Court.

VOTE

9–0, with Justice Tom C. Clark writing the majority opinion for the Court. Joining him were Chief Justice Earl Warren and Justices Hugo L. Black, William O. Douglas, John M. Harlan, William J. Brennan Jr., Potter Stewart, Byron R. White, and Arthur J. Goldberg.

HIGHLIGHTS

Justice Clark, himself a son of the South, had little trouble finding the public accommodations provision of the Civil Rights Act of 1964 constitutional. He found that the law fit comfortably into the tradition of congressional regulation of interstate commerce that the Court had upheld since the case of *Gibbons v. Ogden* in 1824. (See *Gibbons v. Ogden.*)

"Congress was also dealing with what it considered a moral problem" in the 1964 law, Clark wrote. "But that fact does not detract from the overwhelming evidence of the disruptive effect that racial discrimination has had on commercial intercourse." The Court agreed that its 1883 precedent did not apply to the 1964 law, because Congress had been careful to tie its wording to interstate commerce.

The Court again upheld the broad discretion Congress has to legislate in the area of commerce. "It is doubtful if in the long run appellant will suffer economic loss as a result of the Act. Experience is to the contrary where discrimination is completely obliterated as to all public accommodations," the Court said. "But whether this be true or not is of no consequence since this Court has specifically held that the fact that a 'member of the class which is regulated may suffer economic losses not shared by others . . . has never been a barrier' to such legislation."

Justice Douglas, in a concurring opinion, said he would have preferred to uphold the law under the Fourteenth Amendment rather than the commerce clause. He was concerned that by basing the decision on the commerce clause, the Court was guaranteeing "unnecessary litigation" in the future over whether a particular establishment did or did not engage in interstate commerce.

In a companion case involving a Birmingham, Alabama, restaurant called Ollie's Barbecue, which also wanted to remain segregated, the Court said there was less evidence of an interstate clientele, but the food it served had moved in interstate commerce. Partly answering Justice Douglas's point, the Court also said Congress had a "rational basis" for deciding that interstate commerce was involved if an establishment's customers or food had moved or could have moved across state lines.

EXCERPTS

From Justice Clark's majority opinion: "[T]he action of the Congress in the adoption of the Act as applied here to a motel which concededly serves interstate travelers is within the power granted it by the Commerce Clause of the Constitution, as interpreted by this Court for 140 years. It may be argued that Congress could have pursued other methods to eliminate the obstructions it found in interstate commerce caused by racial discrimination. But this is a matter of policy that rests entirely with the Congress, not with the courts. How obstructions in commerce may be removed—what means are to be employed— is within the sound and exclusive discretion of the Congress. It is subject only to one caveat—that the means chosen by it must be reasonably adapted to the end permitted by the Constitution. We cannot say that its choice here was not so adapted. The Constitution requires no more."

IMPACT

The Court's swift and unequivocal decision upholding this provision of the 1964 law was a major civil rights victory. It gave a considerable push to other civil rights legislation.

As for hotels and restaurants, the decision made it clear that old habits had to change. The Justice Department, emboldened by the Court's ruling, took enforcement actions against hundreds of private establishments to require them to serve customers of all races.

Nevertheless, allegations crop up from time to time that a particular establishment or restaurant chain still discriminates against racial minorities. Those reports usually generate negative publicity for the business involved, followed by swift apologies and corrective action. The fact that discrimination in this setting is so universally condemned is a sign of the deep impact the 1964 law—and the Supreme Court decision that upheld it—has had on U.S. society.

United States v. Lopez

Decided April 26, 1995
514 U.S. 549
laws.findlaw.com/US/514/549.html

DECISION

Congress exceeded its constitutional authority to regulate interstate commerce when it passed the Gun-Free School Zones Act of 1990, which forbids possession of firearms within 1,000 feet of a school. Because possession of a gun near a school is not an economic activity with a substantial impact on interstate commerce, Congress has no power to restrict gun possession near schools.

BACKGROUND

In 1990 Congress passed the Gun-Free School Zones Act. The law made it a federal crime to possess a firearm within 1,000 feet of a school. Congress was reacting to the problem of gun violence in school and the horrifying episodes of students shooting other students. To some, these occurrences illustrate the easy availability of guns on school campuses or near them. One government report in the early 1990s indicated that 4 percent of U.S. high school students carried a gun to school at least occasionally.

In 1992 a twelfth grade student named Alfonso Lopez Jr. was arrested in San Antonio, Texas, after arriving at Edison High School with a concealed .38 caliber handgun and five bullets. An anonymous tipster had alerted school officials. At first Lopez was charged under a Texas law banning guns in a school zone, but prosecutors decided instead to cite him for violating the relatively new federal law. Lopez was sentenced to six months in prison.

On appeal, Lopez's lawyers challenged the law as an intrusion on local autonomy. A federal appeals court agreed, asserting that Congress had not made a sufficient connection between gun possession and interstate commerce, which was the only plausible basis for the law.

As the case made its way to the Supreme Court, it took on extra significance. Many conservatives saw the gun law as an another example of what they considered a worrisome trend: Congress, in an effort to please pressure groups, was passing laws in a wide range of areas that once were left to the states. These critics said that Congress was losing sight of the fact that the Constitution limits its powers. Conservatives also felt that since the 1950s the Supreme Court had encouraged Congress in expanding its scope by upholding a range of legislation on "interstate commerce" grounds.

The Rehnquist Court, however, was markedly more conservative than the Court had been under Chief Justices Earl Warren and Warren Burger. If the Court could be persuaded to overturn the gun law, conservatives hoped, Congress might have to think twice about its free-wheeling approach to legislation.

VOTE

5–4, with Chief Justice William Rehnquist writing for the majority. Joining him were Justices Sandra Day O'Connor, Antonin Scalia, Anthony M. Kennedy, and Clarence Thomas. Dissenting were Justices John Paul Stevens, David H. Souter, Stephen G. Breyer, and Ruth Bader Ginsburg.

HIGHLIGHTS

The *Lopez* case sharply divided the Court. It provoked a lengthy and searching debate among the justices about the meaning and extent of the power of Congress to legislate.

To Chief Justice Rehnquist, the case seemed clear. Reviewing the history of the commerce power, Rehnquist said that an activity must "substantially affect" interstate commerce for Congress to regulate it. Possession of guns near schools, he argued, did not meet that standard. As he put it, somewhat sarcastically, "No such substantial effect was visible to the naked eye." Furthermore, Congress had not made the connection between gun possession and commerce through its legislative findings or in any other way.

In arguments before the Court, the Clinton administration had sought to make the link with interstate commerce by arguing that gun possession in or near schools leads to violent crime, discourages travel, and diminishes the educational experience—all of which could have an impact on commerce. But Rehnquist dismissed those arguments out of hand, saying that most of them would apply to other activities usually regulated by the states, such as marriage and family law.

"Under the theories that the Government presents," Rehnquist wrote, ". . . it is difficult to perceive any limitation on federal power, even in areas such as criminal law enforcement or education where States historically have been sovereign. Thus, if we were to accept the Government's arguments, we are hardpressed to posit any activity by an individual that Congress is without power to regulate."

Justice Kennedy, in a concurrence, also raised the specter of an overreaching federal government. "There are over 100,000 elementary and secondary schools in the United States. Each of these now has an invisible federal zone extending 1,000 feet beyond the (often irregular) boundaries of the school property. In some communities, no doubt, it would be difficult to navigate without infringing on those zones. Yet throughout these areas, school officials would find their own programs for the prohibition of guns in danger of displacement by the federal authority unless the State chooses to enact a parallel rule."

Justice Thomas wrote a powerful concurrence, commenting on the Court's own evolution in this area, as well as that of Congress. "I write separately to observe that our case law has drifted far from the original understanding of the Commerce Clause." "The power to regulate 'commerce' can by no means encompass authority over mere gun possession, any more than it empowers the Federal Government to regulate marriage, littering, or cruelty to animals, throughout the 50 States. Our Constitution quite properly leaves such matters to the individual States, notwithstanding these activities' effects on interstate commerce. Any interpretation of the Commerce Clause that even suggests that Congress could regulate such matters is in need of reexamination."

As clear as it was to the majority that the law had nothing to do with commerce, it was equally clear to the dissenters that the law was justified on that ground. "In my view, the statute falls well within the scope of the commerce power as this Court has understood that power over the last half-century," wrote Justice Breyer. "Upholding this legislation would do no more than simply recognize that Congress had a 'rational basis' for finding a significant connection between guns in or near schools and (through their effect on education) the interstate and foreign commerce they threaten." He cataloged dozens of reports and studies that purported to make the connection between school violence, educational quality, and commerce.

Justice Souter also dissented passionately, expressing fear that the majority opinion portended a "backward glance" toward the *Lochner* era, when the Court routinely looked askance at acts of Congress based on interstate commerce. In the 1905 decision *Lochner v. New York,* the Court had struck down a New York law regulating tenement house bakeries, ushering in an era when the Court struck down many regulations on business. "If it seems anomalous that the Congress of the United States has taken to regulating school yards, the act in question is still probably no more remarkable than state regulation of bake shops 90 years ago," Souter said. (See *Lochner v. New York.*)

EXCERPTS

From Justice Rehnquist's majority opinion: "The possession of a gun in a local school zone is in no sense an economic activity that might, through repetition elsewhere, substantially affect any sort of interstate commerce. Respondent was a local student at a local school; there is no indication that he had recently moved in interstate commerce, and there is no require-

ment that his possession of the firearm have any concrete tie to interstate commerce.

"To uphold the Government's contentions here, we would have to pile inference upon inference in a manner that would bid fair to convert congressional authority under the Commerce Clause to a general police power of the sort retained by the States. Admittedly, some of our prior cases have taken long steps down that road, giving great deference to congressional action. The broad language in these opinions has suggested the possibility of additional expansion, but we decline here to proceed any further. To do so would require us to conclude that the Constitution's enumeration of powers does not presuppose something not enumerated and that there never will be a distinction between what is truly national and what is truly local. This we are unwilling to do."

IMPACT

The *Lopez* decision had little practical effect. More than forty states already had passed laws restricting gun possession near schools, so striking down the federal law did not mean that guns were suddenly acceptable on school grounds. Efforts by gun control opponents to invoke *Lopez* in challenging other gun laws were largely unsuccessful.

The Clinton administration, which supported the Gun-Free School Zones Act, reacted to the decision by looking for ways to reenact the law and make it comply with the Court's ruling. In 1996 Congress passed a revised law that was limited to guns that had moved in interstate commerce.

More symbolically, however, the decision sent a chill through Congress, where the lesson of *Lopez* seemed to be that legislators should be more careful to draw a connection between the subject of new statutes and one or more of the powers that the Constitution grants to Congress.

The *Lopez* ruling was followed by a series of decisions in which the Court trimmed back congressional commerce clause power. In the 2000 decision *United States v. Morrison,* the Court struck down parts of the Violence Against Women Act, which enabled victims of gender-motivated violence to seek remedies in federal court. Congress did a better job of documenting the connection between the law and interstate commerce, by showing the cost to the economy of domestic violence. But still the Court found the law unconstitutional because the activity it was regulating was noneconomic and therefore beyond the reach of congressional power.

But by 2005 the trend begun by the *Lopez* decision seemed to have run its course. In *Gonzales v. Raich* the Court said the Commerce Clause did give Congress the power to ban all use of marijuana—including medical—in spite of contrary state laws. Two justices in the 5–4 *Lopez* majority—Anthony Kennedy and Antonin Scalia—defected in the *Raich* case to give federal power a 6–3 win.

Gonzales v. Raich

Decided June 6, 2005
No. 03-1454
laws.findlaw.com/US/000/03-1454.html

DECISION

Under the constitutional power to regulate interstate commerce, Congress has the authority to prohibit the cultivation and medical use of marijuana, even when the marijuana is locally grown and not sold across state lines.

BACKGROUND

In 1996 California voters approved a ballot initiative that allowed seriously ill residents to gain access to marijuana for medical use. Marijuana is illegal for general use, but many medical experts believe it has great medical value in relieving pain and nausea and increasing appetite for those who suffer certain cancers and other diseases, including glaucoma and multiple sclerosis. Under the California law doctors, patients, and those who cultivate marijuana were exempted from state antidrug laws when their use or handling of marijuana was recommended by a physician. Nine other states passed similar laws.

In spite of these laws, federal law enforcement officials insisted that marijuana use for any purpose is still prohibited under the federal Controlled Substances Act (CSA)—as it has been since 1937—and that users were still subject to federal arrest and prosecution. Opponents of medical marijuana also viewed the California initiative and others as a "backdoor" way to loosen drug laws and pave the way for legalization of marijuana for all uses.

The clash between federal and state law was illustrated in 2002 when federal agents and local sheriff's officers raided the Oroville home of Diane Monson, who grew and used marijuana to combat severe back pain. The local officers concluded that she was using marijuana lawfully under California law, but the federal agents seized and destroyed her marijuana plants. She decided to challenge the enforcement of the CSA against her. She was joined by Angel Raich of Oakland, who also used marijuana to relieve pain and lost appetite resulting from several ailments. She had not been arrested but was a crusader on behalf of medical marijuana and did not want her ability to use the drug restricted. The U.S. Court of Appeals for the Ninth Circuit agreed with the two women, ruling that under Supreme Court precedent, enforcing the CSA against state-permitted instate use of marijuana was unconstitutional.

The Bush administration appealed to the Supreme Court, and the case became viewed as an important test of congressional power under the commerce clause—the part of the Constitution Congress invokes to enact laws like the CSA. In the 1995 case *United States v. Lopez* (see *United States v. Lopez*), the Supreme Court had taken a narrow view of that power, striking down a federal law banning gun possession near schools. Since then the Court had given greater weight to the role of states in the U.S. system of government. Medical marijuana supporters hoped that here, too, the Court would find that the federal drug law intruded too much on California's power to fashion and enforce its own laws.

VOTE

6–3, with Justice John Paul Stevens writing the majority opinion, joined by Justices Antonin Scalia, Anthony Kennedy, David Souter, Ruth Bader Ginsburg, and Stephen Breyer. Chief Justice William Rehnquist and Justices Sandra Day O'Connor and Clarence Thomas dissented.

HIGHLIGHTS

Justice Stevens, writing for the Court, sympathized with the women in the case, stating they had "strong arguments" to indicate that marijuana helps their medical conditions. But Stevens said unequivocally, "The CSA is a valid exercise of federal power."

How did Stevens square this conclusion with the *Lopez* decision of ten years earlier and with *United States v. Morrison,* a 2000 decision that struck down a federal law dealing with violence against women? In those cases the Court said that the laws at issue did not truly involve interstate commerce or economic activity.

Stevens said the marijuana case was "at the opposite end of the spectrum." The CSA, he asserted, regulated activities that are "quintessentially economic," namely the trafficking of illegal drugs. And the CSA was part of a systematic, comprehensive set of antidrug laws that the Congress was clearly entitled to enact.

The fact that the marijuana used by the California women was home grown or for personal use, and that it never crossed state lines, was irrelevant in Stevens's view. The cultivation of marijuana in California and nine other states, even for limited purposes, Stevens said, inevitably influences the supply and price of the drug elsewhere. To support this point, Stevens cited *Wickard v. Filburn,* a decision issued by the Court in 1942, at the height of federal power. In *Wickard* the Court said Congress could regulate the price of wheat, even when the wheat was grown for home use and never crossed state lines. The similarities between the two cases, said Stevens, are "striking."

Surprisingly Justice Scalia, one of the five justices who had led the Court's trend toward according states more power in the federal system, joined the majority. He, like Stevens, said the ban was justifiable as part of a comprehensive federal effort to combat drug use. Scalia also looked to another part of the Constitution to justify using the CSA against homegrown marijuana. After specifying the "enumerated powers" of the Congress, Article I of the Constitution gives Congress power to pass all laws "necessary and proper" to carry out its powers— a catch-all phrase that gives Congress a fair amount of leeway.

In dissent, Justice O'Connor said it was impossible to reconcile the majority opinion with the *Lopez* and *Morrison* decisions. Allowing Congress to infringe on state powers just because it is done in the form of a comprehensive antidrug campaign, said O'Connor, "is tantamount to removing meaningful limits on the Commerce Clause." She wrote, "This overreaching stifles an express choice by some states, concerned for the lives and liberties of their people, to regulate medical marijuana differently."

Justice Thomas was even more critical in his dissent. "If Congress can regulate this under the Commerce Clause, then it can regulate virtually anything," he wrote. "If the majority is to be taken seriously, the Federal Government may now regulate quilting bees, clothes drives, and potluck suppers throughout the 50 States."

EXCERPTS

From Justice Stevens's majority opinion: "Given the enforcement difficulties that attend distinguishing between marijuana cultivated locally and marijuana grown elsewhere . . . and concerns about diversion into illicit channels, we have no difficulty concluding that Congress had a rational basis for believing that failure to regulate the intrastate manufacture and possession of marijuana would leave a gaping hole in the CSA. . . .

"One need not have a degree in economics to understand why a nationwide exemption for the vast quantity of marijuana (or other drugs) locally cultivated for personal use (which presumably would include use by friends, neighbors, and family members) may have a substantial impact on the interstate market for this extraordinarily popular substance."

IMPACT

The Court's decision was not necessarily a surprise, but it was a bitter disappointment to those who advocated loosening restrictions on medical marijuana use. Angel Raich said the decision would not keep her from using marijuana to relieve her pain. "If I did not use cannabis, I would die," she said after the opinion was handed down.

But she and other advocates pointed out that while the Court upheld the federal law against marijuana, it was not passing judgment on the law in California and the other states that supported medical marijuana. Given that state and local police are responsible for the vast majority of drug law enforcement nationwide, medical marijuana supporters asserted that the Supreme Court's ruling was unlikely to change what happens at the local level, unless the federal government decided to launch a new campaign to make marijuana arrests.

The Justice Department had little to say about its enforcement plans, but John Walters, the Bush administration's director of the Office of Drug Policy, offered this view: "Today's decision marks the end of medical marijuana as a political issue."

In terms of Supreme Court doctrine, the *Raich* decision may represent a significant turning point in the Court's trend toward limiting congressional power under the commerce clause.

By upholding the congressionally enacted Controlled Substances Act in the face of a state marijuana initiative approved by voters, the decision led some commentators to assert that the Court's federalism trend was over—or at least that it was a "fair-weather" fad without deep roots. The fact that Justice Antonin Scalia, a strong state-power advocate, joined the majority, was also viewed as a sign that the federalism trend might be short-lived. It may be that the Court's federalist justices, who also are its most conservative, simply could not bring themselves to apply their doctrine in a way that would undermine the nation's war on drugs.

In any event, the Court's decision seemed to forecast how it would handle a case that was on its way toward the Supreme Court, involving another clash between a state initiative and federal drug laws. In this case, *Gonzales v. Oregon,* the Court was expected to decide in late 2005 or early 2006 whether the same Controlled Substances Act can be enforced against those who make use of Oregon's Death with Dignity Act. That law allows certain terminally ill patients to obtain prescriptions for drugs that will hasten their death.

COPYRIGHT

The Constitution gives Congress the power to "promote the progress of science and useful arts . . . by securing for limited times to authors . . . the exclusive right to their respective writings." By including this copyright clause, the Framers of the Constitution were acknowledging a basic truth: Authors and artists will have little incentive to create if their works can be copied and they are unable to make money from their creations. This right is basic and has been extended well beyond the written word. But it sometimes conflicts with another democratic ideal related to the freedom of speech: that there should be few barriers to the exchange of ideas, and that the public, not artists alone, should benefit from copyrighted materials, now often described as "intellectual property." Congress and the Supreme Court have struggled with these concepts, especially as new technologies emerge—most recently, Internet file sharing—that make it harder to protect creations from being copied.

63   Metro-Goldwyn-Mayer Studios v. Grokster (2005)

Another related case mentioned in the Copyright section

Sony v. Universal City Studios (1984)

Metro-Goldwyn-Mayer Studios v. Grokster

Decided June 27, 2005
No. 04-480
laws.findlaw.com/US/000/04-480.html

DECISION

Unauthorized peer-to-peer sharing of music and movies over the Internet violates the protection of the copyright laws for the creators of those works. The distributors of software that makes file sharing possible can be held liable for the violations if they actively encourage users to violate copyrights.

BACKGROUND

One of the amazing innovations of the high-speed Internet is the ability for computer users to share files—audio and video as well as written text—with other users almost instantaneously and without loss of quality from the original. File-sharing technology has legitimate uses, but one of its most popular applications has been the massive sharing of copyrighted music and movies, in violation of copyright laws. Where once listeners would purchase CDs, in the late 1990s it became commonplace for computer users, young and old, to acquire hundreds of music files for free through software offered by Napster and other companies.

Alarmed music companies went to court to shut down Napster as a free service, and in 2001 they were successful. But other companies were ready to take Napster's place with software that operates somewhat differently. Instead of using a centralized index that could track how people use the software, StreamCast and Grokster used a more decentralized system that involved them less directly in the so-called "peer-to-peer" file sharing between individual computers. This difference was important for the U.S. Court of Appeals for the Ninth Circuit when these companies were sued. The court ruled that the companies could not be held liable for copyright infringement, because there are legitimate uses for the technology, and because the companies had no actual knowledge of the infringement.

Movie and music companies began suing infringers directly, many of them students on college campuses. But these companies also appealed the ninth circuit ruling to the Supreme Court. In a brief to the Court in early 2005, these companies said piracy of copyrighted materials "has reached epidemic proportions." They estimated that more than 2.6 billion music files and 12 million movies are illegally downloaded every month. Grokster and StreamCast, they alleged, had built their businesses on theft and should be held liable. Though the file sharing was free, Grokster and StreamCast derived in-

come from advertising that users were obliged to view as they were downloading.

But the controversial companies had many allies in the high-tech world. They insisted that file-sharing technology has a growing number of legitimate uses and should not be stifled just because it is misused. Drawing an analogy with an older technology, they said the makers of copy machines are not held liable when people use them to reproduce copyrighted materials, so Grokster and StreamCast should not be held liable either. Supporters reminded the Court that in 1984 the justices resisted similar pleas from the entertainment industry about the copyright threat posed by then-new videocassette recorders. The Court in *Sony v. Universal City Studios* protected VCRs because they had substantial noninfringing uses. It was not long before VCRs spawned a large and lucrative new source of revenue for the entertainment industry. Likewise, high-tech groups said the entertainment industry was already learning to adjust to file sharing and finding ways to profit from it.

VOTE

9–0, with Justice David Souter writing the opinion. He was joined by Chief Justice William Rehnquist and Justices John Paul Stevens, Sandra Day O'Connor, Antonin Scalia, Anthony Kennedy, Clarence Thomas, Ruth Bader Ginsburg, and Stephen Breyer.

HIGHLIGHTS

It was ironic that Justice Souter wrote the majority opinion. By reputation, he was one of the least tech-savvy of all the justices, still writing his opinions without using a computer. But he appeared to be well-versed in file-sharing technology and peppered his decision with computer terminology and even references to music groups such as Modest Mouse.

Souter reviewed and accepted the considerable evidence offered by MGM that Grokster and StreamCast had gone out of their way to encourage infringement and to avoid discouraging infringement. And even though some of the material that can be downloaded is legal—including centuries-old written works that predated copyright laws—Souter said it was obvious the main attraction of the software was to acquire music and movies for free. "Users seeking Top 40 songs, for example, or the latest re-

Rick Carnes, president of the Songwriters Guild of America, demonstrates outside the Supreme Court while the *Metro-Goldwyn-Mayer Studios v. Grokster* case is being heard on March 29, 2005. In that Internet file-sharing decision, the Court ruled that distributors of software that allows users to violate copyright law while downloading music and videos can be held liable for such infringement.

Source: AP/Wide World Photos/Gerald Herbert.

lease by Modest Mouse, are certain to be far more numerous than those seeking a free *Decameron*, and Grokster and StreamCast translated that demand into dollars," Souter wrote.

In this way, Souter said, the file-sharing case was different from the *Sony* VCR decision of nearly twenty-one years before. VCRs were often used for "time-shifting" or taping a television show for viewing later—not a use that violated copyright laws. But in the file-sharing case, there is clear evidence of intent to infringe copyrights, and that is highly relevant in Souter's view. "Nothing in *Sony* requires courts to ignore evidence of intent," Souter wrote.

Though the Court was unanimous in ruling against Grokster, the justices were divided on how strictly to interpret the rule of the *Sony* case. Justices Ginsburg and Kennedy, joined by Chief Justice Rehnquist, wrote a concurring opinion that argued for a strict view under which it was impossible to demonstrate that there were enough legal uses for the Grokster software to pass the *Sony* test. But Justice Breyer, joined by Justices Stevens and O'Connor, urged a more lenient view that would encourage continued innovation and development of a legal market for technology.

EXCERPTS

From Justice Souter's majority opinion: "The argument for imposing indirect liability in this case is . . . a powerful one, given the number of infringing downloads that occur every day using StreamCast's and Grokster's software. When a widely shared service or product is used to commit infringement, it may be impossible to enforce rights in the protected work effectively against all direct infringers, the only practical alternative being to go against the distributor of the copying device for secondary liability on a theory of contributory or vicarious infringement. . . .

"One who distributes a device with the object of promoting its use to infringe copyright, as shown by clear expression or other affirmative steps taken to foster infringement, is liable for the resulting acts of infringement by third parties. We are, of course, mindful of the need to keep from trenching on regular commerce or discouraging the development of technologies with lawful and unlawful potential. Accordingly . . . mere knowledge of infringing potential or of actual infringing uses would not be enough here to subject a distributor to liability. . . . The inducement rule, instead, premises liability on purposeful, culpable expression and conduct, and thus does nothing to compromise legitimate commerce or discourage innovation having a lawful promise."

IMPACT

The entertainment industry was jubilant over its victory. "With this unanimous decision, the Supreme Court has addressed a significant threat to the U.S. economy and moved to protect the livelihoods of the more than 11 million Americans employed by the copyright industries," the Recording Industry Association of America said in a statement. "The Supreme Court has helped to power the digital future for legitimate online businesses—including legal file sharing networks—by holding accountable those who promote and profit from theft."

Supporters of file-sharing and a less-regulated Internet expressed disappointment. "Today the Supreme Court has unleashed a new era of legal uncertainty on America's innovators," said Fred von Lohmann, a lawyer for the Electronic Frontier Foundation. "The newly announced inducement theory of copyright liability will fuel a new generation of entertainment industry lawsuits against technology companies."

As the ruling began to sink in, however, it began to be viewed as something of a compromise. Companies that actively encourage consumers to violate copyright were reined in by the decision, but the file-sharing technology itself was not. And if, as appears to be the case, the marketplace evolves to a point where legal uses of the technology flourish, copyright infringement is unlikely to be found. One thing appeared certain: Expensive litigation aimed at clarifying liability issues will continue.

ENVIRONMENTAL LAW

*T*he Constitution does not guarantee the right to clean air or water or a safe environment. But Congress has legislated extensively in this area, especially when the environmental movement began in the 1960s. The Supreme Court has been called on to interpret those laws, weighing a range of considerations including property rights, interstate commerce, and technical issues such as standing—who has the standing, or right, to sue when government action or inaction leads to environmental harms.

67   Sierra Club v. Morton (1972)

Other related cases mentioned in the Environmental Law section

Lujan v. National Wildlife Federation (1990)
Lucas v. South Carolina Coastal Council (1992)

Sierra Club v. Morton

Decided April 19, 1972
405 U.S. 727
laws.findlaw.com/US/405/727.html

DECISION

An interest group does not have "standing" or the right to sue to protect a wilderness area from government action. To have standing, a plaintiff must be able to show that he or she has been injured or will be injured by the government policy. However, the concept of injury can include "aesthetic and environmental well-being."

BACKGROUND

The Constitution requires that federal courts rule only on "cases or controversies," which the Supreme Court has interpreted to mean those cases in which one side or the other has actually been injured or harmed. This requirement has long been viewed as an important check on the courts, preventing them from deciding hypothetical issues or giving gratuitous advice to the other branches of government. To enforce this requirement, the Court has generally insisted that a person bringing a lawsuit have substantial "standing," which Justice Lewis F. Powell Jr. once defined as "some particularized injury that sets him apart from the man on the street."

For the environment, that standard can be difficult to meet because it could be said that air or water pollution, for example, affect everyone in general but nobody in particular. The issue in this case arose in a controversy over proposed development in Mineral King Valley in California. At the invitation of the U.S. Forest Service, several bidders submitted plans for developing the area for skiing and other recreational uses. In 1969 the government approved a $35 million plan submitted by Walt Disney Enterprises for a resort complex that could accommodate up to 14,000 visitors daily. The plan envisioned ski lifts, new highways, and high-voltage power lines to service a complex of motels and restaurants.

The Sierra Club, an environmental group with special interest in protecting national parks and forests, sued Interior Secretary Rogers Morton, claiming that the development would violate federal laws concerning national forests. A federal judge halted the development, but a federal appeals court panel reversed the judge's action. The appeals panel said it did not believe that the Sierra Club's general concern for national forests, "without a showing of more direct interest, can constitute standing in the legal sense."

VOTE

4–3, with Justice Potter Stewart writing for the majority. He was joined by Chief Justice Warren Burger and Justices Byron R. White and Thurgood Marshall. Justices William O. Douglas, William J. Brennan Jr., and Harry A. Blackmun dissented. Justices Lewis F. Powell Jr. and William Rehnquist, who were not on the Court when the case was argued in November, 1971, did not participate in the case.

HIGHLIGHTS

Cases in which the plaintiff suffered "palpable economic injuries" clearly meet the requirements for standing, Justice Stewart wrote. But the Sierra Club's suit, he said, forces the Court to consider standing for an organization that is claiming noneconomic losses that are widely shared.

Stewart began by recognizing that other kinds of injuries and losses—aesthetic and environmental, for example—could give someone standing to sue. But that alone is not enough, he wrote. Standing, he said, "requires that the party seeking review be himself among the injured."

On that score, the Sierra Club had failed the test, the Court ruled. "The Sierra Club failed to allege that it or its members would be affected in any of their activities or pastimes by the Disney development. Nowhere in the pleadings or affidavits did the Club state that its members use Mineral King for any purpose, much less that they use it in any way that would be significantly affected by the proposed action of the respondents."

The majority was clearly interested in drawing a line so that the courthouse door would not be opened to everyone who objected to a government policy or action, but that was not a concern for the dissenters, especially Justice Douglas. A well-known nature lover and outdoorsman, Douglas even suggested that "inanimate objects" such as trees or the forest itself should have standing to challenge the proposed development at Mineral King Valley. "Contemporary public concern for protecting nature's ecological equilibrium should lead to the conferral of standing upon environmental objects to sue for their own preservation," wrote Douglas. "This suit would therefore be more properly labeled as Mineral King v. Morton."

Because that was not likely, Douglas said the Sierra Club should be entitled to sue on behalf of the forest. "Those who

A dispute over the future of a wilderness area, Mineral King, California, led to *Sierra Club v. Morton* (1972). The Court ruled that an interest group seeking to restrain the federal government from approving the development of a ski resort in a valley of a national park does not have "standing," or the right to sue. In its opinion, however, the Court expanded the concept of injury to include harm to "aesthetic and environmental well-being." *Source: National Park Service.*

standing. He calculated that if the development did attract 14,000 visitors a day, that would mean roughly 300 cars an hour on the roads inside the forest. "Is this the way we perpetuate the wilderness and its beauty, solitude, and quiet?" asked Blackmun.

EXCERPTS

From Justice Stewart's majority opinion: "Aesthetic and environmental well-being, like economic well-being, are important ingredients of the quality of life in our society, and the fact that particular environmental interests are shared by the many rather than the few does not make them less deserving of legal protection through the judicial process. . . .

". . . But broadening the categories of injury that may be alleged in support of standing is a different matter from abandoning the requirement that the party seeking review must himself have suffered an injury. . . .

". . . [A] mere 'interest in a problem,' no matter how long-standing the interest and no matter how qualified the organization is in evaluating the problem, is not sufficient by itself to render the organization 'adversely affected' or 'aggrieved.' The Sierra Club is a large and long-established organization, with a historic commitment to the cause of protecting our Nation's natural heritage from man's depredations. But if a 'special interest' in this subject were enough to entitle the Sierra Club to commence this litigation, there would appear to be no objective basis upon which to disallow a suit by any other bona fide 'special interest' organization, however small or short-lived. And if any group with a bona fide 'special interest' could initiate such litigation, it is difficult to perceive why any individual citizen with the same bona fide special interest would not also be entitled to do so."

hike it, fish it, hunt it, camp in it, frequent it, or visit it merely to sit in solitude and wonderment are legitimate spokesmen for it, whether they may be few or many. Those who have that intimate relation with the inanimate object about to be injured, polluted, or otherwise despoiled are its legitimate spokesmen."

Extolling the virtues of unspoiled lands, Douglas continued, "before these priceless bits of Americana (such as a valley, an alpine meadow, a river, or a lake) are forever lost or are so transformed as to be reduced to the eventual rubble of our urban environment, the voice of the existing beneficiaries of these environmental wonders should be heard."

Less poetically, Justice Blackmun also dissented, suggesting that the majority was being too inflexible in its doctrine on

IMPACT

Even though the Sierra Club lost its battle for standing, the proposed ski resort at Mineral King Valley was never built. In 1978 Congress passed legislation adding the 12,600-acre area to Sequoia National Park, and it remains secluded and largely undeveloped. One travel guide describes the area as "a place where nature, not humans, dominates."

The Court's decision in *Sierra Club v. Morton* was a mixed blessing for the environmental movement. Although it set a high standard for standing, there were ways to comply with it, such as finding plaintiffs who could legitimately complain of a specific injury. In fact, that is what the Sierra Club did in the wake of the Supreme Court's ruling. It amended its lawsuit to allege that its members used Mineral King for recreation. The Supreme Court decision was also an important milestone for the environmental movement in establishing that environmental or aesthetic concerns had some legal significance in justifying legal action by individuals.

As the Court grew more conservative in the 1980s and 1990s, it set the hurdles even higher for standing in environmental cases. In *Lujan v. National Wildlife Federation* (1990) the Court acknowledged that environmental harm could justify standing, but it took a less generous stance on how seriously a plaintiff had to be affected by the harm to justify a suit. Justice Antonin Scalia in particular encouraged the Court in a series of decisions to take a stricter view of standing in such cases.

In June 1999 the Environmental Policy Project at Georgetown University Law Center issued a report criticizing the Supreme Court for seriously eroding the concept of standing since the *Sierra Club* decision. "One of the basic features of our nation's environmental protection system has been the right of citizens to sue in federal courts to force polluters to comply with environmental standards," the report said. "The ability of American citizens to vindicate their legal rights to a clean and healthy environment is rapidly eroding."

Meanwhile, environmental laws came under attack on other grounds. Conservative groups, including the Washington Legal Foundation, argued that when environmental laws deprive property owners of the use of their land, they should be compensated by government under the Fifth Amendment, which says government may not take over private property without paying for it. In the 1992 ruling *Lucas v. South Carolina Coastal Council,* the Court found that a coastal protection law had deprived an owner of all use of his land and therefore amounted to a taking of property by government. When the Supreme Court began in the mid-1990s to limit congressional power under the commerce clause, opponents of environmental laws challenged them on this basis as well. They argued that the Endangered Species Act and other laws were invalid because they did not involve interstate commerce and were therefore beyond the scope of congressional power.

ESTABLISHMENT OF RELIGION

The First Amendment command that "Congress shall make no law respecting an establishment of religion" has proven to be one of the most vexing parts of the Constitution—for the Court as well as for the public. Does it just mean that there should be no official national religion? Or does it mean far more than that, prohibiting any kind of aid to religion? Answering those questions became even more difficult when the Court in 1947 said the establishment clause applies to states as well as to Congress. States and localities set policies for public schools, and that is primarily where establishment clause battles have been fought ever since. The Court has developed several tests aimed at determining when government goes too far in accommodating religion in schools and elsewhere, but none has proved effective in giving the public clear guidance about what is and is not acceptable. It may be that drawing a clear line is simply impossible because the facts and context of each case are different.

Other related cases mentioned in the Establishment of Religion section

Everson v. Board of Education (1947)
Engel v. Vitale (1962)
Murray v. Curlett (1963)
Board of Education of Central School District No. 12 v. Allen (1968)
Epperson v. Arkansas (1968)
Early v. DiCenso (1971)
Wolman v. Walter (1977)
Stone v. Graham (1980)
Marsh v. Chambers (1983)
Wallace v. Jaffree (1985)
Aguilar v. Felton (1985)
Grand Rapids School District v. Ball (1985)
Allegheny County v. ACLU Greater Pittsburgh Chapter (1989)
Lamb's Chapel v. Center Moriches Union Free School District (1993)
Zobrest v. Catalina Foothills School District (1993)
Rosenberger v. Rector and Visitors of Univ. of Virginia (1995)
Mitchell v. Helms (2000)

School District of Abington Township v. Schempp

Decided June 17, 1963
374 U.S. 203
laws.findlaw.com/US/374/203.html

DECISION

Under the First Amendment, which prohibits passage of laws respecting an establishment of religion, public schools may not require the reading of Bible passages or the recitation of the Lord's Prayer. Excusing individual students from attending or participating in these religious activities does not make them constitutional.

BACKGROUND

Just a year before *Schempp* came to the Supreme Court, the justices had decided *Engel v. Vitale,* which said that under the First Amendment, public school officials could not require students to recite a state-sponsored prayer. Before *Engel,* virtually every public school student had begun the school day with some kind of religious observance. The decision in *Engel* touched off a furor among conservatives and some religious leaders, who claimed the Court had "banished God" from the nation's schools.

Rep. L. Mendel Rivers of South Carolina said, "I know of nothing in my lifetime that could give more aid and comfort to Moscow than this bold, malicious, atheistic, and sacrilegious twist by this unpredictable group of uncontrolled despots." New York's Francis Cardinal Spellman, probably the most prominent Roman Catholic leader in the United States, said he was "shocked and frightened" by the decision.

President John F. Kennedy, also a Roman Catholic, indicated support for the Court's ruling, which helped blunt some of the negative reaction. Still, the Court was deluged with more than a thousand letters and hundreds of angry phone calls. Calls for the impeachment of Chief Justice Earl Warren, which had begun after the school desegregation decision in *Brown v. Board of Education,* were renewed.

Given the angry climate, it would have been easy for the justices to pass up the next round of school prayer cases that came to the Court for review. But some Court scholars have suggested that, instead, the Court felt the need to reiterate its views in even stronger terms and show the public that it would not buckle under criticism.

So the justices accepted two cases that were somewhat similar to *Engel v. Vitale,* one from Pennsylvania and the other from Maryland.

In the Pennsylvania case, Abington Senior High School students Roger and Donna Schempp objected to a daily school ritual that was required by state law: the recitation of at least ten Bible verses and the Lord's Prayer. The Schempp family was Unitarian and said at trial that a literal reading of the Bible did not accord with their religious beliefs. The law allowed students not to participate in the recitations, but the Schempps did not want Roger and Donna to be ostracized by fellow students. A lower court agreed with the students that the Pennsylvania law violated the First Amendment.

The companion Maryland case, *Murray v. Curlett,* involved a similar rule in Baltimore. There, every school day began with either a Bible reading or the Lord's Prayer. Atheist Madalyn Mur-

Sidney Schempp holds a Bible as her husband, Edward L. Schempp, and their children, Roger and Donna, look on at their home in Roslyn, Pennsylvania, after the Supreme Court ruled in their favor and against compulsory Bible reading in public schools in *School District of Abington Township v. Schempp* (1963).
Source: AP/Wide World Photos.

ray, later known as Madalyn Murray O'Hair, and her son William objected to the rule. They succeeded in having it amended to allow individual students not to participate, but they also sued to have it overturned on First Amendment grounds. A Maryland court ruled that the law was constitutional.

VOTE

8–1, with Justice Tom C. Clark writing the majority opinion. Joining Clark were Chief Justice Earl Warren and Justices Hugo L. Black, William J. Brennan Jr., William O. Douglas, Arthur J. Goldberg, John M. Harlan, and Byron R. White. Dissenting was Justice Potter Stewart.

HIGHLIGHTS

The main difference between *Engel v. Vitale* and the cases now before the Court was that the New York prayer in *Engel* had been composed and sponsored by the state, whereas the Bible passages and prayers recited in Pennsylvania and Maryland were widely disseminated religious texts.

But to Justice Clark and the Court, that was not an important difference. The constitutional flaw was the same; the school districts in these cases were advancing religion instead of adhering to the neutrality that the Constitution's establishment clause requires, in the Court's view.

"In the relationship between man and religion, the State is firmly committed to a position of neutrality. Though the application of that rule requires interpretation of a delicate sort, the rule itself is clearly and concisely stated in the words of the First Amendment," Clark wrote for the majority.

Clark, for the first time, set out a test by which state laws or regulations could be examined to see if they violated the establishment clause. "To withstand the strictures of the Establishment Clause there must be a secular legislative purpose and a primary effect that neither advances nor inhibits religion," Clark wrote. Under that test, the Pennsylvania and Maryland laws fail.

Clark was mindful of the relationship between the establishment clause and the other religion clause of the First Amendment, which guarantees to all the free exercise of their religion. He also recognized the importance of teaching about religions as part of a well-rounded education. "It certainly may be said that the Bible is worthy of study for its literary and historic qualities," Clark wrote. "Nothing we have said here indicates that such study of the Bible or of religion, when presented objectively as part of a secular program of education, may not be effected consistently with the First Amendment."

Several justices wrote concurring opinions, including Brennan, who was Roman Catholic, and Goldberg, who was Jewish. Brennan wrote, "The history which our prior decisions have summoned to aid interpretation of the Establishment Clause permits little doubt that its prohibition was designed comprehensively to prevent those official involvements of religion which would tend to foster or discourage religious worship or belief." Goldberg concurred in opposing the Bible recitations, but added, "Neither government nor this Court can or should ignore the significance of the fact that a vast portion of our people believe in and worship God and that many of our legal, political and personal values derive historically from religious teachings."

In dissent, Justice Stewart complained that the majority was displaying hostility, rather than neutrality, toward religion. "A refusal to permit religious exercises thus is seen, not as the realization of state neutrality, but rather as the establishment of a religion of secularism, or at the least, as government support of the beliefs of those who think that religious exercises should be conducted only in private."

EXCERPTS

From Justice Clark's majority opinion: "[I]t is no defense to urge that the religious practices here may be relatively minor encroachments on the First Amendment. The breach of neutrality that is today a trickling stream may all too soon become a raging torrent and, in the words of Madison, 'it is proper to take alarm at the first experiment on our liberties.'. . .

". . . [W]e cannot accept that the concept of neutrality, which does not permit a State to require a religious exercise even with the consent of the majority of those affected, collides with the majority's right to free exercise of religion. While the Free Exercise Clause clearly prohibits the use of state action to deny the rights of free exercise to anyone, it has never meant that a majority could use the machinery of the State to practice its beliefs. . . .

"The place of religion in our society is an exalted one, achieved through a long tradition of reliance on the home, the church and the inviolable citadel of the individual heart and mind. We have come to recognize through bitter experience that it is not within the power of government to invade that citadel, whether its purpose or effect be to aid or oppose, to advance or retard."

IMPACT

The decision in *Schempp* reaffirmed the Court's holding in *Engel v. Vitale*. The Court's strong stand did little to calm the controversy over school prayer, however, and it still rages today. Some schools, especially in the South, never heeded the Court's teaching and allow official Bible readings or other religious practices to continue unchallenged. Other ways have been devised to circumvent the ruling. In 1985 the Court in *Wallace v. Jaffree* struck down an Alabama law that called for a "moment of silence" at the start of each day for silent prayer or meditation. The Court found that even though the law appeared neutral on its face, it was intended to advance religion.

Meanwhile politicians continue to accuse the Supreme Court of having removed religion from the public schools. Religious conservatives have pushed Congress repeatedly to approve a constitutional amendment that would require greater accommodation of religious practices in schools and other areas of public life. Following the school shootings in Littleton, Colorado, some members of Congress attempted to pass a law allowing religious observances and memorials on public school grounds to honor people killed in those schools. Opponents pointed out the law would probably be found unconstitutional under *Schempp*. Meanwhile, many other religious advocates say the *Schempp* framework gives schools ample room to include religion as part of their curriculum, if presented in a nonproselytizing way, and to allow students to engage in private religious practices in schools.

The Clinton administration issued guidelines to schools making it clear that certain accommodations to religion can be made and that all mention of religion need not, and should not, be shunned from public schools. "If people had bothered to read the *Schempp* decision, they would have found that the striking-down of state-sponsored religious practices wasn't meant to be hostile toward religion," says Charles Haynes, senior scholar at the Freedom Forum.

Thirty-five years after the *Schempp* ruling, that message was brought home to the Abington School District itself. The school board adopted a new policy allowing students to pray individually or in nondisruptive, noncoercive groups and to form religious clubs. It also allows teachers to include religious material, including the Bible, in their curriculum.

Meanwhile, the leading figure in *Murray v. Curlett* met a mysterious fate. Because of her role in the case and her outspoken views on religion, Madalyn Murray O'Hair became infamous in the 1960s. She continued to espouse atheism and attack religion, even seeking to remove "In God We Trust" from U.S. currency, among other campaigns. In 1995 she disappeared, along with a son, Jon Garth Murray, and adopted daughter, Robin, who was also her granddaughter, the child of another son, William. In 2001 David Waters, who once worked for the family, led police to the shallow grave where their bodies had been buried. Waters was convicted of extortion for his role in the plot that ended in their deaths.

In an ironic twist, O'Hair's son William Murray, who was also involved in the original suit, found religion and became an evangelical preacher.

Lemon v. Kurtzman

Decided June 28, 1971
403 U.S. 602
laws.findlaw.com/US/403/602.html

DECISION

Government programs and laws that aid religious institutions must be evaluated using a three-part test to determine if they violate the First Amendment's ban on government establishment of religion. To be found constitutional, the program's purpose must be secular (nonreligious), its primary effect must not be to advance or inhibit religion, and it must not create excessive entanglement or involvement of government with religion. Under that standard, the Court struck down Pennsylvania and Rhode Island programs that supplemented the salaries of parochial school teachers with public funds.

BACKGROUND

On the question of school-sponsored prayer in public schools, the Warren Court had made its views clear in a series of decisions. The Court said that laws that required prayer or Bible readings in public schools were aimed at, and had the effect of, advancing religion and therefore violated the First Amendment.

But on the related issue of public aid to parochial schools and their students, the Court's rulings seemed to run in the opposite direction. In *Everson v. Board of Education* (1947) the Court quoted Thomas Jefferson's controversial statement that the First Amendment had created a "wall of separation between church and state." The Court nevertheless upheld a New Jersey program that straddled that wall: It reimbursed parents for the costs of transportation to and from schools, including religious schools. The Court said the program gave general aid to parents, not to parochial schools directly.

In its next case on the subject, *Board of Education of Central School District No. 12 v. Allen,* the Court in 1968 upheld a New York program that required local school boards to lend textbooks to parochial schools. Again the Court found that the program benefited parents and children, not schools, and had a nonreligious purpose of improving education for all.

The *Allen* decision encouraged several states to offer a variety of subsidies and assistance programs to financially weak parochial schools. "Parochiaid" programs, as they were known, were politically popular. Public schools were also willing to help because if the parochial schools failed, public schools would have to absorb many extra students.

Two of the programs enacted to help parochial schools were challenged in *Lemon v. Kurtzman,* which originated in Pennsylvania, and in *Early v. DiCenso,* a Rhode Island case. Rhode Island law allowed for parochial school teachers to be given a taxpayer-funded salary supplement. The Pennsylvania program called for reimbursement of the costs of teachers' salaries, textbooks, and school materials for parochial schools. The subsidized teachers could not teach religious subjects in either state's program. Pennsylvania's program was challenged on First Amendment grounds by a taxpayer named Alton Lemon. Lemon filed suit against David Kurtzman, the state superintendent of schools. A lower court struck down Rhode Island's program but upheld Pennsylvania's.

VOTE

8–0, with Chief Justice Warren E. Burger writing the majority opinion. Burger was joined by Justices Hugo L. Black, William O. Douglas, John M. Harlan, Potter Stewart, Harry A. Blackmun, William J. Brennan Jr., and Byron R. White. Justice Thurgood Marshall did not participate.

HIGHLIGHTS

Chief Justice Burger acknowledged at the outset that the Framers of the Constitution had not been as clear as they could have been in drafting the parts of the First Amendment relating to religion. "The language of the Religion Clauses of the First Amendment is at best opaque, particularly when compared with other portions of the Amendment. Its authors did not simply prohibit the establishment of a state church or a state religion, an area history shows they regarded as very important and fraught with great dangers. Instead, they commanded that there should be 'no law respecting an establishment of religion.' "

That ambiguity in the language required careful analysis to determine if a particular government program violated the establishment clause. From prior rulings, the Court had decided on at least two factors that were relevant: whether the program had a "secular purpose," meaning that it had been established to achieve a nonreligious goal, such as improvements in education for all. The second factor was whether the law had the primary effect of advancing or inhibiting religion. On both of these factors the programs at issue seemed to pass. The goal of the programs was general improvement of education, not aiding religion. And because the programs required that funds not be used to teach religious courses, the programs' effect was not to advance religion, the Court concluded.

But those factors were not enough. The Court decided that a third test should determine whether the government program created "excessive entanglement" of the government in the affairs of a religious organization.

Based on this factor, the Court decided the programs would fail. What was the entanglement the Court was concerned about? Noting that the rules of the programs required that none of the publicly subsidized teachers or school materials be used for religious teaching, the Court said, "A comprehensive, discriminating, and continuing state surveillance will inevitably be required to ensure that these restrictions are obeyed and the First Amendment otherwise respected. Unlike a book, a teacher cannot be inspected once so as to determine the extent and intent of his or her personal beliefs and subjective acceptance of the limitations imposed by the First Amendment. These prophylactic contacts will involve excessive and enduring entanglement between state and church."

The Court also expressed more general concerns that if these two programs were allowed to proceed, the relationship of church and state would become an election issue and a constant budget concern for legislators. "The potential for political divisiveness related to religious belief and practice is aggravated in these two statutory programs by the need for continuing annual appropriations and the likelihood of larger and larger demands as costs and populations grow."

No justice dissented from the ruling, but Justice White noted that the three-part test the Court had established was not without problems. The test, White said, "creates an insoluble paradox for the State and the parochial schools. The State cannot finance secular instruction if it permits religion to be taught in the same classroom; but if it exacts a promise that religion not be so taught . . . and enforces it, it is then entangled in the 'no entanglement' aspect of the Court's Establishment Clause jurisprudence." In other words, White felt that satisfying the second prong of the test would almost automatically trigger a violation of the third.

EXCERPTS

From Justice Burger's majority opinion: "Our prior holdings do not call for total separation between church and state; total separation is not possible in an absolute sense. Some relationship between government and religious organizations is inevitable. . . .

"In the absence of precisely stated constitutional prohibitions, we must draw lines with reference to the three main evils against which the Establishment Clause was intended to afford protection: 'sponsorship, financial support, and active involvement of the sovereign in religious activity.' . . .

"The substantial religious character of these church-related schools gives rise to entangling church-state relationships of the kind the Religion Clauses sought to avoid. Although the District Court found that concern for religious values did not inevitably or necessarily intrude into the content of secular subjects, the considerable religious activities of these schools led the legislature to provide for careful governmental controls and surveillance by state authorities in order to ensure that state aid supports only secular education. . . .

". . . Judicial caveats against entanglement must recognize that the line of separation, far from being a 'wall,' is a blurred, indistinct, and variable barrier depending on all the circumstances of a particular relationship."

IMPACT

The so-called Lemon test created in *Lemon v. Kurtzman* has been used in a wide range of cases ever since. In some cases, the government programs at issue have been upheld, while others were struck down. Predicting which programs would pass the Lemon test and which would not has not been easy, however.

In *Wolman v. Walter* (1977) the Court said lending textbooks to parochial schools was permissible, but subsidizing field trips was not. In *Marsh v. Chambers* (1983) the Court upheld the recital of a prayer at Nebraska's state legislative sessions, even though a lower court had said it violated all three parts of the Lemon test. In Chief Justice Burger's opinion for the Court in *Marsh v. Chambers* he contrasted the legislative benediction with school prayer cases. "The individual claiming injury by the practice is an adult," he wrote, "presumably not readily susceptible to 'religious indoctrination' . . . or peer pressure."

In general, however, the Lemon test came to be viewed by many religious conservatives as a tool used to strike down government accommodation of religion more often than not. Now that the liberal justices who were on the Court when it decided *Lemon* have retired, several newer justices have voiced skepticism about the Lemon test. Some say it is too rigid and unworkable—in part because of the "paradox" White identified in his concurring opinion in *Lemon:* any effort to avoid advancement of religion (prong 2) may end up creating excessive entanglement (prong 3). Other critics say the Lemon test is too easily manipulated, enabling both supporters and opponents of a government program to cite it to bolster their argument. In addition, critics viewed the first prong of the test, the "secular purpose" requirement, as too difficult to meet, since there is often a religious motivation, at least in part, behind legislative actions in this area.

Justice O'Connor has argued for a simpler rule that would strike down only those government programs that endorse religion. Some argue that the Lemon test is already dead, but it is not clear what if anything has replaced it.

In the 1993 ruling *Lamb's Chapel v. Center Moriches Union Free School District,* the Court cited the Lemon test in deciding that schools that allow after-hours use of their premises by other civic organizations may not deny access to religious organizations. Justice Scalia mocked the Lemon test bitterly in a concurring opinion. "Like some ghoul in a late-night horror movie that repeatedly sits up in its grave and shuffles abroad after being repeatedly killed and buried, *Lemon* stalks our Establishment Clause jurisprudence once again," Scalia wrote. "The secret of the Lemon test's survival, I think, is that it is so easy to kill. It is there to scare us (and our audience) when we wish it to do so, but we can command it to return to the tomb at will. . . . When we wish to strike down a practice it forbids, we invoke it; . . . when we wish to uphold a practice it forbids, we ignore it entirely. . . . Such a docile and useful monster is worth keeping around, at least in a somnolent state; one never knows when one might need him."

Monster or not, the Lemon test still figured in many church-state decisions more than a decade later. When the Supreme Court in 2005 struck down a Ten Commandments display in county courthouses in Kentucky, the "secular purpose" prong figured prominently, even though several justices said they were not using the Lemon test. The unabashedly religious motivation behind the Kentucky displays proved fatal, even if the displays as they were later modified might have met the other prongs of the Lemon test. (See Ten Commandments Cases.)

Edwards v. Aguillard

Decided June 19, 1987
482 U.S. 578
laws.findlaw.com/US/482/578.html

DECISION

A state law that forbids the teaching of evolution in public schools unless "creation science" is also taught is unconstitutional. The law endorses religion by promoting the teaching of the theory that a supernatural being created the human race. As a result, the law violates the First Amendment, which prohibits laws that relate to "an establishment of religion."

BACKGROUND

For more than a century, scientists, educators, and religious leaders have struggled to reconcile conflicting views of how life began. On one side of the debate are those who believe in the Charles Darwin theory of evolution, which states that life on earth developed and evolved gradually over billions of years, and that man has evolutionary links to other species. On the other side is creationism or creation science, which espouses the biblical view that all living things, including man, were created at once, not through evolution.

Onetime presidential candidate William Jennings Bryan, a fundamentalist, led a campaign in the early part of the twentieth century to pass laws forbidding the teaching of evolution in public schools. Tennessee passed such a law, and, in a sensational 1925 trial, Bryan helped prosecute a teacher, John Scopes, for teaching evolution. Famed defense lawyer Clarence Darrow represented Scopes in the so-called monkey trial. Scopes was convicted, but on appeal the conviction was overturned on a technicality, although the law was upheld.

A handful of other states passed similar laws or resolutions, but several were eventually repealed. By the 1960s only Arkansas and Mississippi had laws that barred the teaching of evolution. In the 1968 decision *Epperson v. Arkansas* the Supreme Court struck down that state's law as a violation of the establishment clause. The sole purpose of the law, the Court said, was to advance the views of a particular religion, a goal that the First Amendment does not allow.

Louisiana legislators tried a different tack, passing a law in 1980 called the "Creationism Act." Instead of banning the teaching of evolution outright, it said evolution could not be taught unless accompanied by instruction in creationism. Neither one was required unless the other was taught. A group of teachers and parents, led by Donald Aguillard, a teacher at Acadiana High School, sued Gov. Edwin Edwards, claiming the law violated the First Amendment. The state defended the law as promoting academic freedom—presenting a range of views—rather than promoting one view over another.

The Court agreed in May 1986 to accept the case. In August seventy-two Nobel Prize–winning scientists and twenty-four scientific organizations—including the National Academy of Sciences—submitted an amicus (friend of the court) brief urging the Court to strike down the Louisiana law. The law, the brief said, threatened "the future of scientific education in this nation." Lawyers for Louisiana argued that the law was intended to foster free inquiry by promoting alternative theories about creation.

VOTE

7–2, with Justice William J. Brennan Jr. writing the majority opinion. Joining him were Justices Thurgood Marshall, Harry A. Blackmun, Lewis F. Powell Jr., John Paul Stevens, Byron R. White, and Sandra Day O'Connor. Dissenting were Justice Antonin Scalia and Chief Justice William Rehnquist.

HIGHLIGHTS

The Court majority used the so-called Lemon test to determine whether the Louisiana law impermissibly advances religion in violation of the Constitution. The test is derived from the 1971 decision in *Lemon v. Kurtzman,* which established standards by which the Court could measure whether a law or government action violated the establishment clause. (See *Lemon v. Kurtzman.*)

The first factor in that test is whether the law was passed with a secular or nonreligious purpose. The Court said the Louisiana law was not, dismissing the state's argument that it was passed to promote academic freedom. "Even if 'academic freedom' is read to mean 'teaching all of the evidence' with respect to the origin of human beings, the Act does not further this purpose," Justice Brennan wrote. "The goal of providing a more comprehensive science curriculum is not furthered either by outlawing the teaching of evolution or by requiring the teaching of creation science."

Instead, the Court agreed, it was clear that the Louisiana law was passed to promote religion. "[W]e need not be blind in this case to the legislature's preeminent religious purpose in enacting this statute," Brennan wrote. "The preeminent purpose of the Louisiana Legislature was clearly to advance the religious viewpoint that a supernatural being created humankind." Based on this analysis, the Court ruled that the law was un-constitutional, without even analyzing the other parts of the Lemon test.

In dissent, Justice Scalia said the Court had gone too far in concluding that Louisiana legislators had improper motives in passing the creationism law. "Our task is not to judge the debate about teaching the origins of life, but to ascertain what the members of the Louisiana Legislature believed," Scalia wrote. "The vast majority of them voted to approve a bill which explicitly stated a secular purpose; what is crucial is not their wisdom in believing that purpose would be achieved by the bill, but their sincerity in believing it would be."

Scalia added, "Our cases interpreting and applying the purpose test have made such a maze of the establishment clause that even the most conscientious governmental officials can only guess what motives will be held unconstitutional. We have said essentially the following: Government may not act with the purpose of advancing religion, except when forced to do so by the free exercise clause (which is now and then); or when eliminating existing governmental hostility to religion (which exists sometimes); or even when merely accommodating governmentally uninhibited religious practices, except that at some point (it is unclear where) intentional accommodation results in the fostering of religion, which is of course unconstitutional."

Donald Aguillard, a teacher at Acadian High School in Scott, Louisiana, filed suit in 1981 against a state law that prohibited the teaching of evolution unless taught along with "creation science." He prevailed when the Court, in *Edwards v. Aguillard* (1987), found the law to be unconstitutional. *Source: AP/Wide World Photos.*

EXCERPTS

From Justice Brennan's majority opinion: "In this case, the purpose of the Creationism Act was to restructure the science curriculum to conform with a particular religious viewpoint. Out of many possible science subjects taught in the public schools, the legislature chose to affect the teaching of the one scientific theory that historically has been opposed by certain religious sects. . . .

"[T]he legislature passed the Act to give preference to those religious groups which have as one of their tenets the creation of humankind by a divine creator. . . .

"We do not imply that a legislature could never require that scientific critiques of prevailing scientific theories be taught. . . . [T]eaching a variety of scientific theories about the origins of humankind to schoolchildren might be validly done with the clear secular intent of enhancing the effectiveness of science instruction. But because the primary purpose of the Creationism Act is to endorse a particular religious doctrine, the Act furthers religion in violation of the Establishment Clause.

"The Louisiana Creationism Act advances a religious doctrine by requiring either the banishment of the theory of evolution from public school classrooms or the presentation of a religious viewpoint that rejects evolution in its entirety. The Act violates the Establishment Clause of the First Amendment because it seeks to employ the symbolic and financial support of government to achieve a religious purpose."

IMPACT

In spite of the ruling in *Edwards v. Aguillard,* controversy still surrounds the teaching of evolution in public schools. Pressure on school boards and textbook publishers, according to a 1998 National Academy of Sciences report, has resulted in the downplaying or elimination of evolution from biology texts and curricula in many schools nationwide. In other schools, evolution is taught as a theory, not fact.

"Many students receive little or no exposure to the most important concept in modern biology, a concept essential to understanding key aspects of living things—biological evolution," the report said. It also cited surveys indicating that fewer than half of Americans believe that humans evolved from earlier species, and more than half of all adults would like to see creationism taught in public schools.

The Christian Coalition, among other groups, has continued to argue that school systems that exclude creationism are improperly failing to reflect the values of the community in the classroom. Critics of creationism call it a "pseudo-science" that does not deserve a place in public school curricula. In August 1999 the Kansas Board of Education adopted new curriculum standards that allow students to graduate from high school without being taught about evolution. In the years since then, school officials in Kansas and elsewhere have considered a variation on this theme that has attracted interest nationwide: intelligent design. Without pinpointing a deity as the designer, this theory argues that the complexity of the natural world must be the result of an "intelligent cause" or design that cannot be explained by natural selection alone.

"Creationists and evolutionists continue to shout past one another, creating confusion about what should be taught at public schools and how it should be taught," wrote Charles Haynes, a scholar with the Freedom Forum, a foundation that promotes First Amendment values. He said it would be appropriate for public school teachers, in describing the views of various religions, to mention creationism and to inform students that some religious groups take issue with the prevailing scientific belief in evolution.

Lee v. Weisman

Decided June 24, 1992
505 U.S. 577
laws.findlaw.com/US/505/577.html

DECISION

Public schools may not include prayer as part of official graduation ceremonies. Because the prayer is officially sanctioned and solicited by school officials, and because students attending may feel coerced into listening or participating, the graduation prayer violates the First Amendment, which bars government establishment of religion.

BACKGROUND

The Supreme Court did not end the national debate over prayer in the public schools with its rulings in the early 1960s in *Engel v. Vitale* and *School District of Abington v. Schempp.* (See *School District of Abington Township v. Schempp.*) Those highly controversial rulings struck down state-sponsored or teacher-led prayers and Bible readings on the grounds that they violated the establishment clause of the First Amendment, which bars government actions "respecting an establishment of religion."

In the decades since, religious conservatives continued to hope that, either through a constitutional amendment or a change in the Supreme Court's views, official prayer could be brought back into the classroom.

Passage of a constitutional amendment proved difficult, but by 1992 chances seemed good for a new take on the issue from a Supreme Court that was drastically different from the one that had ruled in the early 1960s. Two of the justices who had championed separation of church and state—Thurgood Marshall and William J. Brennan Jr.—had retired and had been replaced by justices who seemed open to greater accommodation.

Both David H. Souter and Clarence Thomas had acknowledged during their confirmation hearings the controversy surrounding the so-called Lemon test, the standard for assessing government involvement with religion, first announced in 1971

in *Lemon v. Kurtzman.* The Lemon test has been criticized for building too high a wall of separation between church and state. (See *Lemon v. Kurtzman.*)

Another signal of possible change was the closeness of the vote in a 1989 case, *Allegheny County v. ACLU Greater Pittsburgh Chapter.* That ruling said government could not include a crèche or nativity scene by itself in a holiday season display. Four justices—including the newest, Anthony Kennedy—had dissented, urging a different approach to the establishment clause.

The case that prompted a fresh look at the Court's prayer doctrine involved graduation ceremonies at Nathan Bishop Middle School in Providence, Rhode Island. At the school's 1986 graduation ceremonies, parents Vivian and Daniel Weisman were upset when a Baptist minister offered the benediction, asking the audience to give thanks to Jesus Christ. "It was terribly uncomfortable and inappropriate," Daniel Weisman said.

Three years later, when his next child Deborah was about to graduate from the same school, Weisman found out that the benediction would be given again by a member of the clergy, but this time by a rabbi, someone of Weisman's own faith. School officials had invited the rabbi, and he had composed a prayer with guidelines from the school system. Weisman objected nonetheless, arguing that the ceremony should simply be nonreligious. He went to court to stop the planned benediction, naming principal Robert E. Lee as the defendant. The ceremony was allowed to proceed. The suit continued, however, and lower courts agreed that the graduation prayer violated the Constitution.

When the case reached the Supreme Court it attracted the attention of the first Bush administration, which wanted to urge the Court to reexamine its prayer cases and the Lemon test. The administration hoped for a simpler "coercion" test, one that would strike down government actions only if they actually coerced people to participate in a religious activity.

In the book *The Center Holds,* which examines the Supreme Court of this period, James Simon writes, *"Weisman* seemed well-suited to fulfill the ambitions of Justice Kennedy and the other *Allegheny* dissenters to revise the modern Supreme Court's establishment clause jurisprudence, perhaps once and for all." The government joined in the case on the side of the school board, and Solicitor General Kenneth Starr helped argue it.

As recounted by Simon, the oral arguments did not go smoothly for the school board or Starr. Justice O'Connor suddenly seemed hostile to the coercion test, asking whether under that test it would be constitutional for a state to declare an official religion. Declaring a state bird or state flower was not coercive, she suggested, so perhaps a state religion would also be permissible. (O'Connor was being somewhat facetious here to make the point that the coercion test was too low a standard. As the First Amendment forbids Congress from establishing a religion, it is clear that no state could do so either.) But the school board's lawyer had to concede that such a declaration would be constitutional under the coercion test—an acknowledgment that may have scared justices away. From other questioning as well, a victory for graduation prayer seemed less likely than it had before the arguments.

Daniel Weisman and his daughter, Deborah, challenged the practice of having a member of the clergy deliver invocation and benediction prayers at public school graduation exercises in Providence, Rhode Island. The Supreme Court ruled in their favor in *Lee v. Weisman* (1992). *Source: Providence Journal file photo.*

VOTE

5–4, with Justice Anthony M. Kennedy writing the majority opinion. He was joined by Justices Harry A. Blackmun, John Paul Stevens, Sandra Day O'Connor, and David H. Souter. Dissenting were Chief Justice William Rehnquist and Justices Antonin Scalia, Byron R. White, and Clarence Thomas.

HIGHLIGHTS

To Kennedy, two "dominant facts" dictated the result in the case. First, the graduation prayer, even though spoken by an outsider, was an official part of the public school ceremony, guided and established by school officials. Quoting the Court's decision in *Engel v. Vitale,* Kennedy wrote, "It is a cornerstone principle of our Establishment Clause jurisprudence that it is no part of the business of government to compose official prayers for any group of the American people to recite as a part of a religious program carried on by government, and that is what the school officials attempted to do."

Kennedy added, "The degree of school involvement here made it clear that the graduation prayers bore the imprint of the State, and thus put school-age children who objected in an untenable position." That "untenable position" led to Kennedy's second point about the facts of the *Weisman* case. Even though attendance at the ceremony was not a prerequisite for receiving a diploma, Kennedy said it was virtually mandatory, making it difficult for a dissenting student to avoid the religious aspect of the event.

"The undeniable fact is that the school district's supervision and control of a high school graduation ceremony places public pressure, as well as peer pressure, on attending students to stand as a group or, at least, maintain respectful silence during the invocation and benediction," Kennedy wrote. "This pressure, though subtle and indirect, can be as real as any overt compulsion."

At considerable length, Kennedy examined the peer pressure and other pressures that would make it almost inconceivable for a student not to attend his or her graduation ceremony. "Everyone knows that, in our society and in our culture, high school graduation is one of life's most significant occasions. A school rule which excuses attendance is beside the point. Attendance may not be required by official decree, yet it is apparent that a student is not free to absent herself from the graduation exercise in any real sense of the term 'voluntary.' As a result, based on the Court's prior prayer cases, Kennedy said the graduation prayer was clearly a violation of the First Amendment—so clear that he said it was unnecessary to reexamine the Lemon test.

Kennedy had stepped back from major change in the Court's doctrine and from all the controversy that would have ensued. But among his fellow justices, the decision earned Kennedy a sarcastic dissent from an angry Justice Scalia.

Scalia said it was impossible to have dissented in the *Allegheny* case and come to the conclusion that Kennedy did in the majority. In the *Allegheny* dissent, Kennedy and the other justices said "long-standing traditions" that involved religion could be upheld without violating the First Amendment. Scalia argued that religious invocations were just such a tradition and should be upheld, not eliminated.

"Today's opinion shows more forcefully than volumes of argumentation why our Nation's protection, that fortress which is our Constitution, cannot possibly rest upon the changeable philosophical predilections of the Justices of this Court, but must have deep foundations in the historic practices of our people," Scalia wrote.

Scalia also mocked Kennedy for his "psychojourney" into analyzing the pressures that might compel students to attend the ceremony and not object to the prayer. "The Court has gone beyond the realm where judges know what they are doing," Scalia said.

EXCERPTS

From Justice Kennedy's majority opinion: "If common ground can be defined which permits once conflicting faiths to express the shared conviction that there is an ethic and a morality which transcend human invention, the sense of community and purpose sought by all decent societies might be advanced. But though the First Amendment does not allow the government to stifle prayers which aspire to these ends, neither does it permit the government to undertake that task for itself.

"The First Amendment's Religion Clauses mean that religious beliefs and religious expression are too precious to be either proscribed or prescribed by the State. The design of the Constitution is that preservation and transmission of religious beliefs and worship is a responsibility and a choice committed to the private sphere, which itself is promised freedom to pursue that mission . . . .

"The injury caused by the government's action, and the reason why Daniel and Deborah Weisman object to it, is that the State, in a school setting, in effect required participation in a religious exercise . . . .

" . . . The sole question presented is whether a religious exercise may be conducted at a graduation ceremony in circumstances where, as we have found, young graduates who object are induced to conform. No holding by this Court suggests that a school can persuade or compel a student to participate in a religious exercise. That is being done here, and it is forbidden by the Establishment Clause of the First Amendment."

IMPACT

The *Lee v. Weisman* decision was a bitter disappointment to the Bush administration and to advocates of a return of prayer to schools. Efforts resumed in Congress to pass a constitutional amendment on the subject.

Meanwhile in schools and in lower courts, another tactic was tried and examined—introducing prayer into graduation ceremonies at the initiative of students, rather than the schools themselves. In several schools students were permitted to vote on the content of their ceremonies. If a majority of students voted for an element with religious content, some suggested, then it could be allowed to happen without the same hint of school sponsorship or endorsement.

A federal appeals court upheld this approach in Texas. "Quite unlike the school-directed and school-controlled practice found unconstitutional in *Lee,* the Clear Creek Independent School District's resolution simply permits the students of each graduating class to decide if they do or do not wish to have an invocation as part of their commencement," according to the ruling of the U.S. Court of Appeals for the Fifth Circuit.

But another appeals court struck down the same tactic in New Jersey. In the New Jersey case, the appeals court ruled that even though students initiated the prayer, it was still taking place at an event sponsored and controlled by school officials. "We cannot allow the school district's delegate to make decisions that the school district cannot make," the U.S. Court of Appeals for the Third Circuit said.

In other school districts, private baccalaureate services with religious aspects have been organized totally apart from school sponsorship. In guidelines issued by the Clinton administration in 1995, schools were advised not to organize prayer at ceremonies or to sponsor such baccalaureate services. The administration also said that if school facilities are generally available to private groups, they must also be made available to religious baccalaureate services, but preferably with a disclaimer disavowing school sponsorship.

In 2000 the Court revisited the issue in the context of student-led prayers recited before public school football games in Texas. The Court ruled that, as with the prayer in *Lee v. Weisman,* praying before football games could have the effect of coercing unwilling students to participate in a religious ceremony. (See *Santa Fe Independent School District v. Doe.*)

Agostini v. Felton

Decided June 23, 1997
521 U.S. 203
laws.findlaw.com/US/521/203.html

DECISION

Public schools do not violate the establishment clause of the First Amendment when they provide special education instruction on the premises of parochial schools. The fact that federal funds are spent for programs inside religious schools does not mean or imply government endorsement of religion. School officials can be trusted to fashion rules and guidelines that would avoid excessive entanglement between the public school and the religious group operating the private school.

BACKGROUND

The Supreme Court has struggled for decades to define the constitutionally proper boundary between church and state in the context of public and parochial school education. The Court has allowed some forms of public aid to religious schools, but said other kinds of assistance either create too much entanglement between church and state or imply a government endorsement of religion.

In 1985 the Court drew the dividing line between church and state most sharply, handing down two rulings, *Grand Rapids School District v. Ball* and *Aguilar v. Felton,* that seemed to say that no public funds whatever could be used to provide special instruction within the walls or on the premises of parochial schools. Using the same phrase in both cases the Court ruled that, under Title I of the Elementary and Secondary Education Act of 1965, federal funds for remedial and special education could not be used to send public school teachers into the "pervasively sectarian environment" of parochial schools to provide instruction. Even if they did not participate in any kind of religious instruction, the mere presence of public school teachers within the walls of the parochial school to give instruction amounted to excessive entanglement between church and state.

School systems nationwide responded to these decisions in a variety of ways, ranging from computer-aided instruction to the use of mobile classrooms. New York City claims it spent more than $100 million over a decade to pay for mobile classrooms that would park on city streets just off the premises of the parochial schools so that public school teachers could provide the special services the students needed. Public school officials complained that the decisions placed an unnecessary burden on their budgets to provide these services and that greater numbers of eligible students could be instructed if not for this expense.

Meanwhile, in the years following *Aguilar v. Felton,* the composition of the Supreme Court changed. By the mid-1990s all but one of the justices in the *Aguilar* majority, Justice Stevens, had retired. Several conservative justices sent signals indicating they thought *Aguilar* had gone too far in building a wall between public funding and parochial schools. Eventually, five justices—a majority—gave indications that, to varying degrees, they were ready to reexamine their ruling in *Aguilar.*

Ordinarily, when the Court reexamines one of its doctrines, it does so in the context of a new case with new facts that raise the issue. But in this case, New York City simply asked the Court to reopen the *Aguilar* case. It cited a federal rule of procedure that allows courts to lift injunctions if they have been shown to have inequitable results. Yolanda Aguilar, the school official in the original case, had been replaced by Rachel Agostini. The parents objecting to the program were led by Betty-Louise Felton in both cases.

VOTE

5–4, with Justice Sandra Day O'Connor writing the majority opinion. She was joined by Chief Justice William Rehnquist and Justices Antonin Scalia, Anthony M. Kennedy, and Clarence Thomas. Dissenting were Justices David H. Souter, John Paul Stevens, Ruth Bader Ginsburg, and Stephen G. Breyer.

HIGHLIGHTS

The Court acknowledged that its establishment clause doctrine had, in fact, changed in the decade since *Aguilar.* "What has changed since we decided *Ball* and *Aguilar,*" O'Connor wrote, "is our understanding of the criteria used to assess whether aid to religion has an impermissible effect."

She noted that in the 1993 decision *Zobrest v. Catalina Foothills School District,* the Court already had abandoned one of the premises of *Aguilar,* namely that "public employees placed on parochial school grounds will inevitably inculcate religion or that their presence constitutes a symbolic union between government and religion." In *Zobrest,* the Court had permitted a school district to use public funds for a sign language interpreter for a deaf parochial school student.

The Court also rejected the earlier notion that providing any publicly funded services on parochial school premises represents a "symbolic union" between church and state. "We do not see any perceptible (let alone dispositive) difference in the degree of symbolic union between a student receiving reme- dial instruction in a classroom on his sectarian school's cam- pus and one receiving instruction in a van parked just at the school's curbside," the Court said. "To draw this line based solely on the location of the public employee is neither 'sensi- ble' nor 'sound.' "

Apart from the symbolism, the Court also concluded that there was nothing about the pre-*Aguilar* arrangement, whereby city schoolteachers gave instruction inside parochial schools, that put the public employees in the position of indoctrinating students. "Contrary to our conclusion in *Aguilar,* placing full- time employees on parochial school campuses does not as a matter of law have the impermissible effect of advancing reli- gion through indoctrination."

Finally, the Court said that it was the only institution that could overrule its own decisions—something it feels comfort- able doing, especially in cases interpreting the Constitution. In those cases, no other institution except the Court could fix the Court's mistakes. On the other hand, in cases in which the Court is interpreting laws of Congress, Congress has the ability to correct its own mistakes—or those of the Court—by amend- ing or passing new laws.

EXCERPTS

From Justice O'Connor's majority opinion: "New York City's Title I program does not run afoul of any of three primary criteria we currently use to evaluate whether government aid has the ef- fect of advancing religion: it does not result in governmental in- doctrination; define its recipients by reference to religion; or create an excessive entanglement. We therefore hold that a federally funded program providing supplemental, remedial in- struction to disadvantaged children on a neutral basis is not in- valid under the Establishment Clause when such instruction is given on the premises of sectarian schools by government em- ployees pursuant to a program containing safeguards such as those present here. The same considerations that justify this holding require us to conclude that this carefully constrained program also cannot reasonably be viewed as an endorsement of religion. Accordingly, we must acknowledge that *Aguilar,* as

well as the portion of *Ball* addressing Grand Rapids' Shared Time program, are no longer good law."

IMPACT

The Court's decision in *Agostini* was seen as encouragement to those who favor school voucher programs, in which public funds are given to parents to pay for tuition at private—includ- ing parochial—schools. By sweeping away some of the old as- sumptions about the danger of public funds being used in parochial school settings, the Court, in the view of these advo- cates, was paving the way for a more favorable view of all kinds of public subsidy for parochial school education.

In dissent, Justice Souter warned that the majority opinion would "authorize direct state aid to religious institutions on an unparalleled scale, in violation of the Establishment Clause's central prohibition against religious subsidies by the govern- ment." In fact, the *Agostini* decision was cited frequently when, in 2002, the Court gave its approval to school vouchers in an Ohio case. (See *Zelman v. Simmons-Harris.*)

The *Agostini* ruling also triggered debate over whether the Court's long-standing Lemon test was still viable (see *Lemon v. Kurtzman*). That test for determining whether government actions violate the establishment clause was first enunciated in 1971 and has been attacked by religious advocates who say it raised too rigid a wall of separation between church and state. It asks whether the government action has a religious purpose, has the effect of advancing religion, and involves government too much in religion. (See *Lemon v. Kurtzman.*) The Lemon test had been cited in the original *Aguilar* decision. It was also invoked in *Agos- tini,* but some commentators said its original meaning had been so altered that it was no longer a viable standard.

The *Agostini* ruling was not the final word on how the Court viewed public aid to parochial school students. In the 2000 decision *Mitchell v. Helms,* the Court narrowly approved a program that provided computers and other equipment to parochial schools. The majority cited *Agostini,* but some jus- tices stressed that the program was acceptable because it in- cluded safeguards to prevent the equipment from being used for religious instruction.

Santa Fe Independent School District v. Doe

Decided June 19, 2000
530 U.S. 290
laws.findlaw.com/US/530/290.html

DECISION

Policies allowing prayers to be recited before public school football games amount to establishment of religion and violate the First Amendment, even when the prayers are initiated and led by students.

BACKGROUND

High school football games, especially in small towns in Texas, are major events that draw huge crowds. The teams have avid followers, and the whole experience has been described as a kind of civic religion. In many communities, including Santa Fe, near Galveston, real religion is also involved.

Before 1995 students at Santa Fe High School elected a student council chaplain, whose job it was to recite a prayer or invocation over the public-address system before every home game of the varsity football team.

Parents of students who were Mormon and Roman Catholic objected to the football prayer tradition in this community dominated by Southern Baptists. The parents said their children were subjected to other forms of religious discrimination as well, including one episode in which a teacher berated the Mormon religion after learning that the child was Mormon. The students and parents also objected to the student-led prayers that were part of graduation ceremonies every year.

The parents and students sued the school district, and because they received death threats and criticism within the community, they were allowed to remain anonymous, using the names Jane Doe and John Doe. Before and during the litigation, school district policy on prayer at graduations was revised several times. Just in time for the 1995 high school graduation, a federal district court judge allowed "non-proselytizing" prayer at the ceremony.

After that, the school district further revised its policies, creating a two-step process for dealing with the issue of prayer at football games. Two student elections would be held: the first to decide whether invocations or prayers would be allowed, and the second to elect a student to deliver the prayers. The U.S. Court of Appeals for the Fifth Circuit ruled that, no matter how far the new policy went to put the prayer decision in the hands of students, school officials are present and give permission to the recitation of prayers in a public school setting. Unlike a once-in-a-lifetime graduation ceremony that might justifiably be commemorated by a prayer, football games were routine, the court said.

The school district appealed to the Supreme Court, and to represent it, it called on Jay Sekulow, chief counsel of the American Center for Law and Justice. As he had in previous cases, Sekulow framed the Santa Fe dispute as a fight for freedom of

In *Santa Fe Independent School District v. Doe* (2000), the Court struck down school-organized, student-led prayer at public school football games. Here, football players at a private school, which remained unaffected by the decision, pray before a game in Mississippi in August 2000.
Source: AP/Wide World Photos/Bill Johnson.

speech rather than religion. In this case, he said it was the rights of the students who recite and approve of the prayer that were at stake.

VOTE

6–3, with Justice John Paul Stevens writing the majority opinion, joined by Justices Sandra Day O'Connor, Anthony Kennedy, David Souter, Ruth Bader Ginsburg, and Stephen Breyer. Chief Justice William Rehnquist dissented, joined by Justices Antonin Scalia and Clarence Thomas.

HIGHLIGHTS

In some recent cases the Supreme Court had gone along with the free speech argument that public schools may not discriminate against students who want to deliver a religious message.

But Justice Stevens said pregame prayer at a public school football game was different. Rather than opening a forum to a range of expression, in Santa Fe's case school officials allow a single student to recite a prayer at every home game, under regulations that allow officials to limit the subject and content. In addition, the election process devised by the school system virtually guarantees that minority voices or minority religions are excluded.

Reciting the history and nuances of the school district's policy, Stevens said it was clear that the audiences at school football games would view the prayers as officially approved and even encouraged. The football game, in Stevens's view, was in effect being turned over to students for a single message that would leave adherents of minority religions feeling excluded.

Stevens also dismissed the argument that attendance at football games was optional, unlike graduation ceremonies that were effectively mandatory. Noting the importance of high school football in many communities, Stevens said that for many, "the choice between whether to attend these games or to risk facing a personally offensive religious ritual is in no practical sense an easy one. The Constitution, moreover, demands that the school may not force this difficult choice upon these students."

The dissenters criticized the majority for using the "most rigid version" of the much-criticized standard in *Lemon v. Kurtzman* (see *Lemon v. Kurtzman*) when it determined that the Santa Fe policy has the purpose of advancing religion. School officials revised the policy to give students the choice not to have prayer, Rehnquist noted, and it was never allowed to take effect to see if that would happen.

EXCERPTS

From Justice Stevens's majority opinion: "The District has failed to divorce itself from the religious content in the invocations. It

has not succeeded in doing so, either by claiming that its policy is 'one of neutrality rather than endorsement' or by characterizing the individual student as the 'circuit-breaker' in the process. Contrary to the District's repeated assertions that it has adopted a 'hands-off' approach to the pregame invocation, the realities of the situation plainly reveal that its policy involves both perceived and actual endorsement of religion. In this case, as we found in *Lee*, the 'degree of school involvement' makes it clear that the pregame prayers bear the imprint of the State and thus put school-age children who objected in an untenable position. . . .

"We recognize the important role that public worship plays in many communities, as well as the sincere desire to include public prayer as a part of various occasions so as to mark those occasions' significance. But such religious activity in public schools, as elsewhere, must comport with the First Amendment."

From Chief Justice Rehnquist's dissent: "Even more disturbing than its holding is the tone of the Court's opinion; it bristles with hostility to all things religious in public life. Neither the holding nor the tone of the opinion is faithful to the meaning of the Establishment Clause, when it is recalled that George Washington himself, at the request of the very Congress which passed the Bill of Rights, proclaimed a day of 'public thanksgiving and prayer, to be observed by acknowledging with grateful hearts the many and signal favors of Almighty God.' "

IMPACT

The Court's decision was very unpopular in communities where high school football and prayer had been long intertwined. In September 2000, at the first Santa Fe football game after the ruling, some attendees recited prayer in unison from the stands, but without any school or student direction. In many other less-scrutinized towns, it appeared that traditional student-led prayer before games continued in spite of the decision, or that schools modified prior policies only slightly.

In terms of Supreme Court doctrine, the decision was significant. Even though the Court in general had moved toward greater acceptance of religious practices by government, the *Santa Fe* ruling showed that key justices like Kennedy and O'Connor were still fearful of going too far, especially in school prayer. They still felt that even in settings outside the classroom—like football games—public school students should not feel coerced or compelled to participate in clearly religious activities. In subsequent years the Court was more accepting of optional after-school religious activities on school property (*Good News Club v. Milford*) or government tuition aid going to parochial schools (*Zelman v. Simmons-Harris*) but prayer in school or at major school events seemed to be a line the Court was not yet willing to cross.

Good News Club v. Milford Central School

Decided June 11, 2001
533 U.S. 98
laws.findlaw.com/US/533/98.html

DECISION

Public schools that allow organizations to use their facilities after hours may not discriminate against religious groups in granting access. Excluding religious organizations violates their First Amendment right to freedom of speech.

BACKGROUND

In dozens of communities nationwide, Good News Clubs introduce children ages five to twelve to Christian values and doctrine through songs, games, and prayer. The clubs often meet in homes, but in Milford, New York, Stephen and Darleen Fournier wanted to hold meetings after school in the cafeteria of their local public school.

In compliance with New York law, Milford had a policy allowing community organizations to use public school facilities after hours, so long as they are nonexclusive and open to the general public.

But Milford school officials denied the Fourniers' request on the grounds that what the club planned to do was the equivalent of religious worship—which, under another official policy, could not take place on school grounds. The school board backed up the school officials, stating that the club's purpose was religious instruction, not merely discussing secular topics from a religious standpoint, which would have been permitted.

The Fourniers, their daughter Andrea, and the Good News Club itself challenged the decision in court, claiming that it violated their free speech rights. After first allowing the club to meet for a period, the district court and then the U.S. Court of Appeals for the Second Circuit said Milford's exclusion of the club was constitutional, in part because all religious organizations were excluded, not just some.

As the case went to the Supreme Court, it fit into an increasingly successful strategy adopted by Christian legal groups seeking greater accommodation of religious activities in public places. Instead of casting these cases in terms of the right to free exercise of religion, the American Center for Law and Justice and other organizations used freedom of speech as their legal rallying cry.

VOTE

6–3, with Justice Clarence Thomas writing the majority opinion, joined by Chief Justice William Rehnquist and Justices Sandra Day O'Connor, Antonin Scalia, Anthony Kennedy, and Stephen Breyer. Justice John Paul Stevens, joined by Justices David Souter and Ruth Bader Ginsburg, dissented.

HIGHLIGHTS

Justice Thomas's opinion had two main features. First, adopting the free speech reasoning advanced by the Good News Club, he established that Milford had created a "limited public forum" by adopting a policy that allowed community groups to use its facilities after hours.

In that kind of setting, under past court precedents, Milford does not have to allow all organizations to have equal access—but if it does exclude an organization, it must have a reason other than "viewpoint discrimination." In other words, it cannot exclude a group simply because it does not approve of the message the group will convey to its members or to the public. Thomas cited past decisions including *Rosenberger v. Rector and Visitors of Univ. of Virginia* (1995), in which the Court said that a public university, once it agreed to fund student activities in general, could not exclude from funding a group simply because it had a religious message.

Justice Thomas also dismissed Milford's other argument—that if it allowed the Good News Club to use public facilities it would violate the establishment clause of the First Amendment, in effect giving government endorsement to a religious message. Thomas said that because the policy opened school facilities to all groups in a neutral way, the public would not conclude that Milford was endorsing the religious message of the Good News Club by allowing it to meet in public schools. In fact, he said that excluding the club might give the public a more damaging impression that Milford is hostile to religion.

The dissenting justices said that Milford ought to be able to preserve its vision of what the public schools should be used for by distinguishing between different categories of organizations. For example, Justice Stevens said, a school system might open its doors to political discussion groups but validly bar the Democratic Party or the Ku Klux Klan, which might want to use their meetings to recruit new members. Similarly, he said the town should be allowed to exclude religious groups like the Good News Club, which, he said, hope to recruit young people into religious groups.

EXCERPTS

From Justice Thomas's majority opinion: "What matters for purposes of the Free Speech Clause is that we can see no logical difference in kind between the invocation of Christianity by the Club and the invocation of teamwork, loyalty, or patriotism by other associations to provide a foundation for their lessons. It is apparent that the unstated principle of the Court of Appeals' reasoning is its conclusion that any time religious instruction and prayer are used to discuss morals and character, the discussion is simply not a 'pure' discussion of those issues. According to the Court of Appeals, reliance on Christian principles taints moral and character instruction in a way that other foundations for thought or viewpoints do not. We, however, have never reached such a conclusion. Instead, we reaffirm our holdings . . . that speech discussing otherwise permissible subjects cannot be excluded from a limited public forum on the ground that the subject is discussed from a religious viewpoint. Thus we conclude that Milford's exclusion of the Club from use of the school, pursuant to its community use policy, constitutes impermissible viewpoint discrimination."

From Justice Stevens's dissent: "The particular limitation of the forum at issue in this case is one that prohibits the use of the school's facilities for 'religious purposes.' It is clear that, by 'religious purposes,' the school district did not intend to exclude all speech from a religious point of view. . . . Instead, it sought only to exclude religious speech whose principal goal is to 'promote the gospel.' . . . As long as this is done in an even handed manner, I see no constitutional violation in such an effort. The line between the various categories of religious speech may be difficult to draw, but I think that the distinctions are valid, and that a school, particularly an elementary school, must be permitted to draw them. In short, I am persuaded that the school district could (and did) permissibly exclude from its limited public forum proselytizing religious speech that does not rise to the level of actual worship."

IMPACT

The decision was viewed as a significant victory for those who think religious expression should be permitted on government property and with government financial support. It appeared to erase a line that some lower courts had drawn between organizations that discuss social issues from a religious perspective—which were permitted—and groups that are more overtly conducting religious ceremonies or recruiting attendees into a particular religion, which were not.

In many communities, especially in the South, public schools are used for religious services on the weekend, and they were used that way long before the Supreme Court decided the *Milford* case. But the decision certainly made that arrangement more permissible, and it was cited in resolving several disputes that were pending over Bible clubs and other groups using school facilities.

The ruling was also a boost for the Bush administration in winning support for its so-called faith-based initiative, under which religious organizations could compete along with secular groups for government money to provide social services. The Court's emphasis on neutrality and its disapproval of discriminating against religious groups were good news, as it were, for the administration.

But some school officials and others worried that permitting overtly religious groups to meet right after school on public premises might send a confusing message to students. Said Steven Shapiro, legal director of the American Civil Liberties Union, "In the minds of impressionable young students, today's decision is likely to blur the line between public school and Sunday school."

Zelman v. Simmons-Harris

Decided June 27, 2002
536 U.S. 639
laws.findlaw.com/US/000/00-1751.html

DECISION

An Ohio program that allows needy parents to use taxpayer-funded school vouchers to pay for tuition at religiously affiliated schools does not violate the First Amendment, which bars government establishment of religion.

BACKGROUND

Even a half-century after the Supreme Court ruling in *Brown v. Board of Education* (see *Brown v. Board of Education*), the quality of public schools varies widely throughout the United States. Factors of race and class often affect the educational opportunities children have.

During the 1990s a new alternative gained popularity as a way to combat this problem: school vouchers, also known as school choice. Under these programs, parents—especially those who are poor—would be able to send their children to the public or private school that best suited their needs. These parents would be given a certain amount of government money, in the form of vouchers, that they could then apply toward tuition for private schools, including religious or parochial schools.

In addition to increasing the range of options for parents, these programs were thought to have another benefit, according to advocates: public schools, faced with competition from other public and private schools, would have new incentives to improve their instruction and facilities. The hope was that, as with private enterprise, introducing competition would reward quality programs and force failing schools to become better. Programs were launched in Milwaukee and Cleveland and in Florida.

These programs were instantly controversial for a variety of reasons. For one thing, teacher unions and public school advocates worried that instead of improving troubled schools, voucher programs would just siphon needed funds away from these schools, contributing to a vicious cycle that would result in further deterioration.

Another concern, which became the basis for litigation, was that by including religious schools among the options that parents could pick, these programs have the effect of providing government aid to religion in violation of the First Amendment. For years the uncertain constitutionality of government vouchers going toward religious schools loomed over the school choice movement and slowed its progress.

The city of Cleveland and its troubled public school system became the focal point of the litigation on this issue. With 75,000 mostly poor students in deteriorating schools, and with a high drop-out rate and low student performance, the system was declared by a federal judge to be in a "crisis of magnitude" and placed under the control of the state of Ohio.

As part of the state's response, Ohio launched an experimental voucher program for the city under which poor parents could use state money—up to $2,250 per student—for tuition at private and parochial schools that wanted to participate and met statewide educational standards. Schools also had to promise they would not discriminate against students on the basis of religion or race.

Begun in 1996, the program by 1999 was aiding the parents of 3,700 students—96 percent of whom attended parochial schools. Forty-six of the fifty-six participating schools were religiously affiliated.

Parents who objected to the use of taxpayer funds to support parochial schools challenged the program in state and federal courts as soon as it began. The name of the case resulted from the fact that the parents, led by Doris Simmons-Harris, filed suit against Ohio's superintendent of public instruction, Susan Tave Zelman. In 1999 the U.S. Court of

Left to right, Rosa-Linda Demore-Brown, executive director of the Cleveland Parents for School Choice, and Roberta Kitchen, celebrate the decision in *Zelman v. Simmons-Harris* (2002) in favor of school vouchers for students to attend religious schools. The Court stipulated that the new program must offer a range of religious and secular schools from which to choose.
Source: AP/Wide World Photos/Ron Schwane.

Appeals for the Sixth Circuit struck down the voucher program, finding that it violated the establishment clause of the First Amendment because it had the "primary effect" of advancing religion. The stage was set for the Supreme Court to decide. While the case was pending, the Cleveland program continued in effect.

VOTE

5–4, with Chief Justice William Rehnquist writing the opinion for a majority that included Justices Sandra Day O'Connor, Antonin Scalia, Anthony Kennedy, and Clarence Thomas. Dissenting were Justices David Souter, John Paul Stevens, Ruth Bader Ginsburg, and Stephen Breyer.

HIGHLIGHTS

When the Court examines government programs to see if they violate the establishment clause, it looks first at whether the primary purpose of the program is to advance or endorse a religion. On this point there was little disagreement on the Court; with Cleveland schools in the terrible shape they were in, the voucher program had a valid purpose of trying to improve the education of Cleveland's young people. It was not aimed at subsidizing religious schools.

It was the second inquiry that divided the justices; whether the program had the "primary effect" of advancing religion. Chief Justice Rehnquist said it did not, mainly because the government money did not go directly to Cleveland's parochial schools. Instead—and this was the key to the case— the money went directly to parents who, in turn, gave the money to schools as a result of their "genuine and independent choices." The fact that almost all of these parents were choosing to give their voucher money to religious schools did not make any difference in Rehnquist's view.

In dissent, Justice Souter was adamant that no matter what the method was for getting the money to the parochial schools, the bottom line was that government money was being used to pay for religious instruction at religious schools. Justices Stevens and Breyer also wrote forceful dissents, asserting that in many places around the world, religious and political strife results from lowering the barrier between church and state, as they believed the majority had done in this case.

EXCERPTS

From Rehnquist's majority opinion: "We believe that the program challenged here is a program of true private choice . . . and thus constitutional. . . . [T]he Ohio program is neutral in all respects toward religion. It is part of a general and multifaceted undertaking by the State of Ohio to provide educational opportunities to the children of a failed school district. . . . The program permits the participation of *all* schools within the district, religious or nonreligious. Adjacent public schools also may participate and have a financial incentive to do so. Program benefits are available to participating families on neutral terms, with no reference to religion. The only preference stated anywhere in the program is a preference for low-income families, who receive greater assistance and are given priority for admission at participating schools. . . .

"That 46 of the 56 private schools now participating in the program are religious schools does not condemn it as a violation of the Establishment Clause. The Establishment Clause question is whether Ohio is coercing parents into sending their children to religious schools, and that question must be answered by evaluating *all* options Ohio provides Cleveland schoolchildren, only one of which is to obtain a program scholarship and then choose a religious school."

From Justice Souter's dissent: "In the city of Cleveland the overwhelming proportion of large appropriations for voucher money must be spent on religious schools if it is to be spent at all, and will be spent in amounts that cover almost all of tuition. The money will thus pay for eligible students' instruction not only in secular subjects but in religion as well, in schools that can fairly be characterized as founded to teach religious doctrine and to imbue teaching in all subjects with a religious dimension. Public tax money will pay at a systemic level for teaching the covenant with Israel and Mosaic law in Jewish schools, the primacy of the Apostle Peter and the Papacy in Catholic schools, the truth of reformed Christianity in Protestant schools, and the revelation to the Prophet in Muslim schools, to speak only of major religious groupings in the Republic."

IMPACT

Advocates of school voucher programs rejoiced at the Court's ruling and said it would encourage many more states and localities to create programs similar to the one the Court upheld. Indeed, several states have launched or expanded voucher programs in the wake of the *Zelman* decision.

But the ruling has not cleared all obstacles in the path of school voucher programs. Opposition remains strong from politically powerful groups including public school teachers and some civil liberties organizations.

In addition to political pressure, voucher opponents continued to litigate against voucher programs, in some cases focusing on state constitutions instead of the federal First Amendment.

More than thirty states, it turns out, have constitutional provisions that are far more explicit than the First Amendment in forbidding any government support, direct or indirect, for religious institutions, including schools. Most of these provisions were enacted in the late nineteenth century at a time of strong nativist and anti-Catholic sentiment nationwide. Growing Catholic and immigrant populations protested the Protestant domination of public schools and began demanding public money to support Catholic schools, and states reacted by prohibiting such support outright. Voucher opponents in Florida and elsewhere made use of these state laws and constitutional amendments to argue that even indirect support of religious schools through vouchers is improper.

Elk Grove Unified School District v. Newdow

Decided June 14, 2004
No. 02-1624
laws.findlaw.com/US/000/02-1624.html

DECISION

The Pledge of Allegiance, recited by public school students nationwide every day, is a patriotic exercise. A California father who challenged the words "under God" in the pledge as a First Amendment violation does not have standing or authority to sue, because he does not have legal custody over his daughter who recites the pledge in school.

BACKGROUND

Michael Newdow, an atheist lawyer and physician, says it first dawned on him when he was standing in a grocery store line. He looked at a dollar bill he was about to use and saw the words "In God We Trust" printed on the back. "This is absurd," Newdow said to himself. As an atheist, Newdow was offended by what he saw as government endorsement of a religious view that was contrary to his beliefs.

Thus began a lengthy and quixotic battle in the courts against the religious references that are commonplace in U.S. society. Eventually Newdow's fight focused on the words "under God" in the Pledge of Allegiance. Unlike other references to a deity that go back to the founding of the nation, this one was relatively recent. Congress added the words "under God" to the pledge in 1954, at the height of the cold war when the government wanted to emphasize how the United States contrasted with "godless" communists.

In the U.S. legal system, however, people cannot simply go to court to object to government actions they don't like. They must demonstrate that they themselves have suffered an injury as a result of what the government did. This concept of "standing" posed a problem for Newdow. As an adult, he no longer was compelled to recite the pledge, so he sued on behalf of his daughter, a student at Elk Grove Unified School District near Sacramento, California. But Newdow and the girl's mother never married, and they lived separately. The mother, Sandra Banning, had legal custody over the girl, though court orders allowed the girl to live with Newdow some of the time. Newdow and Banning lived near each other.

In 2002 the U.S. Court of Appeals for the Ninth Circuit, which handles cases from California and other western states, made national headlines when it ruled in Newdow's favor. The court said Newdow, as the girl's biological father, had enough standing to sue, and it also ruled that the pledge violated the establishment clause of the First Amendment, which bars government establishment of religion. At this point the girl's mother informed the court that she alone had the power to make decisions about her daughter's education, and neither she nor the girl, then nine, had any objection to her reciting the pledge. The appeals court then modified its ruling somewhat, but it said Newdow still had standing as a parent to sue.

Amid widespread outcry about the ruling, the school district appealed to the U.S. Supreme Court, and the justices agreed to consider it. The case took an unusual turn when Newdow, who wanted to argue the case himself, petitioned Justice Antonin Scalia to remove himself from consideration of the case. Scalia had given a speech in which he suggested strongly his disagreement with the appeals court ruling, and Newdow filed a motion urging Scalia to recuse. Surprisingly, Scalia agreed, so Newdow faced eight, rather than nine, justices when he argued on March 24, 2004. As is customary, the marshal of the court began the session that day with an opening cry that concludes, "God save the United States and this honorable court."

VOTE

8–0, with Justice John Paul Stevens writing the majority opinion. All eight justices participating agreed that the appeals court ruling should be reversed, but they approached the case differently. Justice Stevens, joined by Justices Anthony Kennedy, David Souter, Ruth Bader Ginsburg, and Stephen Breyer, said Newdow did not have standing to sue, so they did not rule on the merits of his case. Chief Justice William Rehnquist, joined by Justices Sandra Day O'Connor and Clarence Thomas, said Newdow did have sufficient standing, and they said his challenge to the pledge should fail. Justice Scalia did not participate.

HIGHLIGHTS

In deciding to avoid the controversial issue of whether the words "under God" belong in the Pledge of Allegiance, Justice Stevens relied on what he described as the Court's "deeply rooted" commitment to avoid deciding questions of constitutionality unless necessary. Stevens implicitly acknowledged that Newdow had some general standing or interest because he is the girl's father, but because of his complex custody situation, California law did not permit him to sue on her behalf. As a result the Court ruled that Newdow did not have "prudential standing" in the case, a doctrine that relates to the Court's reluctance to reach out and decide issues that are not properly before it.

Stevens also cited the Court's longstanding hands-off policy toward second-guessing state court determinations on family law issues like divorce and custody, which are traditionally defined by state, not federal, law.

While not ruling on the merits of Newdow's challenge, the Stevens opinion did recite briefly the history of the pledge, describing it as a "patriotic exercise designed to foster national unity." This is significant, because Newdow argued that reciting the pledge was a religious, rather than patriotic, exercise.

Chief Justice Rehnquist wrote a separate concurrence to suggest that the majority had created a "novel" doctrine to avoid the merits of the case, when in fact it should have ruled in favor of the current wording of the pledge. The pledge is a "commendable patriotic observance," he said, and reciting it "cannot possibly lead to the establishment of a religion or anything like it."

Justice Thomas also took a different approach. He said that under the Court's precedents, the wording of the pledge was, in fact, unconstitutional—but those precedents were wrong. He said the establishment clause was aimed at keeping Congress from passing laws about religion, but should not be read to keep states from enacting laws such as the California law that requires recitation of the pledge in public school classrooms.

As a result of the various writings of the justices, it was clear that at least three justices—Rehnquist, O'Connor, and Thomas—saw no constitutional problem with keeping the words "under God" in the pledge. More than likely, given Stevens's brief description of the issue, he and the other justices were also unsympathetic toward Newdow's challenge.

EXCERPTS

From Justice Stevens's majority opinion: "The command to guard jealously and exercise rarely our power to make constitutional pronouncements requires strictest adherence when matters of great national significance are at stake. Even in cases concededly within our jurisdiction under Article III, we abide by 'a series of rules under which [we have] avoided passing upon a large part of all the constitutional questions pressed upon [us] for decision.' . . . Always we must balance 'the heavy obligation to exercise jurisdiction,' . . . against the 'deeply rooted' commitment 'not to pass on questions of con-

stitutionality' unless adjudication of the constitutional issue is necessary. . . .

"Nothing that either Banning or the School Board has done, however, impairs Newdow's right to instruct his daughter in his religious views. Instead, Newdow . . . wishes to forestall his daughter's exposure to religious ideas that her mother, who wields a form of veto power, endorses, and to use his parental status to challenge the influences to which his daughter may be exposed in school when he and Banning disagree. The California cases simply do not stand for the proposition that Newdow has a right to dictate to others what they may and may not say to his child respecting religion. . . . The cases speak not at all to the problem of a parent seeking to reach outside the private parent-child sphere to restrain the acts of a third party. A next friend surely could exercise such a right, but the Superior Court's order has deprived Newdow of that status."

IMPACT

The ruling was anticlimactic after the widespread attention paid to Newdow and his controversial objections to the pledge. While turning back Newdow's challenge because of his custody issues, the Court did not completely resolve the issue he raised about the pledge.

Still, supporters of the pledge were quick to proclaim victory. "The Supreme Court has removed a dark cloud that has been hanging over one of the nation's most important and cherished traditions—the ability of students across the nation to acknowledge the fact that our freedoms in this country come from God, not government," said Jay Sekulow, chief counsel for the American Center for Law and Justice.

The Court may have welcomed the chance to avoid an issue that had emotions running high for many people. In an Associated Press poll conducted before the ruling, nearly 90 percent of those responding said the words "under God" should not be removed.

But the issue may return to the Supreme Court. In January 2005 Newdow filed a new challenge to the pledge, joined by several other unnamed parents who did not have similar custody complications.

Newdow also launched other challenges in court, as he had pledged to do. Unsuccessfully, Newdow sued President George W. Bush to prevent him from allowing clergy to offer prayers at his inauguration on January 20, 2005.

Ten Commandments Cases

Van Orden v. Perry
Decided June 27, 2005
No. 03-1500
laws.findlaw.com/us/000/03-1500.html

McCreary County, Kentucky v. American Civil Liberties Union of Kentucky
Decided June 27, 2005
No. 03-1693
laws.findlaw.com/US/000/03-1693.html

DECISION

Displaying the Ten Commandments on public property is permissible under the establishment clause of the First Amendment, depending on the context of the display. A Ten Commandments monument that stands amid other historical displays and has not been challenged for a long period of time is allowed. But when a government body mounts a Ten Commandments display with the clear purpose of advancing religion, it is not permitted, even when the display is later modified to include nonreligious documents.

BACKGROUND

The Ten Commandments express the fundamental doctrines of both Christianity and Judaism. They include basic rules for living, including "Thou shalt not kill," as well as more religious com-

mands, such as, "Thou shalt not take the name of the Lord thy God in vain" and "Remember the Sabbath day, to keep it holy."

For much of the nation's history, displaying the Ten Commandments in public places was not controversial, in spite of their religious content. For example, they were integrated into several parts of the design of the Supreme Court building itself when It opened in 1935. In one of the friezes lining the upper walls of the court chamber, Moses is shown holding the tablets of the Ten Commandments; he is one of seventeen lawgivers depicted.

As late as the early 1960s, a civic group called the Fraternal Order of Eagles distributed hundreds of granite Ten Commandments monuments and paper replicas to state and local governments to display, with the aim of inspiring young people and curbing juvenile delinquency. The movie director Cecil B.

This stone slab bearing the Ten Commandments stands near the Texas Capitol in Austin. In two related separation of church and state decisions—*Van Orden v. Perry* (2005) and *McCreary County, Kentucky v. American Civil Liberties Union* (2005)—the Supreme Court held that the Austin monument did not violate the establishment clause, because of its non-religious context, but ruled against the display of a similar monument at a Kentucky courthouse, on the ground that its erection was for the promotion of religion.

Source: AP/Wide World Photos/ Harry Cabluck.

DeMille helped with the project, partly as a way to promote his forthcoming movie *The Ten Commandments*. Many governmental bodies accepted the displays as gifts without hesitation.

Forty years later, it was one of those monuments, which had been installed in 1961 on the Texas state capitol grounds in Austin, that triggered a dispute that went all the way to the Supreme Court. Thomas Van Orden, a homeless lawyer, noticed the six-foot high monument on his way to the state law library. He sued to have it removed on establishment clause grounds, arguing that its placement on public property amounted to government endorsement of religion. The U.S. Court of Appeals for the Fifth Circuit ruled against Van Orden, finding that a "reasonable viewer" would not conclude from seeing the monument that Texas was endorsing religion or trying to exclude those who do not believe in the Ten Commandments.

The Texas challenge was one of many at the turn of the twenty-first century, reflecting increasing sensitivity over religious symbols and invocations in public places. It was fueled in part by the growing diversity of the population, with more and more adherents to "minority" religions, as well as by mixed signals on the issue from the Supreme Court. (See *Santa Fe Independent School District v. Doe* and *Elk Grove Unified School District v. Newdow*.)

In Kentucky, the local chapter of the American Civil Liberties Union sued to seek removal of newly mounted Ten Commandments displays in the courthouses of McCreary and Pulaski counties. Once the litigation began, the counties modified the displays by surrounding the Ten Commandments with other historical documents with religious references, including a 1983 congressional resolution declaring the Year of the Bible. But county governing boards also passed resolutions defiantly declaring the Ten Commandments as "the precedent legal code" for the laws of Kentucky, and honoring "Jesus Christ, the prince of ethics."

As the controversy continued, the displays were modified again, keeping the Ten Commandments but changing the surrounding documents to include documents with fewer religious references. But the resolutions were not repealed, and the U.S. Court of Appeals for the Sixth Circuit said the displays had to come down. They were placed in the courthouses with a religious objective, the court said, and clearly demonstrated government support for "a single religious influence." With two appeals courts in conflict over the same issue, the stage was set for Supreme Court review.

VOTE

Van Orden v. Perry: 5–4, with Chief Justice William Rehnquist writing a plurality opinion upholding the Texas display, joined by Justices Antonin Scalia, Anthony Kennedy, and Clarence Thomas. Justice Stephen Breyer concurred in the judgment, but for different reasons. Justices John Paul Stevens, Sandra Day O'Connor, David Souter, and Ruth Bader Ginsburg dissented.

McCreary County v. ACLU: 5–4, with Justice David Souter writing the majority opinion disapproving of the Kentucky display. Joining him were Justices John Paul Stevens, Sandra Day O'Connor, Ruth Bader Ginsburg, and Stephen Breyer. In dissent were Justices Antonin Scalia, Chief Justice William Rehnquist, and Justices Clarence Thomas and Anthony Kennedy.

HIGHLIGHTS

The Court's starting point was *Stone v. Graham,* a very cursory 1980 ruling that had invalidated a state law—from Kentucky, ironically—that required the posting of the Ten Commandments in every public school classroom. Using the so-called Lemon test (see *Lemon v. Kurtzman*), the Court said the law lacked a secular or nonreligious purpose and violated the establishment clause.

In the Kentucky cases before the Court this time, that same problem again proved fatal. Even though the county courthouse displays had changed several times, Justice Souter said the original purpose for the displays could not be ignored. Lawyers for the county urged the Court to focus instead on how a reasonable observer would perceive the displays now. "Reasonable observers have reasonable memories," Souter countered.

But in the Texas display, the history was different. Chief Justice Rehnquist, writing for himself and three other justices, specifically stated that he was not using the Lemon test. He focused instead on the "passive" nature of the display and the fact that it was not aimed at schoolchildren—distinguishing it from *Stone v. Graham*. He also cited the many ways in which other government institutions—including the Supreme Court—have recognized the Ten Commandments throughout history.

Justice Breyer provided the fifth vote in favor of the Texas monument, but for different reasons. He called the Lemon test a "useful guidepost," but said "legal judgment" led him to his conclusion. The fact that the monument was a gift from a civic, not religious, group, as well as its placement among many other historical markers, suggest "little or nothing of the sacred." The fact that the monument had gone unchallenged for forty years also indicated that people did not view it as an offensively religious display until Van Orden took it to court. Significantly, Justice Breyer was the only member of the Court in the majority in both cases, favoring the Texas display but finding that the religious purpose behind the Kentucky displays was fatal.

Justice O'Connor, an unpredictable vote on church-state issues, objected to both displays, expressing her preference for enforcing the First Amendment's religion clauses so as to keep religion "a matter for the individual conscience, not for the prosecutor or bureaucrat." By doing so, she said, the

United States has been able to avoid "the violent consequences of the assumption of religious authority by government" around the world.

Justice Scalia bitterly objected to Justice Souter's majority opinion in the Kentucky case. Scalia said there was absolutely nothing wrong with government institutions acknowledging and honoring the nation's religious character. "Publicly honoring the Ten Commandments is . . . indistinguishable, insofar as discriminating against other religions is concerned, from publicly honoring God," Scalia wrote. "Both practices are recognized across such a broad and diverse range of the population—from Christians to Muslims—that they cannot be reasonably understood as a government endorsement of a particular religious viewpoint."

EXCERPTS

From Chief Justice Rehnquist's plurality opinion in *Van Orden v. Perry:* "Of course, the Ten Commandments are religious—they were so viewed at their inception and so remain. The monument, therefore, has religious significance. According to Judeo-Christian belief, the Ten Commandments were given to Moses by God on Mt. Sinai. But Moses was a lawgiver as well as a religious leader. And the Ten Commandments have an undeniable historical meaning. . . . Simply having religious content or promoting a message consistent with a religious doctrine does not run afoul of the Establishment Clause. . . .

"Texas has treated her Capitol grounds monuments as representing the several strands in the State's political and legal history. The inclusion of the Ten Commandments monument in this group has a dual significance, partaking of both religion and government."

From Justice Souter's majority opinion in *McCreary County v. ACLU:* "The reasonable observer could only think that the Counties meant to emphasize and celebrate the Commandments' religious message. This is not to deny that the Commandments have had influence on civil or secular law; a major text of a majority religion is bound to be felt. The point is simply that the original text viewed in its entirety is an unmistakably religious statement dealing with religious obligations and with morality subject to religious sanction. When the government initiates an effort to place this statement alone in public view, a religious object is unmistakable. . . .

"We do not forget, and in this litigation have frequently been reminded, that our own courtroom frieze was deliberately designed in the exercise of governmental authority so as to include the figure of Moses holding tablets exhibiting a portion of the Hebrew text of the later, secularly phrased Commandments; in the company of 17 other lawgivers, most of them secular figures, there is no risk that Moses would strike an observer as evidence that the National Government was violating neutrality in religion."

From Justice Scalia's dissent in *McCreary:* "How can the Court possibly assert that 'the First Amendment mandates governmental neutrality between . . . religion and nonreligion,'. . . and that '[m]anifesting a purpose to favor . . . adherence to religion generally,'. . . is unconstitutional? Who says so? Surely not the words of the Constitution. Surely not the history and traditions that reflect our society's constant understanding of those words. Surely not even the current sense of our society."

IMPACT

The decisions, issued on the same day, gave both sides in the debate over separation of church and state something to praise and something to attack.

"The affirmation of the constitutional principle of government neutrality toward religion is the most important aspect of these rulings," said Ralph Neas, president of the liberal group People For the American Way. "While we disagree with how the Court applied that principle to the facts in Texas, we are very pleased that the Court has rejected efforts to dismantle church-state separation."

Groups on the religious right were angry at the Court, and they said the decisions underscored the need for new justices more attuned to the religious heritage of the nation. "Today's vexing decision highlights the importance of a nomination of a strict constitutionalist to the Bench if there is a possible resignation from a current Justice," said Tony Perkins, president of the Family Research Council.

Conservatives were especially disappointed with Justice O'Connor, a Republican appointee who voted against both Ten Commandments displays. Said the Rev. Louis Sheldon of the Traditional Values Coalition: "If Justice Sandra Day O'Connor retires soon, we will have the opportunity to place someone on the court who appreciates and understands the moral and religious foundations upon which America was founded." When Sheldon spoke, he could not have known that four days later O'Connor would announce her retirement from the Court. O'-Connor's vote in the Ten Commandments displays guaranteed that the church-state views of her successor would be a major issue in the political battle over replacing her.

In terms of Court doctrine, the decisions left many questions unanswered about which Ten Commandments displays would be permitted and which had to be taken down. The Kentucky displays ran into trouble because of the counties' avowed purpose of promoting Christian values at the outset; but does that mean that a government can never mend its ways and renounce that original purpose? The passive display in Texas won the Court's favor in part because it had not been challenged in the first forty years of its existence; but would it have been allowed if it was a newer display and objections were raised quickly?

Overall, though, it appeared that the Court had offered general guidance on how governments could erect Ten Commandments displays that would withstand constitutional scrutiny: Be careful not to use religious language in proposing the display, and surround it with enough nonreligious documents or icons to place the Ten Commandments in a historic context. As Erwin Chemerinsky, the lawyer who argued against the Texas display and lost, put it, "Context is everything."

FREE EXERCISE OF RELIGION

*P*rotecting the right to believe in any religion—or no religion—was one of the main reasons the United States was founded. The First Amendment promises that protection in no uncertain terms by barring Congress from passing any law "prohibiting the exercise" of religion. As absolute as that command seems, the Supreme Court has recognized that it has limits, especially when actions taken in the name of religion affect others. To state an absurd example, if a religion required its believers to rob banks, that activity would probably not be tolerated by the rest of society, or by the law. Most real-life examples are not that easy to resolve, and the Court has struggled to decide when the law should restrict religious activities. Another concern has been that if government backs off and gives religion too much leeway, it will violate the other religious clause of the First Amendment, the establishment clause, by in effect endorsing religion through favored treatment.

Other related cases mentioned in the Free Exercise of Religion section

Marbury v. Madison (1803) (see p. 291)
Minersville School District v. Gobitis (1940)
Jones v. Opelika (1942)
Murdock v. Pennsylvania (1943)
Sherbert v. Verner (1963)
Runyon v. McCrary (1976)
Employment Division v. Smith (1990)
Cutter v. Wilkinson (2005)

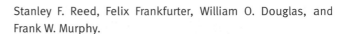

Cantwell v. Connecticut

Decided May 20, 1940
310 U.S. 296
laws.findlaw.com/US/310/296.html

DECISION

A state law that requires religious groups to get prior approval from a government official before they can solicit donations is unconstitutional. The Fourteenth Amendment makes the religion clauses of the First Amendment applicable to state as well as federal action. States may, in a nondiscriminatory way, regulate "the times, the places and the manner" of religious activities and solicitation, but the law at issue improperly gives government the ability to completely prohibit religious activity.

BACKGROUND

Newton Cantwell and his two sons, Jesse and Russell, were arrested on the streets of New Haven and charged with a variety of offenses, including breach of the peace. All three were Jehovah's Witnesses, and they were asking passersby to listen to a recording or take and pay for literature explaining their religion. The recording contained, among other things, some strong anti-Catholic sentiments typical of Jehovah's Witness thinking at the time. On this particular day, they had chosen a heavily Catholic neighborhood of New Haven in which to solicit. Two men agreed when Jesse Cantwell offered to play on his portable phonograph the recording titled "Enemies." They became furious at the sentiments they heard and advised Jesse to move on. He did, but police arrived and arrested the Cantwells on several charges.

Among other things, the Cantwells were convicted of violating a law that required anyone soliciting donations to obtain prior approval for their solicitations from the secretary of the public welfare council. The Cantwells said the requirement violated their freedom of religion, but the Connecticut Supreme Court ruled that the charge was constitutional because it related to solicitation rather than the Cantwells' religious activities.

The case came to the Supreme Court as it was considering a more explosive case involving Jehovah's Witnesses—*Minersville School District v. Gobitis,* testing whether a Jehovah's Witness child could be expelled from school for refusing to participate in the flag salute.

VOTE

9–0, with Justice Owen J. Roberts writing the majority opinion. Joining him were Chief Justice Charles Evans Hughes and Justices James C. McReynolds, Harlan Fiske Stone, Hugo L. Black,

Stanley F. Reed, Felix Frankfurter, William O. Douglas, and Frank W. Murphy.

HIGHLIGHTS

The Court declared that First Amendment prohibitions are made applicable to the states by the Fourteenth Amendment. "The First Amendment declares that Congress shall make no law respecting an establishment of religion or prohibiting the free exercise thereof. The Fourteenth Amendment has rendered the legislatures of the states as incompetent as Congress to enact such laws," said Justice Roberts.

Justice Owen J. Roberts wrote the opinion for the Court's unanimous decision in *Cantwell v. Connecticut* (1940), a case involving religious solicitation by Jehovah's Witnesses. The Court struck down a Connecticut law requiring religious groups to obtain government approval before soliciting donations, but asserted that states may "regulate the times, the places, and the manner" of such activity.

Source: Harris & Ewing, Collection of the Supreme Court of the United States.

Regulating solicitation is normally a constitutional exercise of state power, Roberts continued. But he said the Connecticut law at issue gives state officials absolute power to determine whether an applicant for a license to solicit has a legitimate religious purpose. If so, the license is issued, but if not, the applicant is committing a crime if he or she continues to solicit.

"He [the state official] is authorized to withhold his approval if he determines that the cause is not a religious one," Roberts wrote. "Such a censorship of religion as the means of determining its right to survive is a denial of liberty protected by the First Amendment and included in the liberty which is within the protection of the Fourteenth."

The opinion also examined Cantwell's behavior and found that it was not rude or obnoxious and did not incite others to violence. "On the contrary, we find only an effort to persuade a willing listener to buy a book or to contribute money in the interest of what Cantwell, however misguided others may think him, conceived to be true religion." Justice Roberts added that Cantwell's actions posed no "clear and present danger" that the state would have had the authority to prevent.

EXCERPTS

From Justice Roberts's majority opinion: "[T]he [First] Amendment embraces two concepts—freedom to believe and freedom to act. The first is absolute, but, in the nature of things, the second cannot be. Conduct remains subject to regulation for the protection of society. The freedom to act must have appropriate definition to preserve the enforcement of that protection. In every case, the power to regulate must be so exercised as not, in attaining a permissible end, unduly to infringe the protected freedom. No one would contest the proposition that a state may not, by statute, wholly deny the right to preach or to disseminate religious views. Plainly, such a previous and absolute restraint would violate the terms of the guarantee. It is equally clear that a state may by general and non-discriminatory legislation regulate the times, the places, and the manner of soliciting upon its streets, and of holding meetings thereon; and may in other respects safeguard the peace, good order and comfort of the community, without unconstitutionally invading the liberties protected by the Fourteenth Amendment."

IMPACT

The *Cantwell* decision was the first in which the Supreme Court said that the First Amendment's religion clauses, which bar the establishment of religion and protect the free exercise of religion, apply to actions of the states as well as the federal government. As such, it has been the touchstone for the Court's examination of dozens of state laws and regulations restricting religious practices ever since. *Cantwell* continued a line of cases in which the Court had "incorporated" basic freedoms to apply to the states through the Fourteenth Amendment.

The ruling is notable for another reason. It was the first time it used the time, place, or manner wording to describe the type of limits on First Amendment freedoms that could be permitted without unconstitutionally restricting those freedoms.

That standard also has carried on to today, proving particularly useful in disputes over regulations on speech and expression. It allows governments to say, for example, that using a loudspeaker in a public park is okay at noon but not at midnight, and not permissible at all on someone's doorstep. Generally speaking, regulations that allow government to prohibit a speech or religious activity outright have been struck down, but regulations that are "narrowly tailored" to meet a public safety objective and are not too costly have been allowed.

In a 1992 case, for example, the Court upheld a Minnesota state fair regulation that confined people who wanted to distribute literature to rented booths on the fair grounds. The rule was a reasonable way to prevent disorder and the blockage of foot traffic in a confined area, the Court said, while allowing for communications from booths. Echoing *Cantwell*, Justice Byron White said in that case that the First Amendment "does not guarantee the right to communicate one's views at all times and places or in any manner that may be desired."

As for solicitation by Jehovah's Witnesses, *Cantwell* did not end the Court's scrutiny. In *Jones v. Opelika* (1942) the Court by a 5–4 vote upheld an Alabama ordinance that required Jehovah's Witnesses, like other vendors, to obtain peddler's licenses before soliciting door to door. A year later, the arrival of a new justice on the Court resulted in *Opelika* being overturned. In *Murdock v. Pennsylvania*, Justice Wiley Rutledge, who replaced James Byrnes, joined the dissenters in *Opelika* to form a majority that found that a license fee on Jehovah's Witness solicitors amounted to a tax on the free exercise of religion.

Bob Jones University v. United States

Decided May 24, 1983
461 U.S. 574
laws.findlaw.com/US/461/574.html

DECISION

Private educational institutions that discriminate on the basis of race are not entitled to tax-exempt status. Federal tax law allows the Internal Revenue Service (IRS) to designate charitable organizations as tax-exempt. The government's interest in eliminating racial bias in schools outweighs the schools' First Amendment rights to exercise the religious beliefs behind the discriminatory policy.

BACKGROUND

After the Supreme Court ruled in 1954 that the racial segregation of public schools was unconstitutional, private schools known as "segregation academies" began to spread throughout the South. Because they received no government funds to operate, these schools could exclude blacks if they chose. But such institutions did receive an indirect benefit from government; like other schools, they were tax-exempt.

By 1970 several hundred thousand white students were attending these academies. After a judge ordered the IRS not to give tax-exempt status to several segregated schools in Mississippi, the IRS decided to change its policy and deny tax-exempt status to all schools that discriminated on the basis of race. The commissioner wrote to more than 5,000 schools announcing the change.

Bob Jones University in Greenville, South Carolina, and the Goldsboro Christian Schools in Goldsboro, North Carolina, received letters from the IRS. Established in 1927 by evangelist Dr. Bob Jones Sr., Bob Jones University is a fundamentalist Christian institution with more than 5,000 students; its founder describes it as "the world's most unusual university." The school's sponsors believed that the Bible forbids interracial dating or marriage and accepted no black students. Dancing, card playing, and movie-going were also prohibited. After the IRS policy change, the university changed its racial policy; it accepted black students but only if they were already married to other blacks or if they pledged not to date or marry someone of another race. The policy changed again in 1975, allowing unmarried blacks to attend. But a disciplinary rule said that interracial dating or marriage by students would result in expulsion. The IRS revoked Bob Jones's tax-exempt status in 1975, setting the stage for its lawsuit against the IRS.

Goldsboro Christian Schools, which offered classes from kindergarten through high school, had a longstanding policy of

Bob Jones III, president of Bob Jones University in Greenville, South Carolina, discusses the school's philosophy in 1982. The university's code of ethics at the time prohibited interracial dating and marriage among students. In *Bob Jones University v. United States* (1983), the Court reaffirmed that institutions that discriminate on the basis of race are not entitled to tax exemption.
Source: AP/Wide World Photos.

admitting only whites. The U.S. Court of Appeals for the Fourth Circuit ruled in both cases that to qualify for tax-exempt status, institutions had to show they were "charitable" and did not operate contrary to public policy.

The *Bob Jones* case was notable not only because of what the Court decided but because of the political struggle it provoked. When Bob Jones University lost in the lower court and appealed to the Supreme Court, the Justice Department "acquiesced," acknowledging that the issue was important and needed to be resolved by the nation's highest court. The Solicitor General's Office, which argues the government's cases before the Supreme Court, defended the IRS position.

But top officials in the Reagan administration had a different view. During his presidential campaign, President Ronald Reagan had spoken out against the IRS policy as an "administrative fiat" that went beyond the agency's authority. Others in the Justice Department felt it was important to tell the Court that it was up to Congress, not the IRS commissioner, to decide whether tax-exempt status should be denied to racially discriminatory schools. A major controversy broke out when it became clear that the Reagan administration would change sides and oppose the longstanding IRS policy.

This shift also put the Solicitor General's Office in an awkward position. That office, with a reputation among justices for steadiness and sound legal judgment, rarely if ever reverses itself in a pending case. In a compromise, the office wrote a brief opposing the IRS policy, and Acting Solicitor General Lawrence Wallace, in a footnote, told the Court he did not agree with the new position.

VOTE

8–1, with Chief Justice Warren E. Burger writing the majority opinion. He was joined by Justices William J. Brennan Jr., Byron R. White, Thurgood Marshall, Harry A. Blackmun, Lewis F. Powell Jr., John Paul Stevens, and Sandra Day O'Connor. Justice William Rehnquist dissented.

HIGHLIGHTS

The Court's decision was a forceful reaffirmation of the nation's—and the Court's—determination that racial discrimination in schools be eradicated. It was especially dramatic because its author, Chief Justice Burger, was a conservative who often followed the literal language of a law to reach decisions that were as narrow as possible.

The plain purpose of the law on tax-exempt institutions, as the Court saw it, was to lend support to charitable organizations that serve the public interest and that provide services the government itself cannot or does not provide. "The institution's purpose must not be so at odds with the common community conscience as to undermine any public benefit that might otherwise be conferred," Burger wrote. Citing the nation's long and painful history of racial segregation in schools—and society's efforts to end that discrimination—Burger said unequivocally that schools that discriminate could not fit the criteria for tax-exempt status.

In a concurring opinion, Justice Powell expressed concern that the IRS might use the ruling to enforce a sort of uniformity with government-approved views and punish organizations that espouse controversial views. "Its business is to administer laws designed to produce revenue for the Government, not to promote 'public policy,'" Powell stated.

But Burger expressed no concern about that possible abuse, emphasizing that in this case, the public policy goals of eliminating segregation in schools was deeply held by all three branches of government. "These sensitive determinations should be made only where there is no doubt that the organization's activities violate fundamental public policy."

EXCERPTS

From Justice Burger's majority opinion: "It would be wholly incompatible with the concepts underlying tax exemption to grant the benefit of tax-exempt status to racially discriminatory educational entities, which 'exert a pervasive influence on the entire educational process.' Whatever may be the rationale for such private schools' policies, and however sincere the rationale may be, racial discrimination in education is contrary to public policy. Racially discriminatory educational institutions cannot be viewed as conferring a public benefit within the 'charitable' concept discussed earlier or within the congressional intent."

IMPACT

Bob Jones University continues to exist—and thrive—despite its loss of tax-exempt status. Its Web site, *www. bju.edu,* claims the school has more than 5,000 students and offers more than 150 undergraduate and graduate major subjects. It solicits donations from alumni, but without the promise that the donations are tax-deductible. "While the University has grown, our educational philosophy and religious beliefs have not changed," the university states.

The next question was whether the IRS would continue to enforce the rule upheld by the Supreme Court. In a policy directive in 1999, the IRS noted that this is a "difficult and sensitive tax law area." But it spelled out how the government makes a determination that a school is discriminatory. Attendance records and the determinations of other government agencies are relevant, the policy states. And the fact that a school was established "at the time of local public school desegregation" can also be taken into account.

From time to time, conservative groups that oppose affirmative action have cited the *Bob Jones* case to question the tax-exempt status of schools and foundations that offer scholarships to racial minorities. They argue that if Bob Jones University can be penalized for discriminating against blacks, other institutions should lose their tax-exempt status for discriminating against whites. But usually, these scholarships and other preferences are challenged under other statutes and precedents that do not involve tax status.

Before the South Carolina presidential primary in February 2000, then-Texas governor George W. Bush was criticized for making a campaign appearance at Bob Jones University because of its policy of forbidding interracial dating among students and because of the anti-Catholic sentiments expressed by some of its leaders. After a month of steady criticism, university president Bob Jones III announced that the school was lifting the ban on interracial dating.

Private institutions that discriminate against minorities still exist, but they are vulnerable to lawsuits by anyone excluded from admission. The Supreme Court's 1976 decision in *Runyon v. McCrary,* which bars discrimination in private contracts, arose in the context of a lawsuit filed by black students excluded from a private school in Virginia.

City of Boerne v. Flores

Decided June 25, 1997
521 U.S. 507
laws.findlaw.com/US/521/507.html

DECISION

Congress has the power to enforce the Fourteenth Amendment and other parts of the Constitution, but only the Supreme Court has the ultimate authority to interpret what the Constitution means. For that reason, the Court struck down the Religious Freedom Restoration Act (RFRA), which dictated the standard by which government actions that restrict religious practices should be judged by courts. The Court also said that even though the Fourteenth Amendment allows Congress to pass "remedial" laws that enforce civil rights at the state level, RFRA went too far in telling states what to do.

BACKGROUND

Throughout history the Supreme Court has often been asked to referee disputes in which government has applied seemingly neutral laws in ways that restrict religious practices—from bigamy among the Mormons to home schooling by the Amish. At times the Court has struck the balance in ways that favor religion (the Amish, for example) while at other times it has sided with government enforcement (as it did in the case of Mormon bigamy).

In *Sherbert v. Verner* (1963) the Court established a standard that required government to show it had a "compelling" interest before it could enforce laws against religious practices. In that case the Court reinstated unemployment benefits to a woman who had been fired from her job because of her religion-based refusal to work on Saturdays.

The *Sherbert* standard prevailed for more than two decades, serving in many instances to vindicate controversial religious practices. The Court abruptly abandoned the standard in the 1990 decision, *Employment Division v. Smith.* The Court said Oregon could enforce its narcotics laws against members of a Native American church who used peyote in religious rituals. The

Court said it was no longer necessary for the state to show it had a compelling interest in the restriction. All that was necessary was to show that the law was neutral and generally applicable.

The *Smith* decision, which had the effect of upholding antidrug laws, provoked an angry reaction among religious groups. They were concerned that every ritual from circumcision to the use of sacramental wine could be regulated more easily under the Court's relaxed level of scrutiny.

Congress responded quickly to lobbying by religious organizations. By overwhelming votes—unanimous in the House and only three negative votes in the Senate—Congress passed the Religious Freedom Restoration Act. The law's stated aim was to "restore the compelling interest test as set forth in *Sherbert v. Verner* . . . and to guarantee its application in all cases where free exercise of religion is substantially burdened." The law said that a substantial government restriction on religious practice could be upheld only if it is "in furtherance of a compelling governmental interest and is the least restrictive means of furthering that compelling governmental interest."

Soon, however, scholars and government officials began to criticize the law. States said it was being frequently invoked by prison inmates in defense of allegedly frivolous religious requirements.

In Boerne, Texas, the parishioners of St. Peter the Apostle Catholic Church cited the law to fend off zoning requirements. The congregation had outgrown its stone church, built in 1923. A plan to enlarge the church with a modern building attached to it was rejected by city officials under the city's historic preservation law. The church sued, claiming that enforcement of the historic preservation law against the church violated RFRA. A federal judge struck down the law, but an appeals court panel reversed and said it was constitutional. The stage was set for the Supreme Court's review.

In *City of Boerne v. Flores* (1997), St. Peter the Apostle Catholic Church lost a battle to replace its building after it was declared a historic landmark by the City of Boerne, Texas. The Court's decision in this church-state dispute struck down the Religious Freedom Restoration Act, which Congress had passed in response to *Employment Division v. Smith* (1990).

Source: AP/Wide World Photos/ Tommy Hultgren.

VOTE

6–3, with Justice Anthony M. Kennedy writing for the majority. Joining him were Chief Justice William Rehnquist, John Paul Stevens, Antonin Scalia, Clarence Thomas, and Ruth Bader Ginsburg. In dissent were Justices Sandra Day O'Connor, Stephen G. Breyer, and David H. Souter.

HIGHLIGHTS

Justice Kennedy reached back as far as the landmark case of *Marbury v. Madison* (1803) to remind Congress that "powers of the legislature are defined and limited, and that those limits may not be mistaken, or forgotten." This principle is violated, Kennedy said, when Congress goes beyond enforcing the Fourteenth Amendment and actually seeks to define what the Constitution means. "Congress does not enforce a constitutional right by changing what the right is," Kennedy said. (See *Marbury v. Madison*.)

But he acknowledged he was making a distinction that is hard to define. "While the line between measures that remedy or prevent unconstitutional actions and measures that make a substantive change in the governing law is not easy to discern, and Congress must have wide latitude in determining where it lies, the distinction exists and must be observed," Kennedy wrote.

The reason this line is important, he said, is that the Constitution is not a piece of legislation that is subject to easy change. RFRA, by dictating how the free exercise clause of the First Amendment should be interpreted, amounted to a constitutional amendment. "Shifting legislative majorities could change the Constitution" if RFRA were allowed to stand, Kennedy maintained. Only the Supreme Court can interpret the Constitution, he said.

One reason that RFRA could not be viewed as legitimate "remedial" legislation, Kennedy said, is that there is no record showing that the law was passed to prevent recurrence of any frequent constitutional violations. "The history of persecution in this country detailed in the [congressional] hearings mentions no episodes occurring in the past 40 years," Kennedy wrote. "RFRA is so out of proportion to a supposed remedial or preventive object that it cannot be understood as responsive to, or designed to prevent, unconstitutional behavior. It appears, instead, to attempt a substantive change in constitutional protections."

Justice Stevens, in a brief concurrence, said the law was unconstitutional for a different reason. By displaying what he saw as a "government preference for religion," Stevens said RFRA in fact violated the other religion clause of the First Amendment, which bars Congress from passing a "law respecting an establishment of religion."

Justice O'Connor agreed with the majority on the separation of powers issue, but dissented on the merits. "I remain of the view that [*Employment Division v.*] *Smith* was wrongly decided, and I would use this case to reexamine the Court's holding there. . . . If the Court were to correct the misinterpretation of the Free Exercise Clause set forth in *Smith,* it would simultaneously put our First Amendment jurisprudence back on course and allay the legitimate concerns of a majority in Congress who believed that *Smith* improperly restricted religious liberty."

EXCERPTS

From Justice Kennedy's majority opinion: "Our national experience teaches that the Constitution is preserved best when each part of the government respects both the Constitution and the proper actions and determinations of the other branches. When the Court has interpreted the Constitution, it has acted within the province of the Judicial Branch, which embraces the duty to say what the law is. When the political branches of the Government act against the background of a judicial interpretation of the Constitution already issued, it must be understood that in later cases and controversies the Court will treat its precedents with the respect due them under settled principles, including *stare decisis,* and contrary expectations must be disappointed. RFRA was designed to control cases and controversies, such as the one before us; but as the provisions of the federal statute here invoked are beyond congressional authority, it is this Court's precedent, not RFRA, which must control."

IMPACT

Religious groups reacted with alarm to the Court's decision in *City of Boerne v. Flores,* in part because it was such a resounding repudiation of the political will of Congress that religious practices should be protected. More broadly, the ruling was seen as yet another effort by a conservative Supreme Court to rein in Congress, to remind Congress that it does not have a roving mandate to cure all ills through legislation. Rather, the Court was saying that the Constitution specifies which areas Congress has the power to affect through legislation, and Congress has to stay within those bounds.

Based on the ruling, a religious coalition decided at first to redirect its efforts to state legislatures—an avenue left open by the Supreme Court. A scattering of states have passed laws requiring that state and local government agencies meet a "compelling interest" test before infringing on the exercise of religion.

But religious groups and others also worked with Congress to fashion another federal law to protect religious exercise that would pass constitutional muster with the Supreme Court. In 2000 Congress passed a more limited statute called the Religious Land Use and Institutionalized Persons Act of 2000 (RLUIPA.)

One part of the new law dealt with the kind of dispute that triggered the *Boerne* lawsuit: disagreement between religious institutions and local governments over zoning and land use issues.

The other section said that in government-run institutions such as prisons that receive federal funds, government must not impose rules that restrict religious practices unless they can show a "compelling" reason. In hearings before the bill was passed, Congress heard testimony about arbitrary prison regulations that made it difficult for inmates to practice their religions, especially minority religions.

In the 2005 decision *Cutter v. Wilkinson,* the Supreme Court upheld this section of RLUIPA, ruling in effect that Congress had finally struck the right balance. A group of Ohio inmates led by Jon Cutter had sued under the law to protest regulations that deprived them access to religious literature or kept them from adhering to religious rules and rituals. Ohio responded by asserting the RLUIPA was unconstitutional because it gave religious inmates favored treatment, violating the establishment clause of the First Amendment.

The Supreme Court was unanimous in upholding the law. Justice Ginsburg, writing for the majority, said the law properly balances the religious needs of inmates with the security and order necessary in a prison. There is "play in the joints" between the two religion clauses, she wrote, leaving "some space for legislative action neither compelled by the Free Exercise Clause nor prohibited by the Establishment Clause."

FREEDOM OF ASSOCIATION

The Constitution does not include any explicit guarantee of the right or freedom to associate with people of one's choice. And until the middle of the twentieth century, laws were passed and upheld that restricted membership and activities of organizations viewed as subversive. But gradually, especially in the context of the civil rights movement, the Supreme Court recognized a freedom of association, rooted in the freedom of speech and assembly, as well as general "liberty" interests. But this right sometimes came in conflict with other government interests, such as ending discrimination, posing difficult choices for the Supreme Court.

Other related cases mentioned in the Freedom of Association section

Board of Directors, Rotary International v. Rotary Club of Duarte (1987)
New York State Club Association Inc. v. City of New York (1988)
Hurley v. Irish-American Gay Group of Boston (1995)
Boy Scouts of America v. Dale (2000) (see p. 180)

NAACP v. Button

Decided January 14, 1963
371 U.S. 415
laws.findlaw.com/US/371/415.html

DECISION

Litigation can be a form of political expression protected by the First Amendment. The First Amendment right of association protects legal advocacy. A state law that prohibits organizations from seeking out nonmembers to file lawsuits is unconstitutional under the First Amendment.

BACKGROUND

In the wake of the Supreme Court's *Brown v. Board of Education* decision desegregating public schools in 1954, southern states looked for ways to punish and destroy the National Association for the Advancement of Colored People (NAACP), the noted civil rights group that was behind the school litigation (see *Brown v. Board of Education*). Some states attacked the tax-exempt status of the organization, while others demanded local chapters' membership lists.

Another anti-NAACP strategy was undertaken in Arkansas, Florida, Georgia, Mississippi, South Carolina, Tennessee, and Virginia. In these states, old laws regulating the conduct of lawyers were expanded to prohibit some of the activities of the NAACP.

Among the prohibited activities were two with ancient Anglo-French names: *barratry* and *champerty*. *Barratry* refers to the practice of persistently stirring up or inciting the filing of lawsuits. The related concept of *champerty* involves a person or organization agreeing to finance litigation on behalf of another person in return for a share of whatever damages or penalties are awarded. Both are viewed as illegal or unethical tactics of lawyers.

As part of Virginia's "massive resistance" to school desegregation, the state amended its statutes that defined malpractice by attorneys to make it a crime for an organization to solicit clients for the purpose of filing a lawsuit over an issue that the organization itself has no direct stake in. Through various means including petition-gathering, the NAACP, with 89 branches and more than 13,000 members in Virginia, did in fact look for people who were victims of race discrimination. If their cases had merit and fit into the organization's legal strategy, the NAACP would pay one of its lawyers to file the suit on the person's behalf.

The NAACP challenged the Virginia law by suing state attorney general Robert Y. Button Jr., arguing that enforcing the law against the NAACP would violate the group's First Amend-ment rights of assembly and expression. The law restricted the group's ability to advocate the end of racial discrimination, the NAACP argued. Virginia courts upheld the law, but there was reason for civil rights advocates to hope that the U.S. Supreme Court would be more sympathetic. In several cases, the Court had already struck down efforts by southern states to attack the NAACP by seeking its membership lists and other intrusive tactics.

When the *Button* case was first argued in 1961, Court scholars have revealed, the justices voted 5–4 to uphold the Virginia law. But before the decision was issued Justice Charles Whittaker resigned, and Justice Felix Frankfurter was disabled with a stroke. Both had voted to uphold the law. The Court decided not to issue the opinion and scheduled it to be reargued the following term. By then, President John F. Kennedy had replaced Whittaker with Byron R. White, a Justice Department official with civil rights experience, and Frankfurter with Arthur J. Goldberg, a noted labor lawyer. The stage was set for a far different outcome in *NAACP v. Button*.

VOTE

6–3, with Justice William J. Brennan Jr. writing the opinion for the Court. He was joined by Chief Justice Earl Warren and Justices Hugo L. Black, William O. Douglas, Byron R. White, and Arthur J. Goldberg. Dissenting were Justices John M. Harlan, Tom C. Clark, and Potter Stewart.

HIGHLIGHTS

Justice Brennan was unusually blunt in describing Virginia's likely motivation in passing the new law restricting lawyers' conduct. "We cannot close our eyes to the fact that the militant Negro civil rights movement has engendered the intense resentment and opposition of the politically dominant white community of Virginia; litigation assisted by the NAACP has been bitterly fought," Brennan wrote. "In such circumstances, a statute broadly curtailing group activity leading to litigation may easily become a weapon of oppression, however evenhanded its terms appear."

Regulating the unethical behavior of lawyers was clearly not Virginia's motive in passing the law, Brennan wrote. "Resort to the courts to seek vindication of constitutional rights is a different matter from the oppressive, malicious, or avaricious use of the legal process for purely private gain. Lawsuits attacking racial discrimination, at least in Virginia, are neither very profitable nor very popular."

But Brennan also wanted to make it clear that the Court was not ruling in the NAACP's behalf only because it was litigating on behalf of racial minorities. "That the petitioner happens to be engaged in activities of expression and association on behalf of the rights of Negro children to equal opportunity is constitutionally irrelevant to the ground of our decision," he wrote. "The course of our decisions in the First Amendment area makes plain that its protections would apply as fully to those who would arouse our society against the objectives of the petitioner. For the Constitution protects expression and association without regard to the race, creed, or political or religious affiliation of the members of the group which invokes its shield, or to the truth, popularity, or social utility of the ideas and beliefs which are offered."

And it was clear to the Court that what the NAACP was doing in Virginia was a form of political expression—advocacy—that the First Amendment was designed to protect. The First Amendment does not only protect the expression of abstract ideas, Brennan asserted. Litigation, just as much as a speech at a political rally, deserves a high level of protection as a result.

In dissent, Justice Harlan acknowledged that "litigation is often the desirable and orderly way of resolving disputes of broad public significance, and of obtaining vindication of fundamental rights." But, Harlan said, declaring that litigation is a form of political expression does not mean that it cannot be regulated. "Neither the First Amendment nor the Fourteenth constitutes an absolute bar to government regulation in the fields of free expression and association."

Harlan also said, "Litigation, whether or not associated with the attempt to vindicate constitutional rights, is conduct; it is speech plus. . . . The State may impose reasonable regulations limiting the permissible form of litigation and the manner of legal representation within its borders."

EXCERPTS

From Justice Brennan's majority opinion: "Abstract discussion is not the only species of communication which the Constitution protects; the First Amendment also protects vigorous advocacy, certainly of lawful ends, against governmental intrusion. In the context of NAACP objectives, litigation is not a technique of resolving private differences; it is a means for achieving the lawful objectives of equality of treatment by all government, federal, state and local, for the members of the Negro community in this country. It is thus a form of political expression. Groups which find themselves unable to achieve their objectives through the ballot frequently turn to the courts.

. . . And under the conditions of modern government, litigation may well be the sole practicable avenue open to a minority to petition for redress of grievances.

"The NAACP is not a conventional political party, but the litigation it assists, while serving to vindicate the legal rights of members of the American Negro community, at the same time and perhaps more importantly, makes possible the distinctive contribution of a minority group to the ideas and beliefs of our society. For such a group, association for litigation may be the most effective form of political association.

"These freedoms are delicate and vulnerable, as well as supremely precious in our society. The threat of sanctions may deter their exercise almost as potently as the actual application of sanctions.

". . . Because First Amendment freedoms need breathing space to survive, government may regulate in the area only with narrow specificity. . . .

". . . Precision of regulation must be the touchstone in an area so closely touching our most precious freedoms."

IMPACT

The freedom of association, the freedom to join together with people of one's choice, is not specifically mentioned in the Constitution. But *NAACP v. Button* gave important recognition to it nonetheless as a right that derives from the freedoms of expression and assembly in the First Amendment.

In the context of the 1960s, the decision can also be seen as a crucial endorsement of the basic tactics of the civil rights movement. In a recent essay in the book *Reason and Passion,* Robert L. Carter, general counsel of the NAACP from 1957 to 1968, said of *NAACP v. Button,* "The case gave constitutional protection not only to group litigation efforts but to direct protest activity as well, such as sit-ins at lunch counters and street marches. Such actions were necessary to ensure that the words of the Constitution extended to all, regardless of race, creed, or color."

The decision also came close to declaring a right to file a lawsuit. Often viewed negatively today, lawsuits and litigation were seen in the *Button* decision to be noble and useful tools for advancing constitutional rights.

Perhaps the decision's most lasting legacy, however, is its demand that when government sets out to restrict First Amendment rights, a high standard must be met. Its requirement that "precision of regulation must be the touchstone" in First Amendment cases has been cited by the Supreme Court more than one hundred times since 1963. It means that if a law restricting First Amendment freedoms is too vaguely or too broadly worded, the Supreme Court will strike it down as unconstitutional.

Roberts v. United States Jaycees

Decided July 3, 1984
468 U.S. 609
laws.findlaw.com/US/468/609.html

DECISION

A state law that was used to require the United States Jaycees to admit women as members does not violate the organization's First Amendment freedom of association. The government's compelling interest in eliminating gender discrimination overrides the male members' interests in excluding women.

BACKGROUND

Past decisions by the Supreme Court helped establish the freedom of association, the right to form groups with people of one's choosing. (See *NAACP v. Button.*) One implication of the freedom to associate with certain people is the ability to choose *not* to associate with other people. When that choice is based on categories such as sex or race, however, the freedom of association can turn into a mechanism for exclusion.

Cases dealing with that dilemma started coming to court as those active in the women's rights movement began to view exclusive private organizations as vehicles for perpetuating male dominance in the workplace. Federal statutes outlawed outright discrimination in hiring, but women's rights advocates felt that women could not move up the corporate ladder until they gained access to the private clubs and organizations where business leaders met and networked.

One of those male-dominated organizations that is influential in cities and small towns across the country is the Jaycees—originally named for the initials of Junior Citizens, but now shorthand for the U.S. Junior Chamber of Commerce. Formed in 1920, the group grew as a civic organization for young men ages eighteen to thirty-five. By 1981 it had nearly 400,000 members. Women and older men were allowed associate membership, and women participated in many of the group's events, but they were not permitted to become full members.

Beginning in 1974, the Minneapolis and St. Paul chapters began defying the rule by allowing women to join as full members. The national organization punished the local chapters in various ways, including not allowing its officers to become officers of the national Jaycees. In 1978, when the two chapters were informed their charters would soon be revoked, they filed complaints with a state civil rights agency. They claimed that the national organization, by punishing the local chapters, was violating a Minnesota law that prohibits discrimination in

"public accommodations." Under the law's definitions, that term covered any business or other facility "whose goods, services, facilities, privileges, advantages, or accommodations are extended, offered, sold, or otherwise made available to the public." The state human rights commissioner found "probable cause" that the law had been violated.

The national Jaycees responded by filing suit in federal court against Kathryn Roberts, acting commissioner of Minnesota's Department of Human Rights, asserting that any state effort to force the Jaycees to accept women as members would violate the male members' rights of free speech and association. A federal judge sided with the state officials, but an appeals court panel reversed the decision. The appeals court noted that the Jaycees take political stands on occasion, so that imposing state requirements on its membership policies would interfere with the organization's First Amendment rights.

VOTE

7–0, with Justice William J. Brennan Jr. writing the opinion of the Court. He was joined by Justices Byron R. White, Thurgood Marshall, Lewis F. Powell Jr., John Paul Stevens, Sandra Day O'Connor, and William Rehnquist. Chief Justice Warren Burger and Justice Harry A. Blackmun took no part in the case.

HIGHLIGHTS

Justice Brennan began by identifying two separate kinds of freedom of association. One protects "intimate associations" such as marriage, parenthood, and family. The other protects "expressive associations," in which people join together to exercise First Amendment rights such as speech, religion, and assembly. The nature of the association in a given case, Brennan said, helps determine the extent to which government can restrict or regulate it. "The Constitution undoubtedly imposes constraints on the State's power to control the selection of one's spouse that would not apply to regulations affecting the choice of one's fellow employees," Brennan said.

The Jaycees, he continued, is not the kind of intimate association that deserves maximum protection from government interference. Apart from the criteria of age and sex, no applicants were excluded. "The local chapters of the Jaycees are large and basically unselective groups," said Brennan. "Much of the activity central to the formation and maintenance of the association involves the participation of strangers to that relationship."

If the Jaycees was not an intimate group, the next question for the Court was to decide whether the restrictions imposed by Minnesota amounted to a serious interference with its "expressive" activities.

The Court decided that requiring the Jaycees to allow women as members did not interfere with its ability to express itself. "The Minnesota Act does not aim at the suppression of speech, does not distinguish between prohibited and permitted activity on the basis of viewpoint, and does not license enforcement authorities to administer the statute on the basis of such constitutionally impermissible criteria," Brennan concluded. "Instead . . . the Act reflects the State's strong historical commitment to eliminating discrimination and assuring its citizens equal access to publicly available goods and services. That goal, which is unrelated to the suppression of expression, plainly serves compelling state interests of the highest order."

That compelling interest is not limited to guaranteeing access to businesses that sell products or services, Brennan said. Interpreting the state law to cover civic organizations such as the Jaycees, he wrote, "reflects a recognition of the changing nature of the American economy and of the importance, both to the individual and to society, of removing the barriers to economic advancement and political and social integration that have historically plagued certain disadvantaged groups, including women."

The justices also agreed that the Minnesota law was neither vague nor overly broad, defects that would have compelled the Supreme Court to strike it down. The Court said the state had "used a number of specific and objective criteria—regarding the organization's size, selectivity, commercial nature, and use of public facilities" to determine whether the male-only policy of the Jaycees violated the statute.

EXCERPTS

From Justice Brennan's majority opinion: "An individual's freedom to speak, to worship, and to petition the government for the redress of grievances could not be vigorously protected from interference by the State unless a correlative freedom to engage in group effort toward those ends were not also guaranteed. According protection to collective effort on behalf of shared goals is especially important in preserving political and cultural diversity and in shielding dissident expression from suppression by the majority. . . .

". . . There can be no clearer example of an intrusion into the internal structure or affairs of an association than a regulation that forces the group to accept members it does not desire. Such a regulation may impair the ability of the original members to express only those views that brought them together. Freedom of association therefore plainly presupposes a freedom not to associate.

". . . There is, however, no basis in the record for concluding that admission of women as full voting members will impede the organization's ability to engage in these protected activities or to disseminate its preferred views. The Act requires no change in the Jaycees' creed of promoting the interests of young men, and it imposes no restrictions on the organization's ability to exclude individuals with ideologies or philosophies different from those of its existing members."

IMPACT

Soon after the Supreme Court decision was handed down, the Jaycees voted to change its membership policies and to admit women. A history of the Jaycees on its official Web site describes the change positively as one of several "turning points" during the 1980s.

Civil rights advocates applauded the Court's decision as a sign that the Court understood that discrimination in private organizations had as much impact as did discrimination in the workplace.

The Court reiterated its holding in *Roberts* in a nearly identical case three years later, *Board of Directors, Rotary International v. Rotary Club of Duarte,* and a year after that in *New York State Club Association Inc. v. City of New York.* In the *Rotary Club* case, the Court used the same analysis as in the *Jaycees* decision to conclude that California could require the club to accept women.

The Court's decision in *Roberts v. United States Jaycees* did not, as some had feared, result in a wave of lawsuits seeking to break down barriers at a wide range of private clubs and organizations. By and large, clubs that were active in public and civic affairs heeded the Court's message and changed their restrictive membership policies.

The decision also did not make it impossible for private organizations to make choices about their membership and message. In the 1995 case *Hurley v. Irish-American Gay Group of Boston,* the Supreme Court said that under the First Amendment, the organizers of the annual St. Patrick's Day parade were entitled to exclude a gay Irish group that wanted to march with it and hold a banner. But the Court viewed it as a matter of free speech, not association, ruling that the parade organizers had the right not to be forced to convey a message they disapproved.

Five years later the Court also said the Boy Scouts of America was entitled to prevent an openly gay man from remaining as a scoutmaster. In *Boy Scouts of America v. Dale* the Court said that, unlike in the Jaycees case, allowing state antidiscrimination laws to force the Boy Scouts to accept a gay scoutmaster would interfere with the organization's core message and principles. (See *Boy Scouts of America v. Dale.*)

FREEDOM OF THE PRESS

A free and uncensored press has always been one of the nation's most cherished values. As Thomas Jefferson said in 1787, "Were it left to me to decide whether we should have a government without newspapers or newspapers without a government, I should not hesitate a moment to prefer the latter." But the principle was rarely tested in the Supreme Court until the twentieth century, and it was not until 1964 that the press was given broad protection from being sued for the controversial statements it printed. Thus liberated, the media became a major force in society, sometimes informative and sometimes intrusive; petulant and pervasive at the same time. As a result, it is often unpopular, and while the basic constitutional principles protecting the press are well-established, they are increasingly under challenge.

Other related cases mentioned in the Freedom of the Press section

Gitlow v. New York (1925)

Chaplinsky v. New Hampshire (1942) (see p. 141)

Beauharnais v. Illinois (1952)

Estes v. Texas (1965)

Sheppard v. Maxwell (1966)

Tinker v. Des Moines Independent Community School District (1969) (see p. 150)

United States v. Radio Television News Directors Assn. (1969)

Gertz v. Welch (1974)

Miami Herald Publishing Co. v. Tornillo (1974)

Nebraska Press Assn. v. Stuart (1976)

Federal Communications Commission v. Pacifica Foundation (1978)

Gannett v. DePasquale (1979)

Globe Newspaper Co. v. Superior Court (1982)

Bethel School District No. 403 v. Fraser (1986)

McConnell v. Federal Election Commission (2003) (see p. 168)

Near v. Minnesota

Decided June 1, 1931
283 U.S. 697
laws.findlaw.com/US/283/697.html

DECISION

A Minnesota law that allows a judge to shut down a newspaper that is found to be "malicious, scandalous, and defamatory" amounts to a "prior restraint" on the press and violates the First Amendment to the Constitution. The Court also ruled for the first time that the First Amendment's protection of freedom of the press can be invoked to strike down state laws because of the Fourteenth Amendment to the Constitution.

BACKGROUND

The First Amendment says nothing about "prior restraint"—the legal term for punishing the press before it publishes, rather than afterward. But the notion that prior restraint is a fundamental violation of freedom and a form of censorship is older than the Constitution.

William Blackstone, in describing the English common law that serves as a foundation for the U.S. system, wrote in the eighteenth century, "The liberty of the press is indeed essential to the nature of a free state; but this consists in laying no previous restraints upon publications, and not in freedom from censure for criminal matter when published." In other words, to preserve press freedom, society has to take the risk of allowing controversial publications to come out rather than preventing their appearance. Once published, if the work contains libelous or other material that violates specific laws, then it can be punished—but not before.

A quick scan of any newsstand or supermarket checkout aisle will confirm that sensational newspapers and scandal sheets are common in the United States. It may be less known that similar publications have been just as common throughout U.S. history. Scandal sheets proliferated during the 1920s. Political corruption, industrial growth, and Prohibition-era laws and sentiments provided ample material for these newspapers.

Minnesota generated its share of scandal—and scandalous reporting. The *Rip-saw* in Duluth, for example, offered readers a weekly diet of stories about drunken, corrupt, and lecherous politicians. In 1924 the *Rip-saw* accused a local judge of having a sexually transmitted disease and said a local former mayor had a taste for alcohol and women. Both lost elections, and both went after the publisher, accusing him of criminal libel.

Meanwhile another politician skewered by the newspaper sought revenge in a different way. He persuaded the Min-

nesota legislature to pass a law that declared it was a "public nuisance" to publish or sell a newspaper or periodical that was obscene, lewd, or "malicious, scandalous, and defamatory." A judge who determined that a publication fit that description could enjoin or prevent it from publishing again. The law passed easily in 1925, with no protest and even some support from mainstream Minnesota newspapers.

This law was doomed because of another 1925 event—the Court's decision in *Gitlow v. New York*. Even though the Court upheld Benjamin Gitlow's conviction for violating New York's criminal anarchy act, it also ruled that states were bound by the freedom of speech provision of the First Amendment.

Before the Minnesota law could be used to shut down the *Rip-saw* permanently, its publisher died. But another publication came along to take its place in the crosshairs of other angry politicians. The *Saturday Press* of Minneapolis generated controversy from its first issue. It accused the chief of police of taking payoffs from a local mob figure, who was Jewish. The police chief ordered it off the streets, and the next week its editor Howard Guilford was shot and seriously injured. Guilford later recounted his shooting by writing that he "ran across three Jews in a Chevrolet, stopped a lot of lead and won a bed for myself in St. Barnabas Hospital for six weeks." Reflecting the newspaper's hateful style, Guilford added, "Wherefore, I have withdrawn all allegiance to anything with a hook nose that eats herring."

The paper continued in business with the energetic reporting of its main reporter, Jay Near. Like his editor, Near was anti-Semitic, anti-Catholic, and anti-black, and his writing reflected his sentiments. One piece that discussed the shooting of Guilford blamed it—and most other crime in the city—on "Jew gangsters."

Before long the local county attorney went to a judge to ask that the *Saturday Press* be shut down as a public nuisance that violated the new state law. The judge agreed, and the *Saturday Press* was enjoined from publication.

Near challenged the ruling and the law, but the Minnesota Supreme Court upheld it, likening the newspaper to other public nuisances like brothels. Near next asked for help from the American Civil Liberties Union (ACLU), which, in spite of its distaste for Near's views, took up his cause. Soon, though, the ACLU was effectively elbowed aside by Robert McCormick, wealthy publisher of the *Chicago Tribune* and a First Amend-

In response to writings by Jay Near of the Minneapolis *Saturday Press* and other reporters, Minnesota enacted a law authorizing the suppression of "malicious, scandalous, and defamatory" publications. In *Near v. Minnesota* (1931), the Court ruled that such "prior restraint" violates the First Amendment. This photo of Near, the only one known to exist, appeared on April 19, 1936, in the *Minneapolis Tribune*.
Source: Minneapolis Tribune, *April 19, 1936, Minnesota Historical Society.*

ment champion. McCormick's own paper had made enemies through the years, including automaker Henry Ford, who sued the paper for libel. McCormick took on Near's case as a personal cause, providing Near with much-needed legal help. In April 1930 the Supreme Court announced it would review Near's case.

VOTE

5–4, with the majority opinion written by Chief Justice Charles Evans Hughes. Joining him were Justices Louis D. Brandeis, Owen J. Roberts, Oliver Wendell Holmes Jr., and Harlan Fiske Stone. Dissenting were Justices Pierce Butler, Willis Van Devanter, James C. McReynolds, and George Sutherland.

HIGHLIGHTS

Blackstone's principle of no prior restraint on the press was the basis of the Court's ruling in *Near v. Minnesota*. No prior restraint on publication could be permitted, the majority agreed—except for the rarest of instances, such as preventing the publication of obscenity or of information about troop movements in time of war or of an incitement to violence and the overthrow of the government by force. The Minnesota law was fatally flawed because it was not aimed at punishing past specific publications but was meant to prevent future publication of material critical of public officials. "This is of the essence of censorship," Chief Justice Hughes wrote.

At the same time, however, the Court said the press could be subject to punishment after publication. "Liberty of speech and of the press is also not an absolute right, and the State may punish its abuse."

The most important avenue for punishment after publication, the Court said, is libel litigation. "Public officers, whose character and conduct remain open to debate and free discussion in the press, find their remedies for false accusations in actions under libel laws providing for redress and punishment,

and not in proceedings to restrain the publication of newspapers and periodicals."

The other crucial element of the decision was the definitive statement that the First Amendment's protection of freedom of the press applied to state laws, not just federal laws. Citing the 1925 decision in *Gitlow v. New York* and others, the Court said, "It is no longer open to doubt that the liberty of the press and of speech is within the liberty safeguarded by the due process clause of the Fourteenth Amendment from invasion by state action."

In dissent, Justice Butler accused the Court of far exceeding what the Constitution requires. "It gives to freedom of the press a meaning and a scope not heretofore recognized, and construes 'liberty' in the due process clause of the Fourteenth Amendment to put upon the States a federal restriction that is without precedent."

Butler also objected to the majority's view that obscene publications could be prevented, but a publication like the *Saturday Press* could not. "Both nuisances are offensive to morals, order and good government. As that resulting from lewd publications constitutionally may be enjoined, it is hard to understand why the one resulting from a regular business of malicious defamation may not."

EXCERPTS

From Justice Hughes's majority opinion: "No one would question but that a government might prevent actual obstruction to its recruiting service or the publication of the sailing dates of transports or the number and location of troops. On similar grounds, the primary requirements of decency may be enforced against obscene publications. The security of the community life may be protected against incitements to acts of violence and the overthrow by force of orderly government. . . .

"The fact that for approximately one hundred and fifty years there has been almost an entire absence of attempts to impose previous restraints upon publications relating to the malfeasance of public officers is significant of the deep-seated conviction that such restraints would violate constitutional right. . . .

". . . [T]he administration of government has become more complex, the opportunities for malfeasance and corruption have multiplied, crime has grown to most serious proportions, and the danger of its protection by unfaithful officials and of the impairment of the fundamental security of life and property by criminal alliances and official neglect, emphasizes the primary need of a vigilant and courageous press, especially in great cities. The fact that the liberty of the press may be abused by miscreant purveyors of scandal does not make any the less necessary the immunity of the press from previous restraint in dealing with official misconduct. Subsequent punishment for such abuses as may exist is the appropriate remedy, consistent with constitutional privilege."

IMPACT

The Court's decision was acclaimed widely by U.S. news media, even among those who thought scandal sheets like Near's should not be condoned. Near himself resumed publication for a time with the motto, "The Paper That Refused to Stay Gagged." But the paper faltered, and in 1936 Near died.

Nowhere else was the reaction to the Supreme Court decision as positive as at the offices of the *Chicago Tribune*. "The tower shook with Bertie McCormick's jubilation," wrote Fred W. Friendly in the 1981 book *Minnesota Rag,* a history of the case. "Not since Charlie Root pitched the Chicago Cubs to a pennant in 1929 had there been such a celebration." McCormick ordered up a plaque to memorialize crucial sentences from the decision for the *Tribune*'s lobby. He proclaimed that "the decision of Chief Justice Hughes will go down in history as one of the greatest triumphs for free thought."

Indeed, *Near v. Minnesota* can be viewed as the decision that breathed life into the press freedom clause of the First Amendment. Before *Near,* the press clause had rarely been tested and existed as a more theoretical than practical ideal. The *Near* decision for the first time accorded the press an exalted as well as a practical place in the constitutional landscape. The Court was saying that a critical, even an occasionally obnoxious, press plays a vital role in U.S. democracy, keeping government in check and keeping the electorate informed of things that officials would not themselves reveal. *Near v. Minnesota,* along with the 1964 decision in *New York Times v. Sullivan,* provided the legal cushion that helped embolden the press to take on its dominant role in modern society. (See *New York Times v. Sullivan.*)

The powerful legal influence of the *Near* decision was dramatically demonstrated in 1971, when the *New York Times* began publication of the so-called Pentagon Papers, a secret government history of the Vietnam War. The Nixon administration swiftly went to court to prevent the paper from printing later installments. Within two weeks, the dispute went before the Supreme Court. In a 6–3 decision that relied heavily on *Near v. Minnesota,* the Court said the government had not met the "heavy burden" of justifying prior restraint. (See *New York Times Co. v. United States.*)

New York Times Co. v. Sullivan

Decided March 9, 1964
376 U.S. 254
laws.findlaw.com/US/376/254.html

DECISION

The First Amendment protects the media from libel suits for reports that defame public officials—even when those reports are false—unless it can be shown that the media organization acted with "actual malice." Under that standard, to win money damages, the defamed official must prove that the reporter or organization knew the statement was false or recklessly did not care whether it was true or false.

BACKGROUND

During the early days of the civil rights movement, the white establishment of the South viewed the northern press as an enemy. By reporting on white resistance to integration and on continued mistreatment of blacks by whites, northern journalists helped build up pressure for change.

One way white southern leaders retaliated was to file libel suits against newspapers that "defamed" their communities. By one estimate, white southern politicians filed more than $300 million in claims for libel against media organizations in the early 1960s. The suits were beginning to have an impact; some newspapers, fearing financial losses in libel litigation, began to temper their reporting.

One example of white southern retaliation against the press came in 1960, following the appearance on March 29 of an advertisement in the pages of the *New York Times*. Under the headline "Heed Their Rising Voices," a group of concerned citizens sought support for the efforts of the Rev. Martin Luther King Jr. The ad catalogued recent events in the civil rights movement, including police crackdowns on student civil rights demonstrators in Montgomery, Alabama.

At the time, the *New York Times* sold 650,000 copies daily, 394 of which went to readers in Alabama. But after the *Alabama Journal* printed a story on the advertisement—and on a factual error contained in it—Montgomery City Commissioner L.B. Sullivan wrote to the *Times* demanding a retraction. He called the ad "false and defamatory," and also sent protesting letters to four black Alabama ministers whose names appeared in the ad.

The newspaper responded by letter, indicating it was "somewhat puzzled" by Sullivan's complaint because it was not clear how the ad, which did not mention Sullivan by name or title, could have defamed him. The *Times* letter asked Sullivan for clarification, but he did not respond. Instead, Sullivan filed suit against the newspaper, asking for $500,000 in damages. The governor of Alabama and other officials also sued, and the *Times* faced the possibility of paying out $3 million in damages—payments that could have bankrupted the newspaper. *Times* lawyer James Goodale later said there was some question whether the *Times,* which in 1960 had been "wracked by strikes and small profits," could survive the litigation.

The *Times,* which had a policy of not settling lawsuits out of court, fought the claims in Alabama courts. But after a trial in which the judge instructed the jury that the ad was in fact libelous and that Sullivan had in fact been damaged, the jury brought back a verdict against the *Times* for $500,000.

The Alabama Supreme Court upheld the verdict, offering the view that "The First Amendment of the U.S. Constitution does not protect libelous publications." At the time that assertion was basically correct, and it fell to the *Times* to convince the U.S. Supreme Court that the First Amendment did offer the press protection against libel suits. Even though the advertisement at issue was directed at no one in particular and was not written or edited by any reporter or editor, the case of *New York Times v. Sullivan* was poised to influence the First Amendment rights of journalists nationwide.

VOTE

9–0, with Justice William J. Brennan Jr. writing the opinion of the Court. Joining him were Chief Justice Earl Warren and Justices Hugo L. Black, William O. Douglas, Tom C. Clark, John M. Harlan, Potter Stewart, Byron R. White, and Arthur J. Goldberg.

HIGHLIGHTS

Justice Brennan's opinion in *New York Times v. Sullivan* offers a sweeping history of the value and regulation of free speech in the United States. Brennan went back as far as the Sedition Act of 1798, which made it a crime to write critically about government officials. That law, although never explicitly overturned, had been discredited in "the court of history," Brennan said. Over the years presidents, legislators, and judges alike had developed "a broad consensus that the Act, because of the restraint it imposed upon criticism of government and public officials, was inconsistent with the First Amendment."

The Court had not ruled extensively on the subject of libel, but what it had said in the past did not favor the press. In the 1942 case *Chaplinsky v. New Hampshire,* the Court had included libel in a list of forms of speech that are "no essential part of any exposition of ideas." (See *Chaplinsky v. New Hampshire.*) In the 1952 case *Beauharnais v. Illinois,* the Court said libel is not "within the area of constitutionally protected speech."

Justice Brennan swept aside those precedents by saying, "Those statements do not foreclose our inquiry here." Unlike those decisions, the *Sullivan* case dealt with criticism of public officials, which Brennan said had considerable support in the Constitution and in the nation's history. "It must be measured by standards that satisfy the First Amendment," Brennan insisted. "The general proposition that freedom of expression upon public questions is secured by the First Amendment has long been settled by our decisions."

The First Amendment's protection extends even to erroneous publications, Brennan said, asserting that "erroneous statement is inevitable in free debate, and . . . must be pro-

L. B. Sullivan, second from the right, poses with his lawyers after winning his libel suit against the *New York Times.* The Supreme Court overturned that decision in *New York Times Co. v. Sullivan* (1964), ruling that a higher standard applies to public officials than to private citizens when proving libel. *Source: ©Bettmann/CORBIS.*

tected if the freedoms of expression are to have the 'breathing space' that they need . . . to survive."

That was not just an abstract principle, but had practical effects, Brennan said later in the opinion. "A rule compelling the critic of official conduct to guarantee the truth of all his factual assertions—and to do so on pain of libel judgments virtually unlimited in amount—leads to a comparable 'self-censorship.' "

Brennan's embrace of the role of the press in criticizing the government was not absolute, however. The decision established a rule that would allow a defamed public official to recover damages in the rare instance when he or she could prove that the press had acted with "actual malice." Reviewing the case before the Court, Brennan concluded that the *Times,* while possibly negligent for not checking the facts contained in the ad, had not acted with malice toward Sullivan—especially because Sullivan was not even named in the ad. In fact, Brennan suggested that the Alabama judgment could be overturned on those grounds alone—that the advertisement did not refer with sufficient specificity to Sullivan to be libelous. Brennan chose, and the Court agreed, to fashion a broad constitutional rule.

Brennan's willingness to recognize that the press could, in rare circumstances, be held liable for criticism of a public official led two justices to write separate opinions. Justice Black, joined by Justice Douglas, felt that the First Amendment barred all libel suits by public officials against the media for criticism of their public acts. Black criticized the "actual malice" standard adopted by Brennan, calling malice "an elusive, abstract concept, hard to prove and hard to disprove." Added Black, "State libel laws threaten the very existence of an American press virile enough to publish unpopular views on public affairs and bold enough to criticize the conduct of public officials."

Justice Goldberg also advocated an absolute bar against suing the press in these circumstances, suggesting ways in which the Brennan rule might hamper public debate. "If individual citizens may be held liable in damages for strong words, which a jury finds false and maliciously motivated, there can be little doubt that public debate and advocacy will be constrained," Goldberg wrote. "And if newspapers, publishing advertisements dealing with public issues, thereby risk liability, there can also be little doubt that the ability of minority groups to secure publication of their views on public affairs and to seek support for their causes will be greatly diminished."

EXCERPTS

From Justice Brennan's majority opinion: "[W]e consider this case against the background of a profound national commitment to the principle that debate on public issues should be uninhibited, robust, and wide-open, and that it may well in-

clude vehement, caustic, and sometimes unpleasantly sharp attacks on government and public officials. . . .

". . . The judgment awarded in this case—without the need for any proof of actual pecuniary loss—was one thousand times greater than the maximum fine provided by the Alabama criminal statute, and one hundred times greater than that provided by the Sedition Act. And since there is no double-jeopardy limitation applicable to civil lawsuits, this is not the only judgment that may be awarded against petitioners for the same publication. Whether or not a newspaper can survive a succession of such judgments, the pall of fear and timidity imposed upon those who would give voice to public criticism is an atmosphere in which the First Amendment freedoms cannot survive. . . .

"The constitutional guarantees require, we think, a federal rule that prohibits a public official from recovering damages for a defamatory falsehood relating to his official conduct unless he proves that the statement was made with 'actual malice'— that is, with knowledge that it was false or with reckless disregard of whether it was false or not."

IMPACT

Even though it dealt with a relatively narrow area of the law, *New York Times v. Sullivan* has often been described as the most important decision in the history of freedom of the press. Constitutional scholar Alexander Meiklejohn said the Court's opinion was "an occasion for dancing in the streets."

The Court had recognized, for the first time, that for the press to play its assigned role in a democracy, it needed "breathing space" in which it could boldly criticize government. A press that had to check and recheck all its facts before criticizing a government official would soon become too timid, Brennan said.

The necessary breathing space for the press that Brennan and the Court created includes what has sometimes been described as "the right to be wrong." As long as the press did not act with provable malice or recklessness, it did not need to fear ruinous judgments against it, even if what it published was inaccurate.

The Court's decision has been viewed as a major reason for the development of the U.S. news media into a major force in political life in the last third of the twentieth century. In its increasingly skeptical coverage of the Vietnam War, Watergate, political candidates, and government in general, the press was in a sense fulfilling—or exceeding—the mission for it envisioned by Brennan and the other justices in the majority. "The rise of such investigative journalism would not have been possible if the old law of libel had still shielded officials from criticism," Anthony Lewis wrote in *Make No Law,* a book about the case.

In the view of many historians, the decision also played a crucial role in the civil rights movement. As Lewis also pointed out, Commissioner Sullivan's real target in the lawsuit was "the role of the American press as an agent of democratic change." Sullivan and others wanted to scare off the press through litigation. After the press won the case, it continued to report on the continuing instances of racism in the South, helping create a momentum for change that led to passage of more civil rights legislation in the mid- and late-1960s.

The Court's decision has not been entirely immune from criticism, however. The compromises that Brennan apparently had to make to hold the majority—it went through eight drafts, according to Brennan's papers—left libel litigation intact as a powerful weapon for punishing the press, especially for non-government officials.

As the Court underscored in *Gertz v. Welch* in 1974, private citizens could sue the press more easily than could public officials. In other decisions since 1964, the Court has amended the seemingly simple rule of *New York Times v. Sullivan* to allow libel plaintiffs to win against the press, depending on how private or public they are, how important the subject matter of the defamation was, and what went through the minds of the reporters and editors who prepared the libelous publication. In a 1979 speech, Brennan gently chastised the press for its angry denunciations of post-*Sullivan* Supreme Court rulings that made it harder for the press to win libel suits. "The press, like other institutions, must accommodate a variety of important societal interests," Brennan said.

Throughout the 1980s and 1990s, multimillion-dollar libel verdicts against the media became commonplace, although many were overturned or reduced on appeal. Many news media organizations also became more timid about defending themselves in court, and settled libel disputes before they reached a verdict.

Whatever the modern-day fallout from *New York Times v. Sullivan,* the decision represents an essentially optimistic view of the American public, according to Bruce Sanford, author of the 1999 book *Don't Shoot the Messenger.* The decision, he says, is founded on the belief that the public, without any help from the government, can sort out the torrents of information it receives. The theory behind the decision, writes Sanford, "encompasses the bold idea that falsity is a means of ascertaining truth. Unlike the common law which we inherited from England and which has no tolerance for falsity, the power of our constitutional libel law rests not on the need for government to protect people from false information, but on the conviction that people are capable of discerning the difference between truth and falsity."

Red Lion Broadcasting Co. v. Federal Communications Commission

Decided June 9, 1969
395 U.S. 367
laws.findlaw.com/US/395/367.html

DECISION

Requiring radio and television broadcasters to present both sides of a controversial issue on the air does not violate the First Amendment. Because broadcasters benefit from a scarce public resource, they may be required to serve the public in ways defined by the government.

BACKGROUND

When radio stations began operating in the early part of the twentieth century, they decided for themselves which frequency to use. As the number of stations grew, this practice resulted in chaos, with nearby stations sharing the same or similar frequencies, sometimes interfering with each other's broadcasts.

The Federal Radio Commission was created in 1927 to bring order to radio frequencies through licensing. Shortly thereafter, it also issued a rule requiring stations to foster "free and fair competition of opposing views," when its broadcasts involved issues of public interest.

That obligation continued under the successor organization, the Federal Communications Commission (FCC), and was extended to television. As the regulations evolved, broadcasters were required to provide adequate and fair coverage of issues of public importance. They could not completely ignore news or public affairs programming in favor of entertainment, and the coverage had to be balanced. These policies became known as the "fairness doctrine." In 1969 the FCC added an equal time requirement to the fairness doctrine: when a broadcaster endorsed a political candidate, the candidate's opponent had to be given time to respond, and, when an individual was criticized on the air, that person had to be given the opportunity to respond.

Broadcasters in general did not like the fairness doctrine because it imposed government requirements on content and tended to discourage controversial programming. They claimed that by enforcing the fairness doctrine, the FCC was violating the First Amendment's protection of the freedoms of speech and the press. Government agencies and some civic organizations supported the policy because it compelled broadcasters to give some balanced attention to public affairs, even though often this programming was relegated to Sunday mornings or the middle of the night.

The Court took up the issue in the context of a controversy over a 1964 radio broadcast on a Pennsylvania station, WGCB. Rev. Billy James Hargis, a well-known evangelist broadcaster, was discussing a book about conservative presidential candidate Barry Goldwater, written by journalist Fred Cook. Hargis suggested that Cook had communist leanings and had done things that were ethically questionable. Cook heard the broadcast and demanded free time on the station to reply to the charges. The station, owned by Red Lion Broadcasting Company, refused, prompting Cook to ask for help from the FCC. The FCC ruled that the station had failed to meet its obligations under the fairness doctrine, and a federal appeals court agreed. Meanwhile, in a separate case, a different appeals court struck down the regulations as unconstitutional. The Supreme Court decided that case, *United States v. Radio Television News Directors Assn.*, along with *Red Lion*.

VOTE

7–0, with Justice Byron R. White writing the majority opinion. Joining him were Chief Justice Earl Warren and Justices Hugo L. Black, John M. Harlan, William J. Brennan Jr., Potter Stewart, and Thurgood Marshall. Justice William O. Douglas did not participate for reasons unstated, and Justice Abe Fortas had recently resigned and was not immediately replaced.

HIGHLIGHTS

Justice White's main objective in the decision was to spell out the differences between broadcast and print media and to explain why they justify different treatment under the First Amendment. Unlike print media or one-to-one conversations, which can coexist with each other in almost limitless numbers, broadcasters have to be limited in number for practical reasons, White said. "Without government control, the medium would be of little use because of the cacophony of competing voices, none of which could be clearly and predictably heard," he wrote.

"Where there are substantially more individuals who want to broadcast than there are frequencies to allocate, it is idle to posit an unabridgeable First Amendment right to broadcast comparable to the right of every individual to speak, write, or publish," White said. "It would be strange if the First Amendment, aimed at protecting and furthering communications, prevented the Government from making radio communication possible by requiring licenses to broadcast and by limiting the number of licenses so as not to overcrowd the spectrum." Because of this technological requirement—the so-called "scarcity rationale"—the government has the ability to license broadcasters and impose requirements on them that could not be imposed on traditional media.

White added that this does not mean that the First Amendment plays no role at all in broadcasting. The First Amendment rights to be protected are those of the public, not the broadcaster who holds the license, he said. "The people as a whole retain their interest in free speech by radio and their collective right to have the medium function consistently with the ends and purposes of the First Amendment. It is the right of the viewers and listeners, not the right of the broadcasters, which is paramount."

For these reasons, the Court said the fairness doctrine regulations were within the FCC's power to enact. White expressed some concern that the FCC's rules would discourage controversial broadcasts. But that concern, White said, is "at best, speculative." If it could be shown that the FCC was censoring particular shows because they were critical of the government, the Court said that would raise "more serious First Amendment issues." But that was not the case in the WGCB case, White said.

EXCERPTS

From Justice White's majority opinion: "The history of the emergence of the fairness doctrine and of the related legislation shows that the Commission's action in the Red Lion case did not exceed its authority, and that in adopting the new regulations the Commission was implementing congressional policy, rather than embarking on a frolic of its own. . . .

"In light of the fact that the 'public interest' in broadcasting clearly encompasses the presentation of vigorous debate of controversial issues of importance and concern to the public; the fact that the FCC has rested upon that language from its very inception a doctrine that these issues must be discussed, and fairly; and the fact that Congress has acknowledged that the analogous provisions of [the 1959 amendment to] § 315 [of the Communications Act] are not preclusive in this area, and knowingly preserved the FCC's complementary efforts, we think the fairness doctrine and its component personal attack and political editorializing regulations are a legitimate exercise of congressionally delegated authority. . . .

". . . There is nothing in the First Amendment which prevents the Government from requiring a licensee to share his frequency with others and to conduct himself as a proxy or fiduciary with obligations to present those views and voices which are representative of his community and which would otherwise, by necessity, be barred from the airwaves."

IMPACT

The *Red Lion* decision established, in the clearest terms yet, the constitutional framework for assessing the First Amendment rights of broadcasters. The fact that some kind of government intervention is needed to make broadcast signals heard or seen on a limited spectrum of frequencies makes it constitutionally justifiable to intervene in other ways, the Court said.

Red Lion has been cited in dozens of subsequent decisions to justify a range of regulations of broadcast content that would not likely be upheld if they were applied to print media. Among them is the 1978 decision *Federal Communications Commission v. Pacifica Foundation,* allowing the FCC to sanction the broadcaster of the so-called "seven dirty words" in a monologue by comedian George Carlin. On the issue of fairness, the Court in a 1974 case called *Miami Herald Publishing Co. v. Tornillo* struck down a Florida law that required newspapers to give the same kind of "right of reply" that the Court had upheld for broadcasters in *Red Lion.*

The "scarcity" rationale that underlies *Red Lion* is fading, and broadcasters are happy about that. There are far more broadcast outlets than there are newspapers nationwide—more than 13,000 broadcast outlets, as opposed to fewer than 1,500 daily newspapers. Because there are so many television and radio stations, broadcasters argue, differing views are made available to the public without the need for government regulations.

"The legitimacy of relying on spectrum scarcity as the basis for according broadcasters less freedom than other media rapidly eroded after 1969 and has subsequently disappeared," said noted media lawyer P. Cameron DeVore on behalf of the National Association of Broadcasters.

The FCC itself no longer relies on the scarcity rationale and in 1987 dropped most aspects of the fairness doctrine after President Ronald Reagan vetoed a bill that would have written the doctrine into law. Broadcasters convinced the FCC that the fairness doctrine could no longer be sustained on constitutional grounds and that it had served to stifle, rather than promote, speech.

But broadcasters are still fighting the impact of *Red Lion* in other areas. Even though the FCC repealed other aspects of the fairness doctrine, the "personal attack" rule, requiring broadcasters to give notice and free air time to people attacked on the air, was not struck down until 2000.

Political parties and other groups have also invoked *Red Lion* in seeking to require broadcasters to give free airtime to presidential candidates. Broadcasters reject that proposal as well. In the McCain-Feingold campaign reform law passed in 2002, Congress relied on the stricter regulatory regime that still governs broadcasting to impose several restrictions on radio and television outlets that air political advertising. Those restrictions were upheld or sidestepped by the Supreme Court when, in late 2003, it upheld most provisions of the reform law. (See *McConnell v. Federal Election Commission.*)

New York Times Co. v. United States

Decided June 30, 1971
403 U.S. 713
laws.findlaw.com/US/403/713.html

DECISION

Government must meet a "heavy burden" before it can act to prevent publication of any expression protected by the First Amendment. The Court found that the Nixon administration had not met that burden in seeking to restrain the *New York Times* and the *Washington Post* from publishing a classified government history of the Vietnam War.

BACKGROUND

The *New York Times* edition of Sunday, June 13, 1971, carried an unassuming headline that at first attracted little interest: "Vietnam Archive: Pentagon Study Traces 3 Decades of Growing U.S. Involvement." The next day, however, the story began to trigger a chain of events that resulted in one of the most momentous legal confrontations between the press and the government in U.S. history. The government moved to block publication of future installments in the *Times*'s account of the classified "Pentagon Papers," as they became known. With remarkable speed—a matter of days—the controversy made its way to the Supreme Court. But the dispute had been several years in the making.

Secretary of Defense Robert McNamara commissioned the writing of the Pentagon Papers in 1966. As the Johnson administration became more deeply mired in the Vietnam War, McNamara felt it was important to research and preserve documents that would help explain how and why the United States had gotten involved—and how its policies, over time, had failed. The research project turned into a 7,000-page, 47-volume documentary history that went back to the roots of U.S. Indochina policy in the 1940s. It was completed in 1969 and classified as "top secret." Only fifteen copies were made, and each was strictly accounted for.

One of the dozens of researchers who helped prepare the history was Daniel Ellsberg, a Harvard graduate and U.S. Marines veteran, who had worked for a private consulting firm as well as for the Defense Department under McNamara. As Ellsberg worked on the project, he became convinced that the Pentagon Papers should be made public to expose the deceitful policies of past administrations that had drawn the nation into what seemed like an endless war. For example, the documents showed that at the same time that President Lyndon B. Johnson was criticizing his 1964 Republican opponent Barry Goldwater for advocating a wider war, Johnson was also planning to escalate the war.

Ellsberg, who had top security clearance, secretly photocopied the document and tried to interest antiwar members of Congress in holding hearings and releasing the Pentagon Papers to the public. They balked, and eventually Ellsberg instead brought the papers to the *Times*. Ellsberg's offer to give the papers to the newspaper touched off a contentious debate within the *Times* over the propriety of publishing classified documents. There was considerable fear that the paper would be prevented from publishing or that its executives might be prosecuted under espionage laws. But the newspaper decided that the importance of the disclosures to the public outweighed the risk.

On the first day of publication, reaction from the government was muted. According to David Rudenstine's book on the case, *The Day the Presses Stopped,* President Richard Nixon was initially inclined not to do anything to prevent publication of future installments. One reason was that the history project had ended before Nixon took office, so that its revelations would reflect badly only on his predecessors. Defense Secretary Melvin Laird appeared on a television talk show that Sunday but was not asked a single question about the *Times* story.

A conversation with National Security Adviser Henry Kissinger apparently changed Nixon's mind. Nixon became convinced that publication of the history could compromise intelligence and diplomatic relationships and endanger U.S. troops. He feared that other nations would no longer trust the United States to keep their diplomatic communications private if the *Times* was allowed to publish the Pentagon Papers. Nixon ordered the Justice Department to go to court to prevent further publication of the *Times* stories.

A federal judge in New York issued a temporary restraining order against the *Times*—the first time in U.S. history that a publication had been halted for national security reasons. Several days later, with the assistance of Ellsberg, the *Washington Post* began publishing excerpts as well, and a judge there ordered publication to stop. But after holding hearings on the issues involved, both judges lifted their orders, agreeing that the government had not made a convincing case that publication of the Pentagon Papers was a security threat.

The decisions were quickly appealed, and this time the results were different. The New York federal appeals panel ordered more hearings, but in Washington, D.C., the appeals court agreed that the publications should not be halted.

The issue was immediately appealed to the Supreme Court, which was in the final days of its term, long past the point when it would normally consider new cases. In private conferences, some justices wanted to lift the judges' orders and allow publication immediately, without further debate. Others wanted to put the issue off until the fall. The Court decided instead to hold an extraordinary Saturday session to hear arguments on both sides. It took place on June 26, less than two weeks after the first *Times* story appeared.

According to Bob Woodward and Scott Armstrong's *The Brethren,* the justices were deeply troubled by the case. A copy of the Pentagon Papers was sent to the Court, and the justices read parts that made some of them fear that publication could endanger U.S. troops in Vietnam. During oral arguments, Justice Stewart asked Alexander Bickel, the lawyer for the *Times,* what the Court should do if it determined that disclosure of the papers would directly result in the deaths of U.S. soldiers. Bickel said he doubted that would occur, but conceded that in such a case, "My inclinations to humanity overcome the somewhat more abstract devotion to the First Amendment."

The justices' opinions in the Pentagon Papers case, as well as the urgency with which they considered it, were affected strongly by *Near v. Minnesota* (1931). That decision created a strong and deep presumption against "prior restraint" of expression—in other words, censorship. The First Amendment dictated, in the majority's view, that any harm caused by free expression, such as damaging a person's reputation, be punished after publication, not before. Under the *Near* decision, any government action that prevented a publication for even the briefest period of time was like a ticking constitutional bomb, something that should be defused as rapidly as possible. "The prompt setting of these cases reflects our universal abhorrence of prior restraint," Chief Justice Burger noted, even though he dissented from the majority's decision to allow the publication to proceed.

But the *Near* ruling also spoke of exceptions to the rule against prior restraint, one of which seemed relevant to the Pentagon Papers case. Chief Justice Charles Evans Hughes had suggested that government probably could prevent publication of the "sailing dates of transports or the number and location of troops," especially in wartime. (See *Near v. Minnesota.*)

Daniel Ellsberg speaks to reporters outside the Federal Building in Los Angeles on January 17, 1973, as his co-defendant, Anthony Russo, listens. Ellsberg's public release of the Pentagon Papers, a classified history of U.S. involvement in the Vietnam War, led to *New York Times Co. v. United States* (1971). The Court held that the government did not meet the "heavy burden" necessary to prevent expression protected by the First Amendment.
Source: AP/Wide World Photos.

The justices in the majority concluded that nothing of that nature was involved in publication of the Pentagon Papers. "Only governmental allegation and proof that publication must inevitably, directly, and immediately cause the occurrence of an event kindred to imperiling the safety of a transport already at sea can support even the issuance of an interim restraining order," Justice Brennan wrote.

VOTE

6–3, with the decision expressed in an unsigned (per curiam) opinion. Joining the opinion were Justices William O. Douglas, Potter Stewart, Byron R. White, Thurgood Marshall, Hugo L. Black, and William J. Brennan Jr. Dissenting were Chief Justice Warren Burger and Justices Harry A. Blackmun and John M. Harlan.

HIGHLIGHTS

All the justices wrote separately to express their view of the case. Several recalled the roots and purposes of the First Amendment, asserting that it was intended to prevent, completely and for all time, the sort of government interference with freedom of the press that the government was seeking in this case. "The press was protected so that it could bare the secrets of government and inform the people," wrote Justice Black.

Other justices, notably Stewart and White, took a more moderate position, acknowledging that in some circumstances government would be entitled to protect national security by halting dangerous publications. "Undoubtedly, Congress has the power to enact specific and appropriate criminal laws to protect government property and preserve government secrets," wrote Stewart. White said, "Revelation of these documents will do substantial damage to public interests." But both justices said the government had failed to convince them that halting publication was warranted.

The three dissenting justices lamented the Court's hasty treatment of the case. They said the potential danger to national security, as well as the need for deliberation on such weighty cases, warranted a fuller look than was possible in the time allotted.

"It may well be that if these cases were allowed to develop as they should be developed, and to be tried as lawyers should try them and as courts should hear them, free of pressure and panic and sensationalism, other light would be shed on the situation, and contrary considerations, for me, might prevail," wrote Justice Blackmun. "But that is not the present posture of the litigation."

EXCERPTS

Per curiam: "We granted certiorari in these cases in which the United States seeks to enjoin the *New York Times* and the *Washington Post* from publishing the contents of a classified study entitled 'History of U.S. Decision-Making Process on Viet Nam Policy.'

" 'Any system of prior restraints of expression comes to this Court bearing a heavy presumption against its constitutional validity.' The Government 'thus carries a heavy burden of showing justification for the imposition of such a restraint.' The District Court for the Southern District of New York in the *New York Times* case and the District Court for the District of Columbia and the Court of Appeals for the District of Columbia Circuit in the *Washington Post* case held that the Government had not met that burden. We agree."

Justice Black: "Only a free and unrestrained press can effectively expose deception in government. And paramount among the responsibilities of a free press is the duty to prevent any part of the government from deceiving the people and sending them off to distant lands to die of foreign fevers and foreign shot and shell. In my view, far from deserving condemnation for their courageous reporting, the *New York Times,* the *Washington Post,* and other newspapers should be commended for serving the purpose that the Founding Fathers saw so clearly."

Justice Douglas: "Secrecy in government is fundamentally anti-democratic, perpetuating bureaucratic errors. Open debate and discussion of public issues are vital to our national health. . . .

"The stays in these cases that have been in effect for more than a week constitute a flouting of the principles of the First Amendment as interpreted in *Near v. Minnesota."*

Justice Brennan: "[E]very restraint issued in this case, whatever its form, has violated the First Amendment—and not less so because that restraint was justified as necessary to afford the courts an opportunity to examine the claim more thoroughly. Unless and until the Government has clearly made out its case, the First Amendment commands that no injunction may issue."

Justice Stewart: "[W]hen everything is classified, then nothing is classified, and the system becomes one to be disregarded by the cynical or the careless, and to be manipulated by those intent on self-protection or self-promotion. I should suppose, in short, that the hallmark of a truly effective internal security system would be the maximum possible disclosure, recognizing that secrecy can best be preserved only when credibility is truly maintained."

Justice White: "I do not say that in no circumstances would the First Amendment permit an injunction against publishing information about government plans or operations. Nor, after examining the materials the Government characterizes as the most sensitive and destructive, can I deny that revelation of these documents will do substantial damage to public interests. Indeed, I am confident that their disclosure will have that result. But I nevertheless agree that the United States has not satisfied the very heavy burden that it must meet to warrant an injunction against publication in these cases, at least in the absence of express and appropriately limited congressional authorization for prior restraints in circumstances such as these."

Justice Marshall: "Either the Government has the power under statutory grant to use traditional criminal law to protect the country or, if there is no basis for arguing that Congress has made the activity a crime, it is plain that Congress has specifically refused to grant the authority the Government seeks from this Court. In either case this Court does not have authority to grant the requested relief. It is not for this Court to fling itself into every breach perceived by some Government official nor is it for this Court to take on itself the burden of enacting law, especially a law that Congress has refused to pass."

Chief Justice Burger, in dissent: "To me it is hardly believable that a newspaper long regarded as a great institution in American life would fail to perform one of the basic and simple duties of every citizen with respect to the discovery or possession of stolen property or secret government documents. That duty, I had thought—perhaps naively—was to report forthwith, to responsible public officers. This duty rests on taxi drivers, Justices, and the *New York Times.* The course followed by the *Times,* whether so calculated or not, removed any possibility of orderly litigation of the issue. If the action of the judges up to now has been correct, that result is sheer happenstance."

Justice Harlan, in dissent: "This frenzied train of events took place in the name of the presumption against prior restraints created by the First Amendment. Due regard for the extraordinarily important and difficult questions involved in these litigations should have led the Court to shun such a precipitate timetable."

Justice Blackmun, in dissent: "The First Amendment, after all, is only one part of an entire Constitution. Article II of the great document vests in the Executive Branch primary power over the conduct of foreign affairs and places in that branch the responsibility for the Nation's safety. Each provision of the Constitution is important, and I cannot subscribe to a doctrine of unlimited absolutism for the First Amendment at the cost of downgrading other provisions. First Amendment absolutism has never commanded a majority of this Court. . . .

"I hope that damage has not already been done. If, however, damage has been done, and if, with the Court's action today, these newspapers proceed to publish the critical documents and there results therefrom 'the death of soldiers, the destruction of alliances, the greatly increased difficulty of negotiation with our enemies, the inability of our diplomats to negotiate,' to which list I might add the factors of prolongation of the war and of further delay in the freeing of United States prisoners, then the Nation's people will know where the responsibility for these sad consequences rests."

IMPACT

The decision in *New York Times Co. v. United States* was an extraordinary victory for freedom of the press. In a time of war, in an uncharted area of law, a majority of the Supreme Court had chosen not to believe the government's assertions about the potential danger of publishing these documents. With almost no prior cases to follow or go by, the Court easily could have ruled the other way without being seen as overturning past precedents.

Rudenstine wrote in *The Day the Presses Stopped,* "The newspapers prevailed. The fact that they did in the midst of all these circumstances makes their triumph a matter of exceptional importance not only for the freedom of the American press but for American democracy as a whole."

The newspapers celebrated their victory and resumed publication of stories based on the revelations in the Pentagon Papers. But in all their stories, they recounted only a small part of the original report's contents. Later book versions, including one published by the U.S. government, excluded some of the most sensitive material the government wanted kept secret.

As the months went by the government could not point to any concrete negative effects of the publication of the newspapers' stories. "In hindsight, it is clear to me that no harm was done by publication of the Pentagon Papers," said Erwin Griswold, who had argued the government's case before the Supreme Court as solicitor general.

The disclosures did reenergize the national debate over the wisdom of the Vietnam War. Because the history suggested that President Johnson had misled the public about the war, the Pentagon Papers helped divide, and some would say weaken, the Democratic Party in advance of the 1972 elections.

As for Ellsberg himself, a grand jury indicted him on charges of theft of government property and revealing classified material. The indictment ultimately was dismissed, in part because of Nixon administration tactics in investigating Ellsberg. It was revealed that government employees had participated in a break-in and robbery at the office of Ellsberg's psychiatrist in a search for information to discredit his testimony.

Branzburg v. Hayes

Decided June 29, 1972
408 U.S. 665
laws.findlaw.com/US/408/665.html

DECISION

The First Amendment does not give the press the right to refuse to testify before a grand jury in a criminal investigation. News gathering deserves some protection under the First Amendment, but news organizations' concern about losing their sources does not outweigh the public interest in law enforcement.

BACKGROUND

During the late 1960s, political and social turmoil on college campuses and among racial minorities was accompanied by a resurgence in investigative reporting and alternative news media. To report on dissident movements and social phenomena such as drug use, journalists often had to promise not to reveal the names of their sources, who were fearful of attracting the attention of law enforcement.

Law enforcement officials responded by subpoenaing reporters to testify anyway, on the theory that anyone who has information about illegal activity—no matter how it was obtained—should be compelled to produce it to a grand jury. A clash between the two points of view was inevitable, and it came to the Supreme Court in the form of three separate disputes between the news media and law enforcement.

The first involved Paul Branzburg, an investigative reporter for the *Louisville Courier-Journal.* In 1969 Branzburg wrote an account of two local residents who were making and selling the illegal drug hashish. He had been allowed to interview the two on the condition that he not use their names in the story. When Branzburg was called before a grand jury, he refused to disclose the names, invoking a Kentucky "shield" law that allowed reporters to refuse to identify their sources. The judge ruled the law did not apply when a reporter had actually witnessed illegal acts.

A second case involved Paul Pappas, a television reporter in New Bedford, Massachusetts. The local Black Panther Party allowed Pappas to film its headquarters in anticipation of a police raid but only on the condition that he not show anything but the raid. The raid never materialized, but Pappas was subpoenaed by a grand jury and was asked to reveal what he had seen. He refused, but again judges in Massachusetts said he had no First Amendment right not to testify.

In the third case, the most widely reported, *New York Times* reporter Earl Caldwell was subpoenaed to testify before a grand jury in San Francisco following a series of articles he had written about the Black Panther Party. Caldwell, who is black, had been given unusual access to party leaders Eldridge Cleaver and others, enabling him to report in detail on the organization's strategies and plans. "As I became more deeply involved with the Panthers, I began to keep all kinds of files on them," Caldwell recalled later.

Like the others, Caldwell refused to testify or turn over his files, arguing that to do so would cause an "irreparable breach" with his sources in the Black Panther Party. The government narrowed its request, but Caldwell still resisted. A judge held him in contempt for refusing to testify. On appeal, a panel of judges sided with Caldwell, agreeing that compelling him to testify would restrict the flow of information to the public.

When the Supreme Court agreed to hear the three cases, news media organizations and civil liberties groups met in New York to draft a friend of the court brief supporting the journalists. The press did not argue for an absolute privilege but for a qualified privilege: journalists could be forced to testify only if there is no other source for the information and the reporter's testimony is needed to prevent irreparable damage to life or national security.

VOTE

5–4, with Justice Byron R. White writing the majority opinion. Joining the majority were Chief Justice Warren E. Burger and Justices Harry A. Blackmun, Lewis F. Powell Jr., and William Rehnquist. Dissenting were Justices William O. Douglas, Potter Stewart, William J. Brennan Jr., and Thurgood Marshall.

HIGHLIGHTS

Even as he acknowledged the importance of a free press, Justice White reminded the media that the First Amendment has never been interpreted to allow the press to print anything it wants with impunity or to give the press special access to events that the public may not attend.

Moreover, White said, the First Amendment and the common law give the press no privilege to refuse to testify in circumstances in which any other member of the public would have to testify. "The public . . . 'has a right to every man's evidence,' " White wrote.

"Until now, the only testimonial privilege for unofficial witnesses that is rooted in the Federal Constitution is the Fifth Amendment privilege against compelled self-incrimination," White wrote. "We are asked to create another by interpreting the First Amendment to grant newsmen a testimonial privilege that other citizens do not enjoy. This we decline to do."

The Court rejected arguments from journalists who said that being forced to reveal their confidential sources to a grand jury would discourage those sources from talking to the media, substantially restricting the free flow of information to the public. White said the desire for anonymity by sources who have

These three reporters—left to right, Paul Pappas, Earl Caldwell, and Paul M. Branzburg—fought against revealing information about their sources. The Supreme Court disappointed legal scholars and the media with its ruling in *Branzburg v. Hayes* (1972) that a reporter's First Amendment rights do not protect him or her from being required to give evidence of a crime.

Source: AP/Wide World Photos.

committed crimes, "while understandable, is hardly deserving of constitutional protection." He added, "The crimes of news sources are no less reprehensible and threatening to the public interest when witnessed by a reporter than when they are not." White left room for Congress and the states to enact reporters' privilege laws—some states already had—but he said this did not rise to the level of a constitutional necessity.

The force of White's opinion in opposing a constitutionally based privilege was tempered somewhat by a separate concurring opinion by Justice Powell. "The Court does not hold that newsmen, subpoenaed to testify before a grand jury, are without constitutional rights with respect to the gathering of news or in safeguarding their sources," Powell wrote.

Powell argued for a case-by-case balancing by judges of the conflicting interests in determining whether a reporter should be compelled to testify. Because the vote was 5–4, some have viewed Powell's concurrence as the "controlling" opinion and have cited it since.

Justice Stewart offered a brief but stinging dissent, arguing that the Court's opinion "invites state and federal authorities to undermine the historic independence of the press by attempting to annex the journalistic profession as an investigative arm of government. Not only will this decision impair performance of the press' constitutionally protected functions, but it will, I am convinced, in the long run harm, rather than help, the administration of justice."

EXCERPTS

From Justice White's majority opinion: "We do not question the significance of free speech, press, or assembly to the country's welfare. Nor is it suggested that news gathering does not qualify for First Amendment protection; without some protection for seeking out the news, freedom of the press could be eviscerated. But these cases involve no intrusions upon speech or assembly, no prior restraint or restriction on what the press may publish, and no express or implied command that the press publish what it prefers to withhold. . . . The use of confidential sources by the press is not forbidden or restricted; reporters remain free to seek news from any source by means within the law. . . .

"The sole issue before us is the obligation of reporters to respond to grand jury subpoenas as other citizens do, and to answer questions relevant to an investigation into the commission of crime. Citizens generally are not constitutionally immune from grand jury subpoenas, and neither the First Amendment nor any other constitutional provision protects the average citizen from disclosing to a grand jury information that he has received in confidence."

IMPACT

In spite of the dire predictions of the press, the *Branzburg* decision has not kept confidential sources from talking to the press or kept the press from using them in stories. This may be due in part to the willingness of most journalists to protect their sources, even if it means the reporters go to jail rather than testify. It has become an article of faith among journalists and their newspapers that confidential sources are to be protected.

By the same token, prosecutors still subpoena journalists with regularity. According to the Reporters Committee for Freedom of the Press, news organizations responding to a survey indicated they had received 823 subpoenas in 2001, many of them from prosecutors and police, but many also from parties in civil suits. The *Los Angeles Times* indicated in the survey that prosecutors and private lawyers in civil litigation discuss or issue subpoenas to its reporters two or three times a week. A substantial number of subpoenas are directed at the media even in the more than thirty states that have enacted shield laws, which allow reporters to keep their sources confidential. Justice Stewart's fear that prosecutors would try to turn the press into an "investigative arm of government" has come true, in the view of many in the media.

Disputes over reporters resisting subpoenas made headlines in the early 2000s. In 2001 freelance writer Vanessa Leggett spent 168 days in jail—the longest jail term in U.S. history, apparently, for a journalist—for refusing to reveal her sources for a book she was writing on a Texas murder. Several subpoena controversies were in the news simultaneously in 2005, including that of *Time* magazine reporter Matt Cooper and *New York Times* reporter Judith Miller. They declined to reveal to a grand jury who gave them the name of a Central Intelligence Agency agent. The Supreme Court declined to review their appeals. During this period many news organizations adopted rules discouraging their reporters from using unnamed sources—not just for legal reasons, but because the organizations believed that the use of anonymous sources undermines reader confidence in the accuracy and fairness of the news media.

As for the reporters in the *Branzburg* case, at least one said he destroyed his notes after the case was over. "I erased the tapes and shredded almost every document I had that dealt with the Panthers," Caldwell wrote later. "In America today a reporter cannot save his notes or his tapes or other documents."

Richmond Newspapers, Inc. v. Virginia

Decided July 2, 1980
448 U.S. 555
laws.findlaw.com/US/448/555.html

DECISION

The right of the public and the press to attend criminal trials is guaranteed by the First Amendment. A judge may restrict access only in limited circumstances after making findings that closure is necessary to ensure a fair trial for the defendant.

BACKGROUND

The tradition of openness in criminal trials runs long and deep through the history of Anglo-American law. Early in British history, community leaders were required to attend trials. Even after the requirement was relaxed, the presence of the public at trials was viewed as an important way of guaranteeing that justice was dispensed in an evenhanded fashion. That principle carried over into the laws and practices of courts in the American colonies and the new nation.

The Bill of Rights refers to this principle only briefly, guaranteeing in the Sixth Amendment that those accused of crimes be given "speedy and public" trials. Partly because the Sixth Amendment gives that right to the criminal defendant, rather than to the public or to the press, the question of whether the public or press has a right of access has proved difficult for the courts to resolve. Without access to courts, the press cannot perform the watchdog function on government that is envisioned by the First Amendment.

Especially when the defendant does not want public attention drawn to his or her case, the conflict between the defendant's Sixth Amendment right to a fair trial and the First Amendment freedom of the press can be intractable. In *Nebraska Press Assn. v. Stuart* (1976) the Supreme Court noted that "problems presented by this [conflict] are almost as old as the Republic." That decision struck down a gag order placed on reporters covering a trial and recognized a strong First Amendment interest in the press being able to report on what happens in open court.

In 1979 the Court revisited the issue in *Gannett v. DePasquale,* a 5–4 decision upholding a judge's decision to close a pretrial hearing to the press and public. The Court said the right to a public trial belonged to the defendant and could not be the basis for declaring a public right of access to pretrial hearings. Discussing the sharply divided Court, Bernard Schwartz wrote that at one point in the justices' decisionmaking, a majority did declare a constitutional right of public access to the courts. Justice Lewis F. Powell Jr. changed his mind, however, resulting in the 5–4 decision against the press.

The *Gannett* decision caused an uproar, and lower court judges took it as a cue to shut the press and public out of several criminal trials in the summer of 1979. In public remarks, Chief Justice Warren Burger and others suggested that the decision had been misinterpreted, and that it pertained only to the closing of pretrial hearings, not to trials themselves. It was clear that the Court needed to clarify its views and lay down a clearer rule on public and press access to courts.

A controversy over press access to a Richmond, Virginia, murder trial gave the Court its opportunity. The defendant had been tried three times before for the same crime, and each time the proceedings ended in mistrial. Before the fourth trial began, the defendant's lawyer asked the judge to exclude the press and public. "I don't want any information being shuffled back and forth" about testimony by the witnesses, the lawyer told the judge. The prosecutor went along with the request, and the judge agreed, prompting the local newspaper to sue. The Virginia Supreme Court upheld the closure order. The trial proceeded with the public excluded, and then in a brief announcement the judge informed the public that the defendant was found not guilty.

VOTE

7–1, with Chief Justice Warren E. Burger writing for a plurality of three. Joining his opinion were Justices Byron R. White and John Paul Stevens. Justice William J. Brennan Jr. wrote an opinion concurring in the judgment that was joined by Justice Thurgood Marshall. Justices Potter Stewart and Harry A. Blackmun wrote opinions concurring in the judgment. Justice William Rehnquist dissented. Justice Lewis F. Powell Jr. did not participate for unstated reasons.

HIGHLIGHTS

As with the *Gannett* decision exactly a year earlier, the Court's ruling in the *Richmond Newspapers* case was fractured. Six of the seven justices in the majority wrote separately, each expounding a somewhat different theory about why public and press access to trials was constitutionally guaranteed.

Chief Justice Burger wrote what is known as a plurality opinion, meaning that a majority of the Court agrees with the outcome of the case, but not the legal reasoning behind it. Burger's opinion was joined only by Justices White and Stevens.

Burger expounded on the long history of open courtrooms as a tradition that has value for the public as well as for the defendant. "From this unbroken, uncontradicted history, supported by reasons as valid today as in centuries past, we are bound to conclude that a presumption of openness inheres in the very nature of a criminal trial under our system of justice," Burger wrote.

Burger also said the First Amendment guarantees the right of the public and press to attend trials, even if it does not say so explicitly. The Court has found a right of privacy and a right to travel to be part of the Constitution, even though neither is mentioned in the Constitution, Burger noted. A right to receive information and ideas—and in this context to attend trials—is also part of the First Amendment's promise, Burger said. "Without the freedom to attend such trials, which people have exercised for centuries, important aspects of freedom of speech and 'of the press could be eviscerated,' " he said, quoting from a 1972 case. (See *Branzburg v. Hayes*.)

In the specific case before the Court, Burger said the judge had failed to make any findings to justify excluding the press and public. He had not looked into other possible ways of ensuring fairness without closing the trial, such as sequestering the jury or making sure witnesses do not hear other witnesses' testimony before they take the stand.

Justice Brennan, joined by Justice Marshall, wrote to develop the First Amendment basis for the open court guarantee. "Open trials assure the public that procedural rights are respected, and that justice is afforded equally. Closed trials breed suspicion of prejudice and arbitrariness, which in turn spawns disrespect for law. Public access is essential, therefore, if trial adjudication is to achieve the objective of maintaining public confidence in the administration of justice."

Justice Stewart wrote in his concurrence, "In conspicuous contrast to a military base, a jail, or a prison, a trial courtroom is a public place. Even more than city streets, sidewalks, and parks as areas of traditional First Amendment activity, a trial courtroom is a place where representatives of the press and of the public are not only free to be, but where their presence serves to assure the integrity of what goes on." Justice Stewart also emphasized the First Amendment right of access, but said it was not absolute.

Justice Stevens wrote separately to underline what the Court had decided. "This is a watershed case. Until today, the Court has accorded virtually absolute protection to the dissemination of information or ideas, but never before has it squarely held that the acquisition of newsworthy matter is entitled to any constitutional protection whatsoever." Justices White and

Blackmun also wrote to suggest that the Court could have found a basis for guaranteeing open courts in the Sixth Amendment.

In dissent, Justice Rehnquist said the Court was meddling in an area that should be left to the states to decide. "I do not believe that either the First or Sixth Amendment, as made applicable to the States by the Fourteenth, requires that a State's reasons for denying public access to a trial, where both the prosecuting attorney and the defendant have consented to an order of closure approved by the judge, are subject to any additional constitutional review at our hands."

EXCERPTS

From Justice Burger's plurality opinion: "The historical evidence demonstrates conclusively that at the time when our organic laws were adopted, criminal trials both here and in England had long been presumptively open. This is no quirk of history; rather, it has long been recognized as an indispensable attribute of an Anglo-American trial. . . . [I]t gave assurance that the proceedings were conducted fairly to all concerned, and it discouraged perjury, the misconduct of participants, and decisions based on secret bias or partiality. . . .

"People in an open society do not demand infallibility from their institutions, but it is difficult for them to accept what they are prohibited from observing. When a criminal trial is conducted in the open, there is at least an opportunity both for understanding the system in general and its workings in a particular case. . . .

"The Bill of Rights was enacted against the backdrop of the long history of trials being presumptively open. Public access to trials was then regarded as an important aspect of the process itself; the conduct of trials 'before as many of the people as chuse to attend' was regarded as one of 'the inestimable advantages of a free English constitution of government.' In guaranteeing freedoms such as those of speech and press, the First Amendment can be read as protecting the right of everyone to attend trials so as to give meaning to those explicit guarantees."

IMPACT

The immediate effect of the *Richmond* case was to halt the rash of court closings that had broken out after the *Gannett* decision. "It is gratifying . . . to see the Court wash away at least some of the graffiti that marred the prevailing opinions in *Gannett*," Blackmun wrote in his concurrence. Even though the Court was still divided, the justices in the *Richmond* case agreed that the long tradition of open courts had to be honored and given constitutional force.

Judges today find it considerably more difficult to close trials to the public and press, no matter how sensational the proceedings and how intense the press scrutiny. That doctrine has not always extended to access by broadcast media, which have always been subject to more regulation than print media. (See

Chandler v. Florida.) But the basic principle of open criminal courts is no longer open to question.

Some aspects of civil trials, which are governed by the Seventh Amendment rather than the Sixth, are still routinely closed to public scrutiny by judges. In 1999, however, the California Supreme Court cited the *Richmond Newspapers* case in extending the guarantee of open courts to civil cases as well.

Yale law professor Thomas Emerson pointed to another reason for the symbolic importance of the *Richmond Newspapers* decision. "The *Richmond Newspapers* case was the first in which the Court actually upheld a First Amendment right to obtain information that the government wished to withhold," Emerson wrote in a 1983 book on the Burger Court. The Court has not applied that principle to other fields, but the ruling in *Richmond Newspapers* strengthened the hand of the press in its perennial battles against government secrecy.

The Court did apply the *Richmond Newspapers* decision to other aspects of criminal trials, however. In *Globe Newspaper Co. v. Superior Court* (1982) the Court struck down a law bar- ring the press from juvenile court proceedings. In 1984 and 1986 decisions, the Court said the public and the press had a right of access to jury selection and other pretrial proceedings.

Though the principle of open courts was well settled, news media remained concerned about erosion of courtroom access. Civil cases and settlements sometimes occur outside public view, and in high-profile public trials judges sometimes issue "gag orders" preventing trial participants from talking to the media. More and more, jurors' names are kept secret, presumably to protect the privacy and safety of jurors.

In the aftermath of the September 11, 2001, terrorist attacks, federal officials sought to close administrative hearings on the legal status of immigrants. News organizations challenged the new policy and won the support of the U.S. Court of Appeals for the Sixth Circuit: "The Executive Branch seeks to uproot people's lives, outside the public eye, and behind a closed door. Democracies die behind closed doors." Another appeals court ruled the opposite way, and the Supreme Court declined to resolve the conflicting views.

Chandler v. Florida

Decided January 26, 1981
449 U.S. 560
laws.findlaw.com/US/449/560.html

DECISION

The Constitution does not prohibit states from allowing televised coverage of criminal trials. It has not been shown that the mere presence of cameras in the courtroom harms a defendant's right to a fair trial or to due process.

BACKGROUND

The highly publicized O.J. Simpson murder trial in 1995 may either have been the high point or low point of a trend that has caused controversy since the early twentieth century: the broadcast of courtroom proceedings.

At the beginning of the broadcast era, few people thought twice about allowing cameras and microphones into courtrooms. Radio coverage of the 1925 Scopes "monkey trial," pitting legendary lawyers William Jennings Bryan against Clarence Darrow in a battle over the teaching of evolution, gripped the nation. Ten years later photographers crowded the trial of Bruno Hauptmann for the kidnapping of aviator Charles Lindbergh's son.

The perceived excesses of the media during the Hauptmann trial, however, triggered restrictions on media coverage of trials. In 1937 an American Bar Association committee de- clared that the Hauptmann trial was "the most spectacular and depressing example of improper publicity and professional misconduct ever presented." The American Bar Association (ABA) adopted Canon 35 as part of its code of judicial ethics, barring cameras and microphones inside judicial proceedings. The reasoning behind the restriction was that the presence of the media distorted the proceedings and violated a defendant's Sixth Amendment right to a fair trial.

Most states and the federal courts adopted the ban, and broadcast media presence was effectively eliminated for decades. Only Colorado, Oklahoma, and Texas did not adopt the canon. And it was the televising of a Texas trial that gave the Supreme Court its first chance to rule on the issue. Billie Sol Estes, a well-known Texas financier accused of fraud, was tried in a courtroom that featured a dozen photographers and camerapersons, as well as a tangle of camera cables and microphones.

In the 1965 decision *Estes v. Texas* a divided Supreme Court ruled that the media coverage, over the defendant's objections, was so pervasive that it denied him the due process of law guaranteed by the Constitution. The Court overturned Estes's conviction. But some of the justices' views expressed in the 5–4 decision led to lingering controversy over how far the ruling went. Justice John M. Harlan, viewed as the swing vote in the case, said television coverage violated the constitutional right to a fair trial "at least as to a notorious criminal trial such as this one."

The *Estes* decision slowed what was left of broadcast coverage of courts. A year later, the Court underscored its anti-camera views in *Sheppard v. Maxwell,* which described the extensive coverage of an Ohio murder trial of Dr. Sam Sheppard as "a Roman circus." It was not until the 1970s that experimentation with broadcast coverage resumed. Acting on petitions by Florida broadcasters, the Supreme Court of Florida authorized coverage on an experimental basis in 1977.

The issue returned to the Supreme Court when the defendants in one of the televised trials in Florida challenged the coverage. On trial were Noel Chandler and Robert Granger, two Miami Beach police officers accused of robbing a well-known local restaurant. The chief witness against them was an amateur radio operator who happened to overhear radio transmissions between the officers. These unusual aspects of the trial attracted wide media interest.

Under the rules of the experiment, the defendants could object to television coverage, and they did. Their request was denied, but cameras were allowed to record only the prosecution's presentation, not that of the defense. The officers were found guilty, and they appealed, claiming that the camera coverage spoiled their chances to receive a fair and impartial trial. But appeals courts and the Florida Supreme Court upheld the convictions.

In legal briefs and oral arguments before the U.S. Supreme Court, Florida and various media organizations argued that television technology had changed drastically since the *Estes* case, to the point where trials could be covered unobtrusively. They also asserted that camera coverage educated the public and served as a check on the competence and integrity of the justice system. But lawyers for the defendants argued that "human nature and common sense" dictate that trial participants behave differently when cameras are present, harming the defendants' rights to a fair trial.

VOTE

8–0, with Chief Justice Warren Burger writing the opinion of the Court. Joining him were Justices William J. Brennan Jr., Potter Stewart, Byron R. White, Thurgood Marshall, Harry A. Blackmun, Lewis F. Powell Jr., and William Rehnquist. Justice John Paul Stevens did not participate for unstated reasons.

HIGHLIGHTS

Rather than explicitly overturning the *Estes* decision, the justices chose to interpret it narrowly. The opponents of camera coverage had argued that the decision in *Estes* meant that tele-

vising trials was flatly unconstitutional, no matter what rules or restrictions lessened its effect.

But Chief Justice Burger, focusing on Harlan's views in the *Estes* case, concluded that the Court had not ruled so definitively. "We conclude that *Estes* is not to be read as announcing a constitutional rule barring still photographic, radio, and television coverage in all cases and under all circumstances," Burger wrote. "It does not stand as an absolute ban on state experimentation with an evolving technology, which, in terms of modes of mass communication, was in its relative infancy in 1964, and is, even now, in a state of continuing change."

If *Estes* did not require a flat-out ban on cameras then, Burger said, none was required now—especially since it has not been proven that camera presence always spoils the fairness of a trial. That kind of damage had not even been proven in the case of the police officers before the Court. In the opinion, Burger also pointed to the changes in technology since *Estes* as justification for not banning cameras altogether.

"Not unimportant to the position asserted by Florida and other states is the change in television technology since 1962, when Estes was tried," Burger wrote. "It is urged, and some empirical data are presented, that many of the negative factors found in *Estes*—cumbersome equipment, cables, distracting lighting, numerous camera technicians—are less substantial factors today than they were at that time."

Another powerful argument in favor of allowing the Florida experiment to continue, in Burger's view, was the role of states as "laboratories" in the federal system. He quoted Justice Louis Brandeis, who once encouraged states to "try novel social and economic experiments." Burger concluded, "This concept of federalism . . . must guide our decision."

No justices dissented, but White and Stewart wrote separately to urge that the Court acknowledge that it was, in fact, overturning *Estes*.

EXCERPTS

From Justice Burger's majority opinion: "An absolute constitutional ban on broadcast coverage of trials cannot be justified simply because there is a danger that, in some cases, prejudicial broadcast accounts of pretrial and trial events may impair the ability of jurors to decide the issue of guilt or innocence uninfluenced by extraneous matter. The risk of juror prejudice in some cases does not justify an absolute ban on news coverage of trials by the printed media; so also the risk of such prejudice does not warrant an absolute constitutional ban on all broadcast coverage. A case attracts a high level of public attention because of its intrinsic interest to the public and the manner of reporting the event. The risk of juror prejudice is present in any publication of a trial, but the appropriate safeguard against such prejudice is the defendant's right to demonstrate that the media's coverage of his case—be it printed or broadcast—compromised the ability of the particular jury that heard the case to adjudicate fairly. . . .

"To demonstrate prejudice in a specific case a defendant must show something more than juror awareness that the trial is such as to attract the attention of broadcasters. No doubt the very presence of a camera in the courtroom made the jurors aware that the trial was thought to be of sufficient interest to the public to warrant coverage. Jurors, forbidden to watch all broadcasts, would have had no way of knowing that only fleeting seconds of the proceeding would be reproduced. But the appellants have not attempted to show with any specificity that the presence of cameras impaired the ability of the jurors to decide the case on only the evidence before them or that their trial was affected adversely by the impact on any of the participants of the presence of cameras and the prospect of broadcast. . . .

"Dangers lurk in this, as in most experiments, but unless we were to conclude that television coverage under all conditions is prohibited by the Constitution, the states must be free to experiment. We are not empowered by the Constitution to oversee or harness state procedural experimentation; only when the state action infringes fundamental guarantees are we authorized to intervene. We must assume state courts will be alert to any factors that impair the fundamental rights of the accused."

IMPACT

Chandler was a case in which the Court struck a delicate balance between the Sixth Amendment right of individuals to a fair trial and the First Amendment freedom of the press. The Court did not go so far as to say that broadcasters had a First Amendment right to air court proceedings. It merely said that the Constitution does not automatically bar states from allowing that access.

But that judgment alone was enough to encourage a wide range of experimentation with cameras in courtrooms nationwide. The ABA modified its canon, and by the late 1990s broadcast access was allowed in at least some of the courts in forty-nine states. New York was the holdout, and in June 2005 New York's highest court affirmed the state's policy, finding that the state was under no constitutional obligation to open its courts to cameras. Some states permit cameras only inside appellate courts. In the view of some broadcasters, hearings in those courts are less interesting than actual trials, so broadcasters do not always avail themselves of the privilege. And because *Chandler* did not say camera access was required, judges still have significant authority to restrict and regulate access.

In many areas of the country camera coverage of trials has become a commonplace, if not a daily, occurrence. Ronald L. Goldfarb, author of the 1998 book *TV or Not TV,* also notes that "since 1981, when *Chandler* opened the way for cameras in courts, no verdict has been overturned on the basis of prejudice caused by television."

One sign of how common camera coverage became in the wake of *Chandler* was the launch in 1991 of Court TV, a cable television channel that has aired hundreds of trials, many of them gavel-to-gavel. "Camera coverage of the least misunderstood and most often misportrayed branch of government—and the only branch of government which the Constitution requires to do its business in public—provides a dignified, important view of how the legal system is actually working," wrote Court TV founder Steven Brill in 1995.

Many judges and commentators found reason to disagree with that view in light of the coverage of the O.J. Simpson trial. The nonstop, massive coverage, while it educated an entire generation of viewers about the intricacies of criminal law, also appeared to many to strain the integrity of the trial. Presiding judge Lance Ito and many of the other participants seemed affected by the cameras and the intense scrutiny that accompanied them. Camera advocates, however, said other aspects of the coverage, such as the constant commentary outside the court, were more to blame for any distortions than the cameras inside the courtroom. But in the wake of the Simpson trial, several judges decided to shut cameras out of several high-profile trials, fearing the "O.J. effect."

The Simpson trial also damaged chances that camera access would be allowed any time soon in federal courts. Contrary to the trend in state courts, federal courts, including the Supreme Court, have held to their longstanding resistance to broadcast coverage. Even though Chief Justice Burger wrote the *Chandler* decision, he often said cameras would be allowed into the Supreme Court "over my dead body"—a sentiment echoed more recently by Justice David Souter. That view discouraged the rest of the federal judiciary from experimenting with camera access until after Burger retired in 1986. In 1991, at the urging of members of Congress, the federal courts conducted a limited experiment that, while successful, was not renewed when it expired three years later.

The Supreme Court's resistance stems from the justices' expressed preference for anonymity in an era of celebrity, as well as a more abstract view that federal courts, unlike state courts, should stand apart from politics and daily notoriety. Justice Antonin Scalia once said, "No news is good news" when it comes to the courts, and Justice Anthony Kennedy said after the Simpson trial, "I'm delighted I'm less famous than Judge Ito."

Hazelwood School District v. Kuhlmeier

Decided January 13, 1988
484 U.S. 260
laws.findlaw.com/US/484/260.html

DECISION

School officials have the power to regulate the content of student newspapers that are school supported, so long as their actions are "reasonably related to legitimate pedagogical concerns." The First Amendment does not require public school officials to tolerate student speech that is inconsistent with the school's educational mission.

BACKGROUND

In the Supreme Court's classic description of the rights of students, the opinion in *Tinker v. Des Moines Independent Community School District* (1969) said that students and teachers do not "shed their constitutional rights to freedom of speech or expression at the schoolhouse gate." (See *Tinker v. Des Moines Independent Community School District.*)

But in the years after that decision, the Court and school administrators began to worry that *Tinker* had given students too much license to disrupt or distract fellow students and teachers from the business of school, namely education. A struggle developed to square the promise of *Tinker* with the traditional role of schools as conveyors of moral values and, in many respects, as daytime substitutes for parents themselves. In *Bethel School District No. 403 v. Fraser* (1986), the Court ruled that school officials were entitled to punish a student who used sexual innuendo in a student election speech on behalf of a candidate.

One battleground was student expression in school newspapers, which some saw as posing different issues from the student protest armbands allowed in the *Tinker* decision. Student newspapers are usually school-sponsored in some way, and many are produced as part of the school curriculum in journalism classes. As a result, school administrators felt they were entitled to exert a substantial degree of control over the newspapers' content, even if *Tinker* did not allow them to censor individual students who expressed themselves in ways that did not involve school sponsorship.

A dispute over the student newspaper at Hazelwood East High School in suburban St. Louis, Missouri, brought the issue to the Court. The newspaper, *Spectrum,* was published as part of the journalism curriculum at the high school, and it received funding from the school district.

The newspaper had a stated policy of openness in terms of its contents, except for items that "materially and substantially interfere with the requirements of appropriate discipline," language that was modeled after the *Tinker* decision. The usual practice, once each issue was prepared, was for the journalism teacher to submit page proofs to the principal before the paper was printed.

The proofs for the May 13, 1983, issue of *Spectrum* caught the attention of principal Robert Reynolds. One article told the story of three students' experiences with pregnancy. The article's first sentences read: "Sixteen-year-old Sue had it all—good looks, good grades, a loving family and a cute boyfriend. She also had a seven pound baby boy." Another article dealt with divorce and its impact on students.

The principal had several concerns, as he later stated them. In the article on pregnancy, the girls' real names were omitted to protect their privacy, but Reynolds said he was able to identify them from other details in the story, and he worried that others would recognize them as well. In addition, he felt that some references to sexual activity in the article were inappropriate for younger students. As for the article on divorce, one of the named students who was quoted, a freshman, made critical remarks about her father that Reynolds felt the father should be allowed to rebut. Rather than ordering that the articles be revised, in order to meet publishing deadlines, Reynolds eliminated the pages on which the articles appeared.

Cathy Kuhlmeier and two other students who worked on the newspaper took the school to court, claiming their First Amendment rights had been violated. A federal judge rejected their claim, ruling that school officials had broad leeway to regulate activities that are "an integral part of the school's educational function."

But a federal appeals court ruled in favor of the students. By promising openness to student expression, the school newspaper had become a "public forum," the court said, sharply limiting the authority of school officials to censor it. Censoring these articles could not be justified, the court said, because there was "no evidence in the record that the principal could have reasonably forecast that the censored articles or any materials in the censored articles would have materially disrupted classwork or given rise to substantial disorder in the school." The court relied on the *Tinker* case in its decision. The stage was set for a major reexamination of student First Amendment rights by the Supreme Court.

VOTE

6–3, with Justice Byron R. White writing the majority opinion. Joining White were Chief Justice William Rehnquist and Justices John Paul Stevens, Sandra Day O'Connor, and Antonin Scalia. Dissenting were Justices William J. Brennan Jr., Thurgood Marshall, and Harry A. Blackmun.

HIGHLIGHTS

Justice White began by refuting any notion that the student newspaper was a "public forum," a legal term for a public place where expression generally cannot be suppressed, except for "time, place, or manner" restrictions.

Schools traditionally are not completely open forums, White said, so the newspaper could be regarded as a public forum only if the school had affirmatively defined it that way. Reviewing Hazelwood East's policies and practices, White concluded that "the evidence relied upon by the Court of Appeals fails to demonstrate the 'clear intent to create a public forum.'" As a result, White said, "School officials were entitled to regulate the contents of *Spectrum* in any reasonable manner. It is this standard, rather than our decision in *Tinker*, that governs this case."

To buttress that assertion, White emphasized the difference between a school-sponsored newspaper and the individualistic student expression—wearing an armband—protected in *Tinker*. "The question whether the First Amendment requires a school to tolerate particular student speech—the question that we addressed in *Tinker*—is different from the question whether the First Amendment requires a school affirmatively to promote particular student speech," White wrote. "A school must be able to set high standards for the student speech that is disseminated under its auspices—standards that may be higher than those demanded by some newspaper publishers or theatrical producers in the 'real' world—and may refuse to disseminate student speech that does not meet those standards."

The thrust of White's opinion was not to overturn *Tinker*, but to say that its standard did not apply to school-supported student newspapers. Justice Brennan in dissent argued that the majority had gone further than that and had weakened First Amendment protections for students. "Just as the public on the street corner must, in the interest of fostering 'enlightened opinion,' tolerate speech that 'tempt[s] [the listener] to throw [the speaker] off the street,' public educators must accommodate some student expression even if it offends them or offers views or values that contradict those the school wishes to inculcate," Brennan wrote.

Brennan, a leading champion of freedom of expression, said school officials had in fact created a public forum where students could express their views. The Court, Brennan said, had seriously weakened *Tinker*.

"*Tinker* teaches us that the state educator's undeniable, and undeniably vital, mandate to inculcate moral and political values is not a general warrant to act as 'thought police' stifling discussion of all but state-approved topics and advocacy of all but the official position. . . . The young men and women of Hazelwood East expected a civics lesson, but not the one the Court teaches them today," Brennan wrote.

EXCERPTS

From Justice White's majority opinion: "[W]e hold that educators do not offend the First Amendment by exercising editorial control over the style and content of student speech in school-sponsored expressive activities so long as their actions are reasonably related to legitimate pedagogical concerns.

"This standard is consistent with our oft-expressed view that the education of the Nation's youth is primarily the responsibility of parents, teachers, and state and local school officials, and not of federal judges. It is only when the decision to censor a school-sponsored publication, theatrical production, or other vehicle of student expression has no valid educational purpose that the First Amendment is so 'directly and sharply implicate[d],' as to require judicial intervention to protect students' constitutional rights. . . .

"We cannot reject as unreasonable Principal Reynolds' conclusion that neither the pregnancy article nor the divorce article was suitable for publication in *Spectrum*. Reynolds could reasonably have concluded that the students who had written and edited these articles had not sufficiently mastered those portions of the Journalism II curriculum that pertained to the treatment of controversial issues and personal attacks, the need to protect the privacy of individuals whose most intimate concerns are to be revealed in the newspaper, and 'the legal, moral, and ethical restrictions imposed upon journalists within [a] school community' that includes adolescent subjects and readers. Finally, we conclude that the principal's decision to delete two pages of *Spectrum*, rather than to delete only the offending articles or to require that they be modified, was reasonable under the circumstances as he understood them. Accordingly, no violation of First Amendment rights occurred."

IMPACT

To free speech advocates who had been encouraged by *Tinker*, the *Hazelwood* decision was a turn in the wrong direction. In their view, concern for discipline and order had taken precedence over teaching students the value of robust debate about issues important to their lives.

Student complaints of censorship rose sharply in the wake of *Hazelwood,* reports Mark Goodman, director of the Student Press Law Center, which helps students fight censorship. "At some schools, censorship has become standard procedure; at any school it is a threat," Goodman says. Some schools have responded by closing down student newspapers altogether to avoid litigation and complaints by parents. In other cases, school publications have become bland outlets for officially sanctioned news. *Hazelwood* is being applied to the full and widening range of student media, including yearbooks, drama, and Internet Web pages.

The Student Press Law Center offers suggestions to school newspapers to keep them vigorous in spite of the ruling. First, it urges students not to censor themselves out of fear of *Hazelwood*. It also urges that students seek to have their papers declared public forums or, alternatively, to take their newspapers off campus altogether or at least make them extracurricular. Post-*Hazelwood* rulings in lower courts have indicated that the farther away a publication is from school sponsorship, the easier it is to avoid censorship. Several states have countered *Hazelwood* by passing laws that guarantee free speech rights for students.

The Supreme Court has not indicated that it wants to reconsider *Hazelwood* and return to the days when the *Tinker* decision governed student expression. If anything, there is pressure on courts to expand the reach of *Hazelwood*. The Court in *Hazelwood* explicitly declined to decide whether its ruling covers expression at colleges as well as high schools. But in a 1999 case from Kentucky, a federal judge ruled that *Hazelwood* does apply to college publications. The judge invoked *Hazelwood* to uphold the actions of Kentucky State University in confiscating copies of the student yearbook. The U.S. Court of Appeals for the Sixth Circuit reversed that decision in 2001, finding that colleges are a forum for conflicting ideas and ruling that *Hazelwood* had "little application" to college publications. But in June 2005 the U.S. Court of Appeals for the Seventh Circuit reached the opposite conclusion in *Hosty v. Carter*. Officials at Governors State University in Illinois halted publication of the student newspaper after it printed stories critical of the dean. The appeals court said *Hazelwood* is "generally applicable" to college publications and protected university officials from being sued for their actions. The Supreme Court may be called on to resolve this disagreement among circuit courts.

FREEDOM OF SPEECH

*I*t surrounds us at all times: the raucous, intrusive, exciting, stimulating, and sometimes offensive cacophony of voices, media, and technology that dominate modern society. It is safe to say that without the protection of the First Amendment, this array of speech would be far less robust, far more timid, giving the nation a very different texture and feel. The First Amendment's command against making laws "abridging the freedom of speech," when it has been vigorously defended, keeps the censorious impulses of government in check. The Supreme Court, especially in the twentieth century, has been the leading guardian of freedom of speech. That freedom is challenged often, when issues ranging from national security to the protection of children to reforming elections are at stake. Some restrictions have been upheld, but most are not, and the notion of a "marketplace of ideas" usually prevails: that truth emerges from the competition of ideas, boldly expressed, rather than from government supervision of speech.

Other related cases mentioned in the Freedom of Speech section

Abrams v. United States (1919)
Gitlow v. New York (1925)
Whitney v. California (1927)
Minersville School District v. Gobitis (1940)
Yates v. United States (1957)
Roth v. United States (1957)
Noto v. United States (1961)
Jacobellis v. Ohio (1964)
Ginzburg v. United States (1966)
Redrup v. New York (1967)
United States v. O'Brien (1968)
Red Lion Broadcasting Co. v. Federal Communications Commission (1969) (see p. 120)
Cohen v. California (1971)
Paris Adult Theatre I v. Slaton (1973)
Jenkins v. Georgia (1974)
New York v. Ferber (1982)
Bethel School District v. Fraser (1986)
Hazelwood School District v. Kuhlmeier (1988) (see p. 134)
Boos v. Barry (1988)
United States v. Eichman (1990)
R.A.V. v. City of St. Paul (1992)
Colorado Republican Federal Campaign Committee v. Federal Election Commission (1996)
Ashcroft v. Free Speech Coalition (2002)
Ashcroft v. ACLU (2002)

Schenck v. United States

Decided March 3, 1919
249 U.S. 47
laws.findlaw.com/US/249/47.html

DECISION

The Espionage Act of 1917, which bars acts of insubordination and interference with military recruitment, is constitutional, even when it is used to punish speech that would be permissible in times of peace. The First Amendment is not absolute, and freedom of speech may be restricted when the expression poses a "clear and present danger" to values that Congress is entitled to protect.

BACKGROUND

Before the declaration of war in 1917, the idea of sending U.S. troops to fight the Germans and save the British was not popular with the American people. However, once Congress declared war, there was considerable pressure to stifle dissent about the war. Elihu Root, one of President Woodrow Wilson's advisers, said in early 1917, "We must have no criticism now."

Police surveillance increased, and Americans were encouraged to report their neighbors' "disloyal" acts. Congress enacted the Espionage Act of 1917, which made acts of insubordination and disloyalty punishable by prison terms of up to twenty years. It was the first time since the Alien and Sedition Acts early in the nation's history that criticism of government had been criminalized. Sponsors said that tolerating disloyal public statements might undermine efforts to draft and recruit young people into military service. More than 2,000 people were prosecuted under the act.

One of them was Charles Schenck, general secretary of Philadelphia's Socialist Party. In 1917 the party directed Schenck to prepare a leaflet that would be distributed to young men conscripted in the recently enacted military draft.

The party printed 15,000 copies of Schenck's leaflet, which compared conscription to slavery. It encouraged readers to sign a petition urging Congress to repeal the draft law but did not explicitly tell recipients to resist the draft. After some of the leaflets were mailed, federal officials arrested Schenck and other party officials under the Espionage Act. Schenck was tried, found guilty, and sentenced to six months in jail. His appeal went directly to the Supreme Court because it amounted to a challenge to the constitutionality of a federal law, which the Court could consider without prior review by an appeals court. It fell to Justice Oliver Wendell Holmes Jr. to write the Court's opinion.

The revered Justice Holmes had already given some thought to the Espionage Act. In the summer of 1918, he had a chance encounter with Judge Learned Hand, a federal district court judge who had recently ruled in favor of a magazine called *The Masses* in an Espionage Act case. The two discussed free speech issues and corresponded afterwards. Hand wrote to Holmes, "We must be tolerant of opposite opinions." Holmes replied that freedom of speech was no different from "freedom from vaccination" and could be restricted by a majority.

The exchange did not bode well for Schenck's chances before the justices, who were not immune to the general call to patriotism in wartime. As historian Peter Irons put it in the book *A People's History of the Supreme Court,* "In a symbolic but very real sense, the justices hung up their black robes and donned the khaki uniforms of American soldiers."

Justice Oliver Wendell Holmes Jr. served for twenty-nine years on the Supreme Court, retiring at the age of ninety. He may best be remembered for his opinions in free speech cases, including *Schenck v. United States* (1919), in which he stated that Congress could punish speech that posed a "clear and present danger." In later cases, however, Holmes objected to the Court's use of this standard to uphold convictions.

Source: Library of Congress.

VOTE

9–0, with Justice Oliver Wendell Holmes Jr. writing for the majority. Joining him were Chief Justice Edward D. White and Justices Joseph McKenna, William R. Day, Willis Van Devanter, Mahlon Pitney, James C. McReynolds, Louis D. Brandeis, and John H. Clarke.

HIGHLIGHTS

Justice Holmes's opinion is brief and direct. It deals with the First Amendment issue in just two paragraphs, which have lived on in importance.

The opinion starts by describing, in a disparaging tone, the contents of Schenck's leaflet. "In impassioned language it intimated that conscription was despotism in its worst form and a monstrous wrong against humanity in the interest of Wall Street's chosen few."

How does the leaflet violate the law? Drawing on the "bad tendency" test that courts traditionally had used to evaluate controversial speech, Holmes suggested it was a matter of common sense to conclude that the leaflet was aimed at discouraging conscription. "The document would not have been sent unless it had been intended to have some effect, and we do not see what effect it could be expected to have upon persons subject to the draft except to influence them to obstruct the carrying of it out," Holmes wrote.

Furthermore, Holmes said, showing that the leaflet actually succeeded in encouraging defiance of the draft was not necessary. "If the act (speaking or circulating a paper), its tendency and the intent with which it is done are the same, we perceive no ground for saying that success alone warrants making the act a crime."

Any qualms about restricting speech that ought to be protected by the First Amendment, Holmes concluded, should be alleviated by realizing that in times of war, extraordinary restrictions may be necessary.

EXCERPTS

From Justice Holmes's majority opinion: "We admit that in many places and in ordinary times the defendants in saying all that was said in the circular would have been within their constitutional rights. But the character of every act depends upon the circumstances in which it is done. The most stringent protection of free speech would not protect a man in falsely shouting fire in a theatre and causing a panic. It does not even protect a man from an injunction against uttering words that may have all the effect of force. The question in every case is whether the words used are used in such circumstances and are of such a nature as to create a clear and present danger that they will bring about the substantive evils that Congress has a right to prevent. It is a question of proximity and degree.

When a nation is at war many things that might be said in time of peace are such a hindrance to its effort that their utterance will not be endured so long as men fight and that no court could regard them as protected by any constitutional right."

IMPACT

Justice Holmes's brief ruling in *Schenck* contains some of the most familiar phrases contained in a Supreme Court opinion. "Clear and present danger" and "falsely shouting fire in a theatre" have become shorthand ways of expressing the limits to the protection of speech provided by the First Amendment.

But since Holmes used the phrase "clear and present danger," he and other judges have interpreted it in a variety of

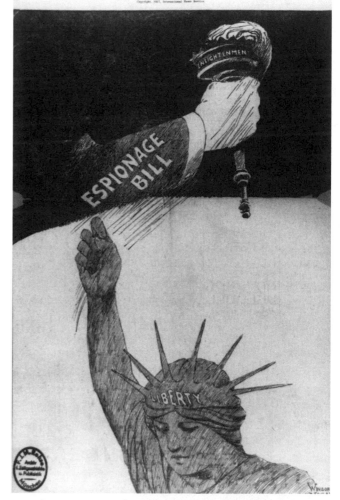

This 1917 wood engraving of the torch of "enlightenment" being snatched from the Statue of Liberty reflects disapproval of the Espionage Act of 1917. In *Schenck v. United States* (1919), the Supreme Court upheld the act, which bars acts of insubordination and interference with military recruitment, although it punished speech that would be permissible in times of peace. *Source: Library of Congress.*

ways—some more protective of speech than others. Chief Justice William Rehnquist, writing in *All the Laws But One,* a 1998 book on civil liberties in wartime, said of *Schenck,* "This notable opinion put some flesh and bones on the First Amendment, but Holmes's formula, like most formulas, raised questions of its own."

In *Schenck,* Holmes seemed to be saying that speech could be restricted if it had the tendency to cause a violation of law. In decisions a week after *Schenck,* one upholding the conviction of Socialist Party leader and presidential candidate Eugene V. Debs, Holmes repeated that view.

By November of that year, however, Holmes, perhaps persuaded by Hand's arguments, changed his opinion. In *Abrams v. United States,* the Court upheld another Sedition Act prosecution, citing *Schenck.* This time Holmes dissented, arguing that to justify restriction of speech, the danger to the country had to be not only "clear and present" but also immediate. Suppress-ing speech when the threat is not imminent would do damage to the "marketplace of ideas" essential to a democracy.

Since *Abrams,* the test has shifted even further to allow all speech except that which can be proven to incite direct and immediate lawlessness. *Schenck* was the Court's starting point on a path that has led to an extraordinary level of protection for even the most unpopular and hateful speech. (See *Brandenburg v. Ohio*; *Texas v. Johnson.*)

One further note: *Schenck* is often described as the first case in which the Supreme Court was asked to overturn a federal law on the basis of First Amendment free speech grounds. Recent scholarship by University of Texas law professor David Rabban, reported in the 1997 book *Free Speech in Its Forgotten Years,* suggests that is not the case. He describes numerous free speech debates and lawsuits that resulted in First Amendment rulings by the Supreme Court and the lower courts in the late nineteenth and early twentieth century.

Chaplinsky v. New Hampshire

Decided March 9, 1942
315 U.S. 568
laws.findlaw.com/US/315/568.html

DECISION

State laws that make it a crime to use words that would provoke a breach of the peace do not violate the First Amendment's protection of free expression if the laws are carefully written to prohibit only the kinds of face-to-face expression that would provoke an average person to fight.

BACKGROUND

The First Amendment appears to be an absolute prohibition on laws regulating speech, as in "Congress shall make no law. . . ." But the Supreme Court has found exceptions to the rule, at times denying certain types of expression—such as obscene or libelous speech—First Amendment protection.

The question before the Court in this case was whether Walter Chaplinsky's words were the kind of speech that warranted First Amendment protection. Chaplinsky, a Jehovah's Witness, was distributing religious literature on the streets of Rochester, New Hampshire, one Saturday afternoon. As he did, he proclaimed that organized religions were a "racket" and made other disparaging remarks about specific religious groups. Offended residents reported him to the police, who at first said Chaplinsky was within his rights.

When the police warned Chaplinsky that residents were getting "restless" about his pronouncements, Chaplinsky called the local marshal a fascist. At some point, a "disturbance" broke out, and Chaplinsky was arrested under a New Hampshire law stating that "no person shall address any offensive, derisive or annoying word to any other person who is lawfully in any street or other public place." He was convicted in a jury trial, but appealed, claiming the law violated the First Amendment. The New Hampshire Supreme Court upheld the law and the conviction.

VOTE

9–0, with Justice Frank Murphy writing the majority opinion. Joining him were Chief Justice Harlan Fiske Stone, Justices Owen J. Roberts, Hugo L. Black, Stanley F. Reed, Felix Frankfurter, William O. Douglas, James F. Byrnes, and Robert H. Jackson.

HIGHLIGHTS

Chaplinsky's main claim was that the New Hampshire law under which he was arrested was unconstitutionally vague—meaning that it was too unclear for people to know when they were disobeying it. The Court dismissed that objection. Justice Murphy cited the New Hampshire court's pronouncement that "the English language has a number of words and expressions which, by general consent, are 'fighting words' when said without a disarming smile. . . . [S]uch words, as ordinary men know, are likely to cause a fight." Words such as *fascist* or *racketeer* clearly fit that category, he said.

Murphy concluded, "A statute punishing verbal acts, carefully drawn so as not unduly to impair liberty of expression, is not too vague for a criminal law."

EXCERPTS

From Justice Murphy's majority opinion: "It is well understood that the right of free speech is not absolute at all times and under all circumstances. There are certain well-defined and narrowly limited classes of speech, the prevention and punishment of which have never been thought to raise any Constitutional problem. These include the lewd and obscene, the profane, the libelous, and the insulting or 'fighting' words—those which, by their very utterance, inflict injury or tend to incite an immediate breach of the peace. It has been well observed that such utterances are no essential part of any exposition of ideas, and are of such slight social value as a step to truth that any benefit that may be derived from them is clearly outweighed by the social interest in order and morality."

IMPACT

Chaplinsky was the last case in which the Court upheld a conviction of someone using "fighting words" when addressing a public official. Subsequent rulings have narrowed it to make it clear that only "in-your-face" pronouncements that cause imminent lawlessness could be barred. Insulting a police officer, which seemed like fighting words to the 1942 Court, would almost certainly not fit that definition today. In the 1971 decision *Cohen v. California,* the Court reversed the conviction of a man who was arrested for wearing inside a courthouse a jacket inscribed with the slogan *Fuck the Draft.* Because the words were not an insult directed to anyone in particular, they could not fit the *Chaplinsky* test, the Court said.

The *Chaplinsky* standard, however, has remained relevant. In the 1980s and 1990s more than 300 college campuses, concerned about discrimination against minorities, enacted "speech codes." The codes generally prohibited offensive or threatening language. Some leading intellectuals and civil rights leaders began to argue that the First Amendment, by protecting racist speech, had become a tool of oppression. Harvard's Henry Louis Gates Jr. wrote an article entitled "Is the First Amendment Racist?" Gates wrote, "Those who would regulate hate speech argue that racist abuse is a variety of . . . the sort of language that the *Chaplinsky* decision declared to be unprotected."

A backlash developed against what some called the "political correctness" of speech codes, and those enacted at state universities were especially suspect, because they amounted to government restrictions on speech that did not meet the *Chaplinsky* standard. Derogatory speech, as hateful as it was, could not often meet the "fighting words" definition of *Chaplinsky.*

The trend toward enacting speech codes slowed in 1992 after the Supreme Court ruled in *R.A.V. v. City of St. Paul* a city ordinance unconstitutional. The ordinance stated, among other things, that anyone who places a burning cross or Nazi swastika, "which one knows or has reasonable grounds to know arouses anger, alarm, or resentment in others on the basis of race, color, creed, religion, or gender commits disorderly conduct and shall be guilty of a misdemeanor."

The case concerned a juvenile known as R.A.V. who, along with two others, burned a cross in the fenced backyard of a black family and was charged with violating the ordinance. When his case reached the U.S. Supreme Court, the justices unanimously declared the ordinance unconstitutional because it singled out for punishment certain forms of expression based on content, but not all kinds of "fighting words."

Justice Antonin Scalia wrote the Court's opinion in *R.A.V.* "St. Paul's brief asserts that a general 'fighting words' law would not meet the city's needs," Scalia wrote, "because only a content-specific measure can communicate to minority groups that the 'group hatred' aspect of . . . speech 'is not condoned by the majority.' The point of the First Amendment is that majority preferences must be expressed in some fashion other than silencing speech on the basis of its content."

West Virginia State Board of Education v. Barnette

Decided June 14, 1943
319 U.S. 624
laws.findlaw.com/US/319/624.html

DECISION

States violate the First and Fourteenth Amendments to the Constitution when they require public school students to stand and recite the Pledge of Allegiance. The First Amendment guarantee of freedom of speech prohibits government from compelling Jehovah's Witnesses or anyone else to declare beliefs that are contrary to their own principles.

BACKGROUND

For a remarkable period during the 1930s and 1940s, members of the Jehovah's Witnesses religion were the targets of widespread persecution and discrimination in the United States. When the Jehovah's Witnesses turned to the courts to vindicate their rights, the ensuing litigation produced several notable Supreme Court decisions—nearly two dozen from 1938 to 1946. Several had a major impact on First Amendment law.

Some of the worst persecution of Witnesses came after the Supreme Court's 1940 decision in *Minersville School District v. Gobitis.* In that 8–1 decision written by Justice Felix Frankfurter, the Court upheld the expulsion of Jehovah's Witnesses from public school for refusing to salute the flag. In the interest of "national unity," Frankfurter argued, the state could enforce the flag salute requirement even if it impacted the Witnesses' religious beliefs.

The ruling came at a time of war nervousness in the United States, when seemingly "disloyal" acts, such as the refusal to recite the pledge, were seen as threats to national security. In 1940 and 1941 anti-Witness violence was reported nationwide, and some historians have traced it to the *Gobitis* decision, which may have been read as license to discriminate against Jehovah's Witnesses generally. "No religious organization has suffered such persecution since the days of the Mormons," the American Civil Liberties Union reported in 1941. It estimated that more than 1,000 Witnesses had been attacked in 236 separate incidents.

In part because of this public reaction, as well as widespread criticism of the *Gobitis* decision in the academic community, several of the justices in the majority had second thoughts about the ruling. In the context of another Jehovah's Witness case in 1942, Justices Black, Douglas, and Murphy joined in an extraordinary separate opinion. "Since we joined in the opinion in the *Gobitis* case," they stated, "we think this is an appropriate occasion to state that we now believe that it was also wrongly decided." Douglas indicated in his memoirs that he had been "naïve" in the *Gobitis* case and had, like other justices, been swayed by the powerful intellect of Justice Frankfurter. "In those days, Felix Frankfurter was our hero," Douglas wrote.

In the meantime, the membership of the Court was also changing. Conservative justice James McReynolds retired and was replaced by James F. Byrnes. Byrnes left sixteen months later and was replaced by Wiley Rutledge, an Iowa law dean known as a civil libertarian. Harlan Stone, who was the lone dissenter in *Gobitis,* was elevated to chief justice. In his place, President Franklin Roosevelt named his attorney general, Robert Jackson, as an associate justice.

With the change in personnel plus the change of heart, it appeared that *Gobitis* was ripe for reversal. The possibility for such action soon emerged from West Virginia, where the state legislature, like many others, had responded to *Gobitis* by requiring schools to promote the "spirit of Americanism" through the curriculum and school activities. The state board of education, in turn, ordered all public school students and teachers to recite the Pledge of Allegiance regularly. Refusal to do so would be viewed as an "act of subordination" and could result in expulsion.

That is what happened to seven children of Jehovah's Witness families who refused to recite the pledge. After the children were expelled, school officials threatened to send them to reformatories for juvenile lawbreakers. Their parents, led by Walter Barnette, whose two daughters had been expelled from elementary school, challenged the action. A three-judge panel, noting that four justices now appeared opposed to *Gobitis,* ordered that the flag salute requirement not be enforced. The stage was set for a second look at the issue of Jehovah's Witnesses and the Pledge of Allegiance.

VOTE

6–3, with Justice Robert H. Jackson writing for the majority. He was joined by Chief Justice Harlan Fiske Stone and Justices Hugo L. Black, William O. Douglas, Francis W. Murphy, and Wiley B. Rutledge. Justices Felix Frankfurter, Owen Roberts, and Stanley Reed dissented.

HIGHLIGHTS

The Court released the *Barnette* decision, aptly enough, on Flag Day of 1943. A Court that had supported the flag salute requirement just three years earlier had changed its mind—one of the swiftest and most dramatic reversals in Supreme Court history.

The Court's majority opinion reached its new view in part by looking at the case as one involving freedom of speech rather than freedom of religion. The salute, the Court decided, "is a form of utterance. Symbolism is a primitive but effective way of communicating ideas. The use of an emblem or flag to symbolize some system, idea, institution, or personality is a shortcut from mind to mind."

Seen in that way, it would have been hard for the Court to uphold a form of forced speech. Jackson wrote, "To sustain the compulsory flag salute, we are required to say that a Bill of Rights which guards the individual's right to speak his own mind left it open to public authorities to compel him to utter what is not in his mind." In addition, analyzing it as a speech case allowed the Court to avoid the need to determine the sincerity of the Jehovah's Witnesses' religious views.

The Court's new opposition to the forced pledge also was founded on a new view of the ability of the First Amendment to limit state and local government as well as federal government actions. In *Gobitis* the Court said it did not want to become "the school board for the country." But now the Court said, "The Fourteenth Amendment, as now applied to the States, protects the citizen against the State itself and all of its creatures—Boards of Education not excepted."

Fundamentally, the decision was based on the Court's notion that forced allegiance to the flag was not the way to achieve national unity. Fostering robust debate and disagreement over important matters was a far more effective way to avoid damaging divisiveness.

Justice Frankfurter, the author of the *Gobitis* decision, was bitter in defeat in *Barnette*. Frankfurter, who was Jewish, wrote, "One who belongs to the most vilified and persecuted minority in history is not likely to be insensible to the freedoms guaranteed by our Constitution. Were my purely personal attitude relevant, I should wholeheartedly associate myself with the general libertarian views in the Court's opinion, representing, as they do, the thought and action of a lifetime. But, as judges, we are neither Jew nor Gentile, neither Catholic nor agnostic. We owe equal attachment to the Constitution. . . . I cannot bring my mind to believe that the 'liberty' secured by the Due Process Clause gives this Court authority to deny to the State of West Virginia the attainment of that which we all recognize as a legitimate legislative end, namely, the promotion of good citizenship, by employment of the means here chosen."

EXCERPTS

From Justice Jackson's majority opinion: "The very purpose of a Bill of Rights was to withdraw certain subjects from the vicissitudes of political controversy, to place them beyond the reach of majorities and officials and to establish them as legal principles to be applied by the courts. One's right to life, liberty, and property, to free speech, a free press, freedom of worship and assembly, and other fundamental rights may not be submitted to vote; they depend on the outcome of no elections. . . .

"National unity as an end which officials may foster by persuasion and example is not in question. The problem is whether under our Constitution compulsion as here employed is a permissible means for its achievement. . . .

"Those who begin coercive elimination of dissent soon find themselves exterminating dissenters. Compulsory unification of opinion achieves only the unanimity of the graveyard. . . .

"If there is any fixed star in our constitutional constellation, it is that no official, high or petty, can prescribe what shall be orthodox in politics, nationalism, religion, or other matters of opinion or force citizens to confess by word or act their faith therein. If there are any circumstances which permit an exception, they do not now occur to us."

IMPACT

The Court's decision in *Barnette,* especially Justice Jackson's words quoted above, stands as one of the most forceful and eloquent statements anywhere of the meaning of freedom and individual liberties in the U.S. system. It has been invoked in more than one hundred cases since—sometimes in dissent, sometimes in majority opinions—as the justification for protecting, even cherishing, unpopular opinions and religions. *Barnette* "has become a hallmark of the freedom of conscience," according to Florida International University constitutional scholar Thomas Baker. The diversity—some would call it cacophony—of American voices today can be traced to the libertarian principles laid down in *Barnette*.

The decision is all the more remarkable because it came during wartime, when governments often clamp down on dissent. The fact that the Court was able to resist nationalistic urges during World War II is a testimony to its independence.

Barnette also established a principle that has evolved since to make it more difficult than ever before for government to justify laws and regulations that impinge on First Amendment freedoms. While most laws can be justified as having a "rational basis," the Court in *Barnette* said legislators needed to meet a higher standard to justify laws that regulate expression or religion. "The right of a State to regulate, for example, a public utility may well include, so far as the due process test is concerned, power to impose all of the restrictions which a legislature may have a 'rational basis' for adopting. But freedoms of speech and of press, of assembly, and of worship may not be infringed on such slender grounds."

Dennis v. United States

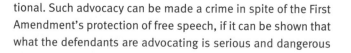

Decided June 4, 1951
341 U.S. 494
laws.findlaw.com/US/341/494.html

DECISION

A federal law that makes it a crime to teach, advocate, or conspire to advocate the overthrow of the government is constitutional. Such advocacy can be made a crime in spite of the First Amendment's protection of free speech, if it can be shown that what the defendants are advocating is serious and dangerous enough to warrant being restricted. The fact that the threat to overthrow the government is not imminent does not mean it cannot be punished.

BACKGROUND

Just before the outbreak of World War II, Congress passed the Smith Act—named for its sponsor, Rep. Howard Smith, D-Va. The Soviet Union had just allied itself with Germany, and Congress thought it was necessary to give the government tools to combat communists and Soviet sympathizers in the United States. The Smith Act made it unlawful "to knowingly or willfully advocate, abet, advise, or teach the duty, necessity, desirability, or propriety of overthrowing or destroying any government in the United States by force or violence." Organizing a group that advocated such acts, or conspiring to commit these acts, was also made a crime.

The law saw little use at first: The course of the war changed, and the Soviet Union became an ally of the United States, not an enemy. When the war ended, however, animosities resumed, and rooting out the "communist threat" became a popular battle cry for U.S. politicians.

In 1948 a grand jury in New York City indicted twelve leaders of the Communist Party of the United States, including Eugene Dennis, the general secretary of the party. Gus Hall, who later became the leader of the Communist Party, was another defendant. By the time the trial began in January 1949, one of the defendants had been separated because of illness, so eleven men stood trial.

Federal judge Harold Medina presided over the trial, which turned into a raucous, highly publicized nine-month proceeding. Demonstrators sympathetic to the communists picketed outside the courthouse protesting what they saw as Medina's biased handling of the case. The evidence presented against the eleven was general in nature, with little proof that these defendants had specifically advocated the overthrow of the government. But all eleven were found guilty, and Medina became a national hero.

The defendants appealed, and their case was ruled on by a panel that included Judge Learned Hand. Thirty years earlier, Hand had debated with Justice Oliver Wendell Holmes Jr. about the "clear and present danger" test Holmes had devised in *Schenck v. United States* (1919) for assessing whether contro-

Eugene Dennis, general secretary of the Communist Party, boards a prison bus in New York City on July 6, 1951. He and other communist leaders were found guilty under the Smith Act of 1940, which made it a federal crime to advocate the forceful overthrow of the U.S. government. Their convictions were upheld when the court judged the law constitutional in *Dennis v. United States* (1951). *Source: AP/Wide World Photos.*

versial speech could be restricted. (See *Schenck v. United States.*)

Since then the definition of "clear and present danger" had evolved considerably, and Hand was again considering its meaning. Earlier, Hand had urged that speech be restricted only if it posed an immediate threat. But now, he seemed to be saying, in grave situations government should not have to wait until the threat was imminent before acting.

In upholding the conviction of the eleven communists, Hand devised a new formula for determining whether speech like theirs could be punished: "In each case, [courts] must ask whether the gravity of the 'evil,' discounted by its improbability, justifies such invasion of free speech as is necessary to avoid the danger." It was a standard that made it easier to prosecute communists even if any threat they posed was not imminent.

The case arrived at the Supreme Court just as anticommunist fervor was reaching an intense level. Sen. Joseph McCarthy, R-Wis., had emerged as an intimidating communist-hunter and was doing his best to keep Americans frightened and suspicious.

VOTE

6–2, with Chief Justice Fred M. Vinson announcing the judgment of the Court. Joining him were Justices Stanley F. Reed, Felix Frankfurter, Robert H. Jackson, Harold H. Burton, and Sherman Minton. Dissenting were Justices Hugo L. Black and William O. Douglas. Justice Tom C. Clark, who was attorney general when the *Dennis* prosecution was initiated, did not participate.

HIGHLIGHTS

Chief Justice Vinson's opinion was a plurality opinion, meaning that a majority of the justices agreed with the decision, but not with the legal reasoning behind it. Vinson began by stating that it was not for the Supreme Court to decide whether the evidence of Smith Act violations presented at the trial of the eleven communists was weak or strong. The Court was obliged to accept the lower courts' view that the defendants' espousal of communism was sufficient to prove a violation of the law. The question before the Supreme Court was whether the law itself was constitutional.

Vinson left no doubt that the goal of protecting the democratically elected government from overthrow justified extraordinary measures. "We reject any principle of governmental helplessness in the face of preparation for revolution, which principle, carried to its logical conclusion, must lead to anarchy," he wrote.

But did the law violate the First Amendment? Not as Vinson read it. He said the law does not restrict debates about the merits of communism—which would be protected speech—but targets the communists' advocacy of overthrowing the government. "It is directed at advocacy, not discussion," Vinson said—a distinction that might be difficult to define.

Reviewing First Amendment doctrine and the clear and present danger test, he concluded it could not mean that the government had to wait until the danger was imminent to act. It adopted Judge Hand's new formula and concluded that even an embryonic effort to advocate the overthrow of government was dangerous. "It is the existence of the conspiracy which creates the danger," Vinson said. On that basis, the convictions were upheld.

Justices Frankfurter and Jackson wrote concurring opinions in which they distanced themselves from Vinson's reasoning, but agreed with the result.

Frankfurter expressed doubts that the Smith Act could be enforced without doing some damage to the First Amendment. "No matter how clear we may be that the defendants now before us are preparing to overthrow our Government at the propitious moment, it is self-delusion to think that we can punish them for their advocacy without adding to the risks run by loyal citizens who honestly believe in some of the reforms these defendants advance." But Frankfurter was willing to set aside his doubts in deference to Congress. "[E]ven when free speech is involved we attach great significance to the determination of the legislature," Frankfurter said.

Justice Jackson, for his part, also doubted the effectiveness of putting communists in prison. "While I think there was power in Congress to enact this statute and that, as applied in this case, it cannot be held unconstitutional, I add that I have little faith in the long-range effectiveness of this conviction to stop the rise of the Communist movement. Communism will not go to jail with these Communists."

Justice Black, known as a First Amendment absolutist, objected strenuously to the majority's view. "The opinions for affirmance indicate that the chief reason for jettisoning the [clear and present danger] rule is the expressed fear that advocacy of Communist doctrine endangers the safety of the Republic," Black wrote in his dissent. "Undoubtedly a governmental policy of unfettered communication of ideas does entail dangers. To the Founders of this Nation, however, the benefits derived from free expression were worth the risk."

"Public opinion being what it now is," Black continued, "few will protest the conviction of these Communist petitioners. There is hope, however, that, in calmer times, when present pressures, passions and fears subside, this or some later Court will restore the First Amendment liberties to the high preferred place where they belong in a free society."

Justice Douglas, a believer in protecting vigorous debate, also dissented. "Some nations less resilient than the United States, where illiteracy is high and where democratic traditions are only budding, might have to take drastic steps and jail these men for merely speaking their creed," said Douglas. "But in America, they are miserable merchants of unwanted ideas; their wares remain unsold."

EXCERPTS

From Justice Vinson's plurality opinion: "Overthrow of the Government by force and violence is certainly a substantial enough interest for the Government to limit speech. Indeed, this is the ultimate value of any society, for if a society cannot protect its very structure from armed internal attack, it must follow that no subordinate value can be protected. If, then, this interest may be protected, the literal problem which is presented is what has been meant by the use of the phrase 'clear and present danger' of the utterances bringing about the evil within the power of Congress to punish.

"Obviously, the words cannot mean that before the Government may act, it must wait until the putsch is about to be executed, the plans have been laid and the signal is awaited. If

Government is aware that a group aiming at its overthrow is attempting to indoctrinate its members and to commit them to a course whereby they will strike when the leaders feel the circumstances permit, action by the Government is required."

IMPACT

The Court's *Dennis* decision served as a green light to the Justice Department, which responded by indicting dozens of other people under the Smith Act.

The Court modified its views on the Smith Act somewhat in the 1957 case *Yates v. United States,* which involved the conviction of fourteen communist leaders. The Court offered a narrower interpretation of the law. "The Smith Act does not prohibit advocacy and teaching of forcible overthrow of the Government as an abstract principle, divorced from any effort to instigate action to that end," the Court said in *Yates*. While

not overturning *Dennis,* it made prosecutions under the law more difficult, and no more were ever pursued.

More broadly, the *Dennis* case represented the Court's willingness to join in the anticommunism wave sweeping the nation. The Court, like the rest of the government, regarded the views espoused by the communists, which might have seemed harmless or fanciful coming from others, as more dangerous and serious because communists were uttering them. That attitude persisted even after Senator McCarthy and his investigations were discredited. As Nat Hentoff wrote of the *Dennis* case in his book *The First Freedom,* "The First Amendment is usually most endangered when the nation is most fearful."

Looking back at the *Dennis* decision, Justice Douglas said in a 1969 speech that it was the culmination of "an all-out political trial which was part and parcel of the cold war that has eroded substantial parts of the First Amendment."

Brandenburg v. Ohio

Decided June 9, 1969
395 U.S. 444
laws.findlaw.com/US/395/444.html

DECISION

State laws that make it a crime merely to advocate the use of violence violate the First Amendment. Only when the advocacy is aimed at inciting "imminent lawless action," and is likely to succeed, may government prohibit it.

BACKGROUND

Following the assassination of President William McKinley in 1901 by an anarchist and the start of the communist movement in 1917, states began passing antisedition laws and so-called "criminal syndicalism" statutes. These laws, passed in thirty-three states, prohibited teaching or advocating the use of violence or crime to bring about political or economic change. The motivation behind the syndicalism laws in most cases was to discourage the spread of socialist or communist anticapitalist views.

In a line of cases beginning with *Schenck v. United States* (1919) and *Abrams v. United States* (1919), the Supreme Court declared that First Amendment freedoms were not absolute. Justice Oliver Wendell Holmes Jr. wrote the Court's opinion in *Schenck,* saying that "if the words used . . . create a clear and present danger," then the freedom of speech and the press may be constrained. (See *Schenck v. United States.*) Holmes, however, dissented in *Abrams*. The leaflet critical of World War I

that resulted in the convictions of Abrams and several fellow anarchists posed no real danger, according to Holmes.

In *Gitlow v. New York* (1925) the Court upheld the conviction of Benjamin Gitlow, who had violated the state's criminal anarchy law by distributing a pamphlet called *The Left Wing Manifesto*. Gitlow's pamphlet called for the overthrow of the capitalist system in the United States. Although he lost his appeal, Gitlow's case is notable because the Court used the due process clause of the Fourteenth Amendment to guarantee freedom of speech against "impairment by the States." This doctrine, known as incorporation, gradually applied most of the freedoms mentioned in the Bill of Rights, which applies only to Congress, to the states. Holmes again dissented, saying that the clear and present danger test should be applied and that Gitlow's pamphlet did not pose such a danger.

In *Whitney v. California* (1927) the Court upheld the conviction of Charlotte Whitney, a California heiress and niece of a former Supreme Court justice, Stephen J. Field. Through her membership in a communist group, Whitney had violated California's syndicalism law, which made it a crime to create and participate in an organization that advocated the overthrow of the government by force. Although the decision was unanimous, Justice Louis Brandeis's stirring concurrence sounded more like a dissent. "Fear of serious injury cannot alone justify suppression of free speech and assembly," he wrote. "Men feared witches and burnt women. It is the function of speech to free men from the bondage of irrational fears. To justify suppression of free speech there must be reasonable ground to fear that serious evil will result if free speech is practiced. There must be reasonable ground to believe that the danger apprehended is imminent. There must be reasonable ground to believe that the evil to be prevented is a serious one. . . . Those who won our independence by revolution were not cowards. They did not fear political change. They did not exalt order at the cost of liberty. To courageous, self-reliant men, with confidence in the power of free and fearless reasoning applied through the processes of popular government, no danger flowing from speech can be deemed clear and present, unless the incidence of the evil apprehended is so imminent that it may befall before there is opportunity for full discussion. . . . Only an emergency can justify repression."

The case decided by the Supreme Court in 1969 concerned not a communist but a leader of the Ku Klux Klan. With the cameras of a local crew running, the red-hooded Clarence Brandenburg spoke to a Klan rally held at a farm in Hamilton County, Ohio. "Personally, I believe the nigger should be re-

Free speech was an area of special concern for Justice Abe Fortas, who was slated to write the opinion in *Brandenburg v. Ohio* (1969) striking down a state law criminalizing the advocacy of violence. Fortas was forced to resign from the Court amid allegations of improper business dealings, and the *Brandenburg* decision was issued per curiam (by the Court).

Source: Harris & Ewing, Collection of the Supreme Court of the United States.

turned to Africa, the Jew returned to Israel," Brandenburg says in one segment of the film. At another point, Brandenburg, taking some liberties with the English language, makes a threat of sorts: "We're not a revengent organization, but if our President, our Congress, our Supreme Court, continues to suppress the white, Caucasian race, it's possible that there might have to be some revengeance."

Based on his speech, Brandenburg was convicted for violating the state's criminal syndicalism law, fined $1,000, and sentenced to one to ten years in prison. He appealed, challenging the law as a violation of his free speech rights. The Supreme Court of Ohio dismissed the appeal, setting the stage for Supreme Court review.

Chief Justice Warren, according to historians, initially assigned the opinion to Justice Abe Fortas, who wrote a draft. Fortas meanwhile became embroiled in a scandal that resulted in his resignation, and, according to Court scholar Bernard Schwartz, Justice William J. Brennan Jr. revised the draft. Perhaps because of these unusual circumstances, the ruling was issued per curiam, or by the Court, rather than under the name of a specific justice.

VOTE

8–0, decided by an unsigned (per curiam) opinion of the Court. The eight were Chief Justice Earl Warren and Justices Hugo L. Black, William O. Douglas, John M. Harlan, William J. Brennan Jr., Potter Stewart, Byron R. White, and Thurgood Marshall. Justice Abe Fortas resigned the month before the ruling was issued and had not yet been replaced.

HIGHLIGHTS

The Court's brief opinion in *Brandenburg* cited the evolving clear and present danger doctrine, first enunciated in *Abrams,* and further refined it. The opinion noted that *"Whitney* has been thoroughly discredited by later decisions," notably *Dennis v. United States.* That 1951 ruling upheld the conviction of U.S. Communist Party leaders based on a modified and looser version of the test. (See *Dennis v. United States.*)

The cumulative effect of these later rulings, in the Court's view, was to lay down the principle that "the constitutional guarantees of free speech and free press do not permit a State to forbid or proscribe advocacy of the use of force or of law violation except where such advocacy is directed to inciting or producing imminent lawless action and is likely to incite or produce such action."

Under that principle, neither the Ohio law nor the *Whitney* decision could stand. The Ohio law criminalized speech whether or not it had any likelihood of actually triggering lawlessness, something the Court said the First Amendment would not tolerate.

Justices Black and Douglas wrote concurring opinions that agreed with the result in *Brandenburg,* but they distanced themselves from the still-controversial clear and present danger test. "I see no place in the regime of the First Amendment for any 'clear and present danger' test, whether strict and tight, as some would make it, or free-wheeling, as the Court in *Dennis* rephrased it," wrote Douglas.

EXCERPTS

Per curiam: "As we said in *Noto v. United States* (1961), 'the mere abstract teaching . . . of the moral propriety or even moral necessity for a resort to force and violence is not the same as preparing a group for violent action and steeling it to such action.' A statute which fails to draw this distinction impermissibly intrudes upon the freedoms guaranteed by the First and Fourteenth Amendments. It sweeps within its condemnation speech which our Constitution has immunized from governmental control.

"Measured by this test, Ohio's Criminal Syndicalism Act cannot be sustained. . . .

". . . [W]e are here confronted with a statute which, by its own words and as applied, purports to punish mere advocacy and to forbid, on pain of criminal punishment, assembly with others merely to advocate the described type of action. Such a statute falls within the condemnation of the First and Fourteenth Amendments. The contrary teaching of *Whitney v. California* cannot be supported, and that decision is therefore overruled."

IMPACT

Although brief and unsigned, the *Brandenburg* decision has been seen as one of the most expansive interpretations of the First Amendment ever announced by the Supreme Court. *New York Times* columnist Anthony Lewis wrote that *Brandenburg* "gave the greatest protection to what could be called subversive speech that it has ever had in the United States, and almost certainly greater than such speech has in any other country."

University of Richmond First Amendment scholar Rodney Smolla has described *Brandenburg* as "one of the genuine lodestars of modern First Amendment jurisprudence." It appeared to add another layer to the clear and present danger test, making it more difficult for government to justify censoring controversial speech. For provocative speech to fall outside the protection of the First Amendment, the Court seemed to be saying, it had to pose not just a clear and present danger of lawful action, but a likely, rather than speculative, danger.

Brandenburg has been invoked as a shield for controversial speech. In *Texas v. Johnson* (1989) Brennan said that if the Court upheld a law banning desecration of the American flag, it would eviscerate *Brandenburg.* More recently, *Brandenburg* has played a role in several lawsuits filed against media organizations claiming that television shows, movies, or books have provoked people to commit suicide, murder, or other dangerous acts. The *Brandenburg* test has bolstered the media's claim that under the First Amendment, they cannot be held liable for those actions.

In 1997 an appeals court ruled that even the *Brandenburg* test could not protect a book that went beyond abstract advocacy to provide detailed instructions on committing a crime. In the Maryland case, the families of three 1993 murder victims sued the publishers of a book called *Hit Man,* an instruction manual for committing murder, which the perpetrator had read. A federal judge initially threw out the suit, citing *Brandenburg* and concluding that the book was protected under the First Amendment because it was not aimed at inciting imminent lawless acts. The Supreme Court in 1998 declined to hear the case, allowing the suit to proceed to trial. In May 1999, however, the parties settled the case, with the publisher agreeing to pay the families an unspecified amount and to stop selling the book.

One sign of the enduring force of the *Brandenburg* decision is, ironically, what did not happen after the terrorist attacks of September 11, 2001. In past wars, presidents to varying degrees have tried to censor speech viewed as subversive to the war effort. By and large that did not occur as the United States went to war in Afghanistan and Iraq. In *Perilous Times,* a 2005 book on free speech in wartime, author Geoffrey Stone asserts that "Although presidents often push the envelope when the law is unclear, they do not defy established constitutional doctrine." *Brandenburg,* he wrote, is an example of one such settled doctrine, established in a nonwartime setting, that keeps presidents in check once a war begins.

Tinker v. Des Moines Independent Community School District

Decided February 24, 1969
393 U.S. 503
laws.findlaw.com/US/393/503.html

DECISION

Students have the First Amendment right to express themselves in public schools so long as they are not disruptive and do not impinge on the rights of others. As a result, students who wore black armbands to protest the Vietnam War should not have been suspended. Their symbolic protest was akin to the kind of "pure speech" that deserves a maximum amount of First Amendment protection.

BACKGROUND

The United States' growing involvement in the Vietnam War in the 1960s triggered nationwide protests, some of which became violent. The protests that triggered the landmark case of *Tinker v. Des Moines Independent Community School District,* however, were low-key.

A group of public school students met one December night in 1965 at the home of high school sophomore Christopher Eckhardt to talk about how to protest the Vietnam War. They decided to wear black armbands, a silent symbol that would demonstrate mourning for people who had died on both sides of the conflict as well as support the call for a Christmas truce in the conflict.

"We didn't think it was going to be that big of a deal," Mary Beth Tinker wrote later in an essay in Peter Irons's book *The Courage of Their Convictions.* But it did turn into a big deal. As word of the planned protest spread, principals of the city's schools met and decided that anyone who wore an armband and refused to take it off when asked would be suspended.

Mary Beth Tinker, an eighth grader; her brother John, who was in high school; and Eckhardt were all suspended for wearing armbands on December 16, 1965. In the local newspaper the next day, the school board president said the armband policy was aimed at preventing "disturbing influences" on the students.

At a subsequent school board meeting packed with parents and others interested in the armband issue, the parents of the suspended students asked that the suspensions be revoked. Students and a lawyer for the Iowa Civil Liberties Union reminded the board that other students had been allowed to wear armbands in other situations, such as to mourn the death of people killed in the civil rights movement. The school board voted 4–3 to continue the ban on armbands.

The parents initiated a lawsuit, and a federal judge was asked to reverse the suspensions on the grounds that the punishment violated the First Amendment rights of the students. The judge said the board was entitled to enact policies to protect "the disciplined atmosphere of the classroom." The federal appeals court divided evenly in the case, which then went to the Supreme Court.

The Court, under Chief Justice Earl Warren, had expanded the protections of the First Amendment, but the *Tinker* case pitted First Amendment interests against the Court's traditional deference to school officials in matters of discipline.

VOTE

7–2, with Justice Abe Fortas writing the majority opinion. Joining Fortas were Chief Justice Earl Warren and Justices William O. Douglas, William J. Brennan Jr., Thurgood Marshall, Potter Stewart, and Byron R. White. Dissenting were Justices Hugo L. Black and John M. Harlan.

HIGHLIGHTS

Justice Fortas, step by step, built a case against the actions of the Des Moines school officials. First, he analyzed what the students did as "akin to pure speech," even though it involved no speech at all. As such, it deserved "comprehensive protection under the First Amendment," Fortas wrote. But do students enjoy the same level of First Amendment protection as adults? They do, Fortas wrote, and not just because they are "persons" under the Constitution.

Teachers and school officials should take special care to protect the First Amendment rights of young people, Fortas said, so that they can learn the importance of constitutional freedoms. He quoted from *West Virginia v. Barnette,* which upheld the right of students to refuse to participate in the flag salute. "That they are educating the young for citizenship is reason for scrupulous protection of Constitutional freedoms of the individual, if we are not to strangle the free mind at its source and teach youth to discount important principles of our government as mere platitudes," the Court had written in 1943. (See *West Virginia State Board of Education v. Barnette.*)

What about the authority of school officials to maintain discipline in the classroom? That is an important value, the Court said, but it was not threatened by what the Des Moines

Mary Beth Tinker and her brother, John, were suspended from their Des Moines, Iowa, high school for wearing black armbands to protest the Vietnam War. In *Tinker v. Des Moines Independent Community School District* (1969), the Court ruled that the suspensions violated the students' First Amendment rights.
Source: The Granger Collection, New York.

students did. "The school officials banned and sought to punish petitioners for a silent, passive expression of opinion, unaccompanied by any disorder or disturbance on the part of petitioners," Fortas wrote.

The lower court had said that even though there was no actual disruption, the school officials were entitled to act to prevent disruption before it happened. But here, too, the Court said the First Amendment prevails. "Any departure from absolute regimentation may cause trouble. Any variation from the majority's opinion may inspire fear," the Court's ruling said. "But our Constitution says we must take this risk."

Not all the justices agreed. Justice Hugo Black, normally a First Amendment absolutist, was swayed by the need to impose discipline in the nation's schools. According to a Black biography by Roger K. Newman, Black's grandson had recently been suspended from high school in New Mexico for writing an article that criticized school administration. The justice did not disapprove of his grandson's suspension, either.

"If the time has come when pupils of state-supported schools, kindergartens, grammar schools, or high schools, can defy and flout orders of school officials to keep their minds on their own schoolwork, it is the beginning of a new revolutionary era of permissiveness in this country fostered by the judiciary," Black wrote. "The truth is that a teacher of kindergarten, grammar school, or high school pupils no more carries into a school with him a complete right to freedom of speech and expression than an anti-Catholic or anti-Semite carries with him a complete freedom of speech and religion into a Catholic church or Jewish synagogue. Nor does a person carry with him into the United States Senate or House, or into the Supreme Court, or any other

court, a complete constitutional right to go into those places contrary to their rules and speak his mind on any subject he pleases. It is a myth to say that any person has a constitutional right to say what he pleases, where he pleases, and when he pleases. Our Court has decided precisely the opposite."

Justice Harlan also dissented, but less vociferously. His concern was taking away the independence of school officials. "I am reluctant to believe that there is any disagreement between the majority and myself on the proposition that school officials should be accorded the widest authority in maintaining discipline and good order in their institutions. To translate that proposition into a workable constitutional rule, I would, in cases like this, cast upon those complaining the burden of showing that a particular school measure was motivated by other than legitimate school concerns—for example, a desire to prohibit the expression of an unpopular point of view, while permitting expression of the dominant opinion."

EXCERPTS

From Justice Fortas's majority opinion: "First Amendment rights, applied in light of the special characteristics of the school environment, are available to teachers and students. It can hardly be argued that either students or teachers shed their constitutional rights to freedom of speech or expression at the schoolhouse gate. . . .

"On the other hand, the Court has repeatedly emphasized the need for affirming the comprehensive authority of the States and of school officials, consistent with fundamental constitutional safeguards, to prescribe and control conduct in the schools. Our problem lies in the area where students in the exercise of First Amendment rights collide with the rules of the school authorities. . . .

"In order for the State in the person of school officials to justify prohibition of a particular expression of opinion, it must be able to show that its action was caused by something more than a mere desire to avoid the discomfort and unpleasantness that always accompany an unpopular viewpoint. . . .

"In our system, state-operated schools may not be enclaves of totalitarianism. School officials do not possess absolute authority over their students. Students in school as well as out of school are 'persons' under our Constitution. They are possessed of fundamental rights which the State must respect, just as they themselves must respect their obligations to the State. In our system, students may not be regarded as closed-circuit recipients of only that which the State chooses to communicate. They may not be confined to the expression of those sentiments that are officially approved. In the absence of a specific showing of constitutionally valid reasons to regulate their speech, students are entitled to freedom of expression of their views. . . .

". . . But conduct by the student, in class or out of it, which for any reason—whether it stems from time, place, or type of behavior—materially disrupts classwork or involves substantial disorder or invasion of the rights of others is, of course, not immunized by the constitutional guarantee of freedom of speech."

IMPACT

In the clearest possible terms, the Supreme Court in *Tinker* declared that public schools are places where freedom of expression must be allowed to thrive. Its declaration that neither students nor teachers "shed their constitutional rights to freedom of speech or expression at the schoolhouse gate" remains a ringing declaration that has helped define the public school environment to this day. Some would call that environment too permissive, while others argue that *Tinker* has been ignored and weakened in the decades since it was handed down.

Historian John W. Johnson, author of a book on the case, says *Tinker* was the "*Roe v. Wade* for public school students." In a thirtieth anniversary article on *Tinker* for the Freedom Forum's Web site, *www.freedomforum.org,* Christopher Eckhardt said, "What George [Washington] and the boys did for white males in 1776, what Abraham Lincoln did to a certain extent during the time of the Civil War for African-American males, what the woman's suffrage movement in the 1920s did for women, the *Tinker* case did for children in America."

For at least fifteen years, in the opinion of Mark Goodman of the Student Press Law Center, the *Tinker* decision provided "ample protections" for students who ran afoul of school authorities in school newspapers, art, drama, and student body politics. Others, including columnist Nat Hentoff, bemoaned the fact that students, teachers and school administrators did not take full advantage of *Tinker,* mainly because of ignorance about its significance. In any event, *Tinker* is often described as the "high-water mark" for student expression.

The water began to recede in the 1980s as the Supreme Court became more conservative and more attuned to the authority of school officials and their desire for order and discipline in the classroom. In a 1986 case, *Bethel School District v. Fraser,* the Court said school officials did not violate the First Amendment when they disciplined Matthew Fraser for giving a speech full of sexual innuendo on behalf of a candidate for student office at a school assembly. Two years later, in *Hazelwood School District v. Kuhlmeier,* the Court cut back on *Tinker* even further, giving school officials greater power to control student speech, this time in the school newspaper, in the interest of "legitimate pedagogical concerns." (See *Hazelwood School District v. Kuhlmeier.*)

Miller v. California

Decided June 21, 1973
413 U.S. 15
laws.findlaw.com/US/413/15.html

DECISION

States do not violate the free speech protections of the First Amendment when they restrict the publication or sale of obscene material. The Court defined obscenity as sexually explicit material that, based on "community standards," appeals to prurient interests, is patently offensive, and lacks artistic, scientific, or political value.

BACKGROUND

One of the best-known lines from a Supreme Court decision expressed Justice Stewart's frustration about the difficulty of defining obscenity. Defining it in words is not easy, Stewart said in the 1964 case *Jacobellis v. Ohio,* but "I know it when I see it."

Because that kind of standard is too subjective for police to apply in enforcing anti-obscenity laws, the Court has tried on many occasions to come up with a clearer and more objective definition. It has proven to be one of the most difficult tasks the Court has undertaken.

It is difficult because, even though the First Amendment says that Congress "shall make no law" limiting the freedom of speech, certain kinds of speech traditionally have been viewed as beyond the pale and undeserving of First Amendment protection. Obscene speech is one of those categories, in the Court's view. But the Court has not found it easy to say what speech is obscene without inadvertently sweeping in more legitimate kinds of expression, such as artistic or medical materials that may include nudity or discussions of sex.

"It is apparent that the unconditional phrasing of the First Amendment was not intended to protect every utterance," the Court said in its first major obscenity case, *Roth v. United States,* in 1957. "We hold that obscenity is not within the area of constitutionally protected speech or press." (The words *obscenity* and *pornography* are often used interchangeably, but under Court doctrine, pornography is a broader term that includes some sexually explicit material that is not obscene. Obscenity is a narrower category that includes hard-core pornography, depictions that are viewed as especially unconventional or depraved.)

The *Roth* case, involving a New York City book dealer, led the Court to establish a test for determining when expressive material is obscene: "Whether, to the average person, applying contemporary community standards, the dominant theme of the material, taken as a whole, appeals to prurient interests." Dissenters said the standard was "too loose, too capricious" to satisfy the First Amendment.

In other obscenity cases, the Court added to the *Roth* standard. In *Jacobellis,* which concerned the showing of a French movie, *Les Amants,* Brennan defined obscenity as material that is "utterly without redeeming social importance." The Court decided the film was not obscene, and the conviction was overturned. In *Ginzburg v. United States* (1966) the Court upheld a conviction violating the federal obscenity statute. Specifically, Ginzburg was convicted of pandering; he sold publications that were openly advertised to appeal to his customers' erotic interest. However, when a newsstand clerk was convicted on a similar charge, the Court reversed the conviction in *Redrup v. New York* (1967). Following *Redrup* the Court struck down more than thirty obscenity convictions. Commentators began to joke about the justices enjoying the obscenity cases too much. The book *The Brethren* indicates the Court held informal "movie days" to review allegedly obscene films in pending cases.

A significantly more conservative Court decided to tackle the problem again in 1973 in *Miller v. California.* According to *The Brethren,* Chief Justice Burger "could hardly wait" to take on the obscenity issue. Marvin Miller was arrested under California's anti-obscenity law for mailing catalogues for his business of selling "adult" books. The catalogues went to some Newport Beach homes, but the residents had not requested them. The catalogues included sexually explicit photographs. Miller was convicted, and his conviction was upheld. The Supreme Court considered the *Miller* case along with *Paris Adult Theatre I v. Slaton,* a Georgia case, in which the theater owner was appealing his conviction for showing obscene films. Because of the difficulty of resolving the issue of obscenity after the first oral argument, the Court ordered the cases reargued the next term.

VOTE

5–4, with Chief Justice Warren E. Burger writing for the majority. Burger was joined by Justices Lewis F. Powell Jr., Byron R. White, Harry A. Blackmun, and William Rehnquist. Dissenting were Justices William O. Douglas, William J. Brennan Jr., Potter Stewart, and Thurgood Marshall.

HIGHLIGHTS

Chief Justice Burger acknowledged the tortured path of past Supreme Court efforts to deal with obscenity. "We have seen 'a variety of views among the members of the Court unmatched in any other course of constitutional adjudication,' " he wrote. But the time had arrived, in Burger's view, to agree on a single set of principles that would not make it impossible to prosecute someone on obscenity charges.

As the doctrine had evolved, Burger said, to win a case the prosecution now had to "prove a negative, i.e., that the material was 'utterly without redeeming social value'—a burden virtually impossible to discharge under our criminal standards of proof." In other words, all it would take for a clever pornographer to get around that rule would be to add something to his work—a social, medical, or artistic comment—that would give it at least a scrap of social value.

In place of that difficult standard, the Court promulgated one that would make it easier for prosecutors to win obscenity cases. It shifted the burden from the prosecutor to the defense; the person accused of violating obscenity laws would now have to prove that the disputed work has "serious literary, artistic, political, or scientific value."

An obscenity violation could also be proved if, according to "community standards," the material was shown to appeal to "the prurient interest," and if it depicts certain specified sexual activity in a "patently offensive" way. The community standard test was perhaps the most significant new element in the *Miller* decision.

Dissenters argued that applying community standards would create different rules in different parts of the country, but Burger rejected the criticism. "Under a National Constitution, fundamental First Amendment limitations on the powers of the States do not vary from community to community, but this does not mean that there are, or should or can be, fixed, uniform national standards of precisely what appeals to the 'prurient interest' or is 'patently offensive,'" Burger wrote. "These are essentially questions of fact, and our Nation is simply too big and too diverse for this Court to reasonably expect that such standards could be articulated for all 50 States in a single formulation, even assuming the prerequisite consensus exists. . . . It is neither realistic nor constitutionally sound to read the First Amendment as requiring that the people of Maine or Mississippi accept public depiction of conduct found tolerable in Las Vegas or New York City."

Justice Brennan, in a dissent written in the companion case, objected to the Court's notion that expression could be suppressed if it did not have "serious" value. Brennan wrote, "Before today, the protections of the First Amendment have never been thought limited to expressions of serious literary or political value."

Brennan also objected to the Court's continued dominance of obscenity regulation, which he indicated would not end with the *Miller* decision. "The problem is . . . that one cannot say with certainty that material is obscene until at least five members of this Court, applying inevitably obscure standards, have pronounced it so."

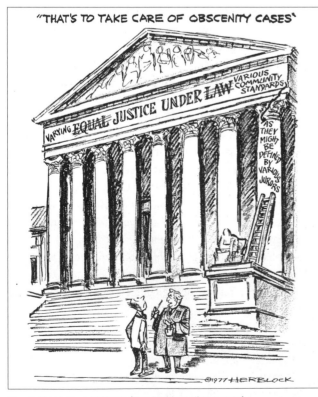

Source: Herblock on All Fronts *(New American Library, 1980).*

Justice Douglas also raised fundamental objections to any kind of obscenity regulation. "The difficulty is that we do not deal with constitutional terms, since 'obscenity' is not mentioned in the Constitution or Bill of Rights. . . . The use of the standard 'offensive' gives authority to government that cuts the very vitals out of the First Amendment."

EXCERPTS

From Justice Burger's majority opinion: "This much has been categorically settled by the Court, that obscene material is unprotected by the First Amendment. We acknowledge, however, the inherent dangers of undertaking to regulate any form of expression. State statutes designed to regulate obscene materials must be carefully limited. As a result, we now confine the permissible scope of such regulation to works which depict or describe sexual conduct. That conduct must be specifically defined by the applicable state law, as written or authoritatively construed. A state offense must also be limited to works which, taken as a whole, appeal to the prurient interest in sex, which portray sexual conduct in a patently offensive way, and which, taken as a whole, do not have serious literary, artistic, political, or scientific value.

"The basic guidelines for the trier of fact must be: (a) whether 'the average person, applying contemporary community standards' would find that the work, taken as a whole, appeals to the prurient interest; (b) whether the work depicts or describes, in a patently offensive way, sexual conduct specifically defined by the applicable state law; and (c) whether the work, taken as a whole, lacks serious literary, artistic, political, or scientific value."

IMPACT

The *Miller* decision triggered an initial crackdown on the sale of obscene materials. One Virginia prosecutor announced he would prosecute anyone selling *Playboy* magazine, because it did not meet community standards. Civil liberties groups predicted the decision would have a chilling effect not only on booksellers and newsstands, but also on authors, publishers, and moviemakers.

But if the Court was hoping that the decision would end its involvement in obscenity cases or end national confusion about what is or is not obscene, it failed. The Court continued to rule in the area. A year after *Miller,* the Court in *Jenkins v. Georgia* intervened to rule that *Carnal Knowledge,* a popular 1971 movie directed by Mike Nichols, could not possibly be viewed as obscene, even under community standards. Juries should not have "unbridled discretion," the Court said.

The concept of "community standards" has continued to divide commentators. "The United States Constitution is a national one," said author Nat Hentoff in the book *The First Freedom.* "If the Sixth Amendment cannot mean one thing in Maine and another in Las Vegas, how can the First Amendment change by crossing state and county lines?"

Depending on the aggressiveness of prosecutors and the sentiments of jurors, adult bookstores and theaters disappeared in some parts of the country, while they thrived in other areas. The Reagan administration in the 1980s mounted a major effort to increase obscenity prosecutions. In general, in more recent years, obscenity prosecutions have been confined to clearly "hard-core" material, while magazines such as *Playboy,* and even more explicit publications, have been safe from legal trouble.

The Court's reluctance to rule more stringently against obscenity, as well as the continued public demand for such materials, has made regulation difficult. But in the 1980s criticism of the Court's approach came from a new direction: feminist theorists argued that the Court has been too permissive, failing to recognize the harm that pornography does, not only to the women depicted in obscene works but to women who suffer abuse at the hands of men who read or view obscene material.

The growth of the Internet has also posed new problems for the Court's obscenity framework. Courts have been asked to consider how to apply the "community standards" test to obscenity on the World Wide Web, which may have originated from Europe but was viewed or downloaded in Maine or Nevada. This question figured prominently in the Supreme Court's 2002 decision *Ashcroft v. ACLU.* At issue was the Child Online Protection Act (COPA), a federal law that used the *Miller* "community standards" test in defining the kind of "harmful to minors" material that would be illegal to post on the Internet. The U.S. Court of Appeals for the Third Circuit, in striking down the law, had ruled that the *Miller* standard did not apply to the Internet because "Web publishers are currently without the ability to control the geographic scope of the recipients of their communications."

But Justice Clarence Thomas said that was no reason for letting Internet publishers off the hook. "If a publisher chooses to send its material into a particular community, this Court's jurisprudence teaches that it is the publisher's responsibility to abide by that community's standards," Thomas wrote. "The publisher's burden does not change simply because it decides to distribute its material to every community in the Nation." Justice Stephen Breyer, in a concurrence, worried that applying *Miller* to the Internet could force Web publishers to water down their content. "To read the statute as adopting the community standards of every locality in the United States would provide the most puritan of communities with a heckler's Internet veto affecting the rest of the Nation," wrote Breyer. But the 2002 ruling did not uphold the law as such, instead sending it back for further review. The case returned to the Supreme Court in 2004. This time, the Court was more critical of the law, but it once again sent the case back to lower courts for further review.

In one area of obscenity law there has been little disagreement: child pornography. In the 1982 case *New York v. Ferber,* the Court said states had broad power to restrict the production and distribution of child pornography, because of the harm it does to the children who are involved in producing it. With the advance of technology in the 1990s, though, concern increased about the spread of child pornography on the Internet. One effort by Congress to address the problem was unsuccessful, however. The Child Pornography Prevention Act of 1996 offered a high-tech definition of child pornography to include material that "appears to be" a minor engaging in sexual conduct. The wording was intended to cover digital "morphing" of images by grafting a minor's face, for example, onto an adult body. But in the 2002 ruling *Ashcroft v. Free Speech Coalition,* the Supreme Court said the law was too broad. The *Ferber* precedent, the Court said, was aimed at protecting the actual children used to produce child pornography. But prohibiting material that used "virtual" children, not real children, would jeopardize legitimate works including movies that use adult actors to portray teenagers.

Buckley v. Valeo

Decided January 30, 1976
424 U.S. 1
laws.findlaw.com/US/424/1.html

DECISION

A federal law that limits the amount of money a candidate for federal office may spend is an unconstitutional violation of the candidate's freedom of speech. Limits on independent expenditures made on behalf of a candidate are also unconstitutional. A limit on the amount of money that individuals and organizations can contribute to a candidate is constitutional

because it serves the important interest of preventing corruption. The Court upheld public funding for presidential primaries, political conventions, and general elections and said limits on expenditures could be imposed on candidates who accept public funding. The Court struck down the method of appointment for members of the Federal Election Commission, which was charged with implementing the law.

BACKGROUND

The Watergate scandal, which led to the resignation of President Richard Nixon in 1974, left Congress and the public eager to find ways of reforming the campaign and election process. Secret and illegal contributions had been made to Nixon's re-election campaign in 1972, and many of those that were not secret were huge. About 140 contributors had donated more than $50,000 each, and one insurance executive had donated $2 million. Some contributions were intended to influence pending government action or to win ambassadorships.

Congress responded by amending a 1971 law that required the reporting of campaign contributions and expenditures. The amendments imposed strict limits on both contributions to candidates and parties and spending by candidates in federal elections. An individual, for example, could give a maximum of $1,000 to a candidate for federal office and $20,000 to a political party. On the spending side, the law limited House candidates to spending $70,000 per election, Senate campaigns to 12 cents per voter, and presidential candidates to $20 million for the general election. It also limited the amount of money a candidate could draw from his or her own funds for a campaign, and limited to $1,000 the amount someone could spend independently to promote or attack a candidate apart from the candidate's campaign. Congress created the Federal Election Commission to implement the law and expanded public funding for presidential elections. Anticipating a challenge to the law, Congress also authorized a fast-track process for the courts to review the law so that regulations could be in place for the 1976 election.

Two senators challenged the law—James Buckley, a conservative from New York, and Eugene McCarthy, a liberal Democrat from Minnesota. They claimed the limits in the law violated their own First Amendment rights as candidates as well as the rights of campaign contributors and political and other organizations. As a formality, they filed suit against Francis Valeo, secretary of the U.S. Senate. An appeals court upheld most of the law, and the challenge moved quickly to the Supreme Court, where it was argued in November 1975.

VOTE

An unsigned (per curiam) opinion announced the ruling. Justices Lewis F. Powell Jr., William J. Brennan Jr., and Potter Stewart were in the majority in all of the votes. Limits on the amount candidates and independent organizations can spend were struck down by a 7–1 vote, with Justice Byron R. White dissenting. Restrictions on what a candidate may spend from his own funds were invalidated by a 7–1 vote, with Justice Thurgood Marshall dissenting. Limits on campaign contributions were upheld by a 6–2 vote, with Chief Justice Warren E. Burger and Justice Harry A. Blackmun dissenting. Public financing of presidential campaigns was upheld by a 6–2 vote, with Burger and Justice William Rehnquist dissenting. Composition of the Federal Election Commission was ruled unconstitutional by an 8–0 vote. Justice John Paul Stevens did not participate in the decision.

HIGHLIGHTS

The Court was under considerable pressure to act quickly; the first federal campaign funds for the 1976 election were due to be paid out to candidates on January 2, 1976. According to Bob Woodward and Scott Armstrong's *The Brethren,* the Court was also distracted by the fact that the ailing William O. Douglas, who had heard the oral arguments but resigned soon after, was attempting to stay with the case and write an opinion. The Court had to remind him finally that retired justices do not have a vote. To speed the opinion writing, the Court decided to assign a committee of justices to draft a per curiam or unsigned decision. Each justice would write a separate section of the decision. But in the end, with several justices also writing separate dissents, the decision turned into one of the lengthiest in Court history.

Although most justices saw First Amendment problems with the broad new regime of campaign regulations, some thought that at least some portions of the law should be upheld. To strike a compromise, the Court made a distinction between campaign contributions—money given by individuals, companies, or political committees to candidates or parties—and campaign expenditures, defined as money spent by the candidates or parties to win votes. It is a distinction that has been questioned ever since, but it was crucial to the Court's resolution of the case because it enabled the Court to treat the two types of transactions differently under the First Amendment.

Campaign spending by candidates and by independent organizations, the Court reasoned, was closely related to political speech, which the Court has always given the highest level of First Amendment protection. The money is spent on flyers, campaign advertising, and generally getting the candidate's message out—all core political speech. Under the Court's First Amendment precedents, the more valuable the speech, the harder it is for government to restrict it, so the Court struck down the spending limits. For the same reason, the limit on candidates' ability to use their own money was also struck down.

But when an individual gives money to a campaign, the Court suggested, its relationship to important protected speech is less direct, and therefore can be regulated more easily. "While contributions may result in political expression if spent by a candidate or an association to present views to the voters, the transformation of contributions into political debate involves speech by someone other than the contributor," the Court said.

The Supreme Court's decision in *Buckley v. Valeo* (1976) has had a profound effect on the way political campaigns raise and spend money. In the 2000 presidential campaign, Republican candidate George W. Bush—top, on board a bus with his wife, Laura, in Derry, New Hampshire in June 1999—declined to accept federal matching funds because doing so would have required him to abide by spending restrictions—the only limitation the Court upheld in *Buckley*. Democratic candidate Al Gore— bottom, campaigning in a Queens, New York, diner in February 2000— chose to accept federal funding. *Source: Reuters/Jim Bourg.*

The Court also saw a stronger connection between the limit on contributions and the political corruption that the law was meant to prevent, making it easier to justify under the First Amendment. The distinction between spending and contributions was supported by five justices, and one—Thurgood Marshall—said in dissent the expenditure of a candidate's own money should be regarded as a contribution that could be regulated.

Other justices weighed in to poke holes in the Court's rationale. "The contribution limitations infringe on First Amendment liberties and suffer from the same infirmities that the Court correctly sees in the expenditure ceilings," Chief Justice Burger wrote.

Marshall said that allowing candidates to spend their own money without limit would have a negative impact on politics. "The perception that personal wealth wins elections may not only discourage potential candidates without significant personal wealth from entering the political arena, but also undermine public confidence in the integrity of the electoral process."

Justice White was the only member of the Court who thought that spending limits in general were constitutional. "It would make little sense to me, and apparently made none to Congress, to limit the amounts an individual may give to a candidate or spend with his approval but fail to limit the amounts that could be spent on his behalf. Yet the Court permits the former while striking down the latter limitation," said White.

The Court struck down the limits on campaign spending, but with an exception. Spending limits were permissible, the Court said, for presidential candidates who agreed to them in exchange for federal funding of their campaigns.

Speaking unanimously, the Court also said that the way Congress structured the Federal Election Commission, with four of its six members appointed by Congress, violated the constitutional separation of powers. The law gave the commission executive branch–type powers, the Court said, so its members had to be appointed by the executive branch, namely the president.

EXCERPTS

Per curiam: "The Act's contribution and expenditure limitations operate in an area of the most fundamental First Amendment activities. Discussion of public issues and debate on the qualifications of candidates are integral to the operation of the system of government established by our Constitution. The First Amendment affords the broadest protection to such political expression in order 'to assure [the] unfettered interchange of ideas for the bringing about of political and social changes desired by the people.' . . .

"The expenditure limitations contained in the Act represent substantial rather than merely theoretical restraints on the quantity and diversity of political speech. The $1,000 ceiling on spending 'relative to a clearly identified candidate' would appear to exclude all citizens and groups except candidates, political parties, and the institutional press from any significant use of the most effective modes of communication. . . .

"By contrast with a limitation upon expenditures for political expression, a limitation upon the amount that any one person or group may contribute to a candidate or political committee entails only a marginal restriction upon the contributor's ability to engage in free communication. A contribution serves as a general expression of support for the candidate and his views, but does not communicate the underlying basis for the support. . . .

"Congress was justified in concluding that the interest in safeguarding against the appearance of impropriety requires that the opportunity for abuse inherent in the process of raising large monetary contributions be eliminated. . . .

"We find that the governmental interest in preventing corruption and the appearance of corruption is inadequate to justify [the] ceiling on independent expenditures. . . .

"The ceiling on personal expenditures by candidates on their own behalf, like the limitations on independent expenditures contained in [the law] imposes a substantial restraint on the ability of persons to engage in protected First Amendment expression. The candidate, no less than any other person, has a First Amendment right to engage in the discussion of public issues and vigorously and tirelessly to advocate his own election and the election of other candidates. . . .

"The major evil associated with rapidly increasing campaign expenditures is the danger of candidate dependence on large contributions. The interest in alleviating the corrupting influence of large contributions is served by the Act's contribution limitations and disclosure provisions, rather than by [its] campaign expenditure ceilings. . . .

"In any event, the mere growth in the cost of federal election campaigns, in and of itself, provides no basis for governmental restrictions on the quantity of campaign spending and the resulting limitation on the scope of federal campaigns. The First Amendment denies government the power to determine that spending to promote one's political views is wasteful, excessive, or unwise. In the free society ordained by our Constitution, it is not the government, but the people—individually as citizens and candidates and collectively as associations and political committees—who must retain control over the quantity and range of debate on public issues in a political campaign."

IMPACT

The most immediate result of the decision was to put the Federal Election Commission out of business, but only temporarily. Congress reconstituted it as a six-member commission, with all of the members appointed by the president.

Abiding by the Court's judgment, Congress also repealed the expenditure limits on all candidates except those who accepted public funding.

The more permanent impact of *Buckley v. Valeo* has been the inability of state legislatures or Congress to find a constitutional way to limit the influence of money in campaigns. "It's the tree in the middle of the ball field," says E. Joshua Rosenkranz of the Brennan Center for Justice, which has urged the Court to reverse *Buckley*. At both the federal and state levels, efforts to restrict campaign expenditures are challenged and usually are struck down because of *Buckley*'s "money-is-speech" rationale.

Critics say that because the *Buckley* decision left campaign spending unregulated, the demand for money in politics has increased uncontrollably, creating incentives to get around the contribution limits. In 1996 more than $2 billion was spent in federal elections. "Soft money"—independent donations to parties that are not regulated by existing laws—skyrocketed to $498 million in the 2000 election. Candidates can be just as beholden to these independent donors as to direct contributors, critics say.

Many organizations and scholars still agree with the Court's view that the First Amendment does and should prevent restrictions on campaign money. At least one current justice, Clarence Thomas, has indicated he thinks that restrictions on contributions as well as spending should be struck down on First Amendment grounds. In *Colorado Republican Federal Campaign Committee v. Federal Election Commission* (1996), Thomas said, "Broad prophylactic bans on campaign expenditures and contributions are not designed with the precision required by the First Amendment, because they sweep protected speech within their prohibitions."

The steady increase in the use of soft money in campaigns, as well as the continuing perception that candidates and elected officials were too easily influenced by big donors and special interests, led Congress to consider new legislation. In 2002 Congress prohibited soft money contributions and imposed a range of other restrictions in the comprehensive Bipartisan Campaign Reform Act (BCRA.) But critics and others—including President George W. Bush—worried that the broad sweep of the law violated the First Amendment's guarantee of freedom of speech. Acting on an expedited appeals schedule, a lower court and then the Supreme Court weighed those concerns. But in December 2003, the Court in *McConnell v. Federal Election Commission* upheld almost all of the law. The Court appeared swayed by evidence of campaign abuses which, the majority said, had caused a "meltdown" of the previous campaign-finance system. (See *McConnell v. Federal Election Commission.*)

Texas v. Johnson

Decided June 21, 1989
491 U.S. 397
laws.findlaw.com/US/491/397.html

DECISION

A state law making it a crime to desecrate the American flag violates the First Amendment's guarantee of freedom of speech. Flag-burning is a form of expressive conduct that deserves First Amendment protection.

BACKGROUND

Few symbols are as important to Americans as the flag. It inspired the national anthem and the pledge of allegiance; it was planted on the moon; and it has been used to rally troops and the public in times of war as well as peace. No wonder, then, that burning the flag is also a powerful symbol, an act of defiance that sends a message of contempt for the country and provokes instant anger in most who observe it.

Gregory Lee Johnson tapped into those emotions on August 22, 1984, during the Republican National Convention in Dallas. The leader of a group called the Revolutionary Communist Youth Brigade, Johnson and roughly one hundred demonstrators went on an unruly march through downtown Dallas to protest Republican ties to big business. Along the way they spray-painted office buildings and overturned planters. One of the protesters grabbed a flag from a bank flagpole and handed it to Johnson. When the demonstrators reached City Hall, Johnson doused the flag with kerosene and set it on fire. "America, the red, white, and blue, we spit on you," the group chanted. A passerby gathered up the ashes of the flag and buried them in his backyard.

An undercover police officer radioed in a report about the flag-burning, and the Dallas police arrested Johnson and charged him under the state law that bars desecration of a "venerated object." The law includes as venerated objects not only the American flag but also the Texas flag and public monuments and burial grounds. It defines desecration as to "deface, damage, or otherwise physically mistreat in a way that the actor knows will seriously offend one or more persons likely to observe or discover his action." At the time, all states except Alaska and Wyoming had similar laws banning flag desecration.

At Johnson's trial the passerby who had collected the ashes testified that he was offended—a necessary element of the crime—and Johnson was found guilty and sentenced to one year in prison. On appeal, a panel of Texas judges overturned the conviction, ruling that Johnson's act was a form of speech protected by the First Amendment. The appeals panel cited the Supreme Court's opinion in *West Virginia Board of Education v. Barnette,* which said the government could not force public school students to salute the flag. The state of Texas appealed, asking the Supreme Court to revive the law. The Court agreed to hear the case, setting the stage for a new confrontation over the meaning of the First Amendment. (See *West Virginia Board of Education v. Barnette.*)

During oral arguments, Kathi Drew, an assistant district attorney from Dallas, argued that Texas had a compelling interest in the "preservation of the flag as a symbol of nationhood and national unity" as well as to prevent a "breach of the peace."

Assistant District Attorney Kathi Drew of Dallas County, Texas, speaks to reporters outside the Supreme Court on March 21, 1989. Drew had earlier argued that flag burners such as Gregory Lee Johnson, left, should be criminally punished. The Court disagreed and in *Texas v. Johnson* (1989) declared that flag-burning deserves First Amendment protection.

Source: AP/Wide World Photos/ Bob Daugherty.

Johnson's lawyer, William Kunstler, known for defending radical causes, noted that the Dallas demonstration was nonviolent and did not even provoke the bystander who said the flag-burning offended him. "One cannot equate serious offense with incitement to breach the peace," Kunstler said.

VOTE

5–4, with Justice William J. Brennan Jr. writing the majority opinion. Joining him were Justices Anthony M. Kennedy, Harry A. Blackmun, Thurgood Marshall, and Antonin Scalia. Dissenting were Chief Justice William Rehnquist and Justices Byron R. White, Sandra Day O'Connor, and John Paul Stevens.

HIGHLIGHTS

This case was not the first one in which the Court had dealt with prohibitions on conduct that also could be viewed as expression. The Court had already established a hierarchy that gives such conduct more or less protection under the First Amendment depending on its expressive content and on how related the restriction was to the expression.

In *United States v. O'Brien* (1968), for example, the Court upheld the law prohibiting the burning of draft cards. The Court found that the law was more related to the conduct than to the expression—protesting the Vietnam War, in this case—making it easier for the government to justify. Preserving draft cards, the Court reasoned, helped in the administration of the draft. Any incidental impact on the free speech of card-burners was acceptable.

Twenty years later, however, in *Boos v. Barry* (1988) the Court ruled that when conduct is targeted for its expressive qualities alone—demonstrating near embassies, in this case—the law restricting it is subjected to "exacting scrutiny" and is very hard for government to defend.

Fitting the burning of the American flag into this existing spectrum was Justice Brennan's main task. With relative ease, Brennan determined first that flag-burning is expressive conduct. "The expressive, overtly political nature of this conduct was both intentional and overwhelmingly apparent," Brennan wrote.

Brennan also concluded that the law prohibiting flag-burning targeted the expression, not the conduct. The justifications the state offered—preserving the national symbol and preventing disturbances—were insufficient, Brennan said. Preserving the flag as a national symbol was a goal related to the expressive aspects of Johnson's act, while preventing breaches of the peace was not even at issue. Brennan noted that under federal law, burning is deemed to be the proper method for disposing of a flag that is torn or dirty. Because Texas outlaws burning a flag only when it offends someone else, Brennan said the prohibition is completely "content-based."

That conclusion brought the flag-burning case outside the framework of the *O'Brien* precedent altogether, and meant that the flag-burning law would have to survive the highest level of scrutiny under the First Amendment to be upheld. And this, the Texas law could not do. Brennan warned about the dangers of restricting unpopular ideas and of enforcing government orthodoxy. "Nothing in our precedents suggests that a State may foster its own view of the flag by prohibiting expressive conduct relating to it," Brennan wrote. "We never before have held that the Government may ensure that a symbol be used to express only one view of that symbol or its referents." Brennan concluded, "We decline . . . to create for the flag an exception to the joust of principles protected by the First Amendment."

The Court's newest justice, Anthony Kennedy, agreed with Brennan but wrote separately to indicate how difficult the decision was for him. "The hard fact is that sometimes we must make decisions we do not like. We make them because they are right, right in the sense that the law and the Constitution, as we see them, compel the result."

In a dissent filled with historic and even poetic references, Chief Justice Rehnquist reviewed the importance of the flag in U.S. culture. "For more than 200 years, the American flag has occupied a unique position as the symbol of our Nation, a uniqueness that justifies a governmental prohibition against flag-burning in the way respondent Johnson did here." Johnson's act, Rehnquist said, was not speech worthy of protection but rather "the equivalent of an inarticulate grunt or roar."

Justice Stevens, like Rehnquist a World War II veteran, also dissented. "The value of the flag as a symbol cannot be measured," Stevens wrote. "The creation of a federal right to post bulletin boards and graffiti on the Washington Monument might enlarge the market for free expression, but at a cost I would not pay. Similarly, in my considered judgment, sanctioning the public desecration of the flag will tarnish its value—both for those who cherish the ideas for which it waves and for those who desire to don the robes of martyrdom by burning it."

Stevens, who took the rare step of reading his dissent from the bench, concluded, "The ideas of liberty and equality have been an irresistible force in motivating leaders like Patrick Henry, Susan B. Anthony, and Abraham Lincoln, schoolteachers like Nathan Hale and Booker T. Washington, the Philippine Scouts who fought at Bataan, and the soldiers who scaled the bluff at Omaha Beach. If those ideas are worth fighting for—and our history demonstrates that they are—it cannot be true that the flag that uniquely symbolizes their power is not itself worthy of protection from unnecessary desecration."

EXCERPTS

From Justice Brennan's majority opinion: "If there is a bedrock principle underlying the First Amendment, it is that the government may not prohibit the expression of an idea simply because society finds the idea itself offensive or disagreeable. . . .

"Texas' focus on the precise nature of Johnson's expression, moreover, misses the point of our prior decisions: their enduring lesson, that the government may not prohibit expression simply because it disagrees with its message, is not dependent on the particular mode in which one chooses to express an idea. If we were to hold that a State may forbid flag-burning wherever it is likely to endanger the flag's symbolic role, but allow it wherever burning a flag promotes that role—as where, for example, a person ceremoniously burns a dirty flag—we would be saying that when it comes to impairing the flag's physical integrity, the flag itself may be used as a symbol—as a substitute for the written or spoken word or a 'short cut from mind to mind'—only in one direction. We would be permitting a State to 'prescribe what shall be orthodox' by saying that one may burn the flag to convey one's attitude toward it and its referents only if one does not endanger the flag's representation of nationhood and national unity. . . .

"It is not the State's ends, but its means, to which we object. It cannot be gainsaid that there is a special place reserved for the flag in this Nation, and thus we do not doubt that the government has a legitimate interest in making efforts to 'preserv[e] the national flag as an unalloyed symbol of our country.' . . . To say that the government has an interest in encouraging proper treatment of the flag, however, is not to say that it may criminally punish a person for burning a flag as a means of political protest. . . .

"We are tempted to say, in fact, that the flag's deservedly cherished place in our community will be strengthened, not weakened, by our holding today. Our decision is a reaffirmation of the principles of freedom and inclusiveness that the flag best reflects, and of the conviction that our toleration of criticism such as Johnson's is a sign and source of our strength. Indeed, one of the proudest images of our flag, the one immortalized in our own national anthem, is of the bombardment it survived at Fort McHenry. It is the Nation's resilience, not its rigidity, that Texas sees reflected in the flag—and it is that resilience that we reassert today.

"The way to preserve the flag's special role is not to punish those who feel differently about these matters. It is to persuade them that they are wrong. . . . We can imagine no more appropriate response to burning a flag than waving one's own, no better way to counter a flag burner's message than by saluting the flag that burns, no surer means of preserving the dignity even of the flag that burned than by—as one witness here did—according its remains a respectful burial. We do not consecrate the flag by punishing its desecration, for in doing so we dilute the freedom that this cherished emblem represents."

IMPACT

After the flag-burning decision came down, Justice Brennan told friends he thought it was nothing new. It followed logically from the Court's First Amendment precedents and broke no new ground, Brennan said. University of Chicago law professor Geoffrey Stone agreed, remarking, "The only astonishing thing is that the opinion was not unanimous."

Members of the public, not so familiar with Court precedent, and the nation's political leaders either embraced the decision or were angered by it. For those who approved of Brennan's decision, the case was a remarkable affirmation of core First Amendment principles. Even preservation of the American flag, the nation's most revered symbol, did not warrant making an exception to the principle of free expression. At a time when the Chinese government was suppressing dissent in Tiananmen Square, the U.S. Supreme Court was telling the world that the U.S. system was strong enough to tolerate even the most obnoxious forms of protest. The decision was remarkable also for winning the support of conservative justices such as Scalia and Kennedy. They were persuaded that the command of the First Amendment could not be ignored.

Those who disapproved turned to their political representatives for help, and reaction to the decision was swift. Both houses of Congress passed resolutions condemning the ruling, and President George Bush called for a constitutional amendment to overturn the Court's decision. First, however, Congress tried the legislative route, passing a law that prohibited any form of desecration of the flag—regardless of whether it is done to offend someone. By making it a broader prohibition, Congress hoped to meet the Court's objection in *Texas v. Johnson* that the Texas law was a "content-based" prohibition.

The new law was also challenged. Less than a year after striking down the Texas law, the Supreme Court, by the same vote, struck down the federal statute in the ruling *United States v. Eichman.* Even though the law's words did not appear to be content-based, Brennan wrote, its purpose was to target expression, again making it subject to the highest level of Court scrutiny. Again, the law failed the test.

Twice defeated in legislation, the groups that wanted to protect the flag from desecration began the more arduous task of launching and ratifying a constitutional amendment. At first the wording for a proposed amendment authorized Congress and the states to pass laws prohibiting the "physical desecration" of the flag. Worried that a patchwork of laws would result, sponsors in later versions of the amendment gave that power to Congress alone.

Under Article 5 of the Constitution, amendments must be approved by a two-thirds vote in Congress, as well as by the legislatures of three-fourths of the states. The Citizens Flag Alliance, created by the American Legion and other veterans' and patriotic organizations, won resolutions favoring such an amendment in forty-nine states.

But it was difficult to convince Congress to approve a flag protection amendment. The House of Representatives approved the amendment by the necessary two-thirds margin seven times in the aftermath of the Supreme Court rulings. In the Senate, the story was different. In 1995 the Senate vote was 63–36, three votes short of the number needed. Two years later the amendment never made it to the floor of the Senate. In March 2000 the amendment failed again in the Senate, this time by a 63-37 vote. Daniel Wheeler of the Citizens Flag Alliance said the repeated shortfalls in the Senate would not deter his group. "We're going to fight until hell freezes over, and then we're going to fight on the ice."

In fact, following the 2004 elections, the campaign to pass a flag-burning amendment gained new strength. The House of Representatives endorsed the amendment in June, 2005, by a 286-130 vote. Many members of Congress invoked the September 11, 2001, terrorist attacks, and the war in Afghanistan and Iraq as reasons to promote patriotic values by passing the amendment. Republicans, with a larger majority in the Senate, were hopeful that the Senate at last would go along with the amendment, but polls of senators indicated the vote would be close. At the same time, public sentiment seemed to turn against the amendment. A May 2005 poll conducted by the Freedom Forum's First Amendment Center indicated that 63 percent of those surveyed opposed amending the Constitution to protect the flag, up from 54 percent the year before.

Reno v. American Civil Liberties Union

Decided June 26, 1997
521 U.S. 844
laws.findlaw.com/US/521/844.html

DECISION

Communications on the expanding medium of the Internet deserve a high level of First Amendment protection from government regulation. A federal law that makes it a crime to knowingly transmit obscene or indecent material to anyone under age eighteen or to display patently offensive material to minors violates the free speech clause of the First Amendment.

BACKGROUND

From the Internet's modest beginnings in 1969 as a way for U.S. defense contractors and government officials to communicate with each other, this medium exploded into widespread popular use in the 1990s. With a computer, a modem, and a telephone line or, increasingly, with broadband access, anyone could send messages or create documents that could be viewed by millions.

As with each new communications medium, the Internet posed a new set of legal and regulatory issues. Because Internet communications emanate from countless sources worldwide rather than a single broadcast antenna or printing plant, many felt that regulation, whether desirable or not, would be nearly impossible. The universality of the Internet also pointed up its value as a medium for free speech.

But to some the Internet was too free—a sort of Wild West in which irresponsible, inaccurate, and even harmful communications were common and difficult to distinguish from their desirable counterparts. The earliest impulses to clamp down on the Internet came, as with other new media, from a desire to protect children. Congress responded when it heard from constituents that children were stumbling inadvertently onto sexually explicit Web sites. Children searching for information on innocent topics sometimes ended up being exposed to what Sen. James Exon, D-Neb., described as the "worst, most vile, most perverse pornography."

Congress tried to remedy the problem by adding some last-minute provisions to a 1996 bill that overhauled regulation of the entire communications industry. One of the measures made it a crime to knowingly transmit obscene or indecent messages to any recipient under eighteen years of age. Another prohibited sending or displaying "patently offensive" material depicting sexual or excretory activities or organs in ways that would make it available to anyone under eighteen. The penalty for violating these laws was a prison term of up to two years. Together, the laws became known as the Communications Decency Act.

The day President Bill Clinton signed the bill became a day of mourning on the Internet. Several Web sites went "dark," with black backgrounds, to protest the law. Just as swiftly, a coalition of civil liberties groups and organizations representing librarians, AIDS counselors, and homosexuals, among others, went to court to challenge the law on its face. They argued that the law was too broad and vague, criminalizing speech that should be protected by the First Amendment. By using terms such as "indecent" and "patently offensive," the law in their view prohibited a broad category of expression that adults had a right to see, and would have a chilling effect on legitimate speech.

A three-judge panel in Philadelphia agreed that the law was unconstitutional. Although the judges acknowledged that obscenity and child pornography were not protected under the First Amendment, the judges said the law as written swept far beyond those categories. Under Supreme Court precedents, the judges said, restrictions on speech must be evaluated in the context of the medium in which they were made. One judge described the Internet as "the most participatory form of mass speech yet developed," therefore deserving "the highest protection from governmental intrusion." The government appealed the decision to the Supreme Court under provisions of the law that called for speedy review of its constitutionality.

Just how the high court would view the case was uncertain because of its conflicting desires to protect children and to foster free expression. One concern among Internet advocates was whether the justices were familiar with the new medium. Some justices were known to be computer literate, while others persisted in writing opinions in longhand. It later became known that the Supreme Court library arranged to demonstrate the use of the Internet for any justice who was interested. Their law clerks, most of them young and well versed in new technology, also helped to educate the justices.

VOTE

7–2, with Justice John Paul Stevens writing the opinion for the Court. Joining Stevens were Justices Antonin Scalia, Anthony M. Kennedy, David H. Souter, Clarence Thomas, Ruth Bader Ginsburg, and Stephen G. Breyer. Justice Sandra Day O'Connor, joined by Chief Justice William Rehnquist, dissented in part.

HIGHLIGHTS

Because the Internet was a "unique and wholly new" medium, Justice Stevens reviewed its history and examined its characteristics to see where it fit in the spectrum of First Amendment protection. One by one, Stevens knocked down the justifications that have been used for the regulation of other media. Radio and television have been regulated because the broadcast spectrum is limited, slots are scarce, and a cacophony of signals would ensue without regulation. (See *Red Lion Broadcasting Co. v. Federal Communications Commission*.) The Internet, Stevens said, "can hardly be considered a 'scarce' expressive commodity. It provides relatively unlimited, low-cost capacity for communication of all kinds."

Offensive broadcasts on radio and television have also been subject to regulation because of the pervasiveness of the media; in other words, listeners and viewers can be subjected to the message by surprise, without choosing to receive it. Again, Stevens found that factor missing with the Internet. "Unlike communications received by radio or television, 'the receipt of information on the Internet requires a series of affirmative steps more deliberate and directed than merely turning a dial.' "

Some restrictions on speech to protect children have been allowed when the regulations still allow adults to receive it. Quoting prior cases, Stevens said that the government may not reduce the adult population to seeing or hearing only what is fit for children, and he concluded that the law on indecency on the Internet would do just that. "Knowledge that, for instance, one or more members of a 100-person chat group will be minor—and therefore that it would be a crime to send the group an indecent message—would surely burden communication among adults," Stevens wrote.

Stevens's analysis led to the conclusion that the Internet belonged on the least restrictive end of the First Amendment spectrum, along with the newspapers and pamphlets that the Framers of the Constitution had in mind when they wrote the Bill of Rights. "Our cases provide no basis for qualifying the level of First Amendment scrutiny that should be applied to this medium," Stevens wrote.

The law has a number of practical problems as well, Stevens said. Current technology makes it impossible or prohibitively expensive to determine the age of the users of a particular Web site or to tag adult content to keep it away from minors. The definitions in the law are so broad, Stevens said, that it could be interpreted to prohibit "discussions about prison rape or safe sexual practices, artistic images that include nude subjects, and arguably the card catalogue of the Carnegie Library."

Stevens was especially critical of one of the government's more novel arguments: that without the law in place, parents and others might avoid using the Internet altogether, thus hampering its growth as an information medium. "The Government apparently assumes that the unregulated availability of 'indecent' and 'patently offensive' material on the Internet is driving countless citizens away from the medium because of the risk of exposing themselves or their children to harmful material," Stevens wrote. "We find this argument singularly unpersuasive. The dramatic expansion of this new marketplace of ideas contradicts the factual basis of this contention. . . . As a matter of constitutional tradition, in the absence of evidence to the contrary, we presume that governmental regulation of the content of speech is more likely to interfere with the free exchange of ideas than to encourage it. The interest in encouraging freedom of expression in a democratic society outweighs any theoretical but unproven benefit of censorship."

Justice O'Connor, joined by Chief Justice Rehnquist, agreed with most of the majority opinion's view that the law prohibited too much speech. She said, however, that the law could be enforced in a constitutional way against an Internet communicator who knew that his or her entire audience was under eighteen. O'Connor also suggested that a law that created, in effect, an adult zone within cyberspace might be constitutional, just as the Court has upheld municipal zoning laws that keep adult bookstores out of residential neighborhoods.

EXCERPTS

From Justice Stevens's majority opinion: "This dynamic, multi-faceted category of communication includes not only traditional print and news services, but also audio, video, and still images, as well as interactive, real-time dialogue. Through the use of chat rooms, any person with a phone line can become a town crier with a voice that resonates farther than it could from any soapbox. Through the use of Web pages, mail exploders,

and newsgroups, the same individual can become a pamphleteer. As the District Court found, 'the content on the Internet is as diverse as human thought.' . . .

"The vagueness of the CDA [Communications Decency Act] is a matter of special concern for two reasons. First, the CDA is a content-based regulation of speech. The vagueness of such a regulation raises special First Amendment concerns because of its obvious chilling effect on free speech. . . .

". . . Second, the CDA is a criminal statute. In addition to the opprobrium and stigma of a criminal conviction, the CDA threatens violators with penalties including up to two years in prison for each act of violation. The severity of criminal sanctions may well cause speakers to remain silent rather than communicate even arguably unlawful words, ideas, and images. . . .

"We are persuaded that the CDA lacks the precision that the First Amendment requires when a statute regulates the content of speech. In order to deny minors access to potentially harmful speech, the CDA effectively suppresses a large amount of speech that adults have a constitutional right to receive and to address to one another. That burden on adult speech is unacceptable if less restrictive alternatives would be at least as effective in achieving the legitimate purpose that the statute was enacted to serve.

"The breadth of the CDA's coverage is wholly unprecedented. . . . [T]he scope of the CDA is not limited to commercial speech or commercial entities. Its open-ended prohibitions embrace all nonprofit entities and individuals posting indecent messages or displaying them on their own computers in the presence of minors. The general, undefined terms 'indecent' and 'patently offensive' cover large amounts of nonpornographic material with serious educational or other value. Moreover, the 'community standards' criterion as applied to the Internet means that any communication available to a nationwide audience will be judged by the standards of the community most likely to be offended by the message. . . .

". . . [T]he strength of the Government's interest in protecting minors is not equally strong throughout the coverage of this broad statute. Under the CDA, a parent allowing her 17-year-old to use the family computer to obtain information on the Internet that she, in her parental judgment, deems appropriate could face a lengthy prison term. Similarly, a parent who sent his 17-year-old college freshman information on birth control via e-mail could be incarcerated even though neither he, his child, nor anyone in their home community found the material 'indecent' or 'patently offensive,' if the college town's community thought otherwise."

IMPACT

Within minutes of being issued, the Court's decision was disseminated widely on the Internet, the very medium the Court was embracing. The ruling was heralded as a bold and protective charter that would greatly help the Internet thrive and grow. First Amendment advocates noted that the Supreme Court had been slow to grasp the full significance and role of other new media of the twentieth century. But in the case of the Internet, they said, the Court "got it" in its very first ruling.

"Today's ruling," said Ann Beeson of the American Civil Liberties Union, "will help insure [sic] that the free speech principles embodied in our Constitution apply with the same force on the Internet as they do in the morning paper, in the town square, and in the privacy of our own homes."

Stevens invoked the colonial imagery of the town crier and the pamphleteer in recognizing that the Internet could be a boon to democracy by allowing the average citizen to make his or her views broadly known at little cost. That democratizing characteristic, in Stevens's view, earned the Internet an honored place in the First Amendment pantheon—a place where restriction or regulation would be exceedingly hard to justify.

But that lofty status did not keep legislators and child safety advocates from trying. "We are essentially back to the drawing board," said Dee Jepsen, president of Enough Is Enough, a group that was a leading supporter of the law struck down by the Court. "This fight to protect America's children is not over."

In 1998 Congress passed the Child Online Protection Act (COPA), which contained many of the same provisions of the earlier law, but was aimed more narrowly at those who made communications to minors "for commercial purposes." Congress and the administration said the new law cured the constitutional defects of the old law and was aimed solely at commercial pornographers, but it too was challenged in court. Civil liberties groups argued that the new law was overbroad, just as the old one had been. For example, the "commercial purposes" limitation in the new law would still leave art gallery and bookstore owners vulnerable to prosecution for legitimate expression. A federal district court judge and the U.S. Court of Appeals for the Third Circuit blocked enforcement of the law, finding that it probably violated the First Amendment. The appeals court ruled that by prohibiting material that failed to meet "community standards," the law imposed an impossible restriction on the Internet, which can be viewed with equal ease in virtually any community in the nation. (See *Miller v. California*.)

The Supreme Court has issued two rulings on COPA, neither one conclusive. In the 2002 ruling *Ashcroft v. ACLU,* the Court said the appeals court had been too quick to reject the law's use of "community standards." It sent the case back to the third circuit, which again found the law too broad. In 2004 the Supreme Court took up the case again and sent it back down again to the appeals court for further review.

Republican Party of Minnesota v. White

Decided June 27, 2002
536 U.S. 765
laws.findlaw.com/US/000/01-521.html

DECISION

It violates the First Amendment for states to prohibit candidates for judicial office from announcing their views about disputed legal or political issues during their campaigns.

BACKGROUND

Like most candidates for office, Minnesota lawyer Gregory Wersal wanted to tell voters his views about issues that might concern them, issues he might be able to do something about.

But because the office he was running for was a seat on the Minnesota Supreme Court, special rules applied. Minnesota, like eight other states, prohibits candidates for judgeships from announcing during their campaigns what their views are about "disputed legal or political issues."

During his 1996 campaign, Wersal in his literature criticized several past decisions of the state supreme court. Some-

one complained to a state ethics board that Wersal had violated the so-called announce clause. The board dismissed the complaint, but Wersal was worried enough about his reputation that he dropped out of the race. Two years later he ran again, but again found himself worried that he would run into ethical trouble if he answered questions about his views from the press and the public.

Believing that the rule violated his First Amendment right to express himself, Wersal challenged the rule in federal court. He was joined by the state Republican Party, which said the rule also violated its First Amendment rights by making it impossible for the party to know whether it should endorse Wersal's candidacy.

Both the district court and the U.S. Court of Appeals for the Eighth Circuit upheld the Minnesota rule, but not without noting the seriousness of the First Amendment issue. The appeals court acknowledged that the rule had the effect of restricting speech that was at the core of the First Amendment—speech by candidates for public office—when it mattered most. But it said the state had identified compelling interests that justified the restriction: preserving the impartiality, and the appearance of impartiality, of the judiciary.

The Supreme Court accepted the Minnesota case, and it quickly evolved into a larger debate over the nature of judging and how—and whether—candidates for judgeships are different from candidates for other offices. The kind of restrictions imposed on Wersal's speech as a candidate for the state supreme court would have been unconstitutional if he had been running for the state legislature. Most of the thirty-one states that elect some or all of their judges had, based on

Greg Wersal, a former candidate for a seat on the Minnesota Supreme Court, challenged state campaign rules, called Canon 5, that prevented judicial candidates from discussing legal and political views. Here he announces the U.S. Supreme Court decision in *Republican Party of Minnesota v. White* (2002), which removed this "ball and chain" on judicial candidates because such prohibitions violate First Amendment rights.
Source: AP/Wide World Photos/Tom Olmscheid.

model rules devised by the American Bar Association, adopted rules restricting judicial campaigns. But are judicial candidates so different that such different rules are warranted?

Ironically, the question was being asked at a time when there was increasing concern that in other ways, judicial elections were becoming too much like other campaigns. In races for judgeships in Alabama, Ohio, Texas, and elsewhere, millions of dollars were being spent by candidates. Much of that money came from special interest groups that wanted voters to elect judges who would rule more favorably toward their viewpoints. Judicial elections had become popular early in the nation's history as a democratizing reform measure that would take the judiciary out of the control of politicians. But some campaign reform groups now felt that elections had become a problem and should be replaced by some form of merit selection by governors.

VOTE

5–4, with Justice Antonin Scalia writing for the majority. Joining him were Chief Justice William Rehnquist, Sandra Day O'Connor, Anthony Kennedy, and Clarence Thomas. Dissenting were Justices John Paul Stevens, David Souter, Ruth Bader Ginsburg, and Stephen Breyer.

HIGHLIGHTS

Justice Scalia examined the Minnesota rule and its state purposes and found it to be a clear violation of the First Amendment. By its terms, the rule goes well beyond a prohibition against making promises about how the candidate would rule in a specific case. "It is clear that the announce clause prohibits a judicial candidate from stating his views on any specific nonfanciful legal question within the province of the court for which he is running," Scalia wrote.

And upholding that kind of rule, Scalia said, would restrict the kind of speech that the First Amendment was intended to protect: speech that would inform voters about candidates for public office. "We have never allowed the government to prohibit candidates from communicating relevant information to voters during an election, Scalia said.

But because the court sometimes will allow speech restrictions that are narrowly tailored and serve a compelling state interest, Scalia examined the concept of judicial impartiality—the goal that Minnesota was striving for in enacting the rule. Assessing all possible definitions of "impartiality," Scalia found the goal unachievable, undesirable, or not well served by the Minnesota rule. For example, Scalia said it would be impossible and undesirable to elect qualified judges who come into office with no preconceptions about the law. But even as he swept away Minnesota's announce clause, Scalia insisted, "we neither assert nor imply that the First Amendment requires campaigns for judicial office to sound the same as those for legislative office." Other restrictions on judicial campaigns that were not challenged in the current case remain in effect.

Justice O'Connor, in her concurrence, addressed the broader issue of how judges are selected across the country. In any state where judges have to stand for election, she said, it is unavoidable that judges, in deciding cases, would have in the back of their minds the impact of their decision on their reelection chances. "If the State has a problem with judicial impartiality, it is largely one the State brought upon itself by continuing the practice of popularly electing judges," O'Connor said.

In dissent Justices Stevens and Ginsburg made impassioned defenses of the concept that judges and judicial candidates are different—and should be treated differently—from candidates for other offices. Ginsburg insisted that judges are not political officials and should not be viewed as politicians. "I would differentiate elections for political offices, in which the First Amendment holds full sway, from elections designed to select those whose office it is to administer justice without respect to persons," she wrote.

EXCERPTS

From Justice Scalia's opinion: "In Minnesota, a candidate for judicial office may not say "I think it is constitutional for the legislature to prohibit same-sex marriages." He may say the very same thing, however, up until the very day before he declares himself a candidate, and may say it repeatedly (until litigation is pending) after he is elected. As a means of pursuing the objective of open-mindedness that respondents now articulate, the announce clause is so woefully underinclusive as to render belief in that purpose a challenge to the credulous."

From Justice O'Connor's concurrence: "We of course want judges to be impartial, in the sense of being free from any personal stake in the outcome of the cases to which they are assigned. But if judges are subject to regular elections they are likely to feel that they have at least some personal stake in the outcome of every publicized case. Elected judges cannot help being aware that if the public is not satisfied with the outcome of a particular case, it could hurt their reelection prospects."

From Justice Ginsburg's dissent: "Legislative and executive officials serve in representative capacities. They are agents of the people; their primary function is to advance the interests of their constituencies. Candidates for political offices, in keeping with their representative role, must be left free to inform the electorate of their positions on specific issues. . . . Judges, however, are not political actors. They do not sit as representatives of particular persons, communities, or parties; they serve no faction or constituency. Thus, the rationale underlying unconstrained speech in elections for political office—that representative government depends on the public's ability to choose agents who will act at its behest—does not carry over to campaigns for the bench."

IMPACT

The decision had an immediate impact in states that had rules similar to Minnesota's. These rules were now invalid, and judges and candidates who were facing punishment for violating them were no longer in trouble.

But the decision also led to challenges of other restrictions on candidates that implicated the First Amendment. Some of these challenges were successful, and to some extent confirmed the dissenters' fears by beginning to treat judicial campaigns in the same way as other campaigns.

For example, a few months after the Supreme Court ruled, the U.S. Court of Appeals for the Eleventh Circuit cited the *White* decision in striking down rules in Georgia that prohibited judicial candidates from making false or misleading statements or soliciting campaign contributions.

Meanwhile on the campaign trail, the Supreme Court's decision did not seem to have a major impact. State judicial elections continued to become more costly, more rancorous, and more noisy. The press and the public seemed somewhat bolder in asking candidates the kinds of questions they would not have asked before, and some candidates were more willing to answer. But many candidates refused to answer, as they had before. The Supreme Court decision made it unconstitutional to prohibit candidates from speaking about important issues, but it did not require them to do so.

McConnell v. Federal Election Commission

Decided December 10, 2003
540 U.S. 93
laws.findlaw.com/US/000/02-1674.html

DECISION

Congress did not violate the First Amendment guarantee of freedom of speech when it passed the Bipartisan Campaign Reform Act (BCRA). The law's restrictions on political parties' use of so-called "soft money" in political campaigns, and on certain kinds of issue advertising before elections, is constitutional. But one restriction in BCRA that makes it illegal for minors to make campaign contributions is unconstitutional.

BACKGROUND

When President George W. Bush signed the Bipartisan Campaign Reform Act into law on March 27, 2002, he said he had misgivings. Several parts of the law, he said, "present serious constitutional concerns." He was not the only one to express such doubts.

Within hours of the signing, opponents of the law led by Sen. Mitch McConnell, R-Ky., filed a First Amendment challenge to the law. It was in the form of a suit against the Federal Election Commission, which applied and enforced the law. Eventually McConnell was joined by more than eighty plaintiffs, each voicing an objection to what was one of the most complex pieces of legislation in congressional history. One opponent of the legislation called it the most sweeping effort to criminalize political speech since the Alien and Sedition Acts passed by Congress more than 200 years before.

That sentiment reflects the strong emotions that preceded passage of the BCRA. The law was the most ambitious effort since the Supreme Court ruling in *Buckley v. Valeo* to deal with the flood of special interest and other money that was dominating—some said corrupting—the U.S. election system. The *Buckley* decision had upheld some of the post-Watergate reforms Congress enacted, but struck down others. Perhaps its most lasting effect was that it treated campaign reforms as potential violations of freedom of speech. Even though the restrictions, strictly speaking, were on the money donated and spent on campaigns, the Court recognized the relationship between money and speech; without money, it is difficult to get a message out.

As a result, the *Buckley* decision—properly so, in the view of many—made it difficult for Congress to fashion additional reforms. Many members of Congress— whether for noble or selfish reasons—cited First Amendment concerns as a reason to oppose reform measures.

But by the end of the twentieth century the cry for reform gained enough strength to overcome constitutional concerns. *Buckley* had restricted campaign donations, but it left campaign spending unregulated. Inevitably, spending increased exponentially, creating almost a hydraulic pressure on parties to find new sources of income. "Soft money" was the answer. Money donated directly to federal campaigns—hard money—was subject to restrictions and disclosure requirements under the post-Watergate reforms embodied in the Federal Election Campaign Act. But other donations—to state parties, for example, or to national parties for general party-building purposes, rather than specific campaigns—were not regulated and became known as soft money. In 1984 soft money accounted for 5 percent of the income and spending of the two major parties. By the 2000 election it accounted for 42 percent—a total of $498 million.

Sen. John McCain, R-Ariz., a longtime reform advocate, led a campaign in Congress to restrict soft money and to enact other reforms. Another big concern had to do with ways in which parties got around another provision of the post-Watergate law. Parties were required to use hard money when they ran advertisements urging people to vote for or against a named candidate. But corporations and unions got around that by paying for ads that used more subtle wording to convey the same message.

McCain's legislation, cosponsored by Sen. Russ Feingold, D-Wisc., dealt with both these issues and many more. In early 2002, to the surprise of many, the legislation passed in both the House and the Senate. Anticipating legal challenges, the bill's sponsors included a fast-track procedure for courts to use to rule on its constitutionality. Sponsors hoped to have the law in place in time for the 2004 presidential campaign.

McConnell said he challenged the law "to defend the First Amendment right of all Americans to be able to fully participate in the political process." The provision regarding advertising seemed especially vulnerable to attack. It prohibited unions and corporations from directly sponsoring "electioneering communications" within sixty days before an election. As the noted First Amendment lawyer Floyd Abrams put it, "Do you really want to limit speech when it matters most?" Supporters of the law said nothing was being censored at all; these kinds of ads could be financed through political action committees that meet disclosure and other requirements.

Republican senator John McCain of Arizona, left, and Democratic senator Russell Feingold of Wisconsin, center, discuss their campaign finance bill in March 2001. The bill became the Bipartisan Campaign Reform Act (BCRA) of 2002, whose provisions were challenged on free speech grounds by their Senate colleague Mitch McConnell of Kentucky in *McConnell v. Federal Election Commission* (2003). The Supreme Court upheld BCRA's restriction on political parties' use of "soft money" and on some kinds of issue advertising but struck down its prohibition of campaign contributors by minors.
Source: Congressional Quarterly/ Scott J. Ferrell.

The fast timetable for considering the challenges almost became undone when a three-judge panel in the District of Columbia took months to hand down its decision. In May 2003 the panel produced a ruling more than 1,600 pages long, upholding some parts of the law and striking down others. The Supreme Court was the next stop, and it agreed to speed its deliberations as well. It scheduled a special September session—a month before its term normally begins—and called for four hours of oral argument. Meanwhile, parties were told to abide by the new laws while their constitutionality was under review.

VOTE

In the main ruling upholding restrictions on soft money and electioneering communications, Justices John Paul Stevens and Sandra Day O'Connor wrote a majority opinion joined by Justices David Souter, Ruth Bader Ginsburg, and Stephen Breyer. Justices Clarence Thomas, Antonin Scalia, and Anthony Kennedy and Chief Justice William Rehnquist authored dissents on different aspects of the majority rulings. The ruling on contributions by minors was unanimous.

HIGHLIGHTS

The Supreme Court's ruling came just as the 2004 presidential campaign was getting underway. To the surprise of many, the Court in its 298-page opinion narrowly upheld all of the provisions of the law that were most important—including the sections viewed as most vulnerable. The ban on soft money was

upheld, as was the ban on directly funded electioneering communications.

The Court in its reasoning went out of its way to defer to Congress, which it said has "particular expertise" in regulating campaigns, and which could fairly undertake efforts to reduce corruption of the political system. Justices Stevens and Breyer succeeded in persuading the majority to leave the law reasonably intact—unlike its 1974 predecessor. They also convinced fellow justices not to second-guess congressional motives. The evidence of corruption was clear enough, the majority agreed, to justify giving Congress wide berth to devise ways to restrict campaign money.

The main Stevens-O'Connor ruling voiced broad suspicion of money in politics that went beyond what it termed "classic quid pro quo" donations that buy the vote of an officeholder or candidate. The two justices recited the "disturbing" findings of the Senate committee that looked into campaign abuses in the 1996 presidential election. The torrent of soft money resulted in a "meltdown" of the campaign finance system, the committee concluded.

With that sentiment underlying the opinion, the justices decided that giving the First Amendment too much weight "would render Congress powerless to address more subtle but equally dispiriting forms of corruption."

Instead of the difficult-to-meet "strict scrutiny" standard the Court usually uses to evaluate government restrictions on speech, the Court adopted a less stringent test, asking only that the law be "closely drawn" to match clearly identified problems.

This more relaxed standard made it easier for the Court to uphold almost all of the law's extensive provisions. It sidestepped ruling on several sections of the law, including those involving broadcast advertising rates and a so-called "millionaire" provision that allows candidates to receiver bigger donations when their opponents use large amounts of their own money in campaigns. The Court said that the challengers to these provisions did not have standing, because any injury they might suffer from these parts of the law was speculative and in the future.

There was only one bright spot in the ruling for First Amendment advocates. The law included an outright ban on campaign contributions by anyone younger than seventeen. Supporters claimed that adults were getting around contribution limits by making donations in their children's names—including infants. But the Court said Congress had based the limit on only "scant evidence" about the problem, insufficient to justify such a broad restriction on the First Amendment rights of minors.

Dissenters said the majority had given short shrift both to the First Amendment and to the positive role played by political parties. "Political parties often foster speech crucial to a healthy democracy," said Rehnquist, who objected to the limits on soft money donation. Justice Scalia attacked what he described as "three fallacious propositions" in the majority ruling.

EXCERPTS

From the Stevens-O'Connor majority opinion: "Just as troubling to a functioning democracy as classic *quid pro quo* corruption is the danger that officeholders will decide issues not on the merits or the desires of their constituencies, but according to the wishes of those who have made large financial contributions valued by the officeholder. Even if it occurs only occasionally, the potential for such undue influence is manifest. And unlike straight cash-for-votes transactions, such corruption is neither easily detected nor practical to criminalize. The best means of prevention is to identify and to remove the temptation. The evidence set forth above, which is but a sampling of the reams of disquieting evidence contained in the record, convincingly demonstrates that soft-money contributions to political parties carry with them just such temptation. . . .

"Many years ago we observed that '[t]o say that Congress is without power to pass appropriate legislation to safeguard . . . an election from the improper use of money to influence the result is to deny to the nation in a vital particular the power of self protection.' . . . We abide by that conviction in considering Congress' most recent effort to confine the ill effects of aggregated wealth on our political system. We are under no il-

lusion that BCRA will be the last congressional statement on the matter. Money, like water, will always find an outlet. What problems will arise, and how Congress will respond, are concerns for another day. In the main we uphold BCRA's two principal, complementary features: the control of soft money and the regulation of electioneering communications."

From Justice Scalia's dissent: "This is a sad day for the freedom of speech. Who could have imagined that the same Court which, within the past four years, has sternly disapproved of restrictions upon such inconsequential forms of expression as virtual child pornography . . . tobacco advertising . . . dissemination of illegally intercepted communications . . . and sexually explicit cable programming . . . would smile with favor upon a law that cuts to the heart of what the First Amendment is meant to protect: the right to criticize the government. For that is what the most offensive provisions of this legislation are all about. We are governed by Congress, and this legislation prohibits the criticism of Members of Congress by those entities most capable of giving such criticism loud voice: national political parties and corporations. . . ."

IMPACT

The Court's complex ruling drew strong reaction from both sides of the debate over campaign reform and the First Amendment. "This opinion represents a landmark victory for the American people in the effort to reform their political system. Now that the court has spoken, we must make sure that the law is properly interpreted and enforced," Senators McCain and Feingold said in a joint statement.

Many commentators were struck by the majority's easy rejection of the importance of freedom of speech during political campaigns. "To me the big picture is the Court's cursory dismissal of First Amendment arguments," wrote Rick Hasen, a professor at Loyola Law School in Los Angeles. Similarly Floyd Abrams, one of the lawyers challenging BCRA, said, "It almost reads like a tax case rather than a First Amendment case. In style, tone and nature, it reads like an opinion about regulation by government of some sort of improper activity."

Charles Cooper, who represented the National Rifle Association during the litigation, lamented that "A politician can attack by name the National Rifle Association, but the NRA cannot utter the attacker's name in its own response. Five justices think that is constitutional, and that is a crying shame."

Sen. McConnell, the leading opponent of the law, said, "This law will not remove one dime from politics. As the majority opinion correctly observed, 'Money, like water, will always find an outlet.'"

McConnell's prediction was borne out, to some extent. Money still flowed into campaigns in huge amounts. According to reports filed with the Federal Election Commission at the end of 2004, more than $1.7 billion from all sources was spent on the campaign. The Democratic and Republican campaigns, deprived of soft money, more than made up for it with hard money donations totaling nearly $400 million each. The highly emotional and hard-fought campaign was credited with bringing new, smaller donors into the process.

A controversial new channel for the flow of money in the 2004 presidential campaign became so-called "527" organizations, named for a section of the Internal Revenue Code. They are tax-exempt groups that are formed to influence elections, but they are not subject to donation limits. Nearly $600 million went to these groups in 2003 and 2004, fueling major ad campaigns on a range of issues including the controversy over Democratic candidate John Kerry's military service in Vietnam. Following the election, some members of Congress introduced legislation to restrict the role of 527s.

GAY RIGHTS

*L*ike many other parts of society, the Supreme Court has been slow to recognize the rights of homosexuals as a group of people who have suffered severe discrimination because of their sexual orientation. Even as the Court expanded the protection of the Constitution for racial minorities and women, and ruled in favor of protecting privacy in intimate relations, it took a long time to extend those doctrines to gays and lesbians. It was not until the mid-1990s that the Court began to write about homosexuals in a respectful tone. The Court's justices, it became apparent, were not immune from the trend in society toward acceptance and tolerance of gays and lesbians. In 2003 the Court took a major step in this area, striking down sodomy laws that had criminalized homosexual behavior. The ramifications of that ruling are still unfolding, but gay rights advocates felt that, while long overdue, the Court's actions had finally given recognition to the rights of a significant segment of society.

Other related cases mentioned in the Gay Rights section

Roberts v. United States Jaycees (1984) (p. 111)
Cook v. Rumsfeld (2004)

Bowers v. Hardwick

Decided June 30, 1986
478 U.S. 186
laws.findlaw.com/US/478/186.html

DECISION

A Georgia law prohibiting sodomy is constitutional. The rights of privacy and liberty, both protected under the Constitution, do not include any right of homosexuals to engage in sodomy, even in a private home with consenting adults.

BACKGROUND

Racial and ethnic minorities and women made considerable strides in their push for equal treatment during the last third of the twentieth century. But homosexual men and women did not enjoy the same success in ending bias against them in the workplace and in society in general. Although homosexuals are more visible and accepted today in the media and in some segments of the culture, they still face discrimination and even violence at the hands of those who disapprove of their lifestyle.

One of the earliest goals of the gay rights movement was to repeal laws that made sodomy a crime. Sodomy, or oral and anal sex, is practiced by heterosexuals as well as by homosexuals, but is frowned upon by religious groups and others. As late as 1961 all fifty states had laws barring sodomy, but by 1986 more than half had repealed them. Although the laws were not consistently or frequently enforced, their mere existence served as a threat to homosexuals and a justification for police raids on gay bars and other establishments.

Georgia's law was still on the books when an Atlanta police officer visited the home of Michael Hardwick in August 1982. Police had a warrant to arrest Hardwick for failure to appear in court to answer charges of drinking in public. He had been arrested for carrying an open beer bottle outside the gay bar where he worked. When the officer came to the house, someone pointed him toward Hardwick's bedroom. The officer opened the bedroom door and saw Hardwick and another man engaged in oral sex. He arrested both on charges of violating the state sodomy law, which prohibits sexual activity involving "the sex organs of one person and the mouth or anus of another." The maximum penalty for violating the law, first passed in 1816, was twenty years in prison.

After the arrest a lawyer for the American Civil Liberties Union contacted Hardwick to see if he wanted to challenge the constitutionality of the sodomy law. Hardwick agreed, even though he knew the resulting publicity would subject him to threats and possible violence.

The local district attorney, however, decided not to present the sodomy charge to a grand jury, apparently preferring to avoid a constitutional confrontation. Hardwick's lawyers continued the suit in federal court, seeking to prevent Michael Bowers, the state attorney general, from enforcing what they said was an unconstitutional law. A federal judge dismissed the suit, but an appeals court ruled that the law violated Hardwick's fundamental constitutional rights. Georgia appealed the decision to the Supreme Court, which had not dealt directly with gay rights before. According to recent scholarship, the Court was at first reluctant to take the case but agreed to hear it.

Justice Lewis F. Powell Jr., in particular, found the case "deeply troubling," according to his biographer, John C. Jeffries Jr., Powell sought help from his law clerks, telling one of them, "I don't believe I have ever met a homosexual." Unknown to Powell, the clerk he was talking to was homosexual. Powell's was the crucial vote, because the other justices were divided 4–4. At first he voted to strike down the law, asserting that imprisoning a person for a private act of sodomy would amount to "cruel and unusual" punishment in violation of the Eighth Amendment. But then, after other justices complained that the Eighth Amendment argument had not been raised in the case before that point, Powell changed his mind. Instead, he joined Justice White's majority opinion.

VOTE

5–4, with Justice Byron R. White writing the opinion for the majority. Joining him were Chief Justice Warren E. Burger and Justices Lewis F. Powell Jr., William Rehnquist, and Sandra Day O'-Connor. Dissenting were Justices Harry A. Blackmun, William J. Brennan Jr., Thurgood Marshall, and John Paul Stevens.

HIGHLIGHTS

Justice White made short shrift of the argument made in Hardwick's behalf that the right of homosexuals to engage in sodomy was akin to the fundamental rights of family intimacy that the Court had declared in other contexts. Over the years the Court has given constitutional protection to family decisions about educating children and about marriage, contraception, and abortion. "We think it evident that none of the rights announced in those cases bears any resemblance to the claimed constitutional right of homosexuals to engage in acts of sodomy that is asserted in this case," White wrote.

Citing the long history of antisodomy laws, White also dismissed any notion that that there was a historical basis for protecting sodomy. "Against this background, to claim that a right to engage in such conduct is 'deeply rooted in this Nation's history and tradition' or 'implicit in the concept of ordered liberty' is, at best, facetious."

Reflecting the Court's conservative approach to interpreting the meaning of the Constitution, the Court also said it would resist pressure to create the new right that Hardwick sought. "The Court is most vulnerable and comes nearest to illegitimacy when it deals with judge-made constitutional law having little or no cognizable roots in the language or design of the Constitution," White wrote. "There should be, therefore, great resistance to expand the substantive reach of [the due process clauses of the Fifth and Fourteenth Amendments], particularly if it requires redefining the category of rights deemed to be fundamental. Otherwise, the Judiciary necessarily takes to itself further authority to govern the country without express constitutional authority. The claimed right pressed on us today falls far short of overcoming this resistance."

The fact that the crime of sodomy seems victimless and occurred in the privacy of Hardwick's home does not make it acceptable, White said, noting that incest and ownership of drugs could also be said to have the same justification. The government, White said, is entitled to make moral judgments in deciding what kinds of behavior to criminalize. Because the case involved homosexual sodomy only, White glossed over Hardwick's assertion that the state was using the law to target homosexuals, even though the same conduct was also illegal for heterosexuals.

Chief Justice Burger wrote a brief concurring opinion to underscore the historical basis for viewing homosexual sodomy as a crime. "To hold that the act of homosexual sodomy is somehow protected as a fundamental right would be to cast aside millennia of moral teaching."

Powell, who could have controlled the decision, instead wrote a two-paragraph concurring opinion. He suggested that a twenty-year prison term for a single act of consensual sodomy would create "a serious Eighth Amendment issue." But because Hardwick was never tried for the violation and never raised the Eighth Amendment issue, Powell said, "this constitutional argument is not before us."

Justice Blackmun wrote a bitter dissent, taking the Court to task for its "almost obsessive focus on homosexual activity" and for ignoring the fundamental constitutional right at stake. "I believe we must analyze respondent Hardwick's claim in the light of the values that underlie the constitutional right to privacy. If that right means anything, it means that, before Georgia can prosecute its citizens for making choices about the most intimate aspects of their lives, it must do more than as-

sert that the choice they have made is an 'abominable crime not fit to be named among Christians.' "

Blackmun also argued against laws that prohibit behavior mainly because it is different or frowned on. "The fact that individuals define themselves in a significant way through their intimate sexual relationships with others suggests, in a Nation as diverse as ours, that there may be many 'right' ways of conducting those relationships, and that much of the richness of a relationship will come from the freedom an individual has to choose the form and nature of these intensely personal bonds."

Finally, Blackmun recalled that it took the Court three years in the 1940s to reverse its view that public school students could be forced to salute the flag. "I can only hope that here, too, the Court soon will reconsider its analysis and conclude that depriving individuals of the right to choose for themselves how to conduct their intimate relationships poses a far greater threat to the values most deeply rooted in our Nation's history than tolerance of nonconformity could ever do."

Justice Stevens also wrote a dissent, arguing that Georgia had offered no acceptable explanation for its selective enforcement of the law against homosexuals. "From the standpoint of the individual, the homosexual and the heterosexual have the same interest in deciding how he will live his own life, and, more narrowly, how he will conduct himself in his personal and voluntary associations with his companions. State intrusion into the private conduct of either is equally burdensome."

EXCERPTS

From Justice White's majority opinion: "No connection between family, marriage, or procreation on the one hand and homosexual activity on the other has been demonstrated, either by the Court of Appeals or by respondent. Moreover, any claim that these cases nevertheless stand for the proposition that any kind of private sexual conduct between consenting adults is constitutionally insulated from state proscription is unsupportable. . . .

"Plainly enough, otherwise illegal conduct is not always immunized whenever it occurs in the home. Victimless crimes, such as the possession and use of illegal drugs, do not escape the law when they are committed at home. . . . And if respondent's submission is limited to the voluntary sexual conduct between consenting adults, it would be difficult, except by fiat, to limit the claimed right to homosexual conduct while leaving exposed to prosecution adultery, incest, and other sexual crimes even though they are committed in the home. We are unwilling to start down that road.

"Even if the conduct at issue here is not a fundamental right, respondent asserts that there must be a rational basis for the law, and that there is none in this case other than the presumed belief of a majority of the electorate in Georgia that homosexual sodomy is immoral and unacceptable. This is said to

Michael Hardwick was arrested for violating the Georgia sodomy statute in 1982. With help from the American Civil Liberties Union, Hardwick sued the state, claiming the law violated his right to privacy. In *Bowers v. Hardwick* (1986), the Supreme Court rejected Hardwick's argument, ruling that the rights to privacy and liberty do not include the right to commit sodomy.
Source: AP/Wide World Photos.

be an inadequate rationale to support the law. The law, however, is constantly based on notions of morality, and if all laws representing essentially moral choices are to be invalidated under the Due Process Clause, the courts will be very busy indeed."

IMPACT

The Court's decision was a major setback for the gay rights movement. In its first full treatment of homosexuality, the Supreme Court in dismissive language refused to accord any legitimacy to the privacy and liberty interests of homosexuals.

As gay right activists continued to press for recognition of their civil rights in a range of areas, the *Hardwick* ruling gave judges and politicians a legal justification for turning a deaf ear, even though it dealt only with sodomy. "Lower courts had treated the *Hardwick* decision as a signal that they, too, should reject the legal claims of gay people challenging discrimination," according to the 1998 book *Strangers to the Law* by Lisa Keen and Suzanne B. Goldberg.

The ruling troubled one justice in particular: Justice Powell, whose vote switch resulted in the Court's decision upholding the law. At a 1990 conference, after his retirement, Powell said of *Hardwick,* "I think I probably made a mistake in that one." Elaborating, Powell said that on reflection, the ruling seemed inconsistent with *Roe v. Wade,* which rooted the right to an abortion in the right to privacy. In later correspondence, Powell also said he thought it was a mistake for the Court to have taken the case at all, given that the Georgia law had not been enforced since 1935 and that Hardwick was never prosecuted.

It was not until the 1996 decision in *Romer v. Evans,* striking down a Colorado antigay constitutional amendment, that the Court began to look at homosexuals in a different light. *Bowers v. Hardwick* was not overturned, but the Court recognized that homosexuals as a group should not be singled out for less-than-favorable treatment. (See *Romer v. Evans.*)

Gay rights groups, including the Lambda Legal Defense and Education Fund, continued to challenge sodomy laws at the state level. By 1999 only fourteen states banned sodomy for both heterosexuals and homosexuals, and five states prohibited it for same-sex couples only.

Ironically, one of the antisodomy laws struck down after legal challenges by gay rights groups was Georgia's. In November 1998 the Georgia Supreme Court said the law violated the state constitution. "We cannot think of any other activity that reasonable persons would rank as more private and more deserving of protection from governmental interference than consensual, private, adult sexual activity," the state court said. "We conclude that such activity is at the heart of the Georgia Constitution's protection of the right of privacy."

Sensing that society's views toward homosexuality had shifted rapidly in the years since *Bowers,* Lambda looked for a new case to bring to the Supreme Court. It found one in a Texas prosecution of a sodomy case, and in 2003 Lambda's gamble paid off. The Court in *Lawrence v. Texas* reversed Bowers—a remarkably quick reversal, in Supreme Court terms. The nation's same-sex antisodomy laws could no longer be used to discriminate against homosexuals. (See *Lawrence v. Texas.*)

Romer v. Evans

Decided May 20, 1996
517 U.S. 620
laws.findlaw.com/US/517/620.html

DECISION

A state constitutional amendment that prohibits passage of laws protecting homosexuals from discrimination violates the Fourteenth Amendment to the U.S. Constitution.

BACKGROUND

Colorado was an early battleground in the fight over gay rights. In 1974 the Boulder City Council enacted a law prohibiting discrimination in the workplace on the basis of sexual orientation, but it created such a controversy that voters repealed it. In 1987 Boulder voters decided to reinstate the ban on discrimination against homosexuals, and Denver and Aspen enacted similar measures. Gov. Roy Romer in 1989 issued an order prohibiting discrimination against people with AIDS, many of whom were homosexual men.

Many Colorado residents with more conservative views were alarmed at these developments, fearing a deterioration of moral and religious principles. They created a group called Colorado for Family Values, with the goal of eliminating state and local antidiscrimination measures. They succeeded in placing a proposed constitutional amendment on the ballot in the fall of 1992. Known as Amendment 2, the measure would repeal existing laws and prevent enactment of future laws that give "protected status" to homosexual or bisexual people. After a

contentious campaign that received national attention, voters approved the measure 53–46 percent.

Before the amendment took effect, gay rights groups and some of the affected municipalities went to state court to challenge it. They claimed the amendment singled out a group of people for disfavored treatment, depriving them of the equal protection of the laws guaranteed by the Fourteenth Amendment. Defenders of the amendment said it merely prohibited special treatment but did nothing to discourage equal treatment.

The case took the name of Richard Evans, a Denver man who served as the mayor's liaison with the local gay community. Governor Romer was named as the defendant in his official capacity as the person who would enforce the amendment, even though he was on record as opposing it.

Colorado courts, including the state supreme court, struck down Amendment 2. "The right to participate equally in the political process is clearly affected by Amendment 2," the state supreme court ruled. "Amendment 2 alters the political process so that a targeted class is prohibited from obtaining legislative, executive, and judicial protection or redress from discrimination."

The state appealed the ruling, setting the stage for a major Supreme Court confrontation on the legal status of homosexuals. The Clinton administration, which had been embroiled in controversy over its policy on gays in the military, decided not to take part in the *Romer v. Evans* case, citing the lack of any federal interest in the dispute.

VOTE

6–3, with Justice Anthony M. Kennedy writing the majority opinion. Joining him were Justices John Paul Stevens, Sandra Day O'Connor, David H. Souter, Ruth Bader Ginsburg, and Stephen G. Breyer. Dissenting were Chief Justice William Rehnquist and Justices Antonin Scalia and Clarence Thomas.

HIGHLIGHTS

One of the challenges for the Court was to determine where homosexuals fit on its spectrum of protection under the Fourteenth Amendment to the Constitution. The Court has reserved its highest level of protection to members of what it has called a "suspect class"—a group with some unchangeable, usually easily identi-

In *Romer v. Evans* (1996), the Supreme Court ruled a Colorado anti-gay rights initiative unconstitutional. Here, after the Court's decision, attorney Jean Dubofsky, right, hugs Priscilla Inkpen, one of the plaintiffs who challenged the measure. Richard Evans, the first named plaintiff in the case, stands at the left.
Source: AP/Wide World Photos.

fied characteristic such as race or ethnic origin. Laws that single out such groups for different treatment are subjected to "strict scrutiny" and are almost always struck down. But with laws that affect groups that the Court has not placed in this category, lower levels of scrutiny are used, enabling some of the laws to be upheld.

In *Romer,* the Court neatly avoided that thicket by asserting that the Colorado amendment failed to survive even the lowest level of scrutiny. That being the case, the Court did not need to decide that homosexuals are a suspect class or where they belonged in its Fourteenth Amendment spectrum.

"If a law neither burdens a fundamental right nor targets a suspect class, we will uphold the legislative classification so long as it bears a rational relation to some legitimate end," Kennedy wrote. "Amendment 2 fails, indeed defies, even this conventional inquiry. First, the amendment has the peculiar property of imposing a broad and undifferentiated disability on a single named group, an exceptional and . . . invalid form of legislation. Second, its sheer breadth is so discontinuous with the reasons offered for it that the amendment seems inexplicable by anything but animus toward the class that it affects; it lacks a rational relationship to legitimate state interests."

The state's argument that the amendment merely puts homosexuals in a position equal to others, Kennedy said, is "implausible." The amendment puts homosexuals far behind others, in terms of being able to call on government to prevent or punish discrimination against them. Kennedy asserted that it does not merely repeal laws specifically protecting homosexuals. A fair, if not necessary, inference, Kennedy said, is that the amendment also prevents homosexuals from invoking general laws against arbitrary government decision making. "The amendment imposes a special disability upon those persons alone," Kennedy wrote.

The Court also dismissed the other justifications the state advanced for the amendment, namely conserving state resources and protecting the freedoms of association and religion of landlords and employers who object to homosexuality. "The breadth of the Amendment is so far removed from these particular justifications that we find it impossible to credit them. We cannot say that Amendment 2 is directed to any identifiable legitimate purpose or discrete objective."

Justice Scalia disagreed angrily with the majority's view. "This Court has no business imposing upon all Americans the resolution favored by the elite class from which the Members of this institution are selected, pronouncing that 'animosity' toward homosexuality is evil. I vigorously dissent."

Scalia noted that the majority had made no mention of the 1986 decision in *Bowers v. Hardwick,* in which the Court had upheld Georgia's law against sodomy. "If it is constitutionally permissible for a State to make homosexual conduct criminal, surely it is constitutionally permissible for a State to enact other laws merely disfavoring homosexual conduct."

Scalia continued, "Today's opinion has no foundation in American constitutional law, and barely pretends to. The people of Colorado have adopted an entirely reasonable provision which does not even disfavor homosexuals in any substantive sense, but merely denies them preferential treatment. Amendment 2 is designed to prevent piecemeal deterioration of the sexual morality favored by a majority of Coloradans. . . . Striking it down is an act not of judicial judgment, but of political will." Under the Court's theory, Scalia said laws against polygamy—having more than one spouse at the same time—could also be challenged.

EXCERPTS

From Justice Kennedy's majority opinion: "Sweeping and comprehensive is the change in legal status effected by this law. So much is evident from the ordinances that the Colorado Supreme Court declared would be void by operation of Amendment 2. Homosexuals, by state decree, are put in a solitary class with respect to transactions and relations in both the private and governmental spheres. The amendment withdraws from homosexuals, but no others, specific legal protection from the injuries caused by discrimination, and it forbids reinstatement of these laws and policies. . . .

". . . Homosexuals are forbidden the safeguards that others enjoy or may seek without constraint. They can obtain specific protection against discrimination only by enlisting the citizenry of Colorado to amend the state constitution or perhaps, on the State's view, by trying to pass helpful laws of general applicability. This is so no matter how local or discrete the harm, no matter how public and widespread the injury. We find nothing special in the protections Amendment 2 withholds. These are protections taken for granted by most people either because they already have them or do not need them; these are protections against exclusion from an almost limitless number of transactions and endeavors that constitute ordinary civic life in a free society. . . .

"It is not within our constitutional tradition to enact laws of this sort. Central both to the idea of the rule of law and to our own Constitution's guarantee of equal protection is the principle that government and each of its parts remain open on impartial terms to all who seek its assistance. . . . A law declaring that in general it shall be more difficult for one group of citizens than for all others to seek aid from the government is itself a denial of equal protection of the laws in the most literal sense. . . .

"We must conclude that Amendment 2 classifies homosexuals not to further a proper legislative end but to make them unequal to everyone else. This Colorado cannot do. A State cannot so deem a class of persons a stranger to its laws. Amendment 2 violates the Equal Protection Clause, and the judgment of the Supreme Court of Colorado is affirmed."

IMPACT

Gay rights advocates instantly applauded the *Romer* decision. In a book about the case called *Strangers to the Law,* authors Lisa Keen and Suzanne B. Goldberg describe it as a "strong, stunning legal victory."

For the first time, the Supreme Court had treated homosexuals and bisexuals as groups that government could not single out for disfavored treatment. It was a ringing and unusual opinion, coming from a conservative Court that ordinarily gave substantial leeway to states to govern themselves as they saw fit. Several weeks after the *Romer* decision, the Court cited it in striking down a similar ordinance that had been passed in Cincinnati.

At first, *Romer* did little to end the debate over the rights of homosexuals. Kennedy's avoidance of any broad statement about or definition of the status of homosexuals, and his avoidance of *Bowers v. Hardwick,* robbed the decision of some of its force. Some scholars have also argued that Kennedy's majority opinion is thinly reasoned and not rooted well enough in Fourteenth Amendment jurisprudence. (See *Bowers v. Hardwick.*)

One sign that the *Romer* decision may have had limited impact came soon after it was handed down. President Bill Clinton announced his support for the Defense of Marriage Act, which was aimed at discouraging state recognition of same-sex marriages. Although gay rights advocates argued it was motivated by the same kind of hostility toward gays that the Court disapproved of in *Romer,* Congress passed the law in 1996.

The *Romer* decision also proved ineffective in the challenges by gay rights groups against the "don't ask, don't tell" policy on gays in the military. Several appeals courts upheld the policy, and the Supreme Court declined to review the issue.

But in 2003 *Romer* became one of the building blocks that helped gay rights advocates reach a major milestone: overturning *Bowers v. Hardwick.* In the ruling in *Lawrence v. Texas,* the Court struck down antisodomy laws aimed at gays, giving new recognition to the privacy interests of homosexuals. The court majority said the *Romer* decision "cast *Bowers*' holding into even more doubt." (See *Lawrence v. Texas.*)

Boy Scouts of America v. Dale

Decided June 28, 2000
530 U.S. 640
laws.findlaw.com/US/530/640.html

DECISION

The government may not force the Boy Scouts to reinstate a gay assistant scoutmaster. Requiring the scoutmaster's reinstatement would violate the Scouts' freedom of association and interfere with its ability to convey its beliefs to its members and to others.

BACKGROUND

As a young boy in New Jersey, James Dale joined the Cub Scouts as soon as he could, and by age eleven he was a full-fledged Boy Scout. He enjoyed the camping and the camaraderie, and even when he turned eighteen—the age limit for Scouts—he stuck with the organization. As he began college at Rutgers University, he became an assistant scoutmaster for his old troop.

While at Rutgers, Dale also "came out" and openly talked about the fact that he was a homosexual. At nineteen he became copresident of the Rutgers University Lesbian/Gay Alliance, and in July 1990 he gave an interview to the *Newark* *Star-Ledger* in which he discussed his sexual orientation and his "double life" in high school.

Though the article did not mention his Scout activities, it ended his avocation as a scoutmaster. Scout officials who read the story immediately invoked a policy in effect since 1978 that barred membership to males who were openly or avowed homosexuals.

Dale, shocked and disappointed, decided to challenge his exclusion from the Scouts and the policy behind it. He sued in state court under a new law that bars discrimination on the basis of sexual orientation in "public accommodations"—places like hotels that offer services to the public. He reasoned that the Boy Scouts, which has an official government charter and often holds meetings and recruits at public schools, qualified as a public accommodation.

After a trial court sided with the scouts, a lengthy appeals process ensued, and finally the New Jersey Supreme Court in 1999 reversed and agreed with Dale. By then Dale had turned twenty-nine. The New Jersey Supreme Court found that the

Former assistant scoutmaster James Dale, left, and his attorney talk with reporters about the Supreme Court's decision in *Boy Scouts of America v. Dale* (2000). The Court ruled that the Boy Scouts were entitled to dismiss Dale, who acknowledged being gay, and upheld the group's right to "freedom of expressive association."
Source: Reuters/Jeff Christensen.

Scouts are a public accommodation and rejected the Scouts' argument that being forced to admit a homosexual would interfere with the organization's ability to communicate its values and views. The state Supreme Court said allowing Dale back as a member would not cause any such interference, because opposing homosexuality is not a central part of the Scouts' message; Scout rules, it noted, discourage any discussion of sexual issues at Scout meetings.

The Boy Scouts, joined by conservative and Christian organizations, appealed to the U.S. Supreme Court. Invoking the part of the Boy Scout oath in which members pledge to be "morally straight," the organization told the court, "Boy Scouting does not have an 'anti-gay' policy, it has a morally straight policy." Gay rights groups viewed the case as an important test of the Supreme Court's latest thinking on discrimination against gays.

VOTE

5–4, with Chief Justice William Rehnquist writing the opinion for the majority. Joining him were Justices Sandra Day O'Connor, Antonin Scalia, Anthony Kennedy, and Clarence Thomas. Dissenting were Justices John Paul Stevens, David Souter, Ruth Bader Ginsburg, and Stephen Breyer.

HIGHLIGHTS

Chief Justice Rehnquist went through several steps to reach the conclusion that requiring the Boy Scouts to accept James Dale in its ranks would violate the Scouts' constitutional rights. Citing the Court's precedents in the area of freedom of association (see *Roberts v. United States Jaycees*), Rehnquist said that

forcing Dale's membership would be unconstitutional if it significantly affected the Scouts' ability to advocate "public or private viewpoints." To determine that, the Court needed to decide first of all what the Scouts' viewpoints were.

Without inquiring too intrusively into those beliefs, Rehnquist said it was clear that—right or wrong—the Scouts have a definite viewpoint that homosexuality is incompatible with its ideal of "morally straight" members and leaders. Courts should not second-guess the validity or consistency of a group's message, Rehnquist added: "We accept the Boy Scouts' assertion. We need not inquire further to determine the nature of the Boy Scouts' expression with respect to homosexuality."

Likewise, Rehnquist deferred to the Scouts' determination that accepting a gay male as a member would impair its ability to express itself about its values or goals. Dale had argued that since the Scouts allow heterosexual members to object to the policy about gay memberships, his own presence would have no effect on the Scouts' message. But Rehnquist said that was "irrelevant," and in any case, "The presence of an avowed homosexual and gay rights activist in an assistant scoutmaster's uniform sends a distinctly different message from the presence of a heterosexual assistant scoutmaster who is on record as disagreeing with Boy Scouts policy."

Having concluded that Dale's presence would significantly interfere with the Scouts' message, Rehnquist's bottom line was that New Jersey's interest in preventing discrimination in public accommodations was far outweighed by the damage to the Scouts' rights caused by forcing the Scouts to accept him.

Justice Stevens, in dissent, said it was astonishing that the Court would give such deference to the Scouts in deciding whether the group had a message that Dale would impair. Quoting from the Scout Oath and other Scout documents, Stevens wrote, "It is plain as the light of day that neither one of these principles—"morally straight" and "clean"—says the slightest thing about homosexuality." Later, Stevens wrote, "Boy Scouts of America is simply silent on homosexuality. There is no shared goal or collective effort to foster a belief about homosexuality at all—let alone one that is significantly burdened by admitting homosexuals."

Stevens also recited some of the history of discrimination against homosexuals and concluded that prejudice against gays "can only be aggravated by the creation of a constitutional shield for a policy that is itself the product of a habitual way of thinking about strangers."

EXCERPTS

From Chief Justice Rehnquist's majority opinion: "The forced inclusion of an unwanted person in a group infringes the group's freedom of expressive association if the presence of that person affects in a significant way the group's ability to advocate public or private viewpoints. . . . Dale, by his own admission, is one of a group of gay Scouts who have 'become leaders in their community and are open and honest about their sexual orientation.' . . . Dale's presence in the Boy Scouts would, at the very least, force the organization to send a message, both to the youth members and the world, that the Boy Scouts accepts homosexual conduct as a legitimate form of behavior. . . .

"We are not, as we must not be, guided by our views of whether the Boy Scouts' teachings with respect to homosexual conduct are right or wrong; public or judicial disapproval of a tenet of an organization's expression does not justify the State's effort to compel the organization to accept members where such acceptance would derogate from the organization's expressive message."

From Justice Stevens's dissent: "His participation sends no cognizable message to the Scouts or to the world. . . . The only apparent explanation for the majority's holding, then, is that homosexuals are simply so different from the rest of society that their presence alone—unlike any other individual's—should be singled out for special First Amendment treatment. Under the majority's reasoning, an openly gay male is irreversibly affixed with the label "homosexual." That label, even though unseen, communicates a message that permits his exclusion wherever he goes. His openness is the sole and suf-

ficient justification for his ostracism. Though unintended, reliance on such a justification is tantamount to a constitutionally prescribed symbol of inferiority."

IMPACT

Gay rights advocates were disappointed that the Court had given the Scouts far more deference and recognition than it gave to James Dale. The ruling also contrasted sharply with the Court's *Romer v. Evans* decisions a few years earlier, in which the majority had disapproved of a ballot initiative that treated homosexuals unequally (see *Romer v. Evans*).

But gay rights advocates were also heartened by the Stevens dissent. The ruling stood as "something of a gay rights milestone, because it revealed four justices are vocal foes of anti-gay discrimination," according to *Courting Justice,* a 2001 book about the Supreme Court and gay rights. "Writing for the dissenters, Stevens spoke out against anti-gay bias more powerfully than any other justice."

Lambda Legal Defense and Education Fund, which represented Dale in his nearly decade-long legal battle, struck a similar note. "The Supreme Court today said that Boy Scouts of America has a right to discriminate, but the Court did not say that discrimination is right," said Lambda senior attorney Evan Wolfson, who argued on Dale's behalf before the Supreme Court.

For the Scouts, the repercussions of the victory were not all positive. With the Scouts' policy against gay membership now officially acknowledged, several government agencies dropped support for the organization. Some barred the Scouts from using city facilities. Connecticut dropped the Scouts from its list of charities that state employees could contribute to through payroll deductions. Some private donors stopped contributing to the Scouts.

Responding to the controversy, the Boy Scouts of America said it would fight for access to schools and to donation programs on a par with other community organizations. In a statement, the Scouts said, "We hope that our supporters will continue to value the Boy Scouts of America's respect for diversity and the positive impact Scouting has on young people's lives. We realize that not every individual nor organization subscribes to the same beliefs that the BSA does, but we hope that all Americans can be as respectful of our beliefs as we are of theirs and support the overall good Scouting does in American communities."

Lawrence v. Texas

Decided June 26, 2003
539 U.S. 558
laws.findlaw.com/US/000/02-102.html

DECISION

The right to liberty embodied in the due process clause of the Fourteenth Amendment makes it unconstitutional for states to make it a crime for two persons of the same sex to engage in intimate sexual conduct.

BACKGROUND

The first time the Supreme Court squarely faced a challenge against laws criminalizing homosexual conduct, it upheld those laws, in *Bowers v. Hardwick.* (See *Bowers v. Hardwick.*) That 1986 decision was a setback for the gay rights community, but it did little if anything to slow the growing acceptance in society of homosexuality. States that had laws like the one upheld in Georgia in *Bowers* moved toward repealing them, and few states enforced them. In spite of the Court's affirmation, people increasingly viewed these laws as an anachronism that did not reflect current attitudes of acceptance toward homosexuality.

Even the Supreme Court did not hold its *Bowers* decision in high regard. In 1990 Justice Lewis Powell Jr. said he had "probably made a mistake" when he voted with the majority in *Bowers*; had he voted against the Georgia law, the decision would have come out the other way.

But still, to gay rights advocates the *Bowers* ruling represented an official rejection of their personhood that remained an obstacle for homosexuals in areas ranging from housing to custody. If they could, by their very lifestyles, be characterized as criminals, they would never attain full equality or dignity.

Yet the Supreme Court rarely reverses itself, and when it does, it usually does so only after a long period of time. In spite of this fact, gay rights advocates in the late 1990s began looking for the right case in which to challenge *Bowers*. They were encouraged when, in the 1996 decision *Romer v. Evans,* the Court struck down a Colorado ballot initiative that prohibited localities from giving legal protection to homosexuals. (See *Romer v. Evans.*) The Court found that initiative to be a form of discrimination against homosexuals that violated the Fourteenth Amendment's equal protection clause.

Soon a Texas case presented itself that would become the vehicle for challenging *Bowers*. Responding to a complaint of a disturbance in 1998, Houston police entered the apartment of John Lawrence. They saw Lawrence and another man, Tyrone Garner, engaging in a sexual act. The two were arrested under the state law that prohibits "deviate sexual intercourse" with a person of the same sex. They challenged the law in court, but the full Texas Court of Appeals for the Fourteenth District, in-

In Houston, Tyrone Garner, left, and John Lawrence, right, celebrate the Supreme Court's decision in *Lawrence v. Texas* (2003), which struck down a Texas sodomy law and reversed *Bowers v. Hardwick* (1986). Gay rights advocates applauded the ruling.
Source: Reuters/Richard Carson.

voking the *Bowers* decision, upheld the convictions and said the law was constitutional. The Lambda Legal Defense and Education Fund, leading strategist in the legal battle for gay rights, appealed the decision to the Supreme Court.

VOTE

5–4, with Justice Anthony Kennedy writing the majority opinion. Joining him were Justices John Paul Stevens, David Souter, Ruth Bader Ginsburg, and Stephen Breyer. Justice Sandra Day O'Connor wrote separately, agreeing with the result but for different reasons. Justice Antonin Scalia, joined by Chief Justice William Rehnquist and Justice Clarence Thomas, dissented.

HIGHLIGHTS

In the majority opinion, Justice Kennedy took the remarkable step of not only overturning *Bowers v. Hardwick,* but asserting that "Bowers was not correct when it was decided, and it is not correct today." He attacked its premises as well as its historical bases, reviewing laws regarding sexual activity and concluding that there was not, in fact, a long U.S. and Judeo-Christian tradition of outlawing homosexual activity. Most of the laws that were passed in this area over history, he said, prohibited certain acts whether they were performed by homosexuals or heterosexuals. Internationally, Kennedy added, decriminalization of sodomy had begun in Europe even before *Bowers* was decided.

"The historical grounds relied upon in Bowers are more complex than the majority opinion and the concurring opinion by Chief Justice Burger indicate. Their historical premises are not without doubt and, at the very least, are overstated," Kennedy wrote.

But just as important, Kennedy said, *Bowers* had trivialized the deeply personal, intimate decisions that homosexual persons make—and, he said, are entitled to make. "Its continuance as precedent demeans the lives of homosexual persons," Kennedy said. He added that it was not the job of the Supreme Court to impose a particular moral code on the nation. Private conduct between consenting adults is beyond the reach of government, he said. The legal basis for his ruling, he said, was the due process clause, which guarantees a sphere of privacy and liberty for everyone—what he described as "liberty of the person both in its spatial and more transcendent dimensions."

Justice O'Connor, writing separately, said the Texas law should be struck down, but for a different reason. The same kind of sexual activity outlawed for homosexuals under the law, she said, is not illegal when it is done by heterosexuals. For that reason, she said the law violated the equal protection clause of the Fourteenth Amendment. As a result she said it was unnecessary to overturn *Bowers.*

Justice Scalia's dissent was an angry denunciation of the majority, which, he said, "has taken sides in the culture war, departing in its role of assuring, as neutral observer, that the democratic rules of engagement are observed." Asserting that he had "nothing against homosexuals," Scalia said it should be up to legislators, not the Supreme Court, to change laws like the one at issue. Justice Thomas said he found the Texas law "exceptionally silly," but he, like Scalia, said it should be up to the legislature to change it.

EXCERPTS

From Justice Kennedy's majority opinion: "Liberty protects the person from unwarranted government intrusions into a dwelling or other private places. In our tradition the State is not omnipresent in the home. And there are other spheres of our lives and existence, outside the home, where the State should not be a dominant presence. Freedom extends beyond spatial bounds. Liberty presumes an autonomy of self that includes freedom of thought, belief, expression, and certain intimate conduct. . . .

"Had those who drew and ratified the Due Process Clauses of the Fifth Amendment or the Fourteenth Amendment known the components of liberty in its manifold possibilities, they might have been more specific. They did not presume to have this insight. They knew times can blind us to certain truths and later generations can see that laws once thought necessary and proper in fact serve only to oppress. As the Constitution endures, persons in every generation can invoke its principles in their own search for greater freedom."

From Justice Scalia's dissent: "Today's opinion is the product of a Court, which is the product of a law-profession culture, that has largely signed on to the so-called homosexual agenda, by which I mean the agenda promoted by some homosexual activists directed at eliminating the moral opprobrium that has traditionally attached to homosexual conduct. . . . [I]f, as the Court coos (casting aside all pretense of neutrality), '[w]hen sexuality finds overt expression in intimate conduct with another person, the conduct can be but one element in a personal bond that is more enduring,' . . . what justification could there possibly be for denying the benefits of marriage to homosexual couples exercising '[t]he liberty protected by the Constitution?' "

IMPACT

Several leaders of the gay rights movement were in the courtroom when the *Lawrence* decision was announced. Some wept as they heard Kennedy's powerful denunciation of the Court's *Bowers* decision and his embrace of the liberty interests underpinning the Court's new interpretation. For the gay rights movement, *Lawrence v. Texas* was the equivalent of *Brown v. Board of Education,* setting aside past discrimination at the highest levels. (See *Brown v. Board of Education of Topeka.*)

Lawrence has had a broad impact that is still unfolding. It immediately called into question other laws and policies that treated gays differently, as well as laws that outlaw other kinds of private behavior. Some viewed the military's "don't ask, don't tell" policy, which still ultimately prohibits declared homosexuals from serving, as jeopardized by *Lawrence*. In late December 2004, a lawsuit entitled *Cook v. Rumsfeld* was filed in federal court in Massachusetts challenging the policy as a violation of *Lawrence* and other constitutional principles. A hearing in the case was held in July 2005.

As Scalia predicted, *Lawrence* also became a major weapon for advocates of same-sex marriage. If the underlying homosexual conduct was no longer illegal, on what basis could same-sex marriage be prohibited? Kennedy's majority opinion specifically stated that the *Lawrence* case "does not involve whether the government must give formal recognition to any relationship that homosexual persons seek to enter."

But when the Supreme Judicial Court of Massachusetts ruled in 2004 that barring same-sex marriage violated that state's constitution, it cited *Lawrence* numerous times nonetheless. Whether *Lawrence* helps spread the legalization of same-sex marriages to other states remains to be seen. But the Supreme Court, with remarkable speed, had changed course on the subject of homosexuality, giving the gay rights movement new momentum to fight future battles against all forms of discrimination.

HABEAS CORPUS

*T*he writ of habeas corpus, known as the Great Writ, is one of the primary protections against tyranny. Literally, the phrase in Latin means "you have the body," and it is in a sense a challenge to government to bring "the body" of a prisoner to court to justify its imprisonment of that individual. It is a backstop guarantee that even when appeals have failed, prisoners have an opportunity to challenge the reasons for keeping them incarcerated. It is not an unlimited right, however, and can be restricted by legislation or even suspended by Congress in cases of "rebellion or invasion," in the words of the Constitution. The Supreme Court has often been called on to rule on the scope of the writ, and in the latter part of the twentieth century, the Court generally sought to rein it in, to prevent successive appeals and bring finality to prison sentences including the death penalty.

Other related cases mentioned in the Habeas Corpus section

Ex parte McCardle (1869)
In re Quirin (1942)
Detainee Cases (2004) (see p. 344)

Ex parte Milligan

Decided April 3, 1866
71 U.S. 2
laws.findlaw.com/US/71/2.html

DECISION

Constitutional protections against illegitimate imprisonment do not disappear in wartime. Neither the president nor Congress may authorize military courts to conduct trials of civilians, at least where civilian courts are open and functioning.

BACKGROUND

One little-known aspect of Abraham Lincoln's presidency was his sweeping suspension of civil liberties during the Civil War. Thousands of sympathizers who disliked the war or who tried to discourage northern efforts to recruit soldiers were arrested with little or no evidence that they had committed any crime.

During his first year as president, Lincoln ordered the suspension of the writ of *habeas corpus,* first between Philadelphia and Washington and then throughout the northeast. *Habeas corpus,* which comes from the Latin phrase "you should have the body," enables someone who is in prison to ask a judge to order the state to bring his or her "body" to court and justify the imprisonment.

At first glance, this may not seem to be a crucial power, but the writ of *habeas corpus,* sometimes called the "great writ," is viewed by many as one of the most important protections against the tyranny of arbitrary government. If a government can be forced to justify in court its imprisonment of individuals, that government is less likely to throw people in prison on a whim.

Article I, Section 9, of the Constitution says the writ shall never be suspended, except for "cases of rebellion or invasion [in which] the public safety may require it." Lincoln felt that the outbreak of civil war was a justification for suspending *habeas corpus* and declaring martial law. The existence of the Republic was at stake, he said, and the temporary suspension of certain civil liberties was a small price to pay. He was anxious to recruit more soldiers and to move troops from the northeast toward Washington, D.C., and dissenters and skeptics were hampering both campaigns. "Must I shoot a simple-minded soldier boy who deserts while I must not touch a hair of a wily agitator who induces him to desert?" Lincoln wrote in a published letter defending suspension of the writ.

Northerners generally appeared to support Lincoln's measures, but there was unease when the military arrested more than 13,000 people—from Baltimore police officials to newspaper publishers. "Arbitrary arrests became a commonplace of Northern life," wrote Civil War historian Allan Nevins.

Few of the arrests were explained, and few were challenged in any court. One, however, made it to the Supreme Court. It involved Lambdin Milligan, an Indiana politician with strong southern sympathies. Milligan and others were suspected of conspiring with the Confederate Army to undermine

President Abraham Lincoln in November 1863. As part of the effort to win the war with the South, Lincoln ordered the suspension of many civil rights, including the right to habeas corpus. In *Ex parte Milligan,* Lincoln appointee Justice David Davis wrote that the president had exceeded his constitutional powers.

Source: Library of Congress.

recruitment of soldiers for the North and to free Confederate prisoners. People like Milligan were called "copperheads," after the poisonous snakes whose coloration enabled them to blend in well with their surroundings.

Milligan and several other members of the group called "Sons of Liberty" were arrested by soldiers in 1864 and brought to trial before a military commission. He could have been tried in civilian federal court, but military leaders apparently did not trust the outcome of a trial before an Indiana jury. The military tribunal found Milligan and the others guilty of inciting insurrection and conspiracy and sentenced them to be hanged. They filed a *habeas corpus* petition challenging the convictions and claiming that it was unconstitutional to try civilians in a military court, especially in Indiana where no combat was under way. Two federal judges split on the case and forwarded it to the Supreme Court.

By the time it got to the Court, President Lincoln had been assassinated. Milligan was assisted by a team of able lawyers, including David Dudley Field, brother of Justice Stephen Field.

Lambdin P. Milligan was a "copperhead," a southern sympathizer, who tried to persuade men not to join the Union army. He was charged with treason and tried by military authorities. In *Ex parte Milligan* (1866) the Court said the president did not have the power to order military trials in areas where civilian courts were operating.

Source: Indiana Historical Society (negative no. C5136).

VOTE

9–0, with Justice David Davis writing for the Court. Joining him were Chief Justice Salmon P. Chase and Justices James M. Wayne, Samuel Nelson, Robert C. Grier, Nathan Clifford, Noah H. Swayne, Samuel F. Miller, and Stephen J. Field.

HIGHLIGHTS

Justice Davis's opinion is "far from a model of logical organization," says Chief Justice William Rehnquist in a 1998 book on civil liberties in wartime called *All the Laws but One.* Nevertheless, Davis quickly stated the magnitude of what was at stake in the *Milligan* case. "The importance of the main question presented by this record cannot be overstated; for it involves the very framework of the government and the fundamental principles of American liberty."

The Court agreed that judicial power belongs to the Supreme Court and lower courts—not to a military tribunal such as the one that tried Milligan. Neither the president nor Congress could authorize such a proceeding, the Court said. "One of the plainest constitutional provisions was, therefore, infringed when Milligan was tried by a court not ordained and established by Congress, and not composed of judges appointed during good behavior," the Court said. Civilian courts in Indiana were fully able to try Milligan, Davis asserted. He also contended that "another guarantee of freedom was broken when Milligan was denied a trial by jury."

Davis acknowledged that wartime could bring limited exceptions to normal constitutional protections. But the only one authorized by the Constitution is suspension of *habeas corpus,* he said. "It is essential to the safety of every government that, in a great crisis like the one we have just passed through, there should be a power somewhere of suspending the writ of habeas corpus." But that did not justify suspension of other constitutional precepts.

Broad declarations of martial law outside a combat zone go against the very purposes of the Declaration of Independence, Davis continued. "Martial law, established on such a basis, destroys every guarantee of the Constitution, and effectually renders the 'military independent of and superior to the civil power.'"

Chief Justice Chase wrote a concurring opinion, joined by Justices Swayne, Miller, and Wayne. They agreed with the majority that Milligan should be released and that the president has no power to order civilians tried by military courts.

But the justices parted company with the majority's view that Congress did not have authority in this area. "We think that Congress had power, though not exercised, to authorize the military commission which was held in Indiana," Chase wrote. "The power to make the necessary laws is in Congress, the power to execute in the President. Both powers imply many subordinate and auxiliary powers. Each includes all authorities essential to its due exercise. But neither can the President, in war more than in peace, intrude upon the proper authority of Congress, nor Congress upon the proper authority of the President."

EXCERPTS

From Justice David Davis's majority opinion: "During the late wicked Rebellion, the temper of the times did not allow that calmness in deliberation and discussion so necessary to a correct conclusion of a purely judicial question. Then, considerations of safety were mingled with the exercise of power, and feelings and interests prevailed which are happily terminated. Now that the public safety is assured, this question, as well as all others, can be discussed and decided without passion or the admixture of any element not required to form a legal judgment. We approach the investigation of this case, fully sensible of the magnitude of the inquiry and the necessity of full and cautious deliberation. . . .

"No graver question was ever considered by this court, nor one which more nearly concerns the rights of the whole people; for it is the birthright of every American citizen when charged with crime, to be tried and punished according to law. The power of punishment is, alone through the means which the laws have provided for that purpose, and if they are ineffectual, there is an immunity from punishment, no matter how great an offender the individual may be, or how much his crimes may have shocked the sense of justice of the country, or endangered its safety. By the protection of the law human rights are secured; withdraw that protection, and they are at the mercy of wicked rulers or the clamor of an excited people. If there was law to justify this military trial, it is not our province to interfere; if there was not, it is our duty to declare the nullity of the whole proceedings. . . .

". . . The Constitution of the United States is a law for rulers and people, equally in war and in peace, and covers with the shield of its protection all classes of men, at all times, and under all circumstances. No doctrine, involving more pernicious consequences, was ever invented by the wit of man than that any of its provisions can be suspended during any of the great exigencies of government. Such a doctrine leads directly to anarchy or despotism, but the theory of necessity on which it is based is false; for the government, within the Constitution, has all the powers granted to it, which are necessary to preserve its existence; as has been happily proved by the result of the great effort to throw off its just authority. . . .

". . . If it was dangerous, in the distracted condition of affairs, to leave Milligan unrestrained of his liberty, because he 'conspired against the government, afforded aid and comfort to rebels, and incited the people to insurrection,' the law said

arrest him, confine him closely, render him powerless to do further mischief; and then present his case to the grand jury of the district, with proofs of his guilt, and, if indicted, try him according to the course of the common law. If this had been done, the Constitution would have been vindicated, the law of 1863 enforced, and the securities for personal liberty preserved and defended. . . .

"It is difficult to see how the safety for the country required martial law in Indiana. If any of her citizens were plotting treason, the power of arrest could secure them, until the government was prepared for their trial, when the courts were open and ready to try them."

IMPACT

The Court's ruling in *Milligan* is often cited as one of its most important, representing the triumph of the civilian rule of law and of the Founders' view that the military should have a limited role in governance of the nation.

"If, in this hemisphere, the United States has been almost unique in avoiding rule by the military throughout its history," wrote Court scholar Bernard Schwartz, "that has been true because of the wall of separation between the civil and the military. . . . *Milligan* is still the great case ensuring that the wall is not breached while civil government is capable of carrying on its functions."

Milligan is also an important statement from the Court that individual freedoms are important even in times of war. "The *Milligan* decision is justly celebrated for its rejection of the government's position that the Bill of Rights has no application in wartime," Rehnquist wrote in his 1998 book.

But at the time of the decision, the Court was roundly criticized for giving aid and comfort to enemies of the victorious north in the Civil War. "The constitutional twaddle of Mr. Justice Davis will no more stand the fire of public opinion than the Dred Scott decision," opined the *New York Herald*. Because the war was over by the time the Court ruled, the decision had little immediate impact.

Many were concerned that the Court's decision would be used to strike down the military governments imposed on the southern states during Reconstruction. Those governments had the authority to try civilians in military courts. In the 1869 case *Ex parte McCardle*, William McCardle, a Mississippi editor arrested under the Reconstruction military regime, had challenged his prosecution, citing *Milligan*. While his case was pending before the Court, Congress passed a law removing the Court's jurisdiction in the case, and the Supreme Court acquiesced.

In the modern era, the Court has not always followed its own rule announced in *Milligan*. In World War II the Court endorsed military trials used to convict Richard Quirin and several other German saboteurs captured as they tried to enter the United States. The Court's 1942 ruling in *Ex parte Quirin* said *Milligan* did not apply because Quirin and the others, unlike Milligan, were actual combatants in the war. The Germans were executed less than a week after the Supreme Court ruled.

From these and other cases, Rehnquist concluded that it is easier for the Supreme Court to favor civil liberties after a war is over than while it is still under way. "It is neither desirable nor is it remotely likely that civil liberty will occupy as favored a position in wartime as it does in peacetime," Rehnquist wrote. "But it is both desirable and likely that more careful attention will be paid by the courts to the basis for the government's claims of necessity as a basis for curtailing civil liberty. The laws will thus not be silent in time of war, but they will speak with a somewhat different voice."

Rehnquist's axiom was borne out, to some extent, after the September 11, 2001, terrorist attacks on the United States. During the combat in Afghanistan and Iraq that followed, both foreign and U.S. citizens were detained by the United States and held for long periods without traditional due process, including access to lawyers. The Bush administration defined the captives as "enemy combatants" rather than prisoners of war, thereby claiming they did not need to abide by international rules for treatment of prisoners of war. With the aid of human rights groups, detainees challenged their detention in U.S. courts, many citing *Milligan*. In a trio of decisions handed down in 2004, the Supreme Court said in general that some kind of due process should be accorded those detained by the United States. The decisions made frequent references to *Milligan*. (See Detainee Cases.)

POWERS OF THE PRESIDENT

The president, like Congress, has a set of specific powers as head of the executive branch of government and as commander-in-chief. It was not until the twentieth century, when the federal bureaucracy grew and the United States became a world power, that the power of the presidency took on outsized, even mythical, dimensions. The president has become viewed as the personification of the United States and as the most powerful individual on earth. But U.S. history is replete with reminders that presidents are human, and that they do not always have the final word. The Supreme Court has on occasion been called on to remind the president that no person is above the law.

Other related cases mentioned in the Powers of the President section

Marbury v. Madison (1803) (see p. 291)
United States v. United Mine Workers (1947)
Nixon v. Fitzgerald (1982)

United States v. Nixon

Decided July 24, 1974
418 U.S. 683
laws.findlaw.com/US/418/683.html

DECISION

A president is not entitled to withhold evidence needed for a criminal trial. An absolute claim of presidential immunity from being subpoenaed cannot be justified by the need for the three branches of government to operate independently or by the need for confidentiality in conversations between the president and his advisers.

BACKGROUND

By the summer of 1974, what had begun as a bungled burglary of Democratic Party offices in Washington, D.C., had turned into a constitutional crisis. The 1972 Watergate burglary was followed by what seemed to be efforts from the White House to protect the burglars and cover up the political motivations for the crime. Prodded in part by media investigations into the Watergate affair, the Nixon administration appointed a special prosecutor to investigate possible criminal acts. At the same time, evidence mounted that seemed to implicate the president. When it became known that President Nixon had secretly taped conversations in the White House, the special prosecutor, Archibald Cox, sought access to several of the tapes.

Nixon refused to give up the tapes, and he ordered Attorney General Elliot Richardson to fire Cox. In a dramatic series of events that became known as the "Saturday night massacre," Richardson refused to fire Cox, as did his deputy, William Ruckelshaus. Both resigned. Robert Bork, the third-ranking Justice Department official, agreed to fire Cox and return the Watergate investigation to the Justice Department. But congressional and public pressure continued, and Leon Jaworski was appointed as the new special prosecutor. Jaworski renewed and expanded the subpoena for the tapes, as calls for Nixon's impeachment or resignation became louder.

The confrontation soon moved to the courts, in spite of offers by Nixon to provide summaries or edited transcripts of the conversations. Jaworski argued that the tapes were needed as evidence to support indictments brought against presidential aides John Mitchell, H.R. Haldeman, John D. Ehrlichman, and others.

Nixon's lawyers based their arguments on the concept of "executive privilege," which they said should protect presidential communications from scrutiny by the other branches of government. Judge John Sirica of the federal district court upheld the subpoena. President Nixon made plans to take the issue to an appeals court panel, but Jaworski, citing the urgency of the issue, asked the Supreme Court to take up the issue directly without waiting for the appeals court to rule.

The justices were impressed with the gravity of the issue; the Court had not agreed to this extraordinary procedure since 1947, when it dealt with issues arising from a nationwide coal strike in *United States v. United Mine Workers*. On May 31, 1974, the Court said it would expedite matters, even though it was preparing to wind up its work for the term. The case was argued July 8. The arguments centered not only on the issue of executive privilege but also on whether the president or the Supreme Court had the authority to determine the constitutional scope of the privilege. When the justices met in conference, it became clear that Nixon's position had no support. It fell to Warren Burger, the man Nixon had named as chief justice, to write the opinion that would rebuff Nixon's effort to save his presidency.

VOTE

8–0, with Chief Justice Warren E. Burger writing the opinion for the Court. Joining him were Justices Lewis F. Powell Jr., Harry A. Blackmun, William J. Brennan Jr., William O. Douglas, Byron R. White, Potter Stewart, and Thurgood Marshall. Justice William Rehnquist, who had been an official in the Nixon Justice Department before joining the Court, did not participate in the case.

HIGHLIGHTS

Before reaching the core issue of executive privilege, the Court dismissed two of the preliminary arguments President Nixon had made suggesting that the Court should not even decide the case. Nixon had argued that because the dispute was between the president and the special prosecutor—both officials of the executive branch—it was not justiciable or suitable for resolution by the courts.

"In light of the uniqueness of the setting in which the conflict arises," the Court countered, "the fact that both parties are officers of the Executive Branch cannot be viewed as a barrier to justiciability. It would be inconsistent with the applicable law and regulation, and the unique facts of this case to conclude other than that the Special Prosecutor has standing to bring this action, and that a justiciable controversy is presented for decision."

The Court also showed no sympathy for Nixon's argument that he alone should be able to determine the scope of executive privilege without interference by the courts. "In the performance of assigned constitutional duties, each branch of the Government must initially interpret the Constitution, and the interpretation of its powers by any branch is due great respect from the others," Burger wrote. "The President's counsel, as we have noted, reads the Constitution as providing an absolute privilege of confidentiality for all Presidential communications. Many decisions of this Court, however, have unequivocally reaffirmed the holding of *Marbury v. Madison,* that '[i]t is emphatically the province and duty of the judicial department to say what the law is.' " Burger continued, "Any other conclusion would be contrary to the basic concept of separation of powers and the checks and balances that flow from the scheme of a tripartite government." (See *Marbury v. Madison.*)

Having asserted its authority to rule in the case, the Court then discussed the privilege issue. The president, the Court agreed, is entitled to great deference in his desire to keep White House communications private so that he can get the best advice possible. "Human experience teaches that those who expect public dissemination of their remarks may well temper candor with a concern for appearances and for their own interests to the detriment of the decisionmaking process," Burger wrote. "Whatever the nature of the privilege of confidentiality of Presidential communications in the exercise of Article II powers, the privilege can be said to derive from the supremacy of each branch within its own assigned area of constitutional duties. Certain powers and privileges flow from the nature of enumerated powers; the protection of the confidentiality of Presidential communications has similar constitutional underpinnings."

The Court went on to create what it called a "presumptive privilege" for presidential communications, a privilege that was at its strongest when the communications involved national security and military matters. But the Court added that the privilege was a limited one that could not take precedence over the needs of the criminal justice system. The truth-seeking nature of the trial process requires maximum access to the necessary evidence, the Court said. "The very integrity of the judicial system and public confidence in the system depend on full disclosure of all the facts, within the framework of the rules of evidence," Burger wrote. "To ensure that justice is done, it is imperative to the function of courts that compulsory process be available for the production of evidence needed either by the prosecution or by the defense."

EXCERPTS

From Chief Justice Warren Burger's majority opinion: "[N]either the doctrine of separation of powers, nor the need for confidentiality of high-level communications, without more, can sustain an absolute, unqualified Presidential privilege of immunity from judicial process under all circumstances. The President's need for complete candor and objectivity from advisers calls for great deference from the courts. However, when the privilege depends solely on the broad, undifferentiated claim of public interest in the confidentiality of such conversations, a confrontation with other values arises. . . .

"The impediment that an absolute, unqualified privilege would place in the way of the primary constitutional duty of the Judicial Branch to do justice in criminal prosecutions would plainly conflict with the function of the courts under Art. III. In designing the structure of our Government and dividing and allocating the sovereign power among three co-equal branches, the Framers of the Constitution sought to provide a comprehensive system, but the separate powers were not intended to operate with absolute independence. . . .

"To read the Art. II powers of the President as providing an absolute privilege as against a subpoena essential to enforcement of criminal statutes on no more than a generalized claim of the public interest in confidentiality of nonmilitary and nondiplomatic discussions would upset the constitutional balance of 'a workable government' and gravely impair the role of the courts under Art. III.

"A President and those who assist him must be free to explore alternatives in the process of shaping policies and making decisions, and to do so in a way many would be unwilling to express except privately. These are the considerations justifying a presumptive privilege for Presidential communications. The privilege is fundamental to the operation of Government, and inextricably rooted in the separation of powers under the Constitution. . . .

"But this presumptive privilege must be considered in light of our historic commitment to the rule of law. . . . We have elected to employ an adversary system of criminal justice in which the parties contest all issues before a court of law. The need to develop all relevant facts in the adversary system is both fundamental and comprehensive. . . . To ensure that justice is done, it is imperative to the function of courts that compulsory process be available for the production of evidence needed either by the prosecution or by the defense. . . .

"In this case, we must weigh the importance of the general privilege of confidentiality of Presidential communications in performance of the President's responsibilities against the inroads of such a privilege on the fair administration of criminal justice. The interest in preserving confidentiality is weighty indeed and entitled to great respect. However, we cannot conclude that advisers will be moved to temper the candor of their remarks by the infrequent occasions of disclosure because of the possibility that such conversations will be called for in the context of a criminal prosecution.

On April 29, 1974, in response to subpoenas from the House Judiciary Committee and special prosecutor Leon Jaworski, President Richard Nixon announced in a televised speech that he would release edited transcripts of conversations with his aides about the Watergate break-in and cover-up. In *United States v. Nixon* (1974), the Supreme Court unanimously ordered Nixon to relinquish the actual recordings of the conversations, rejecting his arguments asserting the need for absolute presidential immunity. *Source: AP/Wide World Photos.*

"On the other hand, the allowance of the privilege to withhold evidence that is demonstrably relevant in a criminal trial would cut deeply into the guarantee of due process of law and gravely impair the basic function of the courts. . . . Without access to specific facts, a criminal prosecution may be totally frustrated. The President's broad interest in confidentiality of communications will not be vitiated by disclosure of a limited number of conversations preliminarily shown to have some bearing on the pending criminal cases."

IMPACT

In Nixon's 1978 memoirs he recalled that his chief of staff, Alexander Haig, called him with the news that the Supreme Court had handed down its decision in the tapes case. "Unanimous. There's no air in it at all," Haig reported. "None at all?" Nixon asked. "It's tight as a drum," Haig replied.

Even though the Court had recognized for the first time that presidential communications deserved confidential treatment, it said unequivocally that, in this case, the privilege had to bow to Jaworski's prosecutorial needs. The Court's unambiguous words prompted Nixon to realize that, tempted as he might have been to ignore or make light of the Court's opinion, "full compliance was the only option."

As the White House moved to comply, the realization settled in that the tapes sought by Jaworski contained the "smoking gun" that would undo Nixon's presidency. Nixon was recorded in

a June 23, 1972, conversation discussing the pros and cons of having the Central Intelligence Agency limit the Federal Bureau of Investigation inquiry into Watergate, not for national security reasons, but for political reasons. Although some argued the conversation could be explained away, even Nixon realized it would be interpreted as obstruction of justice, a serious criminal offense. Meanwhile, the House Judiciary Committee began voting articles of impeachment, and the momentum toward Nixon's removal from office became unstoppable. On August 5, transcripts of the June 23 conversation were made public, and on August 9, less than three weeks after the Supreme Court ruled, Richard Nixon became the first president in U.S. history to resign from office.

Over the years the Court's decision in *United States v. Nixon* has been heralded as proof that no man or woman is above the law in the United States. By echoing the words of *Marbury v. Madison,* the decision also powerfully reasserted the role of the Court in determining the constitutional balance between the branches of the government.

The decision was not the end of the Court's examination of when and whether a president can be subjected to the will of the courts. In *Nixon v. Fitzgerald* (1982) the Court said presidents may not be sued for their official acts. In *Clinton v. Jones* (1997), however, the Court said presidents could not avoid or postpone civil litigation over their unofficial acts. (See *Clinton v. Jones.*)

Clinton v. Jones

Decided May 27, 1997
520 U.S. 681
laws.findlaw.com/US/520/681.html

DECISION

Civil lawsuits against the president of the United States in connection with unofficial conduct may proceed even during the president's tenure in office. Deferring such suits until after the president has left office is not required by the Constitution. If persuaded that the president needs immunity from this kind of lawsuit while in office, Congress could pass a law giving the president such protection.

BACKGROUND

In *Nixon v. Fitzgerald* (1982) the Supreme Court recognized, with some understatement, that the president occupies a "unique position in the constitutional scheme." That unique position, as enforcer of the nation's laws and as an official who is never off duty, has prompted the Court at times to give the president some limited immunity under the law that average citizens do not enjoy.

Part of the reason for granting immunity to a president is the constitutional separation of powers. The three branches of government could not be deemed equal and independent if the courts, one branch of government, could easily intrude on the functioning of the president, the head of another branch.

Another reason is more practical. An essentially full-time president, the Supreme Court has sometimes said, should not be distracted by ongoing litigation or worried that his decisions would trigger lawsuits against him. So in the 1982 *Nixon* case, the Court said the president should enjoy "absolute" immunity from being sued personally for his official acts.

But in other contexts, the Court has said the immunity should be more limited. In an earlier case, *United States v. Nixon* (1974), the Court said the president's immunity must yield to a prosecutor's "particularized need" for evidence in a criminal investigation. That particular investigation concerned the break-in at the Watergate Hotel headquarters of the Democratic National Committee. Less than a month after the decision, President Nixon resigned rather than face almost certain impeachment. (See *United States v. Nixon*.)

With these mixed precedents on the books, it was difficult to predict how the Court would rule on the immunity of a president who had been sued for unofficial acts before or during his presidency.

The issue arose in connection with an embarrassing lawsuit against President Bill Clinton for an incident that allegedly took place when he was the governor of Arkansas. Paula Jones was a low-level employee of the Arkansas Industrial Development Commission in 1991 when Clinton came to the Excelsior Hotel in Little Rock to give a speech to a business conference. Jones was working at the conference registration desk. She alleges that after the speech, a state trooper acting on Clinton's behalf persuaded her to go to a hotel suite reserved for the governor. There, she says Clinton made an "abhorrent" sexual advance toward her, which she repulsed. Afterwards, Jones claims she was treated differently by her superiors, although she did not lose her job.

Jones filed suit against Clinton in 1994, more than a year into his presidency. It was not, strictly speaking, a sexual harassment lawsuit. Instead, she claimed under federal law that Clinton, acting in his official capacity, had violated her constitutional rights. She also made state law claims that Clinton had inflicted "emotional distress" on her and had, along with the state trooper, defamed her by denying the incident took place.

After the suit was filed, Clinton's lawyers, as well as the Justice Department, sought to delay any trial in the case. They argued that presidents should be immune from lawsuits such as Jones's until after they leave office.

Judge Susan Webber Wright—a onetime student of the president when he taught at the University of Arkansas law school—ruled partly in Clinton's favor. She said pretrial matters, such as depositions and fact finding, could continue, but an actual trial would have to wait until Clinton left office. She noted that Jones had filed her suit just days before the statute of limitations had run out, suggesting that an immediate trial was not necessary. An appeals court reversed Wright's decision, ruling that presidents were not entitled to immunity for their unofficial acts. Clinton asked the Supreme Court to reverse that decision.

VOTE

9–0, with Justice John Paul Stevens delivering the Court's opinion. Joining him were Chief Justice William Rehnquist and Justices Sandra Day O'Connor, Antonin Scalia, Anthony M. Kennedy, David Souter, Clarence Thomas, and Ruth Bader

Ginsburg. Justice Stephen G. Breyer filed an opinion concurring in the judgment.

HIGHLIGHTS

As with past decisions on presidential privileges or immunities, the Court once again paid homage to the unique position of the presidency. But this time, the Court was completely unsympathetic toward a president seeking immunity from a suit that involved only his unofficial acts.

The nature of such a lawsuit would give the president none of the rationales the Court had used in prior rulings on presidential immunity. If an unofficial act is at issue, the president's official prerogatives are not being undermined by the conduct of a lawsuit. And because unofficial acts are the focus, a president could not argue that the lawsuit would make him afraid to act boldly in his official duties.

The justices stressed that exposing presidents to lawsuits like that filed by Paula Jones would not be frequent or lengthy enough to take up much of a president's time. Suits against Presidents Theodore Roosevelt and Harry S. Truman had been dismissed before they took office. Two lawsuits stemming from an automobile accident during John F. Kennedy's presidential campaign in 1960 were settled before trial.

Even though Clinton was asking only for a delay in the trial—not that the case be dismissed altogether—the Court found that such a delay infringed on Jones's legal rights. Stevens said delaying the trial was an "abuse of discretion" by Judge Wright.

But Stevens said several times in the opinion that it should not be read to mean that judges can haul presidents into court at will. "Our decision rejecting the immunity claim and allowing the case to proceed does not require us to confront the question whether a court may compel the attendance of the President at any specific time or place," Stevens wrote. "We assume that the testimony of the President, both for discovery and for use at trial, may be taken at the White House at a time that will accommodate his busy schedule, and that, if a trial is held, there would be no necessity for the President to attend in person, though he could elect to do so."

Later, Stevens added, "The high respect that is owed to the office of the Chief Executive, though not justifying a rule of categorical immunity, is a matter that should inform the conduct of the entire proceeding, including the timing and scope of discovery."

EXCERPTS

From Justice John Paul Stevens's majority opinion: "In the more than 200-year history of the Republic, only three sitting Presidents have been subjected to suits for their private actions. If the past is any indicator, it seems unlikely that a deluge of such litigation will ever engulf the Presidency. As for the case at hand, if properly managed by the District Court, it appears to us

Paula Jones, with attorney Joseph Cammarata, left, and her husband, Steve Jones, right, exit the federal courthouse in Little Rock, Arkansas. In *Clinton v. Jones* (1997), the Supreme Court ruled unanimously that civil suits unrelated to official business can be brought against sitting presidents. The decision allowed a suit by Jones against President Bill Clinton to proceed while he remained in office. *Source: Reuters.*

highly unlikely to occupy any substantial amount of petitioner's time. . . .

"Moreover, the availability of sanctions provides a significant deterrent to litigation directed at the President in his unofficial capacity for purposes of political gain or harassment. History indicates that the likelihood that a significant number of such cases will be filed is remote. Although scheduling problems may arise, there is no reason to assume that the District Courts will be either unable to accommodate the President's needs or unfaithful to the tradition—especially in matters involving national security—of giving 'the utmost deference to Presidential responsibilities.' Several Presidents, including petitioner, have given testimony without jeopardizing the Nation's security. In short, we have confidence in the ability of our federal judges to deal with both of these concerns.

"The Federal District Court has jurisdiction to decide this case. Like every other citizen who properly invokes that jurisdiction, respondent has a right to an orderly disposition of her claims. Accordingly, the judgment of the Court of Appeals is affirmed."

IMPACT

There was something profoundly democratic, on the day the decision was handed down, about Justice Stevens describing Bill Clinton as the man who "happens to be President." Stevens's words conveyed unmistakably the notion that presidents are not kings. They must answer to the law like average citizens. Nevertheless, a lawsuit against a president is no ordinary lawsuit, and it can have extraordinary consequences.

With the benefit of hindsight, we now know that the Court's determination that the Paula Jones lawsuit was "highly unlikely" to occupy much of the president's time was a major miscalculation. It was in the context of the *Jones* lawsuit that

President Clinton gave a deposition denying a sexual relationship with White House intern Monica Lewinsky. That, in turn, triggered a chain of investigations and further testimony that resulted in the efforts by Republican lawmakers to remove him from office. President Clinton was impeached by the House of Representatives on December 18, 1998. Following a trial presided over by Chief Justice Rehnquist, the Senate acquitted him of all charges on February 12, 1999. Paula Jones's lawsuit was settled out of court with an agreement that President Clinton would pay her a substantial sum of money.

Beyond the circumstances of the Jones suit and the impeachment, it is difficult to predict how the Supreme Court's decision will affect future presidencies. There is enough deferential language toward presidents in the opinion to suggest that in future cases, judges managing lawsuits against the president will feel compelled to give the chief executive substantial leeway to accommodate his or her busy schedule.

In a speech in the spring of 1999, Justice Stevens defended the decision, noting that the avalanche of lawsuits against the president that some had predicted "hasn't happened yet." Stevens added, "I don't think anyone on the Court would change a word in the opinion if they had to do it over again."

The unanimity of the ruling also symbolized the ability of life-tenured Supreme Court justices to rise above political loyalty in their decision making. Justices Ginsburg and Breyer—Clinton's only two appointees to the Court during his first term—might have been expected by some to take his side in *Clinton v. Jones*. But Ginsburg joined the majority opinion against him, and Breyer wrote a concurring opinion in which he joined in the judgment but stated he was less confident than the majority that a president could remain undistracted by a pending lawsuit against him. As he put it, "The President never adjourns."

PRIVACY

*T*he word *privacy* does not appear in the Constitution, but it has evolved into a right that the Supreme Court has viewed as important to all Americans. Its origins can be found in different parts of the Constitution, including the Fourth Amendment bar against unreasonable searches and seizures, the First Amendment freedom of association, and the liberty and due process protections of the Fifth and Fourteenth Amendments. But privacy is a controversial concept, often targeted as a prime example of judicial activism, because it has been codified by judges rather than by elected legislators. Nonetheless, it is a cherished right, especially in the modern era when technology and the media have intruded in so many ways into individuals' private lives.

Other related cases mentioned in the Privacy section

Union Pacific R. Co. v. Botsford (1891)
Meyer v. Nebraska (1923)
Poe v. Ullman (1961)
Wisconsin v. Yoder (1972)
Doe v. Bolton (1973)
City of Akron v. Akron Center for Reproductive Health (1983)
Bowers v. Hardwick (1986) (see p. 175)
Webster v. Reproductive Health Services (1989)
Planned Parenthood of Southeastern Pennsylvania v. Casey (1992)
Vacco v. Quill (1997)
Washington v. Glucksberg (1997)
Stenberg v. Carhart (2000)

Pierce v. Society of Sisters

Decided June 1, 1925
268 U.S. 510
laws.findlaw.com/US/268/510.html

DECISION

A law that requires young people between the ages of eight and sixteen to attend public school rather than private or religious school violates the Fourteenth Amendment's guarantee of personal liberty. That liberty under the due process clause includes the power of parents to choose their children's schools and to direct their upbringing.

BACKGROUND

In the election of 1922, Oregon voters enacted an unusual law through a ballot initiative. The law made it a crime for parents of children between the ages of eight and sixteen not to send those children to public schools. Exceptions were allowed for the private education of children with physical or mental disabilities and children who lived far from public schools.

The law, apparently unique in the nation, was motivated not by any great support for public education, but rather by an intense dislike of private and parochial schools, especially those operated by the Roman Catholic church. The Ku Klux Klan, which was anti-Catholic as well as antiblack, was behind the initiative. Supporters of the law argued that religious schools promoted religious conflict.

Post–World War I fear of subversive ideas and immigrants also fueled the movement. Compulsory public education was seen as essential to guaranteeing that young people and future citizens would be loyal and patriotic.

The law, which was to take effect in 1926, posed an obvious and immediate threat to private and parochial schools in the state, and they began to lose enrollment. The Society of Sisters, which operated Catholic schools, and the Hill Military Academy, which ran a private school for boys, went to court to challenge the law, filing suit against Oregon governor Walter N. Pierce. A three-judge panel halted enforcement of the law, ruling that it deprived the two school operators of the use of their property without due process of law, a violation of the Fourteenth Amendment. The panel also said parents, as part of their protected liberty, had the right to choose the appropriate schools for their children.

The case went to the Supreme Court at a good time for the opponents of the Oregon law. Two years earlier the Court had struck down a Nebraska law that barred the teaching of foreign languages in the first eight grades. In *Meyer v. Nebraska* the Court had ruled that the law violated the Fourteenth Amendment rights of a German teacher who would be deprived of his job if the law took effect. The Oregon case seemed to involve similar rights and issues.

VOTE

9–0, with Justice James C. McReynolds writing the opinion of the Court. Joining him were Chief Justice William Howard Taft and Justices Oliver Wendell Holmes Jr., Willis Van Devanter, Louis D. Brandeis, George Sutherland, Pierce Butler, Edward T. Sanford, and Harlan Fiske Stone.

HIGHLIGHTS

In the Court's brief, unanimous decision, the justices acknowledged that states have some power to set rules for the education of children. "No question is raised concerning the power of the state reasonably to regulate all schools, to inspect, supervise and examine them, their teachers and pupils; to require that all children of proper age attend some school, that teachers shall be of good moral character and patriotic disposition, that certain studies plainly essential to good citizenship must be taught, and that nothing be taught which is manifestly inimical to the public welfare," the Court said.

But that did not entitle the state to interfere with parents' right to choose between private and public schools. Part of the freedom and liberty that citizens enjoy, the Court said, is the ability to make decisions about raising their children, decisions that are not dictated by the state.

The ruling gave equal emphasis to the property interests of the private and parochial school operators who brought the suit. They too have rights, the Court said. "They have business and property for which they claim protection. These are threatened with destruction through the unwarranted compulsion which appellants are exercising over present and prospective patrons of their schools. And this court has gone very far to protect against loss threatened by such action," the Court said.

Justice McReynolds added, "Appellees asked protection against arbitrary, unreasonable and unlawful interference with their patrons and the consequent destruction of their business and property." He said the businesses were entitled to that protection.

EXCERPTS

From Justice James C. McReynolds's majority opinion: "[W]e think it entirely plain that the Act of 1922 unreasonably interferes with the liberty of parents and guardians to direct the up-

Justice James McReynolds, a conservative on civil liberties, made a departure from his usual position in writing the opinion for *Pierce v. Society of Sisters* (1925), holding that an Oregon law compelling public school education violated parents' Fourteenth Amendment right to personal liberty. The amendment's due process clause guarantees parents the right to choose their children's school.
Source: Library of Congress.

bringing and education of children under their control. As often heretofore pointed out, rights guaranteed by the Constitution may not be abridged by legislation which has no reasonable relation to some purpose within the competency of the state. The fundamental theory of liberty upon which all governments in this Union repose excludes any general power of the state to standardize its children by forcing them to accept instruction from public teachers only. The child is not the mere creature of the state; those who nurture him and direct his destiny have the right, coupled with the high duty, to recognize and prepare him for additional obligations."

IMPACT

The decision in *Pierce*—and *Meyer* before it—came as something of a surprise, especially because Justice McReynolds, a conservative not usually known for his sympathy toward individual liberties, wrote them both. But both decisions were also framed in terms of the property rights of the teacher to keep a job and of the schools to continue their business. The Court found protection of those rights under the due process clause of the Fourteenth Amendment.

Whatever the source for the protection, the Court's decision in *Pierce* has had a lasting impact on civil liberties ever since. In one line of cases, it has been important in protecting the rights of parents to guide the upbringing of their children. In the 1972 decision *Wisconsin v. Yoder,* for example, *Pierce* was cited as the main reason why Amish parents should be able to educate their children privately.

More broadly, however, *Pierce* is cited frequently by the Court as a decision that protects intimate family decisions and relationships from interference by the state. It is one of a handful of decisions the Court has used as building blocks for constructing a "right of privacy." Privacy does not appear in the Constitution, but the Court has found it to be an important component of the liberties that Americans enjoy. In the 1965 decision *Griswold v. Connecticut,* the Court struck down a state law that barred the sale of contraceptives to married couples. *Pierce* was cited by the majority in support of the notion that parents have a privacy right to decide when to have children and how to raise them. Justice Harry Blackmun also invoked *Pierce* in *Roe v. Wade,* his 1973 opinion for the Court that declared a woman's right to an abortion. (See *Griswold v. Connecticut; Roe v. Wade.*)

Griswold v. Connecticut

Decided June 7, 1965
381 U.S. 479
laws.findlaw.com/US/381/479.html

DECISION

States may not make it a crime for anyone to use birth control devices or drugs, or to help others use them or learn about them. Such laws violate the privacy right of married couples. That right of privacy, although not mentioned in the Constitution, is implied by other parts of the Bill of Rights and can be invoked against state laws because of the due process clause of the Fourteenth Amendment.

BACKGROUND

The state of Connecticut had outlawed the use of contraception or birth control devices by anyone—married or unmarried—since 1879. The law was rarely enforced, but It stood as a symbol of an earlier, puritanical era in the state's history.

An earlier effort to have the law struck down had failed before the Supreme Court because of technical flaws in the case. In *Poe v. Ullman* (1961) the Court had turned away a prospective challenge to the law by couples who wanted contraceptive devices but feared they would be prosecuted if they tried to obtain them. By a 5–4 vote, the Court said that the mere prospect of prosecution was "too fragile a foundation" for the Court to decide the constitutionality of the law.

Somewhat emboldened by that decision, Connecticut officials of the Planned Parenthood Federation of America announced plans to offer contraceptive services in the state. Soon after a clinic opened in New Haven, two male police officers visited it. Estelle Griswold, executive director of the Planned Parenthood League of Connecticut, launched into a description of the clinic's services knowing it could lead to her arrest. The police obliged and arrested Griswold and Dr. C. Lee Buxton, the clinic's medical director. Authorities cited the anticontraception law, as well as a companion law that barred aiding others in committing a crime.

The two were convicted and fined $100 each. They challenged the law and its enforcement through the state courts, and the Supreme Court of Errors of Connecticut upheld their convictions. The courts "may not interfere" with state police power to enforce public safety and health, the Connecticut court concluded. Lawyers for Planned Parenthood filed an appeal with the Supreme Court, asserting that the state law violated due process, free speech, and privacy guarantees under the Constitution.

VOTE

7–2, with Justice William O. Douglas writing the majority opinion. Joining him were Chief Justice Earl Warren and Justices Arthur Goldberg, John M. Harlan, Byron White, William Brennan Jr., and Tom C. Clark. Justices Hugo L. Black and Potter Stewart dissented.

HIGHLIGHTS

In deciding that the Connecticut law was unconstitutional, the Court recognized it would have to go beyond the actual words of the Constitution to protect a right that is "unenumerated" in its text. Justice Douglas began by citing prior cases in which the Court had done just that, declaring a range of rights including the right of association, the right to teach children a foreign

In *Griswold v. Connecticut* (1965), the Supreme Court invalidated Connecticut's anticontraception law on the ground that it violated married couples' right to privacy. Estelle Griswold, left, executive director of the Connecticut Planned Parenthood League of Connecticut and appellant in the case, and Cornelia Jahncke, president of the Planned Parenthood League of Connecticut, rejoice over the ruling.

Source: The Granger Collection, New York.

language, and the right to send children to private or parochial schools.

"Specific guarantees in the Bill of Rights have penumbras, formed by emanations from those guarantees that help give them life and substance," Douglas wrote. The right of privacy that was violated by the Connecticut law, Douglas said, could be found by implication in several parts of the Bill of Rights: the First, Fourth, Fifth, and Ninth Amendments, and even the usually overlooked Third Amendment. The Third Amendment bars the quartering of troops in homes without the owner's consent, which Douglas saw as "another facet of that privacy." Douglas used the incorporation doctrine to apply the federal constitutional right to states such as Connecticut through the Fourteenth Amendment.

Other justices in the majority found a different path to the same result. Justice Goldberg, for example, expressed doubt that the Fourteenth Amendment could be used to apply all of the Bill of Rights to the states. But Goldberg, joined by Warren and Brennan, found that the "concept of liberty protects those personal rights that are fundamental," including the right to marital privacy. Justice Harlan rejected the incorporation doctrine and spoke of the "concept of ordered liberty" as the basis for declaring the Connecticut law invalid under the Fourteenth Amendment. Justice White, writing separately, expressed a similar view.

In dissent, Justices Black and Stewart both said they too disapproved of the Connecticut law—Stewart called it "uncommonly silly"—but they could not find it unconstitutional. The remedy, Stewart suggested, was for the voters of Connecticut to persuade their legislators to change the law.

EXCERPTS

From Justice William O. Douglas's majority opinion: "Would we allow the police to search the sacred precincts of marital bedrooms for telltale signs of the use of contraceptives? The very idea is repulsive to the notions of privacy surrounding the marriage relationship.

"We deal with a right of privacy older than the Bill of Rights—older than our political parties, older than our school system. Marriage is a coming together for better or for worse, hopefully enduring, and intimate to the degree of being sacred. It is an association that promotes a way of life, not causes; a harmony in living, not political faiths; a bilateral loyalty, not commercial or social projects. Yet it is an association for as noble a purpose as any involved in our prior decisions."

IMPACT

By striking down a little-used law in a single state, *Griswold* had a tremendous impact on the evolution of individual liberties in the United States. Because it spelled out the right to privacy, the ruling served as the "parent" of *Roe v. Wade,* the 1973 decision that legalized abortion. Some commentators say the *Roe v. Wade* decision would have been impossible if *Griswold* had not been decided as it was. And although the Court was divided on this point, the *Griswold* decision helped extend the force of the Bill of Rights to the state level.

Since *Griswold,* the concept of privacy has taken root in society as a value that is increasingly cherished, even as it is threatened by technology and the media. But in legal terms, privacy has not always been interpreted broadly since *Griswold*. In 1986, for example, the Court indicated the right of privacy did not extend to homosexual couples. (See *Bowers v. Hardwick*.) In 2003, however, the Supreme Court overturned *Bowers,* frequently invoking *Griswold* as it struck down laws that criminalized private homosexual conduct

In part because of *Griswold*'s link to later abortion rulings, the decision also became a symbol of judicial activism, the antithesis of limited decision making. Whereas many conservative jurists think the courts should adhere to the words of the Constitution, Justice Douglas went beyond the words to find new rights in the "penumbras" and "emanations" from the text of the Bill of Rights. During Robert Bork's confirmation hearings in 1987, the conservative appeals judge made it clear he would not be looking in the "penumbras" for new rights such as privacy, but would abide solely by the text of the Constitution. Such statements rallied women's groups and others against him, and the Senate refused to confirm his nomination. In the summer of 2005 women's groups mobilized again on the issue, urging the Senate to determine the views of Supreme Court nominee John Roberts Jr. on privacy.

Roe v. Wade

Decided January 22, 1973
410 U.S. 113
laws.findlaw.com/US/410/113.html

DECISION

A woman's right to an abortion is part of her constitutionally protected right of privacy under the Fourteenth Amendment, although the right is not absolute. Before the end of the first trimester, the decision to abort must be left to the pregnant woman and her physician. During the second trimester, the state may regulate abortion "in ways that are reasonably related to maternal health." Once the fetus is viable, government may restrict or even prohibit abortion, except to preserve the life or health of the mother.

BACKGROUND

The question of abortion—whether and when a woman has the right to end a pregnancy—is one of the most divisive issues ever to come before the Supreme Court. It tests moral, legal, and medical principles in ways that rarely produce easy answers or calm debate. *Abortion: The Clash of Absolutes* is the apt name of a book on the subject by Harvard law professor Laurence Tribe.

For most of U.S. history, however, abortion was not a major issue. "Abortion, at least early in pregnancy, was neither prohibited nor uncommon," writes Tribe. Under common law, abortion was permitted before "quickening," the point when the pregnant woman feels movement by the fetus for the first time—usually the fourth or fifth month of pregnancy.

The push to enact laws restricting abortions came in the nineteenth century, not from religious leaders but from the medical profession. Some have said that doctors were trying to discourage competition from the growing number of abortionists, but other historians claim the motivation was to increase the professionalism of medical practitioners. Doctors also note that the Hippocratic Oath, which guides their profession, bars doctors from giving women a "pessary to produce abortion." The first laws made abortions before quickening a lesser crime than abortions performed after that point, and allowed physicians to make exceptions when the mother's life was endangered.

But by the mid-twentieth century most of those laws had been tightened, and abortion was made broadly illegal, driving the procedure underground. Debate over these laws was revived in the 1960s in part by a rubella epidemic and a highly publicized controversy over so-called thalidomide babies. Rubella or German measles in pregnant women resulted in birth defects for the child, and the use of the tranquilizer thalidomide by the mother produced severe deformities. Sherri Finkbine, a mother who had taken thalidomide before its damaging effects were made public, had to travel to Sweden to get an abortion after a front-page controversy over whether she should be able to have an abortion in the United States. Both episodes, according to Tribe, triggered a reexamination of the issue by doctors and the public. In 1967 the American Medical Association called for the liberalization of abortion laws to allow a greater range of exceptions to bans on the practice.

At the same time, legal doctrines were evolving that encouraged a court challenge to laws restricting abortion. The Court's 1965 decision in *Griswold v. Connecticut,* in particular, had tied together several other precedents to assert a personal right of privacy grounded in different parts of the Constitution. The decision struck down a state law banning the use of contraceptives, even by married couples. That right of privacy, the Court said, shielded a range of personal decisions from intrusion by government. In the book *Liberty and Sexuality,* the definitive work on the issue, author David Garrow suggests that without the *Griswold* decision, the Supreme Court would not have declared a constitutional right to have an abortion. (See *Griswold v. Connecticut.*)

Abortion rights groups in several states began looking for plaintiffs to make a test case of whether antiabortion laws violated women's constitutional rights. Texas lawyers Linda Coffee and Sarah Weddington found a willing plaintiff in Norma McCorvey, an unmarried Dallas carnival worker who wanted an abortion because she could not afford to raise a child. Her desperate search for a way to end the pregnancy led her to the lawyers, and she readily agreed to participate in a suit against the Texas abortion ban, which dated back to 1854. She told the lawyers she had been raped, but years later she said that was not true.

According to her book *I Am Roe,* McCorvey mistakenly believed the lawsuit could be resolved in time for her to have an abortion. "It would be nice to say," she said in the book, "that . . . I realized I was making abortion-rights history. Or changing my life forever. But the honest truth is that nothing like that even occurred to me. I was simply at the end of my rope." Her only request was that she be allowed to remain anonymous, which is why the lawsuit listed her as "Jane Roe." The suit, filed in early 1970, listed Dallas County District Attorney Henry Wade as the defendant because it was his job to enforce the abortion law in Dallas.

A three-judge panel sided with Roe, striking down the Texas law and declaring that the "fundamental right of single women and married persons to choose whether to have children is protected by the Ninth Amendment, through the Fourteenth Amendment." The rarely cited Ninth Amendment reserves to the people those rights not specifically listed in the Constitution. As the case proceeded, McCorvey gave birth to the child and put it up for adoption.

The Texas case, along with a challenge to Georgia's abortion law, arrived at the Supreme Court at an awkward time. Only seven justices were available to consider it. New justices Lewis F. Powell Jr. and William Rehnquist had been confirmed, but not sworn in by the time of oral argument. After oral arguments, Chief Justice Burger assigned the drafting of an opinion to Justice Blackmun, one-time legal counsel to the famed Mayo Clinic. Blackmun toiled for months on the decision, finally sending a draft to his colleagues in May. The draft opinion asserted that the Texas law was unconstitutionally vague. But after several justices suggested the ruling needed to be beefed up, Blackmun urged that it be reargued in the fall, allowing the new justices to participate. He then spent several weeks that summer in the medical library at the Mayo Clinic researching the history of abortion.

Following the second argument in the case, Blackmun produced a stronger draft that reflected his research. With some significant further revisions, the Court's historic ruling was released.

VOTE

7–2, with Justice Harry A. Blackmun writing the opinion of the Court. Joining Blackmun were Chief Justice Warren E. Burger, William O. Douglas, William J. Brennan Jr., Potter Stewart, Thurgood Marshall, and Lewis F. Powell Jr. Dissenting were Justices Byron R. White and William Rehnquist.

HIGHLIGHTS

In major constitutional cases, the Court often gives great weight to how the issue involved was handled at the time of the drafting of the Constitution and relevant constitutional amendments. Heeding that practice, Justice Blackmun spent considerable time in the opinion reviewing the history of abortion in the United States. The history bolstered the Court's main decision in favor of a constitutional right to an abortion.

Blackmun wrote, "At common law, at the time of the adoption of our Constitution, and throughout the major portion of the 19th century, abortion was viewed with less disfavor than under most American statutes currently in effect. Phrasing it another way, a woman enjoyed a substantially broader right to terminate a pregnancy than she does in most States today. At least with respect to the early stage of pregnancy, and very possibly without such a limitation, the opportunity to make this choice was present in this country well into the 19th century. Even later, the law continued for some time to treat less punitively an abortion procured in early pregnancy."

As a preliminary issue, Blackmun also dealt with the touchy question of whether a fetus was a "person" under the Fourteenth Amendment, which guarantees due process and equal protection for "persons born or naturalized in the United States." In Blackmun's view, a fetus was not a person. "The Constitution does not define 'person' in so many words," Blackmun wrote. He then reviewed all the instances in which the word *person* appears in the Constitution. "All this, together with our observation that throughout the major portion of the 19th century prevailing legal abortion practices were far freer than they are today, persuades us that the word 'person,' as used in the Fourteenth Amendment, does not include the unborn."

Blackmun stayed away from another thorny issue. "We need not resolve the difficult question of when life begins.

Norma McCorvey, embracing nine-year-old Meredith Champion, attends an Operation Rescue rally in Dallas in 1997. McCorvey is "Jane Roe" of *Roe v. Wade* (1973), the landmark case declaring that the right to privacy protects a woman's right to terminate a pregnancy. She has since come to oppose abortion.

Source: AP/Wide World Photos/Ron Heflin.

When those trained in the respective disciplines of medicine, philosophy, and theology are unable to arrive at any consensus, the judiciary, at this point in the development of man's knowledge, is not in a position to speculate as to the answer." He went on to say, "We do not agree that, by adopting one theory of life, Texas may override the rights of the pregnant woman that are at stake."

The pregnant woman, Blackmun asserted, has a fundamental right to privacy under *Griswold* and other Court rulings, and making the decision whether to carry a child to birth is part of that right. But that right is not absolute, Blackmun argued; at some point in the pregnancy the state's interest in protecting public health and human lives justifies state regulation or even prohibition of abortions. Because abortions are more dangerous to the woman the later in pregnancy they occur, protecting the health of the woman, as well as the life of the fetus, comes into play.

But determining that point when government intervention is constitutional was difficult. In earlier drafts of the decision, according to Garrow, Blackmun fixed it at the end of the first trimester—three months into pregnancy. Other justices felt that was too early in the pregnancy and feared that if the Court drew the line there, states would prohibit abortions after the first trimester, leaving the rights of many women unprotected.

Blackmun agreed to modify the approach. He kept his reference to the first trimester, noting that up to that point, the abortion procedure is safer in terms of the woman's health than childbirth. After that point, regulations that "reasonably relate" to the mother's health are permitted.

The point at which state interests in the fetus become compelling, Blackmun said, is "viability"—when the fetus could live outside the mother's womb. Blackmun did not say when viability is reached, but at the time it was regarded as being somewhere near the end of the second trimester. After viability, states could regulate or even ban abortions, except to protect the life or health of the mother. In between these two points, Blackmun suggested, the states would have some flexibility in devising regulations.

In a concurring opinion, Chief Justice Burger wrote, "I do not read the Court's holdings today as having the sweeping consequences attributed to them by the dissenting Justices; the dissenting views discount the reality that the vast majority of physicians observe the standards of their profession, and act only on the basis of carefully deliberated medical judgments relating to life and health. Plainly, the Court today rejects any claim that the Constitution requires abortions on demand."

The dissenters argued that the majority opinion had invented a right not contained in the Constitution, and had artificially divided a woman's pregnancy into three parts. If the state had a legitimate interest in fetal health, they reasoned, the interest should last through the entire pregnancy, not just the last third.

Justice White's dissent struck a bitter tone. "The Court, for the most part, sustains this position: during the period prior to the time the fetus becomes viable, the Constitution of the United States values the convenience, whim, or caprice of the putative mother more than the life or potential life of the fetus; the Constitution, therefore, guarantees the right to an abortion as against any state law or policy seeking to protect the fetus from an abortion not prompted by more compelling reasons of the mother. With all due respect, I dissent. I find nothing in the language or history of the Constitution to support the Court's judgment."

Justice Rehnquist wrote in dissent, "The decision here to break pregnancy into three distinct terms and to outline the permissible restrictions the State may impose in each one . . . partakes more of judicial legislation than it does of a determination of the intent of the drafters of the Fourteenth Amendment."

In a second decision issued the same day, *Doe v. Bolton,* the Court also struck down Georgia's less restrictive abortion law.

EXCERPTS

From Justice Harry A. Blackmun's majority opinion: "We forthwith acknowledge our awareness of the sensitive and emotional nature of the abortion controversy, of the vigorous opposing views, even among physicians, and of the deep and seemingly absolute convictions that the subject inspires. One's philosophy, one's experiences, one's exposure to the raw edges of human existence, one's religious training, one's attitudes toward life and family and their values, and the moral standards one establishes and seeks to observe, are all likely to influence and to color one's thinking and conclusions about abortion.

"In addition, population growth, pollution, poverty, and racial overtones tend to complicate and not to simplify the problem. . . .

"The Constitution does not explicitly mention any right of privacy. In a line of decisions, however, going back perhaps as far as *Union Pacific R. Co. v. Botsford* (1891), the Court has recognized that a right of personal privacy, or a guarantee of certain areas or zones of privacy, does exist under the Constitution. . . .

"This right of privacy, whether it be founded in the Fourteenth Amendment's concept of personal liberty and restrictions upon state action, as we feel it is, or, as the District Court determined, in the Ninth Amendment's reservation of rights to the people, is broad enough to encompass a woman's decision whether or not to terminate her pregnancy. . . .

". . . The Court's decisions recognizing a right of privacy also acknowledge that some state regulation in areas protected by that right is appropriate. . . . [A] State may properly assert important interests in safeguarding health, in maintaining medical standards, and in protecting potential life. At some point in pregnancy, these respective interests become sufficiently compelling to sustain regulation of the factors that govern the abortion decision. The privacy right involved, therefore, cannot be said to be absolute. . . .

"We, therefore, conclude that the right of personal privacy includes the abortion decision, but that this right is not unqualified and must be considered against important state interests in regulation. . . .

"With respect to the State's important and legitimate interest in the health of the mother, the 'compelling' point, in the light of present medical knowledge, is at approximately the end of the first trimester. This is so because of the now-established medical fact . . . that, until the end of the first trimester mortality in abortion may be less than mortality in normal childbirth. It follows that, from and after this point, a State may regulate the abortion procedure to the extent that the regulation reasonably relates to the preservation and protection of maternal health. Examples of permissible state regulation in this area are requirements as to the qualifications of the person who is to perform the abortion; as to the licensure of that person; as to the facility in which the procedure is to be performed, that is, whether it must be a hospital or may be a clinic or some other place of less-than-hospital status; as to the licensing of the facility; and the like.

"This means, on the other hand, that, for the period of pregnancy prior to this 'compelling' point, the attending physician, in consultation with his patient, is free to determine, without regulation by the State, that, in his medical judgment, the patient's pregnancy should be terminated. If that decision is reached, the judgment may be effectuated by an abortion free of interference by the State."

IMPACT

The initial reaction to the decision was muted in part because, on the day it was issued, former president Lyndon B. Johnson died, and his death dominated the headlines. Today, most scholars and historians agree that *Roe v. Wade* comes close to *Brown v. Board of Education* as one of the most important Supreme Court decisions in the twentieth century, if not the Court's entire history. The Court declared a constitutional right that had not existed before—a right that has had profound impact on society ever since. (See *Brown v. Board of Education*.)

Laws in virtually every state—except New York, which had already passed a law legalizing abortion—were invalidated overnight. Illegal abortions no longer were necessary, and the number of abortions soon totaled one-quarter of all pregnancies. Alan Guttmacher, president of the Planned Parenthood Federation of America, called *Roe* "a wise and courageous stroke for the right of privacy, and for the protection of a woman's physical and emotional health."

Women's rights advocates applauded the decision because it offered women, for the first time, substantial control over their reproductive lives. No longer would the course of women's lives, education, and careers be determined by an accidental or unwanted pregnancy.

For that same reason, many religious and political leaders bitterly attacked *Roe*. It cheapened human life, they said, making it too easy for women to extinguish a pregnancy if it seemed inconvenient at the moment. More than 1 million abortions are performed every year in the United States according to the latest available statistics. "It is hard to think of any decision in the 200 years of our history which has had more disastrous implications for our stability as a civilized society," said Philadelphia's Cardinal John Krol. Conservative columnist William F. Buckley called it "the Dred Scott decision of the twentieth century."

The decision has been criticized from a legal standpoint by conservatives and as a prime example of judicial activism—legislating from the bench without any firm grounding in the Constitution. Even some liberals have criticized *Roe v. Wade*. Ruth Bader Ginsburg, a women's rights lawyer who later joined the Court as a justice, said the Court "ventured too far." She said the Court should have simply rejected the Texas law without elaboration, rather than issuing an opinion that appeared to many to be "heavy-handed judicial intervention." To defenders of *Roe,* including Blackmun, the decision appeared instead to be a logical extension of the *Griswold* decision.

Rather than ending the abortion debate, *Roe* invigorated the "prolife" movement that opposed abortion rights and transformed abortion into a wrenching political issue. It also brought the Supreme Court, more than ever before, into the political arena; demonstrations against the Court and especially against Justice Blackmun became routine.

Abortion cases became commonplace on the Court's docket, each one provoking controversy and, usually, a fragmented opinion from the Court that reflected its political leanings at the time. In 1976 the Court said the "father" of the fetus could not veto a woman's abortion choice. But in most cases since, the Court has approved of state legislative efforts to restrict the abortion right.

In *City of Akron v. Akron Center for Reproductive Health* (1983) the Court said states could require minors to obtain parental consent before they can have abortions, so long as there is an alternative procedure in cases where trying to obtain parental consent would endanger the pregnant young woman. Significantly in that case, the Court's first woman justice, Sandra Day O'Connor, indicated her misgivings about the *Roe* framework. Noting that medical advances had made fetuses viable outside the womb at earlier and earlier stages, she said the trimester framework of *Roe* was "on a collision course with itself."

In 1989 the appointment of conservative justices brought the Court close to overturning *Roe v. Wade*. In *Webster v. Reproductive Health Services,* the Court by a 5–4 vote upheld several state restrictions on abortion. "A chill wind blows," Blackmun said in a dissent that warned of the possible demise of the abortion right. The Court, he said, was "either oblivious or insensitive to the fact that millions of women, and their families, have ordered their lives around the right to reproductive choice, and that this right has become vital to the full participation of women in the economic and political walks of American life."

Blackmun's fears appeared to be somewhat premature. In 1992 the Bush administration explicitly asked the Court to overturn *Roe v. Wade* in the case *Planned Parenthood of Southeastern Pennsylvania v. Casey,* which again involved state restrictions on abortion, including waiting periods and parental and spousal consent requirements. Surprisingly, the Court turned down the invitation and dramatically embraced *Roe*'s holding.

A joint opinion by Justices O'Connor, David Souter, and Anthony Kennedy held in part that *Roe* had become embedded in the fabric of the nation and could not be jettisoned easily. "An entire generation has come of age free to assume *Roe*'s concept of liberty in defining the capacity of women to act in society, and to make reproductive decisions," these justices wrote. "To overrule under fire in the absence of the most compelling reason to reexamine a watershed decision would subvert the Court's legitimacy beyond any serious question."

In the years since the *Casey* decision, the Court has shown little appetite to revisit the abortion issue, except in the context of restrictions on the sometimes violent demonstrations that have taken place around abortion clinics. The Court has said some regulation of the demonstrations is permissible to protect the safety of patients and staff, but First Amendment considerations make complete bans on such demonstrations unjustifiable.

But abortion rights opponents continued their campaign, urging Congress and the states to pass laws prohibiting what they called "partial-birth" abortions. Abortion rights advocates feared that, depending on how the procedure was defined, the law could cover operations that are fairly common. The Supreme Court in the 2000 ruling *Stenberg v. Carhart* struck down a Nebraska law prohibiting the procedure, in part because it did not make an exception from the ban if the health of the mother was at stake. Significantly, however, the Court's vote striking down the law was 5–4 with Justice Kennedy moving from the camp of abortion rights supporters to oppose the procedure.

For that reason, the abortion issue threatened to reemerge as a national flashpoint in the summer of 2005 when Justice Sandra Day O'Connor announced her retirement. With the departure of O'Connor, who supported abortion rights with limits, and with Kennedy's vote in doubt, the basic *Roe v. Wade* right appeared to some to be in jeopardy again.

Cruzan v. Director, Missouri Department of Health

Decided June 25, 1990
497 U.S. 261
laws.findlaw.com/US/497/261.html

DECISION

States may require "clear and convincing evidence" of a patient's desire to end treatment before allowing the family of a terminally ill patient to disconnect life-support systems and let the patient die. The Court recognized the right of individuals to refuse medical treatment if they are competent to make that decision, but said states are not required to defer to the "substituted judgment" of family members.

BACKGROUND

Because of the medical advances of the twentieth century, a range of techniques and treatments make it possible to keep an individual alive long after the ravages of an illness or accident would have otherwise led to death. Along with their life-saving benefits, these advances have also forced families to face agonizing decisions.

One government study in 1988 indicated that of the 2 million people who die in the United States each year, 80 percent die in hospitals or long-term care facilities. And more than two-thirds of those people die after a decision is made to end further life-sustaining treatment. These decisions involve moral, ethical, and legal factors that made the right to die, living wills, and physician-assisted suicide common topics of discussion in late twentieth-century United States. A Michigan doctor, Jack

Kevorkian, who has helped dozens of ill people commit suicide, is the most provocative and visible symbol of the national debate over these issues.

In the late 1970s Karen Ann Quinlan was the name most associated with the so-called right to die. The New Jersey woman was left in a persistent vegetative state after an auto accident, and her father sought permission to disconnect her respirator and allow her to die. In a controversial 1976 decision, the New Jersey Supreme Court granted permission, citing the young woman's constitutionally protected right of privacy. The U.S. Supreme Court allowed the ruling to stand. Several state legislatures took up the issue, and more than fifty other legal cases entered the courts in the next decade. In many of those cases, judges agreed with family members who argued for their loved ones' right to die.

One of those cases, involving another woman injured in an auto accident, made its way to the Supreme Court. Nancy Cruzan was twenty-five when her car skidded out of control on

Nancy Cruzan, shown here in an undated photograph, suffered irreversible brain damage in a 1983 car accident. In *Cruzan v. Director, Missouri Department of Health* (1990), the Supreme Court determined that states may require "clear and convincing evidence" of an individual's desire to end life-sustaining treatment before allowing family members to discontinue such care. The debate over withdrawing life-support would be revisited fifteen years later in the Terri Schiavo controversy.
Source: AP/Wide World Photos.

an icy road in Jasper County, Missouri, in 1983. She was thrown from her car, and when help arrived, she was not breathing and had no pulse. Paramedics were able to restore her breathing, but too late to prevent permanent brain damage. Cruzan was in a coma for three weeks. At this point her then-husband agreed to have a feeding tube inserted in her stomach to make it easier to feed her. The brain damage proved irreversible, and Cruzan was moved to a long-term care facility where the state paid a reported $130,000 a year to keep her alive in a persistent vegetative state.

More than three years later, with doctors saying that Nancy could live for another thirty years in the same condition, her parents asked hospital officials to remove her feeding and water tubes. They refused to do so without court approval.

A state judge considered the *Cruzan* case, hearing testimony from a friend of Nancy's that she had once said she would never want to live as a "vegetable" if she were injured. Family members also said that Nancy would not have wanted to stay alive in her present circumstances. The judge granted the family's request, but the state of Missouri appealed.

The state supreme court overruled the judge and said Nancy must be kept alive. State policy strongly favors preserving life, the court said, and testimony about Nancy's stated wishes before the accident was "unreliable" in determining if she would really want treatment ended. Possibly because the Missouri decision ran counter to the trend in other state courts, the Supreme Court agreed to hear the case.

As the *Cruzan* case reached the Supreme Court, it took on added significance in part because it raised privacy and autonomy issues that paralleled the debate over abortion rights. The Bush administration argued in support of the Missouri high court decision. If a patient's desire to end treatment could not be clearly determined, the administration argued, the state could opt for preserving life.

VOTE

5–4, with Chief Justice William Rehnquist writing the majority opinion. He was joined by Justices Byron R. White, Sandra Day O'Connor, Antonin Scalia, and Anthony M. Kennedy. Dissenting were Justices William J. Brennan Jr., Thurgood Marshall, Harry A. Blackmun, and John Paul Stevens.

HIGHLIGHTS

Chief Justice Rehnquist tried to make the Court's decision as straightforward as possible. "State courts have available to them for decision a number of sources—state constitutions, statutes, and common law—which are not available to us," Rehnquist wrote. "In this Court, the question is simply and starkly whether the United States Constitution prohibits Missouri from choosing the rule of decision which it did."

He also suggested that the Court did not need to break new ground to reach its decision. A personal "liberty interest" in refusing unwanted medical treatment could be inferred from the Court's prior decisions concerning the due process clause, Rehnquist said.

The difficulty in the *Cruzan* case came because Cruzan's wishes were not entirely clear. In her current state, Cruzan was not competent to state her wishes, so the state was entitled to satisfy itself in other ways about what she wanted to happen. The state has a legitimate interest, the Court found, in preventing abuses by family members who might, because of personal gain, misstate the person's wishes. All agreed that the Cruzans had Nancy's best interests at heart, but in other cases, other family members might be eager to cash in on insurance money.

The Court said the state was acting well within its authority to require "clear and convincing evidence" to prove that a comatose patient would have wanted treatment withdrawn. And Missouri was entitled to come to the conclusion that in Cruzan's case the standard had not been met. The Court's approach was clearly permissive, indicating what states *could* do, rather than what they had to do, in the area of the right to refuse treatment.

But Rehnquist did not go far enough, in Scalia's view, in making clear that courts should not be deciding the question. In a concurring opinion, Scalia wrote, "While I agree with the Court's analysis today, and therefore join in its opinion, I would have preferred that we announce, clearly and promptly, that the federal courts have no business in this field; that American law has always accorded the State the power to prevent, by force if necessary, suicide—including suicide by refusing to take appropriate measures necessary to preserve one's life."

The answers to the moral questions involved, said Scalia, are not "known to the nine Justices of this Court any better than they are known to nine people picked at random from the Kansas City telephone directory."

Dissenters in the case complained that the majority had given short shrift to the deep privacy concerns involved. "Dying is personal. And it is profound. For many, the thought of an ignoble end, steeped in decay, is abhorrent," Brennan wrote. "A quiet, proud death, bodily integrity intact, is a matter of extreme consequence."

Brennan added, "Missouri and this Court have displaced Nancy's own assessment of the processes associated with dying. They have discarded evidence of her will, ignored her values, and deprived her of the right to a decision as closely approximating her own choice as humanly possible. They have done so disingenuously in her name, and openly in Missouri's own."

Justice Stevens also dissented. "There can be no doubt that [Nancy Cruzan's] life made her dear to her family, and to others. How she dies will affect how that life is remembered. The trial court's order authorizing Nancy's parents to cease their daughter's treatment would have permitted the family that cares for Nancy to bring to a close her tragedy and her death. Missouri's objection to that order subordinates Nancy's body, her family, and the lasting significance of her life to the State's own interests. The decision we review thereby interferes with constitutional interests of the highest order."

EXCERPTS

From Chief Justice William Rehnquist's majority opinion: "Determining that a person has a 'liberty interest' under the Due Process Clause does not end the inquiry; 'whether respondent's constitutional rights have been violated must be determined by balancing his liberty interests against the relevant state interests.'

"Petitioners insist that, under the general holdings of our cases, the forced administration of life-sustaining medical treatment, and even of artificially-delivered food and water essential to life, would implicate a competent person's liberty interest. Although we think the logic of the cases . . . would embrace such a liberty interest, the dramatic consequences involved in refusal of such treatment would inform the inquiry as to whether the deprivation of that interest is constitutionally permissible. But for purposes of this case, we assume that the United States Constitution would grant a competent person a constitutionally protected right to refuse lifesaving hydration and nutrition. . . .

"[A]n incompetent person is not able to make an informed and voluntary choice to exercise a hypothetical right to refuse treatment or any other right. Such a 'right' must be exercised for her, if at all, by some sort of surrogate. Here, Missouri has in effect recognized that, under certain circumstances, a surrogate may act for the patient in electing to have hydration and nutrition withdrawn in such a way as to cause death, but it has established a procedural safeguard to assure that the action of the surrogate conforms as best it may to the wishes expressed by the patient while competent. Missouri requires that evidence of the incompetent's wishes as to the withdrawal of treatment be proved by clear and convincing evidence. The question, then, is whether the United States Constitution forbids the establishment of this procedural requirement by the State. We hold that it does not.

". . . As a general matter, the States—indeed, all civilized nations—demonstrate their commitment to life by treating homicide as serious crime. Moreover, the majority of States in this country have laws imposing criminal penalties on one who assists another to commit suicide. We do not think a State is required to remain neutral in the face of an informed and voluntary decision by a physically able adult to starve to death. The choice between life and death is a deeply personal decision of obvious and overwhelming finality.

"... We believe Missouri may legitimately seek to safeguard the personal element of this choice through the imposition of heightened evidentiary requirements. It cannot be disputed that the Due Process Clause protects an interest in life as well as an interest in refusing life-sustaining medical treatment. Not all incompetent patients will have loved ones available to serve as surrogate decisionmakers. And even where family members are present, '[t]here will, of course, be some unfortunate situations in which family members will not act to protect a patient.' . . .

"No doubt is engendered by anything in this record but that Nancy Cruzan's mother and father are loving and caring parents. If the State were required by the United States Constitution to repose a right of 'substituted judgment' with anyone, the Cruzans would surely qualify. But we do not think the Due Process Clause requires the State to repose judgment on these matters with anyone but the patient herself. Close family members may have a strong feeling—a feeling not at all ignoble or unworthy, but not entirely disinterested, either—that they do not wish to witness the continuation of the life of a loved one which they regard as hopeless, meaningless, and even degrading. But there is no automatic assurance that the view of close family members will necessarily be the same as the patient's would have been had she been confronted with the prospect of her situation while competent."

IMPACT

The *Cruzan* decision was a disappointment to those who were seeking a broad pronouncement of the "right to die" from the Supreme Court. "Doctors will remain frightened of making positive decisions because of ancient laws which bear little relationship to modern high-tech medicine," said Derek Humphry of the Hemlock Society on the day of the ruling.

But over time the Court's ruling came to be seen in a more positive light, as a decision that recognized a personal "liberty interest" in refusing unwanted medical treatment. It also gave states considerable leeway in assuring that this interest was not abused. One sign that the Court had not imposed a rigid rule against the right to die came in the resolution of the *Cruzan* case.

Following the publicity surrounding the decision, a few of Cruzan's friends stepped forward to say that on several occasions, Cruzan had made it clear she would not want to be kept alive if an accident or illness left her in a vegetative state. Based on the new testimony, a state judge on December 14, 1990, gave permission to withdraw feeding. Twelve days later, nearly eight years after her accident, Cruzan died at the age of thirty-three.

The *Cruzan* case triggered a wave of interest in "living wills," in which people would make their preferences about end-of-life treatment known in advance. All fifty states now allow for such wills or a similar document, and polls indicate that about 20 percent of Americans have them.

The decision also encouraged right-to-die advocates to push for what they saw as the logical next step: legalization of physician-assisted suicide. If a person had a liberty interest in refusing treatment, they reasoned, why should a doctor's aid not be available? But others saw a clear difference between the more passive withdrawal of feeding and active steps that cause a person's death.

To press their case, right-to-die advocates initiated lawsuits on behalf of terminally ill patients challenging laws against assisted suicide. In cases from New York and Washington, federal appeals courts for differing reasons struck down the laws. Both cases went to the Supreme Court in 1997. In a pair of rulings, *Vacco v. Quill* and *Washington v. Glucksberg,* the Supreme Court reversed the lower courts and upheld the laws. The Court cited society's long tradition of making it a crime to help someone else commit suicide and said the laws served government's "unqualified interest in preservation of life." But, as with *Cruzan,* the Court encouraged the debate over the issue to continue and held out the possibility that in a future case, laws against assisted suicide could be challenged successfully. In 2005 the Court agreed to review an Oregon law that allowed physicians to prescribe death-hastening drugs to terminally ill patients. The George W. Bush administration argued that the law conflicted with federal drug laws. The Court scheduled arguments in the case for fall 2005.

Meanwhile another headline-making controversy in 2005 made it clear that right-to-die issues still provoked strong emotions. Terri Schiavo, a Florida woman who had lapsed into a persistent vegetative state in 1990 for unknown reasons, was the focal point of a tug-of-war between her husband, who believed she would have wanted her feeding tube removed, and her parents, who insisted that she could recover if allowed to live. The ensuing battle eventually involved Congress, which passed an emergency law allowing her parents to seek relief in federal courts. Federal judges reviewed the case but did not disturb earlier rulings that allowed her feeding tube to be removed. She died on March 31, 2005.

PROPERTY RIGHTS

*I*t is no accident that in both the Fifth and Fourteenth Amendments to the Constitution, property is given equal billing with life and liberty as things the government may not take away without due process of law. In our democratic and capitalist system, a person's exclusive use of property has been important as a safeguard against too-powerful government and as an engine driving the economy. But the right to property is not entirely beyond the reach of the state. Government may seize private property to build public roads, for example, and in the twentieth century the courts recognized government zoning power to keep steel mills, for example, from being built next to homes. Calibrating just how much power government can or should have over property has been one of the perennial tasks of the Supreme Court, and the balance has shifted from time to time.

Other related cases mentioned in the Property Rights section

Fletcher v. Peck (1810)
Dartmouth College v. Woodward (1819)
Bunting v. Oregon (1917)
West Coast Hotel v. Parrish (1937)
Berman v. Parker (1954)
Hawaii Housing Authority v. Midkiff (1984)
Nollan v. California Coastal Commission (1987)
Lucas v. South Carolina Coastal Council (1992)
Dolan v. City of Tigard (1994)

Proprietors of Charles River Bridge v. Proprietors of Warren Bridge

Decided February 12, 1837
36 U.S. 420
laws.findlaw.com/US/36/420.html

DECISION

The needs and interests of the public can take precedence over property rights and contracts. A charter given by Massachusetts to build and operate a bridge over the Charles River did not grant an exclusive contract that would prevent construction of another, competing bridge. When the state authorized the second bridge, Massachusetts did not violate the Constitution's contract clause, which prohibits states from impairing contracts.

BACKGROUND

By financing public works, the states played a major role in the economic development of the young nation. The state-built Erie Canal was a boon to the economy of New York. Other states supported transportation through direct aid or through granting charters and subsidies to private companies.

In 1828 the Massachusetts legislature passed a law authorizing a group of Charlestown merchants to build a bridge, known as the Warren Bridge, over the Charles River to Boston. The law may not sound controversial, but behind it was a major political battle. The proprietors of the nearby Charles River Bridge objected vehemently to the plans; they feared competition from the new bridge and claimed that they had exclusive rights to operate a bridge in that area.

Indeed, for decades the Charles River Bridge was the only bridge there. As early as 1740 the colonial legislature had authorized Harvard College to run a ferry from Boston to Charlestown. In 1785 construction of a bridge was authorized under a charter obtained by John Hancock and other leading citizens. The company paid Harvard an annual fee to compensate for its loss of ferry revenue.

The bridge was successful, with tolls generating significant profits for the company. It became a symbol of the power of a monopoly. By the 1820s it also attracted potential competitors who said increased traffic made a new bridge necessary. The Warren Bridge entrepreneurs convinced the legislature that their project was in the public interest, because their plan was to operate it toll-free after construction costs were recovered.

The Charles River Bridge operators went to court to halt the Warren Bridge project. The plea for an injunction was denied, and the bridge was built and opened to the public. But the suit continued to make its way through the courts and became a controversial test of property rights. Both sides argued they were serving the best interest of the public. The Charles River Bridge advocates said private companies would become less interested in undertaking public projects if a monopoly could be ended so easily. The Warren Bridge lawyers argued that monopoly franchises inhibited competition and innovation.

The dispute first went to the Supreme Court in 1831, with Daniel Webster eloquently arguing on behalf of the Charles River Bridge company. But the Court, under Chief Justice John Marshall, was sharply divided. Marshall had traditionally championed property and contract rights, but the Court more recently had given states more power over contracts. The Court announced it could not decide the case, and it was held for reargument. The case was not finally resolved until 1837, soon after President Andrew Jackson appointed Roger Taney as chief justice. Webster argued the case again for the Charles River monopoly, but his legendary powers to persuade the Supreme Court did not work this time.

VOTE

4–3, with Chief Justice Roger B. Taney writing the majority opinion. Joining him were Justices Henry Baldwin, James M. Wayne, and Philip P. Barbour. Dissenting were Justices Joseph Story, Smith Thompson, and John McLean.

HIGHLIGHTS

The length of the opinion—some 230 pages—makes it clear that the Charles River Bridge decision had divided the Court deeply. Justice Story's dissent runs 35,000 words. Chief Justice Taney said that in deciding the case, the justices had to move with "utmost caution; guarding, so far as they have power to do so, the rights of property, at the same time carefully abstaining from any encroachment on the rights reserved to the states." The main constitutional provision at issue was Article I, Section 10, which barred states from passing laws "impairing the obligation of contracts."

Reviewing the history of the ferry and the bridge, the Court found that Massachusetts had not given any exclusive rights to provide transportation across the Charles River—either explicitly or by implication. Public grants are to be construed strictly, Taney wrote. "In charters of this description, no rights are taken from the public, or given to the corporation, beyond those which the words of the charter, by their natural and proper construction, purport to convey."

But Taney also saw a public policy reason for not granting exclusivity. If a monopoly is granted, then improvements and innovations in transportation will occur only when the chartered company feels so inclined. In Taney's view of property rights, the public interest had to be considered, and even made paramount.

As far as the public good is concerned, Justice McLean made the same argument in defense of the power of eminent domain, which gives the state the power to negate property rights altogether for the public good. "The spirit of internal improvement pervades the whole country. There is, perhaps, no state in the Union where important public works such as turnpike roads, canals, railroads, bridges, etc., are not either contemplated, or in a state of rapid progression. These cannot be carried on, without the frequent exercise of the power to appropriate private property for public use. Vested rights are daily divested by this exercise of the eminent domain." Despite these views, McLean sided with the Charles River Bridge argument, and his vote is generally counted as a dissent. He further argued that the Court did not have jurisdiction in the case.

In the principal dissent, Justice Story also invoked the public interest in arguing that the Charles River Bridge contract should be interpreted as an exclusive grant. "If the government means to invite its citizens to enlarge the public comforts and conveniences, to establish bridges, or turnpikes, or canals, or railroads, there must be some pledge that the property will be safe; that the enjoyment will be co-extensive with the grant; and that success will not be the signal of a general combination to overthrow its rights and to take away its profits. The very agitation of a question of this sort is sufficient to alarm every stockholder in every public enterprise of this sort, throughout the whole country."

EXCERPTS

From Chief Justice Roger B. Taney's majority opinion: "[T]he object and end of all government is to promote the happiness and prosperity of the community by which it is established; and it can never be assumed, that the government intended to diminish its power of accomplishing the end for which it was created. And in a country like ours, free, active and enterprising, continually advancing in numbers and wealth, new channels of communication are daily found necessary, both for travel and trade, and are essential to the comfort, convenience and prosperity of the people. A state ought never to be presumed to surrender this power, because, like the taxing power, the whole community have an interest in preserving it undiminished. . . . While the rights of private property are sacredly guarded, we must not forget, that the community also have rights, and that the happiness and well-being of every citizen depends on their faithful preservation. . . .

". . . This act of incorporation is in the usual form, and the privileges such as are commonly given to corporations of that

Massachusetts granted a charter for building the Charles River Bridge that also gave the proprietors the right to collect tolls for use of the bridge. When population growth in the Boston area made construction of another bridge necessary, the proprietors objected to the new construction. In *Proprietors of Charles River Bridge v. Proprietors of Warren Bridge* (1837), the Supreme Court found the state not to be in violation of a contract and held that the needs and interests of the public can take precedence over property rights and contracts.

Source: Library of Congress.

kind. It confers on them the ordinary faculties of a corporation, for the purpose of building the bridge; and establishes certain rates of toll, which the company are authorized to take: this is the whole grant. There is no exclusive privilege given to them over the waters of Charles river, above or below their bridge; no right to erect another bridge themselves, nor to prevent other persons from erecting one, no engagement from the state, that another shall not be erected; and no undertaking not to sanction competition, nor to make improvements that may diminish the amount of its income. Upon all these subjects, the charter is silent, and nothing is said in it about a line of travel, so much insisted on in the argument, in which they are to have exclusive privileges. No words are used, from which an intention to grant any of these rights can be inferred. . . .

". . . Let it once be understood, that such charters carry with them these implied contracts, and give this unknown and undefined property in a line of travelling; and you will soon find the old turnpike corporations awakening from their sleep, and calling upon this court to put down the improvements which have taken their place. The millions of property which have been invested in railroads and canals, upon lines of travel which had been before occupied by turnpike corporations, will be put in jeopardy. We shall be thrown back to the improvements of the last century, and obliged to stand still, until the claims of the old turnpike corporations shall be satisfied; and they shall consent to permit these states to avail themselves of the lights of modern science, and to partake of the benefit of those improvements which are now adding to the wealth and prosperity, and the convenience and comfort, of every other part of the civilized world."

IMPACT

The Charles River Bridge decision was hailed as a blow against monopolies. One pro-Jackson newspaper reported, "The vested-rights class cry out bloody murder."

The decision represented a dramatic change of direction for the Court. In previous decisions, such as *Fletcher v. Peck* (1810) and *Dartmouth College v. Woodward* (1819), the Court had interpreted the Constitution's contract clause to give broad protection to businesses and their contracts.

Now the Court was looking at contracts narrowly, through a lens that took the public interest into account and held it paramount. It was one of the earliest decisions of the Court that established that government has a loosely defined "police power" to promote the public interest through regulations that affect private activities. "The decision in favor of the free public bridge against the private profit-making bridge is one of the constitutional foundations of the social welfare legislation of the twentieth century," wrote historian Leo Pfeffer in *This Honorable Court*.

Although the decision went against business interests, some regard it as a ruling that helped businesses by promoting competition and innovation. It was also in tune with the period of economic growth the nation was beginning. For example, the decision made it easier for railroads to replace toll roads in some instances.

Lochner v. New York

Decided April 17, 1905
198 U.S. 45
laws.findlaw.com/US/198/45.html

DECISION

A New York law limiting the number of hours a bakery worker can be required to work interferes with the Fourteenth Amendment right of businesses and employees to enter into contracts to buy and sell labor. The justices declared that baking is not an unhealthy trade and that the law limiting hours cannot be justified as a legitimate exercise of police powers to protect health and safety.

BACKGROUND

In many large cities at the turn of the twentieth century, the business of baking bread had little to do with home and hearth. It was a grimy, gritty business conducted mainly in the cellars of tenement buildings because the cramped apartments usually were too small to have ovens of their own. The bakers worked extremely long hours, and, because the workplaces were poorly ventilated, the bakers were exposed to flour dust and fumes as well as intense heat. Conditions were often unsanitary: many workers slept, ate, and washed in the same area where bread was prepared. Muckraking journalists and social reformers attempted to expose these conditions. One New York newspaper ran an article in 1894 headlined "Bread and Filth Cooked Together."

At the same time, the labor movement was becoming increasingly militant on the issue of long working hours, not just in bakeries but in many businesses where twelve- or fourteen-hour days, six or seven days a week, were not uncommon. The Haymarket riots in Chicago in 1886 had been triggered by a general strike aimed at generating support for eight-hour work-days. Limiting the number of working hours for laborers was pushed not only as a social benefit but also as a way to gener-ate new jobs and spread employment around more evenly.

In 1895 the New York legislature responded to the reform movement by passing the Bakeshop Act, which said no bakery employees should be "required or permitted" to work more than ten hours per day or sixty hours per week. Unlike similar laws in other states, New York's carried with it criminal penalties.

In April 1901 a Utica bakery owner named Joseph Lochner was accused of violating the law by forcing one of his workers, Aman Schmitter, to work for more than sixty hours a week. Lochner offered no defense except to attack the law, and he was fined $50 in early 1902. Lochner fought the conviction, but the New York appeals courts upheld the conviction and the law.

Lochner's appeal reached the Supreme Court at an oppor-tune time for him. The Court had begun to take the view that the Fourteenth Amendment protected an individual's right to make contracts. More important, the Court was beginning to view the amendment's guarantee of "due process" as not just a right to fair procedure but to substantive fairness—in this context, a limit on states' power to enact laws that interfered with property and contracts.

VOTE

5–4, with Justice Rufus W. Peckham writing the majority opin-ion. Joining him were Chief Justice Melville W. Fuller and Jus-tices David J. Brewer, Henry B. Brown, and Joseph McKenna. Justices John Marshall Harlan, Edward D. White, William R. Day, and Oliver Wendell Holmes Jr. dissented.

HIGHLIGHTS

The Court divided sharply over the constitutionality of the New York law. According to historian Paul Kens's 1998 book on the case, at the time the rumor was that Peckham's majority opin-ion started out as a dissent. Sometimes a dissenting argument can be so convincing that justices in the majority change their minds, turning the opinion on its head.

To strike down the Bakeshop Act, the Court first had to de-cide that the law was not a legitimate exercise of the state's po-lice power, which had been defined over the years to include government's interest in protecting the health, safety, and morals of society.

In a section of the opinion that has been criticized for ig-noring the realities of the working world, the Court said baking was not an unhealthy profession. "The trade of a baker, in and of itself, is not an unhealthy one to that degree which would authorize the legislature to interfere with the right to labor, and

with the right of free contract on the part of the individual, ei-ther as employer or employee."

As a result, the Court concluded that the New York law had nothing to do with the general health of the public. "Viewed in the light of a purely labor law, with no reference whatever to the question of health, we think that a law like the one before us in-volves neither the safety, the morals, nor the welfare, of the public, and that the interest of the public is not in the slightest degree affected by such an act. The law must be upheld, if at all, as a law pertaining to the health of the individual engaged in the occupation of a baker. It does not affect any other portion of the public than those who are engaged in that occupation."

If the law was not intended to protect workers' health, what then was its purpose? The Court concluded, "It seems to us that the real object and purpose were simply to regulate the hours of labor between the master and his employees . . . in a private business. . . . Under such circumstances, the freedom of master and employee to contract with each other in relation to their em-ployment, and in defining the same, cannot be prohibited or in-terfered with without violating the Federal Constitution."

Two forceful dissents make clear how divided the Court was. Harlan said the Court should not have given such short shrift to the motives of the New York legislature. "The rule is universal that a legislative enactment, Federal or state, is never to be disregarded or held invalid unless it be, beyond ques-tion, plainly and palpably in excess of legislative power."

Holmes's dissent asserted that government interferes with personal liberties in a variety of ways that are constitu-tional. "The liberty of the citizen to do as he likes so long as he does not interfere with the liberty of others to do the same, which has been a shibboleth for some well known writers, is in-terfered with by school laws, by the Post Office, by every state or municipal institution which takes his money for purposes thought desirable, whether he likes it or not."

Holmes added, "The Fourteenth Amendment does not enact Mr. Herbert Spencer's Social Statics." This was a sarcas-tic reference to the social Darwinism of economist Spencer, whose views Holmes had summarized. Spencer believed the primary role of government was merely to make sure that indi-vidual liberties were not interfered with any more than neces-sary. Holmes was concerned that Spencer's "laissez-faire" view of government had just been written into constitutional law.

EXCERPTS

From Justice Rufus W. Peckham's majority opinion: "The gen-eral right to make a contract in relation to his business is part of the liberty of the individual protected by the 14th Amend-ment of the Federal Constitution. Under that provision no state can deprive any person of life, liberty, or property without due process of law. The right to purchase or to sell labor is part of the liberty protected by this amendment, unless there are circumstances which exclude the right. There are, however, certain powers, existing in the sovereignty of each state in the Union, somewhat vaguely termed police powers, the exact description and limitation of which have not been attempted by the courts. Those powers, broadly stated, and without, at present, any attempt at a more specific limitation, relate to the safety, health, morals, and general welfare of the public. Both property and liberty are held on such reasonable conditions as may be imposed by the governing power of the State in the exercise of those powers, and with such conditions the 14th Amendment was not designed to interfere."

IMPACT

Lochner v. New York is the only Supreme Court decision that has given its name to an era. The *Lochner* era was a thirty-two-year period in which the Supreme Court and other courts cited this case to strike down a large number of legislative efforts to reform economic conditions through regulations on business. Laws setting minimum wages and prohibiting child labor were invalidated in the name of *Lochner*. A lawyer for the bakery workers said flatly that the *Lochner* decision meant "Everything that furthers the interests of employers is constitutional." Union bakers eventually won shorter working days through collective bargaining.

In a 1910 speech President Theodore Roosevelt—who, as a New York legislator had introduced a bill to regulate the cigar industry—referred to the *Lochner* decision by name as an example of the Supreme Court frustrating popular will. The Court, Roosevelt said, had placed "altogether insurmountable obstacles in the path of needed social reforms." Some recent commentators have said the impact of the decision was more limited, noting that some laws restricting business, especially laws that cited public health and safety, were upheld. In the 1917 decision *Bunting v. Oregon,* for example, the Court upheld an Oregon law establishing a ten-hour workday for industrial workers.

Lochner's force continued to be felt in the early days of Franklin Roosevelt's New Deal legislation. A conservative bloc on the Court helped strike down several pieces of New Deal legislation that regulated businesses, although *Lochner* was not specifically cited.

Gradually, however, the perspective of the Court shifted, and in 1937 the Court effectively buried *Lochner*. In *West Coast Hotel v. Parrish,* in which the Court upheld a state law setting a minimum wage for workers, the majority said, "The Constitution does not speak of freedom of contract." It also adopted a more expansive view of the power of states to regulate businesses. "In dealing with the relation of employer and employed, the legislature has necessarily a wide field of discretion in order that there may be suitable protection of health

Joseph Lochner, owner of Lochner's Home Bakery in Utica, New York, was convicted of violating a law limiting work hours to 10 a day and 60 a week. In *Lochner v. New York* (1905), the Supreme Court ruled in favor of liberty of contract between employer and worker over improved working conditions. Lochner's conviction was overturned. Bakery workers and labor unions assailed the decision, which was based on the Fourteenth Amendment, fearing that it might lead to the reversal of other laws regulating labor.
Source: Collection of Joseph Lochner Jr., by Dante Tranquille.

and safety, and that peace and good order may be promoted through regulations designed to insure wholesome conditions of work and freedom from oppression."

Echoes of the debate over the *Lochner* decision, however, are still heard today. It is criticized not only because of its effect on reform legislation but also because it seems to many to be a conservative brand of judicial activism—imposing an economic theory favored by the Court's majority on the rest of the country, contrary to the expressed view of elected legislators.

Modern-day conservative justices have revisited the concept of economic rights, but in the context of the Fifth Amendment rather than the Fourteenth. In *Nollan v. California Coastal Commission* in 1987, *Lucas v. South Carolina Coastal Council* in 1992, and *Dolan v. City of Tigard* in 1994, the Court gave greater recognition to the takings clause of the Fifth Amendment, though the 2005 decision *Kelo v. City of New London* made it unclear how far this trend would go. (See *Kelo v. City of New London*.) The takings clause prohibits government from taking private property without compensation. "We see no reason why the Takings Clause of the Fifth Amendment, as much a part of the Bill of Rights as the First Amendment or Fourth Amendment, should be relegated to the status of a poor relation," Chief Justice Rehnquist wrote in *Dolan*. As Kens wrote in his book on the case, "*Lochner* is not dead."

Village of Euclid v. Ambler Realty Co.

Decided November 22, 1926
272 U.S. 365
laws.findlaw.com/US/272/365.html

DECISION

Zoning ordinances, which restrict certain uses of land to defined areas, are an appropriate use of government police power, even if a property owner claims that the regulation reduces the value of the land. Courts will not scrutinize challenged zoning ordinances word by word, but will generally uphold them if their validity is "fairly debatable."

BACKGROUND

It is now part of everyday life for U.S. cities and towns to enact and enforce zoning ordinances aimed at regulating the development of land in the interest of safety and aesthetics. That was not always the case. In the mainly rural nineteenth century United States, there was not much perceived need for comprehensive zoning codes. Just as a traffic light is not needed at an intersection until it becomes busy, zoning regulations became popular only when there was enough development to make regulation necessary. The community as a whole benefited from zoning regulations that, for example, kept factories away from residential areas. But zoning was often not popular with property owners who suddenly found they could not use or sell the land the way they had planned.

As zoning laws proliferated, disgruntled property owners challenged many of them in court. They claimed that by preventing the full use of their property, zoning laws violated the Fourteenth Amendment, which says states may not deprive people of their property without due process of law. Municipalities, for their part, defended zoning laws as a valid part of their "police power," a general term for the range of legislation that states may pass under the Constitution to protect the health and well-being of their residents. By the time these disputes made their way to the Supreme Court, most but not all lower courts had ruled in favor of zoning regulation.

The case before the Court involved a comprehensive zoning scheme enacted by the Village of Euclid, a town with fewer than 10,000 residents near Cleveland, Ohio. In 1922 officials passed a zoning law that divided the town into areas in which only industrial, residential, or commercial uses were permitted. Ambler Realty Company owned a sixty-eight-acre parcel of land that encompassed three different zones under the new law. Part of it could be used for industry, but the zoning law limited other parts of the parcel to commercial use, which apparently made it less valuable to the owner when the time came to sell. The realty company sued in federal court. The court found the zoning law unconstitutional and ordered the town not to enforce it.

VOTE

6–3, with Justice George Sutherland writing the majority opinion. Joining him were Chief Justice William Howard Taft and Justices Oliver Wendell Holmes Jr., Louis D. Brandeis, Edward T. Sanford, and Harlan Fiske Stone. Dissenting were Justices Pierce Butler, James C. McReynolds, and Willis Van Devanter.

HIGHLIGHTS

After reciting at length the facts of the case and the history and recent growth of zoning, the Court noted that interpretation of the Constitution also evolves. "While the meaning of constitutional guaranties never varies, the scope of their application must expand or contract to meet the new and different conditions which are constantly coming within the field of their operation," wrote Sutherland. "In a changing world it is impossible that it should be otherwise."

The Court proceeded cautiously to examine the constitutional issues surrounding zoning. Clear lines would be hard to draw, the Court said, because the legitimacy of a particular zoning regulation might be clear in one place, but questionable in another. "It varies with circumstances and conditions," the Court said. "A regulatory zoning ordinance, which would be clearly valid as applied to the great cities, might be clearly invalid as applied to rural communities." Even defining a nuisance would not be easy. "A nuisance may be merely a right thing in the wrong place, like a pig in the parlor instead of the barnyard."

As a result, the Court indicated that governments should be given considerable leeway to decide for themselves what should be regulated and how. The courts should not, Sutherland said, get involved in examining zoning ordinances in detail. Establishing a relatively lax test, the Court said, "If the validity of the legislative classification for zoning purposes be fairly debatable, the legislative judgment must be allowed to control."

Under that test, the Court found it fairly easy to justify the Euclid zoning ordinance and many others. Among the valid police power reasons for enacting a particular ordinance, the Court said, were "promotion of the health and security from injury of children and others by separating dwelling houses from territory devoted to trade and industry; suppression and prevention of disorder; facilitating the extinguishment of fires and the enforcement of street traffic regulations. . . . Another ground is that the construction and repair of streets may be rendered easier and less expensive by confining the greater part of the heavy traffic to the streets where business is carried on."

Significantly, the Court held out the possibility that future cases could present instances in which a zoning ordinance, and the way in which it was applied, could exceed the valid police powers of government and be struck down. The Court, Sutherland said, "has preferred to follow the method of a gradual approach to the general by a systematically guarded application and extension of constitutional principles to particular cases as they arise, rather than by out of hand attempts to establish general rules to which future cases must be fitted."

EXCERPTS

From Justice George Sutherland's majority opinion: "It is said that the Village of Euclid is a mere suburb of the city of Cleveland; that the industrial development of that city has now reached and in some degree extended into the village, and in the obvious course of things will soon absorb the entire area for industrial enterprises; that the effect of the ordinance is to divert this natural development elsewhere, with the consequent loss of increased values to the owners of the lands within the village borders. But the village, though physically a suburb of Cleveland, is politically a separate municipality, with powers of its own and authority to govern itself as it sees fit, within the limits of the organic law of its creation and the state and federal Constitutions. Its governing authorities, presumably representing a majority of its inhabitants and voicing their will, have determined not that industrial development shall cease at its boundaries, but that the course of such development shall proceed within definitely fixed lines. If it be a proper exercise of the police power to relegate industrial establishments to localities separated from residential sections, it is not easy to find a sufficient reason for denying the power because the effect of its exercise is to divert an industrial flow from the course which it would follow, to the injury of the residential public, if left alone, to another course where such injury will be obviated."

IMPACT

The *Euclid* decision for the first time gave constitutional protection to the concept of zoning. With that blessing, zoning ordinances proliferated with little interference from the courts. As the Supreme Court suggested in *Euclid,* courts could and did strike down excessively restrictive ordinances, but it did not happen often. By and large, in fact, the Court has stayed away from zoning cases, viewing the issue, like education, as a matter for local authorities, not courts, to determine.

In the 1990s, however, a growing property rights movement succeeded in bringing a number of zoning-related cases to the Court's attention, and the rulings have gone against zoning. In *Lucas v. South Carolina Coastal Council* (1992) the Court struck down a coastal zoning regulation that had completely eliminated any possible use of a beachfront parcel of land owned by David Lucas. In *Dolan v. City of Tigard* (1994) the Court said the Oregon city could not require a property owner to devote part of his land to public use as a condition for building elsewhere on the land—unless there was a "rough proportionality" between the requirement and the harm posed by the development. Both decisions were based, not on the Fourteenth Amendment but the Fifth Amendment, which bars government from "taking" private property without compensation. These decisions caused some concern among municipal officials that routine zoning decisions would trigger lawsuits and requests for compensation.

Most commentators, however, agree that the rulings have not erased the Court's basic support for zoning as expressed in *Euclid.* That view was confirmed in 2005, when the Court in *Kelo v. City of New London* upheld a government economic development plan that included taking several homes by eminent domain. Justice John Paul Stevens, in his majority opinion, cited the *Euclid* decision in asserting that the courts must defer to state and local governments on matters of planning and zoning. (See *Kelo v. City of New London*.)

Kelo v. City of New London

Decided June 23, 2005
No. 04-108
laws.findlaw.com/US/000/04-108.html

DECISION

Governments do not violate the Fifth Amendment when they take private property and turn it over to other private owners as part of an economic development plan.

BACKGROUND

Even though ownership of private property is a cherished U.S. value, it has long been recognized that governments have the power to seize property for "public use." The classic example is construction of a public highway, where government agencies have the unquestioned ability to take private properties that are in the path of the project, as long as they compensate the owners for their loss.

This concept, known as "eminent domain," is embodied in the Fifth Amendment to the Constitution, a grab-bag amendment that includes many important protections against government power. Its final clause states, "nor shall private property be taken for public use, without just compensation."

The meaning of the phrase "public use" in that clause was the focal point of a dispute in New London, Connecticut. The city had fallen on hard times, especially after a U.S. Navy facility closed in 1996. A state agency designated New London as a "distressed municipality." To revitalize the area, the city, acting through a private economic development corporation, developed a plan that ultimately included a conference center, hotel, various stores and other commercial uses along the waterfront of the Thames River, in an area known as Fort Trumbull. Pfizer Inc., a pharmaceutical company, announced it would build a research facility adjacent to the city's development, bringing many news jobs to New London.

The development plan called for taking several existing private homes by eminent domain. Susette Kelo owned one of the homes, and many of the others were also owned by longtime residents. They challenged the takings, claiming that what New London planned to do with their properties was not a "public use" as required by the Fifth Amendment. The Connecticut Supreme Court upheld the city's plan, and Kelo and the other homeowners took the case to the U.S. Supreme Court.

The Institute for Justice, an energetic public interest group that champions libertarian causes, represented the homeowners and sought to portray them in legal briefs and in the news media as victims of a heartless government that was more interested in increasing tax revenue than in the interests of individual citizens. The institute produced a study documenting 10,000 similar examples of what it called "eminent domain abuse" nationwide. It claimed that if the Supreme Court upheld the Connecticut ruling, then all private property would be vulnerable to taking, because it can almost always be argued that a new use of someone's land will produce more tax revenue than what is currently there.

VOTE

5–4, with Justice John Paul Stevens writing for the majority. Joining him were Justices Anthony Kennedy, David Souter, Ruth Bader Ginsburg, and Stephen Breyer. In dissent were Justices Sandra Day O'Connor, Chief Justice William Rehnquist, and Justices Antonin Scalia and Clarence Thomas.

HIGHLIGHTS

The Supreme Court had already spoken on eminent domain, and those precedents provided strong support for the majority's view. In a 1954 case *Berman v. Parker,* involving an urban renewal project in Washington, D.C., and a 1984 case *Hawaii Housing Authority v. Midkiff* challenging a plan by the state of Hawaii to break up property owned by the original settlers of the islands, the Court decided to defer strongly to other branches of government in determining what the "public use" phrase meant.

As a result, Stevens said in the *Kelo* opinion, it was not for the Supreme Court to substitute its judgment for the officials of New London and Connecticut, who made decisions that led to the taking of the Fort Trumbull homes.

But, said Stevens, the Court's deference did not mean that a government could simply take a property from one owner and turn it over to someone else, nor could it simply make up a pretext for making such a transfer. Pointing to what happened in New London, Stevens seemed to suggest that to meet the "public use" test, a government has to carefully develop a comprehensive plan that "it believes will provide appreciable benefits to the community, including—but by no means limited to—new jobs and increased tax revenue."

Justice Kennedy, who to the surprise of some provided the crucial fifth vote for Stevens's majority, also stressed these factors in his concurrence. He said New London had gone through a careful planning process, and it could not be claimed that the government was corruptly giving over private property to some favored company.

The home of Susette Kelo in New London, Connecticut, became the focal point of that city's exercise of eminent domain to seize private property as part of an economic revitalization plan involving private development. In *Kelo v. City of New London* (2005), the Supreme Court held that the city had not violated property owners' Fifth Amendment rights, emphasizing that such taking of property must "provide appreciable benefits to the community."
Source: AP/Wide World Photos/ Jack Sauer.

But the dissenters said that these cautionary words in the majority meant little, and that the Court's ruling amounted to a green light to almost any kind of eminent domain transfer. The homes of Fort Trumbull were not at all blighted, Justice O'Connor pointed out—unlike the slums at issue in the *Berman* case—nor were they harming society, unlike the monopolistic lock on land ownership involved in *Midkiff*.

Justice Thomas, who also wrote a dissent, lamented that the Court's opinion had ignored the original meaning of the "public use" safeguard in the Fifth Amendment. He also predicted that the impact of the decision would be felt most by the poor. "Allowing the government to take property solely for public purposes is bad enough," Thomas wrote, "but extending the concept of public purpose to encompass any economically beneficial goal guarantees that these losses will fall disproportionately on poor communities. Those communities are not only systematically less likely to put their lands to the highest and best social use, but are also the least politically powerful."

EXCERPTS

From Justice John Paul Stevens's majority opinion: "Those who govern the City were not confronted with the need to remove blight in the Fort Trumbull area, but their determination that the area was sufficiently distressed to justify a program of economic rejuvenation is entitled to our deference. . . . Given the comprehensive character of the plan, the thorough deliberation that preceded its adoption, and the limited scope of our review, it is appropriate for us. . . to resolve the challenges of the individual owners, not on a piecemeal basis, but rather in

light of the entire plan. Because that plan unquestionably serves a public purpose, the takings challenged here satisfy the public use requirement of the Fifth Amendment."

From Justice O'Connor's dissent: "Under the banner of economic development, all private property is now vulnerable to being taken and transferred to another private owner, so long as it might be upgraded—i.e., given to an owner who will use it in a way that the legislature deems more beneficial to the public—in the process. To reason, as the Court does, that the incidental public benefits resulting from the subsequent ordinary use of private property render economic development takings 'for public use' is to wash out any distinction between private and public use of property—and thereby effectively to delete the words 'for public use' from the Takings Clause of the Fifth Amendment. . . . Who among us can say she already makes the most productive or attractive possible use of her property? The specter of condemnation hangs over all property. Nothing is to prevent the State from replacing any Motel 6 with a Ritz-Carlton, any home with a shopping mall, or any farm with a factory."

IMPACT

The Court's decision provoked an unusually broad and mostly negative reaction from the public. Many average citizens viewed the taking of middle-class homes for the benefit of private developers as an injustice. The reaction ran across the political spectrum. Conservatives and libertarians were angry that the Court was retreating from its recent rulings that had seemed to support property rights. Liberals and government reformers felt the Court had given in to corporate interests at the expense of the low- and middle-income property owners who are often the targets of eminent domain takings.

Characteristically, the Institute for Justice rebounded quickly, announcing a campaign to take the fight against eminent domain abuse back to the states. The constitutions of all fifty states have provisions similar, if not identical, to the Fifth Amendment. In several states, legislatures and courts have interpreted their takings clauses more stringently, to require a more substantial "public use" before private homes can be taken. The institute's campaign is aimed at convincing more states to adopt this view.

At the federal level, members of Congress also reacted angrily to the *Kelo* decision. Since most of the controversial takings take place at the state and local level, federal power is limited. But members of both houses of Congress avoided that problem by introducing legislation that would prevent *Kelo*-type takings in any state or local project that receives federal funds.

Some scholars also argued that although the battle over eminent domain was over as far as the Supreme Court was concerned, abuse of the power could be challenged under other constitutional theories involving due process and the "just compensation" clause.

RACIAL DISCRIMINATION

*T*he strife surrounding race relations has been the recurring blemish on this nation's past. And for the early part of U.S. history, neither the Constitution nor the Supreme Court helped improve those relations. The Constitution recognized slavery and the Court upheld it. It was not until ratification of the post–Civil War Amendments, notably the Fourteenth Amendment, that the legal system began to be viewed as a vehicle for combating racial discrimination. But even then progress was slow, and it was not until 1954 that the Court committed itself fully to racial integration in public schools. More than fifty years later, many issues of race still remain on the national agenda.

Other related cases mentioned in the Racial Discrimination section

Ex parte Virginia (1880)
Buchanan v. Warley (1917)
Sweatt v. Painter (1950)
Cooper v. Aaron (1958)
Heart of Atlanta Motel v. United States (1964) (see p. 54)
Green v. County School Board of New Kent County (1968)
Milliken v. Bradley (1974)
Wards Cove Packing Company v. Antonio (1989)
Missouri v. Jenkins (1990)
Oklahoma City Public Schools v. Powell (1991)
Freeman v. Pitts (1992)
Romer v. Evans (1996) (see p. 178)
Smith v. City of Jackson (2005)

United States v. The Schooner Amistad

Decided March 9, 1841
40 U.S. 518
laws.findlaw.com/US/40/518.html

DECISION

The Africans who took over the Spanish schooner *Amistad* were kidnap victims and not the property of their captors. A 1795 treaty with Spain that required the return of property taken on the high seas did not apply to illegally obtained slaves, even if they had taken over the ship.

BACKGROUND

This case decided the fate of fifty-three Africans who, along with a much larger group, had been captured in Sierra Leone and taken to Havana, Cuba, for the slave trade. Spanish planters bought the fifty-three and put them on the *Amistad*, which was destined for coastal estates elsewhere in Cuba. In stormy seas the captives took over the ship and killed the captain and cook.

The ship, which the mutineers thought was on its way back to Africa, had been maneuvered by some remaining Spanish crew members into Long Island Sound instead. Two sea captains who discovered it, as well as the commander of the U.S. cutter that seized it, claimed rights to the ship and its contents. The planters wanted the Africans returned to them. So, from the moment the *Amistad* landed in New London, Connecticut, the saga of the Africans on board became a sensation throughout the United States and a dilemma for the federal courts.

Meanwhile, the Spanish government, backed by the administration of President Martin Van Buren, wanted the ship returned to Spain to allow the Africans to stand trial for murder and mutiny. As the story spread, a group of slavery abolitionists took up the Africans' cause and urged they be set free. It fell to the federal courts, and ultimately to the Supreme Court, to sort out the varying claims on the *Amistad* and its captives, who were held in a New Haven jail.

Roger Baldwin, who later served as a U.S. senator and as governor of Connecticut, argued persuasively on behalf of the Africans that the United States had no authority or obligation to punish them for their mutiny or to return them to Spain, where the slave trade had been abolished. At a celebrated trial in New Haven, one of the captives nicknamed Cinque testified through a translator about his group's steps toward freedom. The federal judge ruled in favor of the Africans. According to Spanish law, they had never legally been slaves, so the judge decided they should be freed and delivered to President Van Buren for return to their native land. As for the ship and its contents, the

judge granted salvage rights to the Coast Guard captain who had brought the ship in.

The Van Buren administration appealed, and in 1841 the case was argued before the Supreme Court. Fearful that the lower court judgment would be reversed, abolitionist supporters of the Africans enlisted former president John Quincy Adams to plead their case.

Oral argument at the Court lasted for eight days. The *National Intelligencer* newspaper reported, "The Supreme Court was yesterday the theater of great interest and attracted a crowded audience" because of Adams's presence. About one day, Adams wrote in his diary, "I spoke four hours and a half, with sufficient method and order to witness little flagging of attention by the judges."

By all accounts, Adams was sharply critical of President Van Buren's support for the Spanish claim. Baldwin, who also argued on behalf of the Africans, was more temperate, asking the Court

This 1839 portrait of Joseph Cinque was painted as Cinque awaited trial in New Haven, Connecticut, for mutiny and murder while leading a revolt among slaves from Sierra Leone aboard the Spanish ship *Amistad*. In *United States v. The Schooner Amistad* (1841)—a case that pitted the Spanish and U.S. governments against the Africans and their representative, former president John Quincy Adams—the justices found that the Africans were kidnap victims, not the property of their captors. The men were set free and returned to Africa.
Source: Library of Congress.

whether the government "can, consistently with the genius of our institutions, become a party to proceedings for the enslavement of human beings cast upon our shores." The importation of slaves to the United States had been abolished in 1808, although commerce in slaves among the states was still permitted.

VOTE

7–1, with Justice Joseph Story writing the majority opinion. Joining him were Chief Justice Roger B. Taney and Justices Smith Thompson, John McLean, James Wayne, John Catron, and John McKinley. Justice Henry Baldwin dissented. Justice Philip Barbour, who died just weeks before the decision, had not yet been replaced.

HIGHLIGHTS

The *Amistad* opinion is dominated by a lengthy description of the intricacies of the case. The facts went to prove the basic holding: The Africans had never been legally enslaved; rather, they had been kidnapped by the Spanish slave traders who had brought them to Cuba in the first place. Because they were not slaves, the Court found, they could not be returned as property. In addition, because they were not legally being held as slaves, the Court said they could not be penalized for rising up and seeking to end their imprisonment. Justice Story affirmed the right of self-defense by people who are held illegally.

Although the Court decided that the Africans should be set free, the *Amistad* ruling was not a true repudiation of slavery. Story's decision was based on the premise that slaves were property. If Spain had been able to prove that the *Amistad* Africans were legally slaves, there is little doubt that the Court would have ordered them returned as slaves. Had they been legally slaves, the Court also would not have given its blessing to the mutiny aboard the *Amistad.*

"By those laws and treaties, and edicts, the African slave-trade is utterly abolished; the dealing in that trade is deemed a heinous crime; and the negroes thereby introduced into the dominions of Spain, are declared to be free," the Court said. "There is no pretence to say the negroes of the *Amistad* are 'pirates' and 'robbers,' as they were kidnapped Africans who, by the laws of Spain itself, were entitled to their freedom." In that sense, the *Amistad* decision reaffirmed that "natural" laws—such as the innate human right to resist illegal imprisonment—could triumph only if there are no "positive" or written laws that contradict them.

Another significant aspect of the ruling was to affirm that free Africans had equal footing with any American to obtain justice in American courts. "They appear here as freemen," Story wrote. "They stand before our courts on equal ground with their claimants; and when the courts, after an impartial hearing, with all parties in interest before them, have pro-

nounced them free, it is neither the duty nor the right of the executive of the United States to interfere with the decision."

EXCERPTS

From Justice Joseph Story's majority opinion: "Upon the merits of the case, then, there does not seem to us to be any ground for doubt that these negroes ought to be deemed free; and that the Spanish treaty interposes no obstacle to the just assertion of their rights. . . .

"When the *Amistad* arrived, she was in possession of the negroes, asserting their freedom; and in no sense could they possibly intend to import themselves here, as slaves, or for sale as slaves. . . .

"Upon the whole, our opinion is, that the decree of the circuit court, affirming that of the district court, ought to be affirmed, except so far as it directs the negroes to be delivered to the president, to be transported to Africa, in pursuance of the act of the 3d of March 1819; and, as to this, it ought to be reversed: and that the said negroes be declared to be free, and be dismissed from the custody of the Court, and go without day [*sic*]."

IMPACT

"The captives are free!" Adams wrote to participants in the case when the decision was handed down. In spite of the somewhat limited scope of the ruling, the abolitionist movement viewed the decision as a significant victory, because its main effect was to set the *Amistad* Africans free. Southerners were not happy with the Supreme Court's decision.

For the captives themselves, as historian Howard Jones put it in *Mutiny on the Amistad,* the decision was "at best a pyrrhic victory in that more than a third of the captives were dead and the survivors had suffered all manner of indignities." They had been held in jail in Connecticut for eighteen months. Private donations financed their trip back to Africa in November 1841.

But the *Amistad* story was not over. The Court ruling remained a sore point for Spain, which sought to be compensated for the loss of the slaves. At various times, members of Congress appeared sympathetic, and a payment of $70,000 was suggested. But no agreement was ever reached, and the issue was effectively dropped once the Civil War began.

Scholars now regard the *Amistad* case as having limited legal significance. As a highly visible controversy that ended with the release of the African captives, however, it can been seen as one of several incidents in the years leading to the Civil War that weakened public support for slavery.

A 1997 movie called *Amistad,* produced and directed by Steven Spielberg, popularized the tale. Retired justice Harry Blackmun played the role of Justice Story in the movie. In the line of succession at the Court, Blackmun had occupied Story's seat. (See Succession Chart of Supreme Court Seats.)

Scott v. Sandford

Decided March 6, 1857
60 U.S. 393
laws.findlaw.com/US/60/393.html

DECISION

Under the Constitution, blacks are not citizens of the United States and may not become citizens. Because they are not citizens, they may not file suit in federal courts. Congress does not have the authority to prohibit slavery in the territories. As a result the Missouri Compromise, which outlawed slavery in parts of the Louisiana Territory, is unconstitutional. Slaves who were moved to territories where slavery had been outlawed were not automatically freed.

BACKGROUND

Before the Civil War, the status of slavery in the new parts of the growing nation was a subject of fervent debate between supporters of slavery and those who wanted to abolish it. Congressional efforts to limit slavery in the territories divided the institution for decades. The newly created Republican Party was devoted to preventing the spread of slavery. In this charged climate, it was perhaps inevitable that both sides would look for a judicial solution. The chance to come up with such a remedy arose in the case of Dred Scott.

Born in Virginia, Scott was sold as a slave to John Emerson, a St. Louis physician. Emerson took Scott along when he joined the military, and in various postings Scott was taken to Illinois, a free state, and to the Wisconsin Territory, which was also free. While in the Wisconsin Territory, Scott married another slave, Harriet Robinson. During a tour in Louisiana, Emerson married Irene Sanford. When Emerson was transferred to Florida, his wife and the Scotts returned to St. Louis. Dr. Emerson died in 1843, after which the Scotts continued to work for his widow and for her brother, John Sanford of New York.

In 1846 the Scotts sued for their freedom, claiming that they had been emancipated when Emerson took them to the slave-free zones of Illinois and the Wisconsin Territory. Their claim, which was consolidated under Dred Scott's name, was supported by the prevailing legal theory in Missouri at the time, which was, "once free, always free." After lengthy delays, the Scotts won at trial, but the state supreme court ruled against them. By now, the case had become well known, and the Missouri Supreme Court may have felt compelled to protect state traditions against outside antislavery influences. The court ruled that in Missouri Scott was still a slave.

Scott's lawyers wanted to appeal the case to the U.S. Supreme Court. For legal and strategic reasons, the best way to do so was to name an out-of-state person as the defendant, thereby triggering federal court jurisdiction over legal disputes between citizens of different states. They chose John Sanford, who was acting as his sister's agent in the litigation anyway. To complete the requirements for federal court jurisdiction, Scott claimed he was a Missouri citizen. The case become known as *Scott v. Sandford* because Sanford's name was misspelled in the records.

A federal trial judge in 1854 agreed with Missouri's high court, finding that Scott was still a slave under Missouri law. The judge also found that Scott was not a citizen of any state, so he could not trigger federal court jurisdiction.

As the case moved to the U.S. Supreme Court, the legal stakes rose, and it became a platform for the broader national debate over slavery. Sanford's lawyers argued for the first time that the Missouri Compromise, which had made the Wisconsin Territory slave free, was unconstitutional and therefore did not have the effect of emancipating Scott. They also questioned whether Scott was a citizen and had any right to sue in federal court.

Reflecting the complexity and tension in the case, the Supreme Court heard arguments in it twice, both in February and December of 1856. The outcome was probably not in doubt: Five of the nine justices on the Court were southerners, several from slaveholding families. Chief Justice Taney, nearly eighty years old, was a Marylander already on record in support of slavery.

Still, there was a considerable amount of behind-the-scenes maneuvering over the case. At first most justices wanted to issue a limited ruling that would avoid the issue of the Missouri Compromise—a law Congress had already repealed with the Kansas-Nebraska Act of 1854, which declared congressional neutrality on the extension of slavery. Instead, these justices would rely on Missouri state law to find that Scott was still a slave. But when two justices said they would dissent and vote to strike down the Missouri Compromise, the rest of the Court agreed the issue needed to be resolved. According to Chief Justice William Rehnquist in a 1998 book, the justices opposing the Missouri Compromise even enlisted President-elect James Buchanan to lobby Justice Robert Grier, a fellow Pennsylvanian, in their effort. Buchanan agreed, and Grier joined the majority. "These machinations, of course, were grossly inappropriate," Rehnquist said.

Finally on March 6, 1857, eleven years after Scott first sued, and two days after the inauguration of President Buchanan, the Court was ready to rule.

Dred Scott, a Missouri slave, sued in federal court to gain his freedom. In *Scott v. Sandford* (1857), the Supreme Court ruled that blacks were not citizens and therefore could not bring suit in federal court. It also held that Congress lacked the authority to restrict slavery in the territories. Although Scott lost the suit, his owner freed him.

Source: Library of Congress.

VOTE

7–2, with Chief Justice Roger B. Taney writing for the Court. He was joined by Justices James M. Wayne, John Catron, Peter V. Daniel, Samuel Nelson, Robert C. Grier, and John A. Campbell. Dissenting were Justices John McLean and Benjamin R. Curtis.

HIGHLIGHTS

The nearly 250 pages of the Court's decision, with separate opinions from all nine justices, are not a model of clarity. Scholars have even debated about which of the justices' writings actually represents the decision of the Court.

It is now generally agreed that Chief Justice Taney's opinion, even though it has been attacked for flawed reasoning and an inaccurate statement of facts, speaks for the Court. Taney's opinion is grounded in his view of the "original intent" of the Framers, namely what the Framers had in mind about slaves and what the status of slaves was at the time of the drafting of the Constitution.

"They were at that time considered as a subordinate and inferior class of beings, who had been subjugated by the dominant race, and, whether emancipated or not, yet remained subject to their authority, and had no rights or privileges but such as those who held the power and the Government might

choose to grant them," Taney wrote. It was a view of the world that presumed that blacks had no basic, natural rights as human beings and that the only rights they could have were those enacted by government. From this perspective, Dred Scott could not be viewed as a citizen of the United States.

Taney acknowledged that the Declaration of Independence declares that "all men are created equal." But, he goes on, "The general words above quoted would seem to embrace the whole human family, and if they were used in a similar instrument at this day would be so understood. But it is too clear for dispute, that the enslaved African race were not intended to be included."

Contrast this view with Justice Curtis's dissent: "Slavery, being contrary to natural right, is created only by municipal law. This is not only plain in itself, and agreed by all writers on the subject, but is inferable from the Constitution and has been explicitly declared by this Court." In other words, Curtis believed that under the laws of nature all human beings have basic rights. Slavery exists only because of laws that are passed in contradiction to those rights, Curtis said, a view of human rights completely opposite from Taney's.

But Taney's view enabled him and the justices in the majority to absolve themselves of responsibility for slavery. That belonged to the legislative bodies that can grant and take away the few rights that slaves are given. Taney wrote, "It is not the province of the court to decide upon the justice or injustice, the policy or impolicy, of these laws. The decision of that question belonged to the political or law-making power, to those who formed the sovereignty and framed the Constitution. The duty of the court is to interpret the instrument they have framed with the best lights we can obtain on the subject, and to administer it as we find it, according to its true intent and meaning when it was adopted."

Taney's assertion also led to one of the Court's main conclusions. Because blacks were not citizens at the time of the framing of the Constitution, they were not entitled to sue in federal courts. So Dred Scott was asking the federal courts to do something they had no jurisdiction to do. Taney also insisted that the Framers of the Constitution viewed slaves as property, not people. "The right of property in a slave is distinctly and expressly affirmed in the Constitution," he wrote.

The next step was for Taney to rule that the Constitution gave Congress no power to enact legislation affecting the territories—certainly not legislation as sweeping as the Missouri Compromise. Taney reached that conclusion by a very narrow and much-disputed reading of the Constitution's provision on territories. So Scott had lost on another score: he could not be free now if he had never been in a free state. Because the Missouri Compromise was illegitimate, Scott's travels to the Wisconsin Territory and to Illinois did not turn him into a free man.

In dissent, Justice Curtis also sharply disputed Taney's version of history at the time of the framing of the Constitution. "To determine whether any free persons, descended from Africans held in slavery, were citizens of the United States under the Confederation, and consequently at the time of the adoption of the Constitution of the United States, it is only necessary to know whether any such persons were citizens of either of the States under the Confederation at the time of the adoption of the Constitution," Curtis wrote. "Of this there can be no doubt. At the time of the ratification of the Articles of Confederation, all free native-born inhabitants of the States of New Hampshire, Massachusetts, New York, New Jersey, and North Carolina, though descended from African slaves, were not only citizens of those States, but such of them as had the other necessary qualifications possessed the franchise of electors, on equal terms with other citizens."

Curtis eloquently attacked the Court majority for basing its decision on an inaccurate view of history and the meaning of the Constitution. "When a strict interpretation of the Constitution, according to the fixed rules which govern the interpretation of laws, is abandoned, and the theoretical opinions of individuals are allowed to control its meaning, we have no longer a Constitution; we are under the government of individual men who for the time being have power to declare what the Constitution is, according to their own views of what it ought to mean."

Justice McLean also dissented, arguing that Scott had rights as a citizen. "Being born under our Constitution and laws, no naturalization is required, as one of foreign birth, to make him a citizen. The most general and appropriate definition of the term citizen is 'a freeman.' Being a freeman, and having his domicil in a State different from that of the defendant, he is a citizen within the act of Congress, and the courts of the Union are open to him."

EXCERPTS

From Chief Justice Roger B. Taney's majority opinion: "The question before us is, whether the class of persons described in the plea in abatement compose a portion of this people, and are constituent members of this sovereignty? We think they are not, and that they are not included, and were not intended to be included, under the word 'citizens' in the Constitution, and can therefore claim none of the rights and privileges which that instrument provides for and secures to citizens of the United States. . . .

"In the opinion of the court, the legislation and histories of the times, and the language used in the Declaration of Independence, show, that neither the class of persons who had been imported as slaves, nor their descendants, whether they had become free or not, were then acknowledged as a part of the people, nor intended to be included in the general words used in that memorable instrument. . . .

Chief Justice Roger B. Taney's opinion in *Scott v. Sandford* (1857) that under the Constitution blacks are not citizens clouded his reputation and hastened the outbreak of the Civil War.
Source: Library of Congress.

". . . [T]he right of property in a slave is distinctly and expressly affirmed in the Constitution. The right to traffic in it, like an ordinary article of merchandise and property, was guarantied to the citizens of the United States, in every State that might desire it, for twenty years. . . .

". . . [I]t is the opinion of the Court that the act of Congress which prohibited a citizen from holding and owning property of this kind in the territory of the United States north of the line therein mentioned, is not warranted by the Constitution, and is therefore void; and that neither Dred Scott himself, nor any of his family, were made free by being carried into this territory, even if they had been carried there by the owner, with the intention of becoming a permanent resident."

IMPACT

It would probably overstate the case to say that the Dred Scott decision triggered the Civil War, but historians agree that it was certainly a contributing factor. The decision made it clear that there would be no easy way, certainly no judicial way, to end slavery or to confine it to the southern states. The Court had declared slavery to be a national institution that Congress could not prohibit in the territories, which represented the future of a growing nation. With no easy end to the strife over slavery in sight, war between North and South became more likely.

Reaction to the ruling was explosive. Abolitionist Horace Greeley's *New York Tribune* said the decision "is entitled to just so much moral weight as would be the judgment of those congregated in any Washington bar room." A Georgia newspaper, on the other hand, boasted that "southern opinion on the subject of southern slavery is now the supreme law of the land."

The decision also was a frequent theme for discussion in the famed Lincoln-Douglas debates that preceded the 1858 Illinois Senate race. Abraham Lincoln said the Supreme Court had been enlisted in a conspiracy to "nationalize slavery," and Stephen Douglas accused Lincoln of declaring war on the Supreme Court. In Lincoln's first inaugural address, delivered moments after Chief Justice Taney swore him in, Lincoln was likely referring to the Dred Scott decision when he said "the people will have ceased to be their own rulers" if the Supreme Court can set national policy.

Decades after the Dred Scott decision, Chief Justice Charles Evans Hughes called it the Supreme Court's greatest "self-inflicted wound." The decision's dogged support of slavery earned it the first place position in Court scholar Bernard Schwartz's list of worst Supreme Court decisions in history. "No decision in our history has done more to injure the reputation of the Court," wrote Schwartz.

Scott v. Sandford was overturned, not by the Court but through the constitutional amendment process. The Thirteenth Amendment, ratified in 1865, abolished slavery altogether, and the Fourteenth Amendment, ratified in 1868, guaranteed citizenship to all persons born or naturalized in the United States, regardless of race or prior servitude.

As a result, in spite of its explosive political impact, the decision had relatively little legal importance, with one exception. Writing on the Missouri Compromise, historian Don Fehrenbacher said, "This was the first instance in which a major federal law was ruled unconstitutional. The decision is therefore a landmark in the development of judicial review and in the growth of judicial power."

Civil Rights Cases

(United States v. Stanley; United States v. Ryan; United States v. Nichols; United States v. Singleton; Robinson and wife v. Memphis and Charleston R. Co.)

Decided October 15, 1883
109 U.S. 3
laws.findlaw.com/US/109/3.html

DECISION

A law passed by Congress banning racial discrimination in privately owned businesses such as inns and theaters is unconstitutional. Neither the Thirteenth Amendment, which banned slavery, nor the Fourteenth Amendment, which barred discrimination by the states, gives Congress the power to enact such a law. Discrimination by innkeepers has nothing to do with slavery, the Court said, and is not a form of state action that can be banned by Congress.

BACKGROUND

Despite the end of slavery, the post–Civil War United States was a place where blacks were still given second-class treatment in a wide range of public accommodations. In all parts of the country, not only the South, hotels, restaurants, and railroads often refused service to blacks or gave them less service than whites.

Passage of civil rights laws and ratification of the Fourteenth Amendment spurred test cases by blacks seeking the same level of service as whites, and in some places they were successful. But instances of discrimination in the Reconstruction-era United States persisted and were the subject of growing national debate.

In 1875 Congress finally responded with a law that guaranteed to all persons "the full and equal enjoyment of the accommodations, advantages, facilities, and privileges of inns, public conveyances on land or water, theatres, and other places of public amusement, subject only to the conditions and limitations established by law and applicable alike to citizens of every race and color, regardless of any previous condition of servitude."

Almost immediately after the law took effect, some hotels shut their doors, while others changed their ways. Blacks were served at the bar of the Willard Hotel in Washington, D.C., for the first time, but blacks who visited restaurants and barbershops in Richmond, Virginia, were turned away. Lawsuits were filed in a smattering of cases.

In November 1879 William Davis Jr., an official of a black New York newspaper, and a lady friend bought tickets and sought admission to a performance of Victor Hugo's *Ruy Blas* at the Grand Opera House in New York City. The famed actor Edwin Booth was performing. Doorkeeper Samuel Singleton turned the couple away because of their race. Davis argued with Singleton, and the police were called. When a police officer told Davis that the owners of the theater did not permit blacks to attend performances, Davis, according to a historical account by Columbia University professor Alan Westin, replied, "The laws of the country do." The next day, Davis filed a criminal complaint, and Singleton was indicted. At trial, Singleton's lawyer argued that the law interfered with the private property rights of New Yorkers. The trial judge referred the constitutional issue to the appeals court, and the appeals judges divided on it.

When the *Singleton* case came to the Supreme Court it was consolidated with several others, which became known as the Civil Rights Cases. The other cases involved hotels in Topeka, Kansas, and Jefferson City, Missouri, and a theater in San Francisco that refused service to blacks. In all the cases, the constitutionality of the 1875 law was at issue.

The solicitor general, representing the United States in the litigation, strongly defended the law before the Supreme Court, noting that it had been passed by a Congress whose members had fought in the Civil War and knew that "every rootlet of slavery has an individual vitality, and to its minutest hair, should be anxiously followed and plucked up."

VOTE

8–1, with Justice Joseph P. Bradley writing for the majority. Joining him were Chief Justice Morrison R. Waite and Justices Samuel F. Miller, Stephen J. Field, William B. Woods, Stanley Matthews, Horace Gray, and Samuel Blatchford. Justice John Marshall Harlan dissented.

HIGHLIGHTS

The decision was a resounding rejection of the government's interpretation of the Fourteenth Amendment. Rather than a broad mandate to reach the behavior of all citizens, the Court said the Fourteenth Amendment was meant only to restrict the actions of states as states. As a result, it gave Congress no power to restrict the private actions of innkeepers and restaurateurs.

"It is state action of a particular character that is prohibited" by the Fourteenth Amendment, Justice Bradley wrote. "Individual invasion of individual rights is not the subject-matter of the amendment. It has a deeper and broader scope. It nullifies and makes void all state legislation, and state action of every kind, which impairs the privileges and immunities of citizens of the United States or which injures them in life, liberty, or property without due process of law, or which denies to any of them the equal protection of the laws."

If any entity was to forbid discrimination in public accommodations, the Court said it was state governments, not the federal government, that civil rights advocates should look to. Once a state government acts, then the Fourteenth Amendment allows Congress and the Supreme Court to pass on what the state had done. But that power could not be expanded, the Court said, to allow Congress to regulate innkeepers directly.

Bradley pointed out that the cases before the Court were different from an 1880 decision, *Ex parte Virginia,* in which the Court said that under the Fourteenth Amendment states could not exclude blacks from juries. Exclusion of blacks from juries was an act of the state, while keeping blacks out of a theater was not.

Similarly, in an analysis of the Thirteenth Amendment, the Court also looked to the issue of state action. The Thirteenth Amendment banned slavery, but the Court said it pertained to slavery sanctioned by the states, not private actions such as the denial of access to a theater. "Should any such servitudes be imposed by a state law, there can be no doubt that the law would be repugnant to the fourteenth, no less than to the thirteenth, amendment, nor any greater doubt that congress has adequate power to forbid any such servitude from being exacted," the Court said. Private discrimination on the basis of color could not be viewed as a form of slavery, the Court reasoned, because at the time of slavery, thousands of blacks were also free and, presumably, discriminated against even though they were not slaves.

Justice Harlan, the Court's only southerner, wrote a dissent that was not only forceful but farsighted. He was a former slaveholder, but had come to the view that the federal government had a responsibility to guarantee full citizenship for blacks. He believed that the Thirteenth and Fourteenth Amendments could fairly be interpreted to permit Congress to enact laws like the one challenged before the Court.

"In every material sense applicable to the practical enforcement of the fourteenth amendment, railroad corporations, keepers of inns, and managers of places of public amusement are agents of the state . . . amenable . . . to public regulation," Harlan wrote. "[A] denial by these instrumentalities of the state to the citizen, because of his race, of that equality of civil rights secured to him by law is a denial by the state within the meaning of the fourteenth amendment."

EXCERPTS

From Justice Joseph P. Bradley's majority opinion: "It [the Fourteenth Amendment] does not invest congress with power to legislate upon subjects which are within the domain of state legislation, but to provide modes of relief against state legislation, or state action, of the kind referred to. It does not authorize congress to create a code of municipal law for the regulation of private rights; but to provide modes of redress against the operation of state laws and the action of state officers, executive or judicial, when these are subversive of the fundamental rights specified in the amendment. Positive rights and privileges are undoubtedly secured by the fourteenth amendment, but they are secured by way of prohibition against state laws and state proceedings affecting those rights and privileges, and by power given to congress to legislate for the purpose of carrying such prohibition into effect, and such legislation must necessarily be predicated upon such supposed state laws or state proceedings, and be directed to the correction of their operation and effect. . . .

"Can the act of a mere individual, the owner of the inn, the public conveyance or place of amusement, refusing the accommodation, be justly regarded as imposing any badge of slavery or servitude upon the applicant, or only as inflicting an ordinary civil injury, properly cognizable by the laws of the state, and presumably subject to redress by those laws until the contrary appears?

"After giving to these questions all the consideration which their importance demands, we are forced to the conclusion that such an act of refusal has nothing to do with slavery or involuntary servitude, and that if it is violative of any right of the party, his redress is to be sought under the laws of the state. . . . It would be running the slavery argument into the ground to make it apply to every act of discrimination which a person may see fit to make as to the guests he will entertain, or as to the people he will take into his coach or cab or car, or admit to his concert or theater, or deal with in other matters of intercourse or business."

From Justice Harlan's dissent: "My brethren say that when a man has emerged from slavery, and by the aid of beneficient legislation has shaken off the inseparable concomitants of that state, there must be some stage in the progress of his elevation when he takes the rank of a mere citizen, and ceases to be the special favorite of the laws, and when his rights as a citizen, or a man, are to be protected in the ordinary modes by which other men's rights are protected. It is, I submit, scarcely just to say that the colored race has been the special favorite of the laws. What the nation, through congress, has sought to accomplish in reference to that race is, what had already been done in every state in the Union for the white race, to secure and protect rights belonging to them as freemen and citizens;

nothing more. The one underlying purpose of congressional legislation has been to enable the black race to take the rank of mere citizens. The difficulty has been to compel a recognition of their legal right to take that rank, and to secure the enjoyment of privileges belonging, under the law, to them as a component part of the people for whose welfare and happiness government is ordained. At every step in this direction the nation has been confronted with class tyranny. . . . The supreme law of the land has decreed that no authority shall be exercised in this country upon the basis of discrimination, in respect of civil rights, against freemen and citizens because of their race, color, or previous condition of servitude. To that decree . . . every one must bow, whatever may have been, or whatever now are, his individual views as to the wisdom or policy, either of the recent changes in the fundamental law, or of the legislation which has been enacted to give them effect."

IMPACT

The white establishment generally applauded the Court's decision in the Civil Rights Cases. That night, news of the decision was announced from the stage of the Atlanta Opera House, which had been sued by a black who had been denied entrance. The audience—except for blacks sitting in the balcony—cheered. Civil rights activist Frederick Douglass said the decision helped southerners put the black man "just where they want him."

The decision had the practical effect of shutting down any hopes for civil rights legislation from Congress for more than a half century. It also encouraged a generation's worth of "Jim Crow" legislation at the state level that required separate facilities for whites and blacks in education, transportation, and public accommodations. Along with a later decision (see *Plessy v. Ferguson*), the Court by its narrow interpretation of the post–Civil War constitutional amendments gave what amounted to a legal imprimatur to a long period of U.S. history in which blacks did not enjoy the full fruits of the emancipation and equality that had been secured by the Civil War.

Ironically, the decision in the Civil Rights Cases also contained the seeds of its demise. In passing, Justice Bradley mentioned that the Court's decision was not based on, and did not affect, other enumerated powers of Congress, including its role in regulating interstate commerce. When society's views about race relations finally shifted in the 1950s and 1960s, Congress again tried to outlaw discrimination in public accommodations. This time, it based the legislation on the commerce power, and this time, in *Heart of Atlanta Motel v. United States* (1964), the Supreme Court found it to be constitutional (see *Heart of Atlanta Motel v. United States*).

Yick Wo v. Hopkins

Decided May 10, 1886
118 U.S. 356
laws.findlaw.com/US/118/356.html

DECISION

The due process clause of the Fourteenth Amendment applies to persons, not just citizens. A law that is neutral on its face but enforced in a discriminatory manner denies the equal protection of the laws and violates the Fourteenth Amendment.

BACKGROUND

Chinese immigration to the United States was unrestricted through most of the nineteenth century, when labor was needed to build railroads and develop the West. By 1882, when Congress passed the first law to restrict the flow of Chinese, more than 75,000 Chinese immigrants lived in California, most of them in San Francisco. Before that, however, local authorities had enacted several regulations to discourage Chinese settlement. A law passed in 1870 limited the number of residents per apartment, and another eight years later cut back on police protection in Chinatown.

In 1880 the local board of supervisors enacted a law clearly aimed at eliminating Chinese participation from the laundry business, one of the Chinese community's principal enterprises. The law required all laundries that did not operate in brick or stone buildings to obtain permission or a license from the board. Brick laundries did not need licenses at all.

The law may have seemed to be a neutral safety regulation, but the situation in San Francisco indicates it was not. Of the 320 laundries in the city at the time, all but 10 were housed in wooden buildings. Chinese immigrants operated about 240 of these laundries. When the licensing regulation took effect, all but one of the Chinese laundry operators who applied were rejected, while all the white owners were given licenses.

Yick Wo, who had been in the laundry business in San Francisco for twenty-two years, was one of the immigrants denied permission to operate in a wooden building, even though his establishment had passed a safety inspection the year before. He continued to keep his doors open to test the law. When he was arrested and ordered to jail, he appealed, challenging the discriminatory enforcement of the law.

A federal judge noted in a related case, "The notorious public and municipal history of the times indicate a purpose to drive out the Chinese laundrymen, and not merely to regulate the business for the public safety." Nonetheless, the California Supreme Court, noting that in some locations the operation of

laundries "may be highly dangerous to the public safety," ruled against Yick Wo. Following his defeat in the California courts, Yick Wo appealed to the U.S. Supreme Court. His appeal took the form of a lawsuit against the man who was officially keeping him in prison: the sheriff of San Francisco, whose name was Hopkins.

VOTE

9–0, with Justice Stanley Matthews writing the majority opinion. Joining him were Chief Justice Morrison R. Waite, Justices Samuel F. Miller, Stephen J. Field, Joseph P. Bradley, John Marshall Harlan, William B. Woods, Horace Gray, and Samuel L. Blatchford.

HIGHLIGHTS

Although agreeing at the outset that the Supreme Court of California was entitled to some deference in interpreting the laws of that state, Justice Matthews boldly asserted that the U.S. Supreme Court is entitled to subject the San Francisco ordinance to "an independent construction, for the determination of the question whether the proceedings under these ordinances, and in enforcement of them, are in conflict with the constitution and laws of the United States."

Unlike the California court, the Supreme Court viewed the ordinance not as an ordinary safety regulation but as an example of "a naked and arbitrary power" that exceeded normal bounds. "The very idea that one man may be compelled to hold his life, or the means of living, or any material right essential to the enjoyment of life, at the mere will of another seems to be intolerable in any country where freedom prevails, as being the essence of slavery itself."

The right not to be subject to such arbitrary treatment belongs to citizens and immigrants alike, the Court agreed. The Court noted the wording of the Fourteenth Amendment: "Nor shall any State deprive any person of life, liberty, or property without due process of law; nor deny to any person within its jurisdiction the equal protection of the laws." Matthews concluded, "The fourteenth amendment to the constitution is not confined to the protection of citizens."

The Court also asserted that the Fourteenth Amendment is violated when a law is enforced in a discriminatory way, even if it is not written in a discriminatory way. Either way, the equal protection of the laws has been denied.

In *Yick Wo v. Hopkins* (1886), a Chinese laundry owner challenged the discriminatory enforcement of a safety regulation that would have closed his business. The Supreme Court ruled that the Fourteenth Amendment protects all persons, not just U.S. citizens, and that a neutral law enforced unevenly denies equal protection of the laws.
Source: Library of Congress.

EXCERPTS

From Justice Stanley Matthews's majority opinion: "[T]he facts shown establish an administration directed so exclusively against a particular class of persons as to warrant and require the conclusion that, whatever may have been the intent of the ordinances as adopted, they are applied by the public authorities charged with their administration, and thus representing the state itself, with a mind so unequal and oppressive as to amount to a practical denial by the state of that equal protection of the laws which is secured to the petitioners, as to all other persons, by the broad and benign provisions of the fourteenth amendment to the constitution of the United States. Though the law itself be fair on its face, and impartial in appearance, yet, if it is applied and administered by public authority with an evil eye and an unequal hand, so as practically to make unjust and illegal discriminations between persons in similar circumstances, material to their rights, the denial of equal justice is still within the prohibition of the constitution."

IMPACT

The *Yick Wo* decision stood in sharp contrast to the Court's earlier interpretation of the Fourteenth Amendment. In *Yick Wo* the Court expanded the meaning of the Fourteenth Amendment by applying its protections to noncitizens. Significantly, it also said the Fourteenth Amendment could be used to restrict the states as well as the federal government. However, it was not until well into the twentieth century that the decision won recognition as a deeply significant statement of the meaning of fair and equal treatment by government.

It has been cited more than 125 times in a range of cases in which arbitrary enforcement of laws is assessed. It was invoked in 1965 in *Griswold v. Connecticut* in connection with a state law forbidding the use of contraceptives. And in *Romer v. Evans* (1996) the Court cited *Yick Wo* in striking down a Colorado law that denied protection to homosexuals. (See *Griswold v. Connecticut* and *Romer v. Evans*.)

Plessy v. Ferguson

Decided May 18, 1896
163 U.S. 537
laws.findlaw.com/US/163/537.html

DECISION

A Louisiana law that required "separate but equal" railroad cars and facilities for black and white passengers is constitutional under the Thirteenth Amendment, which outlaws slavery, and the Fourteenth Amendment, which guarantees equal protection of the laws. Requiring separation of the races, the Court said, does not make them unequal. In addition, the Fourteenth Amendment refers to political equality, not equality in social settings.

BACKGROUND

The post–Civil War amendments and Reconstruction brought about a measure of progress for blacks in their quest for equal treatment, but by the 1890s white domination had returned with passage of Jim Crow laws that enforced racial segregation. An early form of this legislation, enacted throughout the South, required railroads to have separate cars or partitioned areas for black passengers. In 1887 Florida became the first state to pass a separate-car law, and by 1897 all the states of the South had passed similar legislation.

Louisiana was one of the few states in which blacks organized to try to block passage of a segregation law. When the legislation passed anyway, a group of black community leaders mounted a constitutional challenge to it. Albion Tourgée, a famous Reconstruction Republican leader and novelist, agreed to be the lead lawyer for the group, the Citizens' Committee to Test the Constitutionality of the Separate Car Law.

After some false starts, the first real test of the law came in June 1892, when Homer Adolph Plessy boarded the East Louisiana Railroad in New Orleans and took a seat in a car designated for whites. Plessy was a light-skinned black man—one of his eight great-grandparents was black. But railroad officials, apparently alerted that Plessy was coming, asked him to move. When he did not, police, who had also been forewarned, arrested him. Plessy and his lawyers argued before Judge John Ferguson that the separate car law violated the Thirteenth and Fourteenth Amendments. Ferguson ruled against Plessy.

Because of a serious backlog of cases, it took more than three years for the Supreme Court to take up Plessy's appeal. In a brief to the Court, Tourgée asked the justices to imagine how they would feel if they were relegated to a separate railroad car. "What humiliation, what rage would then fill the judicial mind!" he exclaimed. By the time the Court ruled in 1896, public sentiment had, if anything, turned more favorable toward segregation, so it was unlikely that the Court would heed Tourgée's plea.

VOTE

7–1, with Justice Henry B. Brown writing the majority opinion. Joining him were Chief Justice Melville W. Fuller and Justices Stephen J. Field, Horace Gray, George Shiras Jr., Edward D. White, and Rufus W. Peckham. Justice John Marshall Harlan dissented. Justice David J. Brewer did not participate for unexplained reasons.

NEGRO EXPULSION FROM RAILWAY CAR, PHILADELPHIA.

This 1856 wood engraving depicts a black man being expelled from a railway car. Black community leaders in Louisiana mounted a constitutional challenge to racial segregation in *Plessy v. Ferguson* (1896), but the Supreme Court found "separate but equal" facilities for whites and blacks to be constitutional under the Thirteenth and Fourteenth Amendments.
Source: Library of Congress (American Memory Collection).

HIGHLIGHTS

Plessy's lawyers had based their objections to the Louisiana law on both the Thirteenth and Fourteenth Amendments, and the Court rejected both arguments.

Justice Brown found the Thirteenth Amendment issue the easier one to resolve. That amendment outlawed slavery. "That it [the Louisiana law] does not conflict with the thirteenth amendment," Brown said, ". . . is too clear for argument. Slavery implies involuntary servitude—a state of bondage." A law specifying where people should sit on a railroad had nothing to do with slavery, he decided.

On the Fourteenth Amendment, Brown had to decide whether the Louisiana law denied Plessy the privileges or immunities of citizenship and the equal protection of the laws. Brown conceded that "the object of the [Fourteenth] amendment was undoubtedly to enforce the absolute equality of the two races before the law."

But then Brown added a conclusion that has since been attacked as baseless as far as the Fourteenth Amendment is concerned. "In the nature of things, it could not have been intended to abolish distinctions based upon color, or to enforce social, as distinguished from political, equality, or a commingling of the two races upon terms unsatisfactory to either." In other words, Brown was saying that laws making social distinctions between races did not necessarily make them unequal in the eyes of the law. He cited long-accepted laws that segregated schools and outlawed interracial marriages as examples of laws that were acceptable under the Fourteenth Amendment.

In another passage that also has been widely criticized, Brown cited the 1886 decision in *Yick Wo v. Hopkins* in support of the Louisiana statute. The Court in *Yick Wo v. Hopkins* had struck down a regulation that had been aimed at shutting down Chinese-operated laundries in San Francisco. That precedent could have been used to strike down the Louisiana law requiring separate railroad cars for blacks. Instead, Brown said it merely required that regulations that treat races differently must be "reasonable" to be held constitutional.

As a result, Brown said, the *Plessy* case "reduces itself to the question whether the statute of Louisiana is a reasonable regulation, and with respect to this there must necessarily be a large discretion on the part of the legislature. . . . Gauged by this standard, we cannot say that a law which authorizes or even requires the separation of the two races in public conveyances is unreasonable."

The dissent of Justice Harlan, a former slaveholder from Kentucky, is one of the best known in Supreme Court history. On the Thirteenth Amendment issue, Harlan disagreed with the majority. The amendment, he said, bans not only slavery itself but "any burdens or disabilities that constitute badges of slavery or servitude" as well. A law dictating separate rail cars for blacks, Harlan said, was a badge of slavery.

"The white race deems itself to be the dominant race in this country. And so it is in prestige, in achievements, in education, in wealth, and in power. So, I doubt not, it will continue to be for all time, if it remains true to its great heritage and holds fast to the principles of constitutional liberty," Harlan wrote. "But in view of the constitution, in the eye of the law, there is in this country no superior, dominant, ruling class of citizens. There is no caste here."

EXCERPTS

From Justice Henry B. Brown's majority opinion: "A statute which implies merely a legal distinction between the white and colored races—a distinction which is founded in the color of the two races, and which must always exist so long as white men are distinguished from the other race by color—has no tendency to destroy the legal equality of the two races, or re-establish a state of involuntary servitude. . . .

"We consider the underlying fallacy of the plaintiff's argument to consist in the assumption that the enforced separation of the two races stamps the colored race with a badge of inferiority. If this be so, it is not by reason of anything found in the act, but solely because the colored race chooses to put that construction upon it. . . .

". . . Laws permitting, and even requiring, their separation in places where they are liable to be brought into contact, do not necessarily imply the inferiority of either race to the other, and have been generally, if not universally, recognized as within the competency of the state legislatures in the exercise of their police power. The most common instance of this is connected with the establishment of separate schools for white and colored children, which has been held to be a valid exercise of the legislative power even by courts of states where the political rights of the colored race have been longest and most earnestly enforced."

From Justice Harlan's dissent: "Our constitution is colorblind, and neither knows nor tolerates classes among citizens. In respect of civil rights, all citizens are equal before the law. The humblest is the peer of the most powerful. The law regards man as man, and takes no account of his surroundings or of his color when his civil rights as guaranteed by the supreme law of the land are involved. It is therefore to be regretted that this high tribunal, the final expositor of the fundamental law of the land, has reached the conclusion that it is competent for a state to regulate the enjoyment by citizens of their civil rights solely upon the basis of race. . . .

"In my opinion, the judgment this day rendered will, in time, prove to be quite as pernicious as the decision made by this tribunal in the Dred Scott Case."

IMPACT

At first, the *Plessy* decision got little attention, but, eventually, it became the leading case cited in dozens of courts to uphold a broad range of Jim Crow laws and to fortify racial segregation for decades after. With this decision, the Supreme Court became one of the prime obstacles in the path of true racial equality in the United States.

Even Justice Harlan, author of the eloquent dissent in *Plessy,* could not resist the force of the opinion and of public opinion in favor of segregation. Three years after *Plessy,* Harlan wrote a decision in which he saw nothing unconstitutional about racially segregated public schools.

Analytically, *Plessy* has been criticized for faulty logic and basically racist premises, such as the statement that "if one race be inferior to the other socially, the constitution of the United States cannot put them on the same plane." Yale law professor Charles Black said the *Plessy* decision combined "callousness and stupidity." Along with the Dred Scott case before it, *Plessy* is considered one of the Supreme Court's worst decisions. (See *Scott v. Sandford.*)

The long shadow of *Plessy,* upholding separate but equal facilities for blacks and whites, extended well into the twentieth century. Because facilities for blacks were rarely the equal of those for whites, the decision helped maintain white dominance and restricted opportunities for blacks. It was not until the 1954 case of *Brown v. Board of Education* that the separate but equal doctrine was laid to rest. (See *Brown v. Board of Education.*)

As for Plessy himself, in 1897 he paid a $25 fine for his violation of sitting in a white-only railroad car five years earlier.

Shelley v. Kraemer

Decided May 3, 1948
334 U.S. 1
laws.findlaw.com/US/334/1.html

DECISION

So-called "racial covenants," written into real estate sales contracts to keep blacks and other minorities from owning particular pieces of property into the future, may not be enforced by state or federal courts. Buyers and sellers may still make these agreements privately without interference from government.

BACKGROUND

The racial segregation that dominated many cities across the country at the beginning of the twentieth century was often enforced through city zoning laws that kept certain neighborhoods off-limits to blacks. When the Supreme Court in 1917 said in *Buchanan v. Warley* that such zoning laws were unconstitutional, that kind of official endorsement of segregation began to fade.

In its place came a more private arrangement in the form of restrictive covenants. When a piece of property is sold, covenants are sometimes included in the contract as a way for sellers to limit the future use of the property. Racial and religious covenants became popular in both northern and southern cities, barring the future sale of property to blacks and, in some instances, other groups such as Asians or Jews.

Controversy arose over such covenants after World War II, when black war veterans returned home to find themselves unable to buy decent housing. Battling these covenants in court was one of the early legal campaigns of Thurgood Marshall, then counsel for the NAACP and later the first black Supreme Court justice.

A case from Missouri provided the vehicle for Supreme Court review. In 1911 the owners of fifty-seven parcels of land in St. Louis signed agreements pledging that at least for the next fifty years, they would not sell or rent to "people of the Negro or Mongolian Race." At the time of the agreement and for many years later, some of the homes were owned by blacks.

In 1945 a black family—J.D. and Ethel Lee Shelley and their six children—tried to buy a house in the area, apparently unaware of the restrictive covenant. Before the sale went through, a group of neighbors led by Lewis and Fern Kraemer went to court asking the judge to prevent the Shelleys from occupying the house. A lower court declined, but the Missouri Supreme Court said the restrictive agreement did not violate any rights under the federal Constitution. It ordered the Shelleys to leave the house. The Shelleys appealed to the U.S. Supreme Court, which agreed to consider the issue—an issue it had never before faced.

VOTE

6–0, with Chief Justice Fred M. Vinson writing the Court's opinion. Joining him were Justices Hugo L. Black, Felix Frankfurter, William O. Douglas, Harold H. Burton, and Frank Murphy. Justices Stanley F. Reed, Robert H. Jackson, and Wiley B. Rutledge did not participate; all three owned property covered by restrictive covenants.

HIGHLIGHTS

In arguments before the Court in *Shelley v. Kraemer* and a companion case, NAACP lawyers Thurgood Marshall and George Vaughn argued strenuously that by enforcing restrictive covenants, courts were "not a mere arbiter in a contractual dispute" but an arm of government enforcing discrimination.

Marshall also took a gamble by introducing sociological evidence about the harm to public health and safety caused by racial ghettoes. Marshall won support from the Truman administration, with the solicitor general arguing to the Court that whites were "under a heavy debt to colored Americans" because they were brought to this country as slaves. Use of mechanisms like racial covenants, he continued, served to "hold them in bondage" even after slavery was ended. It was apparently the first time the Justice Department filed a brief in support of the NAACP.

The Court ignored the sociological arguments, basing the decision on traditional views of what constitutes the type of "state action" barred by the Fourteenth Amendment. "These are cases in which the States have made available to . . . individuals the full coercive power of government to deny to petitioners, on the grounds of race or color, the enjoyment of property rights in premises which petitioners are willing and

financially able to acquire and which the grantors are willing to sell."

The Court also dismissed an argument made by supporters of covenants, namely that minorities were not being denied equal protection of the laws because state courts could just as easily enforce covenants that kept white people out. "Equal protection of the laws is not achieved through indiscriminate imposition of inequalities," the Court said.

The three justices who did not participate recused themselves because they owned property covered by restrictive covenants.

EXCERPTS

From Chief Justice Fred M. Vinson's majority opinion: "[T]he restrictive agreements standing alone cannot be regarded as violative of any rights guaranteed to petitioners by the Fourteenth Amendment. So long as the purposes of those agreements are effectuated by voluntary adherence to their terms, it would appear clear that there has been no action by the State and the provisions of the Amendment have not been violated. . . .

"We hold that in granting judicial enforcement of the restrictive agreements in these cases, the States have denied petitioners the equal protection of the laws and that, therefore, the action of the state courts cannot stand. We have noted that freedom from discrimination by the States in the enjoyment of property rights was among the basic objectives sought to be ef-

Lewis and Fern Kraemer attempted to prevent J. D. and Ethel Lee Shelley, here with their six children in their St. Louis home, from purchasing a house in their neighborhood. In *Shelley v. Kraemer* (1948), the Supreme Court ruled unanimously that Missouri could not enforce a restrictive covenant (or agreement) among homeowners that they not sell or rent to a non-Caucasian.
Source: George Harris.

fectuated by the framers of the Fourteenth Amendment. That such discrimination has occurred in these cases is clear. Because of the race or color of these petitioners they have been denied rights of ownership or occupancy enjoyed as a matter of course by other citizens of different race or color."

IMPACT

The decision in *Shelley v. Kraemer* was criticized at first as a compromise that went only halfway in disapproving of racial covenants. It said courts could not enforce the covenants, but it allowed them to be made.

Nevertheless, the decision stands as one of the first rulings in which the Court viewed housing discrimination as a constitutional problem. It also kept covenants from spreading further and served as a precursor to the civil rights legislation of the 1960s. In 1968 Congress passed the Fair Housing Act, which bars property owners from refusing to sell or rent housing on the basis of race, color, or national origin.

Brown v. Board of Education of Topeka

Decided May 17, 1954
347 U.S. 483
laws.findlaw.com/US/347/483.html

DECISION

Separate public schools for blacks and whites are inherently unequal. States that maintain racially segregated schools violate the Fourteenth Amendment's guarantee of equal protection of the laws.

BACKGROUND

The North's victory in the Civil War and the constitutional amendments that followed the war did not guarantee equality for blacks in the United States. In ruling on a Louisiana law that required separate facilities for blacks and whites on trains, the Supreme Court upheld the constitutionality of the "separate but equal" accommodations. In this 1896 decision the Court gave its legal blessing to a wide range of segregated services. (See *Plessy v. Ferguson.*) So-called Jim Crow laws embedded segregation deep into the U.S. fabric. Seventeen states and the District of Columbia had laws requiring segregated schools.

Segregation in public schools had condemned generations of black children to lower-quality education because their schools were uniformly neglected, underequipped, and understaffed. But soon after World War II, as black soldiers who had fought hard for their country returned to the United States, demands for an end to segregation, especially in the schools, began to be heard.

Thurgood Marshall, then a young civil rights lawyer and later the Supreme Court's first black justice, believed that the time had come to mount a legal assault on *Plessy v. Ferguson* and on school segregation. Faint signs of hope were beginning to be seen in some Supreme Court rulings. In a 1948 case, *Shelley v. Kraemer,* the Court ruled that states could not enforce racial restrictions on property ownership. (See *Shelley v. Kraemer.*) Two years later, in *Sweatt v. Painter,* the Court told the state of Texas that its law school established for blacks could not be viewed as equal in any way to the all-white University of Texas Law School. The *Sweatt* ruling did not overturn *Plessy,* but it did suggest that public educational institutions for blacks had to be truly equal to those for whites for their separateness to be constitutional. The challenge for Marshall was to show that separate schools could never be equal. He was not at all confident that the Supreme Court would rule that way, but he and the National Association for the Advancement of Colored People (NAACP) decided the effort should be made. "Thurgood Marshall came down for boldness," wrote Richard Kluger in *Simple Justice,* the classic book about the *Brown* case.

In several states and the District of Columbia, courageous African American families began to file highly unpopular lawsuits to challenge school segregation. In the end, five separate cases went before the Supreme Court, and the decision became known by the name of one of them, *Brown v. Board of Education.*

Oliver Brown sued the school board in Topeka, Kansas, on behalf of his daughter, Linda, to challenge that city's segregated system. Linda Brown had to walk between railroad tracks to catch a bus to the all-black Monroe School, even though she lived just a few blocks from the all-white Sumner School. "Sometimes I was just so cold that I cried all the way to the bus stop," she later recalled. In the fall of 1950 Oliver Brown tried to enroll seven-year-old Linda in the third grade at Sumner. When he was turned away, Brown went to the NAACP, which filed suit.

The second case, *Briggs v. Elliott,* was from South Carolina. Harry Briggs Jr. and more than sixty other black parents sued the Clarendon County schools to demand equal school facilities. White children there rode buses to modern schools; black children had to walk as far as five miles to get to sepa-

Linda Brown, fourth from the right in the back row, had to walk a dangerous route to catch a bus to her all-black school although she lived just three blocks from the all-white Sumner School in Topeka, Kansas. The Supreme Court banned segregated schools in *Brown v. Board of Education of Topeka* (1954).
Source: AP/ Wide World Photos/Topeka Capital-Journal/File.

rate, ramshackle schools. In *Davis v. County School Board of Prince Edward County, Virginia,* high school students challenged Virginia's segregated schools. Students at all-black Moton High School in Farmville had staged a highly unusual strike to protest the poor facilities at the school, and 117 of them, led by ninth-grader Dorothy Davis, filed suit. *Gebhart v. Belton* was a Delaware case brought by Ethel Belton and seven other black Claymont parents whose children had to travel to downtown Wilmington to attend an all-black high school that was inferior to the white school. The final case, *Bolling v. Sharpe,* was filed on behalf of twelve-year-old Spotswood Bolling Jr. to challenge segregated schools in Washington, D.C. It was ultimately ruled on separately from the others because of the District of Columbia's status as a federal city not governed by state laws.

In the lower courts the blacks seeking school equality had lost in all but the Delaware case, where schools were ordered desegregated in 1952.

In spite of recent rulings that supported the rights of minorities, the Supreme Court was not eager to take on the issue of public school segregation or to consider overturning *Plessy* outright. Chief Justice Fred M. Vinson, in particular, was reluctant to overturn the settled tradition of separate schools. Hugo L. Black and William O. Douglas were the only two justices eager to overrule *Plessy.*

Lawyers argued the cases over three days in December 1952. Thurgood Marshall made a forceful argument that segregated schools were the result of "an inherent determination that the people who were formerly in slavery . . . shall be kept as near that stage as is possible." In legal briefs, Marshall had cited the work of psychologist Kenneth Clark, who in the 1940s devised a simple test to assess the self-image of young black children. Clark showed the children four dolls—two white and two brown—and asked them to choose the doll they thought looked "nice" or liked the best. Among black children from Massachusetts to Arkansas, a significant majority showed "an unmistakable preference" for the white dolls. To Clark this experiment proved that black children had low self-esteem.

Virginia's attorney general, J. Lindsay Almond Jr., told the justices that an order from the Supreme Court to desegregate schools "would destroy the public school system in Virginia." Almond, like many in the South, thought that local officials would shut down public schools altogether rather than integrate them.

Arguing in the *Briggs* case on behalf of South Carolina's segregated schools was John W. Davis, a former presidential candidate who was perhaps the best known and most accomplished advocate before the Supreme Court of that time. He voiced doubt about whether black families really wanted integration in their schools or even would be better off in integrated schools. He mocked the use of social science evidence—including Clark's doll experiment—by civil rights groups favoring desegregation. "Much of that which is handed around under the name of social science is an effort on the part of the scientist to rationalize his own preconceptions."

Based on the questioning from the justices, Marshall emerged from the arguments worried about whether a majority of the Court was prepared to order school desegregation. As months went by, his concern increased. In May 1953 the Court ordered the case to be reargued in the fall. Justice Frankfurter had urged this course of action after seeing how divided the justices were. The Court also asked the U.S. attorney general to participate in the second set of arguments—a request that forced the new Eisenhower administration to decide where it stood. After some early reluctance, President Dwight Eisenhower agreed that his administration would join the case on the side of desegregation.

Before the cases could be reargued, an unexpected development completely changed the outlook: a new chief justice took over at the Court. In September 1953 Chief Justice Vinson suffered a heart attack and died. Eisenhower named Gov. Earl Warren of California to replace Vinson. What probably would have been a 5–4 majority in favor of overturning *Plessy* turned into a unanimous 9–0 vote because of Warren's determination that the Court present a united front to the nation and his skill in persuading the other justices that it was important to do so. In his memoir, however, Warren insists "there was no dissension within the Court" on the outcome of the *Brown* cases. "There was not even vigorous argument." Warren wrote the decision himself, deliberately keeping it short and devoid of legal jargon so that it could be widely read and understood. To emphasize the Court's unanimity, on the day when the decision was announced Justice Robert Jackson, who had suffered a heart attack, left his sickbed to be on the bench.

VOTE

9–0, with Chief Justice Earl Warren writing the opinion for the Court. Joining him were Justices Hugo L. Black, Stanley F. Reed, Felix Frankfurter, William O. Douglas, Robert H. Jackson, Harold H. Burton, Tom C. Clark, and Sherman Minton.

HIGHLIGHTS

The Court's decision to overturn *Plessy,* after nearly sixty years of living with its "separate but equal" doctrine, could not occur without at least a glance toward history. When the Fourteenth Amendment was ratified in 1868 with its guarantee of equal protection of the laws, did the drafters have public education in mind?

Chief Justice Warren determined, however, that history was of little help on that point. Public education was in its infancy then, and in many states did not exist; where it did exist, blacks were barred outright from benefiting from it. "In approaching this problem, we cannot turn the clock back to 1868, when the Amendment was adopted, or even to 1896, when *Plessy v. Ferguson* was written," Warren wrote. "We must consider public education in the light of its full development and its present place in American life throughout the Nation."

Now, the Court agreed, public education is one of the most important services that government provides. Its impor-

Chief Justice Earl Warren wrote the opinion in *Brown v. Board of Education of Topeka* (1954), a landmark decision of the twentieth century. Anticipating resistance from parts of the country, Warren was determined that the Court present a united front, so he persuaded his colleagues to issue a unanimous decision in striking down school segregation.

Source: Abdon Daoud Ackad, Collection of the Supreme Court of the United States.

tance has transformed public education into a right that should be made available to all equally, in the Court's view.

The crucial next question was whether providing separate schools for blacks and whites is, in itself, a violation of that right to equal education. The Court ruled that unquestionably it did. Separate school facilities for blacks and whites have no place in U.S. society anymore, the Court said. To bolster the point, the Court took the unusual step of citing psychological evidence—notably Kenneth Clark's research, and Gunnar Myrdal's book *An American Dilemma*—to conclude that segregation has a detrimental effect on black children. "Whatever may have been the extent of psychological knowledge at the time of *Plessy v. Ferguson,* this finding is amply supported by modern authority," Warren wrote.

Partly to keep the opinion uncluttered and partly to win over Justice Reed, Warren in the opinion's last paragraph put off any detailed decree or order telling states and school boards what they must do to comply with the Court's ruling. Citing the "considerable complexity" of the task of remedying segregation, the Court scheduled arguments for the fall on the question of "appropriate relief." By avoiding several controversial issues, Warren was able to fashion a unanimous decision that spoke with force, if not specificity.

In the separate opinion, *Bolling v. Sharpe,* handed down the same day, the unanimous Court said segregation was equally unacceptable in District of Columbia schools. "In view of our decision that the Constitution prohibits the states from maintaining racially segregated public schools, it would be unthinkable that the same Constitution would impose a lesser duty on the Federal Government," Warren wrote for the Court.

EXCERPTS

From Chief Justice Earl Warren's majority opinion: "Compulsory school attendance laws and the great expenditures for education both demonstrate our recognition of the importance of education to our democratic society. It is required in the performance of our most basic public responsibilities, even service in the armed forces. It is the very foundation of good citizenship. Today it is a principal instrument in awakening the child to cultural values, in preparing him for later professional training, and in helping him to adjust normally to his environment. In these days, it is doubtful that any child may reasonably be expected to succeed in life if he is denied the opportunity of an education. Such an opportunity, where the state has undertaken to provide it, is a right which must be made available to all on equal terms.

"We come then to the question presented: Does segregation of children in public schools solely on the basis of race, even though the physical facilities and other 'tangible' factors may be equal, deprive the children of the minority group of equal educational opportunities? We believe that it does. . . .

"We conclude that in the field of public education the doctrine of 'separate but equal' has no place. Separate educational facilities are inherently unequal. Therefore, we hold that the plaintiffs and others similarly situated for whom the actions have been brought are, by reason of the segregation complained of, deprived of the equal protection of the laws guaranteed by the Fourteenth Amendment."

IMPACT

With its power and simplicity, the *Brown* decision stands as one of the most important and best known the Court has ever issued. In a single stroke, the Court swept aside centuries of custom, replacing it with a command to work toward the democratic ideal of equality. Where the other branches of government showed ambivalence over issues of race, the Supreme Court spoke firmly.

"This is a day that will live in glory," Justice Frankfurter said in a handwritten note to Warren the day *Brown* was handed down. Thurgood Marshall, who had apparently been tipped off that the decision was coming, was in the Court that day and later recalled, "I was so happy I was numb." By later that day, the euphoria wore off and Marshall realized that "the fight has just begun."

Marshall was correct. Even though the Court had deftly put off the issue of how quickly desegregation should be achieved, it had to deal with that issue again, and it had to face a South that was determined not to change. Many officials in the South labeled the day of the decision "Black Monday." Sen. Harry Byrd of Virginia pledged "massive resistance." Most southern members of Congress signed a "southern manifesto" denouncing the decision.

When the Court reconvened to hear arguments on how to implement *Brown,* it became clear how massive and difficult this endeavor would be. S. Emory Rogers, arguing for segregated schools in South Carolina, said to the Court candidly, "I would have to tell you that right now we would not conform—we would not send our white children to the Negro schools."

On May 31, 1955, the Court handed down what would become known as *Brown II*. Again, the Court spoke with brevity, ordering that the nation's schools desegregate with "all deliberate speed." No specific date was fixed, and many southern states took that as permission to make no progress at all. Some states moved to repeal compulsory attendance laws and to help set up private "academies" that would be able to remain all-white. In many communities, black parents who led efforts to integrate local schools were fired from their jobs and threatened with violence.

In 1957 Gov. Orval Faubus of Arkansas ordered members of the National Guard to physically prevent black students from attending Little Rock's Central High School, defying a post-*Brown* order from a federal judge. Faubus responded to a court order by withdrawing the guard and permitting violence to break out. Reluctantly, President Eisenhower federalized the National Guard and ordered U.S. Army troops to Little Rock to restore order and escort black students to their classes.

Following the turmoil in Little Rock, a federal judge gave permission to the school board to delay full desegregation for two and a half years. The NAACP challenged the delay in court, filing a lawsuit that eventually made its way to the Supreme Court. In the 1958 ruling *Cooper v. Aaron,* all nine justices signed an opinion expressing their anger at the resistance to *Brown* that was being displayed by local officials. "No state legislator or executive or judicial officer can war against the Constitution without violating his undertaking to support it," the Court said.

Other decisions also reaffirmed *Brown,* but resistance continued. Shifts in housing patterns that left many urban neighborhoods dominated by one race or another also kept schools segregated. "Despite all the bends in the road, school desegregation has not retreated," wrote Kluger in *Simple Justice.* Over the years, however, some blacks changed their views about desegregation. They argued that the concept underlying *Brown* was insulting to blacks, because it suggested that any school setting without whites was automatically inferior. Many black families also objected to the long bus rides for their children that were part of many desegregation plans.

In the middle 1990s, encouraged by several rulings from a more conservative Supreme Court, federal judges closed the book on many school district desegregation plans, declaring that local officials had made a good-faith effort to end segregation. Partly because of these developments, decreasing numbers of black students are attending integrated schools. According to Gary Orfield, director of the Harvard Project on School Desegregation, even when minority families move to mostly white suburbs, they often end up attending mostly non-white schools. "Progress toward desegregation in U.S. public schools is being steadily reversed," according to the Harvard project.

Some commentators concluded that in fact little progress had been made toward equality in education for blacks. "Many public schools are as racially isolated and unequal today as when the Supreme Court spoke 45 years ago," wrote *Washington Post* columnist Colbert I. King in 1999. The NAACP Legal Defense and Educational Fund concluded that "over the last 50 years, the segregation of African Americans has actually increased or changed very little."

In a speech marking the forty-fifth anniversary of *Brown,* Secretary of Housing and Urban Development Andrew Cuomo offered an assessment that, in most respects, could have been given before *Brown* was handed down. "The truth is, we are moving to two education systems. . . . You can go into one school in a suburban district, and they have all the tools and all the equipment. They take the first-graders, they bring them in and they put them on the Internet. The other side of town, the urban school district, they don't have a basketball net."

Five years later, in 2004, as the nation celebrated the landmark decision's fiftieth anniversary, many of the same trends were just as apparent. Litigation to address these inequities shifted in many cases to state courts. At the federal level, President George W. Bush had initiated the controversial "No Child Left Behind" school reform effort, aimed in part at reducing the inequality of schools by setting achievement standards and providing extra help for schools that did not measure up.

On May 17, 2004, the Monroe School in Topeka that Linda Brown had to attend because of segregation was dedicated as a national historic site. President Bush, speaking at the dedication, acknowledged that the goals of *Brown* had not yet been fully achieved. "In many ways, the events of those years seemed long ago. We tend to think of them as the distant dramas of a different country. Yet, segregation is a living memory, and many still carry its scars. The habits of racism in America have not all been broken. The habits of respect must be taught to every generation. Laws against racial discrimination must be vigorously enforced in education and housing and hiring and public accommodations."

Loving v. Virginia

Decided June 12, 1967
388 U.S. 1
laws.findlaw.com/US/388/1.html

DECISION

State laws that outlaw interracial marriages make distinctions on the basis of race in violation of the Fourteenth Amendment to the Constitution. In addition, racial classifications are inherently suspect, meaning that they are almost impossible for governments to justify.

BACKGROUND

A ban on interracial marriages, one of the legal legacies of slavery, lasted well into the twentieth century in many parts of the country. These antimiscegenation laws served to stigmatize blacks and to perpetuate state-sanctioned inequality among the races. It was not until 1948 that a state court, California's, found that such a ban violated the Fourteenth Amendment's guarantee of equal protection under the law. Twenty years after that, however, sixteen states—Alabama, Arkansas, Delaware, Florida, Georgia, Kentucky, Louisiana, Mississippi, Missouri, North Carolina, Oklahoma, South Carolina, Tennessee, Texas, Virginia, and West Virginia—still had antimiscegenation laws on their books. A Gallup Poll in 1965 indicated that 42 percent of northern whites and 72 percent of southern whites supported bans on interracial marriages.

Because of Virginia's law, Richard Loving, who was white, and Mildred Jeter, part black and part Native American, traveled to Washington, D.C., to marry in 1958. They returned to Caroline County, Virginia, to live, but five weeks later they were rousted from bed and arrested for violating the state law against miscegenation.

They pleaded guilty and were sentenced to a year in prison. The judge suspended the sentences on the condition that they leave Virginia and stay away for twenty-five years. The judge offered this justification for his ruling: "Almighty God created the races white, black, yellow, malay and red, and he placed them on separate continents. And, but for the interference with his arrangement, there would be no cause for such marriages. The fact that he separated the races shows that he did not intend for the races to mix."

The Lovings moved to Washington, D.C., and had three children. Still, they missed Virginia. They returned to Caroline County, where they lived, somewhat secretly, for five years. But the Lovings were still viewed as criminals in Virginia, so they sought legal help in challenging the antimiscegenation law. According to one account, they wrote to Attorney General Robert F. Kennedy, who turned the plea over to the American Civil Liberties Union.

The ACLU took up their cause and challenged the law through the Virginia courts. But state courts upheld it as a valid way of maintaining "racial integrity." The courts also ruled that marriage law is the sole province of the state government.

Before the Supreme Court, the Lovings' lawyer argued that "these are slavery laws, pure and simple," robbing blacks of their dignity. The state argued that the laws did not violate "equal protection" because they punished blacks and whites equally for the crime of intermarriage.

VOTE

9–0, with Chief Justice Earl Warren writing the opinion of the Court. Joining him were Justices Hugo L. Black, William O. Douglas, Tom C. Clark, John M. Harlan, William J. Brennan Jr., Potter Stewart, Byron R. White, and Abe Fortas.

HIGHLIGHTS

In fairly short order, Chief Justice Warren dismissed one of the few remaining arguments in favor of race-based laws such as antimiscegenation: Because they apply to and punish both white and black offenders equally—both partners in an interracial marriage, in this case—they do not offend the equal protection guarantee of the Fourteenth Amendment. The Court itself had adopted this rationale in an 1883 case that upheld laws punishing interracial sexual relations more severely than between people of the same race. "We reject the notion that the mere 'equal application' of a statute containing racial classifications is enough to remove the classifications from the Fourteenth Amendment's proscription of all invidious racial discriminations," Warren wrote for the Court.

There was no doubt that the Virginia law was an example of invidious racial discrimination, Warren added. "There can be no question but that Virginia's miscegenation statutes rest solely upon distinctions drawn according to race," he wrote. "At the very least, the Equal Protection Clause demands that racial classifications, especially suspect in criminal statutes, be subjected to the 'most rigid scrutiny.' "

This statement marked the first time that the Supreme Court had said flatly that government-created distinctions based on race had to withstand the highest level of scrutiny from the Court—a level that almost no law could survive. The

Court went on to apply the high standard to the Virginia law and found it could not be justified under either the equal protection or the due process clauses of the Fourteenth Amendment.

EXCERPTS

From Chief Justice Earl Warren's majority opinion: "There is patently no legitimate overriding purpose independent of invidious racial discrimination which justifies this classification. The fact that Virginia prohibits only interracial marriages involving white persons demonstrates that the racial classifications must stand on their own justification, as measures designed to maintain White Supremacy. We have consistently denied the constitutionality of measures which restrict the rights of citizens on account of race. There can be no doubt that restricting the freedom to marry solely because of racial classifications violates the central meaning of the Equal Protection Clause. . . .

"Marriage is one of the 'basic civil rights of man,' fundamental to our very existence and survival. To deny this fundamental freedom on so unsupportable a basis as the racial classifications embodied in these statutes, classifications so directly subversive of the principle of equality at the heart of the Fourteenth Amendment, is surely to deprive all the State's citizens of liberty without due process of law. The Fourteenth Amendment requires that the freedom of choice to marry not be restricted by invidious racial discriminations. Under our Constitution, the freedom to marry, or not marry, a person of another race resides with the individual, and cannot be infringed by the State."

IMPACT

In the wake of *Loving v. Virginia,* antimiscegenation laws faded from the legal landscape. Today, to most Americans, they seem antiquated, hateful, and demeaning.

Interracial marriages have become more common throughout the country, although they still comprise less than 1 percent of married couples. According to 2003 census figures, 416,000 of the 58.5 million married couples in the country were a mixture of black and white partners. (In about two-thirds of those interracial marriages, the husband was black.)

Interracial couples still report they are stared at and sometimes discriminated against, and many face disapproval by friends and family. Polls suggest that as many as 20 percent of whites think interracial marriages still should be illegal. But *Loving v. Virginia* made it clear that whatever obstacles interracial couples face, they will not be legal ones.

The day after the Supreme Court announced the decision in *Loving v. Virginia,* President Lyndon Johnson nominated Thurgood Marshall as a justice on the Court. Marshall, the first black named to the Supreme Court, was married to Cecilia Suyat, an Asian American of Philippine heritage. Clarence Thomas, the Supreme Court's second black justice, who suc-

Richard and Mildred Loving, pictured here in 1965, fought to overturn Virginia's law prohibiting interracial marriage. In *Loving v. Virginia* (1967), the Supreme Court unanimously ruled that state laws outlawing such marriages violate the Fourteenth Amendment.
Source: AP/Wide World Photos.

ceeded Marshall twenty-four years later, was a Virginia resident married to Virginia Lamp, a white woman.

The *Loving* decision has been cited in a wide range of cases by both conservative and liberal justices. Conservative justices seeking to strike down affirmative action plans have cited it for the proposition that government has a heavy burden whenever it seeks to justify distinctions based on race—whether for invidious or seemingly benign purposes. Liberal justices have also cited *Loving* to uphold abortion rights, invoking its declaration that fundamental life decisions are beyond the reach of government interference.

The *Loving* decision also attracted new attention from gay rights advocates who hoped that its strong language declaring marriage as a fundamental right could be used to give legal blessing to same-sex marriages as well. Harvard Law School professor Randall Kennedy noted that the Supreme Court had acted to uphold interracial marriages toward the end, not at the

beginning, of the civil rights revolution that began in 1954 with *Brown v. Board of Education.* "If *Loving* is any guide, proponents of same-sex marriage should not look to the Supreme Court for leadership, but should instead seek to persuade people on the grounds of the decency of their position," he wrote. "When the task has largely been done, the Court will come along to offer confirmation."

In fact, when the Supreme Court in June 2003 struck down laws against homosexual activity, the majority did not cite the *Loving* case, and the opinion explicitly avoided the issue of same-sex marriage. (See *Lawrence v. Texas.*) But a few months later, when the Supreme Judicial Court of Massachusetts ruled in favor of same-sex marriage for that state, its ruling, *Goodridge v. Department of Health,* cited *Loving* as proof of the proposition that "the right to marry means little if it does not include the right to marry the person of one's choice."

Griggs v. Duke Power Co.

Decided March 8, 1971
401 U.S. 424
laws.findlaw.com/US/401/424.html

DECISION

The Civil Rights Act of 1964 prohibits employers from requiring job applicants to have high school diplomas or achieve a certain score on general intelligence tests, if those requirements are unrelated to job skills and if they have the effect of disqualifying a disproportionate number of black applicants. As a result, even if it cannot be shown that the employer intended to discriminate against blacks, the employer can be penalized if the test or application process worked to exclude blacks.

BACKGROUND

As with public schools and public accommodations, many private workplaces were racially segregated well into the middle of the twentieth century. The workforce at the Duke Power Company's Dan River Steam Station, a power generating facility in Draper, North Carolina, offered an example of how this segregation operated. Of the ninety-five employees working there in 1965, fourteen were black. All the blacks worked in the labor department of the station, where the highest wages were lower than the lowest salaries among the whites working in the other operating departments of the plant. The discrimination was blatant.

After Congress outlawed workplace discrimination in Title VII of the Civil Rights Act of 1964, Duke Power, along with other

companies, began to change its hiring practices. But instead of opening up hiring, critics say Duke Power looked for new ways to erect barriers to hiring and promoting blacks, under the guise of evenhandedness. In the same way that seemingly neutral literacy tests were used to keep blacks from voting, Duke Power and other employers began requiring applicants for jobs in all departments except the labor department to achieve satisfactory grades on two general intelligence tests before they could be hired. The company also required that anyone seeking to transfer from the labor department into other jobs earn a high school diploma or do well on the intelligence tests. Thirteen of the fourteen blacks working at the plant, led by a man named Willie Griggs, sued the company under the new civil rights law.

After a district court judge ruled in favor of the company, an appeals court also ruled that the company was not in violation of the law because the employer did not intend to discriminate through its hiring policies. When the case reached the Supreme Court, it presented these questions: Does intent matter? If the application process results in the exclusion of most blacks, does that show a violation of the law?

According to the 1979 book *The Brethren,* by Bob Woodward and Scott Armstrong, the Court at first ignored the case. Justice Brennan, who had once represented Duke Power as an attorney, recused himself, but he encouraged Justice Stewart to argue that the Court should accept the case for review. When it came to writing the opinion, Chief Justice Burger, eager to soften his image as a staunch conservative, took the assignment himself in what would prove to be a landmark decision advancing civil rights.

VOTE

8–0, with Chief Justice Warren E. Burger writing for the Court. Joining him were Justices Hugo L. Black, William O. Douglas, John M. Harlan, Potter Stewart, Byron R. White, Thurgood Marshall, and Harry A. Blackmun. Justice William J. Brennan Jr., a former attorney for Duke Power, recused himself.

HIGHLIGHTS

Chief Justice Burger took a remarkably direct, real-world approach to *Griggs v. Duke Power Co.* He was not willing to accept the company's assertions that the testing and diploma requirements at the plant were aimed at generally improving the caliber of employees.

Burger said the job requirements of Duke Power kept blacks from advancing the same way that literacy tests had worked to exclude blacks from voting. "Because they are Negroes, petitioners have long received inferior education in segregated schools," Burger said, adding that far fewer blacks graduated from high school than did whites in North Carolina. Thus, it was a virtual certainty that blacks would have a more difficult time meeting the requirements.

Moreover, the requirements were not closely enough related to the jobs involved to be valid, Burger added, noting that several whites without high school diplomas had performed well in nonlabor departments. "On the record before us, neither the high school completion requirement nor the general intelligence test is shown to bear a demonstrable relationship to successful performance of the jobs for which it was used," Burger wrote.

Under the mandate of Title VII, Burger concluded, these facts were enough to prove a violation, no matter what the motives of the employer. "Good intent or absence of discriminatory intent does not redeem employment procedures or testing mechanisms that operate as 'built-in headwinds' for minority groups and are unrelated to measuring job capability," Burger wrote. "Diplomas and tests are useful servants, but Congress has mandated the commonsense proposition that they are not to become masters of reality."

EXCERPTS

From Chief Justice Warren E. Burger's majority opinion: "The objective of Congress in the enactment of Title VII is plain from the language of the statute. It was to achieve equality of employment opportunities and remove barriers that have operated in the past to favor an identifiable group of white employees over other employees. Under the Act, practices, procedures, or tests neutral on their face, and even neutral in terms of intent, cannot be maintained if they operate to 'freeze' the status quo of prior discriminatory employment practices. . . .

". . . Congress did not intend by Title VII, however, to guarantee a job to every person regardless of qualifications. In short, the Act does not command that any person be hired simply because he was formerly the subject of discrimination, or because he is a member of a minority group. Discriminatory preference for any group, minority or majority, is precisely and only what Congress has proscribed. What is required by Congress is the removal of artificial, arbitrary, and unnecessary barriers to employment when the barriers operate invidiously to discriminate on the basis of racial or other impermissible classification. . . .

". . . The Act proscribes not only overt discrimination, but also practices that are fair in form, but discriminatory in operation. The touchstone is business necessity. If an employment practice which operates to exclude Negroes cannot be shown to be related to job performance, the practice is prohibited."

IMPACT

The Court's unanimous decision came as a welcome surprise to civil rights organizations. Its sweeping language became perhaps the most powerful tool available to minorities and women seeking an end to workplace discrimination. It eliminated the need to prove that employers intended to discriminate against minorities, something that would be difficult to prove in many cases.

The decision was applied most often to invalidate seemingly objective job requirements, such as height and weight requirements for firefighters and police that were not strictly related to the needs of the job. Even less objective requirements, such as job interviews, became subject to scrutiny under *Griggs.* In some ways, *Griggs* also encouraged affirmative action programs by focusing on results, on the actual number of minorities hired, rather than on employers' intentions.

But as the case's ramifications expanded, *Griggs* became increasingly unpopular in the business community. Employers felt they were constantly on the defensive, forced to prove that their hiring practices were fair and that certain job requirements were a "business necessity." Companies were being penalized for setting high standards for hiring. Critics also said that fear of being sued under *Griggs* had led companies to establish minority hiring quotas.

"In the Reagan Administration, the complaints from business officials won a hearing," says David Savage in the book *Turning Right,* published in 1992. In his 1991 book *Order and Law,* former solicitor general Charles Fried says he saw an

Alaska case before the Supreme Court as "our opportunity to tame *Griggs*."

In the 1989 decision *Ward's Cove Packing Company v. Antonio,* the Court did indeed tame *Griggs*. The low number of minorities hired would not alone be enough to prove discrimination, the Court said. And the employees would henceforth have to prove that hiring practices were discriminatory, rather than forcing employers to prove that they were not discriminating.

The *Ward's Cove* decision, along with several others that were seen as cutbacks on civil rights, led Congress to pass a new civil rights law in 1991. Among other things, the law undid the effect of *Ward's Cove* by placing the burden of proof back on the employer.

Echoes of the debate over *Griggs* were heard in 1998 when controversy arose over the Supreme Court's own hiring practices. After it was revealed that the overwhelming majority of Supreme Court law clerks were white males, several justices defended the Court, saying there was no intent to discriminate in hiring and asserting that high standards in hiring were necessary for the Court to do its work. These were some of the same arguments that private sector employers unsuccessfully made in the face of *Griggs*.

In 2005 the Supreme Court extended the *Griggs* rule to the Age Discrimination in Employment Act. The 1967 law, which bars workplace discrimination on the basis of age, was modeled on the Civil Rights Act of 1964. A unanimous Court in *Smith v. City of Jackson* in 2005 cited *Griggs* in ruling that disparate impact claims can be made in age bias cases just as in race cases. Employers were fearful that the ruling would expose them to unwarranted lawsuits when they make manpower and other decisions that inadvertently affect older workers more than younger ones.

Swann v. Charlotte-Mecklenburg Board of Education

Decided April 20, 1971
402 U.S. 1
laws.findlaw.com/US/402/1.html

DECISION

To eliminate lingering racial segregation in public schools, a wide range of methods, including busing, racial ratios, and rearranging school district lines, can be required. Once a school system achieves "unitary" status or desegregation, courts should no longer interfere with local administration of the schools.

BACKGROUND

More than a decade after *Brown v. Board of Education,* many school systems had still not come close to achieving desegregation. Some took the Supreme Court's command to move with "all deliberate speed" as permission to move slowly.

School systems devised ways to look as if they were complying with *Brown* without really changing anything. One popular technique used in several southern systems was to offer both black and white parents "freedom of choice" to send their children to any school they desired. In practice, white parents almost never sent their children to black schools, and black parents rarely sent their children to white schools. They did not want their children to be viewed as interlopers at the white schools. As a result, schools remained segregated.

In 1968 the Supreme Court said the time for slow progress toward desegregation was over. In *Green v. County School Board of New Kent County,* the Court said, "The burden on a school board today is to come forward with a plan that promises realistically to work, and promises realistically to work now." The plan had to remove the remnants of segregation "root and branch," the Court said.

The *Green* decision reenergized efforts by civil rights groups to get school districts to desegregate. In Charlotte, North Carolina, NAACP lawyers moved to reopen the lawsuit that had led to a fairly weak desegregation plan based on freedom of choice. The case was named for a black six-year-old, James Swann, son of Vera and Darius Swann. James had been denied entry to a predominantly white school near his home.

The sprawling Charlotte-Mecklenburg County school system, the forty-third largest system in the nation, had more than 84,000 students, 24,000 of whom were black. About 14,000 black students attended schools that were all black.

A new judge, heeding the command of *Green,* ordered extensive changes, including redrawing school district lines so that schools would bring in students from both inner-city and suburban neighborhoods. The plan required extensive busing of students to achieve the black-white ratios the judge established as goals. The new plan would bus an estimated 13,000 more students than the old plan and would cost more than $1 million to implement. An appeals court panel objected to the plan's extensive busing of elementary school students, but Judge James McMillan stuck to it.

White students board a school bus at Horace Mann Junior High School, formerly an all-black high school, in Little Rock, Arkansas, in 1971. That year, the Supreme Court decided in *Swann v. Charlotte-Mecklenburg Board of Education,* a case from North Carolina, that busing could be among many methods used to achieve school desegregation.
Source: AP/Wide World Photos.

As the case made its way to the Supreme Court, political pressure was building on the justices to call a halt to extensive busing schemes ordered by judges such as McMillan and others in the South. President Richard Nixon issued a policy statement favoring neighborhood schools and indicating that he would not support busing unless told to by the Supreme Court. Some southern political leaders wanted the justices to hold a special summer session so that the Charlotte case could be decided before the next school year began. The Court did not do that, but scheduled the Charlotte case for the first day of the fall term in October.

VOTE

9–0, with Chief Justice Warren Burger writing for the Court. Joining him were Justices Hugo L. Black, William O. Douglas, John M. Harlan, William J. Brennan Jr., Potter Stewart, Byron R. White, Thurgood Marshall, and Harry A. Blackmun.

HIGHLIGHTS

Court historians, notably the late Bernard Schwartz, have documented the extensive behind-the-scenes negotiations and tensions among justices as the Court drafted its opinion in the *Swann* case. Chief Justice Burger viewed the case as possibly the most important decision on race since *Brown v. Board of Education,* and he made it clear from the outset that he hoped for a unanimous decision, just as Chief Justice Earl Warren had done in *Brown.* But he and Justice Black had serious objections to the Charlotte desegregation plan, although the other justices supported it as a necessary, if burdensome, remedy for decades of segregationist policies in the city's school system. Despite Burger's objections to the plan, the chief justice un-

dertook to write the Court's opinion himself, angering several other justices.

In initial drafts of the decision, Burger took a restrictive view of the power of judges to order remedies for school segregation. The other justices objected. As a result, six drafts later, the opinion said extensive remedies were necessary, even if they interfered with the concept of neighborhood schools.

"In default by the school authorities of their obligation to proffer acceptable remedies, a district court has broad power to fashion a remedy that will assure a unitary school system," the Court ruled. But even the final version of the Burger opinion placed some limits on what a judge could do to eliminate school segregation. The remedy had to fit the violation, and there was little a judge could do to correct the larger societal problems—such as segregated housing patterns—that contributed to segregated schools.

"Our objective in dealing with the issues presented by these cases is to see that school authorities exclude no pupil of a racial minority from any school, directly or indirectly, on account of race," the Court said. "It does not and cannot embrace all the problems of racial prejudice, even when those problems contribute to disproportionate racial concentrations in some schools."

The Court also said that strictly meeting goals of a certain percentage of black and white students in each school was not necessary; a limited number of single-race schools could even be tolerated. "The constitutional command to desegregate schools does not mean that every school in every community must always reflect the racial composition of the school system as a whole."

Busing, the Court said, was not a technique to be feared. Nearly 40 percent of U.S. students already traveled to school by bus, Burger said, noting that busing was necessary to bring rural areas out of the era of one-room schoolhouses into more modern, consolidated schools. "We find no basis for holding that the local school authorities may not be required to employ bus transportation as one tool of school desegregation. Desegregation plans cannot be limited to the walk-in school."

Burger cautioned that busing could in some circumstances be too burdensome, especially when young children were involved. "An objection to transportation of students may have validity when the time or distance of travel is so great as to either risk the health of the children or significantly impinge on the educational process."

EXCERPTS

From Chief Justice Warren Burger's majority opinion: "We are concerned in these cases with the elimination of the discrimination inherent in the dual school systems, not with myriad factors of human existence which can cause discrimination in a multitude of ways on racial, religious, or ethnic grounds. The target of the cases from *Brown I* to the present was the dual school system. The elimination of racial discrimination in public schools is a large task and one that should not be retarded by efforts to achieve broader purposes lying beyond the jurisdiction of school authorities. One vehicle can carry only a limited amount of baggage. It would not serve the important objective of *Brown I* to seek to use school desegregation cases for purposes beyond their scope, although desegregation of schools ultimately will have impact on other forms of discrimination. We do not reach in this case the question whether a showing that school segregation is a consequence of other types of state action, without any discriminatory action by the school authorities, is a constitutional violation requiring remedial action by a school desegregation decree. This case does not present that question and we therefore do not decide it. . . .

". . . All things being equal, with no history of discrimination, it might well be desirable to assign pupils to schools nearest their homes. But all things are not equal in a system that has been deliberately constructed and maintained to enforce racial segregation. The remedy for such segregation may be administratively awkward, inconvenient, and even bizarre in some situations and may impose burdens on some; but all awkwardness and inconvenience cannot be avoided in the interim period when remedial adjustments are being made to eliminate the dual school systems. . . .

". . . Neither school authorities nor district courts are constitutionally required to make year-by-year adjustments of the racial composition of student bodies once the affirmative duty to desegregate has been accomplished and racial discrimination through official action is eliminated from the system. This does not mean that federal courts are without power to deal with future problems; but in the absence of a showing that either the school authorities or some other agency of the State has deliberately attempted to fix or alter demographic patterns to affect the racial composition of the schools, further intervention by a district court should not be necessary."

IMPACT

The *Swann* decision was heralded as a firm message to public schools that strong and sometimes controversial measures, including busing, had to be used to end school segregation once and for all. Civil rights leaders returned to courts to force other systems to adopt plans similar to Charlotte-Mecklenburg's, and dozens were adopted. The trend mystified Burger, who thought the Court's decision had limited, not encouraged, the use of busing.

Swann turned out to be the high-water mark of school desegregation rulings. Soon after the decision, the composition of the Court changed. President Nixon, who had reacted to *Swann* by ordering the Justice Department to draft a proposed constitutional amendment to ban busing, named Lewis F. Powell Jr. and William Rehnquist to replace Justices Black and Harlan, respectively.

In 1974 the Court in *Milliken v. Bradley* struck down a Detroit desegregation plan that would have bused children across boundary lines between the city schools and a separate suburban school district. The vote was 5–4, with Nixon's new appointees in the majority. In an angry dissent, Justice Thurgood Marshall, the Court's first black justice who had argued for the NAACP in *Brown v. Board of Education,* said, "After 20 years of small, often difficult steps toward [desegregation], the Court today takes a giant step backwards." In *Missouri v. Jenkins* (1990), *Oklahoma City Public Schools v. Dowell* (1991), and *Freeman v. Pitts* (1992), the Court cut back even further on court-ordered remedies, showing a strong preference for local control of schools. Recent studies indicate that for a variety of reasons, many school districts, especially those in cities, are becoming resegregated, and busing plans are being curtailed.

Ironically, the Charlotte-Mecklenburg case was reopened in 1997. The family of a white first-grade student sued the school district, claiming she was denied admission to a magnet school because she was not black. A federal judge used the suit to reopen the *Swann* case and examine whether the school system should be declared "unitary," putting an end to court-ordered desegregation efforts. In September 1999 the judge decided unitary status had been achieved, which meant that the school system could no longer use race as a criterion in student assignments to schools. The school system and black parents appealed, but after lengthy proceedings, the U.S. Court of Appeals for the Fourth Circuit in 2001 affirmed the unitary status. The Supreme Court declined to review the case.

RIGHT TO COUNSEL

*T*he Sixth Amendment to the Constitution guarantees that anyone accused of committing a crime must have "the assistance of counsel for his defence." The theory behind the guarantee was that if the government is going to use its considerable power to try to put someone in prison for a crime, the defendant ought to have the tools to test the government's case. In the increasingly complex legal world, that means having a lawyer.

It was not until the twentieth century, however, that the Court gave full force to the guarantee by requiring government to pay for legal help for those defendants unable to afford it. And it was not until the 1966 *Miranda* decision—possibly the best-known Supreme Court ruling ever—that police were required to tell criminal defendants that they have a right to counsel.

Other related cases mentioned in the Right to Counsel section

Hurtado v. California (1884)
Norris v. Alabama (1935)
Johnson v. Zerbst (1938)
Betts v. Brady (1942)
Escobedo v. Illinois (1964)
Dickerson v. United States (2000)
Roper v. Simmons (2005) (see p. 25)
Rompilla v. Beard (2005)

Powell v. Alabama

Decided November 7, 1932
287 U.S. 45
laws.findlaw.com/US/287/45.html

DECISION

An accused person has the right to have a lawyer and to have adequate time to prepare a defense, especially in a capital case, where the penalty may be death. If the defendant is unable to hire a lawyer, the state is required to provide a lawyer for him or her. These rights protect defendants in state as well as federal trials under the guarantee of the due process of law provided in the Fourteenth Amendment.

BACKGROUND

During the economic depression of the late 1920s and the early 1930s, it was not uncommon for discontented young people to seek jobs or adventure far from home. Many hitched rides on freight trains, without any clear destination.

A fight broke out between black youths and white youths on one of those trains in March 1931, as it moved through the hills of northern Alabama. The black youths managed to toss most of the whites off the slow-moving train, one by one. By the time the train reached Paint Rock, Alabama, word had been sent ahead to police that a brawl was under way. Authorities boarded the train and arrested nine young black men. Two white women on the train, Victoria Price and Ruby Bates, accused the nine of rape.

The story of the alleged rapes inflamed the local white community around Scottsboro, where the men were jailed. An angry lynch mob arrived on the scene, and a small contingent of National Guard troops was dispatched to help the local sheriff keep the mob from seizing the prisoners, who were removed to Gadsden for safekeeping.

Within a week a grand jury was convened, and it indicted the youths for rape, which at the time carried penalties including death. The presiding judge tried to appoint lawyers to defend the nine, but only one attorney accepted the job. On the morning of the first trial, another lawyer arrived from Chattanooga, home of four of the defendants. The lawyers' contact with their clients in advance of trial was minimal.

Three separate trials proceeded in rapid order, with thousands of people gathering outside the courtroom. The defense was virtually nonexistent. Jurors in one case were clearly aware of the verdict in the preceding case. A brass band played after one guilty verdict. All the defendants were found guilty and sentenced to death. A mistrial was declared in the case of Leroy Wright, who was thirteen years old at the time. The prosecutor asked the jury to sentence Wright to life in prison rather than death because of his age. Because seven of the twelve jurors wanted to put him to death anyway, the judge declared a mistrial.

As the notoriety about the trials of the "Scottsboro Boys" spread, the appeal of the death sentences became politicized. The National Association for the Advancement of Colored People vied with the International Labor Defense, a communist organization, for the authority to file appeals. In March 1932 the Alabama Supreme Court upheld all but one of the convictions, that of Eugene Williams, a minor at the time of his arrest. The Alabama court said the trials were fair. With the backing of the communist legal group, the defendants, led by Ozie Powell, appealed to the U.S. Supreme Court, claiming that the hasty and chaotic conduct of the trial and the last-minute appointment of lawyers to represent the defendants had deprived them of their right to counsel. They also argued that because blacks were systematically excluded from juries in Alabama, the defendants were deprived of their right to an impartial jury of their peers.

VOTE

7–2, with Justice George Sutherland writing the opinion for the Court. Joining him were Chief Justice Charles Evans Hughes and Justices Willis Van Devanter, Benjamin N. Cardozo, Louis D. Brandeis, Owen J. Roberts, and Harlan Fiske Stone. Dissenting were Justices Pierce Butler and James C. McReynolds.

HIGHLIGHTS

U.S. legal history, as recited by Justice Sutherland, appeared to be on the side of the Scottsboro defendants. The American colonies had by and large rejected an English common law rule that had denied the right of counsel to defendants in serious crimes. After reviewing each colony's policies, Sutherland concluded, "It thus appears that in at least twelve of the thirteen colonies the rule of the English common law, in the respect now under consideration, had been definitely rejected and the right to counsel fully recognized in all criminal prosecutions, save that in one or two instances the right was limited to capital offenses or to the more serious crimes." The Sixth Amendment, as well, guarantees the right to counsel in criminal cases.

In sharply critical tones, Sutherland reviewed the hasty and haphazard conduct of the Scottsboro trials. He quoted at length the half-hearted comments to the trial judge by the

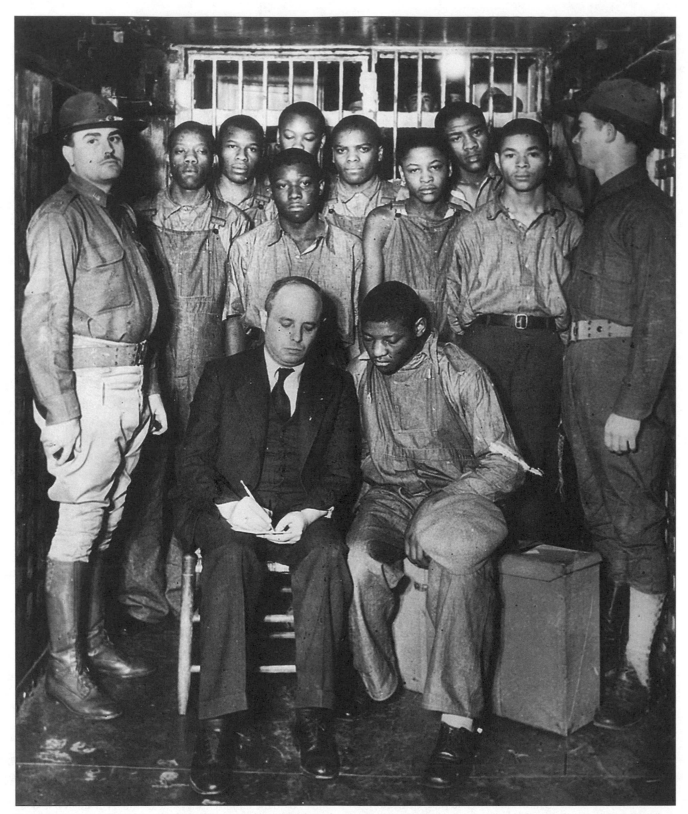

The plight of the nine "Scottsboro Boys," who were arrested in rural Alabama for allegedly raping two white women, spawned numerous legal actions. In *Powell v. Alabama* (1932), the Supreme Court ruled that lack of an effective legal defense violated the defendants' Fourteenth Amendment right to due process of the law. Prominent attorney Samuel Leibowitz handled the defendants' appeals after their original conviction. He is shown here, seated on a chair, conferring with the accused men.

Source: Brown Brothers, Sterling, Pennsylvania.

lawyers who had been reluctantly recruited to defend the nine youths. "The defendants, young, ignorant, illiterate, surrounded by hostile sentiment, haled back and forth under guard of soldiers, charged with an atrocious crime regarded with especial horror in the community where they were to be tried, were thus put in peril of their lives within a few moments after counsel for the first time charged with any degree of responsibility began to represent them."

But that history did not mean that the Supreme Court would automatically rule in favor of the defendants in the *Powell* case. The biggest hurdle was the Court's belief at the time that the guarantees of the Bill of Rights—including the Sixth Amendment right to counsel—applied to actions by the federal government, not state governments. The Court had already begun to apply parts of the First Amendment to the states, but was up to this point reluctant to do the same with other rights.

On the rights of criminal defendants, the Court had ruled in 1884 in *Hurtado v. California* that the federal requirement of indictment by grand juries could not be forced on the states. So in the Scottsboro case, the Court would have to find another way to guarantee the right to counsel in a state trial.

Sutherland achieved the goal by taking a somewhat broader view of the due process clause of the Fourteenth Amendment. That guarantee unquestionably could be applied to the states. If what happened to the Scottsboro defendants violated the Fourteenth Amendment rather than the Sixth, then the Supreme Court could strike down their convictions and order new trials.

At the very least, Sutherland said, due process required that the Scottsboro defendants be given adequate hearing. "What, then, does a hearing include?" Sutherland asked rhetorically. "Historically and in practice, in our own country at least, it has always included the right to the aid of counsel when desired and provided by the party asserting the right. The right to be heard would be, in many cases, of little avail if it did not comprehend the right to be heard by counsel. Even the intelligent and educated layman has small and sometimes no skill in the science of law. . . . He lacks both the skill and knowledge adequately to prepare his defense, even though he have a perfect one. He requires the guiding hand of counsel at every step in the proceedings against him."

By that standard, then, Sutherland concluded that the due process clause had been violated. "In the light of the facts outlined in . . . this opinion—the ignorance and illiteracy of the defendants, their youth, the circumstances of public hostility, the imprisonment and the close surveillance of the defendants by the military forces, the fact that their friends and families were all in other states and communication with them necessarily difficult, and above all that they stood in deadly peril of their lives—we think the failure of the trial court to give them reasonable time and opportunity to secure counsel was a clear denial of due process."

Justice Butler's dissent asserted that, in fact, the Scottsboro defendants had been given adequate representation. Separate trials were given, witnesses were questioned, and the lawyers represented the defendants competently, Butler said. "The record wholly fails to reveal that petitioners have been deprived of any right guaranteed by the Federal Constitution."

EXCERPTS

From Justice George Sutherland's majority opinion: "Under the circumstances disclosed, we hold that defendants were not accorded the right of counsel in any substantial sense. To decide otherwise, would simply be to ignore actualities. . . .

"It is true that great and inexcusable delay in the enforcement of our criminal law is one of the grave evils of our time. Continuances are frequently granted for unnecessarily long periods of time, and delays incident to the disposition of motions for new trial and hearings upon appeal have come in many cases to be a distinct reproach to the administration of justice. The prompt disposition of criminal cases is to be commended and encouraged. But in reaching that result a defendant, charged with a serious crime, must not be stripped of his right to have sufficient time to advise with counsel and prepare his defense. To do that is not to proceed promptly in the calm spirit of regulated justice but to go forward with the haste of the mob. . . .

". . . All that it is necessary now to decide, as we do decide, is that in a capital case, where the defendant is unable to employ counsel, and is incapable adequately of making his own defense because of ignorance, feeble-mindedness, illiteracy, or the like, it is the duty of the court, whether requested or not, to assign counsel for him as a necessary requisite of due process of law; and that duty is not discharged by an assignment at such a time or under such circumstances as to preclude the giving of effective aid in the preparation and trial of the case. To hold otherwise would be to ignore the fundamental postulate, already adverted to, 'that there are certain immutable principles of justice which inhere in the very idea of free government which no member of the Union may disregard.' "

IMPACT

The Court's decision in *Powell v. Alabama* angered white southerners who saw it as an unwarranted federal intrusion into their race relations. But it did not stop Alabama prosecutors from seeking new convictions against the same defendants.

Defense lawyers succeeded in getting the trials moved to a town fifty miles away from Scottsboro, in hopes of finding more impartial jurors. But the results were pretty much the same, and once again appeals traveled back up the court system. This time, the appeal by defendant Clarence Norris caught the Court's eye. He challenged the systematic exclusion of black jurors. In *Norris v. Alabama* (1935) the Court found that the arbitrary exclusion of blacks as jurors violated the defendant's Fourteenth Amendment rights. A third round of trials ensued for some of the defendants; by 1937 four had been convicted and charges against the other five had been dropped. It was not until 1950, with the pardon and release from prison of defendant Andrew Wright, that the legal proceedings against the Scottsboro Nine were completely over.

But beyond the impact on the defendants, the Court's decision was a significant new step in the development of the Fourteenth Amendment as guarantor of individual liberties. Even though the amendment had been enacted after the Civil War to protect the rights of racial minorities, courts had heretofore interpreted the amendment narrowly and in ways that perpetuated discrimination. Now, apparently for the first time, the due process clause had been used to set aside a state criminal conviction on the grounds that the trial had violated the defendant's rights.

At first this precedent too was interpreted narrowly. Because Sutherland's opinion had stressed the unusually chaotic and hasty aspects of the Scottsboro trials, it was applied mainly in capital punishment cases, in which the facts were especially egregious. In 1963, in the landmark case of *Gideon v. Wainwright,* the Court fully extended the reach of the Sixth Amendment and *Powell v. Alabama* to guarantee the right to counsel to noncapital state cases. (See *Gideon v. Wainwright.*)

Gideon v. Wainwright

Decided March 18, 1963
372 U.S. 335
laws.findlaw.com/US/372/335.html

DECISION

A defendant charged with a crime under state law must be provided with an attorney if he is unable to afford one. Having the assistance of a lawyer is so fundamental to the Sixth Amendment right of a fair trial that states can be required to provide lawyers to defendants.

BACKGROUND

The words of the Sixth Amendment to the U.S. Constitution seem clear enough: "In all criminal prosecutions, the accused shall enjoy the right . . . to have the Assistance of Counsel for his defence." No one disputes the right to an attorney, but, historically, it has been the responsibility of the accused to secure a lawyer and pay for the services. The controversy has centered on the rights of those who cannot afford legal assistance.

The historical evidence suggests that the Framers of the Constitution intended to counteract the British common law rule that barred defense lawyers in felony cases. But as the complexity of the law and the cost of hiring lawyers increased, many lawyers—including Supreme Court justices—began to consider the failure to provide counsel in a range of cases to be a fundamental injustice to defendants.

In the 1932 case *Powell v. Alabama,* the Court ruled that at least in cases where the defendant faced the death penalty, the Fourteenth Amendment (not the Sixth Amendment) required that states provide lawyers to defendants. "Even the intelligent and educated layman has small and sometimes no skill in the science of law," the Court said. (See *Powell v. Alabama.*) Six years later, the Court in *Johnson v. Zerbst* said the Sixth Amendment required appointment of counsel in all federal criminal trials.

But in *Betts v. Brady* (1942), the Court said the rule did not have to be extended to state court defendants in non–death penalty cases, except in "special circumstances." The Court was sharply criticized for the *Betts* decision and eventually seemed to take the criticism to heart. From 1950 on, the Court never found a case in which counsel should not have been appointed. The *Betts* standard was defined to protect mentally retarded or illiterate defendants and to provide relief in cases in which there was misconduct by the prosecutor or judge.

By the time Clarence Earl Gideon's case came to the Court, the issue seemed to many legal scholars to be ripe for another look. In *Gideon's Trumpet,* his classic 1964 book on the case, Anthony Lewis says of the right to counsel, "Few legal problems could have been so continuously on the justices' minds and consciences."

It is perhaps ironic that this case made it to the Supreme Court based on an erroneous assumption. Gideon, a fifty-one-year-old drifter, was about to be tried on a petty larceny charge in Florida. He had been charged with breaking into the Bay Harbor Poolroom in Panama City, Florida, in June 1961. According to police, he took some beer and wine, as well as coins from the juke box and cigarette machine. At the beginning of his trial, Gideon stood and asked the judge to appoint a lawyer to represent him, saying flatly, "The United States Supreme Court says I am entitled to be represented by counsel."

Gideon was wrong at the time, and the judge told him so. Only in cases where a defendant faces the death penalty, the judge said, is an indigent defendant entitled to have the state pay for a lawyer to represent him. Because the offense was minor, Gideon's request was denied.

At trial, Gideon conducted his own defense more ably than many nonlawyers might have done. He questioned the government witness and called eight witnesses of his own. But it is clear from the trial transcript that he missed several opportunities to help his case that even a novice lawyer would have exploited. For example, he was not told he could question potential jurors about possible biases, so he did not; nor did he establish any alibi to explain his whereabouts that night. The jury found him guilty and he was sentenced to the maximum prison term of five years.

Gideon, still acting as his own lawyer, appealed his imprisonment to the Florida Supreme Court, which denied his plea. The stage was thus set for his appeal to the U.S. Supreme Court. Gideon wrote the petition in pencil, on prison-sanctioned stationery. It was ungrammatical in places, but powerful as well. "When at the time of the petitioners trial he ask the lower court for the aid of counsel, the court refused this aid," Gideon wrote. Repeating his mistaken notion of the Supreme Court's precedents, he added, "Petitioner told the court that this Court made decision to the effect that all citizens tried for a felony crime should have aid of counsel. The lower court ignored this plea."

Gideon's petition was filed in forma pauperis (Latin for "in the manner of a pauper"), which means that it was accepted without the usual filing fees and without multiple copies. Such petitions often receive only cursory attention from the justices and their law clerks, but it appears that the Court was looking for a case like Gideon's, in which the defendant was not mentally incompetent, but was still tried unfairly because of lack of counsel. "This may be it!" Chief Justice Warren's law clerk wrote at the bottom of his summary of the Gideon petition, according to Ed Cray's 1997 Warren biography. When the Court agreed to hear the case, the Court signaled its importance by asking the parties to argue whether Betts v. Brady should be overturned.

Although Gideon was able to argue his own case in lower courts, the Supreme Court operates differently: only lawyers can argue before the Court. Washington, D.C., attorney Abe Fortas, later a justice himself, was selected to argue on Gideon's behalf. Justice William O. Douglas later said Fortas's advocacy in the Gideon case was "probably the best single legal argument" he had ever heard. Bruce Jacob, an inexperienced assistant Florida attorney general, represented Louie Wainwright, the head of Florida's prisons.

Clarence Earl Gideon, a mechanic sentenced to prison for breaking and entering, thought he should have had the assistance of a lawyer at his trial. Using the prison library, Gideon taught himself enough about the law to petition the Supreme Court to review his conviction. In *Gideon v. Wainright* (1963), a unanimous Court declared that anyone accused of a crime must be guaranteed the right to an attorney, regardless of whether he or she can afford one.
Source: AP/Wide World Photos.

VOTE

9–0, with Justice Hugo L. Black delivering the opinion for Chief Justice Earl Warren and Justices William O. Douglas, Tom C. Clark, John M. Harlan, William J. Brennan Jr., Potter Stewart, Byron R. White, and Arthur J. Goldberg.

HIGHLIGHTS

Justice Black, who had been the chief dissenter in *Betts v. Brady* twenty years earlier, wrote the majority opinion in *Gideon,* which overturned *Betts.* In part to make the decision unanimous, the decision was relatively brief and limited. He made much of the Court's earlier precedents, which he implied were more valid than *Betts.*

Even the *Betts* decision was right in one respect, Black added. "We accept *Betts v. Brady*'s assumption, based as it was on our prior cases, that a provision of the Bill of Rights which is 'fundamental and essential to a fair trial' is made obligatory upon the States by the Fourteenth Amendment. We think the Court in *Betts* was wrong, however, in concluding that the Sixth Amendment's guarantee of counsel is not one of these fundamental rights."

In this way, the Court "incorporated" Sixth Amendment guarantees to bind the states as well as the federal government, through the due process guarantee of the Fourteenth Amendment. The Court did not define the outer limits of its holding. It noted that twenty-two states had urged the Court to overturn *Betts*, while only two states joined Florida in asking that it be retained.

EXCERPTS

From Justice Hugo L. Black's majority opinion: "[R]eason and reflection require us to recognize that in our adversary system of criminal justice, any person haled into court, who is too poor to hire a lawyer, cannot be assured a fair trial unless counsel is provided for him. This seems to us to be an obvious truth. Governments, both state and federal, quite properly spend vast sums of money to establish machinery to try defendants accused of crime. Lawyers to prosecute are everywhere deemed essential to protect the public's interest in an orderly society. Similarly, there are few defendants charged with crime, few indeed, who fail to hire the best lawyers they can get to prepare and present their defenses. That government hires lawyers to prosecute and defendants who have the money hire lawyers to defend are the strongest indications of the widespread belief that lawyers in criminal courts are necessities, not luxuries. The right of one charged with crime to counsel may not be deemed fundamental and essential to fair trials in some countries, but it is in ours."

IMPACT

The *Gideon* decision has become one of the Court's best known rulings. It made its way into popular culture through Anthony Lewis's book and a subsequent movie in which actor Henry Fonda portrayed Gideon. The *Gideon* ruling, along with *Miranda v. Arizona*, symbolized the Warren Court's expansive view of constitutional protections for criminal defendants (see *Miranda v. Arizona*).

Gideon also represented the power of a determined individual to change settled notions about the law. Robert F. Kennedy observed that if

Clarence Earl Gideon handwrote his petition to the Supreme Court seeking a review of his conviction. Gideon filed an in forma pauperis petition that exempted him from paying filing fees and from certain other procedural regulations.

Source: National Archives.

Gideon had not petitioned the Supreme Court when he did, "the vast machinery of American law would have gone on functioning undisturbed. But Gideon did write that letter, the Court did look into his case . . . and the whole course of American legal history has been changed."

Some have said that the practical impact of the *Gideon* ruling may have been more limited than that. In spite of *Betts v. Brady,* most states by the time of *Gideon* were already providing lawyers to indigent defendants, even in non–death penalty cases. But *Gideon* certainly helped to firmly establish publicly funded legal aid and public defender offices throughout the nation.

At first the *Gideon* ruling was interpreted mainly to guarantee lawyers for defendants accused of felonies. But in 1972 the Court expanded the ruling to cover misdemeanor defendants as well. *Gideon* also began a line of cases in which the Court said that at least in a limited way, the Sixth Amendment also guaranteed "the effective assistance of counsel," meaning that if a lawyer's mistakes seriously affected the trial's outcome, a conviction could be overturned. In many appeals of death sentences, death row inmates often include claims that their lawyers did not give them effective assistance. The Supreme Court has responded to some of these claims, especially in death penalty cases. Individual justices have expressed concern about the quality of representation for death row inmates, and the American Bar Association has recruited quality attorneys to take on the often time-consuming and thankless task of aiding inmates on appeal. In the 2005 case *Rompilla v. Beard,* the Court overturned the death sentence of Ronald Rompilla because his attorneys failed to look up files relating to Rompilla's prior crimes, leaving them unable to rebut the prosecutor's statements about his past.

As for Gideon himself, the decision meant a new trial on the larceny charges. With the assistance of a local lawyer, who was able to poke holes in the prosecution's case, Gideon was found not guilty in August 1963.

Miranda v. Arizona

Decided June 13, 1966
384 U.S. 436
laws.findlaw.com/US/384/436.html

DECISION

The Fifth Amendment protects individuals against being forced to give statements that will help the government prove that they committed a crime. Before suspects in police custody can be questioned, they must be informed that they have the right to remain silent, that anything they say may be used against them, that they have the right to have a lawyer present, as well as the right to have a lawyer appointed to defend them if they cannot afford a lawyer.

BACKGROUND

In writing the Bill of Rights, the Framers, who had grown to despise the abusive practices of British criminal prosecutions, placed great emphasis on the rights of the criminally accused. It is no accident, therefore, that four of the first ten amendments to the Constitution deal with the rights of the accused. The Fifth Amendment states, "No person . . . shall be compelled in any criminal case to be a witness against himself." Just how that rule should be enforced has been the subject of dozens of Supreme Court cases. At the end of the nineteenth century, the Court said that for confessions to be admissible in federal court they had to have been given "freely and voluntarily." In 1936 that rule was extended to state cases. The determination of whether a confession was voluntary was made on a case-by-case basis. As a result, cases involving confessions continued to appear on the Court's docket, some of them clearly indicating that police were using "third degree" tactics during interrogations. Justices began to look for cases that would enable the Court to announce a clearer rule for determining if a confession was voluntary.

Two decisions by the Court applying the Sixth Amendment right to the "assistance of counsel" hastened the search. In *Gideon v. Wainwright* (1963) the Court ruled that the right to have the assistance of a lawyer was fundamental for anyone accused of a felony. (See *Gideon v. Wainwright.*) A year later, in *Escobedo v. Illinois,* the Court ruled that if police do not inform a suspect of his right to remain silent, and if they deny the suspect's request to speak with his lawyer, his Sixth Amendment rights have been violated. The defendant in the case, Danny Escobedo, had been questioned for fourteen hours in connection with the murder of his brother-in-law. The Court reversed his conviction.

The *Escobedo* decision was applicable mainly to cases in which a defendant already had a lawyer. According to a biographer, Chief Justice Warren felt that "more needed to be said"

Ernesto Miranda's original conviction on rape and kidnapping charges was thrown out by the Supreme Court in *Miranda v. Arizona* (1966) because police had not informed him of his rights against forced self-incrimination before he confessed to the crimes. His case led to the well-known Miranda warning.
Source: AP/Wide World Photos.

about the issues raised in *Escobedo*. He asked his law clerks to looks for appropriate cases among the 170 that had come to the Court since *Escobedo* raising issues about confessions.

Ernesto Miranda was twenty-three years old when he was arrested in 1963 in Phoenix as a suspect in the kidnapping and rape of a young woman. The victim's 1953 Packard was parked in front of his house, and he matched the general description the woman gave police of her attacker. The victim identified Miranda in a police lineup. In addition, Miranda had a history of arrests for rape and "peeping tom" offenses.

Miranda at first denied any involvement in the rape, but by the end of two hours of questioning by police, he confessed. He signed a statement that included a standard paragraph stating that the confession was voluntarily given. But Miranda had not been told that he had the right to have an attorney present or that he had the right to remain silent. At trial, his lawyer said the confession should not be admitted into evidence, but it was, and Miranda was convicted and sentenced to twenty years in prison. He appealed.

At oral argument before the Supreme Court, Miranda's lawyer conceded the confession had not been coerced, but insisted that Miranda had given up a right that he did not fully appreciate or understand. The Supreme Court was sharply divided over the case, with some justices fearing that any ruling restricting police behavior during interrogations would hamper the police. But Chief Justice Warren, who had once been a district attorney in California, argued forcefully that reform was needed. He noted that he had ordered law enforcement officials in his jurisdiction to warn suspects of their rights against forced self-incrimination. Other justices were also swayed by the fact that the Federal Bureau of Investigation (FBI) and District of Columbia police routinely gave the warnings.

VOTE

5–4, with Chief Justice Earl Warren writing the majority opinion. He was joined by Justices Hugo L. Black, William O. Douglas, William J. Brennan Jr., and Abe Fortas. Justices Tom C. Clark, John M. Harlan, Byron R. White, and Potter Stewart dissented.

HIGHLIGHTS

Supreme Court rulings are often written in ways that provide lower court judges and the general public with few clear rules about how to proceed. Not so with *Miranda,* which speaks boldly and clearly to prosecutors, police, and the public alike. Moreover, the Court normally is inclined to lay down general rules that can be applied with some flexibility to individual situations. But in *Miranda,* the Court said unequivocally that what has come to be known as the Miranda warning is an "absolute prerequisite" for the admissibility of confessions.

"The Fifth Amendment privilege is so fundamental to our system of constitutional rule and the expedient of giving an adequate warning as to the availability of the privilege so simple, we will not pause to inquire in individual cases whether the defendant was aware of his rights without a warning being given." Chief Justice Warren wrote.

The opinion recites the history of the law regarding confessions, as well as established practices within the FBI and in other countries, to reassure the public that its clear rule is neither new nor particularly onerous. In Scotland and India, for example, nearly all confessions made under police interrogation have long been excluded.

While giving Congress and the states some leeway to devise procedures for implementing its rule, the Court said any procedure had to include a warning with four basic elements: You have the right to remain silent; anything you say can and will be used against you; you have the right to talk to a lawyer and have the lawyer present during questioning; if you cannot afford a lawyer, one will be provided to you before questioning can begin.

The opinion also takes pains to spell out when the Miranda rule comes into play. The Court says that police may investigate and ask questions at a crime scene without reading anyone the Miranda warning. But once an individual has been taken into custody "or otherwise deprived of his freedom of action in any significant way," the warning must be given.

That point at which the warning must be given is substantially earlier than when police wanted. Some asserted that the Fifth Amendment privilege applies only when an individual is questioned in court or in some other kind of official proceeding. But the Supreme Court in *Miranda* said in vivid terms that the protection against self-incrimination must be invoked at the custody stage to have any force at all.

"An individual swept from familiar surroundings into police custody, surrounded by antagonistic forces, and subjected to the techniques of persuasion . . . cannot be otherwise than under compulsion to speak," the Court said.

EXCERPTS

From Chief Justice Earl Warren's majority opinion: "The current practice of incommunicado interrogation is at odds with one of our Nation's most cherished principles—that the individual may not be compelled to incriminate himself. Unless adequate protective devices are employed to dispel the compulsion inherent in custodial surroundings, no statement obtained from the defendant can truly be the product of his free choice. . . .

". . . [T]he privilege against self-incrimination—the essential mainstay of our adversary system—is founded on a complex of values. All these policies point to one overriding thought: the constitutional foundation underlying the privilege is the respect a government—state or federal—must accord to the dignity and integrity of its citizens. To maintain a 'fair state-individual balance,' to require the government 'to shoulder the entire load,' to respect the inviolability of the human personality, our accusatory system of criminal justice demands that the government seeking to punish an individual produce the evidence against him by its own independent labors, rather than by the cruel, simple expedient of compelling it from his own mouth. . . .

"Accordingly, we hold that an individual held for interrogation must be clearly informed that he has the right to consult with a lawyer and to have the lawyer with him during interrogation under the system for protecting the privilege we delineate today. As with the warnings of the right to remain silent and that anything stated can be used in evidence against him, this warning is an absolute prerequisite to interrogation. No amount of circumstantial evidence that the person may have been aware of this right will suffice to stand in its stead: only through such a warning is there ascertainable assurance that the accused was aware of this right."

IMPACT

In the decades since *Miranda v. Arizona,* the so-called Miranda warning became familiar to the public, thanks to countless television police shows and movies in which police recite the admonition to arrestees. It also remained controversial. Law enforcement officials and political conservatives attacked it as giving too much weight to the rights of criminal defendants while ignoring the interests of police and crime victims in determining the truth.

In 1968 Congress passed a law aimed at overturning *Miranda*. It allowed confessions to be admitted in federal cases,

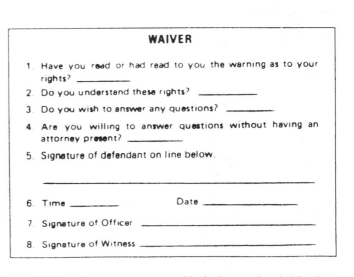

The wording of this Miranda warning is typical of what has become familiar to the public from watching television dramas. Notably, the Supreme Court in *Miranda v. Arizona* (1966) did not specify the exact language to be used when informing a suspect of his or her rights.

even if they were made without Miranda warnings, so long as it could be shown that they were voluntary. But the Justice Department consistently declined to enforce the law, believing that *Miranda* took precedence. Critics of *Miranda* began invoking the dormant law in court cases, however, in hopes that the Supreme Court would uphold the law and effectively nullify its decision.

In 2000 the Court ruled on the issue in the case of *Dickerson v. United States*. By a 7–2 vote the Court said the *Miranda* decision had constitutional dimensions and took precedence over the federal law. Surprisingly Chief Justice William Rehnquist, a longtime critic of the *Miranda* ruling, wrote the Dickerson opinion upholding it. In part, his ruling was a statement of the Court's authority, telling Congress that the Supreme Court, not Congress, decides the meaning of the Constitution. But Rehnquist also recognized how much the *Miranda* decision had become accepted by police and by society. "Miranda has become embedded in routine police practice to the point where the warnings have become part of our national culture," Rehnquist wrote.

Some commentators minimized the importance of the *Dickerson* decision, asserting that the Miranda rule had already been considerably weakened. In the years since *Miranda,* the Supreme Court has chipped away at it and made exceptions, such as allowing police some leeway to make mistakes in interrogations and still have suspects' confessions admitted at trial. But it was significant that the Court refused to reverse course completely on what has become a deeply entrenched procedural rule for police.

Legal scholars dispute *Miranda*'s impact on the ability of police to solve crimes. One conservative scholar, Paul Cassell of the University of Utah—later appointed to a federal judgeship—contends that thousands of criminal cases go unsolved every year because the Miranda rule caused confessions to be tossed out or because suspects refused to talk. Other researchers say the impact is vastly overstated.

Many police officials say they have learned to live with—or even embrace—the Miranda rule. Some say the rule helped police nationwide become more professional, with higher standards of ethics and fairness. Others even suggest that *Miranda* has given police an extra measure of credibility when defendants confess. A substantial percentage of suspects who are given Miranda warnings waive their right to remain silent and continue to talk to police. If the suspect has signed a Miranda waiver, any subsequent confession can be placed into evidence with relative ease.

Critics of police practices say many officers have also developed ways of getting around *Miranda* by advising suspects of their rights, but then telling them they would be better off if they talked.

Miranda was tried and convicted again, this time without using the confession against him. He was imprisoned until 1972 and went back to prison in 1975 after another run-in with the law. After he was released, Miranda was murdered in a fight at a Phoenix bar. According to some reports, he had several Miranda cards, reciting the police warning his case had inspired, in his pockets when he died.

In re Gault

Decided May 15, 1967
387 U.S. 1
laws.findlaw.com/US/387/1.html

DECISION

Juveniles accused of crimes are entitled to many, but not all, of the rights and privileges that adult criminal defendants enjoy. Among the rights that juveniles have are the right to counsel, the right to confront and cross-examine witnesses, and the right not to be forced to incriminate themselves.

BACKGROUND

Before the turn of the twentieth century, juveniles who committed crimes were treated in most respects as if they were adults. Progressive reformers were horrified that children often received long prison terms and were jailed alongside hardened adult criminals.

Reformers believed that society owed it to juveniles to treat them differently, in a parental rather than a punitive manner. Guilt or innocence should no longer be the system's primary concern, they argued, nor should punishment. Rather, the reformers sought to tailor the system to the special needs of children with the goal of rehabilitating them.

Philosophically and constitutionally, the new concept was based on the notion that children, who were ordinarily under the custody of their parents, did not have the same rights of liberty as adults. When the family failed to provide the proper custody of the children, the state could step in and take over.

As the reform movement took hold, an entirely separate juvenile court system developed, but it lacked most of the procedural safeguards that the Bill of Rights gives to adults accused of crime. Rules regarding questioning by police, confessions, trial by jury, and other aspects of the justice system did not apply.

By the 1930s it was clear that this well-intentioned juvenile reform effort, by eliminating procedures and rights enjoyed by adults, had created a new set of problems. Harvard Law School Dean Roscoe Pound in 1937 wrote, "The powers of the Star Chamber were a trifle in comparison with those of our juvenile courts." He was referring to England's infamous seventeenth century Star Chamber, a court that operated in secret and without juries and handed out cruel sentences. The case that went to the Supreme Court seemed to be a prime example of such proceedings.

Fifteen-year-old Gerald Gault and a friend were taken into custody in Gila County, Arizona, in 1964 after a neighbor complained that they made a "lewd" phone call to her. Gault was on probation at the time for a prior offense. Gault's mother was not informed at first that her son had been arrested, and the delinquency hearing the next day occurred without any of the formalities of an adult hearing. Witnesses were not sworn in, and no transcripts were made. There was some dispute about the facts surrounding the phone call, and the juvenile court judge said he would think about the case. Gault was taken to a detention home where he stayed for several days before being released.

After another somewhat ambiguous hearing a few days later, the judge ordered Gault to be committed to the State Industrial School as a juvenile delinquent until his twenty-first birthday—more than five years of confinement. Had an adult committed the same offense, the maximum penalty would have been two months in prison or a $50 fine. The hearings and the judge's decision all happened less than a week after Gault's lewd phone call.

Under Arizona law, no appeal was permitted, but Gault's family filed a habeas corpus petition—a procedure that requires the state to justify its detention of an individual. Arizona courts upheld Gault's punishment and the juvenile justice system. With help from the American Civil Liberties Union, Gault took his case to the U.S. Supreme Court. The state's juvenile court system, he claimed, deprived juveniles of a range of rights, including the right to counsel, the right to confront and cross-examine witnesses, the right not to be forced to incriminate themselves, and the right to appeal.

VOTE

7–2, with Justice Abe Fortas writing the majority opinion for the Court. Joining him were Chief Justice Earl Warren and Justices Hugo L. Black, William O. Douglas, Tom C. Clark, William J. Brennan Jr., and Byron R. White. Justices John M. Harlan and Potter Stewart dissented.

HIGHLIGHTS

"Whatever may be their precise impact, neither the Fourteenth Amendment nor the Bill of Rights is for adults alone." With that pronouncement, the Court ruled in favor of Gerald Gault. Justice Fortas, who had shown a keen interest in juvenile law in earlier decisions, wrote what has been described as a Bill of Rights or Magna Carta for juveniles.

In addition to his concern about the constitutional issue of the lack of adequate procedures for juveniles, Fortas also offered evidence that the special treatment of juveniles in courts had not proved effective. The reformers' belief that fashioning a separate system for juveniles would help nurture them back to a useful role in society had not panned out. "The high crime rates among juveniles . . . could not lead us to conclude that the absence of constitutional protections reduces crime, or that the juvenile system, functioning free of constitutional inhibitions as it has largely done, is effective to reduce crime or rehabilitate offenders." As a result, Fortas concluded that restoring constitutional protections to the system would not damage the juvenile court system.

"The early conception of the Juvenile Court proceeding was one in which a fatherly judge touched the heart and conscience of the erring youth by talking over his problems, by paternal advice and admonition," wrote Fortas. "Then, as now, goodwill and compassion were admirably prevalent. But recent studies have, with surprising unanimity, entered sharp dissent as to the validity of this gentle conception."

At a minimum, the Court agreed, the Constitution required that juveniles be given adequate notice of the charges against them and of their right to counsel, the right to confront and cross-examine witnesses, and the right not to be forced to give testimony against themselves. The Court noted that confessions and admissions by juveniles should not be given full weight, so they should be protected from incriminating themselves.

In dissent Justice Stewart objected that the Court, by transforming juvenile proceedings onto criminal trials, would "invite a long step backwards into the nineteenth century."

EXCERPTS

From Justice Abe Fortas's majority opinion: "[I]t would be extraordinary if our Constitution did not require the procedural regularity and the exercise of care implied in the phrase 'due process.' Under our Constitution, the condition of being a boy does not justify a kangaroo court. The traditional ideas of Juvenile Court procedure, indeed, contemplated that time would be available and care would be used to establish precisely what the juvenile did and why he did it—was it a prank of adolescence or a brutal act threatening serious consequences to himself or society unless corrected?"

IMPACT

Just as earlier reformers had done, the decision in *In re Gault* transformed the nation's juvenile justice system once again. Juvenile courts had to be retooled to take into account due process and constitutional procedures they had long bypassed.

"Gault's adolescent prank had the extraordinary effect of bringing every juvenile court in every state of the Union to a grinding halt so that lawyers and court reporters and all the other trappings of real courtrooms could be put into place," wrote journalist Edward Humes in a 1994 book on the juvenile justice system. "When they started up again, the way in which society dealt with its troubled youth had forever changed. Thirty years later, the system has yet to recover from that one lewd phone call, or from the hidden price tag attached to the reforms it spawned."

Humes and others claim that the reforms stemming from *Gault* have harmed, rather than helped, the fight against youth crime. Before *Gault,* they assert, society could intervene early and take a child away from a harmful environment and away from adult offenders, before his or her offenses became too serious. But since *Gault,* minor offenses have often been treated as just that—minor crimes that do not call for detention when committed by either adults or juveniles. As a result, juveniles are often free to commit further and more serious crimes.

Defenders of the current system say due process and certain punishment—whether the offense is major or minor—is the only constitutional approach to solving juvenile crime, which has reached staggering proportions. According to the Justice Department, law enforcement agencies made an estimated 2.8 million arrests of juveniles in 1997, 19 percent of all arrests made that year.

In recent years, politicians and prosecutors have increased the pressure to handle juveniles in the adult system. In January 2000 the murder trial of Nathaniel Abraham, who was eleven years old when he shot and killed a man, gained national attention. A Michigan judge sentenced the boy to detention until he turns twenty-one. In the fall of 2002, another drama that gripped the nation involved a juvenile offender: Lee Malvo, seventeen, who was accused along with a forty-four-year-old accomplice John Muhammad of shooting ten people, sniper-style, in the Washington, D.C., area. Many political leaders, including Attorney General John Ashcroft, said the two should be executed for their crimes, but a jury in Virginia said Malvo, at least, should not be put to death. In March 2005 the Supreme Court ruled that no one who was younger than eighteen at the time of his or her crime should be put to death. (See *Roper v. Simmons.*)

Nonetheless, for lesser sentences than death, pressure has been strong to have juveniles tried as adults so they could receive adult punishments. Some of the same conditions that spurred reform a century ago, it appeared, were returning.

RIGHT TO TRIAL BY JURY

A jury of one's peers has long been regarded as a crucial safeguard against excessive government power. Juries force prosecutors to present a reasonably solid case before a defendant can be found guilty. And sometimes juries deliver mercy as well as justice—finding defendants not guilty in spite of the facts, when the law being carried out seems unjust or when the defendant seems to deserve a break. In the late twentieth century legislators began looking at whether the sentences judges hand down as a result of jury verdicts vary too greatly from case to case. Congress passed a detailed set of sentencing guidelines, but still left judges with considerable power to decide issues that were once left to jurors. Soon, questions were raised whether the new system had in fact taken too much power away from juries, and the Supreme Court stepped in.

Other related cases mentioned in the Right to Trial by Jury section

Jones v. United States (1999)
Ring v. Arizona (2002)
Blakely v. Washington (2004)
United States v. Booker (2005)

Apprendi v. New Jersey

Decided June 26, 2000
530 U.S. 466
laws.findlaw.com/US/530/466.html

DECISION

In the trial of someone accused of a crime, any fact that increases the penalty for a crime beyond the maximum allowed for that crime must be proved beyond a reasonable doubt before a jury. When a judge alone makes this determination, the defendant's right under the Sixth Amendment to a trial by jury is violated.

Charles Apprendi Jr., here in a New Jersey courtroom in 2000, was convicted of a bias crime for shooting into the home of his black neighbors. In *Apprendi v. New Jersey* (2000), the Supreme Court overturned his 12-year sentence on the grounds that a jury—not a judge alone—must decide (beyond a reasonable doubt) whether bias was the motive. The ruling applies to the determination of any fact that increases the penalty for a crime beyond the maximum allowed by law.

Source: AP/Wide World Photos/Sabina Louise Pierce.

BACKGROUND

Early in the morning of December 22, 1994, Charles Apprendi Jr. fired shots into a home in Vineland, New Jersey. An African American family had just moved into the home and Apprendi, who was white, later said he did not want blacks moving into the neighborhood.

Soon after the shooting, police arrested Apprendi and he confessed. Apprendi was charged with numerous crimes involving the December shooting and earlier incidents that were similar, as well as firearm possession. Under an agreement with prosecutors, Apprendi pleaded guilty to some of the charges. He faced penalties for those crimes of up to twenty years in prison. The agreement was presented to a judge, not a jury, and the judge ratified it after hearing evidence.

Then prosecutors asked the judge for a higher sentence—ten additional years—by alleging that Apprendi's crime was intended to intimidate a racial group. That, prosecutors said, violated New Jersey's hate crime statute under which additional punishment can be given to defendants who commit crimes with biased motivations. The judge then considered evidence from both sides, including testimony by Apprendi himself, who said he was not racially biased but had shot up the house because he was drunk that night. The judge ruled that prosecutors had proven "by a preponderance of the evidence" that Apprendi had violated the hate crime law and deserved a higher sentence. Apprendi was sentenced to a total of twelve years in prison—not as much as he could have been given, but higher than would have been allowed if the hate crime had not been proven to the judge.

The New Jersey Supreme Court upheld the sentence, and Apprendi appealed to the U.S. Supreme Court, claiming that the additional sentence, because it was based on facts that had not been proven to a jury, violated his rights under the Sixth Amendment.

The case arrived at the high court at a point when several justices and other legal experts were expressing concern that plea bargaining and sentencing guidelines had eroded the Sixth Amendment right to a jury trial by giving judges the power to consider factors in sentencing that used to be weighed by juries.

VOTE

5–4, with Justice John Paul Stevens writing for the majority. He was joined by Justice Antonin Scalia, David Souter, Clarence

Thomas, and Ruth Bader Ginsburg. Justice Sandra Day O'Connor dissented, joined by Chief Justice William Rehnquist and Justices Anthony Kennedy and Stephen Breyer.

HIGHLIGHTS

The outcome was, in a sense, forecast by a 1999 decision involving a sentence under federal law. In *Jones v. United States,* the Court said that "under the Due Process Clause of the Fifth Amendment and the notice and jury trial guarantees of the Sixth Amendment, any fact (other than prior conviction) that increases the maximum penalty for a crime must be charged in an indictment, submitted to a jury, and proven beyond a reasonable doubt." That decision did not gain much attention, so the *Apprendi* case gave the Supreme Court the chance to reinforce what it said in *Jones.* The Court did so in the broader context of state laws, where most criminal cases are handled.

Stevens based the decision on the fundamental principle that all Americans accused of crime have the right to have their guilt or innocence decided by a jury of their peers. This was an important safeguard, he said, against the threat of tyranny by government officials. The Framers of the Constitution did not want the government to be able to throw people in jail on phony or trumped-up charges, so the Bill of Rights included the right to a jury trial as an important part of the Sixth Amendment. In a sense, the Framers wanted to make it difficult for government to deprive people of their liberty by putting them in prison.

Equally important, Stevens said, was the strong tradition that a jury must agree that the government had proved the truth of each accusation "beyond a reasonable doubt"—a high level of certainty that the defendant is guilty, not just that he or she was "more likely than not" to have committed the crime. This, too, would force government to make sure it had solid evidence before accusing individuals of a crime.

Both these principles, Stevens said, are undermined when a judge is able to increase a defendant's sentence beyond the ordinary maximum by ruling on accusations made by the prosecutor—and by using a "preponderance of the evidence" standard, which is much easier to meet than "beyond a reasonable doubt."

In dissent, Justice O'Connor said the Court's decision was an example of "pure formalism" that was not supported by history or precedent. Instead she said that the U.S. legal system has a long history of giving judges the kind of discretion in sentencing that the judge in New Jersey used.

But she also warned that the Court's decision would have the effect of calling into question reform efforts that have given judges less discretion as well. In the past three decades, at the federal and state levels, sentencing procedures have changed to ensure that similar defendants found guilty of similar crimes will get similar sentences. Many of these new procedures,

O'Connor said, require judges to make the kinds of sentence-increasing determinations that the *Apprendi* decision seems to reject.

EXCERPTS

From Justice John Paul Stevens's majority opinion: "In his 1881 lecture on the criminal law, Oliver Wendell Holmes, Jr., observed: 'The law threatens certain pains if you do certain things, intending thereby to give you a new motive for not doing them. If you persist in doing them, it has to inflict the pains in order that its threats may continue to be believed.' New Jersey threatened Apprendi with certain pains if he unlawfully possessed a weapon and with additional pains if he selected his victims with a purpose to intimidate them because of their race. As a matter of simple justice, it seems obvious that the procedural safeguards designed to protect Apprendi from unwarranted pains should apply equally to the two acts that New Jersey has singled out for punishment. . . .

"At stake in this case are constitutional protections of surpassing importance: the proscription of any deprivation of liberty without 'due process of law,' . . . and the guarantee that '[i]n all criminal prosecutions, the accused shall enjoy the right to a speedy and public trial, by an impartial jury.' . . . Taken together, these rights indisputably entitle a criminal defendant to 'a jury determination that [he] is guilty of every element of the crime with which he is charged, beyond a reasonable doubt.' "

From Justice Sandra Day O'Connor's dissent: "The apparent effect of the Court's opinion today is to halt the current debate on sentencing reform in its tracks and to invalidate with the stroke of a pen three decades' worth of nationwide reform, all in the name of a principle with a questionable constitutional pedigree. Indeed, it is ironic that the Court, in the name of constitutional rights meant to protect criminal defendants from the potentially arbitrary exercise of power by prosecutors and judges, appears to rest its decision on a principle that would render unconstitutional efforts by Congress and the state legislatures to place constraints on that very power in the sentencing context."

IMPACT

Justice O'Connor described the *Apprendi* decision as a "watershed change in constitutional law" that would have a "colossal" effect on how criminal defendants are sentenced in this country. It did not take long for her prediction to be proven right.

As she predicted, the decision in *Apprendi* was used to attack a broad range of state and federal sentences. In the 2002 case *Ring v. Arizona, Apprendi* was invoked to overturn a death sentence that was imposed based on factors that were determined by a judge, not a jury.

The next significant post-*Apprendi* decision came in June 2004, when the Court struck down sentencing guidelines in Washington. In *Blakely v. Washington,* the Court clarified *Apprendi* in a technical way that nonetheless threatened federal sentencing guidelines as well.

Justice Scalia in *Blakely* wrote that judges simply may not decide any facts that increase a sentence—whether or not the increased sentence was still under the maximum sentence the law would allow. *Blakely* involved a man who had kidnapped his estranged wife, and the sentencing range under state guidelines was fifty-three months. The judge increased the sentence to ninety months, which the state said was allowed even under *Apprendi,* because the punishment for felonies under state law can be as high as ten years or 120 months. Scalia said that maximum did not matter; for constitutional purposes all that mattered was that the judge, not the jury had increased the sentence.

Justice O'Connor warned that this application of *Apprendi* would cast doubt on the sentencing guidelines of many states and the federal government, and again she was right. Throughout the summer after *Blakely* was handed down, challenges to the federal guidelines were brought in federal courts around the country, and Paul Clement, the acting solicitor general of the United States, asked the Court to take up the issue quickly to alleviate the growing chaos in federal sentencing.

The Court did expedite its consideration, and in early October 2004 heard arguments in two drug cases that involved federal sentencing guidelines—a misnomer, really, because the sentencing ranges they set out are in fact mandatory for federal judges. In a complicated decision *United States v. Booker,* issued in January 2005, the Court said that indeed the federal sentencing guidelines were invalid because of the *Apprendi* line of cases. To remedy the situation, however, the Court did not toss out the guidelines altogether. Instead it made them advisory, or optional. This appeared to be a short-term fix. Congress held hearings on how the guidelines should be modified for the long term, and in the meantime a new wave of appeals began testing the meaning of several aspects of the *Booker* decision.

SEARCH AND SEIZURE

*T*he Fourth Amendment to the Constitution declares the "right of the people" to be safe from "unreasonable searches and seizures" both personally and in their "houses, papers, and effects." Deepseated concern about British troops raiding colonial houses at will was behind this sweeping protection. But as the nation grew and technology evolved, the "search and seizure" clause became an important safeguard of personal privacy—not against troops but against police and their increasingly sophisticated methods for investigating suspected crimes. The Supreme Court, in clarifying what is a search and what is "unreasonable," has examined everything from telephone wiretaps to thermal imaging devices.

Other related cases mentioned in the Search and Seizure section

Weeks v. United States (1914)
Olmstead v. United States (1928)
Wolf v. Colorado (1949)
Gideon v. Wainwright (1963) (see p. 260)
Miranda v. Arizona (1966) (see p. 263)
United States v. United States District Court for Eastern District of Michigan (1972)
Goss v. Lopez (1975)
Ingraham v. Wright (1977)
Michigan v. Long (1983)
California v. Ciraolo (1986)
Chandler v. Miller (1997)
Board of Education of Independent School District No. 92 of Pottawatomie County v. Earls (2002)
Hiibel v. Sixth Judicial District Court (2004)
Illinois v. Caballes (2005)

Mapp v. Ohio

Decided June 19, 1961
367 U.S. 643
laws.findlaw.com/US/367/643.html

DECISION

Evidence obtained by searches and seizures in violation of the Constitution is inadmissible in a criminal trial in a state court. The Court extended the so-called exclusionary rule, previously applicable only to federal criminal prosecutions, to state courts.

BACKGROUND

In 1914 the Supreme Court ruled in *Weeks v. United States* that when police use illegal means to obtain evidence against a criminal suspect, that evidence cannot be used against the suspect at trial in a federal court. Without such a rule, the *Weeks* Court found, "The protection of the Fourth Amendment declaring [a defendant's] right to be secure against such searches and seizures is of no value, and, so far as those thus placed are concerned, might as well be stricken from the Constitution."

At the federal level, the exclusionary rule was viewed as an effective way to encourage law enforcement officials to abide by the Fourth Amendment in conducting searches and seizures. If police abuses resulted in the evidence being tossed out at trial, the theory went, then police would think twice about conducting illegal searches. As Judge Benjamin Cardozo put it in a New York case, "The criminal is to go free because the constable has blundered."

But in a series of decisions since *Weeks,* the Court had resisted efforts to extend the rule to state courts, which is, after all, where most people encounter the legal system. The Court argued that the Bill of Rights governed only federal action. As recently as 1949, the Court in *Wolf v. Colorado* had found that state courts did not have to exclude illegally obtained evidence from trials, even though the Fourth Amendment's protection against illegal searches applied to local police as well as to federal agents. Gradually, however, the Court began to "incorporate" the states into protections of other parts of the Bill of Rights such as the First Amendment, by way of the Fourteenth Amendment, which did affect state action.

Indeed, the case that came to the Court appeared to involve a First Amendment issue, not evidence. It concerned a 1957 search by Cleveland police of the apartment of Dollree Mapp, suspected of involvement in an illegal gambling operation. She resisted and asked to see a search warrant. When police waved a piece of paper in front of her, she snatched it and put it down the front of her blouse. Police fought to get it back, and it is not entirely clear whether it was in fact a valid search warrant. None

was produced at the trial. Police proceeded to search the apartment in what the Supreme Court characterized as a "highhanded manner." They found no evidence of gambling, but did find some allegedly obscene literature and photographs in a locked suitcase. Mapp claimed the suitcase belonged to a former boarder, but she was convicted of possessing pornography and sentenced to prison for up to seven years. On appeal, the Ohio Supreme Court ruled that under Ohio law the results of the search were admissible, even though the search was unlawful. Mapp's conviction was upheld.

When the case came to the Supreme Court, Mapp's lawyers argued that the Ohio obscenity law was unconstitutionally vague. An amicus (friend of the court) brief by the American Civil Liberties Union argued that the evidence should be excluded because it was illegally obtained, but that issue was barely mentioned in oral arguments.

As recounted in a biography of Earl Warren by Ed Cray, a majority of the justices agreed in private conference to overturn Mapp's conviction on First Amendment grounds. Chief Justice Warren and Justices Douglas and Brennan indicated they also wanted to reverse the conviction on Fourth Amendment grounds, but no other justices supported them, and the idea was dropped. Later Justice Clark suggested that he too was ready to reverse on that basis as well. Justice Black was persuaded to join them, and Clark was assigned to write the opinion. Justice Frankfurter, who had written the Court's opinion in *Wolf,* was furious when he saw Clark's draft opinion. He argued that the Fourth Amendment issue had not been fully argued and should not be ruled on. But he did not prevail.

VOTE

5–4, with Justice Tom C. Clark writing for the majority. Joining in the majority were Chief Justice Earl Warren and Justices William O. Douglas, William J. Brennan Jr., and Hugo L. Black. Dissenting were Justices John M. Harlan, Felix Frankfurter, Charles E. Whittaker, and Potter Stewart.

HIGHLIGHTS

Justice Clark's main argument was that if the exclusionary rule was an effective constitutional rule at the federal level, it would be illogical, given the Fourteenth Amendment, not to extend the rule to state-sponsored searches as well. "Presently, a federal prosecutor may make no use of evidence illegally seized,

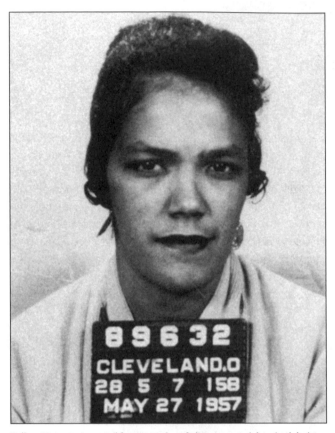

Dollree Mapp was arrested for possession of obscene materials seized during an illegal search. In an amicus curiae brief filed in *Mapp v. Ohio* (1961), the American Civil Liberties Union raised the Fourth Amendment issue on which her case was decided. The Court ruled that illegally obtained evidence could not be used against the accused at trial.
Source: The Granger Collection, New York.

EXCERPTS

From Justice Clark's majority opinion: "Having once recognized that the right to privacy embodied in the Fourth Amendment is enforceable against the States, and that the right to be secure against rude invasions of privacy by state officers is, therefore, constitutional in origin, we can no longer permit that right to remain an empty promise. Because it is enforceable in the same manner and to like effect as other basic rights secured by the Due Process Clause, we can no longer permit it to be revocable at the whim of any police officer who, in the name of law enforcement itself, chooses to suspend its enjoyment. Our decision, founded on reason and truth, gives to the individual no more than that which the Constitution guarantees him, to the police officer no less than that to which honest law enforcement is entitled, and, to the Courts, that judicial integrity so necessary in the true administration of justice."

IMPACT

Justice Clark's offhand remark in an elevator transformed a minor First Amendment case into one of the Warren Court's most significant criminal law decisions. Along with *Gideon v. Wainwright* and *Miranda v. Arizona, Mapp* transformed police practices nationwide. (See *Gideon v. Wainwright* and *Miranda v. Arizona.*) Later Chief Justice Warren said of *Mapp,* "It's hard to say it's a case. It's like a huge cloud from which a lot of things are raining."

Even though the idea of exclusionary rule originated in the *Weeks* case, *Mapp* is far better known and more controversial because it applied the rule to a far broader range of cases. To critics, it exemplified the Warren Court's liberal concern for the rights of defendants as opposed to the needs of law enforcement. Critics and defenders disagree over the impact of *Mapp* on prosecutions, but in 1983 one study indicated that fewer than 3 percent of felony prosecutions were spoiled by improper searches that led to the exclusion of evidence.

As the Court pendulum swung back toward more conservative decisions, *Mapp* came under steady attack. Warren Burger, named by President Richard Nixon to succeed Chief Justice Warren, was critical of *Mapp,* and during the 1970s and 1980s the Court weakened it. In a pair of decisions in 1984, for example, the Court said illegally obtained evidence could be admitted at trial if it could be shown that police would have "inevitably" discovered it without the illegal search, or that police were acting in good faith based on a defective search warrant.

As for Dollree Mapp, she moved to New York where she was convicted in 1974 on charges of selling narcotics. She was sentenced to twenty years to life in prison.

but a State's attorney across the street may, although he supposedly is operating under the enforceable prohibitions of the same Amendment," Clark wrote.

Recalling Cardozo's statement, Clark wrote, "The criminal goes free, if he must, but it is the law that sets him free. Nothing can destroy a government more quickly than its failure to observe its own laws, or worse, its disregard of the charter of its own existence."

Justice Black reached the same conclusion in his concurring opinion, but through the Fourth and Fifth Amendments in tandem, not the Fourteenth.

Justice Harlan's dissent clung to the old arguments against applying the Bill of Rights to actions by the states and accused the majority of abandoning "judicial restraint." The majority's view, Harlan said, "disfigures the boundaries" between the federal and state governments.

Katz v. United States

Decided December 18, 1967
389 U.S. 347
laws.findlaw.com/US/389/347.html

DECISION

The Fourth Amendment's prohibition against unreasonable government searches and seizures applies to the recording of telephone conversations as much as it does to a physical search of a person's home. The scope of the Fourth Amendment does not depend solely on whether there has been a physical intrusion into a constitutionally protected area, such as a person's home. Instead, the Court considered whether the government's action impinged on a person's "reasonable expectation of privacy."

BACKGROUND

The Framers of the Constitution were visionaries, but even they could not have imagined the era of modern communications, from telephones to the Internet. Applying the words of the Constitution to modern circumstances always poses difficult problems for the Supreme Court. How can the document be made relevant to modern concerns without distorting the intentions of the Framers?

Electronic surveillance posed just such a problem. The Fourth Amendment protects "the right of the people to be secure in their persons, houses, papers, and effects, against unreasonable searches and seizures." Telephones and wiretaps do not fit neatly into any of the terms of the amendment.

As telephones—and the ability to intercept conversations on them—developed, the courts at first took the Fourth Amendment literally and decided that government wiretaps were not prohibited. In *Olmstead v. United States* (1928) the Court found that a wiretap was neither a search nor a seizure, because it did not involve police entry into a home or seizure of anything material. Justice Louis Brandeis dissented vigorously in that case, declaring that privacy, or "the right to be let alone," was "the right most valued by civilized men." He added, "To protect that right, every unjustifiable intrusion by the Government upon the privacy of the individual, whatever the means employed, must be deemed a violation of the Fourth Amendment."

Soon after the *Olmstead* decision, Congress acted in part to blunt its effect. In the Federal Communications Act of 1934, Congress prohibited the unauthorized disclosure of intercepted phone conversations. Three years later, the Court interpreted the law to exclude wiretap evidence in federal court trials, although that prohibition was weakened in later decisions. The Federal Bureau of Investigation (FBI) continued to conduct wiretaps, arguing that the law only prohibited divulging the conversations, but did not prevent FBI agents from recording them. Decades later, in the *Katz* case, the Court faced the use of wiretaps in broad constitutional terms.

After trial on an eight-count indictment, Charles Katz was convicted of transmitting wagering information across state lines while telephoning Miami and Boston from Los Angeles. Without first obtaining a warrant, the FBI had attached an electronic listening device to the outside of an enclosed, public phone booth where Katz made the calls. The FBI asserted that it had taken great care to listen only to Katz and only when he was transmitting wagering information. The government also noted that Katz was visible to the public in the glass booth. Katz appealed the conviction, but it was affirmed by the U.S. court of appeals because the FBI had not physically entered the booth.

In his appeals petition, Katz argued that the booth had been electronically entered and that physical penetration was not required for an illegal search to take place under the Fourth Amendment.

VOTE

7–1, with Justice Potter Stewart writing the majority opinion. He was joined by Chief Justice Earl Warren and Justices William O. Douglas, William J. Brennan Jr., John M. Harlan, Byron R. White, and Abe Fortas. Justice Hugo L. Black dissented. Justice Thurgood Marshall did not participate.

HIGHLIGHTS

The Supreme Court chose to abandon the *Olmstead* approach completely. Instead of looking at whether a physical intrusion of a protected place, such as a home, had occurred, the Court declared that "the Fourth Amendment protects people, not places." The Court then decided that the Fourth Amendment could be interpreted to protect privately held conversations even if they are conducted in a publicly visible phone booth.

The Court concluded that Katz's private conversation was protected and that therefore the FBI should have obtained a warrant to intercept it. The FBI asserted that because it had acted on what had been the standard at the time, the conviction should stand. The Court disagreed, saying that no matter how limited the eavesdropping was, it had occurred without the prior approval of a judge, who would have determined whether there was "probable cause" to justify the wiretap. The Court reversed Katz's conviction.

Although Justice Stewart wrote the majority opinion, a concurrence written by Justice Harlan has had more lasting significance. It established that the new framework to use in determining whether a Fourth Amendment violation has occurred is to examine whether the government's action intruded on a person's "constitutionally protected reasonable expectation of privacy."

Justice Black dissented, strenuously maintaining that the Fourth Amendment did not state or imply a protected right to privacy that could be interpreted to include telephone conversations. To Black, the Fourth Amendment quite clearly can only protect describable places, tangible things, and persons from arbitrary search or seizure.

"The Fourth Amendment protects privacy only to the extent that it prohibits unreasonable searches and seizures of 'persons, houses, papers, and effects,' " Black wrote. "No general right is created by the Amendment so as to give this Court the unlimited power to hold unconstitutional everything which affects privacy. Certainly the Framers, well acquainted as they were with the excesses of governmental power, did not intend to grant this Court such omnipotent lawmaking authority as that. The history of governments proves that it is dangerous to freedom to repose such powers in Courts."

EXCERPTS

From Justice Stewart's majority opinion: "[W]hat he [Katz] sought to exclude when he entered the booth was not the intruding eye—it was the uninvited ear. He did not shed his right to do so simply because he made his calls from a place where he might be seen. No less than an individual in a business office, in a friend's apartment, or in a taxicab, a person in a telephone booth may rely upon the protection of the Fourth Amendment. One who occupies it, shuts the door behind him, and pays the toll that permits him to place a call is surely entitled to assume that the words he utters into the mouthpiece

will not be broadcast to the world. To read the Constitution more narrowly is to ignore the vital role that the public telephone has come to play in private communication."

IMPACT

Congress responded to the *Katz* decision by passing, as part of the Omnibus Crime Control and Safe Streets Act of 1968, a provision allowing wiretaps only if approved by a judge through a search warrant. The Nixon administration interpreted the law to allow warrantless wiretaps in cases of national security, but the Supreme Court unanimously rejected that view in *United States v. United States District Court for Eastern District of Michigan* (1972).

The decision in *Katz* did not keep police from wiretapping phone conversations; instead it imposed procedural safeguards that are still in place today. The Administrative Office of the U.S. Courts, which reports annually on the number of judicially authorized wiretaps (*www.uscourts.gov*), said that in 1997, 1,186 wiretaps were authorized at the federal and state levels—an increase of 3 percent over the previous year. Of the 617 authorized by state judges, about 70 percent came from New York, New Jersey, and Florida. Nearly three-quarters of the wiretaps were requested in connection with narcotics investigations.

More broadly, the Harlan standard of "reasonable expectation of privacy" in *Katz* has continued to be used as a benchmark for litigation over government intrusions. At times since *Katz*, that standard has offered little protection in the view of civil liberties advocates. In the 1986 decision *California v. Ciraolo*, for example, the Court said the owner of property surrounded by a ten-foot-high solid wooden fence did not have a reasonable expectation of privacy because any member of the public flying overhead could have seen what the police saw.

On the other hand, in a 2001 case *Kyllo v. United States*, the Court invoked the *Katz* standard to find that police use of thermal imaging devices to detect heat emanating from inside a house constituted a search, and should not occur without a warrant. (See *Kyllo v. United States*.)

Terry v. Ohio

Decided June 10, 1968
392 U.S. 1
laws.findlaw.com/US/392/1.html

DECISION

Police may stop and frisk a person without a search warrant if they reasonably believe their safety or the safety of others is endangered, and if the search is limited to a pat-down of the person's outer clothing. These limited searches are governed by the Fourth Amendment's bar against unreasonable searches and seizures, but can be justified even if police have something less than probable cause to believe the person committed a crime.

BACKGROUND

Led by Chief Justice Earl Warren, the Supreme Court in 1968 had the reputation of protecting the rights of people accused of crime and not being concerned enough about the safety and investigative needs of police. It was in this context that the Court took up *Terry v. Ohio,* a constitutional challenge to the longstanding police practice known as "stop and frisk," which means stopping a suspicious-looking person, not for the purpose of arrest but for a cursory search for weapons.

The case arose from an incident in Cleveland. In October 1963 a police detective saw two men walk back and forth repeatedly in front of a downtown clothing store, occasionally conferring with a third man. "They didn't look right to me at the time," said Detective Martin McFadden, a thirty-nine-year veteran of the force. He suspected they were casing the store for a planned robbery.

When the three men met up again, McFadden took action. He approached them, identified himself as a police officer and asked their names. When they mumbled something, McFadden grabbed one of them—later identified as John Terry—and spun him around. The detective quickly patted Terry down. In the left breast pocket of Terry's overcoat, McFadden felt a pistol. He reached in, but could not remove it. Terry removed his coat and the detective retrieved a .38 caliber revolver. He searched the others and found another revolver in Richard Chilton's pocket. The two were charged with carrying concealed weapons.

At trial, Terry and Chilton sought to prevent the guns from being used as evidence against them, claiming that the police officer obtained them in an illegal search. If the search were in fact illegal, under the so-called exclusionary rule, the guns would have to be excluded as evidence, and the prosecution would have no case against Terry and Chilton. (See *Mapp v. Ohio.*)

The judge ruled that the pat-down search was appropriate, given the police officer's experience, as a way of checking whether these men, involved in a suspicious situation, were armed. The two were convicted, and the convictions were upheld on appeal. In Ohio courts, and then at the Supreme Court, lawyers for the defendants asserted that their clients had been subjected to an illegal search.

VOTE

8–1, with Chief Justice Earl Warren writing the majority opinion. He was joined by Justices Hugo Black, Tom C. Clark, John M. Harlan, William J. Brennan Jr., Potter Stewart, Abe Fortas, and Thurgood Marshall. Justice William O. Douglas dissented.

HIGHLIGHTS

Chief Justice Warren, a onetime district attorney and state attorney general, was nevertheless a strong defender of personal privacy rights. His opinion in *Terry v. Ohio,* therefore, was a careful balancing of both interests. As with his opinion in *Miranda v. Arizona,* written two years earlier, Warren offered the police detailed guidelines on how to conduct a cursory search without violating the Fourth Amendment. (See *Miranda v. Arizona.*)

First, Warren made it clear that the search conducted by Officer McFadden warranted Fourth Amendment scrutiny. "Even a limited search of the outer clothing for weapons constitutes a severe, though brief, intrusion upon cherished personal security, and it must surely be an annoying, frightening, and perhaps humiliating experience," Warren said. "We therefore reject the notions that the Fourth Amendment does not come into play at all as a limitation upon police conduct if the officers stop short of something called a 'technical arrest' or a 'full-blown search.' "

Warren said that in all cases involving the Fourth Amendment, it would be preferable for police to obtain a search warrant from a judge, which requires a showing of probable cause that a crime has been or is being committed. But he acknowledged that obtaining a warrant is not always possible, especially in a situation like the one before the Court, where the officer needed to act quickly to protect himself.

In a footnote, Warren noted that fifty-seven police officers had died in the line of duty in 1966, and 23,851 had been assaulted. "In view of these facts," he wrote, "we cannot blind ourselves to the need for law enforcement officers to protect themselves and other prospective victims of violence in situations where they may lack probable cause for an arrest."

Warren did not want this law enforcement need for self-protection to turn into a broad mandate. "There must be a narrowly drawn authority to permit a reasonable search for weapons for the protection of the police officer, where he has reason to believe that he is dealing with an armed and dangerous individual, regardless of whether he has probable cause to arrest the individual for a crime."

In another cautionary note, Warren said the search must be "confined in scope to an intrusion reasonably designed to discover guns, knives, clubs, or other hidden instruments for the assault of the police officer." Only if these requirements are met, Warren concluded, is the search legal and the fruit of the search admissible at trial.

Justice Douglas, who initially supported the majority, changed his mind and wrote a dissent that criticized the majority for giving police too much power. "Had a warrant been sought, a magistrate would have . . . been unauthorized to issue one, for he can act only if there is a showing of 'probable cause.' We hold today that the police have greater authority to make a 'seizure' and conduct a 'search' than a judge has to authorize such action. We have said precisely the opposite over and over again," wrote Douglas. "To give the police greater power than a magistrate is to take a long step down the totalitarian path."

EXCERPTS

From Justice Warren's majority opinion: "It is quite plain that the Fourth Amendment governs 'seizures' of the person which do not eventuate in a trip to the station house and prosecution for crime—'arrests' in traditional terminology. It must be recognized that whenever a police officer accosts an individual and restrains his freedom to walk away, he has 'seized' that person. And it is nothing less than sheer torture of the English language to suggest that a careful exploration of the outer surfaces of a person's clothing all over his or her body in an attempt to find weapons is not a 'search.'. . . It is a serious intrusion upon the sanctity of the person, which may inflict great indignity and arouse strong resentment, and it is not to be undertaken lightly. . . .

". . . [W]e cannot blind ourselves to the need for law enforcement officers to protect themselves and other prospective victims of violence in situations where they may lack probable cause for an arrest. When an officer is justified in believing that the individual whose suspicious behavior he is investigating at close range is armed and presently dangerous to the officer or to others, it would appear to be clearly unreasonable to deny the officer the power to take necessary measures to determine whether the person is in fact carrying a weapon and to neutralize the threat of physical harm. . . .

". . . Such a search is a reasonable search under the Fourth Amendment, and any weapons seized may properly be introduced in evidence against the person from whom they were taken."

IMPACT

A "Terry stop" or "Terry search" has become a common police and legal shorthand for the type of stop and frisk search authorized by the Court in *Terry v. Ohio*. It is a doctrine that the Court, in the decades since the decision was handed down, has generally reaffirmed and expanded. Although Justice Douglas's dire warning of totalitarianism has not come to pass, it is clear that the *Terry* decision has led to an expansion of police powers during routine encounters with the public.

The *Terry* ruling was limited to pat-downs of a person for possible weapons, but it has been invoked to allow for other types of searches, and other kinds of contraband, as well. In 1972 the Court said an informant's tip was sufficient to trigger a Terry stop. The Court's 1983 decision in *Michigan v. Long* may represent the high-water mark for the power of *Terry*. In that case the Court invoked *Terry* to permit a police search of the passenger compartment of a car. Police found no weapons in the car, but did find marijuana, which was allowed into evidence at trial. "If, while conducting a legitimate Terry search of an automobile's interior, the officer discovers contraband other than weapons, he cannot be required to ignore the contraband," the Court said in *Michigan v. Long*.

At the same time, the Court has been fairly consistent in requiring that police, before they conduct a Terry search, have at least some articulable reason for targeting the individual. In a 1975 case the Court said border patrol agents needed more justification than merely possible Mexican ancestry before searching people. In 1981 the Court said police needed a "particularized and objective basis" for conducting a Terry search, not just a notion that the suspect "looked suspicious" or was in a high-crime area.

A 2004 case clarified a point that was implied, but not stated, in *Terry*. In *Hiibel v. Sixth Judicial District Court*, the Court ruled, "The principles of *Terry* permit a State to require a suspect to disclose his name in the course of a Terry stop."

New Jersey v. T.L.O.

Decided January 15, 1985
469 U.S. 325
laws.findlaw.com/US/469/325.html

DECISION

School officials may search students' belongings for illegal material without a search warrant, so long as the search is reasonable, even though public school students have some expectation of privacy in their belongings.

BACKGROUND

This case began in March 1980 with what is probably an everyday occurrence in U.S. schools: two girls caught smoking in a school bathroom. A teacher at Piscataway High School in suburban New Jersey discovered the girls and sent them to the principal's office. There, under questioning by an assistant vice principal, one girl admitted she had smoked, which was a violation of a school rule. But the other girl, a fourteen-year-old known in the Court papers by her initials T.L.O., denied smoking.

At that point the administrator demanded to see T.L.O.'s purse. He found a pack of cigarettes and a package of cigarette rolling papers—a sign of likely marijuana use. He searched further and found a small amount of marijuana as well as evidence that she was selling marijuana. The school official called her parents and summoned police. The girl was taken to police headquarters, where she confessed to selling marijuana to fellow students. The county prosecutors brought delinquency charges against her, and she was also suspended from school for ten days.

In juvenile court T.L.O.'s lawyers claimed the search of her purse violated the Fourth Amendment, which bars unreasonable searches and seizures. The judge disagreed and sentenced her to a year's probation. On appeal, the New Jersey Supreme Court ruled in favor of the student. The court noted that although smoking is against the school rules, mere possession of cigarettes is not—making the search of T.L.O.'s purse unreasonable. And if the search was unreasonable, then, the court said, the marijuana found during the search could not be used against her. That is because of the "exclusionary rule," under which illegally obtained evidence may not be used at trial. (See *Mapp v. Ohio.*)

The *T.L.O.* case came to the Supreme Court at a time when justices had not yet settled on how much due process or fair procedure children were entitled to in criminal matters. In 1975 the Court had said in *Goss v. Lopez* that students were entitled to only a "rudimentary" level of due process. "Moreover, the Court ignores the experience of mankind, as well as the long history of our law, recognizing that there are differences which must be accommodated in determining the rights and duties of children as compared with those of adults. Examples of this distinction abound in our law," wrote Justice Lewis Powell in *Goss.*

In a 1977 case, *Ingraham v. Wright,* the Court upheld the use of corporal punishment against Florida schoolchildren. It had been challenged as a violation of the Eighth Amendment, which bars cruel and unusual punishment.

VOTE

6–3, with Justice Byron R. White writing the majority opinion for the Court. Joining White were Chief Justice Warren E. Burger and Justices Lewis F. Powell Jr., William Rehnquist, Sandra Day O'-Connor, and Harry A. Blackmun. Dissenting were Justices William J. Brennan Jr., Thurgood Marshall, and John Paul Stevens.

HIGHLIGHTS

One of the difficulties in cases involving searches by school officials was deciding whether these officials should be held to the same constitutional standard as police. If police search an individual, it has been established that under the Fourth Amendment they must have "probable cause" beforehand to suspect that they will find evidence of a crime. In most circumstances, that means they must first obtain a search warrant from a judge.

But many courts had ruled that school principals and teachers were different from police. In the traditional notion of in loco parentis, school officials were often viewed as surrogates or substitutes for parents. And because parents would presumably be allowed to search their children's belongings, so too could school officials.

Justice White found something of a middle ground in his majority opinion. The Fourth Amendment does apply to searches by school officials, not just by police, he said. "Today's public school officials do not merely exercise authority voluntarily conferred on them by individual parents; rather, they act in furtherance of publicly mandated educational and disciplinary policies. In carrying out searches and other disciplinary functions pursuant to such policies, school officials act as representatives of the State, not merely as surrogates for the parents, and they cannot claim the parents' immunity from the strictures of the Fourth Amendment."

White also acknowledged that students share with adults an interest in keeping their belongings private, even at school. "A search of a child's person or of a closed purse or other bag carried on her person, no less than a similar search carried out on an adult, is undoubtedly a severe violation of subjective expectations of privacy."

But on the other hand, White said school administrators must have some leeway to enforce discipline. It would be too much to expect school officials to obtain search warrants for the kind of routine disciplinary actions they must take every day. This is especially true in modern-day schools, where crime and disorder have grown in magnitude, White said. "Against the child's interest in privacy must be set the substantial interest of teachers and administrators in maintaining discipline in the classroom and on school grounds. Maintaining order in the classroom has never been easy, but in recent years, school disorder has often taken particularly ugly forms: drug use and violent crime in the schools have become major social problems."

Against this backdrop, the justices reviewed the circumstances of the search of T.L.O.'s purse and concluded that it was reasonable. In a footnote, White said the ruling did not address the somewhat different issues posed by school searches of lockers or desks, where students might have different expectations of privacy.

In a strongly worded dissent, liberal justices Brennan and Marshall said they "emphatically disagree with the Court's decision to cast aside the constitutional probable-cause standard when assessing the constitutional validity of a schoolhouse search." "Moved by whatever momentary evil has aroused their fears, officials—perhaps even supported by a majority of citizens—may be tempted to conduct searches that sacrifice the liberty of each citizen to assuage the perceived evil. But the Fourth Amendment rests on the principle that a true balance between the individual and society depends on the recognition of 'the right to be let alone'—the most comprehensive of rights and the right most valued by civilized men." Brennan concluded, "Full-scale searches unaccompanied by probable cause violate the Fourth Amendment."

Justice Stevens, also in dissent, said the Court was sending a regrettable message to school students. "Schools are places where we inculcate the values essential to the meaningful exercise of rights and responsibilities by a self-governing citizenry. If the Nation's students can be convicted through the use of arbitrary methods destructive of personal liberty, they cannot help but feel that they have been dealt with unfairly." He concluded, "The Court's decision today is a curious moral for the Nation's youth."

EXCERPTS

From Justice White's majority opinion: "It is evident that the school setting requires some easing of the restrictions to which searches by public authorities are ordinarily subject. The warrant requirement, in particular, is unsuited to the school environment: requiring a teacher to obtain a warrant before searching a child suspected of an infraction of school rules (or of the criminal law) would unduly interfere with the maintenance of the swift and informal disciplinary procedures needed in the schools. Just as we have in other cases dispensed with the warrant requirement when 'the burden of obtaining a warrant is likely to frustrate the governmental purpose behind the search,' we hold today that school officials need not obtain a warrant before searching a student who is under their authority. . . .

". . . [T]he accommodation of the privacy interests of schoolchildren with the substantial need of teachers and administrators for freedom to maintain order in the schools does not require strict adherence to the requirement that searches be based on probable cause to believe that the subject of the search has violated or is violating the law. Rather, the legality of a search of a student should depend simply on the reasonableness, under all the circumstances, of the search. . . .

"This standard will, we trust, neither unduly burden the efforts of school authorities to maintain order in their schools nor authorize unrestrained intrusions upon the privacy of schoolchildren."

IMPACT

The *T.L.O.* decision has become a powerful tool for school administrators who argue for a greater level of surveillance and discipline in schools, especially after several incidents of school shootings by students. How much further it will be extended is unclear, because the Court has established that students are protected by the Fourth Amendment, even if to a lesser degree than adults are.

In the 1995 case *Vernonia School District 47J v. Acton,* the Court built on the *T.L.O.* precedent by allowing random drug testing of student athletes without probable cause to believe that they were involved in drugs. (See *Vernonia School District 47J v. Acton.*)

Some civil libertarians argue that despite the greater need for safety in schools, the Court went too far in *T.L.O.* and *Vernonia* in minimizing the rights of young people. After the Littleton, Colorado, school shootings in 1999, John Whitehead, president of the Rutherford Institute in Charlottesville, Virginia, wrote in a column, "The same students that are being educated about their Constitution and the Bill of Rights in their government classes are being stripped of their own constitutional rights when the bell rings and the class is over."

Vernonia School District 47J v. Acton

Decided June 26, 1995
515 U.S. 646
laws.findlaw.com/US/515/646.html

DECISION

A public school system may require random drug testing for its student athletes. Urine testing is a "search" under the Fourth Amendment, which requires that government searches be reasonable. The random testing of student athletes is reasonable because of the high risk of physical harm to players from drug use and because athletes do not expect privacy in locker rooms. The testing is also justified by the importance of discouraging drug use among children.

BACKGROUND

For years school systems nationwide have struggled to combat the problem of drug use by students. Education about the dangers of drugs and greater police presence within schools have not completely solved the problem, and some school districts have moved aggressively into searching student belongings and lockers, as well as testing students for drug use. The Supreme Court gave some encouragement to the trend in the 1985 ruling *New Jersey v. T.L.O.,* which said school officials

James Acton, center, a high school student from Vernonia, Oregon, leaves the Supreme Court with friends and family members following oral arguments in *Vernonia School District 47J v. Acton* (1995). The Court upheld the school district's requirement that student athletes submit to random drug testing. From left to right are Kathy Armstrong of the American Civil Liberties Union, brother Simon, and parents Judy and Wayne Acton. *Source: AP/Wide World Photos.*

could make unannounced searches of students if they had reasonable suspicion of drug or gun use. (See *New Jersey v. T. L. O.*)

The public schools of Vernonia, Oregon, a small logging community northwest of Portland, were beset by drug and disciplinary problems in the late 1980s, according to school officials. Student athletes, usually viewed as positive role models for their peers, seemed instead to be the leaders in drug use.

The school board responded with a drug-testing program that required students to consent to testing as a condition for participating in interscholastic sports. All student-athletes were tested at the beginning of their sport season, and after that 10 percent of them were selected at random for another test. Under the program, if drug use was detected, a second test would be conducted. If that test was positive, the student would have the choice of entering a supervised treatment program or being suspended from athletics.

The family of seventh-grader James Acton sued the school system in 1991 after he was denied a spot on a school football team. He and his parents had refused to sign the consent forms for the drug-testing program. The family claimed that the rule violated James's Fourth Amendment right against unreasonable searches. The district court ruled in favor of the school system, but the court of appeals reversed the decision. The school district then requested Supreme Court review.

VOTE

6–3, with Justice Antonin Scalia writing the majority opinion. Joining him were Chief Justice William Rehnquist and Justices Anthony M. Kennedy, Clarence Thomas, Ruth Bader Ginsburg, and Stephen G. Breyer. Justices Sandra Day O'Connor, John Paul Stevens, and David H. Souter dissented.

HIGHLIGHTS

Justice Scalia reiterated the rationale for most of the Court's cases regarding students' rights: that schools stand in loco parentis (in the place of parents) during the school day, "permitting a degree of supervision and control that could not be exercised over free adults."

One consequence of that supervision is less privacy than one might expect in other settings. Students receive vaccinations and physical exams in connection with athletics, Scalia noted, also diminishing their expectation of privacy. In one passage, Scalia also said student athletes have even less expectation of privacy than other students do. "School sports are not for the bashful," wrote Scalia. "They require 'suiting up' before each practice or event, and showering and changing afterwards. Public school locker rooms, the usual sites for these activities, are not notable for the privacy they afford."

These factors entered into the Court's determination that drug testing for athletes did not amount to an unreasonable search under the Fourth Amendment. The school system's interest in testing for drugs was also legitimate and important, the Court found. "That the nature of the concern is important—indeed, perhaps compelling—can hardly be doubted," Scalia wrote. "School years are the time when the physical, psychological, and addictive effects of drugs are most severe."

Dissenting justices led by Sandra Day O'Connor were unusually sharp in their criticism of the majority for permitting intrusive searches of individuals who are not suspected of any crime. "For most of our constitutional history, mass, suspicionless searches have been generally considered *per se* unreasonable within the meaning of the Fourth Amendment," O'Connor wrote.

EXCERPTS

From Justice Scalia's majority opinion: "[T]he effects of a drug-infested school are visited not just upon the users, but upon the entire student body and faculty, as the educational process is disrupted. In the present case, moreover, the necessity for the State to act is magnified by the fact that this evil is being visited not just upon individuals at large, but upon children for whom it has undertaken a special responsibility of care and direction. Finally, it must not be lost sight of that this program is directed more narrowly to drug use by school athletes, where the risk of immediate physical harm to the drug user or those with whom he is playing his sport is particularly high. Apart from psychological effects, which include impairment of judgment, slow reaction time, and a lessening of the perception of pain, the particular drugs screened by the District's Policy have been demonstrated to pose substantial physical risks to athletes. . . .

"Taking into account all the factors we have considered above—the decreased expectation of privacy, the relative unobtrusiveness of the search, and the severity of the need met by the search—we conclude Vernonia's Policy is reasonable and hence constitutional.

"We caution against the assumption that suspicionless drug testing will readily pass constitutional muster in other contexts. The most significant element in this case is the first we discussed: that the Policy was undertaken in furtherance of the government's responsibilities, under a public school system, as guardian and tutor of children entrusted to its care. Just as when the government conducts a search in its capacity as employer (a warrantless search of an absent employee's desk to obtain an urgently needed file, for example), the relevant question is whether that intrusion upon privacy is one that a reasonable employer might engage in; so also when the government acts as guardian and tutor the relevant question is whether the search is one that a reasonable guardian and tutor might undertake. Given the findings of need made by the District Court, we conclude that in the present case it is."

IMPACT

Civil liberties groups criticized *Vernonia* as endorsing yet another government intrusion into the privacy of individuals without the usual prerequisite of being suspected of committing a crime. But because the Court confined the decision to student athletes and did not extend it to students in general, the decision's impact has been somewhat limited. Subsequent efforts by school systems to allow random drug testing for all students have been challenged in lower courts, but the Supreme Court has not revisited the issue.

But the *Vernonia* decision did provide the rationale for the Court to allow drug testing in at least one new category of students: those seeking to participate in other extracurricular activities besides sports. In *Board of Education of Independent School District No. 92 of Pottawatomie County v. Earls,* a 2002 decision, the Court said the Oklahoma district's policy of requiring drug tests before students could sign up for extracurricular activities was a "reasonable" method for deterring student drug use.

But beyond the walls of public schools, the *Vernonia* decision did not seem to have much effect. In the 1997 ruling *Chandler v. Miller,* the Court decided not to extend the *Vernonia* decision to candidates for public office. The Court struck down a Georgia law that required drug testing for anyone seeking a place on the ballot in statewide elections.

Kyllo v. United States

Decided June 11, 2001
533 U.S. 27
laws.findlaw.com/US/533/27.html

DECISION

Police who used a thermal imaging device to detect heat inside the home of someone suspected of using heat lamps to grow marijuana indoors violated the Fourth Amendment's ban on unreasonable searches.

BACKGROUND

Danny Kyllo was an indoor gardener. But the plants he grew inside his home in Florence, Oregon, were illegal. They were marijuana plants, cultivated with the help of halide lamps, which emit a lot of heat.

Federal agents in 1991 suspected Kyllo was growing marijuana indoors, and to see if they were correct, they used a thermal imaging device—analogous to a video camera, except that it detects heat rather than visual images. A law enforcement officer parked his car across the street from Kyllo's home and pointed the device at the house. Sure enough, it picked up high levels of heat emanating from one part of Kyllo's house and his garage. Based on that information as well as on tips from informants and Kyllo's high utility bills, a judge agreed to issue a search warrant. The search was conducted, the marijuana plants were found, and Kyllo was charged with manufacturing illegal drugs.

Kyllo's lawyers contended that by using the imaging device before obtaining a search warrant, government had conducted an illegal search of Kyllo's home under the Fourth Amendment. After examining how intrusive the imaging device was, both the federal district court and the U.S. Court of Appeals for the Ninth Circuit said the use of the device was proper, and that Kyllo had no reasonable expectation of privacy regarding the heat that emanated from his house.

The case went to a Supreme Court whose members usually sided with law enforcement on Fourth Amendment issues. But with advances in technology posing an increasing threat to personal privacy—another value to which the high court was sympathetic—Kyllo had a better chance of winning than most drug defendants do before the Supreme Court.

VOTE

5–4, with Justice Antonin Scalia writing for the majority. He was joined by Justices David Souter, Clarence Thomas, Ruth Bader Ginsburg, and Stephen Breyer. Justice John Paul Stevens wrote a dissent, joined by Chief Justice William Rehnquist and Justices Sandra Day O'Connor and Anthony Kennedy.

HIGHLIGHTS

Danny Kyllo's case, even though it involved illegal marijuana growing, clearly appealed to the libertarian impulses of conservative justices Antonin Scalia and Clarence Thomas. Quoting from a 1961 Supreme Court decision, Scalia said that "the right of a man to retreat into his own home and there be free from unreasonable governmental intrusion" is at the core of the Fourth Amendment. In most instances, then, Scalia said, searching a person's home without a search warrant issued by a judge should not be allowed. Having an impartial judge evaluate whether police have a valid reason to search a home is an important check on government intrusion in private lives.

In Kyllo's case, Scalia said the key question was whether a search had in fact occurred. In previous cases the Court had said that when police observe what other people could observe from the street, for example, or even from an airplane above, they are not conducting a search that requires a warrant.

The standard the Court uses in deciding whether a search has occurred comes from *Katz v. United States,* which said police could not place a listening device on the outside of a telephone booth without a search warrant. In that case, Justice John Harlan said the deciding factors are whether the person searched had an expectation of privacy, and whether society regarded that expectation as reasonable. (See *Katz v. United States.*)

In Kyllo's case, Scalia said the use of the thermal imaging device violated Kyllo's reasonable expectation of privacy at its most sacred point: inside the home. The government argued, and the dissenters agreed, that in fact the device gathers information outside the home, namely heat that is detectable on its exterior surfaces. Under that theory, Scalia said, the *Katz* case would have been decided differently, because technically speaking, the listening device only picked up vibrations on the exterior of the phone booth.

For Scalia the key was that the heat data obtained about Kyllo could not ordinarily have been obtained without entering his house. The fact that thermal devices are not widely used or familiar to the general public also bolstered Kyllo's expectation of privacy, in Scalia's view.

EXCERPTS

From Justice Scalia's majority opinion: "We think that obtaining by sense-enhancing technology any information regarding the interior of the home that could not otherwise have been obtained without physical intrusion into a constitutionally protected area constitutes a search—at least where (as here) the technology in question is not in general public use. This assures preservation of that degree of privacy against government that existed when the Fourth Amendment was adopted. On the basis of this criterion, the information obtained by the thermal imager in this case was the product of a search. . . .

"We have said that the Fourth Amendment draws 'a firm line at the entrance to the house'. . . That line, we think, must be not only firm but also bright—which requires clear specification of those methods of surveillance that require a warrant. While it is certainly possible to conclude from the videotape of the thermal imaging that occurred in this case that no 'significant' compromise of the homeowner's privacy has occurred, we must take the long view, from the original meaning of the Fourth Amendment forward."

From Justice Stevens's dissent: "The ordinary use of the senses might enable a neighbor or passerby to notice the heat emanating from a building, particularly if it is vented, as was the case here. Additionally, any member of the public might notice that one part of a house is warmer than another part or a nearby building if, for example, rainwater evaporates or snow melts at different rates across its surfaces. Such use of the senses would not convert into an unreasonable search if, instead, an adjoining neighbor allowed an officer onto her property to verify her perceptions with a sensitive thermometer. Nor, in my view, does such observation become an unreasonable search if made from a distance with the aid of a device that merely discloses that the exterior of one house, or one area of the house, is much warmer than another. Nothing more occurred in this case."

IMPACT

The Court's ruling in *Kyllo* was viewed as an important statement by the Court that government should be cautious as it makes use of newer and more intrusive technologies to investigate crimes.

A few months after the decision the terrorist attacks of September 11, 2001, occurred, and government once again was given a freer hand to conduct investigations. Some commentators even suggested that if *Kyllo* had come to the Court after 9/11, the justices might have ruled differently.

In the years since the decision, *Kyllo* appears not to have imposed major restrictions on police investigations. For example, in the 2005 decision *Illinois v. Caballes,* the Court said it was constitutional for police, during routine traffic stops, to allow drug-detecting dogs to sniff cars that have been stopped, even in the absence of any suspicion of wrongdoing.

The Court majority, including Justices Scalia and Thomas, said the *Caballes* case was different from *Kyllo,* because the dog would detect only illegal materials, whereas the thermal imager can detect both illegal and legal activities—such as a resident taking a sauna or bath.

Other related cases mentioned in the Separation of Powers section

Myers v. United States (1926)
Schechter Poultry Corp. v. United States (1935) (see p. 49)
Cooper v. Aaron (1958)
Bowsher v. Synar (1986)
Morrison v. Olson (1988)
Printz v. United States (1997)
Hamdi v. Rumsfeld (2004) (See Detainee Cases, p. 344)

SEPARATION OF POWERS

The fear of an all-powerful king prompted the Framers of the Constitution to create a government with three branches, each with its own enumerated responsibilities. But the branches are not entirely separate: Each one interacts with the others to ensure that none gets too powerful. The result is a sometimes unwieldy and untidy form of governance that the public grumbles about but is unlikely to alter. "The doctrine of separation of powers was adopted," the late Justice Louis Brandeis wrote, "not to promote efficiency but to preclude the exercise of arbitrary power." The job of refereeing disputes between the branches, and defining those enumerated powers, has fallen to the Supreme Court and resulted in some of its most important decisions.

Marbury v. Madison

Decided February 24, 1803
5 U.S. 137
laws.findlaw.com/US/5/137.html

DECISION

The Supreme Court has the power to review acts of Congress and to declare laws unconstitutional and invalid. The Court struck down a law that increased its authority to issue "writs of mandamus," or orders to government officials.

BACKGROUND

In the early days of the Republic, the Supreme Court did not occupy an exalted position in the government. When the capital city was being built, no one thought to create a separate building or even a chamber for the Court's proceedings. Instead, as an afterthought, the Court was assigned to a "meanly furnished" room on the first floor of the Capitol building. This oversight would not be corrected until 1935, when the Supreme Court building was completed.

The Court was so unimportant to the new nation that John Jay, the first chief justice, resigned to become governor of New York, a job he thought more worthwhile. Jay later complained that the Court position lacked "energy, weight, and dignity."

All that would change under John Marshall, who served as chief justice from 1801 to 1835. The vehicle for this change was *Marbury v. Madison*. Compared with the ultimate importance of the decision in the nation's history, the actual facts of the case were trivial. As Court historian Leo Pfeffer wrote in *This Honorable Court* concerning *Marbury v. Madison,* "A mighty oak has grown out of a quite insignificant acorn, for as important as the decision in the case may have been, so unimportant was the specific law suit which gave rise to it."

The case arose out of the political dispute over the so-called midnight judges, whose commissions were signed by President John Adams on the final night of his administration in 1801. Following Thomas Jefferson's victory over Adams in the election of 1800, Adams's Federalist allies in Congress sought to extend their party's influence by passing legislation that authorized sixteen federal circuit judges and forty-two justices of the peace in Washington, D.C. Congress also reduced the size of the Supreme Court from six to five justices to deprive Jefferson of any quick appointments.

Adams appointed the judges, and the Senate confirmed them. Adams was completing the final paperwork by signing the commissions that would allow the judges to begin work. For reasons still unknown, John Marshall—who was performing the dual task of secretary of state and chief justice at the time—failed to deliver the commissions to all of the appointed judges.

William Marbury and three other appointees who did not receive their commissions petitioned the new president's secretary of state, James Madison, to deliver them. But Jefferson, who was thinking of abolishing the new judgeships, told Madison to hold off. The four appointees in limbo went to the Supreme Court to ask that it order Madison to deliver their commissions.

Marshall, whose initial error launched the case, took a central and confrontational role in resolving it, a situation that would be unheard of today. In December 1801 he ordered the Jefferson administration to respond to Marbury's request at the next session of the Court. The first major test of the power of the Court in relation to the other branches of government was set in motion. The showdown was delayed because Congress, seeking to ward off just such a confrontation, had passed a law putting off the next session of the Court to February 1803, some fourteen months later.

When the Court finally did take up the case, no one appeared to argue on behalf of Madison and the Jefferson administration. Jefferson apparently was content to let the Court rule and deal with the consequences later. The Court took testimony from others, ascertaining that the commissions had been signed but had mysteriously disappeared.

VOTE

4–0, with Chief Justice John Marshall writing the opinion of the Court. Joining him were Justices William Paterson, Bushrod Washington, and Samuel Chase. Justices William Cushing and Alfred Moore did not participate.

HIGHLIGHTS

Chief Justice Marshall faced a dilemma in the case. If he followed his anti-Jefferson inclinations and ordered the commissions delivered to Marbury and the others, Jefferson would almost certainly defy the order, which the Court had no power to enforce. Another possibility was that Jefferson would call for Marshall's impeachment. On the other hand, if the Court dismissed Marbury's plea, it would reaffirm its status as a weakling in the battle among the branches. Marshall, who had probably been weighing his options and even drafting the opinion during the Court's long recess, came up with a third alternative—one

James Madison, the fourth president of the United States, was secretary of state during the events leading to the case of *Marbury v. Madison* (1803). After he refused to deliver the commissions of several federal appointees, William Marbury, one of those appointees, appealed to the Supreme Court for a writ of mandamus ordering Madison to fulfill this duty. Madison is depicted here in a Gilbert Stuart portrait.

Source: Library of Congress.

that asserted the Court's power in general—but not in this particular case.

The Court first ruled that Marbury and the others were in fact entitled to the commissions that had not been delivered to them. "When the officer is not removable at the will of the executive, the appointment is not revocable, and cannot be annulled. It has conferred legal rights" that cannot be revoked, the Court said.

If Marbury's legal rights had been violated, Marshall asserted, he was entitled to some sort of remedy. "The government of the United States has been emphatically termed a government of laws, and not of men. It will certainly cease to deserve this high appellation, if the laws furnish no remedy for the violation of a vested legal right."

The remedy in this instance is a writ of mandamus, Marshall wrote—just the kind of writ that Marbury sought, and just the kind that Congress had authorized the Court to issue when it established the court system in 1789. But—and this is the crux of the decision—Marshall ruled that Congress did not have the power under the Constitution to give the Court that authority. "The authority, therefore, given to the supreme court by the act establishing the judicial courts of the United States, to issue writs of mandamus to public officers appears not to be warranted by the constitution," Marshall wrote.

Congress, Marshall concluded, cannot act outside the Constitution, and the law that gave the Court mandamus power was unconstitutional. Paradoxically, by ruling that the Court was powerless to help Marbury, the Court was asserting its supreme power to rule acts of Congress unconstitutional.

EXCERPTS

From Chief Justice Marshall's majority opinion: "The constitution vests the whole judicial power of the United States in one supreme court, and such inferior courts as congress shall, from time to time, ordain and establish. This power is expressly extended to all cases arising under the laws of the United States; and consequently, in some form, may be exercised over the present case; because the right claimed is given by a law of the United States. . . .

"If it had been intended to leave it in the discretion of the legislature to apportion the judicial power between the supreme and inferior courts according to the will of that body, it would certainly have been useless to have proceeded further than to have defined the judicial power, and the tribunals in which it should be vested. The subsequent part of the section is mere surplusage, is entirely without meaning, if such is to be the construction. If congress remains at liberty to give this Court appellate jurisdiction, where the Constitution has declared their jurisdiction shall be original; and original jurisdiction, where the constitution has declared it shall be appellate; the distribution of jurisdiction made in the constitution, is form without substance. . . .

". . . The constitution is either a superior, paramount law, unchangeable by ordinary means, or it is on a level with ordinary legislative acts, and like other acts, is alterable when the legislature shall please to alter it.

"If the former part of the alternative be true, then a legislative act contrary to the constitution is not law: if the latter part be true, then written constitutions are absurd attempts, on the part of the people, to limit a power in its own nature illimitable. . . .

"It is emphatically the province and duty of the judicial department to say what the law is. Those who apply the rule to particular cases, must of necessity expound and interpret that rule. If two laws conflict with each other, the courts must decide on the operation of each. So, if a law be in opposition to the constitution: if both the law and the constitution apply to a particular case, so that the court must either decide that case conformably to the law, disregarding the constitution; or conformably to the constitution, disregarding the law: the court must determine which of these conflicting rules governs the case. This is of the very essence of judicial duty."

IMPACT

Compared to the number of state and local laws the Court invalidates each year, the number of congressional acts the Court strikes down is small. Even today, the Court usually announces such an opinion with regret. Imagine what it must have been like to do it for the first time. In a young nation where the boundary lines between the branches of government were still uncharted, it was a remarkable—and crucial—assertion of judicial power and independence.

The power of the courts to declare acts of the legislature unconstitutional had its roots in Britain and had been asserted in the *Federalist Papers*. But most scholars think it was essential for the U.S. Supreme Court to state its power explicitly, as a matter of positive law.

The powers of Congress and the president were clear from the start, writes Court scholar Alexander Bickel, but "the institution of the judiciary needed to be summoned up out of the constitutional vapors, shaped and maintained; and the great chief justice, John Marshall—not single-handed, but first and foremost—was there to do it and did."

Historian Charles Warren called *Marbury v. Madison* "the fundamental decision in the American system of constitutional law." Court scholar Bernard Schwartz said the decision is the "*sine qua non* of the American constitutional machinery: draw out this particular bolt, and the machinery falls to pieces."

The decision was not immediately recognized as a landmark, however. Initial press reports focused on the political aspects of the showdown between Jefferson and Marshall. And it took more than fifty years before the Court again struck down an act of Congress. After that, Supreme Court rejection of acts of Congress became less unusual. More than 140 laws have been declared unconstitutional by the Supreme Court—ranging from the Missouri Compromise to the federal income tax to the line item veto.

The ruling was notable for another reason. In the Court's earliest days, it was common for justices to write individual opinions in each case. Marshall decided that the Court should speak with one voice, so *Marbury v. Madison* was written as the single opinion for the entire Court. Justices could still write concurring or dissenting opinions, but one writing stood as the decision of the Court. In 1999 Justice Stephen Breyer raised eyebrows by using the pronoun *I* in a majority opinion, rather than *we*. Breyer later offered assurances in correspondence with law professors that the usage was inadvertent and did not represent a break with the Marshall tradition.

William Marbury, left, brought the suit against James Madison that led to the landmark decision *Marbury v. Madison* (1803). The opinion of Chief Justice John Marshall, right, in the case established the Supreme Court's authority to review the constitutionality of acts of Congress.

Source: left, Maryland Historical Society, Baltimore; right, Library of Congress.

In recent years a slow-simmering debate over the wisdom of *Marbury* had taken place in political and academic circles, though it appears unlikely that such a bedrock precedent would be upended anytime soon. Both liberals and conservatives have questioned the wisdom of *Marbury*'s grant of the power of judicial review to the Supreme Court. In the early 1980s Edwin Meese III, attorney general in the Reagan administration, said the executive branch should not necessarily feel bound by Supreme Court rulings interpreting the meaning of laws. More recently some liberal scholars, including Georgetown University's Mark Tushnet, have argued that judicial review has yielded bad results as often as good ones and is antidemocratic.

"I doubt that there's a good argument—from the point of view of a person who is a democrat and a constitutionalist—for giving the courts the last word on what the Constitution means," Tushnet wrote in an online debate hosted by *Legal Affairs* magazine in 2005. In reply, Duke University law professor Erwin Chemerinsky wrote, "I think that the basic answer came from *Marbury v. Madison*: the limits of the Constitution have no meaning if they are not enforced and the other branches of government see their role as pleasing constituents, not upholding the Constitution. Courts, especially federal judges who are not electorally accountable, are more likely to see their role as enforcing the Constitution."

McCulloch v. Maryland

Decided March 6, 1819
17 U.S. 316
laws.findlaw.com/US/17/316.html

DECISION

Congress has the authority to establish a national bank, and states may not impose taxes on it. Even though the Constitution had created a government of enumerated powers, and creation of a national bank was not one of those powers, the Court said the Constitution gave Congress wide authority to pass laws "necessary and proper" for the execution of its duties.

BACKGROUND

One of the reasons the Framers threw out the Articles of Confederation and replaced them with the Constitution was to create a more effective national government. But even after the Constitution was ratified, conflict persisted among state and national leaders over just how strong the national government should be in relation to the states. As with *Marbury v. Madison* in 1803 on the question of judicial power, it fell to Chief Justice John Marshall to take a major role in resolving this fundamental conflict. (See *Marbury v. Madison*.)

The issue came to the Supreme Court in the form of a dispute over one of the early symbols of federal power: the creation of a national bank, which Secretary of the Treasury Alexander Hamilton and others viewed as necessary to foster development of the new nation. The bank would be a repository of federal funds and would provide the necessary money for national projects such as roads and canals.

Because the Constitution did not mention creation of a national bank in its list of powers granted to Congress, James Madison and Thomas Jefferson opposed it. But at Hamilton's urging, and with the support of George Washington, Congress created a national bank in 1791.

When the bank's charter expired in 1811, the Jefferson-dominated Congress did not renew it. With inflation and economic hardship created by the War of 1812, Congress again saw the need for a national bank. The Second Bank of the United States was chartered in 1816.

Several states worked to undermine the national bank, especially after its policies caused many people to withdraw funds from state banks. Maryland and other states passed laws imposing a tax on the national bank. When James McCulloch, head cashier of the bank's Baltimore branch, refused to pay the $15,000 tax, Maryland took McCulloch to court. Maryland courts sided with state officials, and McCulloch took the case to the Supreme Court.

Because of the high stakes involved, the Court's hearing of the case, which lasted nine days, drew national attention. The legendary Daniel Webster argued for the national bank, while Maryland's attorney general, Luther Martin, argued the other side.

VOTE

7–0, with Chief Justice John Marshall writing the opinion of the Court. Joining him were Justices Bushrod Washington, William Johnson, H. Brockholst Livingston, Thomas Todd, Gabriel Duvall, and Joseph Story.

HIGHLIGHTS

Chief Justice Marshall did not shy away from an undeniable fact: the Constitution did not explicitly authorize Congress to create a national bank. Nevertheless, Marshall concluded that Congress was acting within its powers to create the bank. Just as the Constitution did not authorize the bank, Marshall reasoned, it also did not prohibit it.

"There is no phrase" in the Constitution, Marshall wrote, which "excludes incidental or implied powers; and which requires that everything granted shall be expressly and minutely described." The Constitution explicitly authorized creation of post offices, for example, but did not specifically make it a crime to rob a post office, Marshall noted. But Congress clearly had the power to make such an act a crime. A constitution that spelled out every conceivable power of Congress, Marshall said, would assume "the prolixity of a legal code, and could scarcely be embraced by the human mind."

The power to create a national bank could be implied, Marshall said, from several of the enumerated powers of Congress. "Although, among the enumerated powers of Government, we do not find the word 'bank' or 'incorporation,' we find the great powers, to lay and collect taxes; to borrow money; to regulate commerce; to declare and conduct a war; and to raise and support armies and navies." Most important, Marshall said, the power to create the national bank flowed from the provision of the Constitution (Article I, Section 8) that gave Congress the power to "make all laws which shall be necessary and proper, for carrying into execution the foregoing powers."

Maryland had argued forcefully that because there were other ways to carry out the powers of Congress in this area, creation of a national bank could not be termed "necessary." But Marshall went on at length to make the point that a measure deemed "necessary" did not have to be essential or the only way to reach a goal. Marshall also argued that the necessary

Despite the Supreme Court's decision in *McCulloch v. Maryland* (1819), the Bank of the United States remained under attack. This cartoon by Henry R. Robinson depicts President Andrew Jackson taking on the bank with his veto stick. Vice President Martin Van Buren, center, helps kill the monster, whose heads represent Nicholas Biddle, the bank's president, and directors of the state banks.

Source: Library of Congress.

and proper clause had been added to the Constitution to enlarge congressional power, not to restrict it.

From this analysis, Marshall concluded that if Congress could create the national bank, the state of Maryland could not tax it. "The power to tax involves the power to destroy," Marshall said, and under the federal system states could not endeavor to destroy a federal institution. "The American people have declared their constitution and the laws made in pursuance thereof to be supreme," Marshall said. Allowing Maryland to tax the national bank would "transfer the supremacy, in fact, to the states."

If this tax remained on the books, Marshall said, states could tax other federal institutions as well, which would "defeat all the ends of government. This was not intended by the American people. They did not design to make their government dependent on the states."

EXCERPTS

From Chief Justice Marshall's majority opinion: "This government is acknowledged by all, to be one of enumerated powers. The principle, that it can exercise only the powers granted to it, would seem too apparent, to have required to be enforced by all those arguments, which its enlightened friends, while it was depending before the people, found it necessary to urge; that principle is now universally admitted. But the question respecting the extent of the powers actually granted, is perpetually arising, and will probably continue to arise, so long as our system shall exist. In discussing these questions, the conflicting powers of the general and state governments must be brought into view, and the supremacy of their respective laws, when they are in opposition, must be settled.

"If any one proposition could command the universal assent of mankind, we might expect it would be this—that the government of the Union, though limited in its powers, is supreme within its sphere of action. This would seem to result, necessarily, from its nature. It is the government of all; its powers are delegated by all; it represents all, and acts for all. . . .

". . . [I]t may with great reason be contended that a government, intrusted with such ample powers, on the due execution of which the happiness and prosperity of the nation so vitally depends, must also be intrusted with ample means for their execution. . . .

"We admit, as all must admit, that the powers of the government are limited, and that its limits are not to be transcended. But we think the sound construction of the constitution must allow to the national legislature that discretion, with respect to the means by which the powers it confers are to be carried into execution, which will enable that body to perform the high duties assigned to it in the manner most beneficial to the people. Let the end be legitimate, let it be within the scope of the constitution, and all means which are appropriate, which are plainly adapted to that end, which are not prohibited, but consist with the letter and spirit of the constitution, are constitutional.

"The court has bestowed on this subject its most deliberate consideration. The result is a conviction that the states have no power, by taxation or otherwise, to retard, impede, burden, or in any manner control, the operations of the constitutional laws enacted by congress to carry into execution the powers vested in the general government. This is, we think, the unavoidable consequence of that supremacy which the constitution has declared."

IMPACT

The Court's decision caused an uproar. To many, the national bank, widely reviled and hated, did not seem to deserve the support of the Supreme Court, no matter what the constitutional theory behind it. Ohio defied the decision and continued to collect the tax. In defiance of a federal injunction, an Ohio official went to the bank branch in Chillicothe, where he jumped over the counter and took more than $100,000 from its vaults.

Critics persisted in attacking the decision for years as a usurpation of states' rights. The criticisms prompted Marshall, under a pseudonym, to write several essays defending the decision for a Richmond newspaper. In 1832 President Andrew Jackson vetoed a bill extending the charter of the national bank, and it died. It was replaced at first by federally chartered private banks and then by the Federal Reserve Bank, which still operates today.

With Marshall's elegant writing, *McCulloch v. Maryland* is remembered as much for its eloquence as its doctrine. It would be impossible, however, to overstate its lasting impact on the U.S. government. It forecast many of the constitutional debates that still rage today, and its memorable phrases—such as "the power to tax involves the power to destroy"—are still frequently cited.

Marshall also said, somewhat cryptically, "We must never forget that it is a constitution we are expounding," underlining the Court's role as the prime interpreter of the nation's founding document. But Marshall was also suggesting, in the view of scholars, that the Constitution is not a dry catalogue of laws or codes; rather, it is an organic document that is meant to be adapted to changing national conditions. Conservative scholars dispute that, arguing that the Constitution should be read literally and not elaborated on with speculation about how the Framers would react to a given modern-day dispute.

Those same conservatives also challenge Marshall's other often-quoted lines that seem to give Congress a blank check to intervene in areas not contemplated in the Constitution: "Let the end be legitimate, let it be within the scope of the constitution, and all means which are appropriate, which are plainly adapted to that end, which are not prohibited, but consist with the letter and spirit of the constitution, are constitutional." Those phrases—and the entire decision—inform virtually every act of Congress and every regulation issued by a federal agency.

The current Supreme Court appears to be moving away from Marshall's broad interpretation of the necessary and proper clause and his expansive view of the role of Congress and the national government. Instead, the Court is according more respect for the Tenth Amendment, which reserves undelegated powers to the states. Marshall had given the Tenth Amendment short shrift in *McCulloch v. Maryland,* but it is cited with increasing regularity today. For example, in *Printz v. United States* (1997) the Court struck down a federal law that required local officials to keep records on gun purchasers for the federal government. The law violated the Tenth Amendment by infringing on state sovereignty, Justice Antonin Scalia said, so it was not "proper" under the necessary and proper clause.

Cherokee Cases

Cherokee Nation v. Georgia
Decided March 18, 1831
30 U.S. 1
laws.findlaw.com/US/30/1.html

Worcester v. Georgia
Decided March 3, 1832
31 U.S. 515
laws.findlaw.com/US/31/515.html

DECISION

In *Cherokee Nation v. Georgia,* the Court ruled that it had no jurisdiction under Article III of the Constitution to consider the Cherokees' request to stop the state of Georgia from taking over Cherokee lands. The Cherokee Nation is a "domestic dependent" nation, the Court found, not a sovereign nation. In *Worcester v. Georgia,* the Court modified that view, finding that the Cherokee Nation is a "distinct community" where Georgia laws have no force.

BACKGROUND

From the earliest days of the Republic, the federal government made treaties that recognized the right of Cherokees and other Native American tribes to retain control of their lands in northern Georgia and eastern Tennessee. For several decades, Cherokees, Creeks, and Choctaws in those areas made their livelihood in peace as farmers alongside non–Native American Georgians.

But the state of Georgia wanted to take the Native Americans' land for its own, and it pressured the federal government to support its takeover. Early presidents were reluctant to upset settled treaties and slow to support Georgia. When gold was discovered on Cherokee land in 1829, the Georgia legislature lost its patience and passed laws nullifying the treaties and confiscating Cherokee lands. At the same time Andrew Jackson, whose sympathies were with Georgia, took office as president, so he supported the state's attempts to oust the Cherokees and other tribes. Faced with this bleak political landscape, the Cherokees went to court, hiring as their lawyer former attorney general William Wirt, a Jackson opponent. Forgoing lower federal or state courts, Wirt went straight to the Supreme Court asking it to stop Georgia from enforcing its laws against the Cherokees.

The Court in March 1831 ruled it had no jurisdiction over the dispute, thereby sidestepping the question of the constitutionality of Georgia's laws. The hopes of the Cherokees were dashed. But Marshall's opinion was sympathetic toward the Cherokees, and soon the issue returned to the Court.

In Georgia's campaign to remove the Cherokees, the state became suspicious that a group of New England missionaries was encouraging tribe members not to emigrate. To silence the alleged troublemaking, state officials arrested Samuel Worcester and nine other missionaries for violating one of the new state laws, which required all whites living among the Cherokees to take an oath pledging allegiance to the laws of Georgia. The missionaries refused to take the oath and were sentenced to four years in prison.

Wirt seized on the missionaries' plight to mount a new challenge against Georgia, this time with white plaintiffs rather than the Cherokee Nation. After Georgia courts rejected Wirt's appeal against the law, the Supreme Court heard the case in February 1832. In this case, as with the earlier one, Georgia refused to appear before the Supreme Court to argue its side of the case.

VOTE

Cherokee Nation v. Georgia: 4–2, with Chief Justice John Marshall writing for the majority. Joining him were Justices Henry Baldwin, William Johnson, and John McLean. Dissenting were Justices Smith Thompson and Joseph Story. Justice Gabriel Duvall did not participate.

Worcester v. Georgia: 5–1, with Chief Justice John Marshall writing for the majority, joined by Justices Smith Thompson, Joseph Story, Gabriel Duvall, and John McLean. Justice Henry Baldwin dissented. Justice William Johnson did not participate.

HIGHLIGHTS

In *Cherokee Nation,* Chief Justice Marshall made it clear he thought the Cherokees had gotten a raw deal from Georgia. Marshall sprinkled references to their plight throughout the opinion. But he also, clearly, wanted to avoid getting deeply into the three-way dispute between the Cherokees, the federal government, and Georgia. As the Supreme Court has done before and since, he managed to avoid the main issues by finding that the Court had no jurisdiction over the suit.

The court focused on Article III, Section 2, the part of the U.S. Constitution that lays out the judicial power of the United States. One of the areas to which power extends is cases "between a state . . . and foreign states." Clearly since Georgia is one of the parties, half of the requirement is met. But is the Cherokee Nation a "foreign state?" Although the Cherokees' lawyer made the case that it is a foreign state with "great earnestness and ability," Marshall wrote, the Court was not persuaded. The relationship between a tribe and the United States is unique, he wrote, but in the end he found it to be one "like that of a ward to his guardian," rather than that of two sovereign nations. "They look to our government for protection; rely upon its kindness and its power; appeal to it for relief to their wants; and address the president as their great father," Marshall wrote.

In dissent, Justice Thompson analyzed the relationship differently, primarily because it is defined in treaties. Treaties are made between nations, so for Thompson, it was clear that the Cherokee Nation fit the "foreign states" requirement.

A modern-day Supreme Court justice, Stephen Breyer, has written frequently about the Cherokee cases, and he also wonders why Marshall did not look to a different part of the same section of the Constitution to find that the Court had jurisdiction. Article III, Section 2, also grants judicial power in cases arising under treaties. Even though a Cherokee lawyer invoked

this part of the Constitution, Breyer says that any reference to it was "strangely absent" from Marshall's majority opinion.

Jurisdiction was less of a problem in the second case involving the imprisonment of Samuel Worcester, the missionary. The Judiciary Act creating the Supreme Court said it was the final arbiter of criminal appeals from the states as well as of disputes in which state laws are found to violate treaties.

Marshall went on to review the long history of Native American treaties in which the United States had promised to respect tribal sovereignty and the supremacy of tribal laws, not state laws, inside tribal boundaries. As a result, the Georgia law under which Worcester was arrested is void, and "the judgment a nullity." The court ordered the release of the missionaries.

EXCERPTS

From Chief Justice Marshall's majority opinion in *Cherokee Nation:* "If courts were permitted to indulge their sympathies, a case better calculated to excite them can scarcely be imagined. A people once numerous, powerful, and truly independent, found by our ancestors in the quiet and uncontrolled possession of an ample domain, gradually sinking beneath our superior policy, our arts and our arms, have yielded their lands by successive treaties, each of which contains a solemn guarantee of the residue, until they retain no more of their formerly extensive territory than is deemed necessary to their comfortable subsistence. . . .

"Though the Indians are acknowledged to have an unquestionable, and, heretofore, unquestioned right to the lands they occupy, until that right shall be extinguished by a voluntary cession to our government; yet it may well be doubted whether those tribes which reside within the acknowledged boundaries of the United States can, with strict accuracy, be denominated foreign nations. They may, more correctly, perhaps, be denominated domestic dependent nations. . . .

"The mere question of right might perhaps be decided by this court, in a proper case, with proper parties. But the court is asked to do more than decide on the title. The bill requires us to control the legislature of Georgia, and to restrain the exertion of its physical force. The propriety of such an interposition by the court may well be questioned. It savours too much of the exercise of political power, to be within the proper province of the judicial department."

From Chief Justice John Marshall's majority opinion in *Worcester:* "The Cherokee nation, then, is a distinct community occupying its own territory, with boundaries accurately described, in which the laws of Georgia can have no force, and which the citizens of Georgia have no right to enter, but with the assent of the Cherokees themselves, or in conformity with treaties, and with the acts of congress. The whole intercourse be-

In *Cherokee Nation v. Georgia* (1831) and *Worcester v. Georgia* (1832), the Supreme Court addressed the sovereignty of the Cherokee Nation and Georgia's attempt to confiscate the Cherokees' land. The latter opinion declared the Cherokees to be sovereign, but did little else. Both decisions helped set in motion the chain of events leading to the forced migration known as the Trail of Tears, during which some 4,000 Cherokees died of cold, hunger, and disease on their way to resettlement on western lands. The Trail of Tears is depicted in this 1942 painting by Robert Lindneux.

Source: Woolaroc Museum, Bartlesville, Oklahoma.

tween the United States and this nation, is, by our constitution and laws, vested in the government of the United States. . . .

"If the review which has been taken be correct, and we think it is, the acts of Georgia are repugnant to the constitution, laws, and treaties of the United States.

"They interfere forcibly with the relations established between the United States and the Cherokee nation, the regulation of which, according to the settled principles of our constitution, are committed exclusively to the government of the union.

"They are in direct hostility with treaties, repeated in a succession of years, which mark out the boundary that separates the Cherokee country from Georgia; guaranty to them all the land within their boundary; solemnly pledge the faith of the United States to restrain their citizens from trespassing on it; and recognize the pre-existing power of the nation to govern itself."

IMPACT

The Cherokee cases have been called the Court's most important decisions in determining how Native American nations are regarded under the Constitution. Though the first ruling, with its paternalistic language, describes a relationship of dependency, the second one goes much further toward recognizing the sovereignty of tribal nations. *Worcester v. Georgia* is still often cited in Indian cases to support claims of self-determination by tribes in disputes over everything from water rights to the regulation of casinos. The decisions also established the primacy of federal courts in deciding disputes over Native American sovereignty.

But the Cherokee cases also stand as a symbol of the limits of judicial power, if the other branches of government disrespect what the Supreme Court has done.

Even though the *Worcester* decision waxed eloquent about the independence of the Cherokee nation, it did little to help the cause of the Cherokees. In fact the rulings turned out to be an important link in the chain of events that led to the devastating migration of the Cherokees to Oklahoma along what is now called the Trail of Tears.

Soon after the *Worcester* ruling, as Breyer has written, Justice Story wrote to his friends of his relief at having the case behind him. "Thanks be to God, the court can wash their hands clean of the iniquity of oppressing the Indians and disregarding their rights." But he cautioned that "Georgia is full of anger and violence," and he predicted the state would defy the Court's ruling, with the tacit support of President Jackson. He was correct.

Georgia courts simply refused to obey the Supreme Court's order to release the missionaries. And Jackson did nothing to help. He believed he had as much right to tell the Supreme Court what to do as the other way around. It is part of presidential folklore that Jackson, in response to the *Worcester* ruling, said, "Well, John Marshall has made his decision; now let him enforce it!" But many scholars new believe Jackson never spoke those words.

As the missionaries remained in jail, Marshall wrote to Justice Story, "I yield slowly and reluctantly to the conviction that our Constitution cannot last." Eventually the missionaries were released after they agreed to drop their suit against the state.

As for the Cherokees, Georgia continued to pressure them to leave. In 1835, whether through trickery or not, a small group of Cherokees signed a treaty agreeing to leave Georgia, and the Senate ratified the treaty. In spite of the angry opposition of most Cherokees to the treaty, the U.S. Army moved in to oust the tribe, forcing thousands of Cherokees from their homes. In the thousand-mile march to what is now Oklahoma, an estimated 4,000 Cherokees died.

"There is an obvious winner, the Supreme Court of the United States; an obvious loser, the Cherokee tribe; and an obvious irony, namely that the Supreme Court and the Cherokee tribe were allies," Justice Breyer said in a lecture in 2000 before the Supreme Court Historical Society. The cases also teach another lesson, Breyer said: "the insufficiency of a judicial decision alone to bring about the rule of law."

Breyer drew a parallel between the *Worcester* decision and *Cooper v. Aaron,* the 1958 Supreme Court decision that followed the defiance of another state—Arkansas—against the Court's rulings against school segregation. Breyer wrote, "Perhaps President Jackson's actions helped President Dwight D. Eisenhower to understand both the importance of enforcing a rule of law and the importance of protecting fundamental liberties."

Humphrey's Executor v. United States

Decided May 27, 1935
295 U.S. 602
laws.findlaw.com/US/295/602.html

DECISION

The president does not have the power to remove a member of an independent federal regulatory agency without the consent of Congress. The Court limited the power of the executive branch to control independent agencies through the removal of officers.

BACKGROUND

A Republican member of Congress from 1903 to 1917, William Humphrey of Washington was known as such a fervent protector of business interests that progressives called him "Jesse James." So it was not surprising that Humphrey became an ardent champion of business as soon as President Calvin Coolidge named him to the Federal Trade Commission (FTC) in 1925.

Humphrey's presence changed the commission, which had been created in 1914 in part to rein in monopolistic corporations. His vote in favor of corporations loosened the commission's regulatory grip. "So far as I can prevent it, the Federal Trade Commission is not going to be used as a publicity bureau to spread socialistic propaganda," Humphrey said early in his tenure.

By the time Franklin D. Roosevelt was elected president in 1932, says historian William E. Leuchtenberg, "Humphrey had become a symbol of all that progressives abhorred in the old order." Once Congress had passed Roosevelt's New Deal legislation in the legendary First Hundred Days, the president was eager to shape federal agencies, including the FTC, in ways that would ensure his policies were implemented.

Unfortunately for Roosevelt, Humphrey's term at the FTC was not due to expire until 1938. Unwilling to wait that long, Roosevelt fired him. The commissioner put up a fight, refusing to leave his office, but Roosevelt was adamant. On October 7, 1933, the president sent Humphrey a telegram alerting him that he no longer had a position in the agency. In December Humphrey filed suit in the U.S. Court of Claims, claiming he had been improperly removed from office and asking for $1,251.39 in back pay. In February 1934 Humphrey died of a stroke, but his lawsuit, now entitled *Humphrey's Executor v. United States,* continued.

The Roosevelt administration had every reason to be confident that the challenge to the president's removal power would lose. In *Myers v. United States* (1926) the Supreme Court had ruled that presidents could remove officials such as postmasters. The Court said the power of removal was part of the president's executive power to implement and enforce the laws passed by Congress. But Humphrey's lawyers countered that Congress had intended for the FTC to be an independent agency. If a president could dismiss a commissioner without good cause, that independence would be threatened.

VOTE

9–0, with Justice George Sutherland writing the opinion of the Court. Joining him were Chief Justice Charles Evans Hughes and Justices Willis Van Devanter, Benjamin N. Cardozo, James C. McReynolds, Louis D. Brandeis, Owen J. Roberts, Harlan Fiske Stone, and Pierce Butler.

HIGHLIGHTS

The Court reviewed the legislation creating the FTC, noting its provision that "any commissioner may be removed by the President for inefficiency, neglect of duty, or malfeasance in office." The law also states that no more than three of the five members of the commission could be members of one party. Sutherland concluded from the language that by listing the possible reasons for removal, Congress intended that no other reasons for removal would be permitted.

The Court also said FTC commissioners were not the same kind of government official as postmasters, making the *Myers* decision inapplicable. "The office of a postmaster is so essentially unlike the office now involved that the decision in the *Myers* Case cannot be accepted as controlling our decision here," wrote Sutherland. "A postmaster is an executive officer restricted to the performance of executive functions."

By contrast, the Court said, "The Federal Trade Commission is an administrative body created by Congress to carry into effect legislative policies embodied in the statute in accordance with the legislative standard therein prescribed, and to perform other specified duties as a legislative or as a judicial aid. Such a body cannot in any proper sense be characterized as an arm or an eye of the executive." The commission has some attributes of a judicial agency and some of a legislative body, the Court said, making it inappropriate for a president to remove a member at will.

Recalling the *Marbury v. Madison* decision of 1803, the Court said presidential removal of officers who are not performing strictly executive functions is unconstitutional. Deciding whether a given official wields executive powers and can be removed has to be done on a case-by-case basis, the Court said.

"To the extent that, between the decision in the *Myers* Case, which sustains the unrestrictable power of the President to remove purely executive officers, and our present decision that such power does not extend to an office such as that here involved, there shall remain a field of doubt, we leave such cases as may fall within it for future consideration and determination as they may arise," the Court said.

EXCERPTS

From Justice Sutherland's opinion of the Court: "We think it plain under the Constitution that illimitable power of removal is not possessed by the President in respect of officers of the character of those just named. The authority of Congress, in creating quasi-legislative or quasi-judicial agencies, to require them to act in discharge of their duties independently of executive control cannot well be doubted, and that authority includes, as an appropriate incident, power to fix the period during which they shall continue in office, and to forbid their removal except for cause in the meantime. For it is quite evident that one who holds his office only during the pleasure of another cannot be depended upon to maintain an attitude of independence against the latter's will.

"The fundamental necessity of maintaining each of the three general departments of government entirely free from the control or coercive influence, direct or indirect, of either of the others, has often been stressed and is hardly open to serious question. So much is implied in the very fact of the separation of the powers of these departments by the Constitution, and in the rule which recognizes their essential coequality. The sound application of a principle that makes one master in his own house precludes him from imposing his control in the house of another who is master there. . . .

"The power of removal here claimed for the President falls within this principle, since its coercive influence threatens the independence of a commission, which is not only wholly disconnected from the executive department, but which, as already fully appears, was created by Congress as a means of carrying into operation legislative and judicial powers, and as an agency of the legislative and judicial departments."

IMPACT

The Court's ruling in *Humphrey's Executor* was overshadowed by another decision the Court handed down that day, *Schechter Poultry Corp. v. United States*. The so-called "sick chicken" case was, like *Humphrey's Executor*, a sharp defeat for Roosevelt's New Deal. But *Schechter Poultry* was better known because it struck down major features of the National Industrial Recovery Act, the centerpiece of Roosevelt's effort to bring the nation out of the Great Depression. (See *Schechter Poultry Corp. v. United States*.)

Some scholars now believe that, in fact, Roosevelt was more upset with the decision in *Humphrey's Executor* than with *Schechter Poultry*. The administration felt that the Court had gone out of its way to make it appear that Roosevelt had thumbed his nose at the Constitution when he fired Humphrey, when in fact, the *Myers* decision had given him reason to believe the firing was proper. "I really think the decision that made Roosevelt madder at the Court than any other decision was that damn little case of *Humphrey's Executor v. United States,*" said then–Justice Department official Robert H. Jackson, whom Roosevelt later named to the Court.

In the book *The Supreme Court Reborn,* Leuchtenberg says, "The *Humphrey* ruling went far to persuade the President that, sooner or later, he would have to take bold action against a Court that, from personal animus, was determined to embarrass him and to destroy his program." In 1937 Roosevelt embarked on his ill-fated "Court-packing" campaign, aimed at neutralizing the anti–New Deal Court by increasing its size and filling it with his appointees.

Beyond the immediate political repercussions, the ruling in *Humphrey's Executor* has served as a check on presidential power. Unlike the Court's other anti–New Deal decisions, *Humphrey's Executor* was never reversed and still stands. It has been invoked in several cases in recent years—including the 1988 decision *Morrison v. Olson,* which upheld the independent counsel law—as a framework for deciding whether a president may or may not remove an official who has independent duties.

Youngstown Sheet and Tube Co. v. Sawyer

Decided June 2, 1952
343 U.S. 579
laws.findlaw.com/US/343/579.html

DECISION

President Truman did not have the power under the Constitution or any law to order the seizure of the nation's steel mills to prevent a labor strike. Only Congress, through legislation, could authorize such a seizure.

BACKGROUND

Congress never declared war in the Korean "conflict," but it was a war nevertheless. Repelling the invasion of South Korea by troops from the north, which began in June 1950, was a massive undertaking for the United States, costing more than 33,000 U.S. lives and billions of dollars in arms and equipment.

The U.S. economy was on a war footing to produce the matériel needed for the U.S. troops. So when a labor dispute between the United Steelworkers of America and the steel industry threatened to trigger a strike that would shut down the nation's steel mills, President Harry S. Truman felt the need to act quickly. On April 4, 1952, the union signaled that a strike was imminent. Five days later, after mediation efforts failed, Truman issued an executive order directing a cabinet member, Secretary of Commerce Charles Sawyer, to seize and operate the mills. Truman noted that "steel is an indispensable component of substantially all . . . weapons and materials" needed in the war, making the action essential to the national interest. As soon as the order was issued, the union called off the strike. U.S. flags were hoisted over the steel mills, and production continued as usual.

It was an extraordinary but not unprecedented action. In previous wars, presidents had seized businesses and private facilities deemed necessary for national security, but most of those seizures had been authorized by federal law. The steel

companies affected by the current order, led by the Youngstown firm, went to court claiming that Truman was acting without any congressional or constitutional authorization.

Truman believed his authority to act was based, among other things, on the president's constitutional role as commander in chief. In addition, Truman may have been emboldened by the fact that four of the justices were his own appointees, and some of the others shared an expansive, Roosevelt-era view of the powers of the presidency. Historians have reported that Truman met privately with Chief Justice Fred M. Vinson before issuing the order and received assurances that the seizure was constitutional.

Because of the urgency of the issue, the courts expedited the case. A trial judge ruled against the Truman administration, and an appeals court propelled the case directly to the Supreme Court. On May 12, just over a month after the seizure order was issued, the justices heard oral arguments. As soon as the justices met in conference, it was clear that Vinson's calculations had been wrong.

VOTE

6–3, with Justice Hugo L. Black writing the majority opinion. Joining him were Justices Felix Frankfurter, William O. Douglas, Robert H. Jackson, Harold H. Burton, and Tom C. Clark. Dissenting were Chief Justice Fred M. Vinson and Justices Stanley F. Reed and Sherman Minton.

HIGHLIGHTS

The majority and the dissenters took nearly opposite views of presidential powers and constitutional interpretation. Justice Black took a literal approach, asserting that if neither the Constitution nor any act of Congress authorized the president's action, it could not be permitted. "The President's power, if any, to issue the order must stem either from an act of Congress or from the Constitution itself," Black declared.

As Melvin Urofsky put it in his book *Division and Discord,* Chief Justice Vinson's view was quite the opposite. "The president could, in response to a national emergency, do everything except what had been specifically prohibited."

Black argued that, if anything, Congress had considered and rejected the notion of allowing presidents to seize property as a way of ending labor disputes. When Congress debated passage of the Taft-Hartley Act in 1947, legislators had decided that allowing seizures would interfere with collective bargaining. Instead, the law authorized other ways of preventing harmful strikes, including a "cooling-off" period, an avenue that Truman had not tried in the steel dispute.

No other law authorized the seizure, Black wrote, nor did any provision of the Constitution or the president's general powers as commander in chief. Only Congress, Black concluded, had the power to do what Truman had tried to do. "The power of Congress to adopt such public policies as those proclaimed by the order is beyond question," wrote Black. "It can authorize the taking of private property for public use. It can make laws regulating the relationships between employers and employees, prescribing rules designed to settle labor disputes, and fixing wages and working conditions in certain fields of our economy. The Constitution does not subject this law-making power of Congress to presidential or military supervision or control."

Justice Frankfurter, in a concurring opinion, reviewed the history of other presidential seizures in time of war, and found that most had been authorized by Congress. "A scheme of government like ours no doubt at times feels the lack of power to act with complete, all-embracing, swiftly moving authority," Frankfurter wrote. "No doubt a government with distributed authority, subject to be challenged in the courts of law, at least long enough to consider and adjudicate the challenge, labors under restrictions from which other governments are free. It has not been our tradition to envy such governments. In any event our government was designed to have such restrictions."

Justice Douglas agreed. "We pay a price for our system of checks and balances, for the distribution of power among the three branches of government. It is a price that today may seem exorbitant to many. Today a kindly President uses the seizure power to effect a wage increase and to keep the steel furnaces in production. Yet tomorrow, another President might use the same power to prevent a wage increase, to curb trade-unionists, to regiment labor as oppressively as industry thinks it has been regimented by this seizure."

In another concurrence, Justice Jackson wrote, "When the President takes measures incompatible with the expressed or implied will of Congress, his power is at its lowest ebb. . . . Presidential claim to a power at once so conclusive and preclusive must be scrutinized with caution, for what is at stake is the equilibrium established by our constitutional system."

Chief Justice Vinson's dissent argued that the president's power should be at its height in times of crisis. Under the majority's view, Vinson wrote, "the President is left powerless at the very moment when the need for action may be most pressing and when no one, other than he, is immediately capable of action. Under this view, he is left powerless because a power not expressly given to Congress is nevertheless found to rest exclusively with Congress."

President Harry Truman announces the federal government's takeover of the steel industry on April 8, 1952, in response to a labor dispute that threatened steel production during the Korean conflict. In *Youngstown Sheet and Tube Co. v. Sawyer* (1952), the Court held that only Congress, not the president, could authorize such a seizure.
Source: AP/Wide World Photos.

The Framers of the Constitution, Vinson said, could not have intended to hamstring a president in time of war. "History bears out the genius of the Founding Fathers, who created a Government subject to law but not left subject to inertia when vigor and initiative are required."

EXCERPTS

From Justice Black's majority opinion: "There is no statute that expressly authorizes the President to take possession of property as he did here. Nor is there any act of Congress to which our attention has been directed from which such a power can fairly be implied. . . .

"The order cannot properly be sustained as an exercise of the President's military power as Commander in Chief of the Armed Forces. The Government attempts to do so by citing a number of cases upholding broad powers in military commanders engaged in day-to-day fighting in a theater of war. Such cases need not concern us here. Even though 'theater of war' be an expanding concept, we cannot with faithfulness to our constitutional system hold that the Commander in Chief of the Armed Forces has the ultimate power as such to take possession of private property in order to keep labor disputes from stopping production. This is a job for the Nation's lawmakers, not for its military authorities. . . .

"The Founders of this Nation entrusted the lawmaking power to the Congress alone in both good and bad times. It would do no good to recall the historical events, the fears of power and the hopes for freedom that lay behind their choice. Such a review would but confirm our holding that this seizure order cannot stand."

IMPACT

The so-called "steel seizure" case, and the reaction to it, serves as a case study in the role of the Supreme Court in the national government. Even in time of war and under pressure from the president, the Supreme Court did not hesitate to tell the president he was flat-out wrong. No matter how important the short-term need, the Court said the constitutional framework had to be followed. *The Economist* in London wrote, "The Supreme Court . . . has once more brought to heel the mighty: the President, the union, the industry, and Congress."

President Truman, although unhappy with the decision, did not hesitate to obey it. He returned the steel mills to their owners. The steelworkers went on strike, and the strike was soon settled, with wage increases for the workers and price increases for the producers.

Truman biographer David McCullough wrote that after the decision came down, Justice Black invited the president and other justices to a party at his home in Alexandria, Virginia. At first Truman seemed cool, but after some drinks and food, Truman turned to Black and said, "Hugo, I don't much care for your law, but, by golly, this bourbon is good."

The Court's ruling is often cited not just as a check on presidential power but as a celebration of the checks and balances the Constitution envisioned for the three branches of government. Justice Jackson's formulation in his concurring opinion in *Youngstown Sheet and Tube* is often quoted to make the point that a separate, interdependent, and flexible system works best. "While the Constitution diffuses power the better to secure liberty, it also contemplates that practice will integrate the dispersed powers into a workable government. It enjoins upon its branches separateness but interdependence, autonomy but reciprocity. Presidential powers are not fixed but fluctuate, depending upon their disjunction or conjunction with those of Congress."

That principle returned to the fore in the landmark cases decided by the Court in 2004 stemming from the "war on terror." In *Hamdi v. Rumsfeld,* when Justice Sandra Day O'Connor wrote for the Court that a state of war does not give presidents a "blank check" to violate constitutional principles, she cited *Youngstown* as her main support. (See Detainee Cases.)

Immigration and Naturalization Service v. Chadha

Decided June 23, 1983
462 U.S. 919
laws.findlaw.com/US/462/919.html

DECISION

When Congress passes laws it may not retain for one of its houses the power to veto executive branch decisions implementing the laws. Under the Constitution's design for a national government, that kind of power is legislative in nature and can be exercised only through the approval of both houses of Congress and signature of the president.

BACKGROUND

In the never-ending test of wills between presidents and Congress, the so-called "legislative veto" became an important weapon in the congressional arsenal in the early 1970s. Legislative vetoes, written into many statutes, enabled one or both houses of Congress to veto or disapprove of how the president or an executive or independent agency was implementing the law. Normally, once a law is passed, the executive branch has considerable leeway to decide how it should be carried out or administered. Legislative vetoes, however, gave Congress a way to keep its hand in how its laws were enforced.

Some form of legislative vetoes began creeping into legislation in the 1930s. From the outset, presidents objected to the idea as an infringement on their powers. They occasionally vetoed the laws that Congress sent them because they contained the veto provisions. But it was a low-voltage dispute, partly because Congress enacted only a few each year.

But in the 1970s the debate gained importance because Congress began enacting greater numbers of legislative vetoes into law. This upswing was partly the result of congressional concern over the growing powers of the presidency—the "imperial presidency," as more than one commentator called it. In the 1973 War Powers Act, Congress provided that a resolution of both houses of Congress could force a president to withdraw U.S. troops from an undeclared war. In the International Development and Food Assistance Act of 1975, Congress reserved the right to suspend aid to any country that did not meet human rights standards.

Another impetus for legislative vetoes was the growth of the "administrative state"—the alphabet soup of independent agencies charged with devising regulations on the environment, energy, consumer protection, and workplace safety. Under pressure from lobbying groups and other constituencies, Congress sought to retain the ability to affect the regulatory process. In 1975 Rep. Elliott Levitas of Georgia introduced legislation that would add a legislative veto to regulatory decisions in general. "Where the bureaucrats have gone off the deep end, either house of Congress could veto and reject that unwise standard," Levitas said in defense of the legislation.

One of the areas in which Congress enacted a legislative veto was immigration. A federal law passed in 1924 required that any foreigner who entered the country illegally be deported. But during President Franklin Roosevelt's tenure in office, immigration officials sought the authority to suspend those deportations in cases that would cause severe hardships for families. Congress agreed to allow such suspensions, but attached a legislative veto to that authority. The names of all those whose deportations were being suspended would be submitted to Congress, where a majority vote in either house could disapprove or cancel the suspension. In other words, either house of Congress could require the deportation of a foreigner who had entered or remained in the country illegally, even if executive branch officials had recommended against deportation. From 1952 to 1981 immigration officials suspended the deportation of 5,701 aliens. Congress vetoed 229 of those suspensions.

One of the people who found his deportation suspension vetoed was Jagdish Chadha, an East Indian who was born in Kenya. He had come to the United States in 1966 on a student visa to attend Bowling Green University. When his visa expired in 1972 Chadha believed that changed circumstances in Africa would make it impossible for him to return to Kenya. He tried to remain in the country, but the Immigration and Naturalization Service (INS) ordered him deported. He appealed the decision to an immigration judge who, after reviewing Chadha's case, suspended the deportation order, allowing him to become a resident alien. Chadha's name was then submitted to Congress to allow either house to exercise the legislative veto.

In December 1975 the House of Representatives passed a routine resolution disapproving resident alien status for six aliens, including Chadha. The suspended deportation orders of the six were reinstated, and they were ordered to leave the United States. According to a 1988 book, "no one then or now knows for sure what the reasoning was" for the exercise of the veto in Chadha's case. Author Barbara Hinkson Craig suggests, however, that Chadha and the other five may have been singled out because their claims of hardship were not as serious as others.

But Chadha, believing he had been unjustly treated, decided to challenge the congressional action in court. His lawyers went before an immigration appeals board and then to a federal appeals court claiming that the one-house veto provision was unconstitutional.

By this time the case had begun to attract attention from scholars and litigators who were concerned about the growth of legislative vetoes. Alan Morrison, a lawyer with the Public Citizen Litigation Group and an expert on separation-of-powers issues, offered his help to Chadha's lawyers. Before the appeals court, the INS agreed with Chadha that the law was unconstitutional, and in 1980 the appeals court ruled that in fact the legislative veto violated the constitutional separation of powers.

The case caused considerable debate among the justices, according to Craig. Some were concerned about a decision that could affect the estimated 200 laws on the books that had some form of legislative veto. After hearing arguments in February 1982, the Court held the case until the following term, ordering a second set of arguments in December, apparently to help the justices work through the major constitutional issues involved.

VOTE

7–2, with Chief Justice Warren E. Burger writing the majority opinion for the Court. Joining him were Justices William J. Brennan Jr., Thurgood Marshall, Harry A. Blackmun, John Paul Stevens, Sandra Day O'Connor, and Lewis F. Powell Jr. Dissenting were Justices Byron R. White and William Rehnquist.

HIGHLIGHTS

Chief Justice Burger based his decision on two main provisions of the Constitution, both contained in Article I, Section 7. The

In an effort to obtain legal residency in the United States, Jagdish Chadha, pictured with his wife, Therese Lorentz, and their daughters, challenged the so-called legislative veto, in which a majority vote in either house of Congress could override a presidential veto or disapprove of implementation of a law. Chadha faced deportation under such a circumstance. In *Immigration and Naturalization Service v. Chadha* (1983), the Court declared the legislative veto unconstitutional.

Source: Photo by Terrence McCarthy.

first was the presentment clause, which requires that all legislation passed by Congress be presented to the president for his signature or veto. In the minds of the Framers of the Constitution, Burger wrote, this was not just a minor procedural matter. "Presentment to the President and the Presidential veto were considered so imperative that the draftsmen took special pains to assure that these requirements could not be circumvented." The reason for the procedure, Burger said, was "to check whatever propensity a particular Congress might have to enact oppressive, improvident, or ill-considered measures."

The second provision of the Constitution that Burger noted was the requirement that both houses of Congress pass on legislation. "By providing that no law could take effect without the concurrence of the prescribed majority of the Members of both Houses, the Framers reemphasized their belief . . . that legislation should not be enacted unless it has been carefully and fully considered by the Nation's elected officials."

Justice Powell wrote a concurring opinion that underscored the sweep of the decision: "The breadth of this holding gives one pause. Congress has included the veto in literally hundreds of statutes, dating back to the 1930's."

The scope of the decision inspired a vigorous dissent from Justice White: "Today the Court not only invalidates Section 244(c)(2) of the Immigration and Nationality Act, but also sounds the death knell for nearly 200 other statutory provisions in which Congress has reserved a 'legislative veto.' For this reason, the Court's decision is of surpassing importance. And it is for this reason that the Court would have been well advised to decide the cases, if possible, on the narrower grounds of separation of powers."

White continued, "I regret that I am in disagreement with my colleagues on the fundamental questions that these cases present. But even more I regret the destructive scope of the Court's holding. It reflects a profoundly different conception of the Constitution than that held by the courts which sanctioned the modern administrative state."

EXCERPTS

From Chief Justice Burger's majority opinion: "[T]he fact that a given law or procedure is efficient, convenient, and useful in facilitating functions of government, standing alone, will not save it if it is contrary to the Constitution. Convenience and efficiency are not the primary objectives—or the hallmarks—of democratic government, and our inquiry is sharpened, rather than blunted, by the fact that congressional veto provisions are appearing with increasing frequency in statutes which delegate authority to executive and independent agencies. . . .

"It emerges clearly that the prescription for legislative action in Article I, 1, 7, . . . represents the Framers' decision that the legislative power of the Federal Government be exercised in accord with a single, finely wrought and exhaustively considered, procedure. . . .

"The veto authorized by Section 244(c)(2) doubtless has been in many respects a convenient shortcut; the 'sharing' with the Executive by Congress of its authority over aliens in this manner is, on its face, an appealing compromise. In purely practical terms, it is obviously easier for action to be taken by one House without submission to the President; but it is crystal clear from the records of the Convention, contemporaneous writings and debates that the Framers ranked other values higher than efficiency. . . .

"The choices we discern as having been made in the Constitutional Convention impose burdens on governmental processes that often seem clumsy, inefficient, even unworkable, but those hard choices were consciously made by men who had lived under a form of government that permitted arbitrary governmental acts to go unchecked. There is no support in the Constitution or decisions of this Court for the proposition that the cumbersomeness and delays often encountered in complying with explicit constitutional standards may be avoided, either by the Congress or by the President. With all the obvious flaws of delay, untidiness, and potential for abuse, we have not yet found a better way to preserve freedom than by making the exercise of power subject to the carefully crafted restraints spelled out in the Constitution."

IMPACT

In the life of the Supreme Court, it is a rare and noteworthy event for a decision to overturn an act of Congress. It represents a step that the justices say they take reluctantly: rejecting the will of the people, as carried out by the elected branches of government.

Against that backdrop, the *Chadha* decision had extraordinary significance, striking down parts of more than 200 laws enacted by Congress. As White said in dissent, "Today's decision strikes down in one fell swoop provisions in more laws enacted by Congress than the Court has cumulatively invalidated in its history."

White took the unusual step of reading parts of his dissent from the bench the day the Court handed down the opinion. After that, apparently spontaneously, Chief Justice Burger also spoke, telling the courtroom audience that the justices had agreed that "this is a very difficult and important case."

Court scholar Bernard Schwartz said soon after the decision came down that the Court had made it "all but impossible" for Congress to oversee administrative decision making. That has not proven to be the case: Congress continued to pass laws that contained some form of congressional vetoes, albeit at a slower pace. Alternative ways of involving Congress in reviewing regulatory decisions have developed. Congress passed the Congressional Review Act of 1996, which put in place an expedited procedure for both houses of Congress to pass resolutions disapproving of regulatory actions. Those joint resolutions would then be submitted to the president for signature, conforming to the *Chadha* decision.

The *Chadha* ruling's impact has been to keep congressional power generally in check. In 1985 Congress passed the Gramm-Rudman-Hollings Act, which imposed limits on federal spending. To guarantee that the limits would be heeded, the law empowered the comptroller general to order budget cuts. But the comptroller general is an official under the control of Congress, not the executive branch. In *Bowsher v. Synar* (1986) the Court struck down that aspect of the law. Citing *Chadha,* the Court said Congress could not give a congressional official what amounted to executive branch duties.

As for Chadha himself, he was sworn in as a U.S. citizen in 1984, a step made easier by the fact that he had married a U.S. citizen. The couple had two children, and Chadha became the manager of a music store in San Francisco.

SEX DISCRIMINATION

*A*s with race discrimination, the Supreme Court has not always been at the forefront of the fight for women's equality. As late as 1873, the Court upheld the right of the state of Illinois to refuse to admit Myra Bradwell as a member of the legal profession—with one justice stating that the "timidity and delicacy" of women made them unfit for certain occupations. Slowly but surely, that paternalism faded. The equal protection clause of the Fourteenth Amendment proved to be a powerful tool for women's rights, as it was for racial equality. Still, however, the Court assessed instances of sex discrimination using a slightly less stringent standard than it applied to racial bias. The Court's thinking appeared to be that while there could be no plausible justification for treating blacks worse than whites, there might still be rare instances— having to do with women's unique ability to become pregnant, as well as other physical characteristics—when treating women differently from men might be justified.

Other related cases mentioned in the Sex Discrimination section

Bradwell v. Illinois (1873)
Sweatt v. Painter (1950)
Reed v. Reed (1971)
Mississippi University for Women v. Hogan (1982)
Franklin v. Gwinnett County Public Schools (1992)
Harris v. Forklift Systems (1993)
Oncale v. Sundowner Offshore Services (1998)
Gebser v. Lago Vista Independent School District (1998)
Burlington Industries v. Ellerth (1998)
Faragher v. City of Boca Raton (1998)
Jackson v. Birmingham Board of Education (2005)

Meritor Savings Bank v. Vinson

Decided June 19, 1986
477 U.S. 57
laws.findlaw.com/US/477/57.html

DECISION

Sexual harassment is a form of sex discrimination that is prohibited by Title VII of the Civil Rights Act of 1964. This form of discrimination is illegal not only when it results in the loss of a job or promotion, but also when it creates a "hostile environment" that alters the employee's working conditions.

BACKGROUND

For more than a decade after passage of the Civil Rights Act of 1964, courts resisted the notion that sexual harassment in the workplace was a form of sex discrimination that should be prohibited by the law. As larger numbers of women joined the workforce, however, judicial attitudes began to change. University of Michigan law professor Catharine MacKinnon advanced the view that there were two kinds of illegal sexual harassment: "quid pro quo" harassment, in which a supervisor links job rewards or threats to an employee's acceptance or refusal of sexual advances, and "hostile environment" harassment, in which the sexual advances or conduct are so pervasive or severe that they damage the victim's working conditions.

The Equal Employment Opportunity Commission (EEOC), which enforces Title VII of the Civil Rights Act, adopted this dual formulation in its guidelines, and lower courts began to look more seriously at sexual harassment as a form of discrimination. By the time the issue reached the Supreme Court, this concept had become well established in federal appeals courts.

The Supreme Court took up the case of Mechelle Vinson, who began working for the Capital City Federal Savings and Loan Association in Washington, D.C., in 1974. She began as a teller-trainee but advanced quickly through the ranks, eventually becoming assistant branch manager. In 1978, however, she took sick leave and was then fired for using too much leave time.

Two years later, she sued the bank, since renamed Meritor Savings Bank, claiming she had been the victim of persistent sexual harassment by a bank vice president, Sidney Taylor. She said that ever since she began working at the bank, Taylor had made sexual advances toward her. She agreed to have sex with him many times, but said that it was sometimes under threat of physical force. On several occasions, she claimed, he had raped her. She said she did not report his conduct for fear that she would be fired. Taylor denied doing anything wrong.

A federal judge ruled against Vinson, finding that her relationship with Taylor was voluntary, and that the bank could not

be held liable. But a federal appeals court panel reversed the ruling and sided with Vinson. It said she was the victim of illegal sex discrimination. Even though she had not suffered any job loss, Taylor's behavior had created a "hostile environment." The bank appealed the decision to the Supreme Court.

VOTE

9–0, with Justice William Rehnquist writing the opinion for the Court. Joining him were Chief Justice Warren E. Burger, Byron R. White, Lewis F. Powell Jr., John Paul Stevens, Sandra Day O'-Connor, Thurgood Marshall, William J. Brennan Jr., and Harry A. Blackmun.

HIGHLIGHTS

Rehnquist dismissed the bank's argument that Title VII covered only "tangible" discrimination, in the form of a firing or demotion. The broad wording of the law, Rehnquist said, demonstrates "a congressional intent 'to strike at the entire spectrum of disparate treatment of men and women' in employment."

It is no longer in doubt, Rehnquist said, that "a plaintiff may establish a violation of Title VII by proving that discrimination based on sex has created a hostile or abusive work environment."

The fact that Vinson "voluntarily" had a sexual relationship with Taylor after he made the advances, Rehnquist said, "is not a defense to a sexual harassment suit brought under Title VII." The foundation of any claim, he said, should be that "the alleged sexual advances were 'unwelcome.' The District Court in this case erroneously focused on the 'voluntariness' of respondent's participation in the claimed sexual episodes. The correct inquiry is whether respondent, by her conduct, indicated that the alleged sexual advances were unwelcome, not whether her actual participation in sexual intercourse was voluntary."

At the same time, however, Rehnquist asserted that evidence about the victim's behavior could be introduced at trial. "It does not follow that a complainant's sexually provocative speech or dress is irrelevant as a matter of law in determining whether he or she found particular sexual advances unwelcome. To the contrary, such evidence is obviously relevant."

As for the liability of the company, the Court rejected both extremes. Women's groups argued that the company should be absolutely liable for the actions of its supervisors, and that when Vinson told Taylor to back off, she in effect was telling the bank. Business groups, on the other hand, argued that the bank should not be held liable at all. Because Vinson did not use the established grievance procedure for employees, the company did not know about the misbehavior and could have done nothing to stop it.

"Absence of notice to an employer does not necessarily insulate that employer from liability," the Court said, noting that Meritor Bank's grievance procedures would have required Vinson to complain formally to her supervisor, who in this case was the person harassing her.

EXCERPTS

From Justice Rehnquist's majority opinion: "Without question, when a supervisor sexually harasses a subordinate because of the subordinate's sex, that supervisor 'discriminate[s]' on the basis of sex. . . .

". . . For sexual harassment to be actionable, it must be sufficiently severe or pervasive 'to alter the conditions of [the victim's] employment and create an abusive working environment.'

". . . [W]e reject petitioner's view that the mere existence of a grievance procedure and a policy against discrimination, coupled with respondent's failure to invoke that procedure, must insulate petitioner from liability. While those facts are plainly relevant, the situation before us demonstrates why they are not necessarily dispositive. . . . [T]he bank's grievance procedure apparently required an employee to complain first to her supervisor, in this case Taylor. Since Taylor was the alleged perpetrator, it is not altogether surprising that respondent failed to invoke the procedure and report her grievance to him. Petitioner's contention that respondent's failure should insulate it from liability might be substantially stronger if its procedures were better calculated to encourage victims of harassment to come forward."

IMPACT

Women's rights advocates applauded the *Meritor* decision as a welcome, if tardy, recognition that sexual harassment was a serious problem that could not be dismissed as harmless office "fun." Employers began to take notice and train employees about what kind of behavior is and is not tolerated.

Complaints of harassment filed with the EEOC and with the courts rose steadily, but not just because the *Meritor* case made them possible. Several celebrated episodes highlighted the problem, including accusations of harassment against Sen. Bob Packwood and Supreme Court nominee Clarence Thomas. By 1993 harassment claims had doubled to more than 12,000

annually. In 1998 the EEOC reported that 15,618 new harassment claims were filed, nearly 13 percent by men.

In the years since *Meritor,* the Court has continued to strengthen and expand the decision's scope and meaning. In the 1993 case *Harris v. Forklift Systems,* the Court ruled unanimously that it was not necessary for the victim of harassment to prove that she suffered psychological damage in order to win a lawsuit.

Through the 1980s and early 1990s, business groups complained that the Court's decisions, as well as a welter of lower court rulings, had made it almost impossible for employers to avoid being held responsible for sexual harassment by supervisors. Their lack of knowledge about the conduct, and the existence of strong company policies against harassment did not seem to help companies sued in court.

Three 1998 decisions clarified the Court's doctrine. In *Faragher v. City of Boca Raton* and *Burlington Industries v. Ellerth,* the Court said that in cases where the victim suffered "tangible" job losses, the employer is strictly liable. In cases where there was no penalty to the victim, the employer can avoid responsibility by showing that it took "reasonable care" to prevent harassment and the victim did not make use of complaint procedures. In *Oncale v. Sundowner Offshore Services,* the Court said "same sex" harassment by men against other men or women against women was also illegal under the Civil Rights Act. Women's groups and business groups alike said the Court's rulings benefited both employers and harassment victims by making policies against harassment clear.

In terms of Supreme Court doctrine, the *Meritor* decision was an example of a conservative Court coming to a result that seemed liberal. Led by Rehnquist, a staunch conservative who had just been named by President Ronald Reagan to become chief justice, the Court unanimously upheld an interpretation of civil rights law that was disfavored by conservatives and the business community.

This seeming contradiction can be explained by looking at the law the Court was interpreting. Conservative justices say the Court should not "legislate from the bench," so they adhere to the meaning of federal laws as passed by Congress. If Congress passes a law aimed at achieving liberal goals—the Civil Rights Act of 1964, for example—then the Supreme Court, by interpreting its words literally, ends up sounding liberal as well. The Court also usually makes it a practice to defer to government agencies—the EEOC in this case—in its interpretations of federal laws.

United States v. Virginia

Decided June 26, 1996
518 U.S. 515
laws.findlaw.com/US/518/515.html

DECISION

Excluding women from the state-funded Virginia Military Institute violates the equal protection clause of the Fourteenth Amendment, even though the state offers a leadership program for women at another school. Only an "exceedingly persuasive justification" can make a government gender-based distinction constitutional, and Virginia's justification was inadequate.

BACKGROUND

At the time of the litigation that resulted in this decision, Virginia Military Institute (VMI) in Lexington, Virginia, was the last remaining state-run military college that admitted only men. The Citadel in South Carolina had given in to legal pressure and admitted a female student in 1995, only to see the student withdraw a few days after starting classes.

VMI kept fighting to retain its unique educational techniques, which, it said, would be spoiled if it admitted women. VMI prided itself on its "adversative method" of learning, in which first-year students were tested and hardened through harsh treatment by upperclassmen. Freshmen are tormented on the so-called rat line, and they experience a total lack of privacy—even in bathrooms. This treatment helps bond the class together and, presumably, prepares students to be "citizen soldiers" able to withstand the rigors of combat. The VMI experience also generates intense loyalty to the school among alumni, many of whom have became leaders of industry and government in the state.

When some female students decided they wanted to share in the VMI experience and were denied the chance to do so, the Justice Department filed suit against the state, claiming the male-only policy violated the equal protection clause of the Fourteenth Amendment. A federal district court judge sided with the school, but an appeals court panel said the all-male policy was unacceptable under the Fourteenth Amendment. The appeals court, however, gave the state a chance to remedy the constitutional flaw, either by admitting women, devising a parallel program for women, or ending state support for the institution. Virginia opted for the least painful alternative; the state created the Virginia Women's Institute for Leadership (VWIL) at Mary Baldwin College. That program was also aimed at training "citizen soldiers," but it was significantly different from the VMI program, offering fewer degree programs and less rigorous training. The new program was acceptable to the lower

courts, but the Justice Department went to the Supreme Court to argue that Virginia's differing educational treatment for men and women was still unconstitutional.

The case came to a Supreme Court whose justices were still divided over how to evaluate laws and government actions that discriminated between males and females. Long ago, the Court had found that racial distinctions were presumably unconstitutional and had to be evaluated under a stringent "strict scrutiny" standard, which usually resulted in the government policy being struck down. Its theory was that race was an "immutable" or unchangeable characteristic that should not be used as a reason to treat people differently. Gender, too, is not a matter of choice, but the Court had never given it the same constitutionally protected status as race.

Early in the Court's decision making on issues of gender, the justices had adopted a romantic paternalism toward women that approved of different treatment of females because of women's biological role in bearing children and their traditional role in maintaining households and family matters. In the 1873 decision *Bradwell v. Illinois,* the Court said states could prevent women from practicing law. "Man is, or should be, woman's protector and defender," the Court said in *Bradwell.* As late as 1948, the Court upheld a law that kept a woman from being a bartender unless she was the bar owner's wife or daughter.

A change in the Court's attitude did not come until well after Congress had included gender bias as a prohibited form of discrimination in laws governing the workplace and public education. The 1971 case of *Reed v. Reed* marked the first time the Supreme Court struck down a law because it discriminated against women. The Idaho law in question gave men a preference over women in administering estates when a relative died without leaving a will. The Court said that preference had no rational relationship to the goals of the law, thus establishing a relatively low level standard of scrutiny that was far more lenient toward government than the standard governing racial distinctions. The Court gradually reached an "intermediate" level of scrutiny in the years after *Reed,* a standard that weeded out some but not all gender-based distinctions in the law.

In many rulings on sex discrimination in the 1970s and 1980s, the Court offered few explanations for why it did not guard against gender bias as zealously as it did against racial discrimination. The only rationale appeared to be the fact that

Gussie Ann Lord was one of 23 women attending the Virginia Military Institute (VMI) in 1998. Two years earlier in *United States v. Virginia* (1996), the Supreme Court ruled that excluding women from the state-funded VMI violated the equal protection clause of the Fourteenth Amendment.

Source: AP/Wide World Photos/ Detroit Free Press/Pauline Lubens.

whereas blacks and whites surely had undistinguishable physical capabilities, there were some undeniable differences between men and women—the ability to become pregnant, for example—that could, in rare instances, justify different treatment by government.

VOTE

7–1, with Justice Ruth Bader Ginsburg writing the majority opinion. Joining her were Chief Justice William Rehnquist and Justices John Paul Stevens, Sandra Day O'Connor, Anthony M. Kennedy, David H. Souter, and Stephen G. Breyer. Justice Antonin Scalia dissented. Justice Clarence Thomas did not participate because his son was enrolled at VMI.

HIGHLIGHTS

The Supreme Court had at least one fairly recent precedent to look at in deciding how to judge single-sex public higher education. But that case involved an all-female rather than an all-male institution. In *Mississippi University for Women v. Hogan* (1982) the Court said the school's nursing program could not be reserved for women alone because that unfairly discriminated against men.

In the *Hogan* case the Court offered a variation on the intermediate level of scrutiny used to examine gender-based discrimination. The Court said the government would have to prove it had "exceedingly persuasive justification" for treating men and women differently.

Justice Ginsburg adopted that standard in the VMI case as well, and proceeded to find that Virginia's justifications were not at all persuasive. The Court said the justifications had to be genuine—not invented just to respond to litigation—and could not be based on stereotyped generalizations about men and women's different capabilities.

Virginia had argued, ironically perhaps, that maintaining VMI as an all-male school promoted diversity—at least diversity in educational styles. The Court said that argument was a dubious rationale and did not justify excluding women from benefiting from VMI's unique educational style. "However 'liberally' this plan serves the State's sons, it makes no provision whatever for her daughters. That is not equal protection," Ginsburg wrote.

The state's second argument was that VMI's "adversative" training would have to be drastically changed if women were admitted. The Court acknowledged that some changes would be necessary, especially to protect the privacy of the new students, but those changes did not amount to the "exceedingly persuasive" reasons the *Hogan* precedent demanded.

The Court then turned its attention to the alternate program for women devised by Virginia in response to the lower court's initial order. The Court found the new program inadequate to cure Virginia's basic constitutional violation, namely the exclusion of women from VMI. The women's leadership program is not nearly as rigorous, well-funded, or prestigious as VMI's, the Court said, calling it a "pale shadow" of the VMI program. Drawing an analogy with racial discrimination, Ginsburg recalled the 1950 ruling in *Sweatt v. Painter,* in which the Court said a lackluster law school established for blacks did not cure the state's constitutional violation of excluding blacks from its flagship University of Texas law school.

Justice Scalia wrote an angry dissent. He argued that the Court majority had ignored lower court findings about the benefits of single-sex education for both males and females and about physical differences that make VMI's program inappropriate for women. "The parties to this case could have saved themselves a great deal of time, trouble, and expense by omitting a trial," Scalia said sarcastically.

He added, "The tradition of having government-funded military schools for men is as well rooted in the traditions of this country as the tradition of sending only men into military combat. The people may decide to change the one tradition, like the other, through democratic processes; but the assertion that either tradition has been unconstitutional through the centuries is not law, but politics smuggled into law." The majority opinion, said Scalia, represents "not the interpretation of a Constitution, but the creation of one." He concluded, "It ensures that single-sex public education is functionally dead."

EXCERPTS

From Justice Ginsburg's majority opinion: "[T]he Court has repeatedly recognized that neither federal nor state government acts compatibly with the equal protection principle when a law or official policy denies to women, simply because they are women, full citizenship stature—equal opportunity to aspire, achieve, participate in and contribute to society based on their individual talents and capacities. . . .

" 'Inherent differences' between men and women, we have come to appreciate, remain cause for celebration, but not for denigration of the members of either sex or for artificial constraints on an individual's opportunity. Sex classifications may be used to compensate women 'for particular economic disabilities [they have] suffered,' to 'promot[e] equal employment opportunity,' to advance full development of the talent and capacities of our Nation's people. But such classifications may not be used, as they once were, to create or perpetuate the legal, social, and economic inferiority of women. . . .

". . . [E]ducation, to be sure, is not a 'one size fits all' business. The issue, however, is not whether 'women—or men—should be forced to attend VMI'; rather, the question is whether the State can constitutionally deny to women who have the will and capacity, the training and attendant opportunities that VMI uniquely affords. . . .

". . . The constitutional violation in this case is the categorical exclusion of women from an extraordinary educational opportunity afforded men. A proper remedy for an unconstitu-

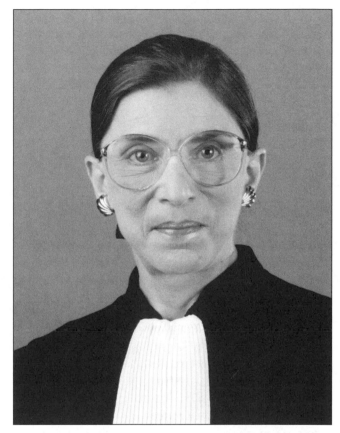

Before being appointed to the Supreme Court, Ruth Bader Ginsburg was known as "the Thurgood Marshall of sex discrimination law." She headed the American Civil Liberties Union's Women's Rights Project and argued and won numerous cases before the Court concerning women's rights. Ginsburg wrote the opinion in *United States v. Virginia* (1996).
Source: Richard Strauss, Collection of the Supreme Court of the United States.

tional exclusion, we have explained, aims to 'eliminate [so far as possible] the discriminatory effects of the past' and to 'bar like discrimination in the future.'. . .

"Virginia chose not to eliminate, but to leave untouched, VMI's exclusionary policy. For women only, however, Virginia proposed a separate program, different in kind from VMI and unequal in tangible and intangible facilities. . . .

"In myriad respects other than military training, VWIL [Virginia Women's Institute for Leadership] does not qualify as VMI's equal. VWIL's student body, faculty, course offerings, and facilities hardly match VMI's. Nor can the VWIL graduate anticipate the benefits associated with VMI's 157-year history, the school's prestige, and its influential alumni network. . . .

"Virginia, in sum, while maintaining VMI for men only, has failed to provide any 'comparable single-gender women's institution.' Instead, the Commonwealth has created a VWIL program fairly appraised as a 'pale shadow' of VMI in terms of the range of curricular choices and faculty stature, funding, prestige, alumni support and influence."

IMPACT

"A savage disappointment" is how VMI superintendent Josiah Bunting described the Court's ruling. For a time, VMI alumni threatened to take the school private. Without public funds, they reasoned, the school could continue its all-male admissions policy. But the costs were high, and soon the school's governing board agreed to face the inevitable and admit women to the school beginning in 1997. Justice Scalia's heated pronouncement in his dissent, "Today the Court shuts down an institution that has served the people of the Commonwealth of Virginia with pride and distinction for over a century and a half," proved incorrect. By the spring of 1998, with twenty-three female students already fitting into campus life, *USA Today* reported, "The fear that had permeated campus since the Supreme Court ordered an end to the 158-year all-male tradition at VMI seems to have dissipated."

Female students reported that the rat line abuse they were subjected to was the same as the males had to endure. Nearly a quarter of the women quit within the first year, but 16 percent of males also left during the same period. In all, the state spent more than $5 million to renovate the school's facilities and hire new staff to accommodate the female students.

Since then, slowly but surely, VMI has embraced its gender diversity, and in 2005 reported that 5 percent of its 1,300 cadets were women. Another sign of the changed atmosphere at VMI came in March 2005 when its admissions office hired Jackie Tugman, one of its alumna from the class of 2002, to help the school reach its goal of having at least 200 female students by 2039. In an article in a VMI publication, she indicated that her biggest challenge was retention—keeping the women who enroll from leaving VMI after a year or two. "I want them to have a clear understanding of what it's like not only to be a cadet but to go through the Rat Line," said Tugman.

It is not yet clear whether the Court's decision will have broader impact on single-sex education, both public and private. Responding to research indicating that some young people perform better in single-sex settings, a number of elementary and secondary schools have experimented with all-male or all-female classes. The Supreme Court's decision did not say all such programs would be unconstitutional, but made them more difficult for school officials to justify.

Women's groups celebrated the VMI decision as a significant victory for equality, but in terms of how the Court views gender-based discrimination, it is unclear whether the ruling represents a major change. As a woman's rights advocate before joining the Court, Ginsburg had argued that the high strict scrutiny standard applied to racial distinctions should also hold for sex discrimination. As a justice, however, her ruling in the VMI case stopped short of that goal. She appeared to use the intermediate level of scrutiny that the Court had used in sex discrimination cases for years. But in describing the standard, she used the *Hogan* variation, requiring that government offer "exceedingly persuasive justification" for treating women differently. Some commentators have suggested that Ginsburg's ruling moved the level of scrutiny closer to strict scrutiny, but probably not all the way.

Davis v. Monroe County Board of Education

Decided May 24, 1999
526 U.S. 629
laws.findlaw.com/US/526/629.html

DECISION

Schools and universities receiving federal funds may be held liable and forced to pay money damages to students who are sexually harassed by other students. To win damages, victims must show that teachers or school officials knew about the harassment but were "deliberately indifferent" to it and that the harassment was so pervasive, persistent, and offensive that it interfered with the victim's access to the education available at the school.

BACKGROUND

The 1972 federal law known as Title IX prohibits discrimination "on the basis of sex" at any educational institution that receives federal financial assistance. Because virtually all public elementary and secondary schools, and many universities, receive federal funds, the law has become a powerful tool for equalizing educational opportunities nationwide. It is best known for increasing access to and spending on athletic programs for females.

In the 1990s women's rights groups sought to expand the application of Title IX into other aspects of school life. The Court's 1992 decision in *Franklin v. Gwinnett County Public Schools* established that schools could be held liable when teachers sexually harass students. The Court limited that ruling somewhat in 1998 in the case of *Gebser v. Lago Vista Independent School District*. In *Gebser* the Court said victims would have to prove that a school official who was in a position to discipline the teacher knew about the harassment but was deliberately indifferent to it.

The next logical step in expanding the scope of Title IX was to address "student-on-student" sexual harassment—an increasingly serious problem by all accounts. Surveys indicate that 80 to 90 percent of female students, and a somewhat smaller percentage of male students, say they have been sexually harassed at school. Sexual banter, some of it harmless and some of it hurtful, is commonplace in the hallways of many public high schools and middle schools. But conservatives who view federal power with skepticism and many school administrators argued that although peer harassment is a problem, it is not a problem that federal law should be called on to solve.

The Court agreed to decide what role Title IX would play in this area when it took up the case of LaShonda Davis. From the facts she and her mother, Aurelia Davis, alleged, LaShonda's experiences at Hubbard Elementary School in Monroe County, Georgia, were far more serious than the occasional taunt a student might typically encounter at school.

Starting in December 1992, an unnamed male student who was in the same fifth-grade classroom as LaShonda started making both physical and verbal advances toward her. Ten-year-old LaShonda and her mother repeatedly complained about the behavior, but, they claimed, nothing was done. At times LaShonda and the boy, labeled in Court papers with the initials "G.F.," were even seated next to each other. LaShonda became distraught, and her grades suffered. "All while this was going on, the school system treated us like the boy who cried wolf," Aurelia Davis said afterward. They complained to police as well, and the harassment ended after five months, when the boy pleaded guilty to sexual battery. The mother then sued the school district under Title IX. Her suit was dismissed, and on appeal a federal appeals court ruled that Title IX did not make it clear to the schools receiving federal funds that they had an obligation to stop student-on-student harassment.

VOTE

5–4, with Justice Sandra Day O'Connor writing the majority opinion for the Court. She was joined by Justices John Paul Stevens, David H. Souter, Ruth Bader Ginsburg, and Stephen G. Breyer. Justice Anthony M. Kennedy wrote a dissenting opinion, joined by Chief Justice William Rehnquist and Justices Antonin Scalia and Clarence Thomas.

Verna Williams, attorney for LaShonda Davis, speaks to reporters outside the Supreme Court in January 1999 after presenting her argument in *Davis v. Monroe County Board of Education*. Davis's father, Leroy, looks on, along with her mother, Aurelia, left, who sued the Monroe County, Georgia, school board and two officials because of the five months of sexual harassment her daughter LaShonda endured from a fellow student. The Supreme Court ruled that schools receiving federal funds may be held liable for failure to address student-on-student sexual abuse. *Source: AP/Wide World Photos/Ron Edmonds.*

HIGHLIGHTS

Justice O'Connor's opinion recognized that schools are not the same as business offices, and that Title IX is not the same kind of broad civil rights law that bars discrimination in the workplace. Title IX, she noted, is tied to federal funding, so it can regulate or punish only the behavior of the entity that received the funds—in this case the Monroe County Board of Education. It was not a law that could be used to punish the harassing student or any individual teachers or school officials who ignored the harassment.

"Where, as here, the misconduct occurs during school hours and on school grounds—the bulk of G.F.'s misconduct, in fact, took place in the classroom—the misconduct is taking place 'under' an 'operation' of the funding recipient. In these circumstances, the recipient retains substantial control over the context in which the harassment occurs." She also noted that schools exert "significant control" over students, so could be held liable for not halting misconduct by students.

But this did not mean that school officials would face lawsuits every time they let a playground argument go unpunished. Again tying the law to the federal funding, the Court said it could punish only actions or inaction by the school board

Associate Justice Sandra Day O'Connor speaks at the National Conference on Public Trust and Confidence in the Justice System in 1999. Days later, O'Connor delivered the opinion in the Title IX sexual harassment case *Davis v. Monroe County Board of Education* (1999).
Source: AP/Wide World Photos/George Bridges.

hold school officials liable for even the most trivial misbehavior by students. "The only certainty flowing from the majority's decision is that scarce resources will be diverted from educating our children and that many school districts, desperate to avoid Title IX peer harassment suits, will adopt whatever federal code of student conduct and discipline the Department of Education sees fit to impose upon them," Kennedy wrote.

Kennedy also saw the decision as a massive intrusion by the federal government into public school education, an area normally controlled at the local and state levels. "The Nation's schoolchildren will learn their first lessons about federalism in classrooms where the federal government is the ever-present regulator. The federal government will have insinuated itself not only into one of the most traditional areas of state concern but also into one of the most sensitive areas of human affairs."

Kennedy continued, "After today, Johnny will find that the routine problems of adolescence are to be resolved by invoking a federal right to demand assignment to a desk two rows away." "The complaint of this fifth-grader survives and the school will be compelled to answer in federal court," he added.

EXCERPTS

From Justice O'Connor's majority opinion: "We consider here whether a private damages action may lie against the school board in cases of student-on-student harassment. We conclude that it may, but only where the funding recipient acts with deliberate indifference to known acts of harassment in its programs or activities. Moreover, we conclude that such an action will lie only for harassment that is so severe, pervasive and objectively offensive that it effectively bars the victim's access to an educational opportunity or benefit. . . .

"Courts . . . must bear in mind that schools are unlike the adult workplace and that children may regularly interact in a manner that would be unacceptable among adults. Indeed, at least early on, students are still learning how to interact appropriately with their peers. It is thus understandable that, in the school setting, students often engage in insults, banter, teasing, shoving, pushing, and gender-specific conduct that is upsetting to the students subjected to it. Damages are not available for simple acts of teasing and name-calling among school children, however, even where these comments target differences in gender."

IMPACT

The Court's ruling was generally welcomed by women's rights advocates, who said it would finally force school administrators to take the issue of sexual harassment as seriously as employers in the workplace do. Gay rights groups also said it would be a valuable tool for combating harassment of gay students in schools and universities.

that had the effect of keeping students from taking advantage of the federally funded programs because of their sex. In other words, the harassment had to be so persistent and serious that victims were prevented from using a school resource. O'Connor offered the example of a group of male students threatening girls on a daily basis every time they tried to use a computer lab or athletic field. If school officials took no action to stop this practice, their behavior would "fly in the face of Title IX's core principles," she asserted.

But O'Connor was also careful to state that the Court did not intend to take away the power of school officials to remedy harassment in the way they see fit. The majority agreed that "courts should refrain from second guessing the disciplinary decisions made by school administrators."

None of these comments satisfied the dissenters, however. Justice Kennedy forecast a flood of lawsuits seeking to

Some civil liberties groups thought that O'Connor went too far to accommodate the dissenters, setting the threshold so high that some incidents of harassment that were serious—but not as persistent or pervasive as the ruling required—would go unpunished. That aspect of the decision pleased school administrators who, like Kennedy, were fearful that the decision might trigger lawsuits over trivial matters. School officials said the ruling would probably accelerate a trend, already under way, of training administrators and teachers to deal with reports of harassment quickly and appropriately.

The Department of Education applauded the decision, and in guidelines for school officials it underscored their duty to take complaints of harassment seriously. As with other Title IX violations, victims may file complaints with the Education Department as well as filing suits privately.

By the time the Supreme Court ruled, LaShonda Davis was a high school junior. Her case was returned to the lower courts to see if it met the requirements set forth in the decision. The case was later settled under terms that have not been disclosed.

In a 2005 case, *Jackson v. Birmingham Board of Education,* the Court expanded on the Davis precedent in an unexpected way. In certain circumstances, the Court said, the right to sue under Title IX even applied to parties who were not the victims of harassment. The ruling supported Roderick Jackson, a male coach for a girls' basketball team, who complained that the team was not treated as well as boys' teams in terms of funding and equipment. When he was fired, he sued the school system under Title IX. The Supreme Court said that firing someone because he complained about sexual discrimination fit Title IX, which bars discrimination "on the basis of sex."

VOTING RIGHTS

The right to vote is fundamental, but the Constitution does not specifically mention it. Decisions about who could vote were left largely to the states, which initially reserved the right mainly to white male property owners. Over decades, the franchise was extended to African Americans and to women and then to young people, and in fact more constitutional amendments are devoted to voting rights or suffrage than any other topic. The Supreme Court played a powerful role in removing barriers to vote for African Americans, but it did not become fully involved in enforcing voting power in general until the *Baker v. Carr* case of 1962. Voting rights cases then became more routine, and the Court found itself examining the redrawing of districts for racial and political reasons. In the dramatic 2000 case of *Bush v. Gore,* the Court even scrutinized the way in which ballots were recounted, and its ruling effectively decided the outcome of a presidential election.

Other related cases mentioned in the Voting Rights section

Chisholm v. Georgia (1793)
Barron v. Baltimore (1833)
Scott v. Sandford (1857) (see p. 231)
Pollock v. Farmers' Loan and Trust Co. (1895)
Nixon v. Condon (1932)
Grovey v. Townsend (1935)
United States v. Classic (1941)
Hirabayashi v. United States (1943)
Colegrove v. Green (1946)
Terry v. Adams (1953)
Gomillion v. Lightfoot (1960)
Gray v. Sanders (1963)
United Jewish Organizations of Williamsburgh v. Carey (1977)
Davis v. Bandemer (1986)
Bush v. Vera (1996)
Shaw v. Hunt (1996)
Hunt v. Cromartie (1999)
Bush v. Palm Beach County Canvassing Board (2000)
Easley v. Cromartie (2001)
Vieth v. Jubelirer (2004)

Smith v. Allwright

Decided April 3, 1944
321 U.S. 649
laws.findlaw.com/US/321/649.html

DECISION

Restricting primary elections to white voters only is a violation of the Fifteenth Amendment to the Constitution, which bars discrimination in voting on the basis of race. Because primaries are part of the process that chooses candidates for state and federal office, these elections amount to state action, even though political parties run them.

BACKGROUND

The Fifteenth Amendment, guaranteeing the right of blacks to vote, was ratified in 1870. But nearly three quarters of a century later, it had proven to be an empty vessel. The federal government did little to enforce it, and the Supreme Court actually had upheld a number of regulations, from poll taxes to literacy tests, that were aimed at keeping blacks from gaining full political power.

In Texas, for example, blacks were allowed to vote in general elections but not in political party primaries. Because Democrats won the general elections virtually all the time, the primary elections were in reality picking the future officeholders, not just candidates for office. Blacks had been cut out of the critical part of the political process.

Moreover, the Court had ruled in 1921 that because political primaries did not exist at the time of the drafting of the Constitution, they could not be regulated. The Court shifted its view in 1923, saying that a Texas law barring blacks from voting in primaries violated the Fourteenth Amendment, though not the Fifteenth. Texas responded by enacting a new law that allowed state party officials to decide membership qualifications—one step removed from the state actually dictating white membership only. That too was struck down in a 1932 case, *Nixon v. Condon.*

The Texas legislature responded to the Court's ruling by repealing the state primary laws. Next, membership by blacks was barred by a convention of the state Democratic Party, rather than the executive committee, which had been viewed as an organ of the state. The party finally had found a winning formula. In *Grovey v. Townsend* (1935) the Supreme Court ruled that membership decisions of the convention of the state party's members could not be viewed as official state action. Setting rules for a private convention, the Court said, was a matter about which "the state need have no concern."

In 1940 the NAACP and its leading legal strategist, Thurgood Marshall, decided it was time to take on the white primary system in the South. As recounted in Juan Williams's biography of Marshall, *American Revolutionary,* Marshall said at an NAACP convention that the place to begin was Texas, "where there are a million Negroes. If we get a million Negroes voting in a bloc, we are going to have some fun."

Some were skeptical because of the Texans' repeated success in fashioning Democratic Party rules to keep all-white primaries from being struck down. But a 1941 Supreme Court decision gave Marshall hope. The Court in *United States v. Classic* had found that fraud in a Louisiana primary was a federal offense, not just a private matter. If primaries were now a matter of federal concern, Marshall thought the Court would take a fresh look at the question of barring blacks from participation in primaries.

Marshall found a test plaintiff in Lonnie Smith, a black physician from Houston who had been repeatedly kept from voting in primaries. S.E. Allwright was the Houston election judge who had barred Smith from voting. The case drew considerable attention, and jazz great Duke Ellington sat in on the proceedings in federal court. But Marshall lost in both the district court and the appeals court, which cited the *Grovey* decision. The Supreme Court accepted it for review in the fall of 1943.

VOTE

8–1, with Justice Stanley F. Reed writing for the majority of the Court. Joining him were Chief Justice Harlan Fiske Stone and Justices Felix Frankfurter, William O. Douglas, Frank Murphy, James F. Byrnes, Robert H. Jackson, and Wiley B. Rutledge. Justice Owen J. Roberts dissented.

HIGHLIGHTS

To hold the white primary system unconstitutional, the Supreme Court first had to find a way to overrule *Grovey v. Townsend,* a fairly recent precedent. Because the Court rarely reverses itself, this task posed a major challenge to Justice Reed, at least in the writing of the decision. The actual vote was not difficult: since *Grovey,* President Franklin D. Roosevelt had replaced seven of the Court's justices.

United States v. Classic provided the key. That decision had cast primary elections in an entirely new light, making it clear that they were not merely the activities of a private club but were an integral part of the election process. "The fusing by the *Classic* case of the primary and general elections into a single instrumentality for choice of officers has a definite bearing on the permissibility under the Constitution of excluding Negroes from primaries," Reed wrote. "Recognition of the place of the primary in the electoral scheme makes clear that state delegation to a party of the power to fix the qualifications of primary elections is delegation of a state function that may make the party's action the action of the state," he continued.

Once Reed made that connection between primaries and elections, it was fairly easy for him to state that the Texas statute violated the Fifteenth Amendment. "It may now be taken as a postulate that the right to vote in such a primary for the nomination of candidates without discrimination by the State, like the right to vote in a general election, is a right secured by the Constitution. By the terms of the Fifteenth Amendment, that right may not be abridged by any state on account of race. Under our Constitution, the great privilege of the ballot may not be denied a man by the State because of his color."

The decision then examined the various ways in which the Texas primary, even though it is a party activity, plays an official role in the electoral process. "When primaries become a part of the machinery for choosing officials, state and national, as they have here, the same tests to determine the character of discrimination or abridgement should be applied to the primary as are applied to the general election."

Justice Roberts's solitary dissent amounts to a stern lecture on the Court's recent practice of overturning precedents. "This tendency, it seems to me, indicates an intolerance for what those who have composed this court in the past have conscientiously and deliberately concluded, and involves an assumption that knowledge and wisdom reside in us which was denied to our predecessors," Roberts wrote.

Noting that the Court had already overturned three precedents in that very term, Roberts said he worried that the trend "tends to bring adjudications of this tribunal into the same class as a restricted railroad ticket, good for this day and train only."

EXCERPTS

From Justice Reed's majority opinion: "We think that this statutory system for the selection of party nominees for inclusion on the general election ballot makes the party which is required to follow these legislative directions an agency of the state in so far as it determines the participants in a primary election. . . .

"The United States is a constitutional democracy. Its organic law grants to all citizens a right to participate in the choice of elected officials without restriction by any state because of race. This grant to the people of the opportunity for choice is not to be nullified by a state through casting its electoral process in a form which permits a private organization to practice racial discrimination in the election. Constitutional rights would be of little value if they could be thus indirectly denied.

"The privilege of membership in a party may be, as this Court said in *Grovey v. Townsend,* no concern of a state. But when, as here, that privilege is also the essential qualification for voting in a primary to select nominees for a general election, the state makes the action of the party the action of the state."

African Americans in Columbia, South Carolina, line up to vote in August 1948 in the state Democratic primary. It was the first time they were allowed to do so since 1876. The Supreme Court ruled in *Smith v. Allwright* (1944) that African Americans could not be denied the ballot in primary elections.
Source: AP/Wide World Photos.

IMPACT

Near the end of his life, Justice Thurgood Marshall declared the *Smith v. Allwright* case as "the greatest one" of his career. It had finally broken the back of segregation in the area of the greatest political power in a democracy—the ballot box.

In spite of the sweep of the decision, some Texans tried yet again to thwart its mandate. The Jaybird Democratic Association, which termed itself a private club, began holding "unofficial" primaries to select candidates for county offices. In *Terry v. Adams* (1953) the Supreme Court struck down the scheme, citing *Smith v. Allwright.* It was the last of the "white primary" cases.

With the all-white primary ended, few tools remained to exclude blacks from voting. Poll taxes and literacy tests persisted, but these too faded and were done away with in the civil rights legislation of the 1960s. The Twenty-Fourth Amendment to the Constitution, ratified in 1964, banned poll taxes in federal elections.

Scholars also cite the *Smith v. Allwright* decision because it took a more practical view of what constituted state action. Under its theory, private organizations that performed essentially state functions could come under constitutional provisions that do not otherwise regulate private relationships.

Baker v. Carr

Decided March 26, 1962
369 U.S. 186
laws.findlaw.com/US/369/186.html

DECISION

Disputes over reapportionment—the drawing of election district boundaries—can be considered by federal courts. Earlier decisions saying that federal courts should stay away from "political questions" such as reapportionment are wrong. The Constitution specifically gives Congress the power to regulate the "times, places or manner" of electing senators and representatives. In addition, the Court said reapportionment has implications for the "equal protection of the laws" guaranteed to individuals by the Fourteenth Amendment to the Constitution, and therefore, reapportionment is an appropriate subject for federal courts to address.

BACKGROUND

When legislative districts contain roughly equal numbers of people, the voting power of the people is also equal. For example, if two districts have approximately 100,000 voters within their boundaries, each individual has roughly the same say in electing the representatives from those districts. But what happens when the population shifts, and one district has 200,000 voters and the next district contains only 50,000? In such a case, a voter in the more populous district has less political power than a voter in the less-populated district.

Such disparities resulted from the migration of large numbers of Americans from rural to urban areas in the early twentieth century, without major changes in election district boundaries. In 1920, for the first time, census figures showed that more Americans lived in urban than rural settings. But for forty more years, lawmakers in many states refused to redraw legislative district boundaries to reflect those changes. Rural in-

terests thereby gained disproportionately greater power in many state legislatures.

Urban interests sought to correct the imbalance, but legislators and the courts turned them down. In *Colegrove v. Green* (1946) the Supreme Court ruled that the courts should stay out of an Illinois dispute over legislative districts in which the disparity between districts was as high as 800,000 people. "Courts ought not to enter this political thicket," wrote Justice Felix Frankfurter, coining a phrase that is still used by the courts. "It is hostile to a democratic system to involve the judiciary in the politics of the people."

The Court had shut the door on deciding these cases, but the problems continued to grow. Los Angeles, California, had one state senator for its 6 million residents, while another California district, with around 14,000 residents, also elected a state senator. Such disparities extended to the congressional districts.

In the view of some political scientists, these disparities were not just abstract problems; rather, they had real-life consequences. State legislatures and Congress were paying scant attention during this period to urban issues—housing and welfare, for example—as well as issues of race, and the dominance of rural interests in state legislatures was partly to blame. It was probably inevitable that the issue would return to the Supreme Court. A case from Tennessee provided an opportunity for the Court to revisit it.

Between 1901 and 1961 the Tennessee legislature had resisted all efforts to change its legislative districts, even though the state had experienced the same shift in population to urban areas that was occurring in other states. Rural residents exercised far more power over state legislative matters than their urban counterparts. By 1960 this disparity reached the point where roughly two-thirds of the state representatives were being elected by one-third of the state's 3.6 million people.

The Tennessee courts were also unsympathetic, ruling that they, like the federal courts, had no power to meddle in what were essentially political determinations about district boundaries. Finally, a group of voters from Memphis, Nashville, and Knoxville led by Charles W. Baker went to federal court with a lawsuit against Joseph Carr, the Tennessee secretary of state. The voters claimed that the disparity in districts reflected an "unconstitutional and obsolete" system that denied them equal protection of the laws. The district court, relying on the Supreme Court's precedents, said federal courts had no jurisdiction over the issues raised in the suit and that those issues were "nonjusticiable," meaning that they were not appropriate for judicial determination.

VOTE

6–2, with Justice William J. Brennan Jr. writing the majority opinion. Joining Brennan were Chief Justice Earl Warren and Justices Hugo L. Black, William O. Douglas, Tom C. Clark, and Potter Stewart. Justices Felix Frankfurter and John M. Harlan dissented. Justice Charles E. Whittaker did not participate.

HIGHLIGHTS

The Supreme Court, by all accounts, struggled with this case. It heard three hours of oral argument on the case during one term and then rescheduled it for another three hours in the next. Justice Clark, in a concurring opinion, said the case "has been most carefully considered over and over again by us in Conference and individually." According to Court watchers Bernard Schwartz (author of *Decision*) and Ed Cray (author of *Chief Justice*), in internal deliberations, the majority was frequently in doubt. It was not until the last moment that it became a 6–2 decision, when Clark changed his mind and voted with the majority.

When the opinion was finally issued, the various writings—three concurring opinions and two dissents, in addition to the main opinion—totaled 163 pages. Frankfurter's dissent, which proved to be his last major opinion, was sixty-four pages. Frankfurter angrily called the majority opinion a "massive repudiation of the experience of our whole past" because it thrust the federal courts into the political realm.

But to Justice Brennan, the result seemed obvious. He avoided the actual merits of the Tennessee case, focusing instead on the threshold question of whether the courts had jurisdiction and the issues involved could be resolved judicially. He said federal courts have jurisdiction because the lawsuit "arises under" a part of the Constitution, namely the Fourteenth Amendment. He also found that the plaintiffs in the case had "standing"—the right to sue—because their right to vote was at stake.

The pivotal part of the ruling was the determination that the issue was "justiciable," which is different from the issue of whether the Court has jurisdiction. For a dispute to be justiciable, the Court has to be able to identify the problem and fashion a remedy that it has the right to impose, using manageable standards to make the determination. In prior cases the Court had decided that two types of disputes were not justiciable: those involving "political questions" and claims that rely on the guaranty clause of the Constitution, under which the federal government guarantees a republican form of government to all states. Brennan swept those obstacles aside, narrowing the definition of political questions that the Court must avoid. Because resolving *Baker v. Carr* did not require the Court to impinge on the separation of powers or to make political judgments, Brennan found the case justiciable. His opinion gave short shrift to the Guaranty Clause, finding that the Fourteenth Amendment's Equal Protection Clause was a valid ground for bringing a reapportionment lawsuit.

EXCERPTS

From Justice Brennan's majority opinion: "Of course, the mere fact that the suit seeks protection of a political right does not mean it presents a political question. Such an objection 'is little more than a play upon words.' Rather, it is argued that apportionment cases, whatever the actual wording of the complaint, can involve no federal constitutional right except one resting on the guaranty of a republican form of government, and that complaints based on that clause have been held to present political questions which are nonjusticiable.

"We hold that the claim pleaded here neither rests upon nor implicates the Guaranty Clause and that its justiciability is therefore not foreclosed by our decisions of cases involving that clause. The District Court misinterpreted *Colegrove v. Green* and other decisions of this Court on which it relied. Appellants' claim that they are being denied equal protection is justiciable. . . .

"We conclude that the complaint's allegations of a denial of equal protection present a justiciable constitutional cause of action upon which appellants are entitled to a trial and a decision. The right asserted is within the reach of judicial protection under the Fourteenth Amendment."

IMPACT

The Court's decision is often associated with the phrase "one person, one vote," which actually did not appear in its text. That standard was announced a year later in *Gray v. Sanders*, a case that built on *Baker v. Carr*. The Court in *Gray v. Sanders* struck down Georgia's "county unit" system of electing state officials because rural counties had more weight than urban counties.

Still, the sweep of *Baker v. Carr* would be difficult to overstate. Chief Justice Warren said in his memoirs that the case was "the most important case of my tenure on the Court"—no small statement from the man who wrote the Court's ruling in *Brown v. Board of Education.*

By the end of 1962, more than sixty lawsuits had been initiated and a dozen state legislatures had met, all with the goal of reapportioning districts to achieve more equal representation. Gradually the nation's electoral map was redrawn, shifting the balance of power toward urban areas and away from rural interests. Reapportionment after every decennial census, only spottily done before the decision, has become routine because of the ruling. The Court has continued to grapple with reapportionment cases ever since, especially on the question of redrawing districts to concentrate the voting power of minorities.

Baker v. Carr has been identified as a major milestone on the Court's road toward greater activism. Frankfurter's view that judges should shy away from the "political thicket" was replaced by Brennan's view that courts had a responsibility to

vindicate constitutional rights, even in areas once viewed as off-limits. It was one of several decisions in which the liberal Brennan sought to give individuals greater access to the courts in the interest of freedom and justice.

The Baker decision played a prominent role in the Court's 2004 decision *Vieth v. Jubelirer,* involving the politically motivated redistricting of Pennsylvania congressional districts after the 2000 census. In a 1986 case *Davis v. Bandemer,* the Court had said courts could scrutinize claims of political gerrymandering, but in the years after that ruling, lower courts struggled to find the proper standard for reviewing such political determinations. In *Vieth,* four justices said the courts should just abandon the enterprise, because the *Baker v. Carr* requirement that there be "manageable standards" for deciding political gerrymandering cases could not be met. Justice Anthony Kennedy, in the decisive fifth vote, said the door should not be closed permanently on the possibility of finding the proper standard under *Baker v. Carr.* But he agreed with the other four justices in the majority that in this case, the Democratic challenge to the Republican-controlled Pennsylvania redistricting should be dismissed.

Oregon v. Mitchell

Decided December 21, 1970
400 U.S. 112
laws.findlaw.com/US/400/112.html

DECISION

Congress acted within its powers when it established an eighteen-year-old minimum-age requirement for national elections. The Constitution prevents Congress from setting the same requirement for state and local elections. The Court upheld a nationwide ban on literacy tests.

BACKGROUND

As the number of young Americans serving in the Vietnam War grew during the 1960s, a parallel movement to lower the voting age to eighteen from twenty-one also gained momentum. Animating the movement was this seeming contradiction: eighteen-year-olds were being drafted to fight for their nation, but they were not entrusted with the right to vote.

Congress responded in 1970 by passing a law—not a constitutional amendment—which, among other things, lowered the voting age in national and local elections to eighteen from twenty-one. It also standardized other kinds of voting requirements, including residency.

The voting age provision caused the greatest controversy, not on the merits of lowering the age, but on the way it was done. Even as President Richard Nixon signed the bill into law, he said he agreed with many constitutional scholars who maintained that Congress did not have the power to make these changes. Nixon agreed that a constitutional amendment was required. Those scholars, and many state officials, believed that the job of setting the rules for state elections belonged to states, not to Congress. Support for this federalism argument was growing among conservatives. Congress, for its part, argued that the Constitution gave it powers to regulate elections even at the state level.

Soon after the 1970 voting rights law was signed, Arizona, Idaho, Oregon, and Texas went directly to the Supreme Court to challenge the voting age provision, as well as other aspects relating to literacy requirements and the length of time residents could be required to live in a state before they could vote. The case was not considered in any lower court, because the Constitution dictates that when states are a party to a suit, their litigation goes directly to the Supreme Court.

With a national election less than two years away, the Supreme Court took up the cases quickly. Two months after hearing arguments in the case, the Court handed down its somewhat fractured opinion.

VOTE

5–4 on the ruling that Congress may not set the voting age for state and local elections, with Justice Hugo L. Black writing the opinion. Joining him were Chief Justice Warren E. Burger and Justices John M. Harlan, Potter Stewart, and Harry A. Blackmun, but these four also said Congress could not set the voting age in federal elections either. Black led a different 5–4 majority in ruling that Congress could set the voting age in federal elections through legislation. Joining Black on that ruling were Justices William O. Douglas, William J. Brennan Jr., Byron R. White, and Thurgood Marshall, but these four also believed Congress could set the voting age in state and local elections. Justice Harlan dissented on the residency issue.

HIGHLIGHTS

The voting breakdown in the case could be characterized as 4–1–4, with Black as the justice in the middle. In such a case, it is that justice's opinion that announces the ruling of the case, even though no other justice agrees with all parts of it.

Black's opinion starts with what appeared to be the easiest part of the case: ruling that Congress, the federal legislative branch, has the power to set the voting age in federal elections. But even that judgment is not clear-cut because of the wording of Article I, Section 4, of the Constitution: "The Times, Places and Manner of holding Elections for Senators and Representatives, shall be prescribed in each State by the Legislature thereof; but the Congress may at any time by Law make or alter such Regulations." The Framers had given both states and the Congress responsibilities in regulating even federal elections.

Black believed that common sense dictated that Congress had the power to intervene in matters such as establishing a voting age in national elections. "The Constitution allotted to

Eighteen-year-old Carol Fulton receives voting machine instructions from Cecil Mitchell, a Franklin County, Ohio, voter registration clerk, in July 1971. According to the Supreme Court's decision in *Oregon v. Mitchell* (1970), Congress had acted within its powers in passing a law—rather than a constitutional amendment—lowering the voting age from twenty-one to eighteen.

Source: AP/Wide World Photos.

the States the power to make laws regarding national elections, but provided that if Congress became dissatisfied with the state laws Congress could alter them. A newly created national government could hardly have been expected to survive without the ultimate power to rule itself and to fill its offices under its own laws."

But to four justices, this conclusion was wrong. Citing the same part of the Constitution, Justice Harlan wrote, "Surely nothing in these provisions lends itself to the view that voting qualifications in federal elections are to be set by Congress."

On the ability of Congress to mandate a lower voting age in state and local elections, Black was also adamant. Congress had no such authority either under the main body of the Constitution or the post–Civil War amendments, which gave Congress the power to enforce civil rights at the state level. No one had argued that setting the minimum age for voters at twenty-one was motivated by racial bias, so those amendments could not be invoked, said Black.

"Since Congress has attempted to invade an area preserved to the States by the Constitution without a foundation for enforcing the Civil War Amendments' ban on racial discrimination, I would hold that Congress has exceeded its powers in attempting to lower the voting age in state and local elections," Black said.

But on this point, a different group of justices disagreed. Justice Douglas said the Civil War Amendments were directed not only at ending racial bias, but also at guaranteeing equal protection of the law for all—a guarantee that would justify congressional legislation establishing a lower minimum age for voting in all elections, not just federal. "It is a reasoned judgment that those who have such a large 'stake' in modern elections as 18-year-olds, whether, in times of war or peace, should have political equality," Douglas wrote.

The Court had an easier time upholding other aspects of the Voting Rights Act provisions, which barred a wider range of literacy tests than had previously been banned and limited the ability of states to impose residency requirements on voters in national elections. Only Harlan dissented on the residency issue, and the Court was unanimous on the literacy test issue.

EXCERPTS

From Justice Black's majority opinion: "I would hold, as have a long line of decisions in this Court, that Congress has ultimate supervisory power over congressional elections. Similarly, it is the prerogative of Congress to oversee the conduct of presidential and vice-presidential elections and to set the qualifications for voters for electors for those offices. It cannot be seriously contended that Congress has less power over the conduct of presidential elections than it has over congressional elections.

"On the other hand, the Constitution was also intended to preserve to the States the power that even the Colonies had to establish and maintain their own separate and independent governments, except insofar as the Constitution itself commands otherwise. . . . No function is more essential to the separate and independent existence of the States and their governments than the power to determine within the limits of the Constitution the qualifications of their own voters for state, county, and municipal offices and the nature of their own machinery for filling local public offices."

IMPACT

The Court's mix-and-match majority may have blunted some of the force of the decision in *Oregon v. Mitchell*. After the opinion was announced, Justice Black reportedly told a law clerk that the ruling reminded him of hunt trips of his childhood where his dogs, instead of searching for birds, would get distracted by the scent of a rabbit and run all over the field. In some of the opinions in the case, Black said, "It just seemed to me that somebody had lost sight of the bird."

But the importance of the decision was clear enough. While eighteen-year-olds could vote in federal elections for president, vice-president, and members of Congress, they could not vote at the same time in the state and local elections of the forty-seven states that said they were too young to vote. The result was that states would need to create dual records and voting machines, a potential administrative nightmare.

The only way to standardize the voting age at all levels of elections was through the constitutional amendment process. With remarkable speed, Congress in March 1971 proposed to the states a constitutional amendment that guaranteed voting rights to all those eighteen and older at the federal and state levels.

Just more than one hundred days later, the necessary three-fourths of the state legislatures had ratified the Twenty-Sixth Amendment—the quickest ratification process of any constitutional amendment in history. The amendment had the effect of giving more than 10 million Americans the right to vote.

It is extremely rare, but not unheard of, for the Constitution to be amended in response to Supreme Court rulings. The Eleventh Amendment, barring citizens from suing states, was a response to *Chisholm v. Georgia* (1793). The Fourteenth Amendment, which became a major guarantor of civil rights, was to some extent a response to two rulings: *Barron v. Baltimore* (1833), which said the Bill of Rights did not apply to states, and *Scott v. Sandford* (1857), which denied citizenship to slaves (see *Scott v. Sandford*). The Sixteenth Amendment, creating the federal income tax, was a response to the 1895 decision in *Pollock v. Farmers' Loan and Trust Co.,* which had struck down a legislatively created tax.

Shaw v. Reno

Decided June 28, 1993
509 U.S. 630
laws.findlaw.com/US/509/630.html

DECISION

White voters are entitled to challenge the boundaries of oddly shaped congressional districts that were created to maximize the number of blacks in those districts. Under the Fourteenth Amendment's guarantee of equal protection of the laws, any use of race as a factor in redistricting must be subjected to "strict scrutiny" to determine if it is narrowly targeted to achieve a compelling government goal.

BACKGROUND

The Voting Rights Act of 1965 succeeded in guaranteeing the right to vote to minorities who had been excluded by literacy tests and other means devised to keep them out of the political process. More than 1 million blacks registered to vote within four years of passage of the law.

The increase in voting strength, however, did not translate into greater numbers of minority candidates elected to office. In many southern states, the location of district boundaries kept black voters in the minority in most jurisdictions. Moreover, even through the 1980s, white voters tended to vote only for white candidates. North Carolina voters, for example, did not elect a single black member of Congress from the post-Reconstruction era through 1990, even though about 20 percent of voting age residents were black.

The Justice Department, which the Voting Rights Act had given unusual supervisory powers over election practices in many states, tried to remedy this situation by urging the creation of "majority-minority" districts. The hope was that if minorities comprised more than one-half of voters in a given district, the chances of electing a minority candidate in that district would be enhanced. Following the 1990 Census, when the states redrew their district lines to reflect new population figures, the Justice Department rejected a North Carolina redistricting plan because it contained only one, not two, majority-minority districts. New boundaries were drawn, and in 1992 both districts sent black representatives to Congress. Nationwide the number of black members of Congress rose sharply, partly because of similar "race-conscious" redistricting.

Ruth Shaw, a white North Carolina voter, went to court to challenge the race-based redistricting of the Twelfth District, where she lived. It was oddly shaped, its boundaries taking sharp turns to incorporate pockets of black residents. In one section, the boundaries followed an interstate highway, prompting one legislator to remark, "if you drove down the interstate with both car doors open, you'd kill most of the people in the district." Shaw and other white voters claimed the district unconstitutionally diminished their voting power. A federal court panel upheld the redistricting, ruling that race-conscious redistricting was permissible as long as its purpose was not to discriminate against whites.

VOTE

5–4, with Justice Sandra Day O'Connor writing the majority opinion. She was joined by Chief Justice William Rehnquist and Justices Antonin Scalia, Anthony M. Kennedy, and Clarence Thomas. Dissenting were Justices Byron R. White, Harry A. Blackmun, John Paul Stevens, and David H. Souter.

HIGHLIGHTS

Once before, the Court had said that using redistricting to create majority black districts was permissible. In the 1977 case *United Jewish Organizations of Williamsburgh v. Carey,* the

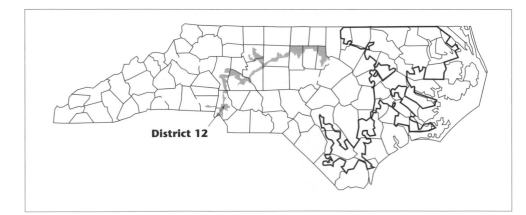

District 12

Congressional redistricting in some states after the 1990 census sought to create so-called majority-minority districts that were likely to elect African Americans. These efforts resulted in such oddly shaped districts as North Carolina's Twelfth District, along Interstate 85. In *Shaw v. Reno* (1993), the Supreme Court placed limits on the use of race as a dominant factor in drawing districts.
Source: CQ Press.

Court upheld a redistricting plan that divided a Hasidic Jewish community in New York into two districts to create majority black districts.

But the Supreme Court of 1993 was different. The Court, as well as the public, was divided over affirmative action—the use of race as a factor to help minorities in the workplace and education. Race-conscious redistricting was, in many ways, an electoral version of affirmative action, aimed at giving minorities a boost at the polling place.

In the *Shaw* case, Justice O'Connor did not overrule the 1977 precedent; instead, she ignored it. She cited instead a line of cases including *Gomillion v. Lightfoot* from 1960 that struck down redistricting efforts by white politicians aimed at excluding blacks. In her view, the use of race as the main factor in both instances was wrong.

"Classifications of citizens solely on the basis of race 'are by their very nature odious to a free people whose institutions are founded upon the doctrine of equality,' " wrote O'Connor, quoting from *Hirabayashi v. United States* (1943). "They threaten to stigmatize individuals by reason of their membership in a racial group and to incite racial hostility. Accordingly, we have held that the Fourteenth Amendment requires state legislation that expressly distinguishes among citizens because of their race to be narrowly tailored to further a compelling governmental interest."

Did the design of North Carolina's Twelfth District meet that test? The Court left that for lower courts to decide. Very few laws or government actions meet that standard, and O'Connor's language made it fairly clear she did not think this one would either. The district at issue, she said, had a "dramatically irregular shape," making it hard to explain on any other basis but race. Racial redistricting, she suggested, created more harms than benefits to race relations. Among other things, she said it would lead elected officials to conclude that they only had to satisfy one race or the other in performing their duties.

In dissent, Justice White asserted that the kind of redistricting at issue in North Carolina did not violate the Fourteenth Amendment because it did not harm or dilute the voting rights of majority white voters. "The Court's approach nonetheless will unnecessarily hinder to some extent a State's voluntary effort to ensure a modicum of minority representation," wrote White. "This will be true in areas where the minority population is geographically dispersed." He concluded, "It involves, instead, an attempt to equalize treatment, and to provide minority voters with an effective voice in the political process. The Equal Protection Clause of the Constitution, surely, does not stand in the way."

EXCERPTS

From Justice O'Connor's majority opinion: " 'The right to vote freely for the candidate of one's choice is of the essence of a de-mocratic society. . . .' For much of our Nation's history, that right sadly has been denied to many because of race. The Fifteenth Amendment, ratified in 1870 after a bloody Civil War, promised unequivocally that '[t]he right of citizens of the United States to vote' no longer would be 'denied or abridged . . . by any State on account of race, color, or previous condition of servitude.'

". . . Our focus is on appellants' claim that the State engaged in unconstitutional racial gerrymandering. That argument strikes a powerful historical chord: it is unsettling how closely the North Carolina plan resembles the most egregious racial gerrymanders of the past. . . .

". . . [W]e believe that reapportionment is one area in which appearances do matter. A reapportionment plan that includes in one district individuals who belong to the same race, but who are otherwise widely separated by geographical and political boundaries, and who may have little in common with one another but the color of their skin, bears an uncomfortable resemblance to political apartheid. It reinforces the perception that members of the same racial group—regardless of their age, education, economic status, or the community in which they live—think alike, share the same political interests, and will prefer the same candidates at the polls. . . .

"The message that such districting sends to elected representatives is equally pernicious. When a district obviously is created solely to effectuate the perceived common interests of one racial group, elected officials are more likely to believe that their primary obligation is to represent only the members of that group, rather than their constituency as a whole. This is altogether antithetical to our system of representative democracy. . . .

"Racial classifications of any sort pose the risk of lasting harm to our society. They reinforce the belief, held by too many for too much of our history, that individuals should be judged by the color of their skin. Racial classifications with respect to voting carry particular dangers. Racial gerrymandering, even for remedial purposes, may balkanize us into competing racial factions; it threatens to carry us further from the goal of a political system in which race no longer matters—a goal that the Fourteenth and Fifteenth Amendments embody, and to which the Nation continues to aspire."

IMPACT

The decision in *Shaw v. Reno* was criticized by civil rights leaders for failing to recognize the impact on minority voting power of the centuries of slavery and discrimination. The Voting Rights Act was aimed at rectifying past discrimination, and the Supreme Court had neutralized an important way of achieving that goal. Civil rights leaders also expressed anger that Justice Thomas, the Court's second black member, had voted with the Court's majority. The number of blacks elected to Congress would decline sharply, civil rights leaders predicted. The Reverend Jesse Jackson predicted an "ethnic cleansing" of Congress.

The decision also guaranteed that litigation over race-conscious redistricting would continue. It offered no clear guidance on just how "bizarre" or oddly shaped a district had to be before it would trigger the high level of scrutiny, nor did it state definitively how much of a factor race could be in the design of a district.

North Carolina's Twelfth District went back to the lower courts for reappraisal under the justices' decision. The lower court found that the district was drawn on the basis of a racial classification, but ruled that it met the "strict scrutiny" standard of *Shaw v. Reno.* When the case returned to the Supreme Court, the justices once again turned down the redistricting scheme and the lower court's view of it. In the 1996 decision, *Shaw v. Hunt,* the Court said the district failed to pass the "strict scrutiny" test. The same day, in *Bush v. Vera,* the Court also threw out three Texas congressional districts.

The issue again returned to the lower courts. When the state legislature redrew the boundaries, the district was somewhat more compact, and there was another difference as well: blacks accounted for only 43 percent of the voting age population. A lower court panel threw out the new district, finding that it, like the previous version, was drawn with race in mind. For a third time, the design of North Carolina's Twelfth District returned to the Supreme Court.

On this go, the Court was not ready to throw out the design. Ruling in *Hunt v. Cromartie* in 1999, the Court said the lower court should not have tossed out the design so quickly, because it was plausible that it had been drawn for political as well as racial reasons. The Supreme Court has long respected traditional redistricting done by a political party to concentrate its members within districts and preserve its dominance. In the latest version

of the Twelfth District, the Supreme Court said the evidence could lead to the conclusion that "the General Assembly did no more than create a district of strong partisan Democrats." This constitutionally permissible motivation was plausible enough that it should be fully considered, not dismissed out of hand. The Court sent the case back to lower courts for yet another look. The district court determined that race in fact was the primary motive for drawing the district, not politics. The case was appealed again to the Supreme Court, which in April 2001 had the final word on North Carolina's Twelfth District. By a 5–4 vote in the case now known as *Easley v. Cromartie,* the Court said the district court's finding of racial motivation was "clearly erroneous." The high correlation between race and party affiliation made it incorrect to conclude that race was the main motive, the majority found. Significantly Justice O'Connor, author of the original *Shaw v. Reno* decision, joined the majority in the latest decision, suggesting that she was finally comfortable with an oddly shaped district drawn mainly for political reasons, even if racial factors were a part of the calculation.

Meanwhile other trends developed in electoral politics that shed new light on *Shaw v. Reno.* Most of the black politicians who had been elected in majority-minority districts after the 1990 Census were reelected even after *Shaw v. Reno* had caused the reduction of black majorities in their districts. These results suggested that white voters in the South were becoming more willing to cast their votes for black candidates, especially incumbents. Some Democratic leaders also had second thoughts about race-based redistricting, because it tended to "rob" black voters from surrounding districts to create a single majority-minority district. Those black voters were needed, some felt, to elect Democrats in the surrounding districts.

Bush v. Gore

Decided December 12, 2000
531 U.S. 98
laws.findlaw.com/US/531/98.html

DECISION

The Florida recount of ballots in the 2000 presidential election must end. The significant differences between counties in the way in which the recount was being conducted amounted to a violation of the Fourteenth Amendment's equal protection clause, and there was no other constitutionally valid way to complete the recount by December 12, which was when Florida needed to submit its vote totals to avoid Electoral College challenges.

BACKGROUND

In the final weeks before the 2000 election, pollsters and analysts predicted it would be a cliffhanger, too close to call. But no one could foresee just how close it would be—and the constitutional chaos it would produce.

Early on election night, based on what turned out to be flawed analysis, television networks put Florida, with its 25 electoral votes, in Democrat Al Gore's column—enough to put him above the 270 electoral votes needed for election. Then the networks switched gears, giving the state to George W. Bush, and Gore prepared to concede the election. But as he traveled to the hall in Nashville where he would make the speech, Gore's political operatives frantically urged him not to concede. With more and more Florida precincts reporting, the gap between the candidates was narrowing, and reports of irregularities increased. Gore shelved his concession speech, and the nation was in for a surreal five-week political roller coaster ride unmatched in U.S. history.

As the news media backpedaled, an automatic recount proceeded in Florida, resulting in an even narrower gap between the candidates that at one point totaled 229 votes out of nearly 6 million cast. Lawyers for both sides of the campaign descended on Florida, and reports of voter intimidation and ballot irregularities fueled angry disagreements over the legitimacy of Florida's election process. The nation soon became familiar with butterfly ballots and hanging chads, which in Palm Beach County appeared to lead many residents to vote twice or to vote inadvertently for conservative Reform Party candidate Pat Buchanan instead of Gore.

Inevitably and within hours, the dispute entered the Florida courts, with angry voters claiming they had been disenfranchised. Democrats clamored for a manual recount in several counties, provided for by Florida law. Republicans, for their part, sought to have the results validated as quickly as possible without any further recounts, which would declare Bush the winner. At this point most commentators still did not see the dispute making its way to the federal courts, much less the Supreme Court. And yet it did. Republicans filed suit in federal court, asking for an injunction to halt the recounts. But the judge refused, stating that resolution of the dispute belonged in the hands of Florida voters, election officials, and courts.

On November 18 Florida Secretary of State Katherine Harris, who had also served as cochair of the Bush campaign in the state, asked the Florida Supreme Court to order a halt in the manual recounts, but it too refused. She proceeded anyway to enforce what she viewed as a specific deadline for accepting late returns in the election. Gore lawyers challenged that decision, and a flurry of further litigation got the case back before the state Supreme Court, which allowed the recounts to continue while the case was pending.

In a historic televised hearing on November 20, the Florida Supreme Court heard the legal arguments for and against extending the deadline for recounts. A few days later, the Florida court ruled that Harris had abused her discretion and said the recounts could continue through Thanksgiving weekend. That decision, in the words of Howard Gillman, who wrote a book on the litigation, was "like a starter's gun triggering at least three simultaneous races": the race to finish the recounts, to enforce

Robert Rosenberg, a Broward County, Florida, election official, examines a ballot as part of the vote recount in the disputed 2000 presidential race. The Supreme Court entered the dispute and in *Bush v. Gore* (2000) decided to stop the Florida recount. Five of the nine justices found that the differences in the way in which counties conducted the recount violated the Fourteenth Amendment's equal protection clause. The decision resulted in George W. Bush defeating Al Gore.
Source: Reuters/Colin Braley.

or undo the Florida ruling, and finally the race to the U.S. Supreme Court.

Before the U.S. Supreme Court, the Bush legal team based its challenge to the recounts primarily on the equal protection clause of the Fourteenth Amendment. But the lawyers also cited a lesser known part of the Constitution that gives state legislatures—not courts—the power to select the state's electors in presidential elections. Suddenly it became possible to imagine that the Supreme Court might have to resolve the dispute. On November 24, the day after Thanksgiving, the Supreme Court announced it would consider the case in oral arguments a week later. In the meantime Florida's Harris certified the election result and declared Bush the winner, but with the Supreme Court's involvement the election dispute was far from over. Litigation continued at the state level even as lawyers prepared for the Supreme Court arguments.

With extraordinary attention focused on the nation's highest court, the technical issues relating to the Florida recount were argued before the justices. And three days later, a unanimous, unsigned decision emerged in the case titled *Bush v. Palm Beach County Canvassing Board*. Although expressing reluctance to intervene in a case in which a state supreme court interpreted the state's own laws, the Court said it was compelled to rule because of its "considerable uncertainty" over the basis for the Florida Supreme Court decision and because the Florida court's ruling raised federal constitutional issues. The Supreme Court sent the case back to Florida for clarification. Some analysts thought the Supreme Court's involvement was over, but that was not the case.

The Florida Supreme Court responded in an unexpected way. On December 8 it ordered recounts to resume statewide under state law allowing for such recounts. Bush lawyers immediately appealed the decision, and the next day the U.S. Supreme Court acted. By a 5–4 vote, with the more liberal justices on the losing side, it issued an injunction halting the recounts pending its own consideration of the recount. In a concurrence Justice Antonin Scalia cast doubt on the legality of the ballots that were to be recounted.

With this injunction the Supreme Court became ground zero in the still-raging election controversy. Liberal commentators said the Court had compromised its image of impartiality by aiding Bush, though opinion polls found most of the public still trusting the Supreme Court as the best arbiter of the dispute.

On the day of the oral argument, December 11, the Supreme Court—usually a zone of quiet and tranquility on Capitol Hill—was surrounded by hundreds of angry partisans of both candidates, many of them shouting at each other. The Court, re-sponding to requests by the media and others, agreed to release the audiotapes of the oral arguments immediately after they ended. Broadcast networks immediately aired the tapes.

VOTE

5–4, with a per curiam opinion agreed to by Chief Justice William Rehnquist and Justices Sandra Day O'Connor, Antonin Scalia, Anthony Kennedy, and Clarence Thomas. Dissenting were Justices John Paul Stevens, David Souter, Ruth Bader Ginsburg and Stephen Breyer.

HIGHLIGHTS

The Court labored to get its decision out quickly. The following day, December 12, was the deadline under law for states to finalize their slate of electors to participate in the Electoral College vote for president December 18. So at 10:00 p.m. on December 12, the day after oral argument, the decision was issued: a relatively brief thirteen-page per curiam or unsigned opinion for the court, along with several concurrences and dissents, for a total of sixty-five pages.

The Court dispensed with it usual syllabus or summary, leaving broadcast journalists frantically flipping through the pages live on television, trying to divine the outcome of the decision. The Court's bottom line, reversing the Florida Supreme Court and remanding it for further proceedings, led some to conclude that there was still hope for Gore. But that was not the case.

Casting aside most of the more technical arguments, the five most conservative justices framed their decision in loftier

Supporters of presidential candidates George W. Bush and Al Gore rally outside the Supreme Court on December 11, 2000, before the Court heard arguments in *Bush v. Gore*. The Court ultimately decided the election when it sided with Bush and ended the Florida ballot recount.

Source: Congressional Quarterly/Scott J. Ferrell.

terms of equal protection of the laws and the principle of "one person one vote" embodied in a long line of voting rights cases. They concluded that the recounts ordered by the Florida Supreme Court could not meet basic equal protection standards under the U.S. Constitution. "Having once granted the right to vote on equal terms, the State may not, by later arbitrary and disparate treatment, value one person's vote over that of another," the opinion stated.

That unequal value placed on the votes of Floridians resulted from the state supreme court's failure to lay down a uniform standard for reviewing disputed ballots. "As seems to have been acknowledged at oral argument, the standards for accepting or rejecting contested ballots might vary not only from county to county but indeed within a single county from one recount team to another," the Court said. "When a court orders a statewide remedy, there must be at least some assurance that the rudimentary requirements of equal treatment and fundamental fairness are satisfied."

The Court seemed to be aware that its intervention in an election matter was unusual, describing it as an "unsought responsibility" thrust on it when the parties took the case to federal courts.

The majority also gently hinted that the time had come for states to update their election machinery. "This case has shown that punch card balloting machines can produce an unfortunate number of ballots which are not punched in a clean, complete way by the voter," the opinion stated. "After the current counting, it is likely legislative bodies nationwide will examine ways to improve the mechanisms and machinery for voting."

In a concurring opinion, Chief Justice Rehnquist, joined by Justices Scalia and Thomas, acknowledged it was unusual for the Court to second-guess state court judgments about that state's own laws. But he said there are occasions when it is necessary, especially when, as in this case, the state court is impeding the role of the state legislature. The court-ordered recounts, he said, would interfere with the legislature's job of certifying electors to participate in the Electoral College.

Even though there were four dissenting justices, the Court's main opinion pointed out that seven of the nine justices had found that the recount posed constitutional problems. Indeed, dissents authored by Justices Souter and Breyer did acknowledge that equal protection claims were the only objections to the Florida recounts worth taking seriously.

But all four of the dissenting justices sharply criticized the majority for usurping the role of state courts and for asserting that there was no time left for the recounts to take place. If needed, there were procedures available under federal law for Congress to resolve the dispute, Souter pointed out. "To recount these manually would be a tall order," Souter said, "but before this Court stayed the effort to do that the courts of Florida were ready to do their best to get that job done. There is no justification for denying the State the opportunity to try to count all disputed ballots now."

Ginsburg scolded the majority for failing to follow its usual practice of respecting a state court's interpretation of its own laws. "The extraordinary setting of this case has obscured the ordinary principle that dictates its proper resolution," Ginsburg wrote. "Federal courts defer to state high courts' interpretations of their state's own law. This principle reflects the core of federalism, on which all agree."

Breyer also noted that states often tolerate a measure of unequal treatment of voters in elections, by delegating to counties the job of running elections. "In a system that allows counties to use different types of voting systems, voters already arrive at the polls with an unequal chance that their votes will be counted."

But Stevens's dissent may have been the most cutting, asserting that the loser in the case was "the Nation's confidence in the judge as an impartial guardian of the rule of law."

EXCERPTS

From the per curiam opinion: "Upon due consideration of the difficulties identified to this point, it is obvious that the recount cannot be conducted in compliance with the requirements of equal protection and due process without substantial additional work. It would require not only the adoption (after opportunity for argument) of adequate statewide standards for determining what is a legal vote, and practicable procedures to implement them, but also orderly judicial review of any disputed matters that might arise. . . .

"The Supreme Court of Florida has said that the legislature intended the State's electors to "participat[e] fully in the federal electoral process," as provided in 3 U.S.C. § 5. . . . That statute, in turn, requires that any controversy or contest that is designed to lead to a conclusive selection of electors be completed by December 12. That date is upon us, and there is no recount procedure in place under the State Supreme Court's order that comports with minimal constitutional standards. Because it is evident that any recount seeking to meet the December 12 date will be unconstitutional for the reasons we have discussed, we reverse the judgment of the Supreme Court of Florida ordering a recount to proceed. . . .

"None are more conscious of the vital limits on judicial authority than are the members of this Court, and none stand more in admiration of the Constitution's design to leave the selection of the President to the people, through their legislatures, and to the political sphere. When contending parties invoke the process of the courts, however, it becomes our unsought responsibility to resolve the federal and constitutional issues the judicial system has been forced to confront."

From Justice Stevens's dissent: "The Constitution assigns to the States the primary responsibility for determining the manner of selecting the Presidential electors. . . . When questions arise about the meaning of state laws, including election laws, it is our settled practice to accept the opinions of the highest courts of the States as providing the final answers. On rare occasions, however, either federal statutes or the Federal Constitution may require federal judicial intervention in state elections. This is not such an occasion. . . .

"What must underlie petitioners' entire federal assault on the Florida election procedures is an unstated lack of confidence in the impartiality and capacity of the state judges who would make the critical decisions if the vote count were to proceed. Otherwise, their position is wholly without merit. The endorsement of that position by the majority of this Court can only lend credence to the most cynical appraisal of the work of judges throughout the land. It is confidence in the men and women who administer the judicial system that is the true backbone of the rule of law. Time will one day heal the wound to that confidence that will be inflicted by today's decision. One thing, however, is certain. Although we may never know with complete certainty the identity of the winner of this year's Presidential election, the identity of the loser is perfectly clear. It is the Nation's confidence in the judge as an impartial guardian of the rule of law."

From Justice Ginsburg's dissent: "In this highly politicized matter, the appearance of a split decision runs the risk of undermining the public's confidence in the Court itself. That confidence is a public treasure. It has been built slowly over many years, some of which were marked by a Civil War and the tragedy of segregation. It is a vitally necessary ingredient of any successful effort to protect basic liberty and, indeed, the rule of law itself. We run no risk of returning to the days when a President (responding to this Court's efforts to protect the Cherokee Indians) might have said, 'John Marshall has made his decision; now let him enforce it!' . . . But we do risk a self-inflicted wound—a wound that may harm not just the Court, but the Nation."

IMPACT

As inscrutable as the Supreme Court's decision might have appeared at first, its immediate meaning was clear: The election of 2000 was finally over. Bush's certified victory in Florida was no longer subject to challenge, and he had enough electoral votes to win nationwide.

The next day Vice President Gore conceded the election, stating in a nationally televised speech that "while I strongly disagree with the court's decision, I accept it." He was praised for placing the rule of law and respect for the Supreme Court above his own interests.

But Gore's statesmanlike response did not keep his supporters and many legal scholars from sharply attacking the decision and its rationale. The Court's conservative majority had long been skeptical of expansive equal protection arguments, some pointed out, yet suddenly it had embraced an extension of equal protection into the unlikely area of election recounts. The same majority usually exalted state sovereignty and shied away from deciding political disputes, but appeared to violate both principles in *Bush v. Gore*. Foreign commentators, mystified by the U.S. system of checks and balances, wondered how judges could end up deciding the outcome of the U.S. presidential election. And a question that may never be answered was often asked in the aftermath of *Bush v. Gore:* What if the shoe had been on the other foot? What if it was candidate Bush who wanted the recounts to continue, and candidate Gore was the one opposing them? Would the Court's conservative majority have ruled the same way? To some, the fact that such a question could even be asked was a sign that the Court's credibility was damaged by its intervention into a presidential election. Yet opinion polls found that the public's view of the Court has changed little. Within months, as the Bush administration took shape, the public seemed to have "moved on."

Some conservative scholars rallied to the Court's defense. Northwestern University law professor John McGinnis said the decision was "an act of statesmanship of high order," made in full knowledge that the media and many academics would oppose it. But another noted conservative, University of Utah professor Michael McConnell—now a federal appeals judge—was not happy with the ruling. "The court did not have the resolution to declare that no recount was necessary, or the patience to declare that a proper recount should proceed," he wrote in a *Wall Street Journal* column. "That means, unfortunately, that Mr. Bush will take office under conditions of continued uncertainty. I do not think that part of the decision did him, or the nation, any favor."

Within the Court, justices said the trauma of the decision did not impair the smooth functioning of their day-to-day relationships. But in spite of the Court's culture of secrecy, some tales of the divisions among the justices during the hectic days of November and December 2000 have been told. A 2004 *Vanity Fair* article, quoting several unnamed law clerks from that term, indicated that Justice Kennedy may have changed his mind during deliberations, and that there was considerable lobbying and discussion among justices and clerks for votes.

The decision will long be remembered as one of the Supreme Court's most momentous, but it may not have cast a long shadow into the future. The opinion explicitly discouraged future litigants from citing it, stating, "Our consideration is limited to the present circumstances, for the problem of equal protection in election processes generally presents many complexities." But *Bush v. Gore* has been cited nonetheless in subsequent election disputes, and if the 2004 election had been closer, it might well have been invoked yet again before the Supreme Court.

WAR POWERS

*T*he power to make war is one of the most awesome duties of government. Both the president and Congress have a role to play, and the Supreme Court has been called on to define the limits the Constitution places on both branches. The Court almost always defers to the other branches and especially to military leaders, mindful that the courts are ill-equipped to second-guess battlefield judgments. The Court has usually heeded the Latin axiom, *Inter arma silent leges,* which means in English: In times of war the law falls silent. But over the decades, as the peacetime Supreme Court has expanded civil liberties, it has been less willing to surrender those rights in wartime.

Other related cases mentioned in the War Powers section

Hirabayashi v. United States (1943)
Ex parte Endo (1944)

Korematsu v. United States

Decided December 18, 1944
323 U.S. 214
laws.findlaw.com/US/323/214.html

DECISION

All laws that limit the rights of people because of their race are automatically suspect and can be justified only very rarely, such as in wartime. However, it was within the war powers of Congress and the president to remove Japanese Americans from areas on the West Coast near military installations in wartime.

BACKGROUND

Following the attack by Japan on the U.S. fleet at Pearl Harbor, Hawaii, on December 7, 1941, a wave of anti-Japanese animosity and panic swept the United States, particularly on the West Coast. Rumors that Japan was planning to attack West Coast military installations, aided by espionage and sabotage by Japanese Americans, fueled the panic.

"The Japanese in California should be under armed guard to the last man and woman right now—and to hell with *habeas corpus* until the danger is over," wrote popular conservative columnist Westbrook Pegler soon after Pearl Harbor. Among those supporting relocation of Japanese Americans was California governor Earl Warren, who would later become chief justice.

President Franklin Roosevelt in February 1942 issued an order authorizing the War Department to exclude anyone—regardless of ethnic heritage—from designated zones around military facilities on the West Coast. His aides later indicated that Roosevelt was not deterred by any constitutional issues. "The Constitution has not greatly bothered any wartime president," wrote Attorney General Francis Biddle, who opposed the order.

Military officials responded first by imposing a curfew on people of Japanese ancestry and then by ordering the "exclusion" of this group altogether. Within months, more than 120,000 people of Japanese descent, 70,000 of them U.S. citizens, were moved to ten relocation centers away from the coast. The fact that many of these detainees had deep ties to the United States and showed not the slightest evidence of sympathy with Japan in the war effort did not deter their removal.

Gen. John DeWitt, justifying the exclusion order before a congressional panel, said, "A Jap's a Jap. It makes no difference whether he is an American citizen or not. I have no confidence in their loyalty whatsoever."

One of those relocated was Fred Korematsu, a Japanese American born in Oakland, California. Korematsu had tried to enlist in the U.S. Army before Pearl Harbor, but was rejected for medical reasons. When the order to evacuate Japanese Americans was issued, he tried to avoid capture by changing his name and having some minor plastic surgery that he hoped would make him appear Hispanic. But he was arrested in San Leandro, California, in May 1942 for remaining in a military zone in violation of the evacuation order. After a jailhouse visit from a lawyer from the American Civil Liberties Union, Korematsu agreed to make a test case to challenge the constitutionality of the evacuation.

While his case was making its way to the Supreme Court, the justices issued a decision upholding the curfew imposed on Japanese Americans. In the May 1943 ruling in *Hirabayashi v. United States*, the Court said the constitutional war power included the "power to wage war successfully," justifying measures such as a curfew. But the Court specifically limited its ruling to the curfew order, avoiding the evacuation issue. Some scholars believe the Court was hoping that the evacuation program would soon be ended, making the constitutional issue moot.

But the program was still in place when the Court considered Korematsu's case in 1944. The U.S. government offered a new justification for the internment program: it protected Japanese Americans from racial hostility they might encounter if they were allowed to return to their homes.

VOTE

6–3, with Justice Hugo L. Black writing for the majority. Joining him were Chief Justice Harlan Fiske Stone and Justices Stanley F. Reed, Felix Frankfurter, William O. Douglas, and Wiley B. Rutledge. Dissenting were Justices Owen J. Roberts, Frank W. Murphy, and Robert H. Jackson.

HIGHLIGHTS

The decision began, ironically, with a ringing condemnation of laws that treat people differently because of racial animosity. "It should be noted, to begin with, that all legal restrictions which curtail the civil rights of a single racial group are immediately suspect. That is not to say that all such restrictions are unconstitutional. It is to say that Courts must subject them to the most rigid scrutiny. Pressing public necessity may sometimes justify the existence of such restrictions; racial antagonism never can."

But the evacuation order and the federal law that backed it up, the Court concluded, were not the product of racial antagonism. Deferring completely to the judgment of military officials, the Court said the evacuation could be justified. "The judgment that exclusion of the whole group was . . . a military imperative answers the contention that the exclusion was in the nature of group punishment based on antagonism to those of Japanese origin." The Court noted that some Japanese Americans had refused to pledge allegiance to the United States, and that some detainees had sought to move to Japan.

The Court also went out of its way to limit the scope of the decision. Although critics of the evacuation order said it could not be distinguished from the accompanying placement of evacuees in relocation centers, the Court said it was ruling only on the former. "Regardless of the true nature of the assembly and relocation centers—and we deem it unjustifiable to call them concentration camps, with all the ugly connotations that term implies—we are dealing specifically with nothing but an exclusion order." The Court said, "it will be time enough to decide" the constitutionality of the detention centers in a separate case.

Justice Frankfurter wrote a concurring opinion that was also deferential toward the military but hinted that he did not necessarily approve of the evacuation of Japanese Americans. "The validity of action under the war power must be judged wholly in the context of war. That action is not to be stigmatized as lawless because like action in times of peace would be law-

less. . . . To find that the Constitution does not forbid the military measures now complained of does not carry with it approval of that which Congress and the Executive did. That is their business, not ours."

The three dissenting justices wrote separately to underline their distaste for the Court's decision. Justice Roberts said that Korematsu had been convicted "as a punishment for not submitting to imprisonment in a concentration camp, based on his ancestry, and solely because of his ancestry, without evidence or inquiry concerning his loyalty and good disposition towards the United States. If this be a correct statement of the facts disclosed by this record, and facts of which we take judicial notice, I need hardly labor the conclusion that Constitutional rights have been violated."

To Justice Murphy, the exclusion order went "over 'the very brink of constitutional power' and . . . into the ugly abyss of racism. . . . Racial discrimination in any form and in any degree has no justifiable part whatever in our democratic way of life. It is unattractive in any setting, but it is utterly revolting among a free people who have embraced the principles set forth in the Constitution of the United States."

Justice Jackson bluntly minimized the "crime" for which Korematsu had been imprisoned. "Korematsu . . . has been convicted of an act not commonly a crime. It consists merely of

During World War II, the federal government forced more than 120,000 Japanese Americans—including native-born and naturalized U.S. citizens—to relocate to internment camps, producing scenes such as this one. In *Korematsu v. United States* (1944), the Supreme Court upheld the constitutionality of the action as a military necessity. Justice Frank Murphy wrote a powerful dissent against the policy, which he described as a "legalization of racism."
Source: Library of Congress.

being present in the state whereof he is a citizen, near the place where he was born, and where all his life he has lived."

EXCERPTS

From Justice Black's majority opinion: "[W]e are unable to conclude that it was beyond the war power of Congress and the Executive to exclude those of Japanese ancestry from the West Coast war area at the time they did. True, exclusion from the area in which one's home is located is a far greater deprivation than constant confinement to the home from 8 p.m. to 6 a.m. Nothing short of apprehension by the proper military authorities of the gravest imminent danger to the public safety can constitutionally justify either. But exclusion from a threatened area, no less than curfew, has a definite and close relationship to the prevention of espionage and sabotage. The military authorities, charged with the primary responsibility of defending our shores, concluded that curfew provided inadequate protection and ordered exclusion. . . .

". . . Citizenship has its responsibilities as well as its privileges, and in time of war the burden is always heavier. Compulsory exclusion of large groups of citizens from their homes, except under circumstances of direst emergency and peril, is inconsistent with our basic governmental institutions. But when under conditions of modern warfare our shores are threatened by hostile forces, the power to protect must be commensurate with the threatened danger.

". . . Korematsu was not excluded from the Military Area because of hostility to him or his race. He was excluded because we are at war with the Japanese Empire, because the properly constituted military authorities feared an invasion of our West Coast and felt constrained to take proper security measures, because they decided that the military urgency of the situation demanded that all citizens of Japanese ancestry be segregated from the West Coast temporarily, and finally, because Congress, reposing its confidence in this time of war in our military leaders—as inevitably it must—determined that they should have the power to do just this."

IMPACT

Korematsu is often ranked, along with *Scott v. Sandford* and *Plessy v. Ferguson,* as one of the Court's worst and most embarrassing decisions. (See *Scott v. Sandford* and *Plessy v. Ferguson.*) Nearly six decades later, it seems inconceivable to many that the Supreme Court would have approved the wholesale evacuation of U.S. citizens chosen solely because of their race and heritage.

Justice Black, who was otherwise known as a defender of civil liberties, was troubled by his authorship of *Korematsu* for the rest of his life, according to biographer Roger Newman. But he persisted in defending it as a correct decision given the necessities of war. In 1967 he told an interviewer, "Had they [the Japanese] attacked our shores you'd have had a large number [of Japanese Americans] fighting with the Japanese troops. And a lot of innocent Japanese-Americans would have been shot in the panic. Under these circumstances I saw nothing wrong in moving them away from the danger area."

The impact of the decision on the evacuation program was limited. By the time *Korematsu* was handed down, the threat of Japanese invasion, if there ever was one, had dissipated. On the same day *Korematsu* was issued, the Court decided a separate habeas corpus case, *Ex parte Endo,* in a seemingly contradictory way. Although it did not pass judgment on the entire relocation program, the *Endo* ruling said that Japanese Americans could not be detained if there was no evidence of their disloyalty to the nation. Perhaps aware that the decision was coming down, the War Department announced a day before the Court acted that detainees "whose records have stood the test of Army scrutiny" would be allowed to return home. The detention centers closed, and Japanese Americans rebuilt their lives and businesses with no further interference.

But the internment had a lasting impact on detainees. In the 1970s Japanese American organizations began pressing Congress for compensation for their wartime deprivations. Congress in 1980 created a commission to look into the issue. It took testimony from hundreds of detainees and recommended that each survivor of the camps be given $20,000 as compensation. The compensation was approved, but by the time the checks were distributed, many of the detainees had died. Under President Ronald Reagan, the nation formally apologized for the internment of Japanese Americans.

At the same time, a legal campaign was launched to overturn Korematsu's conviction. As part of the campaign, political science professor Peter Irons, author of several books on the Supreme Court, obtained the Justice Department's files on the case and several others through the Freedom of Information Act. In the files Irons said he found "smoking guns of legal misconduct," which made it clear that the government had no proof of disloyalty by Japanese Americans before it ordered the evacuation. The government had told the justices otherwise in the *Korematsu* case.

Fred Korematsu's conviction was overturned in 1983. Completing the long saga, President Bill Clinton in 1998 presented Korematsu with the Presidential Medal of Freedom. "Fred Korematsu deserves our respect and thanks for his patient pursuit to preserve the civil liberties we hold dear," Clinton said.

Rosenberg v. United States

Decided June 19, 1953
346 U.S. 273
laws.findlaw.com/US/346/273.html

DECISION

The execution of convicted spies Ethel and Julius Rosenberg may proceed. Their claim that a change in the law on espionage made their death sentence invalid is not significant enough to justify delaying the execution.

BACKGROUND

The Rosenberg trial was one of the flash points of the "red scare" days of the post–World War II period. Communist advances in Eastern Europe, the fall of China, and the outbreak of the Korean War intensified fears that communist spies were infiltrating the United States.

Julius and Ethel Rosenberg, a young New York couple who had been members of the U.S. Communist Party, stood accused of stealing U.S. nuclear weapons secrets and transmitting them to the Soviet Union. Ethel Rosenberg's brother worked in 1945 at the Los Alamos, New Mexico, atomic weapons center where, according to the government, he gave secrets, including a sketch of the atomic bomb, to the Rosenbergs.

Their 1951 New York trial on espionage charges was a nationwide sensation. Director of the Federal Bureau of Investigation J. Edgar Hoover said the Rosenbergs had committed "the crime of the century." The government blamed them for enabling the Soviet Union to build its first atomic bomb. The law under which they were prosecuted, the Espionage Act of 1917, allowed judges to sentence to death anyone found guilty of spying in wartime. After the jury found the Rosenbergs guilty, Judge Irving Kaufman quickly made clear that he would impose the death sentence. Kaufman said the Rosenbergs' acts had led to the Korean War and constituted "a crime worse than murder."

The sentence triggered a worldwide protest. Notable people ranging from scientist Albert Einstein to Pope Pius XII urged that they not be executed. Many people felt that the evidence linking the Rosenbergs to the espionage was weak, and that they were found guilty in part because of the anticommunist hysteria gripping the country.

The Rosenbergs and their supporters mounted several appeals of their sentences, and before it was all over, their case had come before the Supreme Court numerous times. The Court repeatedly declined to review the case, although several justices were privately concerned about the way it was handled. According to the 1983 book *The Rosenberg File,* Justice

Black wanted to hear the case, and Justice Frankfurter said that for him the Rosenbergs' appeals constituted the most anguishing situation he had faced since joining the Court. Frankfurter felt the Court had a responsibility to introduce calm reason into the situation, but most of his colleagues did not agree.

As the date of execution approached, lawyers made one last appeal on the Rosenbergs' behalf. This time they raised a procedural issue that got the attention of Justice Douglas. They argued, in essence, that the Rosenbergs had been improperly sentenced to die. A judge had determined the sentence when in fact, they asserted, the jury should have made that decision.

Douglas heard the Rosenbergs' plea in his chambers and issued a stay on June 17, putting off the execution set for two days later, until the full Court could consider this appeal. Douglas then left town for his summer retreat in the West, later recalling in his memoirs, "Washington was a powder keg" over the Rosenberg case. But Douglas said he had also received a telegram from his hometown in Washington telling him, "If you grant the Rosenbergs a stay, there will be a lynching party waiting for you here."

The Court had recessed for the summer, so the delay could have been for a lengthy period. However, Attorney General Herbert Brownell made a personal plea to Chief Justice Vinson to convene a special session of the Court to act quickly on Douglas's stay. So on June 18, only a day after Douglas issued the stay, the Court held an extraordinary special session to consider the Rosenbergs' case. Douglas, who heard about the special session on his car radio the night before, turned around and made it to the Court in time for the hearing.

VOTE

6–3, with Chief Justice Fred M. Vinson writing the majority opinion. Joining him were Justices Stanley F. Reed, Robert H. Jackson, Harold H. Burton, Tom C. Clark, and Sherman Minton. Dissenting were Justices Felix Frankfurter, Hugo L. Black, and William O. Douglas.

HIGHLIGHTS

As sensational as the Rosenbergs' case was, the actual issue before the Court was a more mundane question of which law should have governed the sentencing of the Rosenbergs. The question stemmed from the fact that the government claimed that the Rosenbergs' conspiracy to commit acts of espionage continued from 1944 through 1950. At the beginning of that period, the Espionage Act applied, and that law gave judges the power to sentence defendants to death. But in 1946 Congress in effect amended the law in a section of the new Atomic Energy Act. Under that amendment, the death penalty could be meted out only if the jury recommended it. So the question the justices had to answer was which sentencing procedure Judge Kaufman should have used.

The Court's opinion concluded that the amended law did not supersede the earlier one, which meant that it was appropriate for the judge to sentence the Rosenbergs to death without jury approval. "We held that this issue raised no doubts of such magnitude to require further proceedings," Chief Justice Vinson wrote.

In a concurring opinion Justice Clark said, "Our liberty is maintained only so long as justice is secure. To permit our judicial processes to be used to obstruct the course of justice destroys our freedom. Over two years ago, the Rosenbergs were found guilty by a jury of a grave offense in time of war. Unlike other litigants, they have had the attention of this Court seven times; each time, their pleas have been denied. Though the penalty is great and our responsibility heavy, our duty is clear."

Ethel and Julius Rosenberg, pictured here in a police patrol car, were sentenced to death after being convicted of espionage in 1951. Justice William O. Douglas issued a stay of execution, but in *Rosenberg v. United States* (1953), the full Supreme Court vacated the stay, rejecting the Rosenbergs' challenge of the sentence's validity. The couple was executed the evening of the decision.

Source: Library of Congress.

The issue did not seem as easy for the dissenters. "It is my view, based on the limited arguments we have heard, that, after passage of the Atomic Energy Act of 1946, it was unlawful for a judge to impose the death penalty for unlawful transmittal of atomic secrets unless such a penalty was recommended by the jury trying the case," wrote Justice Black.

Justice Frankfurter wanted the Court not to decide the case in haste. "I am bound to say that circumstances precluded what to me are indispensable conditions for solid judicial judgment," Frankfurter wrote.

In dissent Justice Douglas wrote, "The Rosenbergs obviously were not engaged in an exchange of scientific information in the interests of science. But Congress lowered the level of penalties to protect all those who might be charged with the unlawful disclosure of atomic data. And if the Rosenbergs are the beneficiaries, it is merely the result of the application of the new law with an even hand."

Douglas argued that the revised law should have governed the sentencing. "It is important that the country be protected against the nefarious plans of spies who would destroy us," Douglas wrote. "It is also important that before we allow human lives to be snuffed out we be sure—emphatically sure—that we act within the law. If we are not sure, there will be lingering doubts to plague the conscience after the event."

EXCERPTS

From Chief Justice Vinson's majority opinion: "This Court has the responsibility to supervise the administration of criminal justice by the federal judiciary. This includes the duty to see that the laws are not only enforced by fair proceedings, but also that the punishments prescribed by the laws are enforced with a reasonable degree of promptness and certainty. The stay which had been issued promised many more months of litigation in a case which had otherwise run its full course.

"The question preserved for adjudication by the stay was entirely legal; there was no need to resort to the fact-finding processes of the District Court; it was a question of statutory construction which this Court was equipped to answer. We decided that a proper administration of the laws required the Court to consider that question forthwith.

"This brought us to the merits. . . . We held that the Atomic Energy Act of 1946 did not displace the Espionage Act."

IMPACT

The Court issued its decision June 19, a day after the arguments. To escape demonstrators, according to biographer Roger Newman, Justice Black left the Court building in a "windowless laundry van." Soon after he got home, lawyers for the Rosenbergs tried to speak with him there, hoping for another delay in the execution. In tears, Black told a family member to turn the lawyers away.

At 8 o'clock that evening, President Dwight D. Eisenhower turned down a final plea for clemency, and the Rosenbergs were executed in the electric chair at Sing Sing prison in New York. It was a Friday, and the Rosenbergs' advocates argued the execution should not take place on the Jewish Sabbath, which starts at sundown, so it was timed to start a few minutes before the sun set. Thousands of pro-Rosenberg protesters in New York City silently awaited word of the execution, while in front of the White House, other demonstrators displayed the opposite view with signs urging "Death to the communist rats."

More than fifty years later, historians still debate the Rosenberg episode. Some argue that while the Rosenbergs were active members of the Communist Party, the government's case against them was flimsy enough that a fair trial should have found them not guilty. Some say their importance in aiding the Soviet atomic weapons program was vastly exaggerated. Others note that at the time the spying began, the Russians were wartime allies, not enemies, of the United States, making execution an excessive punishment. In *The Rosenberg File* authors Ronald Radosh and Joyce Milton conclude, "The fate of the Rosenbergs remains a blot on America's conscience."

Detainee Cases

Hamdi v. Rumsfeld
Decided June 28, 2004
No. 03-6696
laws.findlaw.com/US/000/03-6696.html

Rasul v. Bush *and* Al Odah v. United States
Decided June 28, 2004
No. 03-334
laws.findlaw.com/US/000/03-334.html

Rumsfeld v. Padilla
Decided June 28, 2004
No. 03-1027
laws.findlaw.com/US/000/03-1027.html

DECISION

A U.S. citizen who is captured abroad, classified as an "enemy combatant," and held in the United States has due process rights to challenge his detention before a neutral decision maker. Similarly, foreign citizens captured abroad during hostilities and held at the U.S. facility at Guantanamo Bay, Cuba, are entitled to challenge their imprisonment in U.S. courts.

BACKGROUND

Throughout history the Supreme Court has resolved some aspect of almost every major issue before the American people. So it was only a matter of time before the September 11, 2001, terrorist attacks would produce a case for the Supreme Court.

In fact, four terrorism-related cases went to the Court in the aftermath of September 11, and they were argued in the same month and decided on the same day. Taken together, the cases were a powerful demonstration that even in wartime and in the face of government opposition, the Supreme Court is still the institution that tells the other branches of government how they must treat individual rights and due process.

After the September 11 attacks, Congress passed a joint resolution authorizing President George W. Bush to use "all necessary and appropriate force" against all nations, organizations, and individuals involved in planning the attacks or assisting the effort. President Bush sent troops to Afghanistan to pursue members of the Al Qaeda terrorist organization and the Taliban regime that supported it. This resolution, while not a formal declaration of war, was the justification for the capture by U.S. forces of hundreds of individuals alleged to be aiding Al Qaeda and the Taliban. The cases before the Supreme Court resulted from those detentions.

The first set of cases involved two U.S. citizens, Yaser Hamdi and Jose Padilla, who were detained in the tense months after the September 11 attacks. Hamdi was captured in Afghanistan because, the government alleges, he was helping the Taliban regime fight against U.S. armed forces. Padilla was arrested when he arrived in Chicago on a plane from Pakistan. The government claims Padilla worked with Al Qaeda to plan terrorist attacks on the United States. Both men were eventually classified not as prisoners of war but as "enemy combatants," which, according to the government, meant that they could be held indefinitely by the military without formal charges and without access to lawyers. Both challenged their detention in federal court.

The other set of cases involved foreign nationals captured during the same period and detained at the U.S. naval base at Guantanamo Bay. The base is a geographic oddity: a U.S. military base located on the southeast coast of Cuba, a communist nation that is a longtime adversary of the United States. In the aftermath of the Spanish-American War, more than a century ago, the two nations signed a treaty that gave the United States "complete jurisdiction" over the area that makes up the base, while Cuba retained "ultimate sovereignty."

After undergoing a screening process, many of the people captured by the United States who were deemed to be the most dangerous and those with the highest potential for yielding important intelligence about the enemy were transferred to Guantanamo.

Several of the detainees, including British citizen Shafiq Rasul and Fawzi Khalid Abdullah Fahad Al Odah, a Kuwaiti, initiated these lawsuits, claiming they were not involved in any terrorist activities and had been captured by mistake. They also said they had been prevented from consulting lawyers.

The Bush administration resisted both sets of lawsuits. In the case of the U.S. citizens being held, the administration said the congressional resolution gave it unquestioned authority to remove enemy combatants from the battlefield for the duration of hostilities. In the Guantanamo cases, the administration claimed that because the detainees were being held outside the United States, federal courts had no authority, no jurisdiction, to consider their complaints. The administration in general won its points in lower courts, except that in the case of Padilla, an American captured on U.S. soil, the U.S. Court of Appeals for the Second Circuit said the president did not have the authority to hold him in military prison.

As the disputes went to the Supreme Court, they drew worldwide interest for the issues they raised of human rights as well as wartime military necessity.

In January 2002, the administration of George W. Bush implemented the controversial policy of holding alleged Taliban fighters and Al Qaeda members at the U.S. naval base at Guantanamo Bay, Cuba. In the Detainee Cases (2004), three decisions handed down on the same day, the Supreme Court ruled that so-called enemy combatants—whether citizens or non-citizens—have a right to lawyers, hearings, and other legal protections.
Source: AP/Wide World Photos/U.S. Navy, Shane T.McCoy.

VOTE

Hamdi v. Rumsfeld: 6–3, with Justice Sandra Day O'Connor writing for the majority. Joining her were Chief Justice William Rehnquist, Anthony Kennedy, and Stephen Breyer. Justices David Souter and Ruth Bader Ginsburg concurred in part and dissented in part. Justices Antonin Scalia and John Paul Stevens joined in a dissent, and Justice Clarence Thomas dissented for different reasons.

Rumsfeld v. Padilla: 5–4, with Chief Justice Rehnquist writing for the majority. Joining him were Justices O'Connor, Scalia, Kennedy, and Thomas. Justices Stevens, Souter, Ginsburg, and Breyer dissented.

Rasul v. Bush and *Al Odah v. United States:* 6–3, with Justice Stevens writing the majority opinion. Joining him were Justices O'Connor, Souter, Ginsburg, and Breyer, with Justice Kennedy concurring in the judgment. In dissent were Justices Scalia and Thomas and Chief Justice Rehnquist.

HIGHLIGHTS

In *Hamdi* the Bush administration won on only one point: that the post–September 11 resolution by Congress gave President Bush the power to detain enemy combatants. Five justices—

O'Connor, Rehnquist, Kennedy, and Breyer, plus Thomas who dissented on other aspects of the case—agreed on this point. They cited a World War II precedent, *Ex parte Quirin,* which said that detentions of this kind were justified so as to prevent alleged enemy combatants—even those who were U.S. citizens—from returning to the battlefield to harm Americans again.

But on the other issues before the Court, the justices handed the Bush administration a significant defeat. O'Connor said detentions like that imposed on Hamdi can only last until the end of hostilities. Because the war on terror may never have an ending point, however, O'Connor said that if the government had its way, Hamdi could be detained without being charged and without any due process for the rest of his life—an unacceptable result, in her view. At a minimum, O'Connor said Hamdi was entitled to some kind of review of the reasons for his detention and the ability to refute those reasons. Justices Souter and Ginsburg agreed on that point, but said Hamdi's detention was unauthorized in the first place.

Justices Scalia and Stevens dissented, but not because they supported the Bush administration's position. They asserted that under the Constitution, the only way a U.S. citizen can be imprisoned without being charged with a crime is if Congress votes to suspend the writ of habeas corpus—the doctrine that allows citizens to challenge their imprisonment in court. Congress had done that before in wartime, but Scalia and Stevens insisted that the post–September 11 resolution passed by Congress could not be read as having suspended habeas corpus. Justice Thomas dissented because he felt the Court had no business second-guessing the administration on military matters. Thomas was the only justice who supported the administration's views entirely.

The *Padilla* case was decided separately on a somewhat technical issue. The Court ruled, in essence, that Padilla had filed his suit in the wrong court. Since he was imprisoned in a military brig in South Carolina, he should have sued in federal court there against the warden of the prison rather than in New York federal court against the secretary of defense.

In the Guantanamo cases, which were consolidated into one ruling, Justice Stevens rejected the Bush administration's position and said the detainees there were entitled to some form of due process. He noted that the Guantanamo detainees were not from countries at war with the United States and had not been convicted of any wrongdoing. Equally important, in Stevens's view, was the fact that these prisoners were being held at a base that is under the jurisdiction of the United States. Any American imprisoned at Guantanamo Bay, Stevens pointed out, would be able to sue in U.S. courts, so foreigners should be able to as well.

In dissent Justice Scalia attacked the majority opinion for extending the authority of U.S. courts "to the four corners of the earth." This, he said, puts the courts in the position of reviewing and second-guessing how U.S. forces conduct a foreign war, while and where it is going on.

EXCERPTS

From O'Connor's opinion in *Hamdi:* "While the full protections that accompany challenges to detentions in other settings may prove unworkable and inappropriate in the enemy-combatant setting, the threats to military operations posed by a basic system of independent review are not so weighty as to trump a citizen's core rights to challenge meaningfully the Government's case and to be heard by an impartial adjudicator. In so holding, we necessarily reject the Government's assertion that separation of powers principles mandate a heavily circumscribed role for the courts in such circumstances. . . . We have long since made clear that a state of war is not a blank check for the President when it comes to the rights of the Nation's citizens. . . . Whatever power the United States Constitution envisions for the Executive in its exchanges with other nations or with enemy organizations in times of conflict, it most assuredly envisions a role for all three branches when individual liberties are at stake."

From Justice Thomas's dissent in *Hamdi:* "The Executive Branch, acting pursuant to the powers vested in the President by the Constitution and with explicit congressional approval, has determined that Yaser Hamdi is an enemy combatant and should be detained. This detention falls squarely within the Federal Government's war powers, and we lack the expertise and capacity to second-guess that decision. . . . I do not think that the Federal Government's war powers can be balanced away by this Court."

From Justice Stevens's majority in *Rasul:* "Application of the habeas statute to persons detained at the base is consistent with the historical reach of the writ of habeas corpus. . . . In the end, the answer to the question presented is clear. Petitioners contend that they are being held in federal custody in violation of the laws of the United States. No party questions the District Court's jurisdiction over petitioners' custodians. . . . We therefore hold that [the law] confers on the District Court jurisdiction to hear petitioners' habeas corpus challenges to the legality of their detention at the Guantanamo Bay Naval Base."

From Justice Scalia's dissent: "Today, the Court springs a trap on the Executive, subjecting Guantanamo Bay to the oversight of the federal courts even though it has never before been thought to be within their jurisdiction—and thus making it a foolish place to have housed alien wartime detainees. . . . The Commander in Chief and his subordinates had every reason to expect that the internment of combatants at Guantanamo Bay would not have the consequence of bringing the cumbersome machinery of our domestic courts into military affairs. Congress is in session."

IMPACT

The Court's decisions were immediately viewed as a sharp defeat for the Bush administration, a strong signal from the justices that the Court, and not the executive branch, would have the final say on the scope and reach of the power of the federal judiciary.

But at least at the beginning, the decision's practical effect appeared less dramatic, in part because neither the *Hamdi* nor *Rasul* decisions spelled out in detail what kind of due process or procedure was required. In *Hamdi* O'Connor left it up to lower courts, specifying only that the procedure be "prudent and incremental."

In the Guantanamo cases, the Bush administration picked up on the final paragraph of the Stevens majority opinion, which began, "Whether and what further proceedings may become necessary . . . are matters we need not address now." The government argued that in fact, very limited proceedings, with only a cursory review of the status of Guantanamo detainees, would satisfy the mandate of the *Rasul* decision. It began holding "status hearings" at which detainees would hear a description of why they were detained and would be able to state why they think they should not have been detained. But the detainees were given no right to have a lawyer represent them.

Detainees said these new procedures ignored the spirit of the Court's *Rasul* decision and violated their right to due process. Federal judges in Washington, D.C., were divided on whether the hearings were sufficient. Judge Joyce Hens Green said the procedures deprived the detainees of their fundamental rights, while Judge Richard Leon said the detainees had no basis to complain about the proceedings. The issue was likely to make its way back to the Supreme Court. Meanwhile, both before and after the Court issued its *Rasul* decision, reports emerged alleging that some of the Guantanamo detainees had been abused during interrogations or treated inhumanely during their imprisonment.

For his part, Padilla refiled his case in the proper court in South Carolina. A district court judge ordered the government to charge him with a crime or release him. The U.S. Court of Appeals for the Fourth Circuit ruled in September 2005 that the president has the power to hold Padilla indefinitely. Padilla's appeal returned to the Supreme Court in October.

REFERENCE MATERIALS

Constitution of the United States

We the People of the United States, in Order to form a more perfect Union, establish Justice, insure domestic Tranquility, provide for the common defence, promote the general Welfare, and secure the Blessings of Liberty to ourselves and our Posterity, do ordain and establish this Constitution for the United States of America.

ARTICLE I

Section 1. All legislative Powers herein granted shall be vested in a Congress of the United States, which shall consist of a Senate and House of Representatives.

Section 2. The House of Representatives shall be composed of Members chosen every second Year by the People of the several States, and the Electors in each State shall have the Qualifications requisite for Electors of the most numerous Branch of the State Legislature.

No Person shall be a Representative who shall not have attained to the age of twenty five Years, and been seven Years a Citizen of the United States, and who shall not, when elected, be an Inhabitant of that State in which he shall be chosen.

[Representatives and direct Taxes shall be apportioned among the several States which may be included within this Union, according to their respective Numbers, which shall be determined by adding to the whole Number of free Persons, including those bound to Service for a Term of Years, and excluding Indians not taxed, three fifths of all other Persons.][1] The actual Enumeration shall be made within three Years after the first Meeting of the Congress of the United States, and within every subsequent Term of ten Years, in such Manner as they shall by Law direct. The Number of Representatives shall not exceed one for every thirty Thousand, but each State shall have at Least one Representative; and until such enumeration shall be made, the State of New Hampshire shall be entitled to chuse three, Massachusetts eight, Rhode-Island and Providence Plantations one, Connecticut five, New-York six, New Jersey four, Pennsylvania eight, Delaware one, Maryland six, Virginia ten, North Carolina five, South Carolina five, and Georgia three.

When vacancies happen in the Representation from any State, the Executive Authority thereof shall issue Writs of Election to fill such Vacancies.

The House of Representatives shall chuse their Speaker and other Officers; and shall have the sole Power of Impeachment.

Section 3. The Senate of the United States shall be composed of two Senators from each State, [chosen by the Legislature thereof,][2] for six Years; and each Senator shall have one Vote.

Immediately after they shall be assembled in Consequence of the first Election, they shall be divided as equally as may be into three Classes. The Seats of the Senators of the first Class shall be vacated at the Expiration of the second Year, of the second Class at the Expiration of the fourth Year, and of the third Class at the Expiration of the sixth Year, so that one third may be chosen every second Year; [and if Vacancies happen by Resignation, or otherwise, during the Recess of the Legislature of any State, the Executive thereof may make temporary Appointments until the next Meeting of the Legislature, which shall then fill such Vacancies.][3]

No Person shall be a Senator who shall not have attained to the Age of thirty Years, and been nine Years a Citizen of the United States, and who shall not, when elected, be an Inhabitant of that State for which he shall be chosen.

The Vice President of the United States shall be President of the Senate, but shall have no Vote, unless they be equally divided.

The Senate shall chuse their other Officers, and also a President pro tempore, in the Absence of the Vice President, or when he shall exercise the Office of President of the United States.

The Senate shall have the sole Power to try all Impeachments. When sitting for that Purpose, they shall be on Oath or Affirmation. When the President of the United States is tried, the Chief Justice shall preside: And no Person shall be convicted without the Concurrence of two thirds of the Members present.

Judgment in Cases of Impeachment shall not extend further than to removal from Office, and disqualification to hold and enjoy any Office of honor, Trust or Profit under the United States: but the Party convicted shall nevertheless be liable and subject to Indictment, Trial, Judgment and Punishment, according to Law.

Section 4. The Times, Places and Manner of holding Elections for Senators and Representatives, shall be prescribed in each State by the Legislature thereof; but the Congress may at any time by Law make or alter such Regulations, except as to the Places of chusing Senators.

The Congress shall assemble at least once in every Year, and such Meeting shall [be on the first Monday in December],[4] unless they shall by Law appoint a different Day.

Section 5. Each House shall be the Judge of the Elections, Returns and Qualifications of its own Members, and a Majority of each shall constitute a Quorum to do Business; but a smaller Number may adjourn from day to day, and may be authorized to compel the Attendance of absent Members, in such Manner, and under such Penalties as each House may provide.

Each House may determine the Rules of its Proceedings, punish its Members for disorderly Behaviour, and, with the Concurrence of two thirds, expel a Member.

Each House shall keep a Journal of its Proceedings, and from time to time publish the same, excepting such Parts as may in their Judgment require Secrecy; and the Yeas and Nays of the Members of either House on any question shall, at the Desire of one fifth of those Present, be entered on the Journal.

Neither House, during the Session of Congress, shall, without the Consent of the other, adjourn for more than three days, nor to any other Place than that in which the two Houses shall be sitting.

Section 6. The Senators and Representatives shall receive a Compensation for their Services, to be ascertained by Law, and paid out of the Treasury of the United States. They shall in all Cases, except

Treason, Felony and Breach of the Peace, be privileged from Arrest during their Attendance at the Session of their respective Houses, and in going to and returning from the same; and for any Speech or Debate in either House, they shall not be questioned in any other Place.

No Senator or Representative shall, during the Time for which he was elected, be appointed to any civil Office under the Authority of the United States, which shall have been created, or the Emoluments whereof shall have been encreased during such time; and no Person holding any Office under the United States, shall be a Member of either House during his Continuance in Office.

Section 7. All Bills for raising Revenue shall originate in the House of Representatives; but the Senate may propose or concur with Amendments as on other Bills.

Every Bill which shall have passed the House of Representatives and the Senate, shall, before it become a Law, be presented to the President of the United States; If he approve he shall sign it, but if not he shall return it, with his Objections to that House in which it shall have originated, who shall enter the Objections at large on their Journal, and proceed to reconsider it. If after such Reconsideration two thirds of that House shall agree to pass the Bill, it shall be sent, together with the Objections, to the other House, by which it shall likewise be reconsidered, and if approved by two thirds of that House, it shall become a Law. But in all such Cases the Votes of both Houses shall be determined by yeas and Nays, and the Names of the Persons voting for and against the Bill shall be entered on the Journal of each House respectively. If any Bill shall not be returned by the President within ten Days (Sundays excepted) after it shall have been presented to him, the Same shall be a Law, in like Manner as if he had signed it, unless the Congress by their Adjournment prevent its Return, in which Case it shall not be a Law.

Every Order, Resolution, or Vote to which the Concurrence of the Senate and House of Representatives may be necessary (except on a question of Adjournment) shall be presented to the President of the United States; and before the Same shall take Effect, shall be approved by him, or being disapproved by him, shall be repassed by two thirds of the Senate and House of Representatives, according to the Rules and Limitations prescribed in the Case of a Bill.

Section 8. The Congress shall have Power To lay and collect Taxes, Duties, Imposts and Excises, to pay the Debts and provide for the common Defence and general Welfare of the United States; but all Duties, Imposts and Excises shall be uniform throughout the United States;

To borrow Money on the credit of the United States;

To regulate Commerce with foreign Nations, and among the several States, and with the Indian Tribes;

To establish an uniform Rule of Naturalization, and uniform Laws on the subject of Bankruptcies throughout the United States;

To coin Money, regulate the Value thereof, and of foreign Coin, and fix the Standard of Weights and Measures;

To provide for the Punishment of counterfeiting the Securities and current Coin of the United States;

To establish Post Offices and post Roads;

To promote the Progress of Science and useful Arts, by securing for limited Times to Authors and Inventors the exclusive Right to their respective Writings and Discoveries;

To constitute Tribunals inferior to the supreme Court;

To define and punish Piracies and Felonies committed on the high Seas, and Offences against the Law of Nations;

To declare War, grant Letters of Marque and Reprisal, and make Rules concerning Captures on Land and Water;

To raise and support Armies, but no Appropriation of Money to that Use shall be for a longer Term than two Years;

To provide and maintain a Navy;

To make Rules for the Government and Regulation of the land and naval Forces;

To provide for calling forth the Militia to execute the Laws of the Union, suppress Insurrections and repel Invasions;

To provide for organizing, arming, and disciplining, the Militia, and for governing such Part of them as may be employed in the Service of the United States, reserving to the States respectively, the Appointment of the Officers, and the Authority of training the Militia according to the discipline prescribed by Congress;

To exercise exclusive Legislation in all Cases whatsoever, over such District (not exceeding ten Miles square) as may, by Cession of particular States, and the Acceptance of Congress, become the Seat of the Government of the United States, and to exercise like Authority over all Places purchased by the Consent of the Legislature of the State in which the Same shall be, for the Erection of Forts, Magazines, Arsenals, dock-Yards, and other needful Buildings;— And

To make all Laws which shall be necessary and proper for carrying into Execution the foregoing Powers, and all other Powers vested by this Constitution in the Government of the United States, or in any Department or Officer thereof.

Section 9. The Migration or Importation of such Persons as any of the States now existing shall think proper to admit, shall not be prohibited by the Congress prior to the Year one thousand eight hundred and eight, but a Tax or duty may be imposed on such Importation, not exceeding ten dollars for each Person.

The Privilege of the Writ of Habeas Corpus shall not be suspended, unless when in Cases of Rebellion or Invasion the public Safety may require it.

No Bill of Attainder or ex post facto Law shall be passed.

No Capitation, or other direct, Tax shall be laid, unless in Proportion to the Census or Enumeration herein before directed to be taken.[5]

No Tax or Duty shall be laid on Articles exported from any State.

No Preference shall be given by any Regulation of Commerce or Revenue to the Ports of one State over those of another; nor shall Vessels bound to, or from, one State, be obliged to enter, clear, or pay Duties in another.

No Money shall be drawn from the Treasury, but in Consequence of Appropriations made by Law; and a regular Statement and Account of the Receipts and Expenditures of all public Money shall be published from time to time.

No Title of Nobility shall be granted by the United States: And no Person holding any Office of Profit or Trust under them, shall, without the Consent of the Congress, accept of any present, Emolument, Office, or Title, of any kind whatever, from any King, Prince, or foreign State.

Section 10. No State shall enter into any Treaty, Alliance, or Confederation; grant Letters of Marque and Reprisal; coin Money; emit Bills of Credit; make any Thing but gold and silver Coin a Tender in Payment of Debts; pass any Bill of Attainder, ex post facto Law, or Law impairing the Obligation of Contracts, or grant any Title of Nobility.

No State shall, without the Consent of the Congress, lay any Imposts or Duties on Imports or Exports, except what may be absolutely necessary for executing it's inspection Laws: and the net Produce of all Duties and Imposts, laid by any State on Imports or Exports, shall be for the Use of the Treasury of the United States; and all such Laws shall be subject to the Revision and Controul of the Congress.

No State shall, without the Consent of Congress, lay any Duty of Tonnage, keep Troops, or Ships of War in time of Peace, enter into any Agreement or Compact with another State, or with a foreign Power, or engage in War, unless actually invaded, or in such imminent Danger as will not admit of delay.

ARTICLE II

Section 1. The executive Power shall be vested in a President of the United States of America. He shall hold his Office during the Term of four Years, and, together with the Vice President, chosen for the same Term, be elected, as follows:

Each State shall appoint, in such Manner as the Legislature thereof may direct, a Number of Electors, equal to the whole Number of Senators and Representatives to which the State may be entitled in the Congress: but no Senator or Representative, or Person holding an Office of Trust or Profit under the United States, shall be appointed an Elector.

[The Electors shall meet in their respective States, and vote by Ballot for two Persons, of whom one at least shall not be an Inhabitant of the same State with themselves. And they shall make a List of all the Persons voted for, and of the Number of Votes for each; which List they shall sign and certify, and transmit sealed to the Seat of the Government of the United States, directed to the President of the Senate. The President of the Senate shall, in the Presence of the Senate and House of Representatives, open all the Certificates, and the Votes shall then be counted. The Person having the greatest Number of Votes shall be the President, if such Number be a Majority of the whole Number of Electors appointed; and if there be more than one who have such Majority, and have an equal Number of Votes, then the House of Representatives shall immediately chuse by Ballot one of them for President; and if no Person have a Majority, then from the five highest on the list the said House shall in like Manner chuse the President. But in chusing the President, the Votes shall be taken by States, the Representation from each State having one Vote; A quorum for this Purpose shall consist of a Member or Members from two thirds of the States, and a Majority of all the States shall be necessary to a Choice. In every Case, after the Choice of the President, the Person having the greatest Number of Votes of the Electors shall be the Vice President. But if there should remain two or more who have equal Votes, the Senate shall chuse from them by Ballot the Vice President.][6]

The Congress may determine the Time of chusing the Electors, and the Day on which they shall give their Votes; which Day shall be the same throughout the United States.

No Person except a natural born Citizen, or a Citizen of the United States, at the time of the Adoption of this Constitution, shall be eligible to the Office of President; neither shall any Person be eligible to that Office who shall not have attained to the Age of thirty five Years, and been fourteen Years a Resident within the United States.

In Case of the Removal of the President from Office, or of his Death, Resignation, or Inability to discharge the Powers and Duties of the said Office,[7] the Same shall devolve on the Vice President, and the Congress may by Law provide for the Case of Removal, Death, Resignation or Inability, both of the President and Vice President, declaring what Officer shall then act as President, and such Officer shall act accordingly, until the Disability be removed, or a President shall be elected.

The President shall, at stated Times, receive for his Services, a Compensation, which shall neither be encreased nor diminished during the Period for which he shall have been elected, and he shall not receive within that Period any other Emolument from the United States, or any of them.

Before he enter on the Execution of his Office, he shall take the following Oath or Affirmation:—"I do solemnly swear (or affirm) that I will faithfully execute the Office of President of the United States, and will to the best of my Ability, preserve, protect and defend the Constitution of the United States."

Section 2. The President shall be Commander in Chief of the Army and Navy of the United States, and of the Militia of the several States, when called into the actual Service of the United States; he may require the Opinion, in writing, of the principal Officer in each of the executive Departments, upon any Subject relating to the Duties of their respective Offices, and he shall have Power to grant Reprieves and Pardons for Offences against the United States, except in Cases of Impeachment.

He shall have Power, by and with the Advice and Consent of the Senate, to make Treaties, provided two thirds of the Senators present concur; and he shall nominate, and by and with the Advice and Consent of the Senate, shall appoint Ambassadors, other public Ministers and Consuls, Judges of the supreme Court, and all other Officers of the United States, whose Appointments are not herein otherwise provided for, and which shall be established by Law: but the Congress may by Law vest the Appointment of such inferior Officers, as they think proper, in the President alone, in the Courts of Law, or in the Heads of Departments.

The President shall have Power to fill up all Vacancies that may happen during the Recess of the Senate, by granting Commissions which shall expire at the End of their next Session.

Section 3. He shall from time to time give to the Congress Information of the State of the Union, and recommend to their Consideration such Measures as he shall judge necessary and expedient; he may, on extraordinary Occasions, convene both Houses, or either of them, and in Case of Disagreement between them, with Respect to the Time of Adjournment, he may adjourn them to such Time as he shall think proper; he shall receive Ambassadors and other public Ministers; he shall take Care that the Laws be faithfully executed, and shall Commission all the Officers of the United States.

Section 4. The President, Vice President and all civil Officers of the United States, shall be removed from Office on Impeachment for, and Conviction of, Treason, Bribery, or other high Crimes and Misdemeanors.

ARTICLE III

Section 1. The judicial Power of the United States, shall be vested in one supreme Court, and in such inferior Courts as the Congress may from time to time ordain and establish. The Judges, both of the supreme and inferior Courts, shall hold their Offices during good Behaviour, and shall, at stated Times, receive for their Services, a Compensation, which shall not be diminished during their Continuance in Office.

Section 2. The judicial Power shall extend to all Cases, in Law and Equity, arising under this Constitution, the Laws of the United States, and Treaties made, or which shall be made, under their Authority —to all Cases affecting Ambassadors, other public Ministers and Consuls;—to all Cases of admiralty and maritime Jurisdiction — to Controversies to which the United States shall be a Party; — to Controversies between two or more States; — between a State and Citizens of another State; — between Citizens of different States; — between Citizens of the same State claiming Lands under Grants of different States, and between a State, or the Citizens thereof, and foreign States, Citizens or Subjects.[8]

In all Cases affecting Ambassadors, other public Ministers and Consuls, and those in which a State shall be Party, the supreme Court shall have original Jurisdiction. In all the other Cases before mentioned, the supreme Court shall have appellate Jurisdiction, both as to Law and Fact, with such Exceptions, and under such Regulations as the Congress shall make.

The Trial of all Crimes, except in Cases of Impeachment, shall be by Jury; and such Trial shall be held in the State where the said Crimes shall have been committed; but when not committed within any State, the Trial shall be at such Place or Places as the Congress may by Law have directed.

Section 3. Treason against the United States, shall consist only in levying War against them, or in adhering to their Enemies, giving them Aid and Comfort. No Person shall be convicted of Treason unless on the Testimony of two Witnesses to the same overt Act, or on Confession in open Court.

The Congress shall have Power to declare the Punishment of Treason, but no Attainder of Treason shall work Corruption of Blood, or Forfeiture except during the Life of the Person attainted.

ARTICLE IV

Section 1. Full Faith and Credit shall be given in each State to the public Acts, Records, and judicial Proceedings of every other State. And the Congress may by general Laws prescribe the Manner in which such Acts, Records and Proceedings shall be proved, and the Effect thereof.

Section 2. The Citizens of each State shall be entitled to all Privileges and Immunities of Citizens in the several States.

A Person charged in any State with Treason, Felony, or other Crime, who shall flee from Justice, and be found in another State, shall on Demand of the executive Authority of the State from which he fled, be delivered up, to be removed to the State having Jurisdiction of the Crime.

[No Person held to Service or Labour in one State, under the Laws thereof, escaping into another, shall, in Consequence of any Law or Regulation therein, be discharged from such Service or Labour, but shall be delivered up on Claim of the Party to whom such Service or Labour may be due.][9]

Section 3. New States may be admitted by the Congress into this Union; but no new State shall be formed or erected within the Jurisdiction of any other State; nor any State be formed by the Junction of two or more States, or Parts of States, without the Consent of the Legislatures of the States concerned as well as of the Congress.

The Congress shall have Power to dispose of and make all needful Rules and Regulations respecting the Territory or other Property belonging to the United States; and nothing in this Constitution shall be so construed as to Prejudice any Claims of the United States, or of any particular State.

Section 4. The United States shall guarantee to every State in this Union a Republican Form of Government, and shall protect each of them against Invasion; and on Application of the Legislature, or of the Executive (when the Legislature cannot be convened) against domestic Violence.

ARTICLE V

The Congress, whenever two thirds of both Houses shall deem it necessary, shall propose Amendments to this Constitution, or, on the Application of the Legislatures of two thirds of the several States, shall call a Convention for proposing Amendments, which, in either Case, shall be valid to all Intents and Purposes, as Part of this Constitution, when ratified by the Legislatures of three fourths of the several States, or by Conventions in three fourths thereof, as the one or the other Mode of Ratification may be proposed by the Congress; Provided [that no Amendment which may be made prior to the Year One thousand eight hundred and eight shall in any Manner affect the first and fourth Clauses in the Ninth Section of the first Article; and][10] that no State, without its Consent, shall be deprived of its equal Suffrage in the Senate.

ARTICLE VI

All Debts contracted and Engagements entered into, before the Adoption of this Constitution, shall be as valid against the United States under this Constitution, as under the Confederation.

This Constitution, and the Laws of the United States which shall be made in Pursuance thereof; and all Treaties made, or which shall be made, under the Authority of the United States, shall be the supreme Law of the Land; and the Judges in every State shall be bound thereby, any Thing in the Constitution or Laws of any State to the Contrary notwithstanding.

The Senators and Representatives before mentioned, and the Members of the several State Legislatures, and all executive and judicial Officers, both of the United States and of the several States, shall be bound by Oath or Affirmation, to support this Constitution; but no religious Test shall ever be required as a Qualification to any Office or public Trust under the United States.

ARTICLE VII

The Ratification of the Conventions of nine States, shall be sufficient for the Establishment of this Constitution between the States so ratifying the Same.

Done in Convention by the Unanimous Consent of the States present the Seventeenth Day of September in the Year of our Lord one thousand seven hundred and Eighty seven and of the Independence of the United States of America the Twelfth. IN WITNESS whereof We have hereunto subscribed our Names,

George Washington,
President and deputy from Virginia.

[The language of the original Constitution, not including the Amendments, was adopted by a convention of the states on September 17, 1787, and was subsequently ratified by the states on the following dates: Delaware, December 7, 1787; Pennsylvania, December 12, 1787; New Jersey, December 18, 1787; Georgia, January 2, 1788; Connecticut, January 9, 1788; Massachusetts, February 6, 1788; Maryland, April 28, 1788; South Carolina, May 23, 1788; New Hampshire, June 21, 1788.

Ratification was completed on June 21, 1788.

The Constitution subsequently was ratified by Virginia, June 25, 1788; New York, July 26, 1788; North Carolina, November 21, 1789; Rhode Island, May 29, 1790; and Vermont, January 10, 1791.]

AMENDMENTS

AMENDMENT I

(First ten amendments ratified December 15, 1791)

Congress shall make no law respecting an establishment of religion, or prohibiting the free exercise thereof; or abridging the freedom of speech, or of the press; or the right of the people peaceably to assemble, and to petition the Government for a redress of grievances.

AMENDMENT II

A well regulated Militia, being necessary to the security of a free State, the right of the people to keep and bear Arms, shall not be infringed.

AMENDMENT III

No Soldier shall, in time of peace be quartered in any house, without the consent of the Owner, nor in time of war, but in a manner to be prescribed by law.

AMENDMENT IV

The right of the people to be secure in their persons, houses, papers, and effects, against unreasonable searches and seizures, shall not be violated, and no Warrants shall issue, but upon probable cause, supported by Oath or affirmation, and particularly describing the place to be searched, and the persons or things to be seized.

AMENDMENT V

No person shall be held to answer for a capital, or otherwise infamous crime, unless on a presentment or indictment of a Grand Jury, except in cases arising in the land or naval forces, or in the Militia, when in actual service in time of War or public danger; nor shall any person be subject for the same offence to be twice put in jeopardy of life or limb; nor shall be compelled in any criminal case to be a witness against himself, nor be deprived of life, liberty, or property, without due process of law; nor shall private property be taken for public use, without just compensation.

AMENDMENT VI

In all criminal prosecutions, the accused shall enjoy the right to a speedy and public trial, by an impartial jury of the State and district wherein the crime shall have been committed, which district shall have been previously ascertained by law, and to be informed of the nature and cause of the accusation; to be confronted with the witnesses against him; to have compulsory process for obtaining witnesses in his favor, and to have the Assistance of Counsel for his defence.

AMENDMENT VII

In Suits at common law, where the value in controversy shall exceed twenty dollars, the right of trial by jury shall be preserved, and no fact tried by a jury, shall be otherwise re-examined in any Court of the United States, than according to the rules of the common law.

AMENDMENT VIII

Excessive bail shall not be required, nor excessive fines imposed, nor cruel and unusual punishments inflicted.

AMENDMENT IX

The enumeration in the Constitution, of certain rights, shall not be construed to deny or disparage others retained by the people.

AMENDMENT X

The powers not delegated to the United States by the Constitution, nor prohibited by it to the States, are reserved to the States respectively, or to the people.

AMENDMENT XI (Ratified February 7, 1795)

The Judicial power of the United States shall not be construed to extend to any suit in law or equity, commenced or prosecuted against one of the United States by Citizens of another State, or by Citizens or Subjects of any Foreign State.

AMENDMENT XII (Ratified June 15, 1804)

The Electors shall meet in their respective states and vote by ballot for President and Vice-President, one of whom, at least, shall not be an inhabitant of the same state with themselves; they shall name in their ballots the person voted for as President, and in distinct ballots the person voted for as Vice-President, and they shall make distinct lists of all persons voted for as President, and of all persons voted for as Vice-President, and of the number of votes for each, which lists they shall sign and certify, and transmit sealed to the seat of the government of the United States, directed to the President of the Senate; — The President of the Senate shall, in the presence of the Senate and House of Representatives, open all the certificates and the votes shall then be counted; — The person having the greatest number of votes for President, shall be the President, if such number be a majority of the whole number of Electors appointed; and if no person have such majority, then from the persons having the highest numbers not exceeding three on the list of those voted for as President, the House of Representatives shall choose immediately, by ballot, the President. But in choosing the President, the votes shall be taken by states, the representation from each state having one vote; a quorum for this purpose shall consist of a member or members from two-thirds of the states, and a majority of all the states shall be necessary to a choice. [And if the House of Representatives shall not choose a President whenever the right of choice shall devolve upon them, before the fourth day of March next following, then the Vice-President shall act as President, as in the case of the death or other constitutional disability of the President.—][11] The person having the greatest number of votes as Vice-President, shall be the Vice-President, if such number be a majority of the whole number of Electors appointed, and if no person have a majority, then from the two highest numbers on the list, the Senate shall choose the Vice-President; a quorum for the purpose shall consist of two-thirds of the whole number of Senators, and a majority of the whole number shall be necessary to a choice. But no person constitutionally ineligible to the office of President shall be eligible to that of Vice-President of the United States.

AMENDMENT XIII (Ratified December 6, 1865)

Section 1. Neither slavery nor involuntary servitude, except as a punishment for crime whereof the party shall have been duly convicted, shall exist within the United States, or any place subject to their jurisdiction.

Section 2. Congress shall have power to enforce this article by appropriate legislation.

AMENDMENT XIV (Ratified July 9, 1868)

Section 1. All persons born or naturalized in the United States, and subject to the jurisdiction thereof, are citizens of the United States and of the State wherein they reside. No State shall make or enforce any law which shall abridge the privileges or immunities of citizens of the United States; nor shall any State deprive any person of life, liberty, or property, without due process of law; nor deny to any person within its jurisdiction the equal protection of the laws.

Section 2. Representatives shall be apportioned among the several States according to their respective numbers, counting the whole number of persons in each State, excluding Indians not taxed. But when the right to vote at any election for the choice of electors for President and Vice President of the United States, Representatives in Congress, the Executive and Judicial officers of a State, or the members of the Legislature thereof, is denied to any of the male inhabitants of such State, being twenty-one years of age,[12] and citizens of the United States, or in any way abridged, except for participation in rebellion, or other crime, the basis of representation therein shall be reduced in the proportion which the number of such male citizens shall bear to the whole number of male citizens twenty-one years of age in such State.

Section 3. No person shall be a Senator or Representative in Congress, or elector of President and Vice President, or hold any office, civil or military, under the United States, or under any State, who, having previously taken an oath, as a member of Congress, or as an officer of the United States, or as a member of any State legislature, or as an executive or judicial officer of any State, to support the Constitution of the United States, shall have engaged in insurrection or rebellion against the same, or given aid or comfort to the enemies thereof. But Congress may by a vote of two-thirds of each House, remove such disability.

Section 4. The validity of the public debt of the United States, authorized by law, including debts incurred for payment of pensions and bounties for services in suppressing insurrection or rebellion, shall not be questioned. But neither the United States nor any State shall assume or pay any debt or obligation incurred in aid of insurrection or rebellion against the United States, or any claim for the loss or emancipation of any slave; but all such debts, obligations and claims shall be held illegal and void.

Section 5. The Congress shall have power to enforce, by appropriate legislation, the provisions of this article.

AMENDMENT XV *(Ratified February 3, 1870)*

Section 1. The right of citizens of the United States to vote shall not be denied or abridged by the United States or by any State on account of race, color, or previous condition of servitude.

Section 2. The Congress shall have power to enforce this article by appropriate legislation.

AMENDMENT XVI *(Ratified February 3, 1913)*

The Congress shall have power to lay and collect taxes on incomes, from whatever source derived, without apportionment among the several States, and without regard to any census or enumeration.

AMENDMENT XVII *(Ratified April 8, 1913)*

The Senate of the United States shall be composed of two Senators from each State, elected by the people thereof, for six years; and each Senator shall have one vote. The electors in each State shall have the qualifications requisite for electors of the most numerous branch of the State legislatures.

When vacancies happen in the representation of any State in the Senate, the executive authority of such State shall issue writs of election to fill such vacancies: *Provided,* That the legislature of any State may empower the executive thereof to make temporary appointments until the people fill the vacancies by election as the legislature may direct.

This amendment shall not be so construed as to affect the election or term of any Senator chosen before it becomes valid as part of the Constitution.

AMENDMENT XVIII *(Ratified January 16, 1919)*

Section 1. After one year from the ratification of this article the manufacture, sale, or transportation of intoxicating liquors within, the importation thereof into, or the exportation thereof from the United States and all territory subject to the jurisdiction thereof for beverage purposes is hereby prohibited.

Section 2. The Congress and the several States shall have concurrent power to enforce this article by appropriate legislation.

Section 3. This article shall be inoperative unless it shall have been ratified as an amendment to the Constitution by the legislatures of the several States, as provided in the Constitution, within seven years from the date of the submission hereof to the States by the Congress.][13]

AMENDMENT XIX *(Ratified August 18, 1920)*

The right of citizens of the United States to vote shall not be denied or abridged by the United States or by any State on account of sex.

Congress shall have power to enforce this article by appropriate legislation.

AMENDMENT XX *(Ratified January 23, 1933)*

Section 1. The terms of the President and Vice President shall end at noon on the 20th day of January, and the terms of Senators and Representatives at noon on the 3d day of January, of the years in which such terms would have ended if this article had not been ratified; and the terms of their successors shall then begin.

Section 2. The Congress shall assemble at least once in every year, and such meeting shall begin at noon on the 3d day of January, unless they shall by law appoint a different day.

Section 3.[14] If, at the time fixed for the beginning of the term of the President, the President elect shall have died, the Vice President elect shall become President. If a President shall not have been chosen before the time fixed for the beginning of his term, or if the President elect shall have failed to qualify, then the Vice President elect shall act as President until a President shall have qualified; and the Congress may by law provide for the case wherein neither a President elect nor a Vice President elect shall have qualified, declaring who shall then act as President, or the manner in which one who is to act shall be selected, and such person shall act accordingly until a President or Vice President shall have qualified.

Section 4. The Congress may by law provide for the case of the death of any of the persons from whom the House of Representatives may choose a President whenever the right of choice shall have devolved upon them, and for the case of the death of any of the persons from whom the Senate may choose a Vice President whenever the right of choice shall have devolved upon them.

Section 5. Sections 1 and 2 shall take effect on the 15th day of October following the ratification of this article.

Section 6. This article shall be inoperative unless it shall have been ratified as an amendment to the Constitution by the legislatures of three-fourths of the several States within seven years from the date of its submission.

AMENDMENT XXI *(Ratified December 5, 1933)*

Section 1. The eighteenth article of amendment to the Constitution of the United States is hereby repealed.

Section 2. The transportation or importation into any State, Territory, or possession of the United States for delivery or use therein of intoxicating liquors, in violation of the laws thereof, is hereby prohibited.

Section 3. This article shall be inoperative unless it shall have been ratified as an amendment to the Constitution by conventions in the several States, as provided in the Constitution, within seven years from the date of the submission hereof to the States by the Congress.

AMENDMENT XXII *(Ratified February 27, 1951)*

Section 1. No person shall be elected to the office of the President more than twice, and no person who has held the office of President, or acted as President, for more than two years of a term to which some other person was elected President shall be elected to the office of the President more than once. But this Article shall not apply to any person holding the office of President when this Article was proposed by the Congress, and shall not prevent any person who may be holding the office of President, or acting as President, during the term within which this Article becomes operative from holding the office of President or acting as President during the remainder of such term.

Section 2. This article shall be inoperative unless it shall have been ratified as an amendment to the Constitution by the legislatures of three-fourths of the several States within seven years from the date of its submission to the States by the Congress.

AMENDMENT XXIII *(Ratified March 29, 1961)*

Section 1. The District constituting the seat of Government of the United States shall appoint in such manner as the Congress may direct:

A number of electors of President and Vice President equal to the whole number of Senators and Representatives in Congress to which the District would be entitled if it were a State, but in no event more than the least populous State; they shall be in addition to those appointed by the States, but they shall be considered, for the purposes of the election of President and Vice President, to be electors appointed by a State; and they shall meet in the District and perform such duties as provided by the twelfth article of amendment.

Section 2. The Congress shall have power to enforce this article by appropriate legislation.

AMENDMENT XXIV *(Ratified January 23, 1964)*

Section 1. The right of citizens of the United States to vote in any primary or other election for President or Vice President, for electors for President or Vice President, or for Senator or Representative in Congress, shall not be denied or abridged by the United States or any State by reason of failure to pay any poll tax or other tax.

Section 2. The Congress shall have power to enforce this article by appropriate legislation.

AMENDMENT XXV *(Ratified February 10, 1967)*

Section 1. In case of the removal of the President from office or of his death or resignation, the Vice President shall become President.

Section 2. Whenever there is a vacancy in the office of the Vice President, the President shall nominate a Vice President who shall take office upon confirmation by a majority vote of both Houses of Congress.

Section 3. Whenever the President transmits to the President pro tempore of the Senate and the Speaker of the House of Representatives his written declaration that he is unable to discharge the powers and duties of his office, and until he transmits to them a written declaration to the contrary, such powers and duties shall be discharged by the Vice President as Acting President.

Section 4. Whenever the Vice President and a majority of either the principal officers of the executive departments or of such other body as Congress may by law provide, transmit to the President pro tempore of the Senate and the Speaker of the House of Representatives their written declaration that the President is unable to discharge the powers and duties of his office, the Vice President shall immediately assume the powers and duties of the office as Acting President.

Thereafter, when the President transmits to the President pro tempore of the Senate and the Speaker of the House of Representatives his written declaration that no inability exists, he shall resume the powers and duties of his office unless the Vice President and a majority of either the principal officers of the executive de-partments or of such other body as Congress may by law provide, transmit within four days to the President pro tempore of the Senate and the Speaker of the House of Representatives their written declaration that the President is unable to discharge the powers and duties of his office. Thereupon Congress shall decide the issue, assembling within forty-eight hours for that purpose if not in session. If the Congress, within twenty-one days after receipt of the latter written declaration, or, if Congress is not in session, within twenty-one days after Congress is required to assemble, determines by two-thirds vote of both Houses that the President is unable to discharge the powers and duties of his office, the Vice President shall continue to discharge the same as Acting President; otherwise, the President shall resume the powers and duties of his office.

AMENDMENT XXVI *(Ratified July 1, 1971)*

Section 1. The right of citizens of the United States, who are eighteen years of age or older, to vote shall not be denied or abridged by the United States or by any State on account of age.

Section 2. The Congress shall have power to enforce this article by appropriate legislation.

AMENDMENT XXVII *(Ratified May 7, 1992)*

No law varying the compensation for the services of the Senators and Representatives shall take effect, until an election of Representatives shall have intervened.

Source: U.S. Congress, House, Committee on the Judiciary, The Constitution of the United States of America, as Amended, 100th Cong., 1st sess., 1987, H Doc 10094.

Notes

1. The part in brackets was changed by Section 2 of the Fourteenth Amendment.
2. The part in brackets was changed by the first paragraph of the Seventeenth Amendment.
3. The part in brackets was changed by the second paragraph of the Seventeenth Amendment.
4. The part in brackets was changed by the second paragraph of the Seventeenth Amendment.
5. The Sixteenth Amendment gave Congress the power to tax incomes.
6. The material in brackets was superseded by the Twelfth Amendment.
7. This provision was affected by the Twenty-fifth Amendment.
8. These clauses were affected by the Eleventh Amendment.
9. This paragraph was superseded by the Thirteenth Amendment.
10. Obsolete.
11. The part in brackets was superseded by Section 3 of the Twentieth Amendment.
12. See the Nineteenth and Twenty-sixth Amendments.
13. This amendment was repealed by Section 1 of the Twenty-first Amendment.
14. See the Twenty-fifth Amendment.

The Justices

Baldwin, Henry

Birth: January 14, 1780, New Haven, Connecticut.

Education: Hopkins Grammar School, 1793; Yale College, 1797, LL.D., 1830; attended the law lectures of Judge Tapping Reeve; clerked for Alexander James Dallas.

Official Positions: U.S. representative; chairman, Committee on Domestic Manufactures.

Supreme Court Service: nominated associate justice by President Andrew Jackson January 4, 1830, to replace Bushrod Washington, who had died; confirmed by the Senate January 6, 1830, by a 41–2 vote; took judicial oath January 18, 1830; served until April 21, 1844; replaced by Robert C. Grier, nominated by President James K. Polk.

Family: married Marianna Norton, 1802; died 1803; one son; married Sally Ellicott, 1805.

Death: April 21, 1844, Philadelphia, Pennsylvania.

Barbour, Philip P.

Birth: May 25, 1783, Orange County, Virginia.

Education: read law on his own; attended one session at College of William and Mary, 1801.

Official Positions: member, Virginia House of Delegates from Orange County, 1812–1814; U.S. representative, 1814–1825, 1827–1830; Speaker of the House, 1821–1823; state judge, General Court for the Eastern District of Virginia, 1825–1827; president, Virginia Constitutional Convention, 1829–1830; U.S. district judge, Court of Eastern Virginia, 1830–1836.

Supreme Court Service: nominated associate justice by President Andrew Jackson February 28, 1835, to replace Gabriel Duvall, who had resigned; confirmed by the Senate March 15, 1836, by a 30–11 vote; took judicial oath May 12, 1836; served until February 25, 1841; replaced by Peter V. Daniel, nominated by President Martin Van Buren.

Family: married Frances Todd Johnson, 1804; seven children.

Death: February 25, 1841, Washington, D.C.

Black, Hugo L.

Birth: February 27, 1886, Harlan, Alabama.

Education: Birmingham Medical School, 1903–1904; University of Alabama Law School, LL.B., 1906.

Official Positions: police court judge, Birmingham, 1910–1911; county solicitor, Jefferson County, Alabama, 1914–1917; U.S. senator, 1927–1937.

Supreme Court Service: nominated associate justice by President Franklin D. Roosevelt August 12, 1937, to replace Willis Van Devanter, who had retired; confirmed by the Senate August 17, 1937, by a 63–16 vote; took judicial oath August 19, 1937; retired September 17, 1971; replaced by Lewis F. Powell Jr., nominated by President Richard Nixon.

Family: married Josephine Foster, February 1921; died 1951; two sons, one daughter; married Elizabeth Seay DeMerritte, September 11, 1957.

Death: September 25, 1971, Washington, D.C.

Blackmun, Harry A.

Birth: November 12, 1908, Nashville, Illinois.

Education: Harvard College, B.A., summa cum laude, 1929; Harvard Law School, LL.B., 1932.

Official Positions: clerk, Eighth Circuit Court of Appeals, 1932–1933; judge, Eighth Circuit Court of Appeals, 1959–1970.

Supreme Court Service: nominated associate justice by President Richard Nixon April 14, 1970, to replace Abe Fortas, who had resigned; confirmed by the Senate May 12, 1970, by a 94–0 vote; took judicial oath June 9, 1970; retired August 3, 1994; replaced by Stephen G. Breyer, nominated by President Bill Clinton.

Family: married Dorothy E. Clark, June 21, 1941; three daughters.

Death: March 4, 1999, Arlington, Virginia.

Blair, John, Jr.

Birth: 1732, Williamsburg, Virginia.

Education: graduated with honors from College of William and Mary, 1754; studied law at Middle Temple, London, 1755–1756.

Official Positions: member, Virginia House of Burgesses, 1766–1770; clerk, Virginia Governor's Council, 1770–1775; delegate, Virginia Constitutional Convention, 1776; member, Virginia Governor's Council, 1776; judge, Virginia General Court, 1777–1778; chief justice, 1779; judge, first Virginia Court of Appeals, 1780–1789; delegate, U.S. Constitutional Convention, 1787; judge, Virginia Supreme Court of Appeals, 1789.

Supreme Court Service: nominated associate justice by President George Washington September 24, 1789; confirmed by the Senate September 26, 1789, by a voice vote; took judicial oath February 2, 1790; resigned January 27, 1796; replaced by Samuel Chase, nominated by President Washington.

Family: married Jean Blair, December 26, 1756; died 1792.

Death: August 31, 1800, Williamsburg, Virginia.

Blatchford, Samuel

Birth: March 9, 1820, New York City.

Education: Columbia College, A.B., 1837.

Official Positions: judge, Southern District of New York, 1867–1872; judge, Second Circuit of New York, 1872–1882.

Supreme Court Service: nominated associate justice by President Chester Arthur March 13, 1882, to replace Ward Hunt, who had retired; confirmed by the Senate March 27, 1882, by a voice vote; took judicial oath April 3, 1882; served until July 7, 1893; replaced by Edward D. White, nominated by President Grover Cleveland.

Family: married Caroline Appleton, December 17, 1844.

Death: July 7, 1893, Newport, Rhode Island.

Bradley, Joseph P.

Birth: March 14, 1813, Berne, New York.

Education: Rutgers University, graduated 1836.

Official Positions: none.

Supreme Court Service: nominated associate justice by President Ulysses S. Grant February 7, 1870, succeeding James Wayne, who died in 1867 and whose seat remained vacant by act of Congress until 1870; confirmed by the Senate March 21, 1870, by a 46–9 vote; took judicial oath March 23, 1870; served until January 22, 1892; replaced by George Shiras Jr., nominated by President Benjamin Harrison.

Family: married Mary Hornblower in 1844; seven children.

Death: January 22, 1892, Washington, D.C.

Brandeis, Louis D.

Birth: November 13, 1856, Louisville, Kentucky.

Education: Harvard Law School, LL.B., 1877.

Official Positions: "people's attorney," Public Franchise League and Massachusetts State Board of Trade, 1897–1911; counsel, New England Policyholders' Protective Committee, 1905; special counsel, wage and hour cases in California, Illinois, Ohio, and Oregon, 1907–1914; counsel, Ballinger-Pinchot investigation, 1910; chairman, arbitration board, New York garment workers' labor disputes, 1910–1916.

Supreme Court Service: nominated associate justice by President Woodrow Wilson January 28, 1916, to replace Joseph R. Lamar, who had died; confirmed by the Senate June 1, 1916, by a 47–22 vote; took judicial oath June 15, 1916; retired February 13, 1939; replaced by William O. Douglas, nominated by President Franklin D. Roosevelt.

Family: married Alice Goldmark, March 23, 1891; two daughters.

Death: October 5, 1941, Washington, D.C.

Brennan, William J., Jr.

Birth: April 25, 1906, Newark, New Jersey.

Education: University of Pennsylvania, B.S., 1928; Harvard Law School, LL.B., 1931.

Official Positions: judge, New Jersey Superior Court, 1949–1950; judge, appellate division, New Jersey Superior Court, 1950–1952; associate judge, New Jersey Supreme Court, 1952–1956.

Supreme Court Service: recess appointment as associate justice by President Dwight D. Eisenhower October 16, 1956, to replace Sherman Minton, who had resigned; nominated as associate justice by President Eisenhower January 14, 1957; confirmed by the Senate March 19, 1957 by a voice vote; took judicial oath October 16, 1956; retired July 20, 1990; replaced by David H. Souter, nominated by President George Bush.

Family: married Marjorie Leonard, May 5, 1928, died 1982; two sons, one daughter; married Mary Fowler, March 9, 1983.

Death: July 24, 1997, Arlington, Virginia.

Brewer, David J.

Birth: June 20, 1837, Smyrna, Asia Minor.

Education: Wesleyan University, 1852–1853; Yale University, A.B., 1856; Albany Law School, LL.B., 1858.

Official Positions: commissioner, U.S. Circuit Court, Leavenworth, Kansas, 1861–1862; judge of probate and criminal courts, Leavenworth County, 1863–1864; judge, First District of Kansas, 1865–1869; Leavenworth city attorney, 1869–1870; justice, Kansas Supreme Court, 1870–1884; judge, Eighth Federal Circuit, 1884–1889; president, Venezuela-British Guiana Border Commission, 1895.

Supreme Court Service: nominated associate justice by President Benjamin Harrison December 4, 1889, to replace Stanley Matthews, who had died; confirmed by the Senate December 18, 1889, by a 53–11 vote; took judicial oath January 6, 1890; served until March 28, 1910; replaced by Charles Evans Hughes, nominated by President William Howard Taft.

Family: married Louise R. Landon, October 3, 1861; died 1898; married Emma Miner Mott, June 5, 1901.

Death: March 28, 1910, Washington, D.C.

Breyer, Stephen G.

Birth: August 15, 1938, San Francisco, California.

Education: Stanford University, A.B., 1959; Oxford University, B.A., 1961; Harvard Law School, LL.B., 1964.

Official Positions: Law clerk to Justice Arthur J. Goldberg, 1964–1965; assistant to assistant attorney general, Antitrust Division, U.S. Justice Department, 1965–1967; assistant special prosecutor, Watergate Special Prosecution Force, 1973; special counsel, Senate Judiciary Committee, 1974–1975; chief counsel, Senate Judiciary Committee, 1979–1980; judge, U.S. Court of Appeals for the First Circuit, 1980–1994.

Supreme Court Service: nominated associate justice by President Bill Clinton May 13, 1994, to replace Harry A. Blackmun, who had retired; confirmed by the Senate July 29, 1994, by an 87–9 vote; took judicial oath August 3, 1994.

Family: married Joanna Hare, 1967; two daughters, one son.

Brown, Henry B.

Birth: March 2, 1836, South Lee, Massachusetts.

Education: Yale University, A.B., 1856; studied briefly at Yale Law School and Harvard Law School.

Official Positions: U.S. deputy marshal for Detroit, 1861; assistant U.S. attorney, 1863–1868; circuit judge, Wayne County, Michigan, 1868; federal judge, Eastern District of Michigan, 1875–1890.

Supreme Court Service: nominated associate justice by President Benjamin Harrison December 23, 1890, to replace Samuel Miller, who had died; confirmed by the Senate December 29, 1890, by a voice vote; took judicial oath January 5, 1891; retired May 28, 1906; replaced by William H. Moody, nominated by President Theodore Roosevelt.

Family: married Caroline Pitts, July 1864; died 1901; married Josephine E. Tyler, June 25, 1904.

Death: September 4, 1913, Bronxville, New York.

Burger, Warren E.

Birth: September 17, 1907, St. Paul, Minnesota.

Education: attended the University of Minnesota, 1925–1927; St. Paul College of Law (now William Mitchell College of Law), LL.B., magna cum laude, 1931.

Official Positions: assistant U.S. attorney general, Civil Division, Justice Department, 1953–1956; judge, U.S. Court of Appeals for the District of Columbia, 1956–1969.

Supreme Court Service: nominated chief justice by President Richard Nixon May 21, 1969, to replace Chief Justice Earl Warren, who had retired; confirmed by the Senate June 9, 1969, by a 74–3 vote; took judicial oath June 23, 1969; retired September 26, 1986; replaced as chief justice by William H. Rehnquist, named by President Ronald Reagan.

Family: married Elvera Stromberg, November 8, 1933; one son, one daughter.

Death: June 25, 1995, Washington, D.C.

Burton, Harold H.

Birth: June 22, 1888, Jamaica Plain, Massachusetts.

Education: Bowdoin College, A.B., 1909; Harvard University, LL.B., 1912.

Official Positions: member, Ohio House of Representatives, 1929; director of law, Cleveland, 1929–1932; acting mayor of Cleveland, November 9, 1931–February 20, 1932; mayor of Cleveland, 1935–1940; U.S. senator, 1941–1945.

Supreme Court Service: nominated associate justice by President Harry S. Truman September 19, 1945, to replace Owen J. Roberts, who had resigned; confirmed by the Senate September 19, 1945, by a voice vote; took judicial oath October 1, 1945; retired October 13, 1958; replaced by Potter Stewart, appointed by President Dwight D. Eisenhower.

Family: married Selma Florence Smith, June 15, 1912; two daughters, two sons.

Death: October 28, 1964, Washington, D.C.

Butler, Pierce

Birth: March 17, 1866, Pine Bend, Minnesota.

Education: Carleton College, A.B., B.S., 1887.

Official Positions: assistant county attorney, Ramsey County, Minnesota, 1891–1893; county attorney, 1893–1897.

Supreme Court Service: nominated associate justice by President Warren G. Harding November 23, 1922, to replace William R. Day, who had retired; confirmed by the Senate December 21, 1922, by a 61–8 vote; took judicial oath January 2, 1923; served until November 16, 1939; replaced by Frank Murphy, nominated by President Franklin D. Roosevelt.

Family: married Annie M. Cronin, August 25, 1891; eight children.

Death: November 16, 1939, Washington, D.C.

Byrnes, James F.

Birth: May 2, 1879, Charleston, South Carolina.

Education: St. Patrick's Parochial School (never graduated); studied law privately; admitted to the bar in 1903.

Official Positions: court reporter, Second Circuit of South Carolina, 1900–1908; solicitor, Second Circuit of South Carolina, 1908–1910; U.S. representative, 1911–1925; U.S. senator, 1931–1941; director, Office of Economic Stabilization, 1942–1943; director, Office of War Mobilization, 1943–1945; secretary of state, 1945–1947; governor of South Carolina, 1951–1955.

Supreme Court Service: nominated associate justice by President Franklin D. Roosevelt June 12, 1941, to replace James McReynolds, who had retired; confirmed by the Senate June 12, 1941, by a voice vote; took judicial oath July 8, 1942; resigned October 3, 1942; replaced by Wiley B. Rutledge, appointed by President Roosevelt.

Family: Married Maude Perkins Busch, May 2, 1906.

Death: April 9, 1972, Columbia, South Carolina.

Campbell, John A.

Birth: June 24, 1811, Washington, Georgia.

Education: Franklin College (now the University of Georgia), graduated with first honors, 1825; attended U.S. Military Academy at West Point, 1825–1828.

Official Positions: Alabama state representative, sessions of 1837 and 1843; assistant secretary of war, Confederate States of America, 1862–1865.

Supreme Court Service: nominated associate justice by President Franklin Pierce March 21, 1853, to replace Justice John McKinley, who had died; confirmed by the Senate March 25, 1853, by a voice vote; took judicial oath April 11, 1853; resigned April 30, 1861; replaced by David Davis, nominated by President Abraham Lincoln.

Family: married Anna Esther Goldthwaite in the early 1830s; four daughters, one son.

Death: March 12, 1889, Baltimore, Maryland.

Cardozo, Benjamin N.

Birth: May 24, 1870, New York City.

Education: Columbia University, A.B., 1889; A.M., 1891; Columbia Law School, 1891, no degree.

Official Positions: justice, New York Supreme Court, 1913; judge, New York State Court of Appeals, 1913–1932; chief judge, 1926–1932.

Supreme Court Service: nominated associate justice by President Herbert Hoover February 15, 1932, to replace Oliver Wendell Holmes Jr., who had retired; confirmed by the Senate February 24, 1932, by a voice vote; took judicial oath March 14, 1932; served until July 9, 1938; replaced by Felix Frankfurter, nominated by President Franklin D. Roosevelt.

Family: unmarried.

Death: July 9, 1938, Port Chester, New York.

Catron, John

Birth: ca. 1786, Pennsylvania or Virginia.

Education: self-educated.

Official Positions: judge, Tennessee Supreme Court of Errors and Appeals, 1824–1831; first chief justice of Tennessee, 1831–1834.

Supreme Court Service: nominated associate justice by President Andrew Jackson March 3, 1837, to fill a newly created seat; confirmed by the Senate March 8, 1837, by a 28–15 vote; took judicial oath May 1, 1837; served until May 30, 1865; seat abolished by Congress.

Family: married Matilda Childress.

Death: May 30, 1865, Nashville, Tennessee.

Chase, Salmon P.

Birth: January 13, 1808, Cornish, New Hampshire.

Education: Dartmouth College, 1826.

Official Positions: U.S. senator, 1849–1855, 1861; governor of Ohio, 1856–1860; secretary of the Treasury, 1861–1864.

Supreme Court Service: nominated chief justice by President Abraham Lincoln December 6, 1864, to replace Chief Justice Roger B. Taney, who had died; confirmed by the Senate December 6, 1864, by a voice vote; took judicial oath December 15, 1864; served until May 7, 1873; replaced by Morrison R. Waite, appointed by President Ulysses S. Grant.

Family: married Katherine Jane Garniss, March 4, 1834; died December 1, 1835; married Eliza Ann Smith, September 26, 1839; died September 29, 1845; one daughter; married Sara Belle Dunlop Ludlow, November 6, 1846; died January 13, 1852; one daughter.

Death: May 7, 1873, New York City.

Chase, Samuel

Birth: April 17, 1741, Somerset County, Maryland.

Education: tutored by father; studied law in Annapolis law office; admitted to bar in 1761.

Official Positions: member, Maryland General Assembly, 1764–1784; delegate, Continental Congress, 1774–1778, 1784–1785; member, Maryland Committee of Correspondence, 1774; member, Maryland Convention and Council of Safety, 1775; judge, Baltimore Criminal Court, 1788–1796; chief judge, General Court of Maryland, 1791–1796.

Supreme Court Service: nominated associate justice by President George Washington January 26, 1796, to replace John Blair, who had resigned; confirmed by the Senate January 27, 1796, by a voice vote; took judicial oath February 4, 1796; served until June 19, 1811; replaced by Gabriel Duvall, nominated by President James Madison.

Family: married Anne Baldwin May 21, 1762; seven children, three of whom died in infancy; married Hannah Kitty Giles, March 3, 1784; two daughters.

Death: June 19, 1811, Baltimore, Maryland.

Clark, Tom C.

Birth: September 23, 1899, Dallas, Texas.

Education: Virginia Military Institute, 1917–1918; University of Texas, A.B., 1921; LL.B., 1922.

Official Positions: assistant district attorney, Dallas County, 1927–1932; special assistant, Justice Department, 1937–1943; assistant U.S. attorney general, 1943–1945; U.S. attorney general, 1945–1949; director, Federal Judicial Center, 1968–1970; judge, U.S. Court of Appeals, various circuits, by secial arrangement, 1967–1977.

Supreme Court Service: nominated associate justice by President Harry S. Truman August 2, 1949, to replace Frank Murphy, who had died; confirmed by the Senate August 18, 1949, by a 73–8 vote; took judicial oath August 24, 1949; retired June 12, 1967; replaced by Thurgood Marshall, nominated by President Lyndon B. Johnson.

Family: Married Mary Jane Ramsey, November 8, 1924; one daughter, two sons.

Death: June 13, 1977, New York City.

Clarke, John H.

Birth: September 18, 1857, Lisbon, Ohio.

Education: Western Reserve University, A.B., 1877, A.M., 1880.

Official Positions: federal judge, U.S. District Court for Northern District of Ohio, 1914–1916.

Supreme Court Service: nominated associate justice by President Woodrow Wilson July 14, 1916, to replace Charles Evans Hughes, who had resigned; confirmed by the Senate July 24, 1916, by a voice vote; took judicial oath October 9, 1916; resigned September 18, 1922; replaced by George Sutherland, nominated by President Warren G. Harding.

Family: unmarried.

Death: March 22, 1945, San Diego, California.

Clifford, Nathan

Birth: August 18, 1803, Rumney, New Hampshire.

Education: Haverhill Academy; studied law in office of Josiah Quincy in Rumney; admitted to New Hampshire bar, 1827.

Official Positions: Maine state representative, 1830–1834; attorney general of Maine, 1834–1838; U.S. representative, 1839–1843; U.S. attorney general, 1846–1848; minister to Mexico, 1848–1849.

Supreme Court Service: nominated associate justice by President James Buchanan December 9, 1857, to replace Benjamin R. Curtis, who had resigned; confirmed by the Senate January 12, 1858, by a 26–23 vote; took judicial oath January 21, 1858; served until July 25, 1881; replaced by Horace Gray, nominated by President Chester A. Arthur.

Family: married Hannah Ayer, ca. 1828; six children.

Death: July 25, 1881, Cornish, Maine.

Curtis, Benjamin R.

Birth: November 4, 1809, Watertown, Massachusetts.

Education: Harvard University, graduated in 1829 with highest honors; Harvard Law School, graduated in 1832.

Official Positions: Massachusetts state representative, 1849–1851.

Supreme Court Service: nominated associate justice by President Millard Fillmore December 11, 1851, to replace Justice Levi Woodbury, who had died; confirmed by the Senate December 20, 1851, by a voice vote; took judicial oath October 10, 1851; resigned September 30, 1857; replaced by Nathan Clifford, nominated by President James Buchanan.

Family: married Eliza Maria Woodward, 1833; died 1844; five children; married Anna Wroe Curtis, 1846; died 1860; three children; married Maria Malleville Allen, 1861; four children.

Death: September 15, 1874, Newport, Rhode Island.

Cushing, William

Birth: March 1, 1732, Scituate, Massachusetts.

Education: graduated from Harvard, 1751, honorary LL.D., 1785; honorary A.M., Yale, 1753; studied law under Jeremiah Gridley; admitted to the bar in 1755.

Official Positions: judge, probate court for Lincoln County, Massachusetts (now Maine), 1760–1761; judge, Superior Court of Massachusetts Bay province, 1772–1777; chief justice, Superior Court of the Commonwealth of Massachusetts, 1777–1780, Supreme Judicial Court, 1780–1789; member, Massachusetts Constitutional Convention, 1779; vice president, Massachusetts Convention, which ratified U.S. Constitution, 1788; delegate to electoral college, 1788.

Supreme Court Service: nominated associate justice by President George Washington September 24, 1789; confirmed by the Senate September 26, 1789, by a voice vote; took judicial oath February 2, 1790; served until September 13, 1810; replaced by Joseph Story, nominated by President James Madison.

Family: married Hannah Phillips, 1774.

Death: September 13, 1810, Scituate, Massachusetts.

Daniel, Peter V.

Birth: April 24, 1784, Stafford County, Virginia.

Education: privately tutored; attended Princeton University, 1802–1803.

Official Positions: member, Virginia House of Delegates, 1809–1812; Virginia Privy Council, 1812–1835; lieutenant governor of Virginia, 1818–1835; U.S. district judge, Eastern District of Virginia, 1836–1841.

Supreme Court Service: nominated associate justice by President Martin Van Buren February 26, 1841, to replace Justice Philip Barbour, who had died; confirmed by the Senate March 2, 1841, by a 22–5 vote; took judicial oath January 10, 1842; served until May 31, 1860; replaced by Samuel F. Miller, nominated by President Abraham Lincoln.

Family: married Lucy Randolph, 1809; died 1847; married Elizabeth Harris, 1853; two children.

Death: May 31, 1860, Richmond, Virginia.

Davis, David

Birth: March 9, 1815, Cecil County, Maryland.

Education: graduated from Kenyon College, 1832; Yale Law School, 1835.

Official Positions: Illinois state representative, 1845–1847; member, Illinois Constitutional Convention, 1847; Illinois state circuit judge, 1848–1862; U.S. senator, 1877–1883.

Supreme Court Service: nominated associate justice by President Abraham Lincoln December 1, 1862, to replace John A. Campbell, who had resigned; confirmed by the Senate December 8, 1862, by a voice vote; took judicial oath December 10, 1862; resigned March 4, 1877; replaced by John Marshall Harlan, nominated by President Rutherford B. Hayes.

Family: married Sarah Walker, October 30, 1838; died 1879; one son (two children died in infancy); married Adeline Burr, March 14, 1883; two daughters.

Death: June 26, 1886, Bloomington, Illinois.

Day, William R.

Birth: April 17, 1849, Ravenna, Ohio.

Education: University of Michigan, A.B., 1870; University of Michigan Law School, 1871–1872.

Official Positions: judge, Court of Common Pleas, Canton, Ohio, 1886; first assistant U.S. secretary of state, 1897–1898; U.S. secretary of state, 1898; member, United States delegation, Paris Peace

Conference, 1898–1899; judge, U.S. Court of Appeals for the Sixth Circuit, 1899–1903; umpire, Mixed Claims Commission, 1922–1923.

Supreme Court Service: nominated associate justice by President Theodore Roosevelt February 19, 1903, to replace George Shiras Jr., who had resigned; confirmed by the Senate February 23, 1903, by a voice vote; took judicial oath March 2, 1903; resigned November 13, 1922; replaced by Pierce Butler, nominated by President Warren G. Harding.

Family: married Mary Elizabeth Schaefer, 1875; four sons.

Death: July 9, 1923, Mackinac Island, Michigan.

Douglas, William O.

Birth: October 16, 1898, Maine, Minnesota.

Education: Whitman College, B.A., 1920; Columbia Law School, LL.B., 1925.

Official Positions: member, Securities and Exchange Commission, 1936–1939; chairman, 1937–1939.

Supreme Court Service: nominated associate justice by President Franklin D. Roosevelt March 20, 1939, to replace Louis D. Brandeis, who had retired; confirmed by the Senate April 4, 1939, by a 62–4 vote; took judicial oath April 17, 1939; retired November 12, 1975; replaced by John Paul Stevens, nominated by President Gerald R. Ford.

Family: married Mildred Riddle, August 16, 1923; divorced 1953; one son, one daughter; married Mercedes Hester Davison, December 14, 1954; divorced 1963; married Joan Martin, August 1963; divorced 1966; married Cathleen Ann Heffernan, July 1966.

Death: January 19, 1980, Washington D.C.

Duvall, Gabriel

Birth: December 6, 1752, Prince George's County, Maryland.

Education: classical preparatory schooling; studied law.

Official Positions: clerk, Maryland Convention, 1775–1777; clerk, Maryland House of Delegates, 1777–1787; member, Maryland State Council, 1782–1785; member, Maryland House of Delegates, 1787–1794; U.S. representative, 1794–1796; chief justice, General Court of Maryland, 1796–1802; presidential elector, 1796, 1800; first comptroller of the Treasury, 1802–1811.

Supreme Court Service: nominated associate justice by President James Madison November 15, 1811, to replace Samuel Chase, who had died; confirmed by the Senate November 18, 1811, by a voice vote; took judicial oath November 23, 1811; resigned January 14, 1835; replaced by Philip Barbour, nominated by President Andrew Jackson.

Family: married Mary Brice, July 24, 1787; died March 24, 1790; one son; married Jane Gibbon, May 5, 1795; died April 1834.

Death: March 6, 1844, Prince George's County, Maryland.

Ellsworth, Oliver

Birth: April 29, 1745, Windsor, Connecticut.

Education: A.B., Princeton, 1766; honorary LL.D., Yale (1790), Princeton (1790), Dartmouth (1797).

Official Positions: member, Connecticut General Assembly, 1773–1776; state's attorney, Hartford County, 1777–1785; delegate to Continental Congress, 1777–1784; member, Connecticut Council of Safety, 1779; member, Governor's Council, 1780–1785, 1801–1807; judge, Connecticut Superior Court, 1785–1789; delegate, Constitutional Convention, 1787; U.S. senator, 1789–1796; commissioner to France, 1799–1800.

Supreme Court Service: nominated chief justice by President George Washington March 3, 1796, to replace John Jay, who had resigned; confirmed by the Senate March 4, 1796, by a 21–1 vote; took judicial oath March 8, 1796; resigned September 30, 1800; replaced by John Marshall, nominated by President John Adams.

Family: married Abigail Wolcott, 1771; four sons, three daughters survived infancy.

Death: November 26, 1807, Windsor, Connecticut.

Field, Stephen J.

Birth: November 4, 1816, Haddam, Connecticut.

Education: graduated from Williams College, 1837, class valedictorian; studied law in private firms; admitted to the bar in 1841.

Official Positions: Alcalde of Marysville, 1850; California state representative, 1850–1851; justice, California Supreme Court, 1857–1863.

Supreme Court Service: nominated associate justice by President Abraham Lincoln March 6, 1863, for a newly created seat; confirmed by the Senate March 10, 1863, by a voice vote; took judicial oath May 20, 1863; retired December 1, 1897; replaced by Joseph McKenna, nominated by President William McKinley.

Family: married Sue Virginia Swearingen, June 2, 1859.

Death: April 9, 1899, in Washington, D.C.

Fortas, Abe

Birth: June 19, 1910, Memphis, Tennessee.

Education: Southwestern College, A.B., 1930; Yale Law School, LL.B., 1933.

Official Positions: assistant director, corporate reorganization study, Securities and Exchange Commission, 1934–1937; assistant director, Public Utilities Division, Securities and Exchange Commission, 1938–1939; general counsel, Public Works Administration, 1939–1940, and counsel to the Bituminous Coal Division, 1939–1941; director, Division of Power, Department of the Interior, 1941–1942; under-secretary of the interior, 1942–1946.

Supreme Court Service: nominated associate justice by President Lyndon B. Johnson July 28, 1965, to replace Arthur J. Goldberg, who had resigned; confirmed by the Senate August 11, 1965, by a voice vote; took judicial oath October 4, 1965; resigned May 14, 1969; replaced by Harry A. Blackmun, nominated by President Richard Nixon.

Family: married Carolyn Eugenia Agger, July 9, 1935.

Death: April 5, 1982, in Washington, D.C.

Frankfurter, Felix

Birth: November 15, 1882, Vienna, Austria.

Education: College of the City of New York, A.B., 1902; Harvard Law School, LL.B., 1906.

Official Positions: assistant U.S. attorney, Southern District of New York, 1906–1909; law officer, Bureau of Insular Affairs, War Department, 1910–1914; assistant to the secretary of war, 1917; secretary and counsel, President's Mediation Commission, 1917; assistant to the secretary of labor, 1917–1918; chairman, War Labor Policies Board, 1918.

Supreme Court Service: nominated associate justice by President Franklin D. Roosevelt January 5, 1939, to replace Benjamin Cardozo, who had died; confirmed by the Senate January 17, 1939, by a voice vote; took judicial oath January 30, 1939; retired August 28, 1962; replaced by Arthur Goldberg, nominated by President John F. Kennedy.

Family: married Marion A. Denman, December 20, 1919.

Death: February 22, 1965, Washington, D.C.

Fuller, Melville W.

Birth: February 11, 1833, Augusta, Maine.

Education: Bowdoin College, A.B., 1853; studied at Harvard Law School and read law, 1853–1855.

Official Positions: member, Illinois House of Representatives, 1863–1864; member, Venezuela-British Guiana Border Commission, 1899; member, Permanent Court of Arbitration at the Hague, 1900–1910.

Supreme Court Service: nominated chief justice by President Grover Cleveland April 30, 1888, to replace Morrison R. Waite, who had died; confirmed by the Senate July 20, 1888, by a 41–20 vote; took judicial oath October 8, 1888; served until July 4, 1910; replaced as chief justice by Edward D. White, nominated by President William Howard Taft.

Family: married Calista Ophelia Reynolds, June 28, 1858; died 1864; two daughters; married Mary Ellen Coolbaugh, May 30, 1866; eight children, seven of whom survived childhood.

Death: July 4, 1910, Sorrento, Maine.

Ginsburg, Ruth Bader

Birth: March 15, 1933, Brooklyn, New York.

Education: Cornell University, B.A., 1954; attended Harvard University Law School, 1956–1958; graduated from Columbia Law School, J.D., 1959.

Official Positions: judge, U.S. Court of Appeals for the District of Columbia, 1980–1993.

Supreme Court Service: nominated associate justice by President Bill Clinton June 22, 1993, to replace Byron R. White, who had retired; confirmed by the Senate August 3, 1993, by a 96–3 vote; took judicial oath August 10, 1993.

Family: married Martin D. Ginsburg, 1954; one daughter, one son.

Goldberg, Arthur J.

Birth: August 8, 1908, Chicago, Illinois.

Education: Northwestern University, B.S.L., 1929; J.D., summa cum laude, 1930.

Official Positions: secretary of labor, 1961–1962; U.S. ambassador to the United Nations, 1965–1968.

Supreme Court Service: nominated associate justice by President John F. Kennedy August 29, 1962, to replace Felix Frankfurter, who had retired; confirmed by the Senate September 25, 1962, by a voice vote; took judicial oath October 1, 1962; resigned July 25, 1965; replaced by Abe Fortas, nominated by President Lyndon B. Johnson.

Family: married Dorothy Kurgans, July 18, 1931; one daughter, one son.

Death: January 19, 1990, Washington, D.C.

Gray, Horace

Birth: March 24, 1828, Boston, Massachusetts.

Education: Harvard College, A.B., 1845; Harvard Law School, 1849.

Official Positions: reporter, Massachusetts Supreme Court, 1854–1864; associate justice, 1864–1873; chief justice, 1873–1881.

Supreme Court Service: nominated associate justice by President Chester A. Arthur December 19, 1881, to replace Nathan Clifford, who had died; confirmed by the Senate December 20, 1881, by a 51–5 vote; took judicial oath January 9, 1882; served until September 15, 1902; replaced by Oliver Wendell Holmes Jr., nominated by President Theodore Roosevelt.

Family: married Jane Matthews, June 4, 1889.

Death: September 15, 1902, Nahant, Massachusetts.

Grier, Robert C.

Birth: March 5, 1794, Cumberland County, Pennsylvania.

Education: Dickinson College, graduated 1812.

Official Positions: president judge, District Court of Allegheny County, Pennsylvania, 1833–1846.

Supreme Court Service: nominated associate justice by President James K. Polk August 3, 1846, to replace Justice Henry Baldwin, who had died; confirmed by the Senate August 4, 1846, by a voice vote; took judicial oath August 10, 1846; retired January 31, 1870; replaced by William Strong, nominated by President Ulysses S. Grant.

Family: married Isabella Rose, 1829.

Death: September 25, 1870, Philadelphia, Pennsylvania.

Harlan, John M.

Birth: May 20, 1899, Chicago, Illinois.

Education: Princeton University, B.A., 1920; Rhodes scholar, Oxford University, Balliol College, B.A. in jurisprudence, 1923; New York Law School, LL.B., 1924.

Official Positions: assistant U.S. attorney, Southern District of New York, 1925–1927; special assistant attorney general, New York, 1928–1930; chief counsel, New York State Crime Commission, 1951–1953; judge, U.S. Court of Appeals for the Second Circuit, 1954–1955.

Supreme Court Service: nominated associate justice by President Dwight D. Eisenhower November 8, 1954, to replace Robert Jackson, who had died; confirmed by the Senate March 16, 1955, by a 71–11 vote; took judicial oath March 28, 1955; retired September 23, 1971; replaced by William H. Rehnquist, nominated by President Richard Nixon.

Family: married Ethel Andrews, November 10, 1928; one daughter.

Death: December 29, 1971, Washington D.C.

Harlan, John Marshall

Birth: June 1, 1833, Boyle County, Kentucky.

Education: Centre College, A.B., 1850; studied law at Transylvania University, 1851–1853.

Official Positions: adjutant general of Kentucky, 1851; judge, Franklin County, 1858; state attorney general, 1863–1867; member, Louisiana Reconstruction Commission, 1877; member, Bering Sea Tribunal of Arbitration, 1893.

Supreme Court Service: nominated associate justice by President Rutherford B. Hayes October 17, 1877, to replace David Davis, who had resigned; confirmed by the Senate November 29, 1877, by a voice vote; took judicial oath December 10, 1877; served until October 14, 1911; replaced by Mahlon Pitney, nominated by President William Howard Taft.

Family: married Malvina F. Shanklin, December 23, 1856; six children.

Death: October 14, 1911, Washington, D.C.

Holmes, Oliver Wendell, Jr.

Birth: March 8, 1841, Boston, Massachusetts.

Education: Harvard College, A.B., 1861; LL.B., 1866.

Official Positions: associate justice, Massachusetts Supreme Court, 1882–1899; chief justice, 1899–1902.

Supreme Court Service: nominated associate justice by President Theodore Roosevelt December 2, 1902, to replace Horace Gray, who had died; confirmed by the Senate December 4, 1902, by a voice vote; took judicial oath December 8, 1902; retired January 12, 1932; replaced by Benjamin N. Cardozo, nominated by President Herbert Hoover.

Family: married Fanny Bowdich Dixwell, June 17, 1872.

Death: March 6, 1935, Washington, D.C.

Hughes, Charles Evans

Birth: April 11, 1862, Glens Falls, New York.

Education: Madison College (now Colgate University), 1876–1878; Brown University, A.B., 1881, A.M., 1884; Columbia Law School, LL.B., 1884.

Official Positions: special counsel, New York state investigating commissions, 1905–1906; governor of New York, 1907–1910; U.S. secretary of state, 1921–1925; U.S. delegate, Washington Armament Conference, 1921; U.S. member, Permanent Court of Arbitration, 1926–1930; judge, Permanent Court of International Justice, 1928–1930.

Supreme Court Service: nominated associate justice by President William Howard Taft April 25, 1910, to replace David J. Brewer, who had died; confirmed by the Senate May 2, 1910, by a voice vote; took judicial oath October 10, 1910; resigned June 10, 1916, to become Republican presidential candidate; replaced by John H. Clarke, nominated by President Woodrow Wilson; nominated chief justice February 3, 1930, by President Herbert Hoover, to replace Chief Justice Taft, who had retired; confirmed by the Senate February 13, 1930, by a 52–26 vote; took judicial oath February 24, 1930; retired July 1, 1941; replaced by Harlan F. Stone, nominated by President Franklin D. Roosevelt.

Family: married Antoinette Carter, December 5, 1888; one son, three daughters.

Death: August 27, 1948, Osterville, Massachusetts.

Hunt, Ward

Birth: June 14, 1810, Utica, New York.

Education: graduated with honors from Union College, 1828; attended Tapping Reeve law school.

Official Positions: member, New York Assembly, 1839; mayor of Utica, 1844; member, New York Court of Appeals, 1866–1869; New York State commissioner of appeals, 1869–1873.

Supreme Court Service: nominated associate justice by President Ulysses S. Grant December 3, 1872, to replace Samuel Nelson, who had retired; confirmed by the Senate December 11, 1872, by a voice vote; took judicial oath January 9, 1873; retired January 27, 1882; replaced by Samuel Blatchford, nominated by President Chester A. Arthur.

Family: married Mary Ann Savage, 1837; died 1845; three children; married Marie Taylor, 1853.

Death: March 24, 1886, Washington, D.C.

Iredell, James

Birth: October 5, 1751, Lewes, England.

Education: educated in England; read law under Samuel Johnston of North Carolina; licensed to practice, 1770–1771.

Official Positions: comptroller of customs, Edenton, North Carolina, 1768–1774; collector of customs, Port of North Carolina, 1774–1776; judge, Superior Court of North Carolina, 1778; attorney general, North Carolina, 1779–1781; member, North Carolina Council of State, 1787; delegate, North Carolina convention for ratification of federal Constitution, 1788.

Supreme Court Service: nominated associate justice by President George Washington February 8, 1790; confirmed by the Senate February 10, 1790, by a voice vote; took judicial oath May 12, 1790; served until October 20, 1799; replaced by Alfred Moore, nominated by President John Adams.

Family: married Hannah Johnston, July 18, 1773; two daughters, one son.

Death: October 20, 1799, Edenton, North Carolina.

Jackson, Howell E.

Birth: April 8, 1832, Paris, Tennessee.

Education: West Tennessee College, A.B., 1850; University of Virginia, 1851–1852; Cumberland University, 1856.

Official Positions: custodian of sequestered property for Confederate states, 1861–1865; judge, Court of Arbitration for Western Tennessee, 1875–1879; state legislature, 1880; U.S. senator, 1881–1886; judge, Sixth Federal Circuit Court, 1886–1891, U.S. Circuit Court of Appeals, 1891–1893.

Supreme Court Service: nominated associate justice by President Benjamin Harrison February 2, 1893, to replace Lucius Q. C. Lamar, who had died; confirmed by the Senate February 18, 1893, by a voice vote; took judicial oath March 4, 1893; served until August 8, 1895; replaced by Rufus W. Peckham, nominated by President Grover Cleveland.

Family: married Sophia Malloy in 1859; died 1873; six children, two died in infancy; married Mary E. Harding in April 1874; three children.

Death: August 8, 1895, Nashville, Tennessee.

Jackson, Robert H.

Birth: February 13, 1892, Spring Creek, Pennsylvania.

Education: Local schools in Frewsburg, New York; Albany Law School, 1912.

Official Positions: general counsel, Bureau of Internal Revenue, 1934–1936; assistant U.S. attorney general,

1936–1938; U.S. solicitor general, 1938–1939; U.S. attorney general, 1940–1941; chief U.S. prosecutor, Nuremberg war crimes trial, 1945–1946.

Supreme Court Service: nominated associated justice by President Franklin D. Roosevelt June 12, 1941, to replace Harlan F. Stone, who was promoted to chief justice; confirmed by the Senate July 7, 1941, by a voice vote; took judicial oath July 11, 1941; served until October 9, 1954; replaced by John M. Harlan, nominated by President Dwight D. Eisenhower.

Family: married Irene Alice Gerhardt, April 24, 1916; one daughter, one son.

Death: October 9, 1954, Washington, D.C.

Jay, John

Birth: December 12, 1745, New York City.

Education: privately tutored; attended boarding school; graduated from King's College (later Columbia University), 1764; clerked in law office of Benjamin Kissam; admitted to the bar in 1768.

Official Positions: secretary, Royal Boundary Commission, 1773; member, New York Committee of 51, 1774; delegate, Continental Congress, 1774, 1775, 1777, president, 1778–1779; delegate, New York provincial congress, 1776–1777; chief justice, New York State, 1777–1778; minister to Spain, 1779; secretary of foreign affairs, 1784–1789; envoy to Great Britain, 1794–1795; governor, New York, 1795–1801.

Supreme Court Service: nominated chief justice by President George Washington September 24, 1789; confirmed by the Senate September 26, 1789, by a voice vote; took judicial oath October 9, 1789; resigned June 29, 1795; replaced by Oliver Ellsworth, nominated by President Washington.

Family: married Sarah Van Brugh Livingston, April 28, 1774; died 1802; five daughters, two sons.

Death: May 17, 1829, Bedford, New York.

Johnson, Thomas

Birth: November 4, 1732, Calvert County, Maryland.

Education: educated at home; studied law under Stephen Bordley; admitted to the bar, 1760.

Official Positions: delegate, Maryland Provincial Assembly, 1762; delegate, Annapolis Convention of 1774; member, Continental Congress, 1774–1777; delegate, first constitutional convention of Maryland, 1776; first governor of Maryland, 1777–1779; member, Maryland House of Delegates, 1780, 1786, 1787; member, Maryland convention for ratification of the federal Constitution, 1788; chief judge, general court of Maryland, 1790–1791; member, board of commissioners of the Federal City, 1791–1794.

Supreme Court Service: nominated associate justice by President George Washington November 1, 1791, to replace John Rutledge, who had resigned; confirmed by the Senate November 7, 1791, by a voice vote; took judicial oath August 6, 1792; resigned February 1, 1793; replaced by William Paterson, nominated by President Washington.

Family: married Ann Jennings, February 16, 1766; died 1794; three sons, five daughters, one of whom died in infancy.

Death: October 26, 1819, Frederick, Maryland.

Johnson, William

Birth: December 27, 1771, Charleston, South Carolina.

Education: graduated from Princeton, 1790; studied law under Charles Cotesworth Pinckney; admitted to bar in 1793.

Official Positions: member, South Carolina House of Representatives, 1794–1798; Speaker, 1798; judge, Court of Common Pleas, 1799–1804.

Supreme Court Service: nominated associate justice by President Thomas Jefferson March 22, 1804, to replace Alfred Moore, who had resigned; confirmed by the Senate March 24, 1804, by a voice vote; took judicial oath May 7, 1804; served until August 4, 1834; replaced by James M. Wayne, nominated by President Andrew Jackson.

Family: married Sarah Bennett, March 20, 1794; eight children, six of whom died in childhood; two adopted children.

Death: August 4, 1834, Brooklyn, New York.

Kennedy, Anthony M.

Birth: July 23, 1936, Sacramento, California.

Education: Stanford University, A.B., 1958; London School of Economics, 1957–1958; Harvard Law School, J.D., 1961.

Official Positions: judge, U.S. Court of Appeals for the Ninth Circuit, 1976–1988.

Supreme Court Service: nominated associate justice by President Ronald Reagan November 30, 1987, to replace Lewis F. Powell Jr., who had retired; confirmed by the Senate February 3, 1988, by a 97–0 vote; took judicial oath February 18, 1988.

Family: married Mary Davis, 1963; three children.

Lamar, Joseph R.

Birth: October 14, 1857, Elbert County, Georgia.

Education: University of Georgia, 1874–1875; Bethany College, A.B., 1877; Washington and Lee University, 1877.

Official Positions: member, Georgia legislature, 1886–1889; commissioner to codify Georgia laws, 1893; associate justice, Georgia Supreme Court, 1903–1905; member, mediation conference, Niagara Falls, Canada, 1914.

Supreme Court Service: nominated associate justice by President William Howard Taft December 12, 1910, to replace William Henry Moody, who had retired; confirmed by the Senate December 15, 1910, by a voice vote; took judicial oath January 3, 1911; served until January 2, 1916; replaced by Louis D. Brandeis, nominated by President Woodrow Wilson.

Family: married Clarinda Huntington Pendleton, January 30, 1879; two sons, one daughter.

Death: January 2, 1916, Washington, D.C.

Lamar, Lucius Q. C.

Birth: September 17, 1825, Eatonton, Georgia.

Education: Emory College, A.B., 1845.

Official Positions: member, Georgia House of Representatives, 1853; U.S. representative, 1857–1860, 1873–1877; U.S. senator, 1877–1885; secretary of interior, 1885–1888.

Supreme Court Service: nominated associate justice by President Grover Cleveland December 6, 1887, to replace William Woods, who had died; confirmed by the Senate January 16, 1888, by a 32–28 vote; took judicial oath January 18, 1888; served until January 23, 1893; replaced by Howell E. Jackson, nominated by President Benjamin Harrison.

Family: married Virginia Longstreet, July 15, 1847; died 1884; one son, three daughters; married Henrietta Dean Holt, January 5, 1887.

Death: January 23, 1893, Macon, Georgia.

Livingston, Henry Brockholst

Birth: November 25, 1757, New York City.

Education: graduated from College of New Jersey (Princeton), 1774; honorary LL.D., Harvard (1810), Princeton; studied law under Peter Yates; admitted to bar in 1783.

Official Positions: member, New York Assembly, Twelfth, Twenty-fourth, and Twenty-fifth sessions; judge, New York State Supreme Court, 1802–1807.

Supreme Court Service: nominated associate justice by President Thomas Jefferson December 13, 1806, to replace William Paterson, who had died; confirmed by the Senate December 17, 1806, by a voice vote; took judicial oath January 20, 1807; served until March 18, 1823; replaced by Smith Thompson, nominated by President James Monroe.

Family: married Catharine Keteltas, five children; married Ann Ludlow, three children; married Catharine Kortright, three children.

Death: March 18, 1823, Washington, D.C.

Lurton, Horace H.

Birth: February 26, 1844, Newport, Kentucky.

Education: Douglas University (University of Chicago), 1860; Cumberland Law School, L.B., 1867.

Official Positions: chancellor in equity, 1875–1878; judge, Tennessee Supreme Court, 1886–1893; judge, U.S. Court of Appeals for the Sixth Circuit, 1893–1909.

Supreme Court Service: nominated associate justice by President William Howard Taft December 13, 1909, to replace Rufus W. Peckham, who had died; confirmed by the Senate December 20, 1909, by a voice vote; took judicial oath January 3, 1910; served until July 12, 1914; replaced by James C. McReynolds, nominated by President Woodrow Wilson.

Family: married Mary Francis Owen, September 1867; three sons, two daughters.

Death: July 12, 1914, Atlantic City, New Jersey.

McKenna, Joseph

Birth: August 10, 1843, Philadelphia, Pennsylvania.

Education: Benicia Collegiate Institute, graduated in 1864; admitted to the bar in 1865.

Official Positions: district attorney, Solano County, California, 1866–1870; member, California Assembly, 1875–1876; U.S. representative, 1885–1892; judge, U.S. Ninth Judicial Circuit, 1892–1897; U.S. attorney general, 1897.

Supreme Court Service: nominated associate justice by President William McKinley December 16, 1897, to replace Stephen J. Field, who had retired; confirmed by the Senate January 21, 1898, by a voice vote; took judicial oath January 26, 1898; retired January 5, 1925; replaced by Harlan F. Stone, nominated by President Calvin Coolidge.

Family: married Amanda Frances Bornemann, June 10, 1869; three daughters, one son.
Death: November 21, 1926, Washington, D.C.

McKinley, John

Birth: May 1, 1780, Culpeper County, Virginia.
Education: read law on his own; admitted to the bar in 1800.
Official Positions: Alabama state representative, sessions of 1820, 1831, and 1836; U.S. senator, 1826–1831 and 1837; U.S. representative, 1833–1835.
Supreme Court Service: nominated associate justice by President Martin Van Buren September 18, 1837, for a newly created Supreme Court seat; confirmed by the Senate September 25, 1837, by a voice vote; took judicial oath January 9, 1838; served until July 19, 1852; replaced by John A. Campbell, nominated by President Franklin Pierce.
Family: married Juliana Bryan; married Elizabeth Armistead.
Death: July 19, 1852, Louisville, Kentucky.

McLean, John

Birth: March 11, 1785, Morris County, New Jersey.
Education: attended local school; privately tutored; read law with John S. Gano and Arthur St. Clair Jr.
Official Positions: examiner, U.S. Land Office, 1811–1812; U.S. representative, 1813–1816, chairman, Committee on Accounts; judge, Ohio Supreme Court, 1816–1822; commissioner, General Land Office, 1822–1823; U.S. postmaster general, 1823–1829.
Supreme Court Service: nominated associate justice by President Andrew Jackson March 7, 1829, to replace Robert Trimble, who had died; confirmed by the Senate March 7, 1829, by a voice vote; took judicial oath January 11, 1830; served until April 3, 1861; replaced by Noah H. Swayne, nominated by President Abraham Lincoln.
Family: married Rebecca Edwards, 1807; died 1840; four daughters, three sons; married Sarah Bella Ludlow Garrard, 1843; one son, died at birth.
Death: April 3, 1861, Cincinnati, Ohio.

McReynolds, James C.

Birth: February 3, 1862, Elkton, Kentucky.
Education: Vanderbilt University, B.S., 1882; University of Virginia, LL.B., 1884.
Official Positions: assistant U.S. attorney, 1903–1907; U.S. attorney general, 1913–1914.
Supreme Court Service: nominated associate justice by President Woodrow Wilson August 19, 1914, to replace Horace H. Lurton, who had died; confirmed by the Senate August 29, 1914, by a 44–6 vote; took judicial oath October 12, 1914; retired January 31, 1941; replaced by James F. Byrnes, nominated by President Franklin D. Roosevelt.
Family: unmarried.
Death: August 24, 1946, in Washington, D.C.

Marshall, John

Birth: September 24, 1755, Germantown, Virginia.
Education: tutored at home; self-taught in law; attended one course of law lectures at College of William and Mary, 1780.
Official Positions: member, Virginia House of Delegates, 1782–1785, 1787–1790, 1795–1796; member, Executive Council of State, 1782–1784; recorder, Richmond City Hustings Court, 1785–1788; delegate, state convention for ratification of federal Constitution, 1788; minister to France, 1797–1798; U.S. representative, 1799–1800; U.S. secretary of state, 1800–1801; member, Virginia Constitutional Convention, 1829.
Supreme Court Service: nominated chief justice by President John Adams January 20, 1801, to replace Oliver Ellsworth, who had resigned; confirmed by the Senate January 27, 1801, by a voice vote; took judicial oath February 4, 1801; served until July 6, 1835; replaced by Roger B. Taney, nominated by President Andrew Jackson.
Family: Married Mary Willis Ambler, January 3, 1783; died December 25, 1831; ten children.
Death: July 6, 1835, Philadelphia, Pennsylvania.

Marshall, Thurgood

Birth: July 2, 1908, Baltimore, Maryland.
Education: Lincoln University, A.B., cum laude, 1930; Howard University Law School, LL.B., 1933.
Official Positions: judge, Second Circuit Court of Appeals, 1961–1965; U.S. solicitor general, 1965–1967.
Supreme Court Service: nominated associate justice by President Lyndon B. Johnson June 13, 1967, to replace Tom C. Clark, who had retired; confirmed by the Senate August 30, 1967, by a 69–11 vote; took judicial oath

October 2, 1967; retired October 1, 1991; replaced by Clarence Thomas, nominated by President George Bush.

Family: married Vivian Burey, September 4, 1929, died February 1955; married Cecilia Suyat, December 17, 1955; two sons.

Death: January 24, 1993, Bethesda, Maryland.

Matthews, Stanley

Birth: July 21, 1824, Cincinnati, Ohio.

Education: Kenyon College, graduated with honors, 1840.

Official Positions: assistant prosecuting attorney, Hamilton County, 1845; clerk, Ohio House of Representatives, 1848–1849; judge, Hamilton County Court of Common Pleas, 1851–1853; member, Ohio Senate, 1855–1858; U.S. attorney for southern Ohio, 1858–1861; judge, Superior Court of Cincinnati, 1863–1865; counsel, Hayes-Tilden electoral commission, 1877; U.S. senator, 1877–1879.

Supreme Court Service: nominated associate justice by President Rutherford B. Hayes January 26, 1881, to replace Noah Swayne, who had retired; no action by Senate; renominated by President James A. Garfield March 14, 1881; confirmed by the Senate May 12, 1881, by a 24–23 vote; took judicial oath May 17, 1881; served until March 22, 1889; replaced by David J. Brewer, nominated by President Benjamin Harrison.

Family: married Mary Ann Black, February 1843; died 1885; eight children; married Mary Theaker, 1887.

Death: March 22, 1889, Washington, D.C.

Miller, Samuel F.

Birth: April 5, 1816, Richmond, Kentucky.

Education: Transylvania University, M.D., 1838; studied law privately; admitted to the bar in 1847.

Official Positions: justice of the peace and member of the Knox County, Kentucky, court, an administrative body, in the 1840s.

Supreme Court Service: nominated associate justice by President Abraham Lincoln July 16, 1862, to replace Peter V. Daniel, who had died; confirmed July 16, 1862, by a voice vote; took judicial oath July 21, 1862; served until October 13, 1890; replaced by Henry B. Brown, nominated by President Benjamin Harrison.

Family: married Lucy Ballinger, November 8, 1842; died 1854; three children; married Elizabeth Winter Reeves, widow of his law partner, 1857; two children.

Death: October 13, 1890, Washington, D.C.

Minton, Sherman

Birth: October 20, 1890, Georgetown, Indiana.

Education: Indiana University, LL.B., 1915; Yale University, LL.M., 1917.

Official Positions: public counselor, Public Service Commission, 1933–1934; U.S. senator, 1935–1941; assistant to president, 1941; judge, Seventh Circuit Court of Appeals, 1941–1949.

Supreme Court Service: nominated associate justice by President Harry S. Truman September 15, 1949, to replace Wiley B. Rutledge, who had died; confirmed by the Senate October 4, 1949, by a 48–16 vote; took judicial oath October 12, 1949; retired October 15, 1956; replaced by William J. Brennan Jr., nominated by President Dwight D. Eisenhower.

Family: married Gertrude Gurtz, August 11, 1917; two sons, one daughter.

Death: April 9, 1965, in New Albany, Indiana.

Moody, William H.

Birth: December 23, 1853, Newbury, Massachusetts.

Education: Harvard College, A.B., cum laude, 1876; Harvard Law School, 1876–1877; read law with Richard Henry Dana.

Official Positions: city solicitor, Haverhill, 1888–1890; district attorney, Eastern District of Massachusetts, 1890–1895; U.S. representative, 1895–1902; secretary of the Navy, 1902–1904; U.S. attorney general, 1904–1906.

Supreme Court Service: nominated associate justice by President Theodore Roosevelt December 3, 1906, to replace Henry B. Brown, who had retired; confirmed by the Senate December 12, 1906, by a voice vote; took judicial oath December 17, 1906; retired November 20, 1910; replaced by Joseph R. Lamar, nominated by President William Howard Taft.

Family: unmarried.

Death: July 2, 1917, Haverhill, Massachusetts.

Moore, Alfred

Birth: May 21, 1755, New Hanover County, North Carolina.

Education: educated in Boston; studied law under his father; received law license, 1775.

Official Positions: member, North Carolina legislature, 1782, 1792; North Carolina attorney general, 1782–1791;

trustee, University of North Carolina, 1789–1807; judge, North Carolina Superior Court, 1799.

Supreme Court Service: nominated associate justice by President John Adams December 6, 1799, to replace James Iredell, who had died; confirmed by the Senate December 10, 1799, by a voice vote; took judicial oath April 21, 1800; resigned January 26, 1804; replaced by William Johnson, nominated by President Thomas Jefferson.

Family: married Susanna Eagles.

Death: October 15, 1810, Bladen County, North Carolina.

Murphy, Francis W.

Birth: April 13, 1890, Sand (now Harbor) Beach, Michigan.

Education: University of Michigan, A.B., 1912, LL.B., 1914; graduate study, Lincoln's Inn, London, and Trinity College, Dublin.

Official Positions: chief assistant U.S. attorney, Eastern District of Michigan, 1919–1920; judge, Recorder's Court, Detroit, 1924–1930; mayor of Detroit, 1930–1933; governor general of the Philippines, 1933–1935; U.S. high commissioner to the Philippines, 1935–1936; governor of Michigan, 1937–1939; U.S. attorney general, 1939–1940.

Supreme Court Service: nominated associate justice by President Franklin D. Roosevelt January 4, 1940, to replace Pierce Butler, who had died; confirmed by the Senate January 16, 1940, by a voice vote; took judicial oath February 5, 1940; served until July 19, 1949; replaced by Tom C. Clark, nominated by President Harry S. Truman.

Family: unmarried.

Death: July 19, 1949, Detroit, Michigan.

Nelson, Samuel

Birth: November 11, 1792, Hebron, New York.

Education: graduated from Middlebury College, 1813.

Official Positions: postmaster, Cortland, New York, 1820–1823; presidential elector, 1820; judge, Sixth Circuit of New York, 1823–1831; associate justice, New York Supreme Court, 1831–1837; chief justice, New York Supreme Court, 1837–1845; member, Alabama Claims Commission, 1871.

Supreme Court Service: nominated associate justice by President John Tyler February 4, 1845, to replace Justice Smith Thompson, who had died; confirmed by the Senate February 14, 1845, by a voice vote; took judicial oath February 27, 1845; retired November 28, 1872; replaced by Ward Hunt, nominated by President Ulysses S. Grant.

Family: married Pamela Woods, 1819; died 1822; one son; married Catherine Ann Russell, ca. 1825; two daughters, one son.

Death: December 13, 1873, Cooperstown, New York.

O'Connor, Sandra Day

Birth: March 26, 1930, El Paso, Texas.

Education: Stanford University, B.A., 1950, Stanford University Law School, LL.B., 1952.

Official Positions: deputy county attorney, San Mateo, California, 1952–1953; assistant attorney general, Arizona, 1965–1969; Arizona state senator, 1969–1975, majority leader, state Senate, 1973–1974; judge, Maricopa County Superior Court, 1975–1979; judge, Arizona Court of Appeals, 1979–1981.

Supreme Court Service: nominated associate justice by President Ronald Reagan August 19, 1981 to replace Potter Stewart, who had retired; confirmed by the Senate September 21, 1981, by a 99–0 vote; took judicial oath September 26, 1981; announced retirement July 1, 2005.

Family: married John O'Connor, 1952; three sons.

Paterson, William

Birth: December 24, 1745, County Antrim, Ireland.

Education: graduated from College of New Jersey (Princeton), 1763; M.A., 1766; studied law under Richard Stockton; admitted to the bar, 1769.

Official Positions: member, New Jersey Provincial Congress, 1775–1776; delegate, New Jersey State Constitutional Convention, 1776; New Jersey attorney general, 1776–1783; delegate, U.S. Constitutional Convention, 1787; U.S. senator, 1789–1790; governor, New Jersey, 1790–1793.

Supreme Court Service: nominated associate justice by President George Washington March 4, 1793, to replace Thomas Johnson, who had resigned; confirmed by the Senate March 4, 1793, by a voice vote; took judicial oath March 11, 1793; served until September 9, 1806; replaced by Henry B. Livingston, nominated by President Thomas Jefferson.

Family: married Cornelia Bell, February 9, 1779; died 1783; three children; married Euphemia White, 1785.

Death: September 9, 1806, Albany, New York.

Peckham, Rufus W.

Birth: November 8, 1838, Albany, New York.

Education: Albany Boys' Academy; studied privately in Philadelphia.

Official Positions: district attorney, Albany County, 1869–1872; corporation counsel, City of Albany, 1881–1883; judge, New York Supreme Court, 1883–1886; judge, New York Court of Appeals, 1886–1895.

Supreme Court Service: nominated associate justice by President Grover Cleveland December 3, 1895, to replace Howell E. Jackson, who had died; confirmed by the Senate December 8, 1895, by a voice vote; took judicial oath January 6, 1896; served until October 24, 1909; replaced by Horace H. Lurton, nominated by President William Howard Taft.

Family: married Harriette M. Arnold, November 14, 1866; two sons.

Death: October 24, 1909, Altamont, New York.

Pitney, Mahlon

Birth: February 5, 1858, Morristown, New Jersey.

Education: College of New Jersey (Princeton), A.B., 1879; A.M., 1882.

Official Positions: U.S. representative, 1895–1899; New Jersey State senator, 1899–1901; president, New Jersey Senate, 1901; associate justice, New Jersey Supreme Court, 1901–1908; chancellor of New Jersey, 1908–1912.

Supreme Court Service: nominated associate justice by President William Howard Taft February 19, 1912, to replace John Marshall Harlan, who had died; confirmed by the Senate March 13, 1912, by a 50–26 vote; took judicial oath March 18, 1912; retired December 31, 1922; replaced by Edward T. Sanford, nominated by President Warren G. Harding.

Family: married Florence T. Shelton, November 14, 1891; two sons, one daughter.

Death: December 9, 1924, Washington, D.C.

Powell, Lewis F., Jr.

Birth: September 19, 1907, Suffolk, Virginia.

Education: Washington and Lee University, B.S., 1929; Washington and Lee University Law School, LL.B., 1931; Harvard Law School, LL.M., 1932.

Official Positions: president of the Richmond School Board, 1952–1961; member, 1961–1969, and president, 1968–1969, Virginia State Board of Education; president of the American Bar Association, 1964–1965; president, American College of Trial Lawyers, 1968–1969.

Supreme Court Service: nominated associate justice by President Richard Nixon October 22, 1971, to replace Hugo L. Black, who had retired; confirmed by the Senate December 6, 1971, by an 89–1 vote; took judicial oath January 6, 1972; retired June 26, 1987; replaced by Anthony Kennedy, nominated by President Ronald Reagan.

Family: married Josephine M. Rucker, May 2, 1936; three daughters, one son.

Death: August 25, 1998, Richmond, Virginia.

Reed, Stanley F.

Birth: December 31, 1884, Minerva, Kentucky.

Education: Kentucky Wesleyan University, A.B., 1902; Yale University, A.B., 1906; legal studies, University of Virginia and Columbia University (no degree); graduate studies, University of Paris, 1909–1910.

Official Positions: representative, Kentucky General Assembly, 1912–1916; general counsel, Federal Farm Board, 1929–1932; general counsel, Reconstruction Finance Corporation, 1932–1935; special assistant to attorney general, 1935; solicitor general, 1935–1938.

Supreme Court Service: nominated associate justice by President Franklin D. Roosevelt January 15, 1938, to replace George Sutherland, who had retired; confirmed by the Senate January 25, 1938, by a voice vote; took judicial oath January 31, 1938; retired February 25, 1957; replaced by Charles E. Whittaker, appointed by President Dwight D. Eisenhower.

Family: married Winifred Elgin, May 11, 1908; two sons.

Death: April 2, 1980, New York City.

Rehnquist, William

Birth: October 1, 1924, Milwaukee, Wisconsin.

Education: Stanford University, B.A., 1948, M.A., 1948; Harvard University, M.A., 1950; Stanford University Law School, LL.B., 1952.

Official Positions: law clerk to Supreme Court Justice Robert H. Jackson, 1952–1953; assistant U.S. attorney general, Office of Legal Counsel, 1969–1971.

Supreme Court Service: nominated associate justice by President Richard Nixon October 21, 1971, to replace John M. Harlan, who had retired; confirmed by the Senate December 10, 1971, by a 68–26 vote; took judicial oath January 7, 1972; nominated chief justice by President Ronald Reagan June 20, 1986; confirmed by the Senate 65–33, September 17, 1986; took judicial oath September 26, 1986; replaced as associate justice by Antonin Scalia; served until September 3, 2005; replaced by John G. Roberts Jr., nominated by President George W. Bush.

Family: married Natalie Cornell, August 29, 1953; died October 17, 1991; one son, two daughters.

Death: September 3, 2005, Arlington, Virginia.

Roberts, John G., Jr.

Birth: January 27, 1955, Buffalo, New York.

Education: Harvard University, B.A., 1976; Harvard Law School, LL.B., 1979.

Official Positions: law clerk to Justice William H. Rehnquist, 1980–1981; special assistant to Attorney General, William French Smith, U.S. Justice Department, 1981–1982; associate counsel to President Ronald Reagan, 1982–1986; judge, U.S. Court of Appeals for the District of Columbia Circuit, 2003–2005.

Supreme Court Service: nominated associate justice by President George W. Bush July 19, 2005, to replace Sandra Day O'Connor, who announced her retirement on July 1, 2005; elevated to chief justice nominee upon death of Chief Justice William H. Rehnquist September 3, 2005; confirmed as chief justice by the Senate September 29, 2005, by a 78–22 vote; took judicial oath September 29, 2005.

Family: married Jane Marie Sullivan, 1996; one daughter, one son.

Roberts, Owen J.

Birth: May 2, 1875, Germantown, Pennsylvania.

Education: University of Pennsylvania, A.B. with honors, 1895; LL.B. cum laude, 1898.

Official Positions: assistant district attorney, 1903–1906; special deputy attorney general, Eastern District of Pennsylvania, 1918; special U.S. attorney, 1924–1930; umpire, Mixed Claims Commission, 1932; chairman, Pearl Harbor Inquiry Board, 1941–1942.

Supreme Court Service: nominated associate justice by President Herbert Hoover May 9, 1930, to replace Edward T. Sanford, who had died; confirmed by the Senate May 20, 1930, by a voice vote; took judicial oath June 2, 1930; resigned July 31, 1945; replaced by Harold H. Burton, nominated by President Harry S. Truman.

Family: married Elizabeth Caldwell Rogers, 1904; one daughter.

Death: May 17, 1955, West Vincent Township, Pennsylvania.

Rutledge, John

Birth: September 1739, Charleston, South Carolina.

Education: privately tutored; studied law at the Middle Temple in England; called to the English bar February 9, 1760.

Official Positions: member, South Carolina Commons House of Assembly, 1761–1776; South Carolina attorney general pro item, 1764–1765; delegate, Stamp Act Congress, 1765; member, Continental Congress, 1774–1776, 1782–1783; president, South Carolina General Assembly, 1776–1778; governor, South Carolina, 1779–1782; judge of the Court of Chancery of South Carolina, 1784–1791; chief, South Carolina delegation to the Constitutional Convention, 1787; member, South Carolina convention to ratify U.S. Constitution, 1788; chief justice, South Carolina Supreme Court, 1791–1795; member, South Carolina Assembly, 1798–1799.

Supreme Court Service: nominated associate justice by President George Washington September 24, 1789; confirmed by the Senate September 26, 1789, by a voice vote; took judicial oath February 15, 1790; resigned March 5, 1791; replaced by Thomas Johnson, nominated by President Washington. Later sworn in by virtue of recess appointment as chief justice August 12, 1795; appointment not confirmed, and service terminated December 15, 1795.

Family: married Elizabeth Grimke, May 1, 1763; died 1792; ten children.

Death: July 18, 1800, Charleston, South Carolina.

Rutledge, Wiley B.

Birth: July 20, 1894, Cloverport, Kentucky.

Education: University of Wisconsin, A.B., 1914; University of Colorado, LL.B., 1922.

Official Positions: judge, U.S. Court of Appeals for the District of Columbia, 1939–1943.

Supreme Court Service: nominated associate justice by President Franklin D. Roosevelt January 11, 1943, to replace James F. Byrnes, who had resigned; confirmed by the Senate February 8, 1943, by a voice vote; took judicial oath February 15, 1943; served until September 10, 1949; replaced by Sherman Minton, nominated by President Harry S. Truman.

Family: married Annabel Person, August 28, 1917; two daughters, one son.

Death: September 10, 1949, York, Maine.

Sanford, Edward T.

Birth: July 23, 1865, Knoxville, Tennessee.

Education: University of Tennessee, B.A. and Ph.B., 1883; Harvard, B.A., 1884, M.A., 1889; Harvard Law School, LL.B., 1889.

Official Positions: special assistant to the U.S. attorney general, 1906–1907; assistant U.S. attorney general, 1907–1908; federal judge, U.S. District Court for the Middle and Eastern Districts of Tennessee, 1908–1923.

Supreme Court Service: nominated associate justice by President Warren G. Harding January 24, 1923, to replace Mahlon Pitney, who had retired; confirmed by the Senate January 29, 1923, by a voice vote; took judicial oath February 19, 1923; served until March 8, 1930; replaced by Owen J. Roberts, nominated by President Herbert Hoover.

Family: married Lutie Mallory Woodruff, January 6, 1891; two daughters.

Death: March 8, 1930, Washington, D.C.

Scalia, Antonin

Birth: March 11, 1936, Trenton, New Jersey.

Education: Georgetown University, A.B., summa cum laude, 1957; Harvard Law School, LL.B., magna cum laude, 1960.

Official Positions: general counsel, White House Office of Telecommunications Policy, 1971–1972; chairman, Administrative Conference of the United States, 1972–1974; assistant attorney general, Office of Legal Counsel, 1974–1977; judge, U.S. Court of Appeals for the District of Columbia Circuit, 1982–1986.

Supreme Court Service: nominated associate justice by President Ronald Reagan June 24, 1986, to replace William H. Rehnquist, who had been promoted to chief justice; confirmed by the Senate September 17, 1986, by a 98–0 vote; took judicial oath September 26, 1986.

Family: married Maureen McCarthy, 1960; nine children.

Shiras, George, Jr.

Birth: January 26, 1832, Pittsburgh, Pennsylvania.

Education: Ohio University, 1849–1851; Yale University, B.A., 1853, honorary LL.D., 1883; studied law at Yale and privately; admitted to the bar in 1855.

Official Positions: none.

Supreme Court Service: nominated associate justice by President Benjamin Harrison July 19, 1892, to replace Joseph P. Bradley, who had died; confirmed by the Senate July 26, 1892, by a voice vote; took judicial oath October 10, 1892; retired February 23, 1903; replaced by William R. Day, nominated by President Theodore Roosevelt.

Family: married Lillie E. Kennedy, December 31, 1857; two sons.

Death: August 2, 1924, Pittsburgh, Pennsylvania.

Souter, David H.

Birth: September 17, 1939, Melrose, Massachusetts.

Education: Harvard College, B.A., 1961; Oxford University (Rhodes Scholar), 1961–1963; Harvard University Law School, LL.B., 1966.

Official Positions: assistant attorney general, New Hampshire, 1968–1971; deputy attorney general, New Hampshire, 1971–1976; attorney general, New Hampshire, 1976–1978; associate justice, New Hampshire Superior Court, 1978–1983; associate justice, New Hampshire Supreme Court, 1983–1990; judge, U.S. Court of Appeals for the First Circuit, 1990.

Supreme Court Service: nominated associate justice by President George Bush July 23, 1990, to replace William J. Brennan Jr., who had retired; confirmed by the Senate October 2, 1990, by a 90–9 vote; took judicial oath October 9, 1990.

Family: Unmarried.

Stevens, John Paul

Birth: April 20, 1920, Chicago, Illinois.

Education: University of Chicago, B.A., 1941; Northwestern University School of Law, J.D., magna cum laude, 1947.

Official Positions: law clerk to Justice Wiley B. Rutledge, 1947–1948; associate counsel, Subcommittee on the Study of Monopoly Power, House Judiciary Committee, 1951; member, U.S. Attorney General's National Committee to Study the Antitrust Laws, 1953–1955; judge, Seventh Circuit Court of Appeals, 1970–1975.

Supreme Court Service: nominated associate justice by President Gerald R. Ford November 28, 1975, to replace William O. Douglas, who had retired; confirmed by the Senate December 17, 1975, by a 98–0 vote; took judicial oath December 19, 1975.

Family: married Elizabeth Jane Sheeren, 1942, divorced 1979; one son, three daughters; married Maryan Mulholland Simon, 1980.

Stewart, Potter

Birth: January 23, 1915, Jackson, Michigan.

Education: Yale College, B.A., cum laude, 1937; Yale Law School, LL.B., cum laude, 1941; fellow, Cambridge University, Cambridge, England, 1937–1938.

Official Positions: member, Cincinnati, Ohio, city council, 1950–1953; vice mayor of Cincinnati, 1952–1953; judge, Sixth Circuit Court of Appeals, 1954–1958.

Supreme Court Service: received recess appointment as associate justice by President Dwight D. Eisenhower October 14, 1958, to replace Harold H. Burton, who had retired; nominated associate justice by President Eisenhower January 17, 1959; confirmed by the Senate May 5, 1959, by a 70–17 vote; took judicial oath October 14, 1958; retired July 3, 1981; replaced by Sandra Day O'Connor, nominated by President Ronald Reagan.

Family: married Mary Ann Bertles, April 24, 1943; two sons, one daughter.

Death: December 7, 1985, Hanover, New Hampshire.

Stone, Harlan Fiske

Birth: October 11, 1872, Chesterfield, New Hampshire.

Education: Amherst College, A.B., 1894, M.A., 1897, LL.D., 1913; Columbia University, LL.B., 1898.

Official Positions: U.S. attorney general, 1924–1925.

Supreme Court Service: nominated associate justice by President Calvin Coolidge January 5, 1925, to replace Joseph McKenna, who had retired; confirmed by the Senate February 5, 1925, by a 71–6 vote; took judicial oath March 2, 1925; nominated chief justice by President Franklin D. Roosevelt June 12, 1941, to replace Chief Justice Charles Evans Hughes, who had retired; confirmed by the Senate June 27, 1941, by a voice vote; took judicial oath July 3, 1941; served until April 22, 1946; replaced by Fred M. Vinson, nominated by President Harry S. Truman.

Family: married Agnes Harvey, September 7, 1899; two sons.

Death: April 22, 1946, Washington, D.C.

Story, Joseph

Birth: September 18, 1779, Marblehead, Massachusetts.

Education: attended Marblehead Academy; graduated from Harvard, 1798; LL.D., 1821; read law under Samuel Sewall and Samuel Putnam; admitted to bar, 1801.

Official Positions: member, Massachusetts legislature, 1805–1808; Speaker of the House, 1811; U.S. representative, 1808–1809; delegate, Massachusetts Constitutional Convention, 1820.

Supreme Court Service: nominated associate justice by President James Madison November 15, 1811, to replace William Cushing, who had died; confirmed by the Senate November 18, 1811, by a voice vote; took judicial oath February 3, 1812; served until September 10, 1845; replaced by Levi Woodbury, nominated by President James K. Polk.

Family: married Mary Lynde Oliver, December 9, 1804; died June 1805; married Sarah Waldo Wetmore, August 27, 1808; seven children.

Death: September 10, 1845, Cambridge, Massachusetts.

Strong, William

Birth: May 6, 1808, Somers, Connecticut.

Education: Yale College, A.B., 1828; M.A., 1831.

Official Positions: U.S. representative, 1847–1851; Pennsylvania Supreme Court justice, 1857–1868.

Supreme Court Service: nominated associate justice by President Ulysses S. Grant February 7, 1870, to replace Robert C. Grier, who had retired; confirmed by the Senate February 18, 1870, by a voice vote; took judicial oath March 14, 1870; retired December 14, 1880; replaced by William B. Woods, nominated by President Rutherford B. Hayes.

Family: married Priscilla Lee Mallery, November 28, 1836; died 1844; two daughters, one son; married Rachel Davis Bull, a widow, November 22, 1849; two daughters, two sons.

Death: August 19, 1895, Lake Minnewaska, New York.

Sutherland, George

Birth: March 25, 1862, Buckinghamshire, England.

Education: Brigham Young (University) Academy, 1879–1881; University of Michigan Law School, 1882.

Official Positions: Utah state senator, 1896–1900; U.S. representative, 1901–1903; U.S. senator, 1905–1917; chairman, advisory committee to the Washington Conference for the Limitation of Naval Armaments, 1921; U.S. counsel, Norway–United States arbitration, The Hague, 1921–1922.

Supreme Court Service: nominated associate justice by President Warren G. Harding September 5, 1922, to replace Justice John H. Clarke, who had resigned; took judicial oath October 2, 1922; confirmed by the Senate September 5, 1922, by a voice vote; retired January 17, 1938; replaced by Stanley F. Reed, nominated by President Franklin D. Roosevelt.

Family: married Rosamund Lee, June 18, 1883; two daughters, one son.

Death: July 18, 1942, Stockbridge, Massachusetts.

Swayne, Noah Haynes

Birth: December 7, 1804, Frederick County, Virginia.

Education: studied law privately; admitted to the bar in Warrenton, Virginia, in 1823.

Official Positions: Coshocton County (Ohio) prosecuting attorney, 1826–1829; Ohio state representative, 1830 and 1836; U.S. attorney for Ohio, 1830–1841; Columbus city councilman, 1834.

Supreme Court Service: nominated associate justice by President Abraham Lincoln January 21, 1862, to replace John McLean, who had died; confirmed by the Senate January 24, 1862, by a 38–1 vote; took judicial oath January 27, 1862; retired January 24, 1881; replaced by Stanley Matthews, nominated by President Rutherford B. Hayes and renominated by President James A. Garfield.

Family: married Sarah Ann Wager, 1832; four sons, one daughter.

Death: June 8, 1884, New York City.

Taft, William Howard

Birth: September 15, 1857, Cincinnati, Ohio.

Education: Yale University, A.B., class salutatorian, 1878; Cincinnati Law School, LL.B., 1880.

Official Positions: assistant prosecuting attorney, Hamilton County, Ohio, 1881–1883; assistant county solicitor, Hamilton County, 1885–1887; judge, Ohio Superior Court, 1887–1890; U.S. solicitor general, 1890–1891; judge, U.S. District Court for the Sixth Circuit, 1892–1900; chairman, Philippine Commission, 1900–1901; governor general of the Philippines, 1901–1904; secretary of war, 1904–1908; president of the United States, 1909–1913; joint chairman, National War Labor Board, 1918–1919.

Supreme Court Service: nominated chief justice by President Warren G. Harding June 30, 1921, to replace Chief Justice Edward D. White, who had died; confirmed by the Senate June 30, 1921, by a voice vote; took judicial oath July 11, 1921; retired February 3, 1930; replaced by Chief Justice Charles Evans Hughes, nominated by President Herbert Hoover.

Family: married Helen Herron, June 19, 1886; two sons, one daughter.

Death: March 8, 1930, in Washington, D.C.

Taney, Roger Brooke

Birth: March 17, 1777, Calvert County, Maryland.

Education: graduated from Dickinson College in Pennsylvania, 1795, honorary LL.D.; read law in office of Judge Jeremiah Chase in Annapolis.

Official Positions: member, Maryland House of Delegates, 1799–1800; Maryland state senator, 1816–1821; Maryland attorney general, 1827–1831; chairman, Jackson Central Committee for Maryland, 1827–1828; U.S. attorney general, 1831–1833; acting secretary of war, 1831; U.S. secretary of the Treasury, 1833–1834 (appointment rejected by Senate).

Supreme Court Service: nominated chief justice by President Andrew Jackson December 28, 1835, to replace John Marshall, who had died; confirmed by the Senate on March 15, 1836, by a 29–15 vote; took judicial oath March 28, 1836; served until October 12, 1864; replaced by Salmon P. Chase, nominated by President Abraham Lincoln.

Family: married Anne Phoebe Carlton Key, January 7, 1806; died 1855; six daughters; one son died in infancy.

Death: October 12, 1864, Washington, D.C.

Thomas, Clarence

Birth: June 23, 1948, Pin Point, Georgia.

Education: Immaculate Conception Seminary, 1967–1968; Holy Cross College, B.A., 1971; Yale University Law School, J.D., 1974.

Official Positions: assistant attorney general, Missouri, 1974–1977; assistant secretary of education for civil rights, 1981–1982; chairman, Equal Employment Opportunity Commission, 1982–1990; judge, U.S. Court of Appeals for the District of Columbia, 1990–1991.

Supreme Court Service: nominated associate justice by President George Bush July 1, 1991, to replace Thurgood Marshall, who had retired; confirmed by the Senate October 15, 1991, by a 52–48 vote; took judicial oath October 23, 1991.

Family: married Kathy Grace Ambush, 1971; one son; divorced 1984; married Virginia Lamp, 1987.

Thompson, Smith

Birth: January 17, 1768, Dutchess County, New York.

Education: graduated from Princeton, 1788; read law under James Kent; admitted to the bar, 1792; honorary law doctorates from Yale, 1824; Princeton, 1824; and Harvard, 1835.

Official Positions: member, New York state legislature, 1800; member, New York Constitutional Convention, 1801; associate justice, New York Supreme Court, 1802–1814; appointed to New York State Board of Regents, 1813; chief justice, New York Supreme Court, 1814–1818; secretary of the Navy, 1819–1823.

Supreme Court Service: nominated associate justice by President James Monroe December 8, 1823, to replace Brockholst Livingston, who had died; confirmed by the Senate December 19, 1823, by a voice vote; took judicial oath February 10, 1823; served until December 18, 1843; replaced by Samuel Nelson, nominated by President John Tyler.

Family: married Sarah Livingston, 1794; died September 22, 1833; two sons, two daughters; married Eliza Livingston; two daughters, one son.

Death: December 18, 1843, Poughkeepsie, New York.

Todd, Thomas

Birth: January 23, 1765, King and Queen County, Virginia.

Education: graduated from Liberty Hall (now Washington and Lee University), Lexington, Virginia, 1783; read law under Harry Innes; admitted to bar in 1788.

Official Positions: clerk, federal district for Kentucky, 1792–1801; clerk, Kentucky House of Representatives, 1792–1801; clerk, Kentucky Court of Appeals (Supreme Court), 1799–1801; judge, Kentucky Court of Appeals, 1801–1806; chief justice, 1806–1807.

Supreme Court Service: nominated associate justice by President Thomas Jefferson February 28, 1807, to fill a newly created seat; confirmed by the Senate March 3, 1807, by a voice vote; took judicial oath May 4, 1807; served until February 7, 1826; replaced by Robert Trimble, nominated by President John Quincy Adams.

Family: married Elizabeth Harris, 1788; died 1811; five children; married Lucy Payne, 1812; three children.

Death: February 7, 1826, Frankfort, Kentucky.

Trimble, Robert

Birth: November 17, 1776, Berkeley County, Virginia.

Education: Bourbon Academy; Kentucky Academy; read law under George Nicholas and James Brown; admitted to the bar in 1803.

Official Positions: Kentucky state representative, 1802; judge, Kentucky Court of Appeals, 1807–1809; U.S. district attorney for Kentucky, 1813–1817; U.S. district judge, 1817–1826.

Supreme Court Service: nominated associate justice by President John Quincy Adams April 11, 1826, to replace Thomas Todd, who had died; confirmed by the Senate May 9, 1826, by a 27–5 vote; took judicial oath June 16, 1826; served until August 25, 1828; replaced by John McLean, nominated by President Andrew Jackson.

Family: married Nancy Timberlake, August 18, 1803; at least ten children.

Death: August 25, 1828, Paris, Kentucky.

Van Devanter, Willis

Birth: April 17, 1859, Marion, Indiana.

Education: Indiana Asbury University, A.B., 1878; University of Cincinnati Law School, LL.B., 1881.

Official Positions: city attorney, Cheyenne, 1887–1888; member, Wyoming territorial legislature, 1888; chief justice, Wyoming Territory Supreme Court, 1889–1890; assistant attorney general, Department of the Interior, 1897–1903; judge, U.S. Court of Appeals for the Eighth Circuit, 1903–1910.

Supreme Court Service: nominated associate justice by President William Howard Taft December 12, 1910, to replace Edward D. White, who became chief justice; confirmed by the Senate December 15, 1910, by a voice vote; took judicial oath January 3, 1911; retired June 2, 1937; replaced by Hugo L. Black, nominated by President Franklin D. Roosevelt.

Family: married Dellice Burhans, October 10, 1883; two sons.

Death: February 8, 1941, Washington, D.C.

Vinson, Frederick Moore

Birth: January 22, 1890, Louisa, Kentucky.

Education: Kentucky Normal College, 1908; Centre College, A.B., 1909; LL.B., 1911.

Official Positions: commonwealth attorney, Thirty-second Judicial District of Kentucky, 1921–1924; U.S. representative, 1924–1929, 1931–1938; judge, U.S. Court of Appeals for the District of Columbia, 1938–1943; director, Office of Economic Stabilization, 1943–1945; administrator, Federal Loan Agency, 1945; director, Office of War Mobilization and Reconversion, 1945; secretary of the Treasury, 1945–1946.

Supreme Court Service: nominated chief justice by President Harry S. Truman June 6, 1946, to replace Chief Justice Harlan F. Stone, who had died; confirmed by the Senate June 20, 1946, by a voice vote; took judicial oath June 24, 1946; served until September 8, 1953; replaced by Earl Warren, nominated by President Dwight D. Eisenhower.

Family: married Roberta Dixson, January 24, 1923; two sons.

Death: September 8, 1953, Washington, D.C.

Waite, Morrison R.

Birth: November 27, 1816, Lyme, Connecticut.

Education: graduated from Yale College, 1837.

Official Positions: Ohio state representative, 1850–1852; representative to the Geneva Arbitration, 1871; president of the Ohio Constitutional Convention, 1873–1874.

Supreme Court Service: nominated chief justice by President Ulysses S. Grant January 19, 1874, to replace Salmon P. Chase, who had died; confirmed by the Senate January 21, 1874, by a 63–0 vote; took judicial oath March 4,

1874; served until March 23, 1888; replaced by Melville W. Fuller, nominated by President Grover Cleveland.

Family: married his second cousin, Amelia C. Warner, September 21, 1840; five children.

Death: March 23, 1888, Washington, D.C.

Warren, Earl

Birth: March 19, 1891, Los Angeles, California.

Education: University of California, B.L., 1912; J.D., 1914.

Official Positions: deputy city attorney, Oakland, California, 1919–1920; deputy district attorney, Alameda County, 1920–1925; district attorney, Alameda County, 1925–1939; California attorney general, 1939–1943; governor, 1943–1953.

Supreme Court Service: nominated chief justice by President Dwight D. Eisenhower September 30, 1953, to replace Chief Justice Fred M. Vinson, who had died; confirmed by the Senate March 1, 1954, by a voice vote; took judicial oath October 5, 1953; retired June 23, 1969; replaced by Warren E. Burger, nominated by President Richard Nixon.

Family: married Nina P. Meyers, October 14, 1925; three sons, three daughters.

Death: July 9, 1974, Washington, D.C.

Washington, Bushrod

Birth: June 5, 1762, Westmoreland County, Virginia.

Education: privately tutored; graduated from the College of William and Mary, 1778; read law under James Wilson; member, Virginia bar; honorary LL.D. degrees from Harvard, Princeton, and University of Pennsylvania.

Official Positions: member, Virginia House of Delegates, 1787; member, Virginia convention to ratify U.S. Constitution, 1788.

Supreme Court Service: nominated associate justice by President John Adams December 19, 1798, to replace James Wilson, who had died; confirmed by the Senate December 20, 1798, by a voice vote; took judicial oath February 4, 1799; served until November 26, 1829; replaced by Henry Baldwin, nominated by President Andrew Jackson.

Family: married Julia Ann Blackburn, 1785.

Death: November 26, 1829, in Philadelphia, Pennsylvania.

Wayne, James M.

Birth: 1790, Savannah, Georgia.

Education: College of New Jersey (Princeton University), 1808, honorary LL.B., 1849; read law under three lawyers including Judge Charles Chauncey of New Haven; admitted to the bar January 1811.

Official Positions: member, Georgia House of Representatives, 1815–1816; mayor, Savannah, 1817–1819; judge, Savannah Court of Common Pleas, 1820–1822; Georgia Superior Court, 1822–1828; U.S. representative, 1829–1835; chairman, Committee on Foreign Relations.

Supreme Court Service: nominated associate justice by President Andrew Jackson January 7, 1835, to replace William Johnson, who had died; confirmed by the Senate January 9, 1835 by a voice vote; took judicial oath January 14, 1835; served until July 5, 1867; replaced by Joseph Bradley, nominated by President Ulysses S. Grant.

Family: married Mary Johnson Campbell, 1813; three children.

Death: July 5, 1867, Washington, D.C.

White, Byron R.

Birth: June 8, 1917, Fort Collins, Colorado.

Education: University of Colorado, B.A., 1938; Rhodes Scholar, Oxford University, 1939; Yale Law School, LL.B., magna cum laude, 1946.

Official Positions: law clerk to Chief Justice Fred M. Vinson, 1946–1947; deputy U.S. attorney general, 1961–1962.

Supreme Court Service: nominated associate justice by President John F. Kennedy March 30, 1962, to replace Charles E. Whittaker, who had retired; confirmed by the Senate April 11, 1962, by a voice vote; took judicial oath April 16, 1962; retired June 28, 1993; replaced by Ruth Bader Ginsburg, nominated by President Bill Clinton.

Family: married Marion Stearns, 1946; one son, one daughter.

Death: April 15, 2002, Denver, Colorado.

White, Edward D.

Birth: November 3, 1845, Lafourche Parish, Louisiana.

Education: Mount St. Mary's College, Emmitsburg, Maryland, 1856; Georgetown College (University), Washington, D.C., 1857–1861; studied law at University of Louisiana (Tulane) and with Edward Bermudez; admitted to the bar in 1868.

Official Positions: Louisiana state senator, 1874; associate justice, Louisiana Supreme Court, 1878–1880; U.S. senator, 1891–1894.

Supreme Court Service: nominated associate justice by President Grover Cleveland February 19, 1894, to replace Samuel Blatchford, who had died; confirmed by the Senate February 19, 1894, by a voice vote; took judicial oath March 12, 1894. Nominated chief justice by President William Howard Taft December 12, 1910, to replace Melville Fuller, who had died; confirmed by the Senate December 12, 1910, by a voice vote; took judicial oath December 19, 1910; served until May 19, 1921; replaced as chief justice by former president Taft, appointed by President Warren G. Harding.

Family: married Virginia Montgomery Kent, November 1894.

Death: May 19, 1921, in Washington, D.C.

Whittaker, Charles E.

Birth: February 22, 1901, Troy, Kansas.

Education: University of Kansas City Law School, LL.B., 1924.

Official Positions: judge, U.S. District Court for Western District of Missouri, 1954–1956; judge, Eighth Circuit Court of Appeals, 1956–1957.

Supreme Court Service: nominated associate justice by President Dwight D. Eisenhower March 2, 1957, to replace Stanley Reed, who had retired; confirmed by the Senate March 19, 1957, by a voice vote; took judicial oath March 25, 1957; retired March 31, 1962; replaced by Byron R. White, nominated by President John F. Kennedy.

Family: married Winifred R. Pugh, July 7, 1928; three sons.

Death: November 26, 1973, Kansas City, Missouri.

Wilson, James

Birth: September 14, 1742, Caskardy, Scotland.

Education: attended University of St. Andrews (Scotland); read law in office of John Dickinson; admitted to the bar in 1767; honorary M.A., College of Philadelphia, 1776; honorary LL.D., 1790.

Official Positions: delegate, first Provincial Convention at Philadelphia, 1774; delegate, Continental Congress, 1775–1777, 1785–1787; delegate, U.S. Constitutional Convention, 1787; delegate, Pennsylvania convention to ratify U.S. Constitution, 1787.

Supreme Court Service: nominated associate justice by President George Washington September 24, 1789; confirmed by the Senate September 26, 1789, by a voice vote; took judicial oath October 5, 1789; served until August 21, 1798; replaced by Bushrod Washington, nominated by President John Adams.

Family: married Rachel Bird, November 5, 1771; died 1786; six children; married Hannah Gray, September 19, 1793; one son died in infancy.

Death: August 21, 1798, Edenton, North Carolina.

Woodbury, Levi

Birth: December 22, 1789, Francestown, New Hampshire.

Education: Dartmouth College, graduated with honors, 1809; Tapping Reeve Law School, ca. 1810.

Official Positions: clerk, New Hampshire Senate, 1816; associate justice, New Hampshire Superior Court, 1817–1823; governor, New Hampshire, 1823–1824; Speaker, New Hampshire House, 1825; U.S. senator, 1825–1831, 1841–1845; secretary of the Navy, 1831–1834; secretary of the Treasury, 1834–1841.

Supreme Court Service: nominated associate justice by President James K. Polk December 23, 1845, to replace Justice Joseph Story, who had died; confirmed by the Senate January 3, 1846, by voice vote; took judicial oath September 23, 1845; served until September 4, 1851; replaced by Benjamin R. Curtis, nominated by President Millard Fillmore.

Family: married Elizabeth Williams Clapp, June 1819; four daughters, one son.

Death: September 4, 1851, Portsmouth, New Hampshire.

Woods, William B.

Birth: August 3, 1824, Newark, Ohio.

Education: attended Western Reserve College for three years; graduated from Yale University, 1845.

Official Positions: mayor of Newark, Ohio, 1856; Ohio state representative, 1858–1862, Speaker in 1858–1860 and minority leader in 1860–1862; chancellor, middle chancery district of Alabama, 1868–1869; U.S. circuit judge for the Fifth Circuit, 1869–1880.

Supreme Court Service: nominated associate justice by President Rutherford B. Hayes December 15, 1880, to replace William Strong, who had retired; confirmed by the Senate December 21, 1880, by a 39–8 vote; took judicial oath January 5, 1881; served until May 14, 1887; replaced by Lucius Q. C. Lamar, nominated by President Grover Cleveland.

Family: married Anne E. Warner, June 21, 1855; one son, one daughter.

Death: May 14, 1887, Washington, D.C.

Source: Adapted from Joan Biskupic and Elder Witt, *Congressional Quarterly's Guide to the U.S. Supreme Court,* 3rd ed. (Washington, D.C.: Congressional Quarterly, 1997), 855–962. Updated by the author.

Succession Chart of Supreme Court Seats

Year	Chief Justice	Seat 2	Seat 3	Seat 4	Seat 5	Seat 6	Seat 7	Seat 8	Seat 9	Seat 10
1789	Jay	Rutledge, J.	Cushing	Wilson	Blair					
1790–1791						Iredell				
1791–1793		Johnson, T.								
1793–1795		Paterson								
1795	Rutledge, J.									
1796–1798	Ellsworth				Chase, S.					
1799				Washington						
1800						Moore				
1801–1803	Marshall, J.									
1804–1806						Johnson, W.				
1807–1810		Livingston					Todd			
1811			(vacant)							
1811–1823			Story		Duvall					
1824–1826		Thompson								
1826–1828							Trimble			
1829							McLean			
1830–1834				Baldwin						
1835						Wayne				
1836	Taney				Barbour					
1837–1841								Catron	McKinley	
1841–1843					Daniel					
1844		(vacant)								
1845		Nelson		(vacant)						
1846–1851			Woodbury	Grier						
1852			Curtis							
1853–1857									Campbell	
1858–1860			Clifford							
1861					(vacant)					
1862					Miller		Swayne		Davis	
1863–1864										Field
1865	Chase, S.P.									
1866–1867								(seat abolished)		
1868–1869						(vacant)				

Succession Chart of Supreme Court Seats *(Continued)*

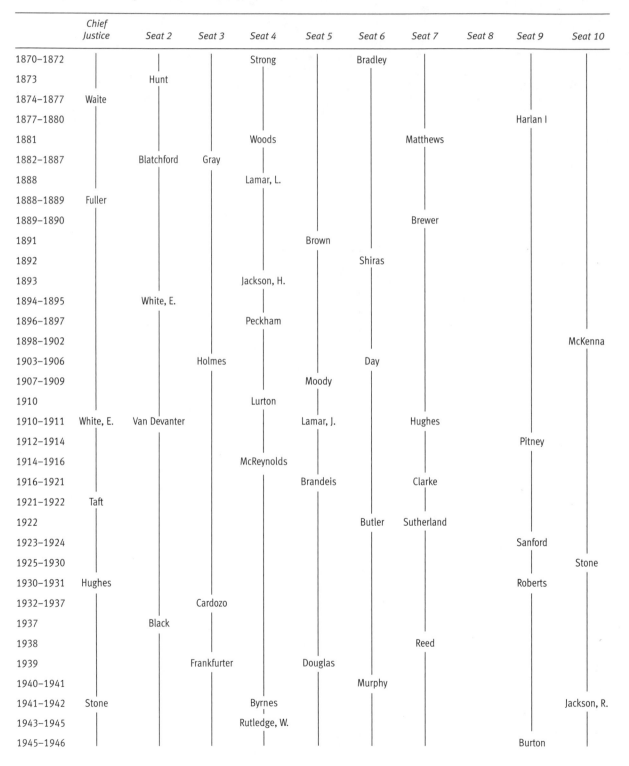

	Chief Justice	Seat 2	Seat 3	Seat 4	Seat 5	Seat 6	Seat 7	Seat 8	Seat 9	Seat 10
1870–1872				Strong		Bradley				
1873		Hunt								
1874–1877	Waite									
1877–1880									Harlan I	
1881				Woods			Matthews			
1882–1887		Blatchford	Gray							
1888				Lamar, L.						
1888–1889	Fuller									
1889–1890							Brewer			
1891					Brown					
1892						Shiras				
1893				Jackson, H.						
1894–1895		White, E.								
1896–1897				Peckham						
1898–1902										McKenna
1903–1906			Holmes				Day			
1907–1909					Moody					
1910				Lurton						
1910–1911	White, E.	Van Devanter			Lamar, J.		Hughes			
1912–1914									Pitney	
1914–1916				McReynolds						
1916–1921					Brandeis		Clarke			
1921–1922	Taft									
1922						Butler	Sutherland			
1923–1924									Sanford	
1925–1930										Stone
1930–1931	Hughes								Roberts	
1932–1937			Cardozo							
1937		Black								
1938							Reed			
1939			Frankfurter		Douglas					
1940–1941						Murphy				
1941–1942	Stone			Byrnes						Jackson, R.
1943–1945				Rutledge, W.						
1945–1946									Burton	

Succession Chart of Supreme Court Seats *(Continued)*

	Chief Justice	Seat 2	Seat 3	Seat 4	Seat 5	Seat 6	Seat 7	Seat 8	Seat 9	Seat 10
1946–1949	Vinson									
1949–1953				Minton		Clark				
1953–1954	Warren									
1955–1956										Harlan II
1957–1958				Brennan			Whittaker			
1959–1962									Stewart	
1962–1965			Goldberg				White, B.			
1965–1967			Fortas							
1967–1969						Marshall, T.				
1969	Burger		(vacant)							
1970–1971			Blackmun							
1971–1975		Powell								Rehnquist
1975–1981					Stevens					
1981–1986									O'Connor	
1986–1987	Rehnquist									Scalia
1988–1990		Kennedy								
1990–1991				Souter						
1991–1993						Thomas				
1993–1994							Ginsburg			
1994–2005			Breyer							
2005–	Roberts									

Thumbnail Sketch of the Supreme Court's History

Court Era	Chief Justices	Defining Characteristics	Major Court Cases
Developmental Period (1789–1800)	John Jay (1789–1795) John Rutledge (1795) Oliver Ellsworth (1796–1800)	Low prestige: spotty attendance by justices, resignations for more "prestigious positions," hears about fifty cases Business of the Court: largely admiralty and maritime disputes Use of seriatim opinion practice	*Bingham v. Cabbot* (1795) *Bingham v. Cabot* (1798)
The Marshall Court (1801–1835)	John Marshall (1801–1835)	Establishment of Court's role in governmental process Strong Court support for national powers (especially commerce) over states' rights Use of "Opinions of the Court," rather than seriatim practice Beginning of systematic reporting of Court opinions Despite the importance of Court opinions interpreting the Constitution, the business of the Court continues to involve private law issues (maritime, property, contracts)	*Marbury v. Madison* (1803) *Fairfax's Devisee v. Hunter's Lessee* (1813) *Martin v. Hunter's Lessee* (1816) *McCulloch v. Maryland* (1819) *Gibbons v. Ogden* (1824) *Cherokee Nation v. Georgia* (1831) *Worcester v. Georgia* (1832) *Wheaton v. Peters* (1834) *Proprietors of Charles River Bridge v. Proprietors of Warren Bridge* (1837)
Taney and Civil War Courts (1836–1888)	Roger Taney (1836–1864) Salmon Chase (1864–1873) Morrison Waite (1874–1888)	Continued assertion of federal power over states (with some accommodation for state police powers) Growing North–South splits on the Court Court showdowns with Congress at the onset and conclusion of the Civil War Growth of Court's caseload, with the majority of post–Civil War cases involving private law issues and war litigation Congress fixes Court size at nine	*United States v. Libellants and Claimants of the Schooner Amistad* (1841) *Luther v. Borden* (1849) *Dred Scott v. Sandford* (1857) *Ableman v. Booth* (1859) *Ex parte Vallandigham* (1864) *Ex parte Milligan* (1866) *Cherokee Tobacco Case* (1871) *The Butchers' Benevolent Association of New Orleans v. The Crescent City Livestock Landing and Slaughterhouse Co.* (1873) *Esteben v. Louisiana* (1873) *Bradwell v. Illinois* (1873) *Minor v. Happersett* (1875) *Reynolds v. United States* (1879) *United States v. Stanley* (1883) *United States v. Ryan* (1883) *United States v. Nichols* (1883) *United States v. Singleton* (1883) *Robinson and Wife v. Memphis and Charleston Railroad Co.* (1883) *Yick Wo v. Hopkins* (1886)

Court Era	Chief Justices	Defining Characteristics	Major Court Cases
Conservative Court Eras (1889–1937)	Melville Fuller (1888–1910) Edward White (1910–1921) William Howard Taft (1921–1930) Charles Evans Hughes (1930–1937)	But for a brief period reflecting progressivism, the Courts of this era tended to protect business interests over governmental police powers Court sets "civil rights" policy of "separate but equal" Congress relieves justices of circuit-riding duty Congress, in 1925 Judiciary Act, gives Court greater discretion over its docket Despite Judiciary Act, Court's docket continues to grow, with many cases reflecting economic issues (for example, congressional power under the commerce clause) Some important construction of Bill of Rights guarantees (protection of rights increases after WW I) Showdown with FDR over New Deal legislation: Court continues to strike down New Deal, leading the president to propose a Court-packing plan	*In re Neagle* (1890) *Fong Yue Ting v. United States* (1893) *Pollock v. Farmer's Loan and Trust Co. I* (1895) *Pollock v. Farmer's Loan and Trust Co. II* (1895) *In re Debs* (1895) *Plessy v. Ferguson* (1896) *Williams v. Fears* (1900) *De Lima v. Bidwell* (1901) *Downes v. Bidwell* (1901) *Lone Wolf v. Hitchcock* (1903) *Lochner v. New York* (1905) *Patterson v. Colorado* (1907) *Loewe v. Lawlor* (1908) *Berea College v. Kentucky* (1908) *Muller v. Oregon* (1908) *Standard Oil Co. of New Jersey v. United States* (1911) *Lawlor v. Loewe* (1915) *Frank v. Magnum* (1915) *Caminetti v. United States* (1917) *Buchanan v. Warley* (1917) *Goldman v. United States* (1918) *Hammer v. Dagenhart* (1918) *Schenck v. United States* (1919) *Debs v. United States* (1919) *Abrams v. United States* (1919) *Adkins v. Children's Hospital* (1923) *Pierce v. Society of Sisters* (1925) *Gitlow v. New York* (1925) *Village of Euclid v. Ambler Realty Co.* (1926) *Nixon v. Herndon* (1927) *Buck v. Bell* (1927) *Whitney v. California* (1927) *United States v. Macintosh* (1931) *Near v. Minnesota* (1931) *Nixon v. Condon* (1932) *Powell v. Alabama* (1932) *Nebbia v. New York* (1934) *Norris v. Alabama* (1935) *Humphrey's Executor v. United States* (1935) *Schechter Poultry Corp. v. United States* (1935) *United States v. Butler* (1936) *National Labor Relations Board v. Jones and Laughlin Steel Corp.* (1937)

Court Era	Chief Justices	Defining Characteristics	Major Court Cases
The Roosevelt and World War II Court Eras (1937–1953)	Charles Evans Hughes (1937–1941) Harlan Fiske Stone (1941–1946) Fred Vinson (1946–1953)	With the "switch in time that saved nine" the Court begins to uphold federal regulations under the commerce clause, as well as state use of police powers Expansion of rights and liberties, until WW II and ensuing cold war Increases in nonconsensual behavior (dissents and concurrences) among the justices	Cantwell v. Connecticut (1940) Minersville School District v. Gobitis (1940) Bridges v. California (1941) Chaplinsky v. New Hampshire (1942) Ex Parte Quirin (1942) Parker v. Brown (1943) West Virginia State Board of Education v. Barnette (1943) Hirabayashi v. United States (1943) Smith v. Allwright (1944) Korematsu v. United States (1944) Screws v. United States (1945) Bridges v. Wixon (1945) In re Yamashita (1946) Louisiana ex rel. Francis v. Resweber (1947) Sipuel v. Oklahoma State Board of Regents (1948) Shelley v. Kraemer (1948) Dennis v. United States (1951) Youngstown Sheet and Tube Co. v. Sawyer (1952)
The Warren Court Era (1953–1969)	Earl Warren (1953–1969)	Expansion of rights, liberties, and criminal justice Establishment of the right to privacy Emergence of Court as national policy maker Continued increase in Court's docket, with steady growth in the number of in forma pauperis petitions Growth in the percentage of constitutional cases on Court's plenary docket First black justice (Marshall) appointed to the Court	Rosenberg v. United States (1953) Brown v. Board of Education of Topeka (1954) Bates v. City of Little Rock (1960) Mapp v. Ohio (1961) Baker v. Carr (1962) Engel v. Vitale (1962) NAACP v. Button (1963) Gideon v. Wainwright (1963) School District of Abingdon Township v. Schempp (1963) New York Times Co. v. Sullivan (1964) Bell v. Maryland (1964) Reynolds v. Sims (1964) Heart Of Atlanta Motel v. United States (1964) United States v. Seeger (1965) Griswold v. Connecticut (1965) United States v. Price (1966) Miranda v. Arizona (1966) Time, Inc. v. Hill (1967) Loving v. Virginia (1967) In re Gault (1967) Katz v. United States (1967) Epperson v. Arkansas (1968)

Court Era	Chief Justices	Defining Characteristics	Major Court Cases
The Warren Court Era (Continued)			*Terry v. Ohio* (1968)
			Tinker v. Des Moines Independent Community School District (1969)
			Red Lion Broadcasting Co. v. Federal Communications Commission (1969)
			Brandenburg v. Ohio (1969)
			Powell v. McCormack (1969)
			Goldberg v. Kelly (1970)
			Oregon v. Mitchell (1970)
Republican Court Eras (1969–)	Warren Burger (1969–1986) William Rehnquist (1986–2005) John G. Roberts Jr. (2005–)	Attempts in some areas (for example, criminal law) to limit or rescind Warren Court rulings Expansion of women's rights, including right to abortion Some attempt to increase state power Legitimation of affirmative action policies Court increasingly called on to resolve intergovernmental disputes involving separation of powers or the authority of one branch of government over another Appointment of first woman (O'Connor) to the Court Rejection of race-based legislative districting Increased recognition of gay rights Intervention in the 2000 presidential election Further definition of reasonable accommodation under Americans with Disability Act Recognition of legal limits on technology to investigate crimes Continued focus on political campaign finance Reviews of due process rights for enemy combatants in terrorism-related cases Rulings on public displays of religious symbols	*Griggs v. Duke Power Co.* (1971) *Swann v. Charlotte-Mecklenburg County Board of Education* (1971) *Lemon v. Kurtzman* (1971) *New York Times Co. v. United States* (1971) *Reed v. Reed* (1971) *Sierra Club v. Morton* (1972) *Wisconsin v. Yoder* (1972) *Flood v. Kuhn* (1972) *Furman v. Georgia* (1972) *Branzburg v. Hayes* (1972) *Roe v. Wade* (1973) *San Antonio Independent School District v. Rodriguez* (1973) *Frontiero v. Richardson* (1973) *Miller v. California* (1973) *Cleveland Board of Education v. LaFleur* (1974) *Gertz v. Robert Welch* (1974) *Miami Herald v. Tornillo* (1974) *United States v. Nixon* (1974) *Buckley v. Valeo* (1976) *Dothard v. Rawlinson* (1977) *Regents of the University of California v. Bakke* (1978) *Richmond Newspapers, Inc. v. Virginia* (1980) *Chandler v. Florida* (1981) *Kissinger v. Halperin* (1981) *Plyler v. Doe* (1982) *Nixon v. Fitzgerald* (1982) *Bob Jones University v. United States* (1983) *Immigration and Naturalization Service v. Chadha* (1983) *Roberts v. United States Jaycees* (1984) *New Jersey v. T.L.O.* (1985) *Wallace v. Jaffree* (1985)

Court Era	Chief Justices	Defining Characteristics	Major Court Cases
Republican Court Era (Continued)			*Meritor Savings Bank v. Vinson* (1986)
			Bowers v. Hardwick (1986)
			Johnson v. Transportation Agency, Santa Clara County (1987)
			Edwards v. Aguillard (1987)
			Hazelwood School District v. Kuhlmeier (1988)
			Hustler Magazine, Inc. v. Falwell (1988)
			Thompson v. Oklahoma (1988)
			DeShaney v. Winnebago County Department of Social Services (1989)
			Price Waterhouse v. Hopkins (1989)
			Texas v. Johnson (1989)
			Employment Division, Dept. of Human Resources of Oregon v. Smith (1990)
			Cruzan v. Director, Missouri Department of Health (1990)
			Hodgson v. Minnesota (1990)
			Lee v. Weisman (1992)
			Church of the Lukumi Babalu Aye, Inc. and Ernesto Pichardo v. City of Hialeah (1993)
			Shaw v. Reno (1993)
			United States v. Lopez (1995)
			Vernonia School District 47J v. Acton (1995)
			Shaw v. Hunt (1996)
			Romer v. Evans (1996)
			United States v. Virginia (1996)
			Clinton v. Jones (1997)
			Agostini v. Felton (1997)
			City of Boerne v. Flores (1997)
			Vacco v. Quill (1997)
			Reno v. American Civil Liberties Union (1997)
			Davis v. Monroe County Board of Education (1999)
			Hunt v. Cromartie (1999)
			United States v. Playboy Entertainment Group, Inc. (2000)
			Santa Fe Independent School District v. Doe (2000)
			Apprendi v. New Jersey (2000)
			Boy Scouts of America v. Dale (2000)
			Bush v. Gore (2000)
			Easley v. Cromartie (2001)
			PGA Tour v. Martin (2001)
			Kyllo v. United States (2001)

Court Era	Chief Justices	Defining Characteristics	Major Court Cases
Republican Court Era (Continued)			
			Good News Club v. Milford Central School (2001)
			Zelman v. Simmons-Harris (2002)
			Republican Party of Minnesota v. White (2002)
			Lawrence v. Texas (2003)
			Grutter v. Bollinger (2003)
			McConnell v. Federal Election Commission (2003)
			Elk Grove Unified School District v. Newdow (2004)
			Al Odah v. United States (2004)
			Hamdi v. Rumsfeld (2004)
			Rasul v. Bush (2004)
			Rumsfeld v. Padilla (2004)
			Roper v. Simmons (2005)
			Gonzalez v. Raich (2005)
			Kelo v. City of New London (2005)
			McCreary County, Kentucky v. American Civil Liberties Union of Kentucky (2005)
			MGM v. Grokster (2005)
			Van Orden v. Perry (2005)

Source: Adapted from Lee Epstein and Thomas G. Walker, *Constitutional Law for a Changing America: Rights, Liberties, and Justice,* 5th ed. (Washington, D.C.: CQ Press, 2004).

Online Sources of Decisions

y using the Internet, one can read the full text of Supreme Court decisions and listen to oral arguments from historic cases. The following sites are some of the best.

U.S. Supreme Court Web site

supremecourtus.gov

The U.S. Supreme Court's Web site opened April 17, 2000. Opinions are available the day they are handed down, although the Cornell University or FindLaw sites are often quicker. In addition to opinions, the site contains useful docket information as well as basic information about the Court and its operations: rules, argument calendars, bar admission forms, visitors' guides, and a small number of photographs and historical materials.

Cornell Legal Information Institute

supct.law.cornell.edu/supct/index.html

Although several Internet sites provide Supreme Court opinions, the Cornell Legal Information Institute is a popular choice because it is so easy to use.

Cornell offers the full text of all Supreme Court decisions from May 1990 to the present. Decisions are posted the same day the Court releases them and can be accessed by using the name of the first party, the name of the second party, keyword, date, or other variables.

The site also provides nearly 600 historic Supreme Court decisions dating back to the Court's beginnings on such topics as school prayer, abortion, administrative law, copyright, patent law, and trademarks. Cases can be accessed by topic, party name, or opinion author.

The site also has the full text of the Supreme Court Rules, the Court calendar for the current term, the schedule of oral arguments, biographical data about current and former justices, and a glossary of legal terms.

liibulletin

Send an email message to listserv@listserv.law.cornell.edu

The liibulletin is a free mailing list that alerts subscribers when new Supreme Court decisions are placed on the Internet. The list provides syllabi of new decisions, in addition to instructions about how to obtain the full text. Cornell Law School's Legal Information Institute operates the site.

To subscribe, send an email message to listserv@listserv.law.cornell.edu and leave the subject line blank. In the message area type: subscribe liibulletin *firstname lastname,* where *firstname* and *lastname* are replaced by your first and last names.

Oyez Oyez Oyez: A U.S. Supreme Court Database

oyez.org

This site offers recordings of oral arguments from about 1,000 Supreme Court cases. The site is operated by Northwestern University, and the recordings are digitized from tapes in the National Archives.

Listening to the cases requires RealAudio software. Oyez offers a link to another Internet site where the software can be downloaded for free. A recent addition to the site is a growing number of Podcasts of arguments.

The database can be searched by title, citation, subject, and date. For each case, the site provides recordings of oral arguments and text listing the facts of the case, the constitutional question involved, and the Court's conclusion.

Oyez also provides brief biographies of all current and former justices and a virtual tour of the Supreme Court building.

FindLaw

findlaw.com/casecode/supreme.html

This site provides the full text of all Supreme Court decisions from 1893 to the present. The database can be browsed by year and *U.S. Reports* volume number, and it also can be searched by citation, case title, and keywords. The decisions are in HTML format, and many have hyperlinks to citations from previous decisions.

The site also offers the full text of the U.S. Constitution, with annotations by the Congressional Research Service, and links to cited Supreme Court cases. FindLaw, a legal publisher, operates the site.

FedWorld/FLITE Supreme Court Decisions

fedworld.gov/supcourt/index.htm

FedWorld's database contains the full text of all Supreme Court decisions issued between 1937 and 1975. The database was originally compiled by the U.S. Air Force and has been placed online by the National Technical Information Service.

The more than 7,000 decisions are from volumes 300 to 422 of *U.S. Reports.* They can be searched by case name and keyword. The decisions are provided in ASCII text format.

Sources: Bruce Maxwell, *How to Access the Federal Government on the Internet: Washington Online,* 4th ed. (Washington, D.C.: Congressional Quarterly, 1999); Kenneth Jost, ed. *The Supreme Court A to Z,* 3rd ed. (Washington, D.C.: CQ Press, 2003), 545–546. Updated by the author.

How to Read a Court Citation

The official version of each Supreme Court decision and opinion is contained in a series of volumes entitled *United States Reports,* published by the U.S. Government Printing Office.

Although there are several unofficial compilations of Court opinions, including *United States Law Week,* published by the Bureau of National Affairs; *Supreme Court Reporter,* published by West Publishing Company; and *United States Supreme Court Reports, Lawyers' Edition,* published by Lawyers Cooperative Publishing Company, it is the official record that is generally cited. An unofficial version or the official slip opinion might be cited if a decision has not yet been officially reported.

A citation to a case includes, in order, the name of the parties to the case, the volume of *United States Reports* in which the decision appears, the page in the volume on which the opinion begins, the page from which any quoted material is taken, and the year of the decision.

For example, *Griswold v. Connecticut,* 381 U.S. 479, 482 (1965) means that the Supreme Court decision in the case of Griswold against the state of Connecticut can be found in volume 381 of *United States Reports* beginning on page 479. The number 482 refers to the page where the specific quotation in question can be found. The date is the year the opinion was issued.

All of the cases in this book use the official U.S. cite, even though early cases were cited in a different way. Until 1875 the official reports of the Court were published under the names of the Court reporters, and it is their names, or abbreviated versions, that appear in cites for those years; U.S. volume numbers have been assigned to them retroactively. A citation such as *Marbury v. Madison,* 1 Cranch 137 (1803) means that the opinion in the case of Marbury against Madison is in the first volume of reporter Cranch beginning on page 137. (Between 1875 and 1883 a Court reporter named William T. Otto compiled the decisions and opinions; his name appears on the volumes for those years as well as the *United States Reports* volume number, but Otto is seldom cited.)

The titles of the volumes to 1875, the full names of the reporters, and the corresponding *United States Reports* volumes are:

1–4 Dall.	Dallas	1–4 U.S.
1–9 Cranch or Cr.	Cranch	5–13 U.S.
1–12 Wheat.	Wheaton	14–25 U.S.
1–16 Pet.	Peters	26–41 U.S.
1–24 How.	Howard	42–65 U.S.
1–2 Black	Black	66–67 U.S.
1–23 Wall.	Wallace	68–90 U.S.

Source: Adapted from Kenneth Jost, ed., *The Supreme Court A to Z,* 3rd ed. (Washington, D.C.: CQ Press, 2003), 534.

Glossary of Common Legal Terms

Accessory. In criminal law, a person not present at the commission of an offense who commands, advises, instigates, or conceals the offense.

Acquittal. Discharge of a person from a charge of guilt. A person is acquitted when a jury returns a verdict of not guilty. A person may also be acquitted when a judge determines that there is insufficient evidence to convict him or that a violation of due process precludes a fair trial.

Adjudicate. To determine finally by the exercise of judicial authority to decide a case.

Affidavit. A voluntary written statement of facts or charges affirmed under oath.

A fortiori. With stronger force, with more reason.

Amicus curiae. A friend of the court, a person not a party to litigation, who volunteers or is invited by the court to give his views on a case.

Appeal. To take a case to a higher court for review. Generally, a party losing in a trial court may appeal once to an appellate court as a matter of right. If he loses in the appellate court, appeal to a higher court is within the discretion of the higher court. Most appeals to the U.S. Supreme Court are within the Court's discretion. However, when the highest court in a state rules that a U.S. statute is unconstitutional or upholds a state statute against the claim that it is unconstitutional, appeal to the Supreme Court is a matter of right.

Appellant. The party that appeals a lower court decision to a higher court.

Appellee. One who has an interest in upholding the decision of a lower court and is compelled to respond when the case is appealed to a higher court by the appellant.

Arraignment. The formal process of charging a person with a crime, reading him the charge, asking whether he pleads guilty or not guilty, and entering his plea.

Attainder, Bill of. A legislative act pronouncing a particular individual guilty of a crime without trial or conviction and imposing a sentence upon him.

Bail. The security, usually money, given as assurance of a prisoner's due appearance at a designated time and place (as in court) to procure in the interim his release from jail.

Bailiff. A minor officer of a court usually serving as an usher or a messenger.

Brief. A document prepared by counsel to serve as the basis for an argument in court, setting out the facts of and the legal arguments in support of his case.

Burden of proof. The need or duty of affirmatively proving a fact or facts that are disputed.

Case Law. The law as defined by previously decided cases, distinct from statutes and other sources of law.

Cause. A case, suit, litigation, or action, civil or criminal.

Certiorari, Writ of. A writ issued from the Supreme Court, at its discretion, to order a lower court to prepare the record of a case and send it to the Supreme Court for review.

Civil law. Body of law dealing with the private rights of individuals, as distinguished from criminal law.

Class action. A lawsuit brought by one person or group on behalf of all persons similarly situated.

Code. A collection of laws, arranged systematically.

Comity. Courtesy, respect; usually used in the legal sense to refer to the proper relationship between state and federal courts.

Common law. Collection of principles and rules of action, particularly from unwritten English law, that derive their authority from longstanding usage and custom or from courts recognizing and enforcing these customs. Sometimes used synonymously with case law.

Consent decree. A court-sanctioned agreement settling a legal dispute and entered into by the consent of the parties.

Contempt (civil and criminal). Civil contempt consists in the failure to do something that the party is ordered by the court to do for the benefit of another party. Criminal contempt occurs when a person willfully exhibits disrespect for the court or obstructs the administration of justice.

Conviction. Final judgment or sentence that the defendant is guilty as charged.

Criminal law. That branch of law which deals with the enforcement of laws and the punishment of persons who, by breaking laws, commit crimes.

Declaratory judgment. A court pronouncement declaring a legal right or interpretation but not ordering a specific action.

De facto. In fact, in reality.

Defendant. In a civil action, the party denying or defending itself against charges brought by a plaintiff. In a criminal action, the person indicted for commission of an offense.

De jure. As a result of law, as a result of official action.

Deposition. Oral testimony from a witness taken out of court in response to written or oral questions, committed to writing, and intended to be used in the preparation of a case.

Dicta. *See Obiter dictum.*

Dismissal. Order disposing of a case without a trial.

Docket. *See Trial docket.*

Due process. Fair and regular procedure. The Fifth and Fourteenth Amendments guarantee persons that they will not be deprived of life, liberty, or property by the government until fair and usual procedures have been followed.

Error, Writ of. A writ issued from an appeals court to a lower court requiring it to send to the appeals court the record of a case in which it has entered a final judgment and which the appeals court will now review for error.

Ex parte. Only from, or on, one side. Application to a court for some ruling or action on behalf of only one party.

Ex post facto. After the fact; an ex post facto law makes an action a crime after it has already been committed, or otherwise changes the legal consequences of some past action.

Ex rel. Upon information from; usually used to describe legal proceedings begun by an official in the name of the state, but at the instigation of, and with information from, a private individual interested in the matter.

Grand jury. Group of twelve to twenty-three persons impaneled to hear in private evidence presented by the state against persons accused of crime and to issue indictments when a majority of the jurors find probable cause to believe that the accused has committed a crime. Called a "grand" jury because it comprises a greater number of persons than a "petit" jury.

Grand jury report. A public report released by a grand jury after an investigation into activities of public officials that fall short of criminal actions. Grand jury reports are often called "presentments."

Guilty. A word used by a defendant in entering a plea or by a jury In returning a verdict, indicating that the defendant is legally responsible as charged for a crime or other wrongdoing.

Habeas corpus. Literally, "you have the body"; a writ issued to inquire whether a person is lawfully imprisoned or detained. The writ demands that the persons holding the prisoner justify his detention or release him.

Immunity. A grant of exemption from prosecution in return for evidence or testimony.

In camera. "In chambers." Refers to court hearings in private without spectators.

In forma pauperis. In the manner of a pauper, without liability for court costs.

In personam. Done or directed against a particular person.

In re. In the affair of, concerning. Frequent title of judicial proceedings in which there are no adversaries, but rather where the matter itself—as a bankrupt estate—requires judicial action.

In rem. Done or directed against the thing, not the person.

Indictment. A formal written statement based on evidence presented by the prosecutor from a grand jury decided by a majority vote, charging one or more persons with specified offenses.

Information. A written set of accusations, similar to an indictment, but filed directly by a prosecutor.

Injunction. A court order prohibiting the person to whom it is directed from performing a particular act.

Interlocutory decree. A provisional decision of the court that temporarily settles an intervening matter before completion of a legal action.

Judgment. Official decision of a court based on the rights and claims of the parties to a case that was submitted for determination.

Jurisdiction. The power of a court to hear a case in question, which exists when the proper parties are present, and when the point to be decided is within the issues authorized to be handled by the particular court.

Juries. *See Grand jury and Petit jury.*

Magistrate. A judicial officer having jurisdiction to try minor criminal cases and conduct preliminary examinations of persons charged with serious crimes.

Mandamus. "We command." An order issued from a superior court directing a lower court or other authority to perform a particular act.

Moot. Unsettled, undecided. A moot question is also one that is no longer material; a moot case is one that has become hypothetical.

Motion. Written or oral application to a court or a judge to obtain a rule or an order.

Nolo contendere. "I will not contest it." A plea entered by a defendant at the discretion of the judge with the same legal effect as a plea of guilty, but it may not be cited in other proceedings as an admission of guilt.

Obiter dictum. Statement by a judge or justice expressing an opinion and included with, but not essential to, an opinion resolving a case before the court. Dicta are not necessarily binding in future cases.

Parole. A conditional release from imprisonment under conditions that if the prisoner abides by the law and other restrictions that may be placed upon him, he will not have to serve the remainder of his sentence. But if he does not abide by specified rules, he will be returned to prison.

Per curiam. "By the court." An unsigned opinion of the court or an opinion written by the whole court.

Petit jury. A trial jury, originally a panel of twelve persons who tried to reach a unanimous verdict on questions of fact in criminal and civil proceedings. Since 1970 the Supreme Court has upheld the legality of state juries with fewer than twelve persons. Because these small juries comprise fewer persons than "grand" juries, they are called "petit" juries.

Petitioner. One who files a petition with a court seeking action or relief, including a plaintiff or an appellant. But a petitioner is also a person who files for other court action where charges are not necessarily made; for example, a party may petition the court for an order requiring another person or party to produce documents. The opposite party is called the respondent.

When a writ of certiorari is granted by the Supreme Court, the parties to the case are called petitioner and respondent in contrast to the appellant and appellee terms used in an appeal.

Plaintiff. A party who brings a civil action or sues to obtain a remedy for injury to his rights. The party against whom action is brought is termed the defendant.

Plea Bargaining. Negotiations between prosecutors and the defendant aimed at exchanging a plea of guilty from the defendant for concessions by the prosecutors, such as reduction of charges or a request for leniency.

Pleas. *See Guilty and Nolo contendere.*

Presentment. *See Grand jury report.*

Prima facie. At first sight; referring to a fact or other evidence presumably sufficient to establish a defense or a claim unless otherwise contradicted.

Probation. Process under which a person convicted of an offense, usually a first offense, receives a suspended sentence and is given his freedom, usually under the guardianship of a probation officer.

Quash. To overthrow, annul, or vacate; as to quash a subpoena.

Recognizance. An obligation entered into before a court or magistrate requiring the performance of a specified act— usually to appear in court at a later date. It is an alternative to bail for pretrial release.

Remand. To send back. In the event of a decision being remanded, it is sent back by a higher court to the court from which it came for further action.

Respondent. One who is compelled to answer the claims or questions posed in court by a petitioner. A defendant and an appellee may be called respondents, but the term also includes those parties who answer in court during actions in which charges are not necessarily brought or in which the Supreme Court has granted a writ of certiorari.

Seriatim. Separately, individually, one by one.

Stare decisis. "Let the decision stand." The principle of adherence to settled cases, the doctrine that principles of law established in earlier judicial decisions should be accepted as authoritative in similar subsequent cases.

Statute. A written law enacted by a legislature. A collection of statutes for a particular governmental division is called a code.

Stay. To halt or suspend further judicial proceedings.

Subpoena. An order to present one's self before a grand jury, court, or legislative hearing.

Subpoena duces tecum. An order to produce specified documents or papers.

Tort. An injury or wrong to the person or property of another.

Transactional immunity. Protects a witness from prosecution for any offense mentioned in or related to his testimony, regardless of independent evidence against him.

Trial docket. A calendar prepared by the clerks of the court listing the cases set to be tried.

Use immunity. Protects a witness against the use of his own testimony against him in prosecution.

Vacate. To make void, annul, or rescind.

Writ. A written court order commanding the designated recipient to perform or not perform acts specified in the order.

SELECTED BIBLIOGRAPHY

Abraham, Henry J., and Barbara A. Perry. *Freedom and the Court: Civil Rights and Liberties in the United States.* 8th ed. Lawrence: University Press of Kansas, 2003.

Abrams, Floyd. *Speaking Freely: Trials of the First Amendment.* New York: Viking, 2005.

Amar, Akhil Reed, and Alan Hirsch. *For the People: What the Constitution Really Says about Your Rights.* New York: Free Press, 1998.

Baker, Thomas E. *The Most Wonderful Work: Our Constitution Interpreted.* St. Paul: West Publishing, 1996.

Ball, Howard. *Bakke Case: Race, Education, and Affirmative Action.* Lawrence: University Press of Kansas, 2000.

———. *A Defiant Life: Thurgood Marshall and the Persistence of Racism in America.* New York: Crown Publishers, 1999.

Barth, Alan. *Prophets with Honor: Great Dissents and Great Dissenters in the Supreme Court.* New York: Viking, 1974.

Berger, Raoul. *Death Penalties: The Supreme Court's Obstacle Course.* Lincoln, Neb.: iUniverse, 1999.

Blasi, Vincent, ed. *The Burger Court: The Counter-Revolution That Wasn't.* New Haven: Yale University Press, 1983.

Bloch, Susan Low, and Thomas Krattenmaker. *Supreme Court Politics: The Institution and Its Procedures.* St. Paul: West Publishing, 1994.

Bolick, Clint. *Voucher Wars: Waging the Legal Battle over School Choice.* Washington, D.C.: Cato Institute, 2003.

Bugliosi, Vincent. *No Island of Sanity: Paula Jones v. Bill Clinton: The Supreme Court on Trial.* New York: Ballantine Publishing Group, 1998.

Burger, Warren E. *It Is So Ordered: A Constitution Unfolds.* New York: William Morrow, 1995.

Caplan, Lincoln. *The Tenth Justice: The Solicitor General and the Rule of Law.* New York: Alfred A. Knopf, 1987.

Choper, Jesse, ed. *The Supreme Court and Its Justices.* 2nd ed. Chicago: American Bar Association, 2000.

Clark, Hunter R. *Justice Brennan: The Great Conciliator.* New York: Birch Lane Press, 1995.

Clayton, James E. *The Making of Justice: The Supreme Court in Action.* New York: Dutton, 1964.

Commission on the Bicentennial of the United States Constitution. *The Supreme Court of the United States: Its Beginnings and Its Justices, 1790–1991.* Washington, D.C., 1992.

Cottrol, Raymond J., Raymond T. Diamond, and Leland B. Ware. Brown v. Board of Education: *Caste, Culture, and the Constitution.* Lawrence: University Press of Kansas, 2003.

Craig, Barbara Hinkson. *Chadha: The Story of an Epic Constitutional Struggle.* Berkeley: University of California Press, 1988.

Cray, Ed. *Chief Justice: A Biography of Earl Warren.* New York: Simon and Schuster, 1997.

Curtis, Michael Kent. *No State Shall Abridge: The Fourteenth Amendment and the Bill of Rights.* Durham: Duke University Press, 1986.

Cushman, Clare, and Melvin I. Urofsky. *Black, White, and Brown: The Landmark School Desegregation Case in Retrospect.* Washington, D.C.: CQ Press, 2004.

Davis, Martha F. *Brutal Need: Lawyers and the Welfare Rights Movement, 1960–1973.* New Haven: Yale University Press, 1995.

Davis, Sue C. *Justice Rehnquist and the Constitution.* Princeton: Princeton University Press, 1989.

Douglas, William O. *The Court Years, 1939–1975.* New York: Random House, 1980.

Dreyfuss, Joel, and Charles Lawrence III. *The* Bakke *Case: The Politics of Inequality.* New York: Harcourt Brace Jovanovich, 1979.

Eisler, Kim Isaac. *A Justice for All: William J. Brennan Jr. and the Decisions That Transformed America.* New York: Simon and Schuster, 1993.

Epstein, Lee, and Joseph F. Kobylka. *The Supreme Court and Legal Change: Abortion and the Death Penalty.* Chapel Hill: University of North Carolina Press, 1992.

Foner, Eric. *The Story of American Freedom.* New York: W.W. Norton, 1999.

Frank, John P. *Marble Palace: The Supreme Court in American Life.* New York: Alfred A. Knopf, 1958.

Fried, Charles. *Order and Law: Arguing the Reagan Revolution— A Firsthand Account.* New York: Simon and Schuster, 1991.

Friendly, Fred. *Minnesota Rag: The Dramatic Story of the Landmark Supreme Court Case That Gave New Meaning to Freedom of the Press.* New York: Random House, 1981.

Garraty, John A., ed. *Quarrels That Have Shaped the Constitution.* Rev. ed. New York: Harper Perennial, 1989.

Garrow, David J. *Liberty and Sexuality: The Right of Privacy and the Making of* Roe v. Wade. Berkeley: University of California Press, 1998.

Gillman, Howard. *The Votes That Counted: How the Court Decided the 2000 Presidential Election.* Chicago: The University of Chicago Press, 2001.

Goldstein, Robert Justin. *Flag Burning and Free Speech: The Case of* Texas v. Johnson. Lawrence: University Press of Kansas, 2000.

Graham, Fred. *Happy Talk: Confessions of a TV Newsman.* New York: W.W. Norton, 1990.

Gunther, Gerald. *Learned Hand: The Man and the Judge.* New York: Alfred A. Knopf, 1994.

Hall, Kermit L., ed. *The Oxford Companion to the Supreme Court of the United States.* 2nd ed. New York: Oxford University Press, 2005.

———. *The Oxford Guide to United States Supreme Court Decisions.* New York: Oxford University Press, 1999.

Hentoff, Nat. *The First Freedom: The Tumultuous History of Free Speech in America.* New York: Delacorte Press, 1980.

Hughes, Charles Evans. *The Supreme Court of the United States: Its Foundation, Methods, and Achievements: An Interpretation.* Garden City, N.Y.: Garden City Publishing, 1936.

Hull, N.E.H., and Peter Charles Hoffer. Roe v. Wade: *The Abortion Rights Controversy in American History.* Lawrence: University Press of Kansas, 2001.

Hutchinson, Dennis J. *The Man Who Once Was Whizzer White: A Portrait of Justice Byron R. White.* New York: Free Press, 1998.

Irons, Peter. *The Courage of Their Convictions: Sixteen Americans Who Fought Their Way to the Supreme Court.* New York: Free Press, 1988.

———. *A People's History of the Supreme Court.* New York: Viking, 1999.

Jeffries, John C., Jr. *Justice Lewis F. Powell Jr.* New York: Charles Scribner's Sons, 1994.

Johnson, John W. Griswold v. Connecticut: *Birth Control and the Constitutional Right of Privacy.* Lawrence: University Press of Kansas, 2005.

———. *The Struggle for Student Rights:* Tinker v. Des Moines *and the 1960s.* Lawrence: University Press of Kansas, 1997.

———, ed. *Historic U.S. Cases, 1690–1990: An Encyclopedia.* New York: Garland Publishing, 1992.

Jones, Howard. *Mutiny on the Amistad.* New York: Oxford University Press, 1987.

Jost, Kenneth. *The Supreme Court A to Z.* 3rd ed. Washington, D.C.: CQ Press, 2003.

———, ed. *The Supreme Court Yearbook.* Washington, D.C.: CQ Press, annual series, 1992–2001.

Keen, Lisa, and Suzanne B. Goldberg. *Strangers to the Law: Gay People on Trial.* Ann Arbor: University of Michigan Press, 1998.

Kens, Paul. Lochner v. New York: *Economic Regulation on Trial.* Lawrence: University Press of Kansas, 1998.

Kluger, Richard. *Simple Justice: The History of* Brown v. Board of Education *and Black America's Struggle for Equality.* Rev. ed. New York: Alfred A. Knopf, 2004.

Labbé, Ronald M., and Jonathan Lurie. *Slaughterhouse Cases: Regulation, Reconstruction, and the Fourteenth Amendment.* Abridged. Lawrence: University Press of Kansas, 2005.

Lazarus, Edward P. *Closed Chambers.* New York: Times Books, 1998.

Leuchtenberg, William E. *The Supreme Court Reborn: The Constitutional Revolution in the Age of Roosevelt.* New York: Oxford University Press, 1995.

Lewis, Anthony. *Gideon's Trumpet.* New York: Vintage, 1964.

———. *Make No Law: The Sullivan Case and the First Amendment.* New York: Random House, 1991.

Lieberman, Jethro K. *A Practical Companion to the Constitution: How the Supreme Court Has Ruled on Issues from Abortion to Zoning.* Berkeley: University of California Press, 1999.

McCorvey, Norma. *I am Roe: My Life,* Roe v. Wade, *and Freedom of Choice.* New York: Harper Collins, 1994.

Meisel, Alan. *The Right to Die.* 2nd ed. New York: Aspen, 1995.

Monk, Linda R. *The Bill of Rights: A User's Guide.* 4th ed. Alexandria, Va.: Close Up Publishing, 2004.

Murdoch, Joyce, and Deb Price. *Courting Justice: Gay Men and Lesbians v. The Supreme Court.* New York: Basic Books, 2001.

Murphy, Bruce Allen. *Fortas: The Rise and Ruin of a Supreme Court Justice.* New York: William Morrow, 1988.

Nelson, William E. Marbury v. Madison: *The Origins and Legacy of Judicial Review.* Lawrence: University Press of Kansas, 2000.

Newman, Roger K. *Hugo Black: A Biography.* New York: Pantheon Books, 1994.

O'Brien, David M. *Storm Center: The Supreme Court in American Politics.* 6th ed. New York: W.W. Norton, 2002.

O'Connor, Sandra Day. *The Majesty of the Law: Reflections of a Supreme Court Justice.* New York: Random House, 2003.

Ogletree, Charles J., Jr. *All Deliberate Speed: Reflections on the First Half-Century of* Brown v. Board of Education. New York: W.W. Norton and Company, 2004.

Pearson, Drew, and Robert S. Allen. *The Nine Old Men.* Garden City, N.Y.: Doubleday, Doran, 1936.

Perry, Barbara A. *The Priestly Tribe: The Supreme Court's Image in the American Mind.* Westport, Conn.: Praeger Publishers, 1999.

Perry, H.W., Jr. *Deciding to Decide: Agenda Setting in the United States Supreme Court.* Reprint. Cambridge: Harvard University Press, 2005.

Peters, Shawn Francis. *Judging Jehovah's Witnesses.* Lawrence: University Press of Kansas, 2000.

Pfeffer, Leo. *This Honorable Court: A History of the United States Supreme Court.* Boston: Beacon Press, 1965.

Rabban, David M. *Free Speech in Its Forgotten Years.* Cambridge, England: Cambridge University Press, 1997.

Radosh, Ronald, and Joyce Milton. *The Rosenberg File.* New York: Holt, Rinehart, and Winston, 1983.

Rehnquist, William H. *All the Laws but One: Civil Liberties in Wartime.* New York: Alfred A. Knopf, 1998.

———. *The Supreme Court: How It Was, How It Is.* New York: William Morrow, 1987.

Rosenkranz, E. Joshua, and Bernard Schwartz, ed. *Reason and Passion: Justice Brennan's Enduring Influence.* New York: W.W. Norton, 1997.

Rowan, Carl T. *Dream Makers, Dream Breakers: The World of Justice Thurgood Marshall.* Boston: Little, Brown, 1993.

Rudenstine, David. *The Day the Presses Stopped: A History of the Pentagon Papers Case.* Berkeley: University of California Press, 1996.

Salokar, Rebecca Mae. *The Solicitor General: The Politics of Law.* Philadelphia: Temple University Press, 1992.

Sanford, Bruce W. *Don't Shoot the Messenger: How Our Growing Hatred of the Media Threatens Free Speech for All of Us.* New York: Free Press, 1999.

Savage, David G. *Guide to the U.S. Supreme Court.* 4th ed. Washington, D.C.: CQ Press, 2004.

———. *Turning Right: The Making of the Rehnquist Supreme Court.* New York: John Wiley and Sons, 1992.

Schwartz, Bernard, ed. *The Ascent of Pragmatism: The Burger Court in Action.* Reading, Mass.: Addison-Wesley, 1990.

———. *A Book of Legal Lists: The Best and Worst in American Law.* New York: Oxford University Press, 1997.

———. *The Burger Court: Counter-Revolution or Confirmation?* New York: Oxford University Press, 1998.

———. *Decision: How the Supreme Court Decides Cases.* New York: Oxford University Press, 1996.

———. *A History of the Supreme Court.* New York: Oxford University Press, 1993.

———. *Swann's Way: The School Busing Case and the Supreme Court.* New York: Oxford University Press, 1986.

Schwartz, Herman. *The Burger Years: Rights and Wrongs in the Supreme Court, 1969–1986.* New York: Viking, 1987.

Simon, James F. *The Center Holds: The Power Struggle Inside the Rehnquist Court.* New York: Simon and Schuster, 1995.

Smolla, Rodney A., ed. *Free Speech in an Open Society.* New York: Alfred A. Knopf, 1992.

———. *A Year in the Life of the Supreme Court.* Durham: Duke University Press, 1995.

Starr, Kenneth W. *First Among Equals: The Supreme Court in American Life.* New York: Warner Books, 2002.

Sunstein, Cass R. *One Case at a Time: Judicial Minimalism on the Supreme Court.* Cambridge: Harvard University Press, 1999.

Tribe, Laurence H. *Abortion: The Clash of Absolutes.* New York: W.W. Norton, 1990.

Tushnet, Mark V. *A Court Divided: The Rehnquist Court and the Future of Constitutional Law.* New York: W.W. Norton, 2005.

———. *Making Constitutional Law: Thurgood Marshall and the Supreme Court, 1961–1991.* New York: Oxford University Press, 1997.

Urofsky, Melvin I. *The Continuity of Change: The Supreme Court and Individual Liberties, 1953–1986.* Belmont, Calif.: Wadsworth Publishing, 1991.

——. *Division and Discord: The Supreme Court under Stone and Vinson, 1941–1953.* Columbia: University of South Carolina Press, 1997.

——, ed. *The Douglas Letters.* Bethesda, Md.: Adler and Adler, 1987.

——. *One Hundred Americans Making Constitutional History.* Washington, D.C.: CQ Press, 2004.

——. *Public Debate over Controversial Supreme Court Decisions.* Washington, D.C.: CQ Press, 2005.

Van Sickel, Robert W. *Not a Particularly Different Voice: The Jurisprudence of Sandra Day O'Connor.* New York: Peter Lang Publishing, 1998.

Warren, Charles. *The Supreme Court in United States History.* 2 vols. Rev. ed. Boston: Little, Brown, 1926.

Warren, Earl. *The Memoirs of Earl Warren.* Garden City, N.Y.: Doubleday, 1977.

Wilkinson, J. Harvie III. *From Brown to Bakke.* New York: Oxford University Press, 1979.

——. *One Nation Indivisible: How Ethnic Separatism Threatens America.* Reading, Mass.: Addison-Wesley, 1997.

Williams, Juan. *Thurgood Marshall: American Revolutionary.* New York: Times Books, 1998.

Woodward, Bob, and Scott Armstrong. *The Brethren: Inside the Supreme Court.* New York: Simon and Schuster, 1979.

Yarbrough, Tinsley E. *The Rehnquist Court and the Constitution.* New York: Oxford University Press, 2000.

Zelden, Charles L. *Battle for the Black Ballot: Smith v. Allwright and the Defeat of the Texas All-White Primary.* Lawrence: University Press of Kansas, 2004.

AUTHOR BIOGRAPHY

Tony Mauro has covered the Supreme Court for twenty-five years, first for Gannett News Service and *USA Today* and then for *Legal Times* and American Lawyer Media. He is also a contributing author to four books: *A Year in the Life of the Supreme Court* (1995), *Reason and Passion: Justice Brennan's Enduring Influence* (1997), *The Burger Court* (1998), and *A Year at the Supreme Court* (2004). In 1999 the American Bar Association awarded him a certificate of merit for his Supreme Court coverage, and *Washingtonian* magazine included him on its list of top fifty journalists in Washington, D.C., in 2001.

INDEX

Note: page numbers followed by *p* refer to photographs